WORLD WIDE ENDEAVOR

The Story of the
Young People's Society of Christian Endeavor

BY
Rev. Francis E. Clark, D.D.

President of the United Society of Christian Endeavor

Illustrated with Magnificent full - page half - tone Illustrations and a beautiful collection of other Fine Engravings

First Fruits Press
Wilmore, Kentucky
c2015

World wide endeavor: the story of the Young People's Society of Christian Endeavor, from the beginning and in all lands, by Francis E. Clark.

First Fruits Press, ©2015
Previously published: Philadelphia and Chicago: Gillespie & Metzgar, 1895.

ISBN: 9781621713517 (print), 9781621713524 (digital)

Digital version at http://place.asburyseminary.edu/christianendeavorbooks/38/

First Fruits Press is a digital imprint of the Asbury Theological Seminary, B.L. Fisher Library. Asbury Theological Seminary is the legal owner of the material previously published by the Pentecostal Publishing Co. and reserves the right to release new editions of this material as well as new material produced by Asbury Theological Seminary. Its publications are available for noncommercial and educational uses, such as research, teaching and private study. First Fruits Press has licensed the digital version of this work under the Creative Commons Attribution Noncommercial 3.0 United States License. To view a copy of this license, visit http://creativecommons.org/licenses/by-nc/3.0/us/.

For all other uses, contact:

First Fruits Press
B.L. Fisher Library
Asbury Theological Seminary
204 N. Lexington Ave.
Wilmore, KY 40390
http://place.asburyseminary.edu/firstfruits

Clark, Francis E. (Francis Edward), 1851-1927.
    World wide endeavor: the story of the Young People's Society of Christian Endeavor, from the beginning and in all lands / by Francis E. Clark.
    561 pages: illustrations, portraits, facsimiles ; 21 cm.
    Wilmore, Ky. : First Fruits Press, ©2015.
    Reprint. Previously published: Philadelphia : Gillespie & Metzgar, 1895.
    ISBN: 9781621713517 (pbk.)
    1. International Society of Christian Endeavor -- History. 2. United Society of Christian Endeavor -- History. 3. Church work with young people -- History I. Title.
BV1424 .C6 2015

Cover design by Jonathan Ramsay

asburyseminary.edu
800.2ASBURY
204 North Lexington Avenue
Wilmore, Kentucky 40390

First Fruits Press
The Academic Open Press of Asbury Theological Seminary
204 N. Lexington Ave., Wilmore, KY 40390
859-858-2236
first.fruits@asburyseminary.edu
asbury.to/firstfruits

Sincerely Your Friend
Francis E. Clark.

World Wide Endeavor

THE STORY OF THE

Young People's Society of Christian Endeavor

FROM THE BEGINNING AND IN ALL LANDS

BY

Rev. Francis E. Clark, D. D.

President of the United Society of Christian Endeavor

WITH WORDS OF GREETING BY

Rev. Russell H. Conwell, Rev. Theodore L. Cuyler, Rev. M. Rhodes, Rev. David J. Burrell, Rev. B. B. Tyler, Rev. E. R. Dille, Rev. W. H. McMillan, Rev. J. K. McLean, Rev. J. F. Cowan, Rev. Canon Richardson, Rev. F. B. Meyer (London), Rev. Theo. Monod (Paris), Count Bernstorff (Berlin).

Illustrated with Magnificent full-page half-tone Illustrations and a beautiful collection of other Fine Engravings

---

SOLD ONLY BY SUBSCRIPTION

GILLESPIE & METZGAR,
PUBLISHERS,

PHILADELPHIA, PA.   CHICAGO, ILL.

Entered according to Act of Congress in the year 1895, by
GILLESPIE, METZGAR & KELLEY,
In the office of the Librarian of Congress, at Washington.
All rights reserved.

ALL PERSONS ARE WARNED NOT TO INFRINGE UPON OUR COPYRIGHT BY USING EITHER THE MATTER OR THE PICTURES IN THIS VOLUME.

GRATEFULLY DEDICATED

TO MY WIFE

THE FIRST FRIEND OF THE FIRST SOCIETY OF CHRISTIAN ENDEAVOR, AND
MY CONSTANT AND DEVOTED HELPER IN ALL SUBSEQUENT
ENDEAVORS IN MANY LANDS FOR CHRIST
AND THE CHURCH.

A PRELIMINARY TALK WITH THE READER.

I DO not like the formality of a preface, which is too often the unopened receptacle for an author's hopes and fears and apologies for his literary offspring; so I will not dignify these few prefatory remarks with the name "preface," lest my readers should be tempted to skip them altogether. Moreover, a formal preface is very little needed in a book of this nature, which aims to be simply a plain, unvarnished tale of Christian Endeavor from its humble beginning fourteen years ago to the present time.

I need not rehearse the various motives which have combined to induce me to write this book. It is true, that many friends, by their urgent advice, have had not a little to do with my decision to undertake the task. My publishers, too, whom I am also glad to count among my friends—a classification which an author cannot always make—have also, by their urgency, led me to undertake and persevere in the undertaking; but, more than all, my own strong impression that it was time to write a history of the early days of Christian Endeavor led me to undertake the task.

Every year the traditions of these early days are growing more and more dim. Though only fourteen short years have passed, several minor questions in regard to the early days of the movement are already debated. The place and time of the formation of the first society in some of the States is even now in some cases an unsettled question. The longer any such attempt as this, to set forth a comprehensive history of Christian Endeavor, is delayed, the more of these mooted questions will arise.

In my own mind I had found that the memory of some facts connected with the early days of the first society were already growing dim until it was refreshed by consultation of reports and newspaper accounts and journals kept during those early days.

On some accounts it would seem more fitting and modest to put off writing the history of such a movement until it had larger time to make history; but in these pages I hope no word will be found that savors of boasting, as though Christian Endeavor was putting off the harness instead of putting it on.

While writing every page of the book I have realized that there is much yet for the Endeavor Society to learn, many unscaled heights for it to climb, much of devotion and consecration for it yet to attain, a larger and fuller knowledge of God's word and will for it to seek, while, at the same time, in writing every page I have had occasion

A PRELIMINARY TALK WITH THE READER.

to acknowledge God's goodness and guiding hand in the wonderfully rapid growth and extension of Christian Endeavor principles into every land.

If it should still seem to some, as I must say it seemed to me when first confronted with the proposition to write this history, that it would be better to put it off for fifty or a hundred years, until a succeeding generation could weigh more impartially the substantial value of this new movement, I can only say that those who should write the history in the succeeding years would be further removed from the beginnings, and while they could weigh its value more impartially, perhaps, they could not so accurately tell the impulses and purposes which gave birth to the society, or so carefully follow the growth of the movement during its formative years. If the Christian Endeavor Society has the future before it which many of us hope and pray for, this history is but the first of a series, written by many hands perhaps, which will tell of its subsequent progress. But this volume may have its own value in being the story of an eye-witness of much that happened during the first decade and a half of Christian Endeavor. I have striven to be accurate in every detail, and, though doubtless minor inaccuracies will be found and corrections will be made in subsequent editions, yet at least it can be said that the utmost care has been taken to have every statement correct, and such that future writers may trust.

My one peculiar sorrow in writing these pages has been that so much must be left out which I should be glad to include; that the names of so many good friends who have been most active and efficient in promoting the advance of Christian Endeavor could not be recorded; that so many important services rendered could not be given even a line; that so many well-known faces must be omitted from the groups of Christian Endeavorers, and faces of those who have done quite as much, perhaps, for the cause as many of those who are here shown to the readers; but in a movement that counts its adherents by millions and whose centres of influence are found in every State and province, and every foreign land as well, such omissions are absolutely inevitable.

They do not tell by any means of my lack of appreciation of the workers, for some of the unrecorded ones are among the best exponents of Christian Endeavor, as well as among the dearest friends I have on earth. And now this volume is given to the world, trusting that it may show to the world something of the heroism of youth; something of the power of the simple gospel; something of the efficacy of covenant vows when taken upon the lips of generous, high-minded young men and women; something of the vigor and vitality of the religion of Jesus Christ as it appeals to the ingenuity and resourceful tact of consecrated young hearts.

F. E. C.

HILLCREST, AUBURNDALE, MASS.

WORDS OF GREETING.

BAPTIST TEMPLE,
   REV. RUSSELL H. CONWELL, PASTOR.

THE Christian Endeavor Society is the sail of a small church and the rudder of a large one. In a weak mission or in a feeble church such a society trains the unskilled laborers into efficient speakers and workers, and gives courage to those who hesitate to join the uncertain enterprise. But, in the large congregation, of which I may speak with a more valuable experience, the Christian Endeavor organizations are a necessity to spiritual growth or efficient work. The regular prayer-meetings and the stated public service, where thousands regularly attend, is no place to train the new convert, nor for the practical arrangement of Christian enterprises. Only a few can so speak as to be heard in such large gatherings, and they necessarily deliver addresses upon great principles. If every Christian in our week-day prayer-meetings, with the average attendance, were to speak for five minutes, it would take five days and nights of a continuous session. If we were to depend on the general prayer-meeting for training in prayer or exhortation, or if we were to act only on the suggestions Christians make there, we would be much weaker than a small church; but the Christian Endeavor societies, multiplying as the need presses, divide the masses into sections, which are small enough and large enough to worship and work effectively. They keep up the working forces in discipline and zeal, and they develop individually the genius and enthusiam of hundreds who would otherwise be lost in the monotonous crowd. He was indeed an apostle who obeyed the call of God and went bravely forward in organizing the Christian Endeavor societies for enormous development of Christian power, and for the most practical Christian union of the churches.

Russell H. Conwell

PHILADELPHIA.

LAFAYETTE AVENUE PRESBYTERIAN CHURCH,
REV. THEODORE L. CUYLER, D. D., PASTOR.

I AM delighted to hear, my dear Brother Clark, that you are preparing the history of the Christian Endeavor Society. The men who make history are the best men to write it. To you and to our friend, Sir George Williams, of London, God has vouchsafed the peculiar honor and privilege of founding great organizations, and also the joy of seeing them spread over the whole Christian world. Both go to the root of things—the salvation, education, and development of the young.

During the dozen years of my Brooklyn pastorate, before the inauguration of your first Christian Endeavor Society at Portland, I had been witnessing the immense power and indispensableness of a Young People's Association in my own church. It was and is just as important a part of the church's spiritual machinery as the Sabbath-school. Your Christian Endeavor societies occupy precisely that same place in every church that is wise enough to introduce them, and has grace enough to conduct them. A church that does not rear its youth for Jesus Christ, has no future in this world; it is dying at the top, and sapless at the roots. The Master has no place for such cumberers of His ground.

My chief solicitude for the Christian Endeavor societies is that they be kept strongly and tightly to their cardinal purpose, viz., the conversion and training of souls for the Master; aggressive work for Him can alone keep the organization sweet, hale, and spiritually athletic. The social must be only a road to the spiritual. All roads must lead to Christ. Then, we of the various denominations can go singing and shouting along the road, "One in our Master, and all we be brethren."

Your admirable movement has already survived the peril of being a "novelty." There is a cemetery for religious and benevolent enterprises just at that point where novelty dies out, and plenty of them have had Christian burial in that "Potter's field." By God's good guidance and rich blessing the Christian Endeavorers have left that fatal spot far behind, and are marching on two million strong. May your societies live on, even if you don't, to march into the millennial morning with colors flying and the dear name of the Crucified on every ensign.

Theodore L. Cuyler

BROOKLYN, N. Y.

FIRST CHURCH OF THE DISCIPLES OF CHRIST.
Rev. B. B. Tyler. D. D.. Pastor.

THAT the Christian Endeavor movement is a child of Providence but few, if any, who understand its spirit, methods, aims, and results will deny or even question. There is no such aid to the pastor in his arduous and multiform work—especially in large cities—as a well organized Society of Christian Endeavor. It may fittingly be characterized among human agencies as his cunning and strong right hand. To the wide-awake, consecrated pastor this unique organization has come to be an essential factor in the promotion of spiritual life and in the prosecution of aggressive evangelistic efforts.

The Pledge requires daily reading of the Bible and prayer. This covenant kept makes spiritually-minded young people. The keeping of this part of the Pledge helps the members of a Society of Christian Endeavor not only to do whatever the Lord Jesus would like to have them do, but to be whatever He would like to have them be. The Church also, according to the Pledge, is to be supported in every way, but especially by attendance on the regular Lord's Day and mid-week services. But the daily devotional exercises to which Christian Endeavorers are pledged unfit them for the silent attendance on the mid-week prayer and conference-meeting, and when they participate their participations must of necessity be bright, pointed, practical, spiritual, helpful.

To obtain, however, the largest and most satisfactory results, the pastor must be in genuine sympathy with his young people in their desire to be and to do whatever the Lord Jesus would like to have them be and do. For myself, I would be at a loss as to how to proceed with my work without the hearty co-operation of the intelligent and spiritually-minded young people in my Society of Christian Endeavor.

B. B. Tyler

New York City.

ST. MARK'S EVANGELICAL LUTHERAN CHURCH,
   REV. M. RHODES, PASTOR.

GOD'S method in the development and advancement of His kingdom is often singular. Where we can note the beginnings, how small they often are. "The kingdom of God cometh not with observation." The Divine method, so far as it takes on any material form, is always lowly, in contrast with the pretense and display of all individual or organized apparition. There is no flourish of trumpets, no glitter of shields, no waving of banners. It was so at Advent, so at Pentecost, so at the Reformation, so at the birth of the Young People's Society Christian Endeavor.

There was a great, noble, but idle multitude to be inspired and equipped for God. It was more than any ordinary undertaking. The instrumentality seemed limited, but through God it became adequate; and now, after less than a decade and a half of years, we look back to exclaim, "What hath God wrought!"

I have been especially pleased to note the efficiency of the movement in the development of the young people. How it has promoted the apostolic injunction, "Neglect not the gift that is in thee." What a noble company of lay-workers it is training for the great demands of the twentieth century! There will be abler ministers of the Word for it. There will be better informed and more interested men and women in missionary enterprise. There will be a purer, stronger citizenship in every way. The movement is making the Church more and more the busy, fruitful vineyard of the Lord.

Anything that will rightly serve to interpret to the largest number, the spirit, methods, and purpose of this society cannot be other than a blessing to the Church and the world.

I sincerely pray that it may move on in its noble work until the vision of the Seer shall become the supreme fact of the ages, when our eyes shall look upon "that great city, the holy Jerusalem, descending out of Heaven from God, having the glory of God; her light like unto a stone most precious, even like a jasper stone, clear as crystal."

M. Rhodes

ST. LOUIS, MO.

MARBLE COLLEGIATE REFORMED CHURCH,
REV. DAVID JAMES BURRELL, D. D., PASTOR.

A BOOK on the Endeavor movement is demanded; and who but Dr. Francis E. Clark shall write it? To him belongs the honor of launching the ship, and, still further, of standing by her tiller until now. Tell us, good skipper, of the voyage.

The coming historian will characterize the nineteenth century as *The Age of New Forces*. He will make mention of steam and electricity, and of their wonderful application and adjustments in the industrial world. He will have something to say about dynamite and of the part it played in enforcing peace. But he will dwell with vastly greater emphasis on certain new forces and new adjustments of religious things; such as the Sunday-School, the Missionary Propaganda, the Temperance Reform, Women's Work, and the Endeavor Movement. Nor is the last the least. It stands for the transfusion of youthful blood; it means the mobilization of the Christian Army; it marks an awakening as distinct as the Crusades and immensely more momentous. Millions of young people training for service; what does that mean? The future will tell. But the Church can never more be what it used to be; rather, a labor guild, a hive of industry, a living organism of wheels within wheels, each in place, and the Spirit directing the whole. This is the shibboleth of the future, "All at it, always at it, altogether at it."

David Jas. Burrell

NEW YORK CITY.

CENTRAL METHODIST EPISCOPAL CHURCH, SAN FRANCISCO, CAL.
REV. E. R. DILLE, D. D., PASTOR.

A LITTLE more than fourteen years ago a pastor in a quiet town in Maine, having had a revival in his church and feeling the need of getting his young converts to work by organizing a young people's society, set in motion the most marvelous religious movement of the nineteenth century—nay, the grandest Christian movement since the Reformation, except the second Reformation under the Wesleys and Whitefield.

Said Charles Kingsley, "The first open look of young eyes upon the condition of the world is one of the chief regenerative forces of humanity;" and so this movement, which now rallies in the various organizations of young people three millions of youth in thirty-two religious denominations, has in it the promise and potency of the millennial glory.

And sober history will record down to the last syllable of time that, whatever form the young people's movement may take in the coming years, the acorn was dropped by Francis E. Clark's hand, that now, in fourteen years, has produced a mighty forest that shakes like Lebanon and covers the whole earth.

"A man may boast of a stately mansion he builds, or of a statue he carves, but he may not boast of the oak tree that grows in his grounds. God built that. Men may build a house; God builds a tree. Men may organize a society; God starts a movement."

No ecclesiastical authority called the Young People's Society of Christian Endeavor into being; no church council decreed it; it had the same quiet origin as had the Sunday-school movement, the missionary movement, the temperance crusade—the same quiet origin as had the movement called Methodism and the movement called Christianity. "The kingdom of God cometh not with observation."

The founders of this society labored in discouragement and obloquy often, but they labored with a sublime optimism and an invincible faith in God that never faltered. They had no precedents to guide them, and while they may have made mistakes, I agree with the judgment of the late Dr. C. F. Deems, of precious memory: "No management in America is, all things considered, less open to adverse criticism than that of the Society of Christian Endeavor. I know that is a good deal to say, but when I think of the dangers that beset its founders and promoters, and of the wonderful success of the movement that might so easily have been wrecked upon any one of the thousand rocks that lay in its course, I record the above judgment as, before God, my deliberate conviction."

Long may the Young People's Society of Christian Endeavor live, blessing and blest; and long may its founder live!

Elbert R. Dille

SECOND UNITED PRESBYTERIAN CHURCH, ALLEGHENY, PA.
REV. W. H. MCMILLAN, D. D., PASTOR.

LOOKING at the Christian Endeavor Society both as a pastor and a Christian, I have found it to be worthy of unqualified approval. It is just what the churches need to train their young disciples for the service of the Lord, and to put them in right relations with all His other followers. And a Christian soldier may put on the "whole armor," but that will avail nothing if he is not drilled in the "manual of arms" and the movements of battle. The young can be taught; they furnish plastic material to be formed into excellent shapes for the Master's use. The Lord is ready to do great things by means of common people, and the Christian Endeavor is putting such into His hands, consecrated and prepared unto every good work.

The Christian Endeavor Society is a university; it furnishes an "all-around" training for Christian workers. The field is the world. The fruits of the Spirit are many. The places of duty are many, and as various as the manifold places of life; this society is so designed as to be sure to train somebody for everything to be done. It was the defect of former organizations of young people that they were too narrow in their scope to cover all the work to be done, or to furnish all the training needed to do it well. A young people's missionary society developed a spirit of beneficence, and that was all. A young men's prayer-meeting gave them courage to let their voices be heard in the larger meeting, but that was all. Christian Endeavor adjusts itself to the capacities and circumstances of all, and develops all in their peculiar graces and prepares them for their appropriate work.

That this society has been wonderfully designed of God to meet the wants of young Christians, is proved by the fact that denominational societies formed out of the inspiration of this movement, but for sectarian purposes, have been made close copies of this organization. Those who did not want the interdenominational fellowship of the Christian Endeavor Society did desire to copy its plan.

The name Christian Endeavor is also to be cherished, because it stands for a distinct and wonderful voice of God, in His Providence calling upon all His people to be one. It is true that this interdenominational fellowship promotes Christian unity. If there are those who are more "Separatists" than they are "Unionists," they should stand aloof from this society, and they doubtless will do so as long as their "Distinctives" bulk so large before them.

But Christian Endeavor does not seek a forced unity. It promotes first of all the unity of the Spirit, and then, through the truest loyalty to personal convictions and ecclesiastical affinities, it seeks, by bringing all nearer to the Lord and into the clearer light of His presence, to have them realize that "One is their Master, even Christ, and that they all are brethren."

W. H. McMillan.

PACIFIC THEOLOGICAL SEMINARY (CONGREGATIONAL), OAKLAND, CAL.
Rev. J. K. McLean, D. D., President.

THE Young People's Christian Endeavor movement is a prophecy in part fulfilled and partly unfulfilled. It is an accomplishment of Joel's prediction: "Afterward I will pour out my spirit upon all flesh; and your sons and your daughters shall prophesy; and your young men shall see visions; and also upon the servants and the hand-maidens in those days will I pour out my spirit." This spontaneous, widely-extended, astonishing uprising of young people—of all orders, conditions, qualities, circumstances, and out of so many nations—into Christian faith and service, is unprecedented and unapproached in religious history. Its unambitious originator and leader must have credit upon the human side for a movement which, for the time it has been in operation, reveals a greater potency for high results than any other spiritual movement of the nineteenth century.

But I am fain to believe that the chief power of the movement is yet undisclosed. It is like a magnificent tree, wonderfully grown and yielding choice fruitage already, but whose principal work has been developing itself substantially and gathering up vital forces for generations to follow. Except unforeseen blight shall fall upon it, the present gigantic movement carries within itself in large degree the power to solve the problem of the Christian ages—the conquest of the world for Jesus. Let it have fair and full trial. Shield it from the frosts of unfounded suspicions. Guard it from the cankerworm of false criticism. Environ it with the warm atmosphere of hope, confidence, and prayer. Let every hand which is laid upon it be of furtherance and upholding help. Let us prune it lovingly of surplusage and excrescence. Enrich its soil by manifested appreciation and encouragement. Above all, let us by faithful supplication secure for its continuance of the out-poured Spirit in which it had its birth. If ever the Young People's Society of Christian Endeavor shall fail, I verily believe it will be through lack of the old people's Christian endeavor on its behalf.

J. K. McLean.

SUNDAY-SCHOOL PERIODICALS OF THE METHODIST PROTESTANT CHURCH.
REV. J. F. COWAN, D. D., EDITOR.

I AM asked to briefly relate my experience with Christian Endeavor. I have an old Irish friend who pronounces it "expayrience." The new word which his revised version of the second syllable produces exactly expresses my estimate of the Christian Endeavor movement in my denomination. It is one of the best *paying* investments the church has ever made. I speak of it as an investment, but really it cost us nothing. It came to us like an obliging, generous-hearted neighbor, who offers his service on moving day; was given elbow-room; pitched in and made itself indispensable, and then asked our benediction. Of course, we gave it, but not in dismissal. It has our blessing, for we have been blessed by our societies. For we have been blessed over a thousand times, for we have over a thousand societies, and every one of them is a strictly denominational young people's society. We have made them so by the action of our General Conference. Denominational first, then interdenominational. First the cars, and then the coupling-links of the train. In the beginning, before Christian Endeavor came to us, we were looking around trying to devise a hard and fast denominational young people's society. But we are now of the opinion that we could not have devised one which could have filled the bill better than the Young People's Society of Christian Endeavor. It is just as denominational as the local churches of which it is a part, and as the Sunday-schools of the same local churches.

Personally, no one Christian institution or organization has been such a Godsend to me as the Young People's Society of Christian Endeavor. It has been an eye-opener and broadener. It has helped me to find a great deal to respect and love in my fellow-Christians of other names, where before I was disposed to mistrust and hold aloof. It has torn up the rails of my narrow-gauge Christianity and spiked down a wider and heavier track. I do not now connect at the junction of half-finger fraternity, but go through on the main track with the apostles, martyrs, and saints of all ages. My world is several times larger in circumference than it used to be. I begin to realize what Paul meant when he said, "All things are yours." I used to claim only the Methodists were mine; but the Presbyterians, the Baptists, the Congregationalists, Episcopalians, the Lutherans—all are mine. If I am discouraged over my own failures, I am encouraged over their success. If I am small and weak, they are great and strong, and my fraction is being added to theirs in the great common denominator, Christian Endeavor fellowship, so that Christianity is coming to have a unity, a solidarity, which it never had before in my conception. I can say of it and Dr. Clark as Paul did of the Philippians: "I thank my God for every remembrance of you, always, in every prayer of mine for you all, making requests with joy for your fellowship in the gospel from the first day until now."

J. F. Cowan

MEMORIAL CHURCH, LONDON, ONTARIO.
Rev. Canon Richardson, M. A., Rector.

IT is with much gratification that I avail myself of an opportunity to bear some testimony for Christian Endeavor as introductory to a work by its honored founder, Rev. Dr. Clark, designed as it is to present a general view of the wonderful movement in all lands. I rejoice to know that the church of which I am a clergyman is gradually coming to adopt Christian Endeavor, and in every instance where it has been introduced it is cordially approved and heartily indorsed. The Young People's Society of Christian Endeavor is felt by us to be a great God-inspired movement to win the young men and maidens of the professing church to Christ, and to interest them in Christian service and the spiritual work of the church.

Born by no sect, the pet child of no ecclesiastical authority, actuated by one great impulse and controlled by one prevailing idea—for Christ and the Church—it is fulfilling its blessed mission quietly and unostentatiously, and so effectively that it has already captured the nations of the earth. It has to-day more than 40,000 societies and a membership that aggregates more than two and a half millions. Persons who do not think seriously of religion and Christian life pause and ponder when they see the great tide of enthusiastic young people that are known everywhere as Christian Endeavorers, and when there is heard the refrain that comes from thousands and hundreds of thousands of young voices throughout Christendom, from America, England, Alaska, Africa, Australia, China, Japan, Spain, Germany, Turkey, India, and Samoa; a united company singing the sweet hymns of the one Church of Christ, and with fervency and zeal worshiping the One Common Lord and Master, at once curiosity passes into wonder and wonder into adoration of the "Lord and Saviour of Life," and the indifferent, the doubting, the worldly-minded are constrained to say that, after all, Christianity is not decadent nor the Bible a last year's almanac, that there is verily something in the religion of the Lord Jesus Christ.

Yes, this is the Society of Christian Endeavor, and there has been nothing like it since the establishment of the Christian Church.

J. B. Richardson

CHRIST CHURCH, WESTMINSTER BRIDGE, LONDON, ENG.
REV. F. B. MEYER, PASTOR.

THE Christian Endeavor movement in this country is growing by leaps and bounds, and is proving itself one of the greatest possible boons to the Christian church. The wonder now is that we have been expending ourselves so largely on literary and mutual improvement societies instead of appealing to the spiritual forces that were lying unawakened in so many young natures. The hour, however, came, and the man, to give expression to one of the thoughts of God, and to carve a channel through which rivers of consecration and devotion might flow to make glad the city of God. The admixture of the sexes, under the holy influences of these societies; the influence which Christian girls and youths may exert on each other; the training which the movement gives for speaking, praying, organization, and committee work, is of the highest value. The church life of the future will be healthier, gladder, more enterprising, as our Endeavorers pour into the churches, to assume, as they certainly will do, positions of great responsibility. Two perils—the Scylla and Charybdis—of the movement are to be feared; first, lest the worldly spirit should intrude and the mere social element become too absorbing; secondly, lest false doctrine should be imbued by young souls, eager for all that God can give. There are no safeguards against these other than prayer, the holding of conventions, where the Holy Spirit is honored, and right doctrines about His gracious influences are propounded, and the careful interest in the movement of the most devoted and earnest men in the churches.

But may we not specially rely on His gracious interposition, to whom the whole movement, in its origin and conduct up till now, is so evidently due?

F. B. Meyer

REV. THEODORE MONOD, D. D., PARIS.

(Translated from the French.)

CONCERNING the Christian Endeavor organization of parochial activity in my own church, where it has been on trial for more than a year, I am happy to say that it gives entire satisfaction.

The formation of that little nucleus of young believers, meeting every week for prayer and every month for renewed consecration to God's service and apportionment to every worker of his share in the common task, has been to us what "the balmy breezes" of spring are to field and forest. The influence has been felt by the whole parish. The old channels have been filled with water and other channels have been dug beside them. The Sunday-school, the visitation of the poor and sick, the attendance at public worship, the service of song, the efforts to evangelize, the increase of fellowship between church-members, our newly-instituted social meeting for the parish, all these are their progress to what we call our " grouped *activité Christienne*."

The new institution commends itself to me by proving itself at once spiritual and practical, strong and supple; I appreciate its unity and variety, and, finally, its high value as developing simultaneously a spirit of ecclesiastical loyalty and of Christian solidarity, the latter being symbolized by the common title which unites all your societies under one wide banner, while it leaves to each of them perfect liberty. I therefore give thanks to you, dear and honored brother, while I unite with you in giving thanks to Him who, through your hands, has been pleased to sow the humble seed that has grown into so large a tree.

Th. Monod.

COUNT BERNSTORFF, BERLIN.

THE Christian Endeavor Society can look back on such a great development in the United States of America that this alone makes it a duty for all earnest Christians to give the matter a conscientious consideration. We are therefore very grateful to Dr. Clark, that with his great experience in this matter he means to give a full historical sketch of what the society has hitherto achieved.

In Germany only a very short time has elapsed since we can speak of small beginnings, but even in this limited period a number of objections have already been overcome. In our age we want whole-hearted Christians; we must therefore welcome everything which helps to lead youth to a living, active Christianity. Now, it seems to us that these societies help to win young men and women to take a decided standing for the cause of the Lord. This will not only be a great blessing to the young people themselves and afford them a hold, but also be of incalculable value to the churches in gaining for them members who know in whom they believe, and who take an active part in church work. We earnestly recommend the perusal of the book to all who have the Lord's cause at heart.

A. G. v. Bernstorff.

CONTENTS.

CHAPTER I.
ENDEAVORERS BEFORE THE ENDEAVOR SOCIETY.

Who Was the Original Endeavorer?—Early Young People's Prayer-Meetings—The Ore in the Mountain—Cotton Mather's Proposals—An Early Consecration Meeting—Two Hours and Two Prayers—Young People Should be Seen and Not Heard—From an Old Record Book—Some Spartan Bands—The Amusement Idea—The Succulent Oyster, a Gastronomic Plummet, ... 43

CHAPTER II.
THE CRADLE OF THE CHRISTIAN ENDEAVOR MOVEMENT.

The Streets of Gloucester—The Cradle of Christian Endeavor—How Williston Got Its Name—A Pun and What Came of It—The Pastor's Class a Forerunner of the Endeavor Society—The Sunday-School Prayer-Meeting—The Mizpah Circle—A Revival and Its Consequences—The Week of Prayer and the Endeavor Society—Some Serious Questions—How They Were Answered, ... 49

CHAPTER III.
THE BIRTHDAY OF THE SOCIETY.

February 2, 1881—A Northern Winter Scene—Savory Odors—A Pastor's Fears—The First Constitution—An Underscored Paragraph—Then and Now—The Persistence of the Original Type—No Mincing of Words—The Original Strenuousness of the Pledge—A Deathly Stillness—Not Many Mighty—No Prigs, ... 56

CHAPTER IV.
THE HEART OF THE SOCIETY.

The Prayer-Meeting Idea—At the "Usual Hour"—The Deacon's Prayer—Winking at Gray Hairs and Wrinkles—The Warm Spot in the Room—A Service for Instruction—The Fetish of the Prayer-Meeting—A New Conception of the Prayer-Meeting—Inspiration and Fellowship Rather than Instruction—Something for Thomas and Harry, and Mary and Susan—Showing His Colors—A Place for Every One, ... 66

CHAPTER V.
EARLY DAYS AND EARLY WAYS.

A Brief Record—The First Prayer-Meeting—Doubts and Fears—The First Leader—The First Boy Leader—No Attempt at Eloquence—From America to Berlin—He Kept His Pledge—How the Boys Hold Out—The Influence of that Prayer-Meeting, . . 71

CONTENTS.

CHAPTER VI.
THE CHARTER MEMBERS.

Reading Character from Chirography—Supplementing the Reader's Insight—Some of the Charter Members, and What has Become of Them—Earnest Workers in Williston Church—Christian Workers in Other Fields—Some "Local Unions"—Y. M. C. A. Workers—Letters from College Boys—What a Brown University Student Says of College Boys—A Letter from the First President—"What Christian Endeavor Has Done for Me"—Answered by Mr. William H. Pennell, ... 74

CHAPTER VII.
THE GRAIN OF MUSTARD SEED, AND HOW IT GREW.

The New Williston Church—Some Records from My Journal—Monotony of the Records a Good Sign—How the Seed Germinated—Rev. Charles A. Dickinson—The First Newspaper Article—The Second Society—Rev. Charles Perry Mills—From Port to Port—The Third Society and its Pastor, ... 84

CHAPTER VIII.
EARLY FRIENDS OF EARLY DAYS.

The New Broom, and How it Swept—The First Anniversary—Inter-denominational Already—The Second President—The Newspaper Reports—Why it Grew—The Hectograph Pad, and How it Was Used—Its Own Recommendation, ... 89

CHAPTER IX.
OBJECTORS AND OBJECTIONS.

The Advantages of Criticism—The "Pooh-pooh," the "Bow-wow," and the "Hear-hear" Stages—Hot-House Green Peas—Aminidab Pinpoint—"Sucking the Life Blood of the Church"—An "*Imperium in Imperio*"—An Editorial—"All Society and Very Little Christian Nurture"—How Objections Have Been Refuted—"Veritas" and "Senex," and What They Had to Say—The Societies' Defenders, ... 94

CHAPTER X.
THE FIRST CONVENTION.

The Multitudinous Convention of the Present Day—A Contrast—The Throngs in England—The Societies Represented—How Far They Came Then—How Far They Come To-day—The Subjects Discussed—The Secretary—Some Early Endeavor Worthies, and What They Talked About—"Hampden '83"—The Spirit of Prophecy, . . 98

CHAPTER XI.
THE BATTLE-GROUND OF THE SOCIETY.

Some Objections to the Pledge—The Young Man and the Imaginary Desert Island—Silence in Heaven by the Space of Half an Hour—The Anxious Parent—How the Pledge Won the Victory—Its Scripturalness—The Strenuousness of the Psalmist's Pledges—The Bane of Christian Work—Duty *Versus* Feeling—Speechmakers Not Wanted—The All-Sufficient Excuse, ... 103

CONTENTS.

CHAPTER XII.
THE DISEASES OF CHILDHOOD.

Light Mortality Among the Christian Endeavor Societies—Not Decreed by Ecclesiastics—Growth from a Seed—Weakness of the Spinal Column—The Backbone Deliberately Broken by Some Pastors—How It Has Been Mended—The *Magnum Caput*—The Young Man Who "Knew It All"—Died of Severe Cold—Some Churches of the Holy Refrigerator—The Good Deacon and "the Singin' School"—The Rash of Petty Criticism—Societies That Have Been Starved to Death—Fatal Results of the Lack of Exercise—A Superabundance of Adipose Tissue—Ecclesiastical Opposition, . . 115

CHAPTER XIII.
THE SECOND CONVENTION.

An Invitation That Was Not Accepted—The Hospitable Second Parish Church—The Societies Represented—The Questions Discussed—Seven Good Rules for the Social Committee—The Right Use of Personal Pronouns—Seven Classes of People Who Should Not Be Members of the Endeavor Society—Our Rules; Are They Too Strict?—What Young Ladies May Do—The Fifty-six Societies and Where They Were Located—The Largest Two Societies—The Baby Society—The Invitation for Next Year, ... 120

CHAPTER XIV.
ENDEAVOR PIONEERS.

An Important Ally from Vermont—What He Did For the Society—A Prophecy and Its Fulfillment—Another Friend from New York—The Pioneer in the Dutch Reformed Church—A Beloved Leader of Congregationalism—A Helper from the Pacific—Some Early Friends from the Great Interior—The Free Baptist Pioneer—Good News from Societies Nearer Home—Mr. Adriance's Testimony, ... 125

CHAPTER XV.
THE EARLIEST LITERATURE OF CHRISTIAN ENDEAVOR.

Printers' Ink and What it Has Done for the Movement—A Convenient and Inexpensive Agency—Children and Church-Going—"Begin Early"—The First Article About the Endeavor Movement—"How One Church Cares for Its Young People"—How Wings were Given to this Article—*The Sunday-School Times* Contains an Article—The *Golden Rule*, *The Christian Mirror*, and the *Christian Union* Open their Columns—"How do the Boys and Girls Hold Out?"—*The Christian at Work* and the *Illustrated Christian Weekly* and Their Part in the Work—In Many Lands and Many Languages, ... 130

CHAPTER XVI.
THE FIRST BOOK ON CHRISTIAN ENDEAVOR.

A Little Tract, and What Led to it—The Work of a Summer Vacation—A Dedication from the Heart—Not a Sectarian Organization—Dr. Goodell's Testimony—Bringing in Honey—Growth Rather Than Conquest—A Lesson from Napoleon—Dr. Bushnell's Stimulating Book—Jerusalem Full of Boys and Girls—The Testimony of Eminent Divines—Practical Questions Answered—How the Book Was Circulated—Reprinted in England—Revised in 1887—A Significant Change—Principles Unchanged, . 135

CONTENTS.

CHAPTER XVII.
CHAINED LIONS.

Objections and Objectors—Honest Difficulties—Captious Criticisms—The Test of Time—"Bring Them All Into One Great Prayer-Meeting"—The Bold and Brazen Type of Piety!—Naturalness Cultivated—Scaring, Coaxing, Melting—Old Objections Reappearing—How they Melt Away—Time and Experience the Best Allies of the Endeavor Society, ... 139

CHAPTER XVIII.
THE THIRD CONVENTION.

Outside the State of Maine—The Number of Societies in 1884—A Two Days' Convention—One Hundred and Forty-two Delegates—A Connecticut Pioneer—Massachusetts' Large Delegation—Proportionate Representation—The Society in Nineteen States, One Territory, and the Dominion of Canada—Massachusetts Now the Leader—Denominational Representation—The Constitution Not Too Strict—The Papers Read and Subjects Discussed—Can We Improve the Name?—Some Stirring Addresses, 143

CHAPTER XIX.
NEWS FROM ACROSS THE SEAS.

Foo Chow and Honolulu—Good News from Ceylon—Precious Pearl—Christian Endeavor Hens and Trees—Beginnings in Hawaii—The First Society in Honolulu—Its Vicissitudes and Its Victories—The Beginning of the Work in China—Mr. Ling and His Address, ... 148

CHAPTER XX.
OUR EARLY FELLOWSHIP.

Inevitable and Natural—The Use of Anniversaries—Geographical and Municipal Lines—State Pride and Patriotism—Natural Divisions—The Earliest State Unions—The Beginning of City Unions—A Simple Program—Autumn Leaves in Vallambrosa—The Roots of these Union Meetings—"That they all may be one"—The Beginning of State and Local Unions—Their Prominent Place in Christian Endeavor—Where the First State Union was Formed—The First Little Convention—The Call of the Pastor and Presidents—How Mr. Manchester was "Loaded"—How the Name was Obtained—Dr. Twitchell's Account of the First Local Union—The Birthplace—How the Idea Spread—The Advantages of Local Unions—To God be the Glory, ... 151

CHAPTER XXI.
AN EPOCH-MAKING CONVENTION.

At Ocean Park—Two Hundred and Fifty-three Societies—Massachusetts Still in the Lead—Why the Convention was Memorable—The Beginnings of the United Society—A Matter of Far-reaching Influence—The Guiding Hand of God—No Forced Growth—No Preconcerted Boom—The Need of a General Secretary—The Chosen Man—How Mr. Hill Distinguished Himself—Generous Societies—The First President of the United Society—Passing into History, ... 158

CONTENTS.

CHAPTER XXII.

GAINING FRIENDS.

Why the First Secretary Resigned—Who was Chosen in His Place—A Faithful Friend—Mr. Hill's Address—Prophecy as Well as Definition—His Assistant Pastor—The Treasurer of the United Society and how he was Qualified for his Work—Mr. Grose and Mr. Brokaw—How Dr. Boynton Signalized his Advent to the Endeavor Field—Other Friends of the Movement—In the Cumberland Presbyterian Denomination—Men who Deserve the Thanks of all Christian Endeavorers, ... 165

CHAPTER XXIII.

AN EFFECTIVE ORGANIZATION—THE UNITED SOCIETY.

No Ecclesiastical Functions—A Very Simple Organization—Not a Board of Control—A Bureau of Information—What the United Society has Done—The Movement Saved from Disaster—Business Reduced to a Minimum—Entire Harmony—Eminent Men who have Seen Eye to Eye—No Desire for Personal Aggrandizement—The First Quarters of the United Society—Subsequent Removal—The Board of Trustees and its Meeting—Other United Societies—Early Financial Struggles—Not Wrapped in the Lap of Luxury—Some Well-to-do Friends—A Generous Subscription—The Largest Contributors—Constituting Life Members—Precious Pearl a Life Member—The Ingenuity of the Finance Committee—The Deepest Financial Straits—A Dark Outlook—A Happy Thought and what Came of it—Christian Endeavor Day and its Contributions—What is Done with the Money—Modest Expenses—A Missionary Day—Living Up to Our Principles—Giving Through the Regular Channels, ... 171

CHAPTER XXIV.

THE FIRST SARATOGA CONVENTION.

Heaven-Breathing Devotion—"Do You Remember Saratoga?"—A Fragrant Memory—The Strength of Christian Endeavor—No Local or Provincial Affair—Eight Denominations in Christian Endeavor—From the Land of Steady Habits—Dr. Deems' Sermon—Some Notable Addresses—Keep Your Colors Flying—An Improbable Prophecy and How It Was Fulfilled—Self-Entertainment—The First Early Morning Prayer-Meeting, ... 178

CHAPTER XXV.

THE SOCIETY'S MOTHER AND HER SISTERS.

The Traditional Stepmother—Part of the Mother's Life—Not a Poor Relation or a Young Relation—What is the Church?—Why the Constitution was Amended—Over-Tired Workers—Has the Sunday Evening Service Been Reinforced?—Is the Prayer-Meeting Stronger?—Facts and Figures Which Bear on the Subject—Some Sisters of the Society—A Hundred Years Ago—Robert Raikes and His Endeavor—The Sunday-School Committee and What It May Do—The Mission Circle—Enthusiasm for Missions—The Mothers' Endeavor Society—The Best-Loved Little Sister of All—A Brotherly Sister—The Y. M. C. A. and Christian Endeavor—The Brotherhood of Andrew and Philip, ... 184

CONTENTS.

CHAPTER XXVI.
THE SECOND SARATOGA CONVENTION.

Good-Natured Rivalry—Dr. Hoyt's Inspiring Sermon—Other Friends Added to the Movement—Rev. B. Fay Mills and His Address—High Ideals—Old Friends as well as New—An Important Action—The Trend of Events—An Unmistakable Call of Providence—Saying Good-bye to the Pastor—Twenty-three Hundred and Fourteen Societies Recorded—Six Thousand Dollars Raised—The Connecticut Penny—Another Pleasant Incident, ... 193

CHAPTER XXVII.
THE GOLDEN RULE AND OTHER ENDEAVOR PAPERS.

Mr. Boynton's Resolution—The Checkered Experience of a Newspaper—Things Which Cost Money—The Change from a Blanket Sheet—Early Editors and What They Did for the Paper—Large Accessions to the Editorial Force—The Junior *Golden Rule*—What the Papers Have Done for the Cause—Deacon Burnham's Connection With the Paper—Other Endeavor Papers, ... 200

CHAPTER XXVIII.
ENDEAVOR SONGS AND SINGERS.

At the Cross, at the Cross—" Faith is the Victory "—The Use of Hymn-Singing—Silence Not a Virtue to Be Cultivated—Dr. Rankin's Endeavor Hymn—Mr. Dickinson's Beautiful Hymn—How It Happened to Be Written—How They Sing in Australia—A Lesson Which America May Learn, ... 211

CHAPTER XXIX.
THE SOCIETY AND THE YOUNG MEN.

Incredible Statements—Young Men and the Endeavor Pledge—Young Men in the First Society—No End of Prigs—The Great Conventions and Young Men—"A Little Chariot for a Pony Team "—The Gap Between the Sunday-School and the Church—No Wheedling, Coaxing Tones—Not for Ice-Cream and Syllabub—" Pie and Cake Affairs "—Outspoken Devotion to Christ, ... 217

CHAPTER XXX.
THE SOCIETY AND THE YOUNG WOMAN.

More Young Women Than Young Men—Prejudice Against Union Meetings—The Young Man of Constantinople and His Ungallant Remark—The Spiritual Tact of Women—Her Work on the Lookout Committee—The Young Woman and the Missionary Committee—Taking Part in Meeting—How a Heroic Young Woman Kept Her Pledge—Miss Sewall's Words to Her Sisters—Some Ladies Who Have Made Endeavor Meetings Memorable—New Chapters in the Acts of the Apostles—Dr. Wayland Hoyt's Memorable Address—How St. Paul Has Been Misinterpreted—The Evil of a Wrong Interpretation of Scriptures—Corinthian Women and American Women—A Typical Prayer-Meeting of Old—The Women Were Present—Do Not Let the Women Lal, Lal, Lal—Teaching and Usurping Authority—What She Actually Does in the Christian Endeavor Prayer-Meeting—Read Again the First Chapter of Acts, ... 221

CONTENTS.

CHAPTER XXXI.
THE FIRST CAMPAIGN IN ENGLAND.

Slight Variations in Color and Odor—The Similarity of Christian Endeavor—The First Invitation from Across the Seas—" An American Fad "—" English Stolidity and American Precocity "—Some Pioneers in England—Christian Endeavor and Lawn Tennis—A Missionary's Testimony—A Meeting in the City Temple—Some Startling Figures from a Member of Parliament—How They Can Be Explained—The Meeting of the Boundary Lane Society—An Excruciating Pause—In Manchester—A Meeting in Action—An Invitation from Mr. Spurgeon—What Amused the Students—The Sunday-school Union and Its Efficient Aid—The Earliest Champion of Christian Endeavor in England—Sympathetic English Audiences—A Brief Visit to Paris—Dr. McAll and Mr. Greig, ... 230

CHAPTER XXXII.
THE FIRST GREAT CONVENTION.

In Battery D—Forebodings and Headshakings—Westward the Star of Christian Endeavor—Some Magnificent Addresses—Pansy's Story—Encircling the Globe—New York in the Lead—Three Hundred and Ten Thousand Members—Reports from Different Sections—Our Emigrant Population—Five Million Boys Wanted—Systematic Bible Study—" Not to be Ministered Unto, But to Minister," 240

CHAPTER XXXIII.
BADGES AND BANNERS.

The Badge and Its Significance—Mr. Grose's Story of the Badge—Mr. Woolley's Part—Ribbon Badges—The Badge-Banner and Its Significance—Captured by New York—Taken by Pennsylvania—Sent Across the Sea—Pennsylvania's Consolation—Oklahoma and Delaware—The Real Significance of the Badge-Banners, ... 248

CHAPTER XXXIV.
THE SOCIETY AS AN EVANGELIST.

The Traditional Picture of Evangelist—How Many Endeavorers Have Joined the Churches—The Idea of Associate Membership—No List of Black Sheep—An Honor to Be an Associate Member—Yet Only the First Step—Are You Facing Up Hill or Down?—How Pastors Have Used the Pledge—A Large Pond to Fish In—No Extravagant Claim—Special Evangelistic Efforts—Pointing Young People to the Wicket Gate, 253

CHAPTER XXXV.
INTERDENOMINATIONALISM.

A New Word—Not Undenominational—The Difference Between the Terms—Interdenominationalism a Modern Fad—What Sectarians Think of It—Looking Over the Denominational Fences—In Honor Preferring One Another—No Doctrinal Union—No Union on the Basis of Church Government—But a Union for Service—The Two Most Widely Sung Songs—Christ's Wonderful Prayer—When the Society Became Interdenominational—Sectarian Objections—Extraordinary Misstatements—Jaundice and Untruthful Remarks—Their Refutation—The Denominations Which Lead—The Society Perfectly Adapted to All Denominations—Testimonies at the Pastors' Hour—A Glorious Consecration Meeting, ... 257

CONTENTS.

CHAPTER XXXVI.

THE DEVELOPMENT OF STATE SPIRIT.

"Our State for Christ"—A Distinctive Feature of the Great Conventions—How the Badges and Banners Contribute—Maryland's Song—"Old Kentucky Home"—Washington's Invitation Song—"Tramp, Tramp, Tramp"—Baltimore's Song—California, '95—The Massachusetts Christian Endeavor Hymn—A Stirring Convention Rally Song—Affectionate Pride in the State—Our Country for Christ, ... 265

CHAPTER XXXVII.

THE PHILADELPHIA CONVENTION.

Great Expectations—Over 7,000 Societies—New York Still the Banner State—A Cordial Address of Welcome—New Friends who have Since been Prominent—The Convention Sermon—Wonderful Progress in Every Direction—What the Papers Had to Say of the Convention—"The Largest Delegate Religious Assembly that Christendom Has Yet Witnessed "—The City Taken by Storm—The President and the Postmaster-General—General Howard's Address—Some " Philadelphia Mintings," 272

CHAPTER XXXVIII.

THE RISE OF THE MISSIONARY SPIRIT.

The World for Christ—Dr. Pierson's Remarkable Statement—Mr. Robert T. Wilder on the Missionary Uprising—Dr. Gifford's Stirring Words—Mr. Mershon's Missionary Sum in Arithmetic—A Great Awakening—Two Cents a Week for Missions—An Enthusiasm Which Never Wanes — $250,000 in 1893-4 — A Million for Missions—What the Societies Are Doing for Missions—A Montreal Society—Boys and Girls in Mission Schools and Colleges—A Revered and Beloved Leader—What a Society Did—Dr. Gordon's Plan—A Wise Suggestion—How the Denominations are Carrying it Out—Many Missionary Enterprises—The Significance of These Facts—Presbyterian Efforts —What the Reformed Dutch Endeavorers are Doing—Christian Endeavor Churches —The Disciples of Christ and Their Endeavor Enterprises—The Work of the Young Congregationalists—Sunday-school Endeavor Missionaries—At the Fountain Head, ... 281

CHAPTER XXXIX.

WORK FOR THE BOYS AND GIRLS.

The Necessity of the Movement—Tabor, Iowa, and What Occurred There—The Germ of the Junior Movement—The Faithful Pastor and His Work—His Own Account of the First Society—Why Should There be Junior Societies—What the Junior Society is Not—Primary Sunday-School Methods Not Adapted—Not for Pouring in but for Drawing Out—Not Playing at Work but Work—Some Junior Leaders—A Leader in New Jersey—A Leader from St. Louis—A Wisconsin Leader—A Connecticut Leader Transplanted to New York—The Better Half Again—Too Numerous to Mention—A Splendid Society in Australia—Some Missionary Juniors—" The Dear Home Land Across the Sea "—The Junior Society of Two—The Prayer Shelf—Five Pennies as Good as a Nickel, ... 292

CONTENTS.

CHAPTER XL.
THE ATTITUDE OF THE DENOMINATIONS.

Not Spoiled by Flattery—Beginning to Receive Recognition—The Harder Struggles of Sunday-Schools to Obtain a Footing—A Day of Fasting and Prayer Against Sunday-Schools—The Y. M. C. A. and Its Early Struggles—The Presbyterian Church and Its Attitude Toward Christian Endeavor—The Friends as Cordial Allies—The Reformed Presbyterians in Christian Endeavor—The Cumberland Presbyterians always Cordial—Methodist Protestants and Their Kindly Attitude—The Disciples of Christ and How They Accepted the Society—Denominational Leaders Identified with Christian Endeavor—The African Churches in the Movement, ... 309

CHAPTER XLI.
ST. LOUIS CONVENTION.

The Two Rival Claimants—How the Question Was Decided—From 7,600 to Over 11,000—The Graphic Report of the Opening Scene—The Sermon again a Great Event—Some Eloquent Addresses—The Advent of the New Secretary—His Introduction to the Work—The Marriage of the Flags, ... 314

CHAPTER XLII.
TEN YEARS OLD.

The Tenth Birthday and How It Was Celebrated—Going Back Home—Williston Church on the Night of the Anniversary—The Cradle In Which the Child Was Rocked—The Early Prayer-Meeting—Some Admirable and Fraternal Speeches—Mr. Pratt's Address—Dr. Burrell's Famous Poem, ... 328

CHAPTER XLIII.
ON ENGLISH SOIL ONCE MORE.

Slow Progress in the Mother Land—The Fostering Care of the Sunday-School Union—Another Invitation—A Run Through Italy—The First English Convention—Some English Endeavorers—An Address With the Right Ring—The Significance of this Convention—The Outlook for the Future—Some Devoted Endeavorers—The Two Weeks' Campaign—Going our Several Ways—Mr. Dickinson's Appointments—Mr. Boynton's Work—Mr. Hill's Tour—Coming Together in Cumberland—Under the Pines of Keswick—English and American Audiences—The Reflex Influence on America—The Endeavor Society No Temporary and Provincial Affair, ... 335

CHAPTER XLIV.
THE CONVENTION OF THE TWIN CITIES.

The Actual Registration—The Opening Scene of the Convention—A Growing Task—Some Hearty Addresses of Welcome—The Secretary's Report an Inspiring Document—The Great Increase of the Past Year—Why the Color Came to His Cheeks—The Famous Pastor's Hour—Thrilling Addresses—Dr. Rondthaler's Open Parliament—His Flowery Remark—Dr. Deems on the "Soo" Line—"Beautiful Oklahoma"—The Next Convention—Good-Natured Montrealers—An Historic Thunderstorm—No Panic in an Endeavor Convention, ... 341

CONTENTS.

CHAPTER XLV.
THE SIGNS OF NEW IDEAS.

Invented or Adopted—From the Standard Dictionary—" Endeavor," " Endeavorer," etc.—" Lookout "—" Sunshine Committee "—The Signs of New Ideas—Combinations of Words—" The Surprise Committee "—" Floating Societies "—" Barrack Societies "—Phrases of Work That Tell of Spiritual Energy—Endeavor Outside of the Endeavor Society—Introducing the Principles Into Other Church Work—What the Society Has Done for the Church Prayer-Meeting—Sometimes Saving it from Decay—A Christian Endeavor Church, not a Christian Endeavor Denomination—The Burlington Plan, 351

CHAPTER XLVI.
ON SEA AND SHORE.

A Wild Prediction—Some Touching Stories—The Wreck of the "Galatin "—How He Saved His Pledge—The Japanese Society and the Floating Society—Miss Antoinette P. Jones and Her Work—How the Work Began, How It Extended,—Another Clause in the Pledge—Introduction Cards—An Endeavor Social for Jack Tar—Throw Out the Life-Line—Ringing Them Up—Mr. Wood and His Mission—Junior Endeavorers of the Navy Yard—The Character of the Sailor, ... 358

CHAPTER XLVII.
IN UNEXPECTED PLACES.

Neglected Mission Districts—In the Slums—A State Prison Society—A Pathetic Message—in Asylums and Hospitals—Among New York Policemen—Among the Life Savers—Some Earnest Workers—Christian Endeavor in the Army—Good News from the Frontier—Among the National Guards—Commercial Travelers and Their Endeavor—The Travelers' Union—What the Members Promise—A Touching Testimony—For the Deaf and Dumb—Among the Italians and Bohemians—Hungarians and Poles—Mexicans and Chinese—Mr. Ju Hawk's Address—" God Be With You " in Cree—Christianizing White People—What Some Christian Endeavor Indians Are Doing, 368

CHAPTER XLVIII.
LATER LITERATURE OF THE MOVEMENT.

" Young People's Prayer-Meetings in Theory and Practice "—" Ways and Means for Christian Endeavor "—" Danger Signals "—" Looking Out on Life "—" The Mossback Correspondence "—" Christian Endeavor Saints "—" How " and " Why "—" The Philosophy of the Christian Endeavor Movement "—" Golden Rule Meditations "—" Social Evenings "—" Business "—" Endeavor Day Exercises "—" Foreman Jennie "—" Endeavor Doin's Down to the Corners "—Pansy's Books—" Our Town "—" The Iron-Clad Pledge "—Mrs. Hill's Works—" Attractive Truths in Lesson and Story "—" A Decade of Christian Endeavor "—Many Useful Pamphlets—The Society's Critic—The Hundredth Man—A Damnable Heresy—An Awkward and Meaningless Term—Unitarian Tendency—Perversion of Facts—A Theological Professor and What He Has to Say—Objecting to the International Bible—A Curious Leaflet—It Wags the Dog—Sectarian Criticism—The Impotency of Such Attacks—A Welcome Kind of Criticism, . . 377

CONTENTS.

CHAPTER XLIX.

THE NEW YORK CONVENTION.

A Magnificent Meeting—Opening Scenes—How the Endeavorers Came In—Some of the Distinguished Speakers—A Ripple of Excitement—Some Distinguished Statesmen—The Postmaster-General and the Secretary of State—Hon. Chauncey Depew—"Cleveland, '94"—The World Around—Simultaneous Meetings—Denominational Rallies—A Marvelous Consecration Meeting, ... 393

CHAPTER L.

SOME CONVENTIONS BENEATH THE SOUTHERN CROSS.

An Invitation and What Came of It—Cordial Greetings Everywhere—Six Delightful Weeks—A Christian Endeavor Pennant—Elaborate Programs—The *Australian Christian World's* View of the Meetings—The *Golden Link* and Its Account of the Victoria Convention—Delightful Meetings in Adelaide—A Comparison with the Salvation Army—The Importance of the Pledge—A Pioneer of South Australia—In Queensland's Capital—The Singing of Australian Endeavorers—The Monster Tea, ... 402

CHAPTER LI.

TYPICAL ENDEAVOR SCENES ON FOREIGN SHORES.

The Same Enthusiasm the World Around—A Glimpse in Canton—Some Beautiful Emblems—How Mr. Yeung Led the Meeting—A Glimpse in Shanghai—A Printers' Endeavor Society—No Printers' Devils—The Juniors of the South Gate—The Junior Society and the Baby Towers—A Glimpse in Japan—Some Things That a Traveler Learns—Is Christian Endeavor Fitted for Japan?—Some Reasons for Believing That It Is—A Glimpse in India—The Constitution and Its Translation—A Scene in the Woman's Union Mission—Some Endeavorers of Bombay—In the Land of the Sultan—Some Queer Hieroglyphics—How an American Endeavor Society Multiplied Itself—Think of the Possibilities—A Scene in San Sebastian—A Meeting in Paris—Union of French and English in Christian Endeavor—A Harmonious Variety, ... 410

CHAPTER LII.

THE MONTREAL CONVENTION.

The Title of the Chapter—The Montreal Convention—The Preliminary Meetings—The Opening Session—The Wise and Witty Welcomes—The Booming Cannon, and What They stood For—Junior Society Work and Its Importance—The Statistics of the Past Year—Some Eloquent Addresses—The First Signer of the Junior Pledge—An Unhappy Incident—All's Well that Ends Well—Some Memorable Consecration Meetings—A Sudden Death—Generous Endeavorers—The White Caps, and What They Did—The Press Committee—A Delightful Excursion—A Happy End, ... 424

CONTENTS.

CHAPTER LIII.
THE GOOD CITIZENSHIP MOVEMENT.

How It Began—How National Conventions Sound the Keynote—The Keynote of the Montreal Convention—What Endeavorers May Do—Not Boycotters—Law-Abiding Citizens—" Go Tell That Tiger "—A Fluttering Bit of Paper—An Endeavorer on Duty—At the Dram-Shop—On Guard Respecting the Sabbath—" God is Marching On "—How the Fire Kindled—Dr. Parkhurst's Probe—Robert Ross, of Troy—Good Citizenship Clubs, ... 436

CHAPTER LIV.
A MISSIONARY REVIVAL.

A Great Impetus to Missionary Earnestness—Another Important Enlargement—Come Over and Help Us—A New Crusade—Missionary Literature—A Missionary Meeting—Joseph and His Brethren—" Give, Give, Give "—Maintaining Our Institutions—Missions and Modern Civilization—The Missionary Extension Course—Golden-Rule Mission Clubs—Quarter of a Million Dollars for Missions—The Reflex Influence on American Life, 443

CHAPTER LV.
THE CLEVELAND CONVENTION.

Unfavorable Omens—The Hard Times and the Strike—Eugene V. Debs or Grover Cleveland—No Postponement—A Bitter Disappointment—A Graphic Report—The Preliminary Meetings—Governor McKinley's Welcome—Some New Features—Something for the Eye as Well as the Ear—Banners and Diplomas—The Roll of Honor—An Address in Chinese—Jonas Spotted Bear—The Sermons Once More—What the Papers Thought of It—Something More than Gush—Farewell Words, ... 448

CHAPTER LVI.
THE DEVELOPMENTS OF 1894.

A Year of Great Conventions—Secretary Baer's Journey—In the Far South—" The Best Convention Ever Held "—Nuggets from the Different States—England's Whitsuntide Convention—Denominational Endeavors—The Missionary Extension Course—Good Citizenship Work—A Break in Health, and What Came of It—Two Months of Complete Rest—Beginnings in Germany—A Visit to Scandinavia—In the Metropolitan Tabernacle Again—In Wales—In Ireland and Scotland—Home Once More, . . . 463

CHAPTER LVII.
PRACTICAL WORK AND PRACTICAL WORKERS.

Saying Verses and Singing Hymns—No Mean Accomplishment—The Widening Scope of Christian Endeavor—Some Loving Efforts—Some Odd Committees—A Famous Sunday Breakfast Association—How it Works and What it Has Accomplished—Comfort Bags for the Life Savers—Many Services Sustained—A Good Idea from Rochester—Saving the Stranger—An Evangelistic Committee and its Work—What the Ushers Did—Helpers in the Song Service—A Jubilant Hymn, ... 470

CONTENTS.

CHAPTER LVIII.

CHRISTIAN ENDEAVOR IN EUROPE AND AUSTRALIA.

The Story as Told By the Workers Themselves—Early Days and Early Ways in Great Britain—The British Birthplace of the Society—A Christian Endeavor County—The Influence of "Pansy"—The First Christian Endeavorer of Great Britain—The Pathetic Letter From His Death-Bed—The Advance of Christian Endeavor in the Land of the Covenant—Progress in Ireland—Fitted to the Welsh Character—Beginnings in France—Great Advance of Recent Years—The Action of the General Synod—How the Work Began in Germany—Interesting Meetings in Berlin—Fitted to Hungary and Its Needs—Christian Endeavor in Spain—In Switzerland—Mrs. Gulick's Interesting Account—The Wonderful Advance in Australia—Endeavorers Under the Southern Cross—The Welcome to Endeavor in the Land of the Kangaroo, ... 477

CHAPTER LIX.

CHRISTIAN ENDEAVOR IN ASIA AND AFRICA.

Beginnings in China—The Story as Told by One of the First Endeavorers—Great Advances in Foo Chow—A Wider Outlook by the Secretary—Constantly Increasing Success—The Work in Japan—Told by the President of the United Society for Japan—"Wherever Formed They Prove a Blessing"—Christian Endeavor in India—An Evangelistic Committee and Its Work—In Madura and the Marathi Missions—Good News from Calcutta—The Interest of the Redcoats—A Few Words from Persia—From the Land of Persecution—The Sultan's Objection to Christian Endeavor—Beginnings in Africa—Good News from Cape Colony—How Christian Endeavor Flourishes in Liberia, . 490

CHAPTER LX.

IN MEXICO, SOUTH AMERICA, AND THE ISLANDS OF THE SEA.

A Natural Grouping—Pioneers in Mexico—Nine Years to a Day—Still Making Progress—A Creditable Periodical—Difficulties in South America—The First Society in Chile—The Spread of the Cause—In the Sandwich Islands—Good News from Honolulu—Societies in Honolulu's Schools—On the Other Islands of the Group—In the South Seas—The First Samoan Endeavor Society—Its Perils and Its Triumphs—The Blessings of the Prayer Chain—The Work Still Advancing, ... 506

CHAPTER LXI.

THE BOSTON CONVENTION OF 1895.

The Story of the Boston Convention—A Difficult Story to Tell—The Inadequacy of the English Language—Boston's First Great Convention—How Things Worked Together for Good—The Public Gardens and Boston's Decorations—The Convention Weather—The Boston Papers and Their Welcome—The Motormen and the Police—A Little Story from a Saloon—Historic Pilgrimages—The Jingo Spirit and Why it was Absent—Many Delegates from Abroad—The Wonderful Evangelistic Services—Christian Citizenship and Reform—A Missionary Convention—The World's Union and How it was Formed—A Brief Story of the Days—Tents "Williston" and "Endeavor"—The Growth of the Year—The Denominational Rallies—The Responsibilities of Success—Some Rare Excursions—A Quiet Sabbath—The Scholarship of the World for Christ—The Greatest of Conventions—"Arouse Ye, Arouse Ye, O Servants of God," 512

CONTENTS.

CHAPTER LXII.
WASHINGTON, '96.

Its Distinguishing Characteristic—Spiritual Power—Difficulties in the Way—The Wrecked Tent—The Registration—A Delightful Conference—Strong Resolutions—Mr. Baer's Eloquent Figures—How the Denominations Stand—The Roll of Honor—Before the Capitol—A Wonderful Sight—Men's Meetings and Women's Meetings—The Closing Day—The World's Unions—A Deaf and Dumb Forerunner—Crystallizations—Our Platform, ... 533

LIST OF ILLUSTRATIONS.

	PAGE
Autographs of Charter Members,	75, 77, 79
Austin, Mrs. George G.,	81
Armstrong, Carrie,	83
Agge, Franklin,	90
Aminidab Pinpoint, Ph. D.,	95
Active Membership Pledge,	104
Adriance, Rev. S. W.,	165
Alden, Mrs. ("Pansy"),	224
Audrews, Prof. W. W.,	323
Atkinson, F. G.,	343
Alameda County Delegates, California,	363
Allen, J. W.,	400
Ayer, A. A.,	427
Ames, H. B.,	427
Arrival of Michigan Delegation (Cleveland Convention),	450
Allen, Charles E.,	306
Allen, Thomas H.,	307
Atkinson, C. J.,	326
Altemus, Edward,	327
Alexander, William G.,	327
Allen, J. Burns,	334
Anderson, T. G.,	388
Austin, E. C.,	376
A Christian Endeavor Family, Japan,	497
Burrell, Rev. David,	42
Birthplace of Young People's Society Christian Endeavor,	59
Barker, Mrs. J. L.,	81
Barnes, Harris,	83
Bennett, Abbie,	83
Brokaw, Rev. R. W.,	127
Burnham, Rev. M.,	147
Boynton, Rev. N.,	168
Burnham, Deacon Choate,	206
Berner, Rev. G.,	208
Barrows, Rev. John H.,	242
Beckley, Rev. J. T.,	272
Bowers, Henry M.,	273
Benson, Gustavus S. J.,	273
Bender, William A.,	273
Baldwin, Tom C.,	274
Baer, Mrs. John Willis,	293
Brooks, Raymond C.,	297
Bradshaw, Miss Ida,	301
Brookfield, Miss Caroline M.,	301
Boys' Junior Society, Bethany Presbyterian Church,	305
Bitting, Rev. W. C.,	318
Baer, John Willis,	320
Breg, William G.,	343
Brown, Miss Jessie H.,	380
Barraclough, W. H.,	404
Bird, Rev. Alfred,	404
Barnard, H. A.,	427
Bell, Arthur F.,	427
Barton, Rev. J. H.,	306
Belt, W. H. G.,	306
Belt, W. G.,	306
Barber, Rev. Clarence H.,	306
Barber, T. P.,	306
Blincoe, William,	306
Ball, Fred S.,	306
Bishop, Frank O.,	307
Burns, J. H.,	307
Boughner, H. D.,	307
Buwer, Rev. W. W.,	326
Bagly, Rev. Edw. B.,	326
Belt, Mary E.,	326
Binford, Rev. M. M.,	326
Black, Miss Sadie E.,	327
Black, Rev. Wm. H.,	327
Breed, J. Howard,	334
Bitting, W. W.,	334
Babcock, Rev. Maltbie B.,	388
Bryon, Benjamin,	388
Blackwell, H. S.,	388
Barker, Herbert W.,	388
Bacon, Miss Carrie L.,	401
Blecher, Rev. Frederick,	483
Bentley, Rev. W. P.,	493
Buss, Fanny,	507
Bartholomew, W. F.,	513
Cuyler, Rev. Theodore L.,	47
Chapel where First Christian Endeavor Meeting was held,	67
Cousins, Miss Carrie J.,	81
Cruzan, Rev. J. A.,	149
Childs, W. H.,	153
Congress Park, Saratoga, N. Y.,	193
Coleman, George W.,	207
Chapman, Rev. J. Wilbur,	278
Christian Endeavor Church No. 4, Grand Rapids, Mich.,	289
Christian Endeavor Church No. 2, Wakonda, South Dakota,	290
Coleman, Mrs. George W.,	293
Cowan, Rev. J. W.,	295
Cannon, J. M.,	315
Conant, Edw. M.,	343
Catlin, Lieutenant E. H.,	371
Caldwell, Charles,	399
Cole, Parsells,	399
Cruikshank, James A.,	399
Closs, Rev. W. J. L.,	648
Clark, Rev. William,	404
Chinese Doctor,	417
Chinese Junior Society,	413
Comstock, Anthony,	432
Christian Endeavor Exhibit at the World's Fair,	442
Cleveland Convention Tent (Exterior),	451

LIST OF ILLUSTRATIONS.

	PAGE
Cleveland Convention Tent (Interior),	451
Cheesman, J. E.,	455
Crawford, Rev. C. H.,	306
Chamberlain, E. G.,	306
Caskey, Robert,	306
Conner, L. A.,	306
Curtis, F. A.,	306
Cassels, A. Gordon,	307
Collier, Mrs. Robert,	307
Coates, W. A.,	326
Conibear, Rev. G. A.,	326
Carlisle, Rev. John W. F.,	326
Cromer, Rev. J. C.,	326
Cristy, Rev. A. B.,	326
Clark, Frank N.,	327
Carier, Rev. W. O.,	327
Cutts, Charles,	327
Carr, H. Willis,	327
Chapman, Joseph, Jr.,	327
Clark, Ester A.,	327
Clark, E. B.,	327
Croxall, F. H.,	388
Chapman, W. H.,	388
Craft, Mrs. Josephus,	401
Clarke-Duncas, S. C.,	376
Chaplin, Rev. W. Knight,	478
Chinese Delegates, California State Convention,	493
Chinese Christian,	493
Convention in China (June, 1894),	493
Christian Endeavor Convention, China (June, 1894),	493
Christian Endeavorers, Kobe School, Japan,	495
Christian Endeavorer, Tottori, Japan,	496
Christian Endeavor in Liberia,	504
Christian Endeavor Society of Kamahamaha Seminary, Honolulu,	509
Capen, Samuel B.,	513
Crockett, A. J.,	513
Committee of '96,	532
Church, W. A. H.,	532
Clark, Charles S.,	532
Capitol, The,	533
Dille, Rev. E. E.,	42
Dickinson, Rev. Charles A.,	42
Darby, Rev. W. J.,	42
Dunning, Miss Bessie,	81
Dodge, Miss Annie L.,	81
Davis, Mrs. Alice P.,	83
Dwight Place Church, New Haven, Conn.,	157
Deems, Rev. C. F.,	180
Doyle, Rev. S. H.,	210
Dickinson, Mrs. Charles A.,	293
Dunning, Rev. A. E.,	331
Daniels, Franc B.,	342
Dean, Fred W.,	343
Dixon, Rev. A. C.,	394
Davis, H. M.,	399
Darsie, Rev. S. L.,	455
Driscoll, Rev. E. A.,	306
Deland, Rev. William C.,	306
Douglas, Miss Maud P.,	307
Darnell, Mrs. J. H.,	307
Dart, Charles B.,	307
Dill, H. E.,	307
Dewhurst, A. E.,	307
Dawes, W. R.,	307
Dillon, R. W.,	326

	PAGE
Deland, Rev. William C.,	326
Dowman, Rev. C. E.,	327
Davis, H. M.,	388
Denis, L. B.,	388
Dodson, Rev. J. R.,	388
Doane, Rev. John,	401
Davidson, F. F.,	513
Dixon, H. G.,	513
Ellis, William T.,	205
Exposition Building, St. Louis, Mo.,	314
Excursion Steamers, St. Louis, Mo.,	321
Essenwein, Rev. J. Berg,	381
Ellis, John D.,	306
Ewton, John A.,	307
Elderdice, Rev. Hugh L.,	326
Evans, Samuel C., Jr.,	326
Ellis, Elwood O.,	326
Ellis, Mrs. Bessie De Morse,	327
Eliot, Willard,	327
Eshman, Prof. A. W.,	327
Eaton, Mrs. James D., Chihuahua, Mexico,	506
Fac simile of Original Constitution,	61, 62, 63, 64, 65
Fac simile of Pledge, Japanese,	106
Fac simile of Pledge, Telugu,	106
Fac simile of Pledge, Armeno-Turkish,	108
Fac simile of Pledge, Tamil,	108
Fac simile of Pledge, Dakota-Indian,	109
Fac simile of Pledge, Danish,	110
Fac simile of Pledge, Malagasy,	110
Fac simile of Pledge, Dutch,	111
Fac simile of Pledge, Spanish,	111
Fac simile of Pledge, Bohemian,	112
Fac simile of Pledge, Bengali,	112
Fac simile of Pledge, Chinese,	113
Fac simile of Pledge, Swedish,	113
Fac simile of Pledge, Urdu,	114
Fac simile of Pledge, German,	114
Free Baptist Camp Grounds,	159
First Methodist Episcopal Church, Saratoga, N. Y.,	179
Fac simile of Hymns,	214
Fac simile of Hymns,	215
Fallows, Bishop,	242
Frederick, A. H.,	276
First Regiment Armory (Interior),	279
Fulton, Rev. A. A.,	284
Farnam, Mrs. Dr.,	293
Fowle, Mrs. J. L.,	293
Ferguson, W. S.,	313
Floating Society Program,	358
Frye, Charles J.,	399
Fergusson, G. Tower,	306
French, Rev. C.,	306
Fuller, C. C.,	306
France, Charles L.,	307
Fisher, Lillian M.,	307
Fitch, N. B.,	307
Fodtheringham, T. T.,	326
Foss, V. Richard,	326
Fiske, William T.,	326
Fowle, Rev. J. L.,	326
Furbeck, Rev. George W.,	326
Foster, P. S.,	326
Fraser, Rev. J. G.,	326
Fleck, Rev. E. Lee,	326
Fuller, C. C.,	327
Freeman, W. W.,	388

LIST OF ILLUSTRATIONS.

	PAGE
French, Charles W.,	388
Flaws, Anna W.,	376
First Japanese Convention,	495
First M. E. Church, Monrovia, Liberia,	504
Fac simile of Samuel Francis Smith's Hymn,	530
Floral Design in Public Gardens, Boston, Mass.,	531
Grose, Rev. H. B.,	42
Garland, Edmund,	81
Garland, Miss Anna M.,	81
Gould, Samuel C.,	83
Goodwin, George E.,	83
Goodell, Dr. C. L.,	127
Gifford, Rev. O. P.,	164
Grose, Prof. H. H.,	168
Golden Rule Office,	202
Golden Rule Office,	203
Graff, George B.,	207
Gordon, Dr. A. J.,	285
Gruman, Grove A.,	343
Great Northern Bridge and Falls of St. Anthony (Minneapolis),	345
Gates, President Merrill E.,	394
Gray, George,	404
Gray, Randolph S.,	404
Grafton, A. B.,	427
Grieg, Robert,	427
George, Rev. R. A.,	455
Ganner, John H.,	306
Grotthouse, H. H.,	307
Goodell, Miss Nellie C.,	307
Gipson, Miss Mary F.,	307
Gordon, Rev. J. B.,	326
Grubb, Rev. M. B.,	326
Gale, Rev. S. M.,	327
Gibson, W. B.,	327
Gipson, Miss Mary F.,	327
Garrett, Rev. D. C.,	327
Guy, W. R.,	327
Gillespie, W. A.,	334
Graham, G. T.,	376
General View of Lausanne,	486
Girls' School Christian Endeavor Society, Tottori, Japan,	497
Group of Christian Endeavorers, Monrovia, Liberia,	504
Goll, Rev. George P.,	504
Gomien, Charles,	507
Gilman, E. A.,	513
Howe, Prof. James Lewis,	42
Henson, Rev. P. S.,	42
Harper, President William R.,	42
Hamlin, Rev. Teunis S.,	42
Hight, Clarence A.,	81
Hanson, Charles,	83
Howard Avenue Church, New Haven, Conn.,	154
Hill, Rev. James L.,	163
Home of Robert Raikes, Gloucester,	190
Hoyt, Rev. Wayland,	194
Harwood, F. J.,	195
Headquarters, Saratoga Convention,	198
Haus, Miss Kate H.,	225
Hightown Church, Crewe, England,	236
Harper, President,	243
Hudson, M. A.,	245
Howard, Gen. O. O,	278
Hill, Mrs. James L.,	293

	PAGE
Hammon, W. H.,	315
Huntoon, Lew A.,	343
Hill, Mrs. Grace Livingston,	380
Heely, A. B.,	399
Hulse, Levi S.,	455
Hills, Norman E.,	455
Hitchcock, J. V.,	455
Hamilton, R. B.,	455
Hamlyn, Rev. W.,	306
Hartman, John P., Jr.,	306
Hunt, Charles N.,	306
Hulett, W. I.,	306
Holbrook, Miss Carrie,	307
Harmon, Elder M. F.,	307
Hull, Louis Burt,	307
Holland, Miss Luella E.,	307
Hoobler, B. R.,	307
Hill, Rev. E. M.,	326
Hardy, E. A.,	326
Hudson, M. A.,	326
Hughes, John Silver,	326
Hunter, Rev. R. B.,	326
Hathaway, Alfred C.,	326
Holdredge C. B.,	327
Haskell, F. P., Jr.,	388
Higgins, Lincoln,	388
Horsfall, Frank L.,	388
Hawkins, W. J.,	376
Hitchcock, Howard,	488
Hubbard, Rev. George H.,	493
Hubbard, Mrs. George H.,	493
Harada, Rev. E.,	498
Hamadan Church, Persia,	500
Hamadan Christian Endeavorers, Persia,	501
Hill, Mrs. A.,	507
Israel, Edward E.,	315
Interior of Foo Chow City Church,	493
Interior of Tent Endeavorer,	523
Interior of Tent Williston,	523
Jewett, Frank W.,	83
Junior Society East Orange, N. J.,	299
Junior North Platte, Nebraska,	303
Jayne, Trafford N.,	343
Jones, Miss Antoinette P.,	359
Jackson, J. B.,	404
Japanese Endeavor Paper,	416
Jones, Miss Antoinette P.,	306
Jennings, Rev. C. A. B.,	306
Jones, Thomas,	306
Jostin, John,	307
Jurney, Miss Lucy,	307
Jarvis, S. J.,	326
Jackson, W. B.,	326
Johnson, T. M.,	327
John, Rev. L. F.,	327
Junior Rally, Pennsylvania State Convention, York,	271
Jessup, Henry W.,	388
Jaccard, Rev. M. C.,	485
Jenanyan, Rev. H. S.,	491
Japanese Convention, 1895, Osaka, Japan,	497
Jaffna Native Christian Endeavorers,	499
Jenanyan, Mrs. Helene R., Asia Minor,	502
Kelly, Rev. Gilby C.,	42
Kidder, Fred H.,	42
Kenworthy, Miss Eliza,	81

37

LIST OF ILLUSTRATIONS.

Name	PAGE
Kenworthy, Maria,	83
Kirk Street Church, Lowell, Mass.,	143
Kerr, Rev. T. J.,	194
Kinney, Rev. H. N.,	195
Kinports, Harry A.,	343
Kemp, F.,	404
Kelly, Dr. Elmer E.,	306
Kinzer, Rev. A. D.,	306
Kirkpatrick, Judge L. J.,	306
Kelly, Prof. D. S.,	306
Kilbourne, A. E.,	307
Krause, Rev. J. C.,	326
Kephart, Rev. C. J.,	326
Kentucky State Convention Hall, Hopkinsville, Ky.,	271
Kilgour, Robert,	388
Kieffer, Edw. H.,	401
Karmarkar, Rev. Sumatrao Vishnu,	491
Kobe Kindergarten, Japan,	497
Kilborn, Charles H.,	513
Lowden, Rev. J. M.,	42
Leavitt, Rev. Burke F.,	51
Libby, George F.,	73
Lean, Mrs. E.,	81
Leavitt, Mrs. Helen S.,	81
Lord, Fred,	83
Lowden, Rev. J. M.,	128
Leitch, Miss Margaret,	148
Ling, Mr.,	150
Lee, Lewis S.,	273
Lindsay, L. F.,	315
Littlefield, Milton R., Jr.,	399
Lighthall, George R.,	427
Lake View Park, Cleveland,	442
Lewis, F. Melville,	455
Lawson, Robert,	306
Lewis, Rev. Richard W.,	306
Leffingwell, Alton G.,	306
Leach, Frank A.,	307
Lund, Frank W.,	307
Lee, Edwin F.,	326
Little, James A.,	326
Lewis, W. J.,	326
Lucas, J. M.,	327
Loose, E. P.,	327
Landreth, Ira,	327
Lewis, W. H.,	327
Langdale, F. G.,	327
Lane, A. W.,	327
Lincoln, H. C.,	334
Lynch, Miss M. F.,	388
Leason, William,	507
Leet, Grant,	532
McMillan, Rev. W. H.,	42
Mizpah Circle,	52
Maine Blizzard,	57
Musans, Mrs. William T.,	81
Morris, George P.,	81
McCullough, Mrs.,	81
Mills, Rev. C. P.,	86
McKenzie, Rev. Alex.,	147
Manchester, Eli, Jr.,	154
Miller, Rev. Rufus W.,	192
Mills, Rev. B. Fay,	196
Mershon, S. L.,	196
McAll, Dr.,	238
Matthews, J. D.,	287

Name	PAGE
Montgomery, Mrs. Mary,	293
March of the Nations (Boston Convention),	294
Middleton, Ida M.,	301
Merritt, Miss May C.,	301
McClain, W. H.,	315
Minneapolis Convention Hall (Exterior),	341
Minneapolis Convention Hall (Interior),	342
McDonald, Willis M.,	343
Mission Launch, Vineyard Sound, Mass.,	361
Madison Square Garden Building,	391
Madison Square Garden Building (Interior),	394
Madison Square Garden Building (Exterior),	394
McEwen, Rev. H. T.,	400
McCutcheon, W. B.,	404
Madanapalle Christian Endeavor Society,	419
Murray, Edith M.,	469
Murray, Mary Ethel,	469
Murray, Jessie M.,	469
Miller, Rev. W. P.,	306
McCauley, Rev. W. F.,	306
Moulton, H. A.,	306
McDonald, Rev. C. D.,	306
McCrory, Rev. J. T.,	446
Magee, R. A.,	306
Meeser, Rev. S. B.,	306
Marsden, Edward,	306
Mellish, Roland,	307
Milligan, Miss Mabel,	307
McIntosh, James,	307
McCurdy, Rev. J. F.,	307
Murphy, J. H.,	307
Morris, Thomas, Jr.,	307
Masson, Miss Jennie T.,	307
MacDonald, George,	307
Morrow, W. H.,	307
McGillivary, Rev. J. A.,	326
McMillan, Rev. John,	326
Morse, R. J.,	326
McEwen, Mrs. H. T.,	326
McDill, Rev. D. F.,	326
Mason, Rev. A. De W.,	326
Mason, Thomas J.,	326
Miars, Rev. Mary E.,	326
MacLaurin, Ella B.,	326
McMill, C. C.,	327
McElfresh, H. T.,	327
McColl, Prof. J. R.,	327
Manning, Myra A.,	327
Morse, Rev. E. L.,	327
Murphy, J. A.,	327
More, Rev. J. B.,	327
Miller, Edwin S.,	327
MacFarland, Margaret,	327
Merritt, C. Z.,	327
Merriam, W. Stewart,	327
Michigan State Convention, 1895,	271
MacRae, Miss,	388
Mansfield, Dr. A. D.,	388
Marion, Elizabeth,	388
Mills, F. D.,	376
Morgan, Rev. A. R.,	491
McCutcheon, W. B.,	491
Muhlenberg Chapel, Liberia,	504
Manhood, Carrie,	507
MacDonald, James,	507
Magwood, R. H.,	513
Mechanics' Hall,	527
Mechanics' Hall (Front),	527
Morgan, John D.,	532

LIST OF ILLUSTRATIONS.

	PAGE
North Church, Newburyport, Mass.,	87
Noyes, Rev. E. N.,	245
Neesima, Mrs.,	293
New York Port Floating Society,	361
Neale, A. W.,	455
Noell, W. L.,	306
Nash, Rev. F. L.,	306
Nicholson, Allan,	307
Nabers, Rev. J. H.,	326
Nisbitt, Thomas B.,	326
Needham, O. M.,	327
Needham, Mrs. O. M.,	327
Old Book by Cotton Mather,	44
Oklahoma Banner,	251
Osgood, E. G.,	306
Ottman, Rev. F. C.,	326
Ohrenschall, Frederick,	388
Officers Christian Endeavor Society, Girls' Boarding-School, Foo Chow, China,	493
Officers of Foo Chow Society,	493
Okayama Orphan Asylum, Japan,	497
Okayama Church, Japan,	497
Okayama Christian Endeavor Society, 1895, Japan,	497
Old North Meeting-House,	517
Patterson, Rev. Wm.,	42
Page of Rules from Cotton Mather's Manual,	45
Parlor in which Society was formed,	59
Patterson, Mrs. George T.,	81
Plummer, Mrs. Charles A.,	81
Pennell, Wm. H.,	82
Pennell, Mrs. Nannie,	83
Plumb, Rev. A. H.,	147
Potts, Rev. A. W.,	232
Pratt, Rev. Dwight M.,	328
Police Endeavor Society,	371
Prince, Miss Jeannette,	307
Protzman, Miss Sallie M.,	307
Pratt, Paul,	307
Phelps, Rev. Lawrence,	326
Peck, W. J.,	326
Penfield, Rev. Thornton B.,	326
Pierson, Rev. J. Judson,	326
Proudfit, Rev. Alex.,	326
Porter, F. R. W.,	327
Parnell, R. J.,	327
Palmer, E. A.,	327
Parsons, C. H.,	327
Patton, Thomas R.,	334
Perkins, Wm. C.,	388
Patterson, Francis E.,	388
Page, Frank E.,	388
Prominent Workers of the Toronto Union,	376
Priestnal, W.,	491
President Kozaki, Kioto, Japan,	497
President Baptist Y. P. S. C. E., South Africa,	503
Patriotic Meeting, Boston Common,	523
Patriotic Song Service,	541
Platform—Junior Rally (Washington Convention),	543
Rhodes, Rev. M.,	42
Richardson, Rev. Canon J. B.,	42
Robinson, Marietta,	81
Rankin, Rev. J. E.,	182
Raikes, Robert,	189
Randall, George M.,	273

	PAGE
Roth, John H.,	315
Roads, Rev. Charles,	380
Rose, Rev. S. P.,	427
Ross, Robert,	442
Roblee, A. E.,	455
Riggle, Mrs. Mary R.,	306
Richardson, Rev. A. F.,	306
Robertson, Peyton,	307
Race, Miss Mattie E.,	307
Rogers, Rev. Anderson,	326
Reynolds, Rev. A. L.,	326
Rees, Rev. Levi,	326
Reyser, Rev. Leander S.,	326
Rodgers, Rev. W. T.,	327
Robb, Dunbar,	327
Roby, L. L.,	327
Radford, J. D.,	327
Ransom, George,	327
Ragan, George A.,	327
Richardson, Rev. N. F.,	327
Richardson, Mrs. L. V. C.,	334
Robinson, J. B.,	334
Rigdon, R. L., M. D.,	388
Read, John N.,	491
Reed, Miss Mary,	491
Randall, Rev. C. E.,	491
Reception at Secretary Baer's Home,	527
Robinson, W. H.,	532
Staples, Granville,	71
Sayward, Miss Rose M.,	81
Scolfield, Mrs. Josie P.,	83
Sayward, Mrs. Hattie J.,	83
Sleeth, Agnes A.,	83
St. Lawrence Street Church, Portland, Maine,	93
Stephenson, James W.,	99
Sayward, Edward L.,	100
Second Church, Portland, Maine,	121
Smith, Augustus R.,	144
Scene at Old Orchard,	158
Shaw, William,	167
Scene in Saratoga,	178
Sherwood, Rev. H. W.,	195
Sewell, Rev. J. L.,	204
Scudder, Miss Alice May,	225
Sunday-School Union Building, 56 Old Bailey, London,	231
Spurgeon, Rev. Charles H.,	236
Sketches of Christian Endeavor Badge,	249
Shumway, Rev. Walter B.,	273
Scott, John B.,	273
Smith, J. S.,	276
Shaw, Mrs. William,	293
Sleeper, Rev. W. W.,	301
Spooner, Rev. A. W.,	301
Sheldon, J. W.,	315
Stimson, Rev. Henry A.,	319
Southgate, Rev. C. M.,	332
Smith, W. H. H.,	348
Stewart, Rev. George B.,	348
Solano County Delegates, California,	363
Santee Training School (Y. P. S. C. E.),	375
Santee Agency (Y. P. S. C. E.),	375
Sidney, Margaret,	379
Stebbins, George C.,	398
Stevens, W. F.,	399
Scott, Rev. W.,	404
Smith, Miriam C.,	455
Signing the Pledge,	456

LIST OF ILLUSTRATIONS.

	PAGE
Sængerfest Hall (Cleveland Convention),	459
Society of Three Sisters,	468
Sunday Breakfast Association,	470
Spooner, H. H.,	306
Strong, W. H.,	306
Smith, John S.,	306
Scott, Rev. Harry O.,	306
Sleman, John B.,	307
Stewart, O. W.,	307
Soper, Ben. H.,	307
Shively, Miss Myrtie,	307
Skelton, Miss Bessie E.,	307
Siddall, G. Ward,	326
Shearer, Rev. Wm. B. A.,	326
Sommerville, R. M.,	326
Schuyler, Miss Carrie M.,	326
Swengel, Rev. N. F.,	326
Sykes, Rev. G. S.,	326
Sinclair, Robert B.,	326
Shupe, Rev. H. F.,	326
Sommerbell, Rev. Martyn, D. D.,	326
Stewarts, E. Belle,	327
Stephenson, O. L.,	327
Scudday, Rev. H. G.,	327
Smith, Mrs. Floyd N.,	327
Siser, H. L.,	327
Stevens, C. L.,	327
Scott, Rev. Harry Omar, D. D.,	327
Strayer, Paul M.,	388
Sweet, W. E.,	388
Scouler, Miss Bessie,	388
Scott, W. H.,	388
Stockwell, Miss Netta A.,	401
Scotland for Christ,	478
Scotch National Council,	481
Stevens, Rev. J.,	493
Sanderson, Thomas,	507
Santiago English Christian Endeavor Society,	507
Somerby, George K.,	513
Street Decorations, Boston, Mass.,	527
State Headquarters, Mechanics' Building,	527
Shand, Miles M.,	532
Stowell, W. R.,	532
Sleman, John E.,	532
Street Decorations (Washington Convention),	536
Section of State Headquarters, Armory Hall (Washington Convention),	538
Tilton, Miss Inez,	81
Tolman, Mrs. Charles,	81
Twitchell, Dr.,	156
Tabernacle, Ocean Park,	160
Tabernacle, Ocean Park (Interior),	161
Thrall, Rev. J. B.,	245
The Royal Legion,	246
Towner, E. E.,	276
Two in One,	294
Tonner, F. W.,	315
Temple, Rev. W. H. G.,	319
Thwing, J. E.,	343
Thompson, J. E.,	404
Town Hall, Sidney, Australia,	404
Tea Meeting, Melbourne Town Hall,	404
Tamil Christian Endeavorers,	418
The Smallest Young People's Society Christian Endeavor in the World,	421
Three Forward Movements,	437
Tyler, Rev. J. Z.,	455
Trustees at Cleveland (Stillman House),	462

	PAGE
Thaeler, Rev. A. D.,	306
Townsend, James R.,	306
Towner, E. E.,	307
Timmons, R. W.,	307
Tolles, H. N.,	307
Thompson, Rev. H. A.,	307
Thomas, Miss Bessie,	326
Tracy, Rev. William,	326
Taylor, William P.,	327
Turkle, Rev. A. J.,	327
Turner, W. L.,	334, 543
Tent Williston,	523
Tent Endeavor,	523
Taylor, A. S.,	532
Van Patten, W. J.,	125
Van Patten, Mrs. W. J.,	293
Van Hook, Mrs. M. Jolly,	307
Williston Chapel,	49
Wyer, Charles,	83
Wilcox, Miss Nellie,	83
Wyer, Addie,	83
Williston Church (from the North),	84
Wright, Rev. A. H.,	101
Ward, George M.,	166
Worden House, Saratoga, N. Y.,	181
Wilcox, Miss Lillian A.,	204
Wells, Prof. Amos R.,	204
Willard, Frances E.,	224
Waters, Charles,	231
Walker, Matthew W.,	273
Wallace, Richard H.,	273
Wanamaker, John,	277
Wilder, Rev. Robert T.,	282
Ong Tsin Chong,	286
Wells, Mrs. Amos R.,	293
Wishard, Miss Harriet J.,	293
Wainright, Thomas W.,	301
Westminster Junior Endeavorers,	302
Williston Souvenir,	329
Wells, Rev. J. H.,	344
Wood, J. M.,	364
Wing, F. D.,	372
Wray, Josiah R.,	400
Wootton, H. E.,	405
Wilson, A. S.,	405
Wesley Church, Sidney, Australia,	405
Wells, Rev. J. Lester,	472
Wollam, J. M.,	306
Williams, Rev. M. J.,	306
Whitfield, Miss Nellie,	307
Warner, Archie B.,	307
Waldron, Rev. O. W.,	326
Weeks, Rev. T. S.,	326
Williams, Rev. J. H.,	326
Whitney, J. R.,	326
Wright, Rev. J. H.,	327
Wheeler, F. C.,	327
Watts, W.,	327
Waller, Mrs. Edith Meeker,	327
Waller, William S.,	327
Wilcox, W. Beach,	327
Wood, Miss Gertrude L.,	389
Watt, Rolla V.,	389
Williams, Miss Jessie,	389
Wilson, S. A.,	389
Wickson, A. Frank,	388
Warren, J. G.,	401

LIST OF ILLUSTRATIONS.

	PAGE
Waugh, Rev. A. J.,	401
Wiggins, Lottie E.,	376
Wootton, H. E.,	491
Wilson, Fanny,	507
Wilson, Rev. J. C.,	507
Wilson, Mrs. J. C.,	507
Walsh, F. W., Jr.,	513
Washington Elm, Cambridge, Mass.,	517
White Lot, The (Washington Convention),	535
Young Men's Christian Association Building, Sidney,	404
Young, Rev. S. Edward,	473
Young, Rev. E. K.,	326
Young People's Society of Christian Endeavor, Okayama, Japan,	497
Zartman, Rev. P. E.,	327

THE OFFICERS AND TRUSTEES OF THE UNITED SOCIETY OF CHRISTIAN ENDEAVOR.

1. Pres. Francis E. Clark, D. D.
2. Gen. Sec'y, John Willis Baer.
3. Treasurer, William Shaw.
4. Rev. J. Z. Tyler, D. D.
5. Rev. Ralph W. Brokaw.
6. Rev. W. J. Darby, D. D.
7. Rev. H. B. Grose.
8. Bishop Samuel Fallows, D. D.
9. Rev. J. F. Cowan.
10. Rev. M. Rhodes, D. D.
11. Rev. J. T. Beckley, D. D.
12. Rev. M. M. Binford.
13. Rev. James L. Hill, D. D.
14. Rev. Chas. A. Dickinson.
15. Rev. Wm. Patterson.
16. Rev. J. M. Lowden.
17. Prof. Jas. Lewis Howe, Ph. D.
18. Rev. Canon J. B. Richardson.
19. Rev. H. C. Farrar, D. D.
20. Rev. P. S. Henson, D. D.
21. Rev. W. W. Andrews, Ph. D.
22. Rev. N. Boynton.
23. Wm. R. Harper, LL. D.
24. Hon. John Wanamaker.
25. Rev. Gilby C. Kelly, D. D.
26. W. J. Van Patten, Esq.
27. Rev. David J. Burrell, D. D.
28. Auditor, Fred. H. Kidder.
29. Rev. Teunis S. Hamlin, D. D.
30. Rev. Wayland Hoyt, D. D.
31. Rev. Rufus W. Miller.
32. Rev. John Henry Barrows, D. D.
33. W. H. Pennell, Esq.
34. Rev. W. H. McMillan, D. D.
35. Rev. E. E. Dille, D. D.
36. Williston Church, Portland, Me.

CHAPTER I.

ENDEAVORERS BEFORE THE ENDEAVOR SOCIETY.

Who Was the Original Endeavorer?—Early Young People's Prayer-Meetings—The Ore in the Mountain—Cotton Mather's Proposals—An Early Consecration Meeting—Two Hours and Two Prayers—Young People Should be Seen and Not Heard—From an Old Record Book—Some Spartan Bands—The Amusement Idea—The Succulent Oyster, a Gastronomic Plummet.

IT must not be supposed that there were no Endeavorers before the first Endeavor Society was formed. By Endeavorers, I do not mean simply Christian workers, zealous and faithful, for of these from the time when our Lord ascended up into the heavens there has been a constantly increasing host. But I mean young people and others who were not only imbued with the spirit of Christian Endeavor, but who believed in its principles, though they had not been formulated or the constitution of the society written out.

If we were in any danger of forgetting this fact we are constantly reminded of it on public platforms and from private letters. Nearly all the saintly characters of the Bible from Adam down have been quoted as the "original Endeavorer," while every now and then some one claims for himself the distinction of having been the first Christian Endeavorer when, as a boy, he made some good resolve to serve the Lord and confess Him before men.

The fact seems to be that a multitude of Christian people all over the world, but more particularly in America, have been imbued with the spirit of this idea before it was formulated. Ten thousand pastors were eagerly desiring some method better than they had known before of reaching and training their young people for Christ's service.

Tens of thousands of young people gathered every week in prayer-meetings whose lack of vitality and frequent long periods of lethargy were a constant surprise and mortification to the faithful few, who concluded, at last, in many cases that there was something incongruous between a hearty, joyous Christian life and the average young person, and that a prayer-meeting was not adapted to his nature.

But the most remarkable example of Endeavorers before the Endeavor Society is found in a short-lived movement which began nearly two centuries ago in the churches of Massachusetts.

Just as the ore lies in the mountain for hundreds of centuries before it is discovered, so the ore of consecration and pledged service has lain in the lives of young people in all the Christian ages. It was only waiting for the Christian Endeavor Society to unearth it and mold it into many beautiful forms for the Master's use. A very rare pamphlet by Cotton Mather, published in 1724, is entitled "Proposals for the Revival of Dying Religion by well Ordered Societies for that Purpose." This pamphlet bears this quaint impress:

"Boston: Printed by S. Kneeland, for John Phillips, and Sold at his Shop over against the South-side of the Town-House. 1724."

This pamphlet goes on to urge the animating and regulating of private meetings of religious people for the exercises of religion.

With as much truth as quaintness the distinguished author remarks at the beginning: "It is very certain That where such Private Meetings under a good Conduct have been kept alive, the Christians which have composed them, have like so many Coals of the Altar kept one another alive, and kept up a lively Christianity in the neighborhood. Such Societies have been tried, and proved to be strong Engines, to uphold the Power of Godliness. The throwing up of such Societies has been accompanied with a Visible Decay of Godliness. The less Love to them, the less Use of them, there has been in a Place, the less has Godliness flourished there; the less there has been of the Kingdom of God."

Here are some splendid Endeavor principles from these forerunners of the Endeavor movement. "Such a meeting," writes Cotton Mather, "should look upon themselves as bound up in one bundle of love, and count themselves obliged in very close and strong bonds to be serviceable one to another."

Here is something that looks very much like our consecration meeting:

Religious Societies.

PROPOSALS
For the REVIVAL of
Dying Religion,
BY WELL-ORDERED
Societies
FOR THAT PURPOSE.

With a brief DISCOURSE, Offered unto a RELIGIOUS SOCIETY, on the First Day of their Meeting.

1 Theff. V. 11. *Edify one another*

BOSTON:
Printed by S. KNEELAND, for JOHN PHILLIPS, and Sold at his Shop over against the South-side of the Town House. 1724.

TITLE-PAGE OF AN OLD BOOK BY COTTON MATHER.

"Let the List be once a Quarter called over; and then, If it be observed, that any of the Society have much absented themselves, Let there be some sent unto them, to inquire the Reason of their Absence; and if no Reason be given, but such as intimates an Apostacy from good Beginnings, Let them upon Obstinacy, after loving and faithful Admonitions, be Obliterated."

And here, too, is the provision for the missionary committee translated into the old-fashioned language of the beginning of the eighteenth century, and yet this was nearly a century before organized missionary effort was known in the churches of America. "Once in three months," says the sixth article of this constitution, "Let there be, if need be, a Collection, out of which the necessary Charges of the Society shall be defrayed, and the rest be employed upon such Pious Uses as may be agreed upon."

There were some provisions in this society, however, which would scarcely commend themselves to modern Christian Endeavorers, as for instance, article 1st, which says: "Let there be two Hours at a Time set apart, and let there be two Prayers made by the Members of the Society, in their Turns; between which let a SERMON be repeated; and there should be the Singing of a PSALM annexed."

This seed dropped by Cotton Mather evidently bore much fruit, and if the churches had been ready to welcome and foster such an agency who knows but the Endeavor movement would not have begun five generations before it actually did commence, and five generations of earnest young Christians been trained for Christ and the church, as they were not trained by the repressive methods which the churches soon adopted. But alas! this movement was not looked upon with much favor; the pernicious maxim prevailed that young people should be seen and not heard in religious service; the tithing man

---

II. LET all the Members of the *Society* Resolve to be *Charitably watchful* over one another : never to Divulge one anothers *Infirmities* ; always to *inform* and *advise* one another of every thing that may appear to call for an *Admonition*, and to *take it kindly*, when they are Admonished.

III. LET all who are to be admitted, as Members of the *Society*, be accompanied by two or three of the rest, unto the *Minister* of the Place, that they may receive his holy Counsels and Charges, and that every thing may be done with his Approbation ; and so let their *Names* be added unto the *Roll*.

IV. IF any Person thus enrolled among them, fall into a *Scandalous Iniquity*, Let the *Rebukes* of the *Society* be dispensed unto him, and let them forbid him to come any more among them, until he bring suitable Expressions and Evidences of *Repentance* with him.

V. LET the List be once a *Quarter* called over ; and then, If it be observed, that any of the *Society* have much absented themselves, Let there be some sent unto them, to inquire the *Reason* of their *Absence* ; and if no *Reason* be given, but such as intimates an *Apostacy* from good Beginnings, Let them upon obstinacy, after loving and faithful Admonitions, be *Obliterated*.

VI. ONCE in three Months, Let there be, if need be, a *Collection*, out of which the *necessary Charges* of the *Society* shall be defrayed, and the rest be employed upon such *Pious Uses* as may be agreed upon.

VII. ONCE

A PAGE OF RULES FROM COTTON MATHER'S MANUAL.

was more in evidence than the lookout committee to keep the young people in the right way.

The church acted the part of the traditional stepmother rather than of the loving parent to this new organization, and it was soon crushed out, and, after a few years, we hear very little further about it.

In its day and generation, however, it accomplished a good work, and quite a number of societies, mostly in Massachusetts, but to some extent in other colonies, were established on the basis of Cotton Mather's constitution.

Rev. Otis Carey, an honored missionary in Japan, in looking over an old record book of the North Parish of Bridgewater, now Brocton, Mass., finds that an agreement was made June 17, 1741, between those who " thrue the grace of god have been awackened in the days of our yuth to be consarned about the things that belonge to our everlasting peace and that wolde remember our Creator in the days of our yuthe."

Among the articles of this society, which was evidently based on the rules laid down by Cotton Mather, are the following, which we give verbatim, with all their quaint disregard for orthography :

" 1 it shall be our endeaveare to spend the tow ourse frome seven to nine of every lords day eveneing in prayer togathare by turnse the one to begine and the outhear to conclud the meting and betwene the tow prayers haveing a sarmon repeated whereto the singing of a psalm shall be anexed and ef aftear the stated exersise of the eveneing are ovear if theare be any residue of time we will aske one a nothare questions out of the catecism or some questions in divinyty or have such reliagus conversation as we shall best sarve for the edefication of the sosiety."

" 2 that we will bare with one anothare infarmitys and not upbrad tharwith nor deulge any thing of what natur soever to that is done at our meetings to the pregedic of it."

" 3 we do oblige our sevels to come directly from the pelaces whare we do live to our metings and to returne directly as sone as the meting is done oure homes without going any othour places or into any othar company."

" 4 if any one of our sosiety do fall into any scandelus iniquity or he has bene reproved for smaller miscariges don't reforme we will admonish of his evel and suspend him from coming among us for a longer or shorter space of time acording to the nater of the ofence nor shall he be againe reseved without credibel expreshones of his repentance but in such a case and in othears that may seem to require it we will nót act without the advis and aprobation of our ministear."

" 5 We would perticulur be consarned those of us that have not yet aproch to the tabel of Christ to git and keepe a ful sence of the bonds we are under by our baptism and covenant professing, and so be preparing for the timle and solem recognicion of them in our aproching the tabel of christ."

" 6 once in tow monthes we will read over our articals at our metings and call over our lest that if any have been absent that may by one of the sosiety be asked the reson tharfore."

To come down to more modern times, it must be said that the old-fashioned young people's prayer-meetings, sparsely attended and uninteresting as they usually were, undoubtedly prepared the way for the Christian Endeavor movement.

In many churches was a little Spartan band of devoted young people who, as best they could, let their light shine before men, and when the simple and efficient methods of the Endeavor Society were proposed, they were all ready to accept them and to pour the accumulated strength of years of service into this new channel.

In many churches, too, conspicuously in the Lafayette Avenue Church of Brooklyn, of which the honored Dr. Cuyler was pastor, were strong and vigorous young people's associations, which, though they did not have the distinguishing characteristics of the Christian Endeavor Society of to-day, nevertheless accustomed the mind of the Christian public to the idea of organized activity among the young people of the churches.

Too many of these associations, however (I am not speaking of the one in the Lafayette Avenue Church), exalted some phase of the entertainment idea. They were musical societies, or debating societies, or societies for literary culture and mutual improvement, and the religious idea, as represented in the prayer-meeting, often had rather an inconspicuous place.

In short, the distinctively religious thought was subordinated to the amusement idea, without which it was supposed to be impossible to draw young people into the church.

REV. THEODORE L. CUYLER, D. D.

At a meeting of ministers held in Boston shortly before the Endeavor Society was begun, the perennial subject was discussed, "How can we win our young people to Christ?"

The frequency with which this theme occurred for many years in ministerial conferences shows the longing desire on the part of a multitude of ministers for a practical solution of this question of questions, the problem of Christian nurture.

At this particular meeting of which I am speaking, one young minister arose and with an air of assurance and complete conviction, exclaimed: " Brethren, I have solved the difficulty. I have learned how to win my young people, and I have accomplished it with the aid of the succulent oyster. I called the boys together and gave them an oyster stew, and now they are all on the side of the church; and then I got the girls together and gave them an oyster supper, and now they are on my side."

I was woefully disappointed by this young doctor's prescription, and as the years have gone by, I have come to have less and less faith in any such cheap and easy way of winning young souls for the kingdom.

The depths of these young natures cannot be sounded by any such gastronomic plummet as the oyster. Nor can their depths be stirred by a "pink tea" or a "pop-corn sociable." These things are all well in their place, but their place is a subordinate one to the distinctively religious idea.

It was not upon such principles that the Endeavor Society was established. What its principles are and how they have been wrought out will be related in another chapter.

CHAPTER II.

THE CRADLE OF THE CHRISTIAN ENDEAVOR MOVEMENT.

The Streets of Gloucester—The Cradle of Christian Endeavor—How Williston Got Its Name—A Pun and What Came of It—The Pastor's Class a Forerunner of the Endeavor Society—The Sunday-School Prayer-Meeting—The Mizpah Circle—A Revival and Its Consequences—The Week of Prayer and the Endeavor Society—Some Serious Questions—How They Were Answered.

THE birthplace of any movement or of any man that has been conspicuously used of Providence is always of interest. A small fortune would be paid for the rough pine cradle in which Abraham Lincoln was rocked.

WILLISTON CHAPEL.

The streets of Gloucester are forever hallowed, in the imagination of the Christian world, because out of them Robert Raikes gathered the living material for the first modern Sunday-school; and an interest which would not otherwise attach to the Williston Church in Portland, Me., gathers around it because here, in the Providence of God, the first Society of Christian Endeavor was started.

This church was admirably suited to the purpose for which God designed it. It was a young church; only eight years from its organization when the first Endeavor Society was begun. It was composed very largely of young people, and those whose gray hairs showed that they could no longer claim this title were young in heart and in Christian enthusiasm and enterprise.

It was founded in 1873 as an offshoot of State Street Church, whose members for a long time had maintained a Sunday-school in a neglected part of the city.

After a number of years a chapel was built to accommodate this Sunday-

WILLITS CHURCH.

school, which, in honor of the maiden name of the beloved wife of Rev. George Leon Walker, D. D., then the pastor of State Street Church, was called Williston Chapel. Gradually the enterprise gained strength and secured the sympathy of the people in the vicinity, and, in 1873, a church was formed of which Rev. Burke F. Leavitt, now an honored minister in Massachusetts, was the first pastor. After three years of faithful service Mr. Leavitt resigned, and a young theological student, who has since, because of a pun upon his initials, very absurdly become known as "Father Endeavor Clark," was called to take charge of the enterprise.

In the fall of 1876 he was ordained and installed, and for seven years, as pastor of the people, received their loving support and warm sympathy in his efforts for young and old.

REV. BURKE F. LEAVITT, THE FIRST PASTOR OF WILLISTON CHURCH.

The church rapidly grew from a membership of something like fifty to nearly four hundred. The Sunday-school was proportionately prosperous, and, within less than two years a new and beautiful brick and stone edifice was erected by the members of Williston Church, the building which was destined to be known as the birthplace of the Christian Endeavor movement.

The pastor devoutly believed in young people, in their earnestness and faithfulness, their devotion and self-sacrifice. He tried in every way to interest them and draw them to the church, and in all these efforts he was most heartily upheld by the church and always affectionately and loyally seconded by the one, who, with far more reason than usual, may be called his "better half."

A debating society was started for the young people of the church very soon after the new pastorate began. For a few weeks it ran well, but like other efforts of the kind it proved to have very little *staying* power. Numerous entertainments were projected and carried out with greater or less success. Some money was brought into the treasury of the church and a languid interest in the church and its affairs was excited in the hearts of the young people who participated in them, but they accomplished little permanent good.

The pastor's class was inaugurated, which filled the place occupied by many Junior Societies of Christian Endeavor to-day. In fact, a brief and simple pledge not unlike the Junior pledge was adopted for that class, beginning, as almost every Christian Endeavor pledge begins to-day, "Trusting in the Lord Jesus Christ for strength, I promise Him that I will strive to do whatever He would like to have me do."

Topics related to the Christian life were studied. *Pilgrim's Progress* was read through by the pastor and his class together. The church creed simplified and brought down to the understanding of the young converts occupied the class for one year, and from this class many graduated into the church each year who were all ready, when the first Endeavor Society was started, to form the nucleus of a strong and enduring organization.

Much help, too, was found in a series of Sunday-school prayer-meetings, held immediately after the Sunday-school session, for a few weeks following the Week of Prayer. In these evangelistic services many young people were led to commit themselves to Christ.

Another forerunner of the Endeavor Society was the "Mizpah Mission Circle," a company of girls and boys which met every week at the pastor's house, under the care of Mrs. Clark, to talk about mission subjects, to pray for the extension of the kingdom, and to sew and work in various ways for the mission cause.

Almost all the girls and boys of this mission circle became members of the first Endeavor Society.

It is very pleasant in these days of missionary enthusiasm to remember that one of the elements which made possible the first Endeavor Society was a mission circle, and a mission circle which bore the name of the benediction with which hundreds of thousands of Christian Endeavorers every week close their meeting: "The Lord watch between me and thee when we are absent one from another."

THE MIZPAH CIRCLE (OLDER SECTION).

Late in the year 1880 an unusual interest began to manifest itself among the young people of Williston Church. The young people's prayer-meeting, which had enjoyed rather a spasmodic life, was more largely attended, and some voices were heard in it beyond the regulation three or four. This interest was deepened and quickened by the meetings of the Week of Prayer, which was always observed in that church with much earnestness and deep devotion.

MRS. F. E. CLARK.

As a result of this Week of Prayer, in January, 1881, supplemented by the Sunday-school prayer-meetings and the pastor's class, and the influence of the Mizpah Circle under the direction of the pastor's wife, many young hearts were given to the Lord Jesus Christ; a new song was put into their mouths, and their eager impulse was, as is always the impulse of new converts, to do something for Him whom they have begun to love. After the Week of Prayer was over special meetings were held, and in all some twenty or thirty young converts were born into the kingdom of God.

It was felt that this was a very serious and critical time with them. They would receive impressions and form religious habits during the first few weeks after conversion which would never be lost. The first three months would set their stamp of consistent devotion to Christ or sluggish indifference to His claims on the whole of their subsequent Christian lives.

Some of their brothers and sisters had in previous years come to the church, and too many of them had, metaphorically, taken back seats, and folded their hands, and were seldom heard and not always seen in the prayer-meetings of the church or in any of its spiritual activities. Should this be the history of these young converts? Should they pattern after the example of the faint-hearted Christians who had gone before them? Should they add simply to the numerical strength of the church by placing their names on the roll without adding to its spiritual vitality?

These were questions which weighed heavily upon the hearts of the pastor and his wife, and doubtless upon the hearts of many others in that church. Inwardly they resolved that these questions must not be answered in the affirmative; that these new converts must not be left to haphazard growth and spasmodic service; but that the way must be made plain and easy for them to confess their Lord before men, to renew this confession often enough to make sure that they should not forget their obligations, and that something should be given to each one of them to do for Him whom, with trembling aspiration, they had thus begun to love. Frequent public confession of Christ and constant appropriate work for Him they believed were the two panaceas for spiritual idleness and inactivity.

That church had the usual means of grace, the ordinary appliances of a church. The Sunday-school was vigorous and vital, the prayer-meeting was of more than average interest, the preaching services were well attended, the missionary activities were well developed, especially among the women of the church; the pastor and people were closely united in ties of sympathy and affection.

But still there was not in that church, nor was there in any other church, to my knowledge, a sufficient opportunity for young people to express their devotion or to utilize their enthusiastic love and bounding aspirations in their service of Christ. It was the rarest thing in the world to hear a young voice in the weekly prayer-meeting of the church, and the very rarity of such an occurrence placed a seal on the lips of most young people.

The youngest could not teach in the Sunday-school because they were too inexperienced. The so-called young people's prayer-meeting was, as was usual in most churches, in the hands of the more experienced and more fluent young people, and the average convert could not find there a place for his first stumbling confession of Christ, nor was there any appropriate work for him to do, even if his heart were warmed to desire a larger service.

How to change this state of affairs; how to provide some natural outlet for these young energies; how to furnish appropriate work which should not be merely playing at work but actually accomplishing something for Christ and the Church, was the great problem of the hour.

To solve this problem the pastor of the church drew up the constitution of a young people's society, and asked these recent converts, together with some who had been longer in the church, to come to his house on Wednesday evening, the second day of February. But the story of this meeting and what came of it must be reserved for another chapter.

CHAPTER III.

THE BIRTHDAY OF THE SOCIETY.

February 2, 1881—A Northern Winter Scene—Savory Odors—A Pastor's Fears—The First Constitution—An Underscored Paragraph—Then and Now—The Persistence of the Original Type—No Mincing of Words—The Original Strenuousness of the Pledge—A Deathly Stillness—Not Many Mighty—No Prigs.

THE second day of February, 1881, proved to be one of the most bitterly cold days in the calendar of the year, and Maine knows something about cold weather every year, as my readers who have the good fortune to live in the Pine Tree State can testify. Snow covered the ground and the housetops, and glittering icicles like stalagmites of diamonds hung on the eaves.

The crisp snow creaked under the runners of the flying sleighs, and the coasting and skating were excellent. But, in spite of these out-door attractions of a Northern winter, the young people of whom I have before spoken accepted the invitation of their pastor and his wife to come to the parsonage.

Various savory odors from the kitchen were wafted upwards to the pastor's study throughout the morning of that day, for the Mizpah Circle were coming to tea, and the pastor's wife desired to treat them with due hospitality.

In the afternoon some forty girls and boys, with a few young ladies, gathered for the usual meeting of the Mizpah Circle, and, after tea, were joined by their older brothers and sisters. Conspicuous among the older ones were Mr. W. H. Pennell and his fine Sunday-school class of young men. After a little general conversation as to the importance of starting right, of working for the church, and of showing one's colors for Christ on all occasions, the pastor, with a good deal of hesitation, produced a constitution whose germs had lain in his mind for a long while, but which he had written out for the first time that day.

He was afraid that its strenuous pledge would not commend itself to the young people; that they would be afraid of its strictly religious character; that they would not find enough of the oyster supper and pink tea element in it to win their approval; but, ever since, his weak faith and lack of knowledge of young hearts has been rebuked by their acceptance of this constitution and by the loyal adhesion to it of millions of like-minded youth.

It was proposed in this document, which the minister that evening brought down from his study, that the society should be called the "Williston Young People's Society of Christian Endeavor." Its object was declared to be "to promote an earnest Christian life among its members, to increase their mutual acquaintance, and to make them more useful in the service of God." It was provided also that there should be two classes of members, "active and associate," the active members being those who sincerely desired to accomplish the results above specified, and the associate members those who were not willing to consider themselves decided Christians, but who desired the privileges and companionships of the society.

It was specified in this constitution that there should be a president, vice-president, and secretary; also a prayer-meeting committee, lookout committee,

AFTER A MAINE BLIZZARD.

social committee, missionary committee, Sunday-school committee, and flower committee, each consisting of five members.

These committees were defined in the same way that they are now defined in the constitution of the society, and it was provided that they should make a report to the society at the monthly business meeting concerning the work of the past month. But, as in these days, so also in that early day, everything pivoted on the prayer-meeting. The most important clause of the constitution related to the prayer-meeting, which stated, "*It is expected that all the active members of this society will be present at every meeting unless detained by some absolute necessity, and that each one will take some part, however slight, in every meeting.*" This sentence was underscored, and when the constitution was printed it was put in italics, which symbolizes the way in which it has been engraved, underscored, and italicized on the heart of the Christian Endeavor movement from that day to this.

Moreover, this article concerning the prayer-meeting went on to state that once each month an experience meeting should be held, at which meeting "each member shall speak concerning his progress in the Christian life for the past month." "If any one chooses, he can express his feelings by an appropriate verse of Scripture." "It is expected, if any one is obliged to be absent from this experience meeting, he will send his reason for absence by some one who attends." Moreover, at the close of the monthly experience meeting, the constitution specified that "the roll shall be called, and the response of the active members who are present shall be considered a renewed expression of allegiance to Christ." "If any member of the society is absent from the monthly experience meeting and fails to send an excuse, the Lookout Committee is expected to take the name of such a one, and, in a kindly and brotherly spirit, to ascertain the reason of the absence. If any member of this society is absent and unexcused from three consecutive experience meetings, such a one ceases to be a member of the society, and his name shall be stricken from the list of members."

It will be noticed that, word for word, this original constitution has, in almost every important particular, been followed by the vast majority of the almost numberless millions of copies of constitutions printed since. The object of the society was defined in the same way then as now. The two classes of members were distinguished from each other by the same definition. The committees, so far as they were outlined at all, were assigned the same duties in that original constitution as they now assume.

The prayer-meeting pledge was made strenuous and binding from the beginning, although in its expanded form it was not then fully written out, but it was understood that every member who signed that constitution promised to attend the young people's meeting and take some part aside from singing, "unless prevented by some absolute necessity." There was no mincing of words or shading off of the idea, and, though it was discovered afterward that some less stalwart souls found a gap in the pledge in the words "it is expected," through which they crawled into the seductive playground of indolence and ease—a gap which, by the way, was soon stopped up—yet, in purpose and spirit, the prayer-meeting pledge was as strenuous then as it always has been since.

The provision for the consecration meeting was complete from the first, and the same words are used now as then, with the exception that it was in those days called an "experience meeting," a name which was often applied to it for some years, but which was afterward dropped for the broader and more significant term "consecration."

THE BIRTHPLACE OF THE YOUNG PEOPLE'S SOCIETY OF CHRISTIAN ENDEAVOR.

THE PARLOR IN WHICH THE SOCIETY WAS FORMED.

This then was the document which the pastor, on that cold February evening, brought down-stairs to his young people. No wonder that he felt in some doubt as to whether they would accept its strong and iron-clad provisions. With a good deal of natural hesitation he presented it to them and read the constitution through, page by page.

A deathly stillness fell upon the meeting. Those strict provisions were evidently more than the young people had bargained for. They had not been accustomed to take their religious duties so seriously. Nothing of the sort had ever been heard of in that church, or, to their knowledge, in any church, before. To some of them it seemed that more was expected of them than of the deacons even, and other officers of the church, and they felt keenly their own inexperience and awkwardness in Christian service.

It was simply a company of average young people. Not many mighty, not many learned, were there, but this company was another of the weak things which God used to confound the mighty. These young men and women were as bashful, as timid and retiring, as any similar company, probably. Among them was not a single unpleasantly precocious young Christian. There was no prig in all that room, imbued with the smug consciousness that he was "not as other men."

They were active, energetic, fun-loving young people, just such as can be gathered in any church to-day.

But they were *Christian* young people. Their hearts were touched by love for Him who gave Himself for them, and they sincerely desired to do His will.

As I said, a considerable and painful silence fell upon the meeting when this constitution with its serious provisions was proposed. It seemed as though the society would die still-born, and be simply a creature of the pastor's imagination. But God ordered it otherwise. In that company were two who were especially influential and helpful in launching the little craft. These were Mr. W. H. Pennell, before mentioned, and the pastor's wife. Seeing that the matter was likely to fall through, at least for that meeting, Mr. Pennell affixed his signature to the constitution and called upon his class of young men to do the same. Mrs. Clark quietly circulated among the girls of the Mizpah Circle, persuading them that it was not such a "dreadful" promise to make as they at first supposed, telling them that the provisions of this constitution any earnest young Christian could live up to, and promising herself to be a member, though at first she shrunk from the pledge as much as any of them.

One by one the young men and women affixed their names to the document, a few more minutes were spent in conversation, a closing prayer was offered, and a hymn sung, and the young people went out into the frosty night to their homes with many a merry "Good-night," "Good-night" to each other, and the first society of Christian Endeavor was formed.

Fac-Simile of Original Constitution.

Name. This Society shall be called the Williston Young Peoples Society of Christian Endeavor

Object. Its object shall be to promote an earnest Christian life among its members, to increase their mutual acquaintance, and to make them more useful in the service of God.

Membership. The members of this society shall consist of all young people who sincerely desire to accomplish the results above specified. They shall become members upon being ~~the~~ elected by the society and by signing their names on this book.

Officers — The Officers of this Society shall be a President, Vice President & Secretary ~~Treasurer~~
There shall also be a Prayermeeting Committee of ~~five~~
A Social Committee of ~~three~~
and a Lookout Committee of ~~three~~

Duties of Officers
The duties of the President Vice President, & Secretary shall be those that usually fall to those officers
The Prayermeeting Committee shall have in charge the Friday evening prayermeetings shall see that a topic is assigned & a leader provided for each meeting.

<u>The Prayermeeting</u>
It is expected that all the members of the Society will be present at every meeting unless detained by some absolute necessity, & that each one will take some part however slight in every meeting. The meetings will be held just one hour and, at their close, some time may be taken for introductions & social intercourse if desired.

Once each month an experience meeting shall be held at which each member shall speak concerning his or her progress in the Christian life for the past month. If any one chooses he can express his feelings by an appropriate verse of Scripture. It is expected that if any one is obliged to be absent at this monthly meeting he will send the reason of his absence by someone who attends

Social Committee

It shall be the duty of the Social Committee to provide for the mutual acquaintance of the members by occasional Sociables for which any Entertainment that may be deemed best may be provided.

Lookout Committee

It shall be the duty of the Lookout Committee to bring new members into the Society, to introduce them to the work & to affectionately look after & reclaim any that seem to be indifferent to their duties.

Meetings & Elections

Business meetings can be held at the close of the Friday evening meeting or at any other time in accordance with the call of the President. An election of Officers & Committees shall be held once in six months. Names may be proposed by a nominating committee appointed by the President —

Miscellaneous

Any other committees may be added and duties assumed by this Society which may in the future seem best. This Constitution can be amended by a two third vote of the society.

CHAPTER IV.

THE HEART OF THE SOCIETY.

The Prayer-Meeting Idea—At the "Usual Hour"—The Deacon's Prayer—Winking at Gray Hairs and Wrinkles—The Warm Spot in the Room—A Service for Instruction—The Fetish of the Prayer-Meeting—A New Conception of the Prayer-Meeting—Inspiration and Fellowship Rather than Instruction—Something for Thomas and Harry, and Mary and Susan—Showing His Colors—A Place for Every One.

SINCE so much of the life of the Christian Endeavor movement centres in the prayer-meeting, it is important that the prayer-meeting idea which is cultivated by this movement should be thoroughly understood.

If it has conferred one conspicuous blessing upon the churches above every other, it has been, I believe, in reviving the true idea of the church prayer-meeting, which in many cases was in danger of being utterly lost. In many thousands of churches the prayer-meeting had degenerated into a lecture by the minister, supplemented, perhaps, by one or two long and able petitions by the brethren. The following picture of the prayer-meeting of old will be recognized by many:

The notice was given from the pulpit, "The prayer and conference meeting will be held at the usual hour." When the "usual hour" arrived, a sparse congregation of from six to twenty-six would spread themselves out over the vestry, occupying as much of the floor space as possible that the poverty of attendance might not be too evident. The pastor would give out a long hymn, the organist would play the tune all through, chorus and all, upon an asthmatic organ; the scattered congregation would pipe through five or six verses of the hymn; then would come a long prayer from the pastor and an abbreviated sermon of from twenty to thirty minutes in length; the venerable deacon (God bless him!) who for years had borne the burden and heat of the day, would offer a long, long prayer, not forgetting the Jews, even though he sometimes did forget the commonplace members of the Sunday-school connected with his own church. Another long hymn and prayer, and the time to close would come, much to the relief of the majority of the audience.

Many of my readers will recognize this description as in no sense a caricature of the prayer-meeting a generation back.

The so-called young people's prayer-meeting was scarcely more attractive. The attendance was still smaller, and, though the average age was somewhat younger than in the other prayer-meeting of the church, yet it required a great stretch of courtesy and an extensive winking at gray hairs and wrinkles to consider the majority of those present any longer young people, except by brevet.

The only warm spot in the room was often found in the air-tight stove.

One of the more elderly young men usually occupied the chair. By no

THE CHAPEL OF WILLISTON CHURCH WHERE THE FIRST CHRISTIAN ENDEAVOR MEETING WAS HELD.

possibility was it a young woman, and there were many most excruciating pauses which could only be filled up by a frequent resort to the over-worked hymn book.

I am far from saying that all young people's meetings, or all church prayer-meetings, are accurately described in the foregoing paragraphs; but, without hesitation, I can call a multitude of my readers to witness that a great many meetings could thus be described without a particle of exaggeration.

Very evidently there was a fault somewhere, and I do not hesitate to say that this fault was a radical one, lying at the very basis of the prayer-meeting idea in many churches.

It was a service for instruction rather than for inspiration. It was the place where young people and others should study the map of the celestial city and hear about the positions of the guide-posts which pointed to it, but a meeting where they were not expected to take many forward steps in the direction of that city.

Of course, if it were to be a meeting for instruction, it must naturally drift into the hands of those who were able to instruct. The pastor, the aged deacon, venerable in years and ripe in experience; the college graduate, the glib and gifted speaker, found a place in the prayer-meeting for the exercise of their gifts, but there was no place in such a meeting for young Thomas and Harry, and Mary and Susan. They were not wise. They had little experience. If they spoke at all, it must be in a stumbling and hesitating way. Perhaps they would break down if they even attempted to repeat a verse of Scripture. What place then for their active participation would there be in such a meeting?

For generations the idea of edification was the fetish of the prayer-meeting. No one was expected to take part who could not speak to edification, and the remnants of this idea, frayed and torn as they are, are still the bane of many a prayer-meeting in all parts of the world.

The Society of Christian Endeavor started with another conception of the prayer-meeting. It was not a place for instruction from man so much as for instruction from God. It was not the place for the exposition of a body of divinity or for indoctrination in the fine points of theology. It was a place for *practice* rather than for preaching, for inspiration and fellowship rather than for instruction. A place for the participation of all the average two-talent people, rather than of the exceptional ten-talent man and woman.

The idea of instruction was not ignored, but the leaders of this new society contended that the prayer-meeting was not the place for instruction in the ordinary sense of the word, and that there is ample room for instruction in other services of the church.

The Sunday morning service is for instruction. The Sunday evening service is for instruction. The Sunday-school is for instruction. The pastor's catechetical class is for instruction. The missionary concert is for instruction. The religious newspaper is for instruction. In fact, there are few departments of church life which have not this for their central idea. But the Christian Endeavor Society has always believed that the prayer-meeting was for another order of service, and that this other service is quite as necessary to the development of spiritual activities as the service of instruction.

And so it happens that the whole idea of participation is changed. There is something for Thomas and Harry and Mary and Susan to do, as well as for their respective and respected fathers and grandfathers. There is an appropriate and modest part which the youngest believer in Christ can have in the weekly prayer-meeting as well as the pastor and oldest saint. And, moreover, it is not only fitting for them to participate, but it is obligatory upon them to confess their Lord, if they would grow in His grace and knowledge.

It is not sufficient for them to confess Christ before men by baptism and by publicly joining the church of Christ, but frequent, nay, constant, confession of Him alone insures their growth in grace.

And what more appropriate or delightful place for such a confession of Christ is there than the prayer-meeting—especially for the new convert, the young people's prayer-meeting? Here his trembling voice may at once be heard in acknowledgment of his Saviour's love. If he hesitates and stumbles in his speech, it is of no consequence, for he is not making an oration or polishing a well-rounded sentence, or giving instruction to his elders. That would indeed be absurd and the height of priggishness.

But he can rise to his feet and say : " I love Him because He first loved me." He can offer the Publican's trembling prayer, " God be merciful to me a sinner," or the Psalmist's humble petition, " Create within me a clean heart, O God." He can show his colors, and at least stand up to be counted on Christ's side.

Now if any young brother is urged to participate in the meeting, he cannot find a convenient excuse in the fact that he is inexperienced and cannot speak to the edification of the assembly.

The timid brother who has been a little troubled in his conscience because his voice is so seldom heard in the house of prayer cannot salve his conscience with the thought that he cannot speak to edification.

The women who have been restrained by a misinterpretation of Paul's command uttered eighteen hundred years ago to their rude, half-Christianized sisters in Corinth, who were told by the great apostle not to chatter in church while the services were going on, can no longer keep silence by hiding behind this misinterpretation. They can at least repeat a verse of Scripture or a favorite hymn which expresses their heart's devotion without any let or hindrance from the most rigid divine of the oldest school.

In short, the society of Christian Endeavor is built upon this radical idea, that in the prayer-meeting there is a place for every one ; a word, a testimony, or a prayer ; that it is a necessary part of the Christian life to confess the Lord, and that no one can grow in grace as he should when he neglects this aid to an outspoken Christian life.

The monthly consecration services still further emphasizes this idea, for at this meeting it is provided that the names shall be called ; that some response shall be given by every one; that the absent members shall send at least a verse of Scripture to show that they have not forgotten their vows; and continual attendance and participation in this meeting is made a test upon which continuance in the society depends.

This idea has very largely pervaded the meetings of older members of the church, at least in many sections of America. It has rejuvenated ten thousand lifeless young people's prayer-meetings, has poured life blood into ten thousand more mid-week services of the church, and has proved, I think it can be claimed without immodesty, an immeasurable blessing to the spiritual activities of every church where the idea has been adopted.

CHAPTER V.

EARLY DAYS AND EARLY WAYS.

A Brief Record—The First Prayer-Meeting—Doubts and Fears—The First Leader—The First Boy Leader—No Attempt at Eloquence—From America to Berlin—He Kept His Pledge—How the Boys Hold Out—The Influence of that Prayer-Meeting.

THE only record which I find in a brief diary kept in those days concerning the beginning of the Christian Endeavor Society reads as follows: "Feb. 2, 1881. The boys and girls take tea with us, about thirty-five of them, and we form a young people's society, with Granville Staples for President."

Two days later, Feb. 4, is this record: "First young people's meeting conducted by the new association. Very successful."

I remember far more about this meeting than this hasty diary records. I went to it, I remember, with a good deal of anxiety. I had begun to feel almost hopeless concerning any new plan for the nurture of the young people, so many had been tried with unsatisfactory results. I feared that this new society would go the way of all the others, and that the promise which the members had made at their pastor's house, two days before, would seem so onerous and burdensome that they could not fulfill it.

GRANVILLE STAPLES.

The first prayer-meeting of the newly fledged society, held Feb. 4, 1881, was led by Mr. Granville Staples, who two days before had been elected president of the society. He was a young man of two or three and twenty years of age, perhaps, who was then employed as clerk in his brother's dry goods store in Portland. A most earnest Christian, and, unusually gifted in the prayer-meeting, it was but natural that he should have this duty assigned to him. A letter received from Mr. Staples confirming my own recollection of the matter settles beyond dispute the fact.

The second prayer-meeting, held a week later, was conducted by Master Henry B. Pennell, the eleven-year-old son of the first signer of the constitution. Some have wondered that a lad of that age should have been chosen for this service, but Henry Pennell was a boy of unusual maturity, and I desired to emphasize the fact that this was a young people's society, and that a lad could lead a meeting if only the older ones would support him and take their part according to the Christian Endeavor pledge.

According to my recollection he led the meeting modestly and well. The others, seeing one of their youngest companions in the chair, rallied to his support, and in every way the meeting was a conspicuous success.

The pastor of the society was surprised and delighted with the result of that first Christian Endeavor prayer-meeting. His little faith in young people was increased, and he went home from the meeting with a new song in his heart and a new hope for the future of the young people of the church.

Yet there was no attempt at eloquence in that prayer-meeting, not a single remark was made that will be recorded in history or treasured up by future generations. Many of the testimonies were hesitating and awkward, very likely. Some of them possibly were ungrammatical. The prayers contained few well-rounded periods or flights of eloquence, but the members were faithful to their pledge, many new voices were heard that had never been heard before, and which never would have been heard but for their prayer-meeting promise, and many young hearts were strengthened in their purpose to serve with all their might the Lord whom they had begun to confess.

Most of those present on that first evening are still young men and women. Some of the older ones are verging toward middle age. The boys have grown up and gone into business or the trades. Some of them have graduated at college and are established in their professions. But I will venture to say that there is not one of them but has been a better man and woman during all these years than otherwise he or she would have been had it not been for that confession of Christ and other confessions which followed in the prayer-meeting room of Williston Church.

A few months since, in the American Church in Berlin, a young man spoke to me after the service whom I very speedily recognized, though I had not seen him for many years, as one of the earliest Endeavorers of Williston Church, George F. Libby by name, who was either present at the very first meeting or one of the meetings which immediately followed.

He was then one of the youngest of all the society, a boy of twelve or thirteen years perhaps. He has gone through the public schools and through college. He is a graduate in medicine and has established himself in a lucrative position in his native city. When I saw him he was taking special studies in the capital of Germany, but he was the same simple-minded, earnest young Christian that I knew fourteen years before in Williston Church.

In Berlin I heard from his lips the same loving testimony to the goodness of his Saviour that he gave as a boy in the old church home, better expressed to be sure, deeper and richer in experience, but still the same testimony of love, the same aspiration for service. He still wears his Christian Endeavor badge, and he told me that never had the influence of the Endeavor pledge lost its

GEORGE F. LIBBY (1881).

DR. GEORGE F. LIBBY (1892).

hold upon him, and that, whether in Germany or America, Berlin or Portland, he endeavored to do whatever Christ would like to have him to do, and to confess His name before men.

Such is the history of many of the earliest members of the Endeavor Society, I believe. Their early love, faith, and loyalty is maintained in these later years with unflagging zeal, and their chief joy is still found in service for Christ and the Church.

CHAPTER VI.

THE CHARTER MEMBERS.

Reading Character from Chirography—Supplementing the Reader's Insight—Some of the Charter Members, and What has Become of Them—Earnest Workers in Williston Church—Christian Workers in Other Fields—Some "Local Unions"—Y. M. C. A. Workers—Letters from College Boys—What a Brown University Student Says of College Boys—A Letter from the First President—"What Christian Endeavor Has Done for Me"—Answered by Mr. William H. Pennell.

IN the *fac similes* of the autographs of the first signers of the original constitution, my readers, if they are expert at deciphering character from handwriting, will find employment for a leisure hour. But perhaps they will be glad to have me help them in their task of character reading by telling them something of the subsequent history of these charter members of the Society of Christian Endeavor. These members all signed their names, evidently, with the pastor's stylographic pen, so that the character cannot be detected as easily as if each one had used his own favorite quill. So I will supplement my reader's insight with the following facts:

The names of many of these earliest signers of the constitution have already appeared and will appear in other chapters of this book, and the mention here made of them must be very brief.

I regret that I do not know something of all of these earliest members, and that I have not the pictures of all of them. It is only fair to say that there were some who joined the society a few days or a few weeks later who were just as devoted Christians and just as worthy of honor as any who signed their names on the first evening.

To all intents and purposes they, too, were charter members of the first society, but were detained from that first meeting by illness, or by some other imperative duty.

Through the kindness of Mrs. E. L. Sayward I am able to give my readers on another page the faces of some of these earliest members. On still another page will be found the faces of some others who did not happen to be among the first signers.

Of the first name that appears on this roll of honor, Wm. H. Pennell, I

Names of Members
Active Members

1. Wm. H. Pennell
2. Chas. S Thorndike
3. Edw L. Sayward
4. John C. B. Shrafe
5. C. W. Dearborn
6. B H Farnsworth
7. Geo. L. Osgood
8. C. C. Cryder
9. Henry P. Pennell
10. Charles F. Johnson
11. Isa Pennell
12. Cora Rand
13. Gracie Burrowes
14. Anna M Garland
15. Annie P. Merrill
16. Carrie B Howes
17. Alice Carter
18. Carrie J Cousins
19. Charles K. Isaac
20. Frank C Pibber

have already spoken, and, in subsequent pages, his name will appear more than once. His Christian devotion and entire loyalty to Christian Endeavor ideas are too well known to require further comment.

Mr. Edward L. Sayward, the first young man who signed the constitution, is an active and successful business man of Portland. A prominent member of Williston Church still, of whose Sunday-school he has been the efficient superintendent. His pastor can still count upon him as in days of old for faithful service. His wife, who at the time of this chronicle was Miss Hattie L. Jordan, though not able to be present at this meeting, became a member within a week or two, and is a worthy helpmate of her husband in every good work. She was one of Mrs. Clark's most efficient and trusted helpers in the Mizpah Circle, and has greatly assisted me in preparing these brief biographies.

Miss Carrie B. Howes is the wife of one of Colorado's most devoted Endeavorers, Mr. Edward B. Clark, who is now the President of the Denver Christian Endeavor Union, and who for many years has been prominent in the work throughout the Centennial State. What more appropriate than that he should marry one of the original Endeavorers.

Of Henry B. Pennell we speak in another connection. With his sister, Isabel Pennell, he lives in Jamaica Plain, Mass., and both, I am sure, are devoted to the work of Christ and His Church.

Alice M. Carter has changed her name to Mrs. Geo. L. Patterson. She now lives in New York City. She is an earnest and devoted Christian, as she always was while in Williston Church.

Carrie J. Cousins is still an active member of the Williston Society, earnest in every good work.

Helen A. Sampson, now Mrs. Helen A. Leavitt, lives in Bowdoinham, Maine, where she has resided since her husband's death with her two children. She is a woman of most lovable nature, as all her friends predicted when she was a girl, and is as earnest and devoted in her Christian work as ever.

Miss Florence M. Safford has become Mrs. Geo. G. Austin. She still lives in Portland, where she has for a number of years attended a Methodist Church.

Lillian Armsby lives in Portland still and is an active and loyal member of Williston Church and society.

Millie E. Libby has become Mrs. Osgood T. Lean and lives at Millis, Mass. She is the mother of three little girls, who doubtless will be earnest Christian Endeavorers in good time.

Miss Marietta Robinson still lives in Portland, but having moved to another part of the city attends the West End Congregational Church.

Miss Eloise Bragdon is now Mrs. Elmer Bachelder of Portland.

THE CHARTER MEMBERS.

Active Members

21. Helen A. Sampson.
22. Alma G. Bennett.
23. Florence M. Safford.
24. Lillian Armsbey
25. Millie E. Libby.
26. Manilla Robinson
27. Eloise Bragdon.
28. Iny F. Tilton.
29. Will. J. Knight.
30. Clarence A. Hight.
31. Edmund T. Garland.
32. Bessie E. Pine.
33. Connie E. Johnson.
34. Annie L. Dodge.
35. Bessie A. Rand.
36. Bessie Dunning
37. Eliza A. Kenworthy
38. Clara V. Sprague
39. Josie A. Hutchins.
40. Nellie A. Jordan.
41. Amelia Kenworthy
42. Fred Waterman
43. Henry. Fabyan

THE CHARTER MEMBERS.

Miss Inez Tilton lives in Haverhill, Mass., carrying with her no doubt the good influences of Williston society.

Clarence A. Hight is a rising young lawyer of the city of Portland. He is now an attendant at St. Stephen's Episcopal Church, and says that "next to the instruction of his parents the Williston society has been the most prominent formative factor in his life."

Edmund T. Garland is now the Secretary of the Y. M. C. A. of Portland and is looked upon as one of the most successful secretaries as well as one of the most devoted Christian young men of Maine.

Carrie E. Johnson still lives in Portland and is now a member of High Street Church.

Annie L. Dodge is now Mrs. E. Garland of Saco. She is now as always a most devoted Christian.

Misses Eliza and Amelia Kenworthy are still active workers in Williston Church and society, ever ready, as of old, for any good work.

Miss Clara B. Sprague is a teacher in one of the public schools of Minneapolis, and from her we shall hear in a later portion of this chapter.

Miss Nellie M. Jordan is now Mrs. Charles A. Plummer, and is still active in Williston Church, as in days of yore.

George P. Morris lives in Portland, and is still actively connected with the church of his first love.

Miss Jennie M. Hayes is one of the most earnest and consecrated workers in Williston Church and Sunday-school, and is assistant superintendent in the infant department of the Sunday-school.

Miss Maude Burrows has become Mrs. J. L. Barker, but is still connected with the church of her childhood.

Miss Lola Jefferds is an invalid living in Livermore Falls, Maine, where her parents reside.

Miss Rose Sayward is still an active member in the Williston Church and Endeavor society.

Two more of the earliest members of the Williston Society concluded to unite their fortunes for life, and a few years ago formed a "local union," as it has been felicitously called. These two are Mr. Charles S. Thorndike and Miss Hattie Littlefield, who are now living in Worcester, Mass.

Miss Carrie Knight has become Mrs. William T. Musans, and has wandered farther from the home church than any of the others, so far as I know, for she is now living in San Francisco, having spent many years on the Pacific coast.

Miss Jennie L. Sampson is now Mrs. Charles Tolman of Portland, and is, as of old, an active and earnest member of Williston Church.

The fourteenth anniversary of the Williston Society, held February 3,

THE CHARTER MEMBERS.

44. Willie Hutchinson
45. Granville Staples
46. Geo. P. Morris
47. Jennie Hayes.
48. Maud Burrowes
49. Lola Jefferds.
50. Rose Sayward.
51. Lizzie Wilson.
52. Addie Libby.
53. Jennie Sampson.
54. Emma Young.
55. Sterling T. Dow.
56. Chas. B. Newton
(a) F. J. Bragdon
57. Hattie Littlefield

1895, was an occasion of peculiar interest to all its members. The society, vigorous and flourishing as ever, doing a better work, according to its pastor's testimony, than ever before within his knowledge, received hearty messages and affectionate greetings from many of its earliest and long absent members.

Some of these members belong to the special roll of honor whose autograph signatures are here given, and some joined the society shortly afterward. We must make room in this chapter for a few extracts from these delightful letters which tell of the faithfulness and constancy and joyous devotion of these early members.

Miss Henrietta H. Stanwood, one of the earliest members, who was afterward one of the editors of *The Congregationalist*, wrote: "It is an honor to be a pioneer in such a movement as you now celebrate. I shall always be glad that I saw the first link formed of the blessed chain of Christian Endeavor which to-day encircles the world. Those first days brought us very near each other as we prayed and trusted."

Mr. Edmund T. Garland, Secretary of the Portland Y. M. C. A., wrote: "I owe everything to the Williston Society. It was through its influence and inspiration that I became a Christian and first learned how to do Christian work."

Rev. Clayton D. Boothby, who with his wife were later members of the society, wrote from Thomaston, Maine, where he is a pastor, that he had just organized a society in his church where there had never been one before, and that his wife had organized a Junior society, and that both societies were most promising factors of the church.

Another of the early, though not earliest, members of Williston Society, Arthur H. Chamberlain, wrote from Brown University, where he is a college boy, the following glowing message:

BROWN UNIVERSITY, Jan. 31, 1895.
DEAR WILLISTON Y. P. S. C. E.

To tell all that Christian Endeavor has done for me would be impossible. Probably I do not realize in any full degree how much influence has been brought to bear upon my life by work in and for Christian Endeavor by the atmosphere of its meetings, by association with its members, and, most of all, by the very spirit and inspiration of the movement. I always have believed that Christian Endeavor was the strongest organized force in the religious world, and especially is this noticeable here at college. Almost all the most earnest Christian men and Y. M. C. A. workers here at Brown are Christian Endeavorers, and I believe it is so among young people almost everywhere.

ARTHUR H. CHAMBERLAIN.

Another Williston boy who is now in college, Henry R. Holden, of Yale University, wrote, that "through the earlier years of my Christian life the Young People's Society of Williston Church was of the greatest benefit to me, and it did more than any other influence toward keeping my feet in the right path. Its name is always mentioned in my prayers, and I hope that you as constantly remember your absent members."

Chas. F. Johnson, the General Secretary of the Y. M. C. A. of Milford, Mass., wrote: "The early training I received as an early member of your society was the foundation of the work the Master called me to nine years ago."

Miss Clara V. Sprague, a teacher in Minneapolis, declared: "I know that the society has done me untold good. Whatever there may be of character in me I feel confident comes from my Christian experience. That has been largely helped and strengthened by my connection with Christian Endeavor."

A GROUP OF CHARTER MEMBERS (WILLISTON SOCIETY).

1. Rev. F. E. Clark.
2. Mrs. F. E. Clark.
3. Granville Staples.
4. William H. Pennell.
5. Miss Florence Safford, now Mrs. Geo. G. Austin.
6. Miss Jennie L. Sampson, now Mrs. Charles Tolman.
7. Carrie M. Knight, now Mrs. Wm. T. Musatre.
8. Miss Inez Tilton.
9. Miss Eliza Kenworthy.
10. Marietta Robinson.
11. Geo. P. Morris.
12. Miss Alice M. Carter, now Mrs. Geo. T. Patterson.
13. Miss Rose M. Sayward.
14. Edward L. Sayward.
15. Miss Carrie Jackson Cousins.
16. Miss Millie E. Libby, now Mrs. I. Lean.
17. Miss Helen A. Sampson, now Mrs. Helen Samp. Leavitt.
18. Edmund T. Garland.
19. Miss Bessie Dunning.
20. Miss Annie L. Dodge (1881).
21. Miss Nellie N. Jordan, now Mrs. Charles A. Plummer.
22. Geo. A. Libby.
23. Clarence A. Hight.
24. Miss Anna M. Garland.
25. Miss Maud Burrows, now Mrs. J. L. Barker.
26. Miss Annie L. Dodge, now Mrs. E. Garland (1895).
27. Edmund T. Garland (1895).
28. Miss Annie P. Merrill, now Mrs. McCullough.

Fred A. Lord, one of the youngest members of the society in its early days, wrote from Biddeford, Me.: "Although at the time I joined I was such a little fellow that I hardly knew the significance of the step I was taking, yet the helpful start received from the society, coupled with constant watchfulness on the part of my dear home friends, has resulted in making me a Christian young man. I love the name of Christian Endeavor and all that it means."

Mrs. Annie L. Garland wrote from Saco: "My thoughts go back to a little gathering at the home of our pastor fourteen years ago. I feel that no greater honor can ever come to me than that of being a charter member of the Christian Endeavor Society."

WILLIAM H. PENNELL.

Mr. Henry B. Pennell answered: "Present in heart and spirit, in delightful memories and earnest prayers that the future of Williston Society may be as fruitful as the past."

Mr. Granville Staples sent his greetings as the first president of the society. "Little did we know," he wrote, "on that Wednesday evening fourteen years ago what a mighty work God was to do through us. I wish I could take you to some of the meetings of the Philadelphia Union and show you what Christian Endeavor is doing here."

I cannot present this sheaf of living messages to my readers in any better way than by binding them all together with the following letter from Mr. William H. Pennell, known everywhere as the first signer of the constitution:

WASHINGTON, D. C., January 29, 1895.

DEAR FRIENDS OF WILLISTON C. E. SOCIETY:

You ask what has Christian Endeavor done for me—and it would take a volume to tell the story. It has kept me in touch with Christian work. It has helped me to accomplish some little for the glory of God and the help of mankind. It has brought me into close relationship with many of the Christian workers in the country and among all denominations. It has shown me that sectarian differences are very flimsy barriers to keep brethren apart, and that when these brethren meet upon the common ground of the Fatherhood of God and the Brotherhood of Men, as taught and practiced by our Saviour, Jesus, the world is made better by every Christian life.

It has shown me that young people have a strong desire to make the world better by their lives, and that they are willing and glad to leave all theological discussions and denominational diversions to those who can be profited by them. With the motto given us by our beloved President, Dr. Clark, "For Christ and the Church," each one is willing to devote all energies to building up their own church home, that in that way Christ may be exalted. All this Christian Endeavor is teaching me. And may God help us all to live the life that shall best glorify our Saviour. Truly yours, W. H. PENNELL.

SOME EARLY MEMBERS OF THE WILLISTON SOCIETY.

1. Mrs. Alice Pote Davis.
2. Samuel C. Gould.
3. Charles Wyer.
4. Mrs. Nannie B. Pennell.
5. Geo. E. Goodwin.
6. Harris Barnes.
7. Abbie Bennett.
8. Maria Kenworthy.
9. Frank W. Jewett.
10. Mrs. Josie P. Scofield.
11. Charles Hanson.
12. Miss Nellie Wilcox.
13. Addie Wyer.
14. Carrie Armstrong.
15. Mrs. Hattie Jordan Sayward.
16. Fred. Lord.
17. Agnes A. Sleeth.

CHAPTER VII.

THE GRAIN OF MUSTARD SEED, AND HOW IT GREW.

The New Williston Church—Some Records from My Journal—Monotony of the Records a Good Sign—How the Seed Germinated—Rev. Charles A. Dickinson—The First Newspaper Article—The Second Society—Rev. Charles Perry Mills—From Port to Port—The Third Society and its Pastor.

IT may be of interest to note that four days after the Society of Christian Endeavor was formed, and two days after the first prayer-meeting under its auspices was held, the beautiful new Williston Church was dedicated.

It had been built some two years and a half before, and had been occupied since about the 1st of September, 1878, but it was not dedicated until the debt incurred in building the church was not only pledged but all paid in, so that the dedicatory exercises were postponed till February 6, 1881.

The same earnestness and zeal which characterized the first meeting was shown in the subsequent meetings of the society.

The allusions that I find in my journal to those early young people's prayer-meetings are very brief, but all are encouraging. They were held on Friday evenings, from half-past seven to half-past eight. Here are some of the records:

"Feb. 11, 1881. Young people's prayer-meeting held. A very good one."

WILLISTON CHURCH (FROM THE NORTH).

"Feb. 25. Young people's meeting. An experience meeting and a very good one."

"April 1. A very good young people's meeting in the evening conducted by Edward Sayward."

"April 8. Young people meet in the evening, and all do well."

"April 15. A hard, driving snow-storm. Wind very strong, snow deep and drifting. Young people's meeting in the evening."

So it seems that even a Maine blizzard could not interfere with a Christian Endeavor prayer-meeting.

The very monotony of these reports speaks well for the steadfastness of the early Endeavorers. The meetings had no history to record, because they were so uniformly good. The pastor had no discouraging and hopeless comments to make, because the young people were faithful to their vows and their covenant obligations.

REV. CHARLES A. DICKINSON.

For many weeks and months nothing was said to the outside public about this new organization in Williston Church. Not a line concerning it found its way into the local papers, much less into the religious journals of the day. But life cannot long be hidden. The little seed that quietly germinates under the soil is bound to push its way up and out into the world by and by. It is sure to attract the attention of the passer-by sooner or later, if it has the germ of life within it.

So it was that this Society of Christian Endeavor could not, even if it desired, hide its light under a bushel, and this it did not wish to do. Yet for many months it was allowed to work out its own problems unheralded by men.

Even the members of the church with which it was connected knew little about it except that there was a young people's meeting held every week, of which notice was given from the pulpit—a meeting which the pastor always attended, and in which he took especial delight and pride.

A brother minister of Portland was the first, to my knowledge, to speak a word of hopefulness and cheer concerning this new organization.

The Rev. Charles A. Dickinson, whose name is now honored and beloved by Endeavorers everywhere, was then the pastor of the old Second Parish Church of Portland. This historic church enjoyed in its early days the ministrations of that remarkable man, the devout Edward Payson, who, perhaps, more than any other man of this century, has left his impress upon the churches of New England.

The Church is often called the Payson Memorial Church.

This young pastor, now the leader of the Institutional Church movement throughout America, then as now believed in young people, loved them, and desired to find new methods of usefulness for them.

Meeting him upon the street one day, for I knew him familiarly as an old friend of school-boy days, I asked him to come to our young people's meeting some time, since I thought he would enjoy it. He accepted my invitation, and one evening quietly took a back seat, coming in a little late, so that I did not know that he was there. He was very much moved by the meeting, though it was an ordinary Endeavor prayer-meeting, such as those so summarily dismissed in my journal every week. But the evident sincerity and child-like faith of the young people, their earnest prayers and frequent testimonies touched his heart, and he has told me since that he could scarcely keep back the tears of joy as he heard the outspoken confession of these young friends, and he resolved that, as soon as possible, he would have a Society of Christian Endeavor in his own church.

REV. C. P. MILLS.

The way was not open for him, however, just then to form such a society, and consequently the second society was formed, not in the Second Parish Church of Portland, but in the North Church of Newburyport, Mass.

In August, 1881, I wrote an article which was published in *The Congregationalist*, entitled "How One Church Cares for Its Young People." This was a description of the methods and plans of the Society of Christian Endeavor. It emphasized the prayer-meeting and the committee work and the consecration meeting. The article was reprinted in *The Sunday School Times*, and in other papers in this country and England. It immediately fell under the eye of Rev. Charles Perry Mills, pastor of the North Church of Newburyport, who, during all these years, has remained the beloved pastor of the same people, and has the distinction of being for the longest number of years the pastor of the same Endeavor Society of any man in the world. But I will let him tell in his own words how he came to form the second Society of Christian Endeavor and what the result was, only entering a *caveat* against his too complimentary allusions to the author of this history:

The Young People's Society of Christian Endeavor of the North Congregational Church of Newburyport, Mass., was organized, according to the record, October 18, 1881, eight months after the original society in the Williston Church at Portland. In the first voyage that the Young Christian Endeavor child undertook it passed successfully from port to port, from Portland to Newburyport, where it was warmly adopted because of its comely beauty and promising vigor. That Christian Endeavor was of spiritual origin and destined to become a Providential movement may be gathered from the similarity of the occasions that called into existence the first and second societies. The Newburyport pastor, Charles Perry Mills, the first winter of his pastorate, 1881, had the happiness to see a revival that resulted in the conversion of a goodly number of young people, a revival that was simultaneous with the one that occurred in the Portland Church, that produced similar results, and that led to the formation of the first society, and then, when the plan of the first was known, to the second. The spiritual chords were vibrating in unison all unconsciously between these two seaport cities seventy miles apart on the Atlantic coast. It is a sign of great spiritual movements that God selects His choice man to be founder and leader; but the same divine breath prepares the hearts of kindred spirits to second and augment the movement. It was divinely given to Dr. Clark to originate the motion; the Newburyport pastor has always felt special gratitude that his life has been signalized by the opportunity given him to second the motion. If a motion is made and not seconded, that is one sign that it is without wisdom, or that the time is not ripe; but when the motion is seconded, it is then open for discussion and adoption. The Williston plan was seconded because it was *motion*, an advanced method over existing organizations for the training of the young. There was no special organization at the time, aside from the Sunday-school, for the care of the young in the Newburyport Church. A half-dozen constitutions of various societies for young people in other places were studied and compared, with the instant result that the Christian Endeavor Constitution, as struck off by Dr. Clark's inspiration, was accepted as superior to any or all. It was religious, as distinguished from the literary, musical, or social; it was organized, as distinguished from loose societies whose parts did not fit compactly together; it provided for a prayer-meeting with the distinctive feature of the pledge. It was felt that the Prime Mover of such a motion was the Spirit of God. At the tenth anniversary of this society the young man who was president, and who had started with its start and grown with its growth, said: "To-day we celebrate not only *our* anniversary, but also the decennial of the transplanting of this movement into Massachusetts soil, and its great growth shows how wonderfully it was adapted to this soil. The

NORTH CHURCH, NEWBURYPORT, MASS.

motion made in Portland and seconded in Newburyport, has been most unanimously carried throughout the world. Our society is the best school ever provided for the training of the young in the Christian life, and if true to our pledge, our growth in grace must be constant, and ever shall exert a mighty influence for good upon the coming generations in the church." The young man who made that utterance now faithfully handles money in the bank on week-days, and as faithfully handles the word of life in the pulpit on Sundays, and, together with his utterance, may be taken as a typical instance of the kind of result which Christian Endeavor turns out. A Junior Society to-day occupies the place in the North Church which was originally taken by the Young People's Society, and side by side with both there exists a Woman's Society of Christian Endeavor, most efficient and helpful, and filling for one sex at least the idea of a Senior Society, which the pastor advocated at the Montreal Convention.

The Newburyport Society, in addition to being the second society, and thus commending the motion to general acceptance, has another pleasant point of connection with the great movement of all the societies that is worthy of historical record. Among his early appointments where Dr. Clark advocated the cause from the platform, he accepted one to address this North Church Society at one of its anniversaries, and there he was given for the first time the appellation by the Newburyport pastor of "Father Endeavor." The pastor reported his own gentle witticism in *The Golden Rule*, from which this appellation was immediately taken up and used as a term of honor and endearment until it has become familiar as the name of Christian Endeavor. Dr. Clark has since pleasantly retorted that the pastor who perpetrated that stroke that carried the suggestion of such age in it should be known as "the man who fired the *joke* heard round the world;" but it was more than a joke. It was the recognition of what the great host of Christian Endeavorers, yea, what the Christian world now rejoices to acknowledge, that God had chosen His own prophet and made him the father of this movement. It was said with the same reverence and affection that led this same pastor to say at the decennial of the society, in speaking of W. H. Pennell, the first man who signed the Christian Endeavor constitution, remembering that in Hebrew *El* means God, that he was the *pen of God*. If this pastor should outlive Dr. Clark he would like to enter a claim upon these historic pages to head the list of contributors for some fitting memorial that will perpetuate the name, influence, and distinctive work of our "Father Endeavor."

The location of the third society is, so far as known, in the Christian Church of Scituate, R. I.; the fourth, in the St. Lawrence Street Church, of Portland, Me., a church situated at the other end of the city from the Williston Church; and the fifth, in the Winooskie Avenue Church, of Burlington, Vt. Other societies within a few months were formed in the Second Parish Church, in Portland; the West Church, of the same city; in Bath and Hampden, in Maine.

Thus, gradually, the work grew, and societies were multiplied, and Christian people began to say to themselves, "Is it not possible that God has a work for the Society of Christian Endeavor to do of which we have not as yet even dreamed?"

CHAPTER VIII.

EARLY FRIENDS OF EARLY DAYS.

The New Broom, and How it Swept—The First Anniversary—Inter-denominational Already—The Second President—The Newspaper Reports—Why it Grew—The Hectograph Pad, and How it Was Used—Its Own Recommendation.

THUS the early days of the first Endeavor Society went by.

The little faith of the pastor of the church was rebuked week by week as he saw the constancy and faithfulness of the young Christians.

Constantly and delightfully has he been surprised almost every week of his life since, by the same traits in the young people in all parts of the world. Everywhere he has found that when their hearts are touched by the love of Christ there are few things that they will not do and bear for His dear sake.

In the Williston Church the broom which he feared would only sweep clean while it was new, showed no signs of wearing out. In fact, the society gained in efficiency and well-regulated zeal as the days went by. New plans were adopted as new plans were needed, but still the great principles involved in the pledge, the consecration meeting, and the work of the different committees, were adhered to as strictly as at first, and in these features were found the life and virility of the society.

The records concerning the meetings are delightfully monotonous and uniformly tell of good work. Week by week new friends were won for the cause; especially in the fall of 1881 and the early winter of 1882, as the reports of the success of the first society became known and newspaper articles were multiplied describing its simple organization and its complete success.

When February 2, 1882, came around again the young society was quite vigorous enough to observe its anniversary and to rejoice that it had lived to see its first birthday.

Moreover, it called in its still younger brothers to rejoice with it, for by this time I find, on consulting the records of the day, that it is thought that there were at least twenty societies which were modeled on the basis of the Williston constitution. The usually published figures which declare that there were seven societies in 1882, refer to the first day of the new year. The widespread interest in the society which had arisen since the second society was established in October, 1881, may be understood from the fact that when the anniversary exercises were held in February, 1882, societies were known to exist in Dubuque, Ia.; Canandaigua, N. Y.; Hollis and Nashua, N. H.; Muir, Mich.; Goderich, Can., as well as those already mentioned. Most of these latter were but a few days or weeks old, and the exact date of their birth is not always known.

There were now two other societies in the parent city of Portland: One in the St. Lawrence Street Church, and one, if I am not mistaken, in the West Church. They had begun to be heard of, too, in other denominations besides the Congregational, even before the first society was a year old; and there is a record of one formed in a Baptist Church—in the Free Will Baptist Church of Augusta, Me.—besides the Christian Church of Scituate, R. I.

FRANKLIN AGGE.

Thus, before the first society could celebrate its first anniversary the movement had already become inter-denominational and inter-state, a prophecy this of the great work God designed it to accomplish in bringing together the young people of all countries and all denominations, not into a new denomination, not into organic unity, but into a spiritual unity, which from that day to this has increasingly marked the Christian Endeavor movement in all lands.

The first anniversary could scarcely have been a very stirring occasion, for I find in my journal under date of February 2, 1882, only the record "Anniversary of the Young People's Society."

From a newspaper clipping, however, which has been preserved, it seems that the Williston Society then had one hundred and thirty active members and some fifteen or twenty associate members. It seems, also, that it held a prayer-meeting every Friday evening, which, according to this newspaper, "is very largely attended, the vestry being frequently filled, and a large proportion of the active members take some part in every meeting."

"Monthly socials," the report goes on to say, "have also been held throughout the year, in which the young people have become acquainted with each other."

At this anniversary, remarks were made by the President, Mr. Franklin Agge, who, on the retirement of Mr. Granville Staples, had been elected the second President of the society. Mr. Agge was a young machinist of brilliant parts and great energy, who has since made a large place for himself in his chosen profession.

As a constructor of city water-works he has become well known in his line of business throughout the country, and frequently makes long journeys to distant parts of our own land and even to the countries across the sea to superintend the establishment of water-works.

He is still a devoted member of Williston Church, and for a number of years has been an honored deacon of the church. One of the addresses on this anniversary occasion was naturally made by Mr. Agge, another by Mr. Granville Staples, as the first President, who, having moved to the other end of the city, was by this time connected with the St. Lawrence Church, near his home, and with the Endeavor Society of that church.

A third address was by Mr. W. H. Pennell, the genial first signer of the constitution, of whom we have before spoken, and the fourth was by the pastor.

The reports of this anniversary were printed in the Portland daily papers, *The Christian Mirror*, *The Congregationalist*, and *The Golden Rule*, which was then especially friendly to the movement, though not in any way officially connected with it until a number of years after.

These reports greatly increased the interest which was already felt in the society, and doubtless resulted in turning the attention of many pastors to this form of work, who afterward adopted the principles and name of this new organization. It would be interesting to trace in more minute detail the beginnings of the first score or two of societies, but space will not allow; neither is the data at hand for such a history; but it is very plain that the society grew then, as it has since, because of its own inherent worth.

There was no attempt to crowd it upon public attention. There was no organization to print or circulate its literature. There was no money in its treasury to pay for the circulation of books or leaflets concerning the matter. In fact, it had no treasury at all except the private purses of one or two people who were frequently called to dip into them to pay for the postage stamps and the letter paper required in answering the very numerous requests for information which began to be received.

In the first place, it was not thought necessary even to print the constitution of a society so ephemeral as it was supposed the Endeavor Society would be. A hectograph gelatine pad was obtained and copies were made of the original constitution to the number perhaps of seventy or eighty. These copies, together with a personal letter of explanation, were sent to those who made inquiries concerning the society, and, in this work, I am glad to gratefully acknowledge that I was very ably seconded and assisted by Mr. W. H. Pennell, whose name has already figured in these records.

Not a few of the circulars and early letters went out from his home, and in the work he was assisted by his two older children, Henry and Isabel. At this time the society had no influential friends in any part of the world; no extraneous influences gave it prestige and currency. It spread simply because

> *Name.* This society shall be called the Williston Young People's Society of Christian Endeavor. (Portland, Me.)
>
> *Object.* Its object shall be to promote an earnest Christian life among its members, to increase their mutual acquaintance, and to make them more useful in the service of God.
>
> *Membership.* The members of this society shall consist of all young people who sincerely desire to accomplish the result above specified. They shall become members upon being elected by the society and by signing their names in this book.
>
> *Officers.* The officers of this society shall be a President, Vice President and Secretary. There shall also be a Prayer-meeting Committee of five, a Social Committee of five and a Lookout Committee of five.
>
> *Duties of Officers.* The duties of the President, Vice President and Secretary shall be those that usually fall to those offices. The Prayer-meeting Committee shall have charge of the Friday evening prayer-meetings; shall see that a topic is assigned & leader provided for each meeting.
>
> *The Prayer-meeting.* It is expected that all the members of the society will be present at every meeting unless detained by some absolute necessity, and that each one will take some part however slight in every meeting. The meeting will be held just one hour and at the close some time may be taken for introductions and social intercourse if desired. Once each month an experience meeting shall be held at which each member shall speak concerning his or her progress in the Christian life for the past month. If any one chooses he can express his feelings by an appropriate verse of scripture. It is expected that if any one is obliged to be absent at this monthly meeting he will send the reason of his absence by some one who attends.
>
> *Social Committee.* It shall be the duty of the Social Committee to provide for the mutual acquaintance of the members by occasional socials for which any entertainment that may be deemed best may be provided.
>
> *Lookout Committee.* It shall be the duty of the Lookout Committee to bring new members into the society, to introduce them to the work & to affectionately look after & reclaim any that seem to be indifferent to their duties.
>
> *Meetings & Elections.* Business meetings can be held at the close of the Friday evening meeting or at any other time in accordance with the call of the President. An election of officers & committees shall be held once in six months. Names may be proposed by a nominating committee appointed by the President.
>
> *Miscellaneous.* Any other committee may be added and duties assumed by this society which may in the future seem best. This constitution can be amended by a two thirds vote of the society.

REDUCED FAC SIMILE OF HECTOGRAPH PAD COPY OF THE CONSTITUTION SENT OUT IN ANSWER TO INQUIRIES BEFORE THE CONSTITUTION WAS PRINTED.

God had a work for it to do. The society was its own recommendation. Wherever a band of these faithful, devoted young soldiers of Christ gathered together, subscribed to the pledge, and showed their faith by their works and their outspoken confession of Christ in the prayer-meeting, the fact necessarily made itself known. Their light could not be hid. No bushel measure, with which some churches and ministers tried to hide it, was so opaque that some gleams of the spiritual life of the society could not shine through.

Wherever one society was started, another was very sure to spring up in a little while, and that reproduced itself in another, and that one in another; and so the work spread and multiplied, until north and east and west, in many different denominations, the Society of Christian Endeavor began to be known.

ST. LAWRENCE STREET CHURCH, PORTLAND, ME. (WHERE FOURTH SOCIETY WAS FORMED).

For several years the movement grew in this way alone without any systematic efforts to advance its principles, for it was not until 1885 that, as a matter of absolute necessity, the United Society was organized and a responsible bureau was created for the publishing of the literature, and for the spreading of the idea. But of this important era in the Christian Endeavor movement we will tell in a later chapter, when we shall have traced the history of the society beyond its infancy and into its sturdy childhood.

CHAPTER IX.

OBJECTORS AND OBJECTIONS.

The Advantages of Criticism—The "Pooh-pooh," the "Bow-wow," and the "Hear-hear" Stages—Hot-House Green Peas—Aminidab Pinpoint—"Sucking the Life Blood of the Church"—An "*Imperium in Imperio*"—An Editorial—"All Society and Very Little Christian Nurture"—How Objections Have Been Refuted—"Veritas" and "Senex," and What They Had to Say—The Societies' Defenders.

IT is scarcely to be expected that an organization like the Society of Christian Endeavor, working on lines so radically different, in some respects, from any other religious organization, could escape without criticism. In fact, it would not be well that it should thus escape. Absence of criticism would mean indifference and a lack of vitality and energy which would bode no good to the infant organization.

As a matter of fact, the society did not escape searching and even bitter criticism. It was laughed at and sneered at and contemptuously put one side in some quarters. It was seriously objected to from the standpoint of orthodoxy, from the ground of Biblical criticism, and from almost every imaginable standpoint.

A new movement, as an English author has wittily said, must always pass through three stages: The "pooh-pooh stage" of contemptuous indifference, the "bow-bow stage" of barking criticism, before it comes to the "hear-hear stage" of general and hearty acceptance.

This has been the history of this society in all lands where it has gained a foothold. Under date of February 12, 1882, I find the following record: "Meeting of the Cumberland Association of ministers and churches in Williston Church. I give some account of our young people's society. All approve of it except Mr. ——. He doesn't believe in 'hot-house green peas,' and is very bitter toward the society."

In about the same proportion have the objectors existed ever since. Almost all of my ministerial brethren, as well as the great majority of the laymen of the churches, have heartily and enthusiastically approved of the society, its aims and its methods, but with them has always come the objector. Sometimes he has been kindly and at other times severe. Sometimes gentle in his reproof and admonition, at other times, hostile and biting; but, on the whole, he has done the society quite as much good as its enthusiastic friends. He has not meant to help it forward, but he has undoubtedly done so, making it cautious and conservative, critical in its examination of itself and of any new plans that it might advocate.

The Endeavor Society has always courted investigation in the fullest possible way, and it has never been harmed, except temporarily and locally, by the severest criticism. A cartoon representing Aminidab Pinpoint, Ph. D., pictures very graphically some of the critics of the society, as seen by Rev. A. Mossback of *The Golden Rule*. He, according to Mr. Mossback's story, is so eagerly intent on the fact that the S is wrong side up in the good citizenship banner, that he cannot see any lay excellencies or hopeful signs in this great uprising of young people.

The most common objection in the early days related to its connection with the church. It was considered in many quarters, where it was not understood, a parasite that would suck the life blood of the church. Ungracious flings were often thrown out against "these new-fangled societies outside of the church which were invented to do the very thing for which the church was established;" and when it was proved beyond a doubt that this society, unlike some others, was not outside  of the church, but was *in* the church and *of* the church and *for* the church, in fact, a very integral part of the church, like the Sunday-school or the mid-week prayer-meeting, then the critics changed their tone and deplored the existence of a "little church within the church."

Sometimes they would drop into Latin, and my friends would solemnly shake their heads, and, in deep bass voices, warn the public of the dangers of an *imperium in imperio*.

A leading religious paper, in the fall of 1882, after printing an article by me concerning the society as a means of promoting Christian nurture, goes on editorially to express the fears of many Christian people in a forcible and vigorous way, and in a more kindly spirit than was sometimes exhibited.

We will quote a few paragraphs from this editorial, for it shows the kind and nature of the criticisms which the society encountered and lived down in its early years:

"Christian nurture is as old as the church. It has been a need; it is a need, and it will be a need. We want it, must have it; we die daily without it; but how are we to get it? We are afraid of the society plan. That is the standing American way of doing things—to get up a society and have grand co-operative action; but this is a case where one may be better than many, and co-operation not so good as operation. Fill the country with societies, and nothing would be done until individuals began to do their individual duty. Why not begin in this way? A great society will not create opportunities. Good sense, a pair of open eyes, and a faithful heart make the best Society of Christian Endeavor in the world. Get your little world around you and begin operations at once. Have your circle, your meetings, your little societies.

"The society for carrying on so simple a duty is pretty sure to be all society, and very little Christian nurture. As far as association is needed, the church is all that is required. What is the church good for if not to guide and support Christian nurture and to call out Christian endeavor? It furnishes every required opportunity, and the use of its agencies will not require a multiplication of agencies nor an increase of machinery.

"If organization is required, there is every chance in the world to organize through the church. . . . Young people should not be crowded too far, nor into a kind of mature work they are not fit to do; to exhort and preach when their minds are callow and their judgments unformed. . . . The sum of it is, we want the Christian nurture and the Christian endeavor, but we want them writ small, and not in capitals. We do not object to societies, but we are afraid of the Society of Christian Endeavor."

These objections sound rather peculiar, in view of the developments of the dozen years since they were written.

"Good sense, a pair of open eyes and a faithful heart make the best Society of Christian Endeavor in the world." Indeed! But there have been people with good sense, open eyes and faithful hearts since the foundation of the world, but still in the Providence of God something seems to have been left for the society of Christian Endeavor to accomplish.

"The society for carrying on so simple a duty is pretty sure to be all society and very little Christian nurture."

And yet since these lines were penned, out of the associate ranks of the Society of Christian Endeavor, influenced in part, at least, by these society methods of Christian nurture, more than 800,000 young people have come into the evangelical churches of America, and are to-day working for the Master.

Since these lines were written more than three millions of young people have received training and help from this organization, as they would every one gladly testify, and nearly two millions and a half of them are to-day in the ranks of this society, which, according to this editorial, and in the opinion of many others in those early days, had no excuse for existence.

"Happily in this nineteenth century," this article goes on to say, "where the sun shines, there will be light, and where a Christian man lives, there will be a Society of Christian Endeavor and Christian nurture in full operation."

This was the cheap and easy solution of this paper of the whole mighty problem of the Christian training of youth. Many other editors and pastors agreed with him, and tried in every way to write small the word Endeavor and the society which bore this name.

The inference must not be drawn, however, that all editors or the great majority of pastors shared the views herein expressed. To be sure, many religious papers in the early days seemed to take substantially the same ground. Many were the flings admitted to their columns, and the communications from this or that disgruntled subscriber, "Veritas" or "Senex," who seemed to think that the whole order of nature, or at least the Church of Christ, was to be overthrown by this simple organization.

But while the society provoked these antagonisms it also secured a host of defenders and friends. The great majority of ministers who were in actual fields of labor, and who were in closest touch with their young people, at once saw the undoubted advantages of this systematic plan of Christian nurture. They were ready to stand for it enthusiastically, and the more they knew of the society and its actual workings among their young people, the more eager they were to testify to its advantages. They were always ready to reply to "Veritas," and "Senex," and the other brethren who criticised the society from the standpoints of their inner consciousness in the religious press.

They were ready to address anniversaries and conventions, too, and to stand for the society in which they had come to believe, in conferences and associations and ministerial gatherings.

For every objector who appeared, a dozen advocates and defenders of the society at once came to the fore, ready to speak out of their personal knowledge and experience the kind of testimony which very soon silenced if it did not convert the objector.

As a matter of fact, many of those who in the first place found the greatest number of theoretical objections to the society, after a little, when by some personal experience they came to know its working, were transformed into its most ardent and enthusiastic friends.

Not a few of those who are foremost in the work of the society to-day are willing to own that at first they were prejudiced against it, and sought to prejudice others, until they saw what it could do for their own young people in unsealing their lips and unfettering their hands in confession and work for Christ.

CHAPTER X.

THE FIRST CONVENTION.

The Multitudinous Convention of the Present Day—A Contrast—The Throngs in England—The Societies Represented—How Far They Came Then—How Far They Come To-day—The Subjects Discussed—The Secretary—Some Early Endeavor Worthies, and What They Talked About—"Hampden '83"—The Spirit of Prophecy.

THE annual conventions of the Society of Christian Endeavor have become such notable and multitudinous events that it is of special interest to note the small beginnings from which they sprang. To-day the largest cities in the Union can scarcely contain the eager throngs that attend the Annual International Convention for the United States and Canada. No one place of meeting in any part of America begins to be large enough to contain the throngs. Halls that seat from five to ten thousand can accommodate but a small fraction of the vast numbers that come together.

Even the Annual State Conventions frequently number their delegates by thousands instead of by hundreds. The largest halls in the largest cities have been unable to contain them, and they overflow into all the neighboring churches. The same characteristics mark the Endeavor Conventions in other lands.

In England, where the convention-going spirit is not indigenous to the soil, the numbers who come together are often scarcely less than in America. The Metropolitan Tabernacle cannot hold the Endeavorers of London alone, and Birmingham greeted several thousand young men and women from all parts of the United Kingdom at a British National Convention.

In Australia the same convention scenes are duplicated, and I have seen the great town hall in Melbourne with a seating capacity of over three thousand, the town hall of Adelaide, and the Centennial Hall of Sydney filled to overflowing with the Endeavorers of the Colonies.

So in China the same spirit prevails, and the recent convention in Shanghai seemed to inspire Chinese hearts with the same enthusiasm and zeal. These facts of later years make the first annual convention of the Societies of Christian Endeavor of peculiar interest. If a *fac simile* of the modest program could be here reproduced, it would be seen that the convention—"a conference" it was then called—was held on the second of June, 1882, in the Williston Church, and that an afternoon and evening session sufficed for the business and fellowship of the convention.

At this convention six societies were represented, all but two of them belonging to churches in the city of Portland.

The Williston Society reported 168 members, the Second Parish Society 75 members, the West Church Society 38 members, the St. Lawrence Street Society 63 members, the Society in the Winter Street Church of Bath 75 members, and the Hampden Society 62 members. In all 481 members in the six societies. If my memory is not at fault five of these societies were represented by actual delegates, and the other one, connected with the church at Hampden, Maine, sent a letter of greeting and a report of its progress.

It was not thought at all strange that no one came from such a vast distance as Hampden to attend the convention! In fact, it would have been thought singular if any one had thought it worth while to spend the time and money necessary to come so far. The delegates from Bath, some thirty-five miles from Portland, were received with open arms, and their devotion to the cause in coming so far was considered not a little remarkable. To the conventions held in these days, delegates are glad to come, though it involves the long journey from Australia.

To the Cleveland Convention, Mr. J. G. Thompson started from Sydney, Australia, expecting to make the journey to Cleveland and back, a distance of eighteen thousand miles or more, for the sole purpose of attending the Thirteenth International Convention.

JAMES W. STEPHENSON.

When he had accomplished seven thousand miles of his journey and had reached San Francisco, he found that the railroad strike absolutely barred his progress further eastward, so, since he could not get to Cleveland, he turned around and sailed back in the next steamer to Sydney. He is not discouraged, however, but expects to attend the next Endeavor Convention, for which he will have to make a journey of twenty thousand miles.

But small, comparatively, as was this first convention, and limited as the area from which the delegates were drawn, it was, nevertheless, a meeting of power and promise, and prophesied large things for the future. After the organization, the devotional exercises and the Secretary's report of the societies represented, a discussion was held concerning "Our Work."

Our work was divided into four sub-heads: The Prayer-Meeting, discussion of which was opened by Mr. James W. Stephenson of the Second Parish Society; The Experience Meeting, opened by Mr. Granville Staples; The Sociables, by Mr. W. H. Pennell; and The Lookout Committee Work by Miss Anna Garland of the Williston Society.

This, with the election of officers and committees for the next year, constituted the program of the afternoon session.

Mr. Stephenson, who opened the first question, had been from that day to this an ardent worker and supporter of the society. A genuine Scotchman with a charming brogue, a forcible speaker and a most devoted Christian, we cannot

EDWARD L. SAYWARD (1881).

EDWARD L. SAYWARD (1895).

wonder that he was chosen the Secretary of the Convention and of the Conference of Societies for the coming year.

For many years after the Maine State Union was formed, he was the Secretary of the Union, and his presence and counsel has always been helpful to the societies from the beginning.

Miss Garland, who opened the discussion of the Lookout Committee work, was a young lady of exceptional devotion and sweetness of spirit, wholly bound up in the Master's work. Her influence was widely and always beneficially felt until, a few years ago, her busy hands were stilled in death.

So far as I know all the others who took prominent part in that first Conference are still living and active in the work of the society.

The oldest minister of Portland, Dr. Holbrook, who was then acting pastor of the West Church, was chosen Chairman of the Conference, thus showing what

THE FIRST CONVENTION.

the society has proved a thousand times since, that it welcomes to its ranks and to its work all those who have young hearts, no matter how white their locks or long their years. The Secretary of the Convention was Edward L. Sayward, a boy of fourteen or fifteen years of age then, who had the honor of being the first young person to sign the constitution, his signature coming immediately after Mr. W. H. Pennell. He was a bright, intelligent lad. He is now connected with one of the leading mercantile houses of Portland, and is still an honor to the church and the society where he received his early religious training.

At the evening session the discussion centered around the two words "Our Society." "Its Object" was discussed by Rev. C. A. Dickinson, the dear friend of my boyhood and manhood as well, who was then the pastor of the Second Parish Church. "Its Spirit" was discussed by Rev. A. H. Wright, pastor of the St. Lawrence Street Church of Portland, the church of which he is still the beloved and honored pastor. In his spirit Mr. Wright is often thought by his brethren to resemble more than any other man they know the Apostle John, and doubtless the discussion of the spirit of the society was tinged by his own Christlike life.

REV. A. H. WRIGHT.

The last address of the evening was given by myself upon the rules of the society, in which the pledge, consecration meeting, and provision for dropping delinquent members were enlarged upon.

Not only did the Hampden Society send its greetings, but these salutations were supplemented by an invitation for the conference to meet in Hampden in 1883. In this invitation, too, there was a prophecy of future years, for now to every convention come pressing invitations from many cities in all parts of the country, and banners and streamers and State songs impress upon the convention-goers the attractions of "Washington for '96" and "California for '97," and Louisville and Baltimore and Saratoga and Philadelphia, and half a score of other cities, perhaps, for '98.

In England, too, is the same generous rivalry, and Birmingham and Bristol and Liverpool are in the field for the coming conventions.

I regret to say that it was never possible to hold a convention in Hampden. It is a pity that the cordial invitation could not be accepted, but it was thought when 1883 came around that it was best to hold another meeting in the city of Portland, where was still the chief stronghold of the society. The officers for the conference for the following year were as follows: President, Mr. Wm. H. Pennell; Vice-Presidents, Messrs. L. W. Buckman, C. E. Bolton, W. W. Robinson, S. C. Merrill, Edmund S. Garland; the latter being a younger brother of the Miss Garland I have before mentioned, now the Secretary of the Y. M. C. A. of Portland.

The Secretary of the organization then formed was Mr. J. W. Stephenson, and the Executive Committee, Rev. F. E. Clark, H. H. Burgess, Esq., a prominent merchant of Portland, and Rev. C. A. Dickinson.

In a pleasant account of this conference, written by Miss Etta H. Stanwood for the *Christian Mirror*, of which she was the assistant editor, we read the following closing paragraph: "May the time speedily come when every church in our land shall cherish in its midst one of these societies of earnest Christian Endeavor full of faithful young workers, which, in turn, shall add beauty and strength to its pillars, and prove an honor to the church roll."

This large wish seemed to be uttered in the spirit of prophecy rather than that of present expectation, when we think of the six little societies that made up this first conference, or of the straggling score which already existed in different parts of the country; but it also indicates the hopefulness and energy, the enthusiasm and the large anticipations of the youthful Society of Christian Endeavor.

CHAPTER XI.

THE BATTLE-GROUND OF THE SOCIETY.

Some Objections to the Pledge—The Young Man and the Imaginary Desert Island—Silence in Heaven by the Space of Half an Hour—The Anxious Parent—How the Pledge Won the Victory—Its Scripturalness—The Strenuousness of the Psalmist's Pledges—The Bane of Christian Work—Duty *Versus* Feeling—Speechmakers Not Wanted—The All-Sufficient Excuse.

I HAVE already spoken of some of the objections which were urged against the infant society, largely from a theoretical point of view. But the chief battle-ground of the society has been the field of its largest success, and its widest influence as well, namely, the prayer-meeting pledge.

From the beginning this pledge has been objected to by many. It has been carefully scrutinized and picked to pieces, sentence by sentence and word by word. Every imaginable bugbear has been conjured up.

Some pastors have objected to it, some parents have disapproved of it, and a multitude of young people have shrunk from it, as something that was altogether too stringent for them to subscribe to.

But in spite of all these objections and difficulties the pledge has been adhered to faithfully and religiously. Its efficacy and vital importance to a society of Christian Endeavor has never been for a moment doubted by any leader in the movement, and the utmost pains has been taken to inculcate the reasonableness, the Scripturalness, and the vital necessity of the pledge, wherever the principles of the Endeavor Society have penetrated.

Many of the objections to the pledge have been purely childish, like the refusal of the young lady to join the society because its pledge would always prevent her from going away on her summer vacation, since she could not attend and take part in every meeting unless she stayed at home every week of the year.

Another fearful young soul seriously objected to the pledge because he conjured up in his imagination a desert island on which he might be wrecked. In his imagination his trunk had gone to the bottom of the sea, and in his trunk was his Bible, so how could he fulfill his promise to read the Bible every day, to say nothing of attending and taking part in a Christian Endeavor meeting.

Another brother who was discussing this subject in Australia objected to it on the ground that it was unscriptural, and went on to prove his somewhat astonishing statement by saying that the Bible said that there was silence in heaven by the space of half an hour, whereas the Christian Endeavor pledge did not provide for any silence in the Endeavor meeting.

This gentleman was answered by a young man who spoke immediately afterward, who very quietly remarked that doubtless the angels in heaven had an excuse which they could conscientiously give to the Master for their silence by the space of half an hour, and this excuse was specifically admitted to be a good one in the very heart of the pledge.

Moreover, he went on to say, "as half an hour is to eternity, so the silence

Active Member's Pledge.

TRUSTING in the Lord Jesus Christ for strength, I promise Him that I will strive to do whatever He would like to have me do; that I will make it the rule of my life to pray and to read the Bible every day, and to support my own church in every way, especially by attending all her regular Sunday and mid-week services, unless prevented by some reason which I can conscientiously give to my Saviour; and that, just so far as I know how, throughout my whole life, I will endeavor to lead a Christian life.

As an Active Member, I promise to be true to all my duties, to be present at and to take some part, aside from singing, in every Christian Endeavor prayer meeting, unless hindered by some reason which I can conscientiously give to my Lord and Master. If obliged to be absent from the monthly consecration meeting of the Society, I will, if possible, send at least a verse of Scripture to be read in response to my name at the roll-call.

Signed ....

Date .... Residence ....

allowed in the young people's prayer-meeting should be to a whole hour devoted to the prayer-meeting." Whatever may be thought of the answer, it can at least be said that it was as good as the objection.

Another pastor tells in print of a father with whom he sympathized, who sent his children to Europe that they might be rid of the baleful influence of the prayer-meeting pledge. Unhappy man! He must needs go in these days to Kamskatka or Nova Zembla to be sure of escaping all contamination from the Endeavor movement.

But there were other and more serious objections brought against the pledge. It has been said that it tends to a formal and narrow conception of the religious life, that the duties prescribed are performed to fulfill the promise and not from love to Christ, that it is likely to kill spontaneity and individuality in the meetings and to foster insincerity. A long train of unspeakable ills it has been supposed by some would follow in its train.

The simple and sufficient answer to all these objections is the answer of experience. Louder than ten thousand theories and in clearer tones does the experience of all these years prove that the pledge is not only reasonable and Scriptural but absolutely essential to the continued growth and development of a Christian Endeavor society.

I can say deliberately that, looking back over all the history of all these years, I remember no society except those which have been crowded out of their churches by ecclesiastical interference and denominational jealousy that has not done a conspicuously good work for Christ and the church that has adhered heartily to the spirit of the prayer-meeting pledge.

I have never known of a society to fail except those before specified, whose failure could not be traced directly or indirectly to an unwillingness on the part of its members to accept this pledge or live up to it.

As to the Scripturalness of the pledge, it seems strange that any one can have even a casual acquaintance with the Old Testament, which is so full of covenants and promises between God and His people without believing in the pledge idea which is nothing but the covenant idea, and not one of these covenants has been abrogated or set one side by the New Testament.

Listen to the grand strenuousness of the Psalmist's pledges: "If I forget thee, O Jerusalem, let my right hand forget her cunning. If I do not remember thee let my tongue cleave to the roof of my mouth, if I prefer not Jerusalem above my chief joy." Over and over again are these covenants repeated with solemn emphasis.

In fact it would take a volume larger than the present one to discuss adequately the subject of Bible pledges.

But has the pledge made the religious life of the young people, formal, narrow, and mechanical?

A great crowd of witnesses from all parts of the world can be summoned to say that the result has been exactly the reverse.

The fulfilling of the pledge of the Christian Endeavor Society has made every other duty easier. Because everything done for Christ opens the way to some other service for Him. The only path to the tablelands of love lies over the hard and rugged mountains of duty. He who only takes part in prayer-meeting when he feels like taking part, he who only does his duty when impelled to do it by some irresistible impulse will seldom speak for God or work for humanity. The bane of the prayer-meeting for centuries was that participation in it was a matter of feeling and impulse. Very few *felt* like offering a prayer or giving their testimony or quoting a verse of Scripture and so

Christian Endeavor in Foreign Languages.

當撰證明書

フレッド、シー、クライン氏

右本年四月四日夜開會セシ名古屋美普教會青年共勵会総會ニ於テ本年七月加奈太モントリール府ニ開カル、基督教徒共勵會大會ヘ出席スベキ本會ノ代員ニ撰擧セラレタルコヲ証明ス

紀元千八百九十三年四月四日

會長 丸山 愿

書記 児島亀士

CREDENTIALS OF REV. FRED C. KLEIN TO THE MONTREAL CONVENTION.

CARD OF MEMBERSHIP.

వాగ్దానము.

యేసుక్రీస్తును రక్షణార్థముగా నాధారముచేసికొని దేవుడు బలమునిచ్చునని నమ్ముకొని నేను ఆయనయెదుట ప్రమాణము చేయడమేమనగా: ఆయన నన్ను నేమిచే నిచ్ఛయించునో దాని చేయుటకు యత్నించెను. ప్రతిదినము ఆయనకు ప్రార్థనచేయుచు, సత్యవేదమును చదువుకొనుచు, ఆయన దయవల్ల నాజీవితకాలమంతయు క్రీస్తుధర్మము ననుసరించి నడుచుకొనుటకు పోరాడెదను.

నేను కారకసమాజకుడనై సమాజబద్ధతుల ప్రకారము నడుచుకొనెదనని మాటనిచ్చుచున్నాను. మరియు నా ప్రభువును యజమానుడునగు యేసుక్రీస్తుయెదుట చెప్పకొనతగిన ఆటంకము కలిగితే నేగాని నేను ప్రతికూటమునకువచ్చి కూటమును జరిపించుటయందు పాడుట మాత్రమేగాక, మరియేదో ఒక సహాయము చేసెదనని మాటనిచ్చుచున్నాను. నెలకు జరుగు ప్రతిష్ఠకూటమునకు వచ్చుటకు వల్లపడని పక్షమందు శక్యమైనయెడల నేను రానినంగతిని సమాజమునకు ముందుగా తెలియచేసెదను.

స్థలము __________ చేవ్రాలు __________

తేది __________

TELUGU.

the meeting drifted into the hands of a few specially glib or especially conscientious ones.

The poison which has entered into Christian work of all kinds has been this same false notion that impulses and feelings and not duty must be considered, in Christ's service. As a consequence in many churches very little was done or attempted except in seasons of especial emotional interest.

The antidote to this poison is found I believe in the idea of the pledge. The idea of duty for duty's sake, if we are not prompted by the gentler spirit of love "for Christ's sake."

Duty done will lead to love. It is the very shortest path. The societies of Christian Endeavor are living examples of the absolute necessity of the principle embodied in the pledge. The prayer-meeting is the pivot on which they revolve. It is the centre of all their work. It is not only the thermometer that registers the heat, it is the furnace that generates the warmth of their religious life, and of the prayer-meeting the pledge is the very backbone. Without it the prayer-meeting soon languishes, falls into ruts and either drags out a poor, dying existence or is given up altogether.

Instead of promoting a precocious spirit of glib and wordy religiosity, as some have feared, the pledge has operated in exactly the opposite direction.

Just here has been a very serious misapprehension in regard to the pledge in many minds. It has been thought that it demanded a *speech* in each prayer-meeting from every immature convert or at least a well-rounded prayer. The editorial from which I have quoted in a previous chapter falls into this error. "Young people," it says, "should not be crowded to exhort and preach when their minds are callow and their judgments unformed."

The Endeavor Society never contemplated anything of the sort, and has never accomplished anything of the sort. It is expected that each member will confess his Lord in some appropriate way like the repetition of a verse of Scripture or a hymn, a sentence prayer or a simple testimony. Such confession is obligatory upon the youngest disciple as upon the oldest and most experienced.

Nor does any reasonable excuse for the non-performance of these duties fail of recognition in the prayer-meeting pledge. These promises are made to be fulfilled "unless prevented by a reason which I can give to the Lord Jesus Christ." If a young person has such an excuse he has an all-sufficient excuse. If he has not one that he can conscientiously give to Christ he ought to be ashamed to give any. The matter is left to his own conscience. It is to be settled between himself and God. Neither the lookout committee, the president or the pastor decides the matter for him. He must bring every question which arises to the bar of conscience. In this way the pledge has been of immense value to a multitude of hearts.

Fac Simile of Pledges in Foreign Languages.

ARMENO-TURKISH.

CARD OF MEMBERSHIP.

வாக்.ருத்தத்தம்.

என் ஆத்தும இரட்சிப்புக்காக கர்த்தராகிய இயேசுகிறிஸ்துவின்மேல் பற்றுதல் வைத்து, தேவ ஒத்தாசையை நம்பி, நான் என்ன செய்யவேண்டுமென்று அவர் இத்தங்கொள்வாரோ அதைச் செய்ய முறபடுவேன் என்றும், நாள்தினம் அவசர் கோவில் ஜெபித்து வேதம் வாசித்துவருவேன் என்றும், என் ஜீவகால மெல்லாம் அவர் கிருபையிலும் இதிக்ர ஜீவனருசெய்ய முறபசெய்வேன் என்றும் வாக்குக்கொடுக்கிறேன். ஒரு பிரியா அவுலமாக என் கடமைகளேயும் உண்மையாய் நிறைவேற்றவும், என் கர்த்தரும் ஆண்டவருமாகிய இயேசு கிறிஸ்துவினிடம் மனச்சாட்சியின்படி சொல்லத்தக்க யாதொரு காரணத்தால் தடைப்பட்டாலன்றி ஒவ்வொரு கூட்டத்திற்கும் வந்த பாவேதைத்தவிர வேறே தாவியும் பங்குபெறவும் வாக்குக்கொடுக்கிறேன். மாதாந்தர தற்பிரிஷ்டுடை கூட்டத்திற்கு வரமலிருக்க வேண்டியதாயிருக்கும்பொழுது, கடேமானுள் அப்படி வராமலிருக்கும் காரணத்தைச் சங்கத்தாருக்குத் தெரிவிப்பேன்.

இருப்பிடம்_____ கையெழுத்து_____

தேதி_____

TAMIL.

THE BATTLE-GROUND OF THE SOCIETY.

But, as I said before, the best argument for the pledge is found in the lives of the multitude of young Christians who have been quickened and strengthened and made Christlike. The sweetness, naturalness, joy, and strength of their lives forever answer the theoretical objections to the pledge.

At the beginning many societies tried to weaken the pledge or tone it down. They tried to leave loop-holes in it through which the less conscientious could escape from their duty. But such societies gradually weakened and waned and revived only when reorganized on the basis of the strict pledge.

Once or twice the pledge has been changed in some slight particulars, but only with the purpose and result of making it more strenuous and binding upon each young heart.

I well remember some days of prayer and solicitude, when, with my friend of college days, Rev. S. Winchester Adriance, whose connection with the society will hereafter be spoken of, I went over the pledge word by word and phrase by phrase.

This scrutiny resulted in the "revised pledge," as it is now called, which is adopted by societies all over the world; but the story of this revised pledge, and especially of its relations to the work of the church, must be reserved for a succeeding chapter.

THE WOOPE KIN (DAKOTA INDIANS) PLEDGE.

V. Tona Htani opapi heca on caje en aupi kin hena woiciconze kin de yutanwicakiyapi kte.

Jesus Htakiniwacinskanpi kin en owape cin decen miciconza:

1. Anpetu otoiyohi wowapi wakan mdawa kte.
2. Anpetu otoiyohi Jesus Messiya cewakiye kta.
3. Wocekiye Omniciye owasin en waun kte, qa, dowanpi ikapeya, omniciye owasin en onspa ecamon kta, taku awicakehan kagimaye sni kinhan.* Qa Piya iciconzapi Omniciye kin en waun kta owakihi sni kinhan, wowapi wicawaqu kte, Wowapi Wakan oehde wanjidan esta, qa cajemayatapi hehan he miciyaotaninpi kte.
4. Jesus Messiya Itancan kin towasake wacinwaye ca taku kasta Jesus ecawecon kta iyokipi kin hena ecamon wacanmi kta. Qa token owakahnige cin, Jesus wacinyanpi wicohan ohna mihduhe kta, tohanyan ni waun hehanyan. Decen miciconza.

* Taku kag imaye cin he decen wake: Taku Wakantanka itokam owahdake owakihi ehantanhans.

V. PLEDGE.

Candidates for Active membership shall be required to sign the following pledge:

As an Active Member of the Christian Endeavor Society, I promise:

1st. To read the Bible every day.
2d. To pray every day.
3d. To be present at every regular prayer-meeting of the Society, unless detained by some absolute necessity.* To take some part, aside from singing, in every meeting. If absent from the monthly Consecration Meeting, to send at least a verse of Scripture to be read in answer to my name at roll-call.
4th. Trusting in the Lord Jesus Christ for strength, I promise Him that I will strive to do whatever He would like to have me do; and just so far as I know how, throughout my whole life, I will endeavor to lead a Christian life.

* Meaning by this, some reason which with a clear conscience I can present to God.

Fac Simile of Pledges in Foreign Languages.

Aktive Medlemmers Løfte.

Stolende paa, at den Herre Jesus Kristus vil forlene mig Styrke, lover jeg Ham, at jeg vil stræbe at gjøre hvadsomhelst, han ønsker mig at gjøre; at jeg vil gjøre det til mit Livs Regel at bede og at læse Guds Ord hver Dag; at jeg vil støtte min egen Menighed i alle Ting, især ved at være tilstede ved alle Søndags- og Hverdags-Gudstjenester, med mindre jeg hindres af Aarsager, jeg samvittighedsfuldt kan fremføre for min Frelser; samt at jeg i hele mit Liv vil stræbe efter bedste Evne at leve et kristeligt Liv. Som et aktivt Medlem lover jeg at være tro i Udførelsen af mine Pligter, at være nærværende ved og foruden i Sang tage nogen Del i hvert af Foreningens Bønnemøder, med mindre jeg hindres af nogen Grund, som jeg kan samvittighedsfuldt fremføre for min Herre og Mester. Om jeg nødsages til at være fraværende fra den maanedlige Sammenkomst til Helligelse til Herren, lover jeg, at jeg, om muligt, vil indsende idetmindste et Skriftsted til Oplæsning ved Opraabet af mit Navn.

Underteanet..

Datum........................... Bovæl...........................

DANISH.

"HO ANY KRAISTY SY NY FIANGONANY."

FIKAMBANAN' NY KRISTIANA TANORA
AÔ AMBOHIPOTSY.

FANEKENA.

(1) Noho ny fahatokisako any Jesosy Kraisty Mpamonjy ahy sy ny fitiavako Azy dia manolo-tena ho mpanompony aho ka manaiky hanao izay tiany hataoko mandrakariva.

(2) Manaiky hamaky ny Soratra Masina sy hivavaka amin' Andriamanitra isan-andro aho.

(3) Manaiky hanao izay azoko atao aho hitaona ny sasany ho Kristiana, ary hitady izay asa ho any Jesosy Kraisty Tompoko tandrifin' ny ho any ny tenako.

(4) Satria voaray ho isan' ity Fikambanana ity aho, dia manaiky ho tonga amy ny fotoam-pivavahana isan-kerinandro ka hahavita izay tokony ho anjarako amin' izany, raha tsy misy sampona lehibe izay atoako ho ampy hahafa-tsiny ahy aminy Jesosy Kraisty Tompoko. Ary raha misy mahasampona ahy, dia manaiky hampandre ny sekretary aho.

Hoy _____

_____ 189

MALAGASY.

Fac Simile of Pledges in Foreign Languages.

Formule voor werkend Lidmaatschap.

MET opzien aar den Heere Jezus Christus voor kracht, beloof ik Hem dat ik trachten zal in alles naar Zijnen Wensch te handelen; dat ik het de wet mijns levens wil maken elken dag te bidden en den Bijbel te lezen: dat ik in elk opzicht de Kerk wil bijstaan, voornamelijk door het geregeld bijwonen van alle hare zondagsche en wekelijksche diensten, tenzij verhinderd om redenen, die ik met een goed geweten mijnen Zaligmaker geven kan; en dat ik streven zal, voor zooverre ik dat versta, gedurende mijn geheele leven een Christelijk pad te bewandelen.

Als een werkend lid beloof ik getrouw te zijn aan alle mijne verplichtingen, tegenwoordig te zijn en, behalve in gezang, werkdadig deel te nemen in elken Christelijk-streven bidstond, tenzij verhinderd om redenen die ik met een goed geweten mijnen Heer en Meester geven kan. Indien verplicht afwezig te zijn van den maandelijkschen toewijdings-bidstond, dan zal ik, indien mogelijk, minstens een Schriftuurplaats zenden, die in antwoord op mijn naam op het appèl kan worden voorgelezen.

Geteekend ....

Woonplaats ....

DUTCH.

Voto de los Miembros Activos.

CONFIADO en que el Señor Jesu-Cristo me ayude, le prometo que procuraré hacer todo lo que Él quiera que yo haga; que será regla de mi vida hacer oración y leer la Biblia todos los dias, y sostener mi iglesia de todas las maneras que me sea posible, especialmente asistiendo á los cultos, tanto en el domingo como entre semana, á no ser impedido por algún motivo que pueda presentar en conciencia á mi Salvador, y que hasta donde me lo permita mi inteligencia, y durante toda mi vida, procuraré vivir como cristiano verdadero. Como miembro activo de la Sociedad de Esfuerzo Cristiano, prometo asistir y tomar alguna parte (á más de cantar) en todos los cultos de oración, siempre que no sea impedido por alguna razón que pueda presentar por justa á mi Señor y Maestro. Si me veo obligado á estar ausente de la reunión de consagración, haré lo posible por enviar un texto de la Escritura para que sea leido en respuesta á mi nombre al llamar la lista.

Firmado, ...

Fecha, ... Residencia, ...

SPANISH.

Fac Simile of Pledges in Foreign Languages.

❧ Slib činného člena. ❧

Spoléhaje v Spasitele svého Ježíše Krista, jakožto svoji posilu slibuji Jemu, že se budu snažiti abych činil vše, co se Jemu líbí; dále že se budu každodenně modliti i čísti písmo svaté a pokud mi možno bude po celý svůj život po křesťansku žíti. Jakožto činný člen slibuji býti přítomnu a účastnu v každé schůzi nenaskytne-li se mi nějaká překážka, kterou bych se mohl svědomitě omluviti před svým Pánem, Ježíšem Kristem. Bude-li mi nemožno dostaviti se do posvěcující měsíční schůze, chci poslati omluvu svojí nepřítomnosti dozorčímu výboru.

Jméno: ....

Dne .... *18* *Adresa* ....

BOHEMIAN.

শ্রীষ্টীয় উদ্যোগ-সমিতির প্রকৃত সভ্যের প্রতিজ্ঞা।

শক্তির জন্যে প্রভু যীশু খ্রীষ্টেতে নির্ভর করিয়া, আমি প্রতিজ্ঞা করিতেছি যে, তাঁহার অভিপ্রায় অনুসারে কার্য্য করিতে প্রাণপণে চেষ্টা করিব ; এবং প্রতিদিন বাইবেল শাস্ত্র পাঠ ও প্রার্থনা করাই আমার জীবনের উদ্দেশ্য হইবে। আমি যে মণ্ডলীভুক্ত সেই মণ্ডলীর উন্নতি সাধ্যানুসারে চেষ্টা করিব; বিশেষতঃ যীশুর নিকট যে প্রকার বাধার আপত্তি থাটিতে পারে এমন বাধা না থাকিলে, মণ্ডলীর রবিবাসরিক ও সাপ্তাহিক প্রত্যেক সভায় উপস্থিত হইব, এবং আপন জ্ঞান অনুসারে মৃত্যু পর্যন্ত খ্রীষ্টীয় জীবন যাপন করিতে চেষ্টা করিব।

প্রকৃত সভা বলিয়া আমার যাহা কর্তব্য, তাহাই করিব। সমিতির প্রত্যেক প্রার্থনা সভায় যে প্রকার বাধার আপত্তি আমার প্রভুর নিকটে থাটিবে এমন বাধা না থাকিলে, আমি গীত গান ছাড়া কোন না কোন কার্য্য করিয়া সভার সাহায্য করিব। মাসিক আয়োজনসভের সভায় উপস্থিত হইতে না পারিলে, আমি শাস্ত্রের কোন একটী পদ লিখিয়া পাঠাইয়া দিব, যেন, আমার নাম ডাকিবার সময়ে সেই পদটী পড়া যাইতে পারে।

সভ্যের নাম _____

তারিখ _____ বাড়ী ⎫
বা ⎬ _____
ঠিকানা ⎭

BENGALI.

Fac Simile of Pledges in Foreign Languages.

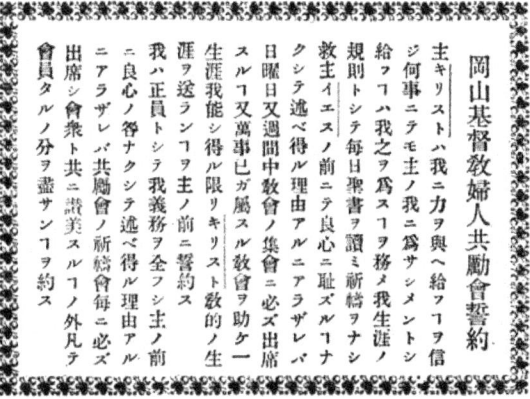

JAPANESE.

LÖFTESKORT FÖR AKTIVT MEDLEMSKAP.

I förtröstan att Herren Jesus Kristus vill förläna mig styrka dertill lofvar jag Honom härmed att troget utföra hvad Han vill hafva mig att göra; att jag vill göra det till mitt lifs regel att dagligen läsa i Bibeln och bedja till honom; att på allt sätt verka för och understödja den församling jag tillhör, isynnerhet lofvar jag att vara närvarande vid församlingens alla reguliära söndags- och veckomöten, såvida icke sådane hinder deremot uppkomma, hvilka jag samvetsgrant kan såsom skäl för min frånvaro framlägga för min Frälsare samt att så långt möjligt är vill jag söka lefva ett sannt kristligt lif.

Som en aktiv medlem af Ungdomsföreningen för kristlig verksamhet lofvar jag att troget utföra alla mina förbindelser och skyldigheter; att närvara vid och på något sätt, jämte sång, deltaga i föreningens möten, såvida ej hinder deremot möta, hvi ka jag samvetsgrant kan uppgifva till min Herre och Frälsare såsom orsak till bortovaron. Om tvingande skäl afhålla mig från att närvara vid det månadtliga bekännelsemötet, skall jag om möjligt, åtminstone sända en bibelvers till mötet att uppläsas då mitt namn upprepas.

Underskrift, ...

Bostad, ...

SWEDISH.

Fac Simile of Pledges in Foreign Languages.

Membership Pledge Card.

IQRAR-NÁMA I SHARÁKAT.

MAIN Khudáwand Yisú Masíh se naját ká ummedwár hoke aur Khudá kí madad par takiya karke yih wada kartá hún kí main us kí marzí ke muwáfiq chalne kí hatt-ul-maqdúr koshish karúngá, main har noz dua karúngá, aur har roz Baibal parhá karúngá, aur us ke fazl ke wasíle apní tamám umr bhar Masíhána taur par rahne kí justojú karúngá, aur chúnki main mustaid sharík hún, main wada kartá hún kí main apne tamám faráizon ko thík thík tarah se adá karúngá, aur jab tak ki main kisí kháss wajah se roká na jáún jis ká sirf Khudá hí gawáh rahegá, main har ek Míting men barábar házir rah ke sáre kámon men sharík hoúngá. Agar main máhwárí jalsa i Taqdís se gair-házir ho jáún to main apne maqdúr bhar Anjuman ko apni gair-házirí ke sabab se ágáh karúngá.

DASTKHATT_____

URDU.

GERMAN.

CHAPTER XII.

THE DISEASES OF CHILDHOOD.

Light Mortality Among the Christian Endeavor Societies—Not Decreed by Ecclesiastics—Growth from a Seed—Weakness of the Spinal Column—The Backbone Deliberately Broken by Some Pastors—How It Has Been Mended—The *Magnum Caput*—The Young Man Who "Knew It All"—Died of Severe Cold—Some Churches of the Holy Refrigerator—The Good Deacon and "the Singin' School"—The Rash of Petty Criticism—Societies That Have Been Starved to Death—Fatal Results of the Lack of Exercise—A Superabundance of Adipose Tissue—Ecclesiastical Opposition.

EVERY infant organization has to contend with the diseases incident to childhood, and the great majority of them succumb to these diseases. In fact, the mortality among societies, clubs, leagues, and associations of all kinds is far greater than among infants of the human race, and a society that can survive the first five years of its existence and grow stronger each year, especially when it has no nurture and care from other organizations, gives proof of intense vitality.

The Society of Christian Endeavor has well stood this test. The mortality, even in the local organizations, which have been planted under the most unfavorable auspices, has been surprisingly small. Especially when it is remembered that the society had no influential foster-parent and no powerful god-father to stand sponsor for it, the significance of this light mortality is still more fully understood.

It must always be borne in mind that the Society of Christian Endeavor, unlike many other organizations, was not decreed into existence by any ecclesiastical council or church court. It was not fostered by any powerful denomination, nor did it express the will of ecclesiastics who should cause it to live, whatever its inherent vitality.

In fact, it has grown in spite of the opposition of the official authorities of one or two denominations who have done much to hamper and hinder it.

It sprang from a little seed dropped into the soil of a single church in a down-east city, and it has been marked throughout all its history by its wonderful providential guidance and preservation.

Still, even such an organization could not altogether escape the ills of infancy.

Some societies have suffered much and some have died from a weakness of the spinal column. In fact, this has been the most fatal illness.

The pledge when adopted has sometimes been tampered with and weakened. The clause relating to attendance upon and participation in the young people's prayer-meeting has either been left out altogether, or it has been so toned down as to have but little binding force upon the consciences of those who sign it.

Almost always has this resulted in spiritual atrophy or death, though, I am glad to say, in the vast majority of cases, societies saw the evils of a weak and meaningless pledge, and reorganized on a better basis before it was too late to save themselves from total extinction.

Sometimes, strange to say, the backbone has been deliberately broken by pastors or other influential church-members, even when the society started with a good spinal column and good prospects for success.

The pastor has sometimes considered the rules too strict, the pledge too binding, has preached against it or discouraged the young people from fulfilling it, and at times has even gone so far as to compel them to drop it. These cases I am glad to say among the forty thousand societies have been very rare.

Another disease from which some societies have suffered would be called, I suppose, by Latin school boys the "*magnum caput.*" Sometimes the society has contained a young man, more rarely a young woman, "who knew it all."

It was impossible to teach these youths anything from the experience of the past. They insisted upon forming their societies without a pledge or without a consecration meeting or without a lookout committee, and would blandly inform those who had long experience in the work that such rules and regulations, though they might be well enough for some, seemed childish to them, and "could not be adopted by our young people."

Almost invariably these large-headed societies have yielded to the fatal disease that was born in them and have died a natural death, usually, however, to be resuscitated on a more modest, humble, and reasonable spirit.

Still other societies have died of the severe cold. They belonged to churches of the "Holy Refrigerator" order. They have been left out altogether of the interest and prayers of church and pastor.

The cold shoulder has been turned upon them in every way and after a short existence they have given up the ghost.

"You call yourself an Endeavor Society," sneeringly said a prominent pastor of a western city to his modest, earnest young people, who for a year or two had found great strength and help in the Endeavor organization. "You call yourself an Endeavor Society," he said, "I would like to know what you are endeavoring to do."

They modestly replied that they were endeavoring to lead earnest, Christian lives, that they were endeavoring to speak for the Lord Jesus in their weekly meetings, to get better acquainted with one another, to help each other in the Christian life, and that they would be glad to do anything they could for the church if he would tell them how.

"O that's what you call endeavoring, is it?" he replied, "saying verses in meeting and singing hymns! Go down into the slums of the city and start a mission, that's what I should call endeavoring."

They replied that they would be very glad to do anything of the sort that he directed, and that they existed for just that purpose. But his sneering commands went no further. He pointed out no way for them to expend their energies, but simply laughed at their present efforts. No wonder that the society was soon frozen out.

Another Endeavor Society of which I know, was forbidden the use of the vestry or any room in the church building for its meetings by the church officers unless they paid a larger rent for the same than they would be obliged to pay for a public hall in the town, in which to hold their meetings.

Another clear case of death from cold and exposure.

I was once called upon by a good deacon who was in a very indignant frame of mind and who almost ordered me in tones that sounded very imperative, to come to his town and "straighten out" the young people of the church.

When I inquired what they did that was so objectionable I could not learn of any serious charges except that they had their own young people's meeting, which, as it drew in many young people that were not Christians, was more popular and more largely attended than the other prayer-meeting of the church.

"Moreover," the good deacon went on to say, "I went into one of those e'er young people's meetings, and what do you think they did? They sang nine times in the course of the hour."

"But did they not sing Gospel hymns?" I inquired.

"Yes," said he, "I suppose they did, but I ain't goin' to any more singin' schools like that."

Whereupon he stalked off apparently quite indignant that I would not go and put a stop to "the singing school."

Other societies have died of a distressing rash induced by constant though often petty criticism. Little pin points have been stuck into them over and over and over again, until at last they got quite tired of living.

The whole society was criticised for the negligence of a few of its members, or because some overworked Christians went away before the Sunday evening service to which they thought they could not stay even though they had strength for the young people's meeting, the whole society was blamed.

Because of the back row of gigglers and whisperers who perhaps did not belong even to the associate membership of the society another pin of criticism was stuck into the sensitive flesh.

Because John and Mary, who were beginning to "keep company" together, sat together in the prayer-meeting, it was termed a "courting-society," and the critic would wax merry over his small witticism that "C. E. stood for Courting Endeavor."

Because all the young people of the community who could be induced to go to the young people's meeting, could not be induced to go to the mid-week meeting the criticism has been made that the society drained the life-blood of the mid-week meeting, though perhaps three times as many young people attended this same meeting as ever before.

I have even heard the boys of a Junior Society criticised by their elders because they snowballed each other on the way to the Junior meeting, though the meeting was held on Saturday afternoon, and the snow was temptingly soft.

Another disease from which many societies have suffered has been lack of nutrition, anemia, I suppose modern physicians would call the disease.

They have been literally starved to death. Hundreds of societies have been starved out of the ranks of the churches in this way.

They were not recognized or in any way welcomed. They were shown that their efforts were not desired and that they were in the way of another organization which the ecclesiastical authorities desired to have supplant them. The inter-denominational features of the society were feared and opposed, ministers who stood for the society were suspected of disloyalty to the denomination, and their position made in a variety of ways uncomfortable.

In many cases the evident object of this course of treatment has been successful, and the society has been literally starved to death by the lack of recognition and encouragement as well as open and secret opposition.

Other societies have suffered from lack of exercise. The committees have been few and their work feeble. There has been no one to crowd work upon them or to teach them the blessedness of doing for Christ. The way in has been made too wide and easy, and, as a consequence, many members have come into the society who never ought to come as active members. They have settled down at their ease to do nothing for Christ, and the society has suffered from a super-abundance of flesh and a sad lack of activity. Like the inevitable fat woman in the show they have been about the most worthless organization in existence. They have suffered from a superabundance of adipose tissue.

Their rolls have been swelled by a list of names that stood for no genuine endeavor, and the only way for them to accomplish good work has been to reduce their size, to give the drones a chance to get out, and to give to all the active members a reasonable amount of earnest work to do for the Master. This course of treatment has almost always saved the life of overgrown societies.

It must not be supposed, however, from this somewhat startling list of maladies that the mortality among Christian Endeavor Societies has been very large. On the contrary it has been surprisingly small. Every one of the earliest societies so far as I know is still in existence and doing a good work.

Comparatively few of those formed in later days since the rules have been better understood have even been afflicted with the diseases of childhood, and had it not been for ecclesiastical opposition to Christian Endeavor in some quarters, the mortality among all the societies that have been formed would be at most an infinitesimal fraction of one per cent.

CHAPTER XIII.

THE SECOND CONVENTION.

An Invitation That Was Not Accepted—The Hospitable Second Parish Church—The Societies Represented—The Questions Discussed—Seven Good Rules for the Social Committee—The Right Use of Personal Pronouns—Seven Classes of People Who Should Not Be Members of the Endeavor Society—Our Rules; Are They Too Strict?—What Young Ladies May Do—The Fifty-six Societies and Where They Were Located—The Largest Two Societies—The Baby Society—The Invitation for Next Year.

AS was said in a previous chapter, the society in the church of Hampden, Me., one of the first half-dozen, had invited the Convention of 1883 to meet with them, but Hampden being somewhat remote from the centre of Christian Endeavor work, it was thought best by the executive committee to hold the second convention as well as the first in Portland, so the hospitable Second Parish Church, of which Rev. C. A. Dickinson had been pastor, but who, during the previous year, had become pastor of the Kirk Street Church in Lowell, opened its doors to the convention.

In numbers, interest, and power, this convention, though still in the days of small things, was a decided advance over its predecessors.

Three sessions were held, morning, afternoon, and evening, instead of two as at the previous convention, and this meeting was considered of enough importance to have its proceedings printed in pamphlet form.

An interesting little volume of forty-seven pages contains the records, the list of societies represented with the names of the delegates, the leading papers that were read and the answers given to the questions of the question box.

The list of delegates, though printed in large type, occupied only about one page of the minutes, and, if my count is correct, there were in all seventy-one, though of course others came to the meeting who did not consider themselves delegates.

The number of societies represented had grown most encouragingly during the year. We do not find Hampden on the list sending delegates this year, or Bath, but the other societies of last year are represented, and in addition to these the First Baptist and the Casco Street Free Baptist of Portland, Woodfords, Kennebunk, Cumberland Centre, Bucksport, Biddeford, Freeport, Limington, and

Norway, Me.; Burlington, Vt.; Great Falls and Milton, N. H.; Kirk Street Church, Lowell, Mass., and the Immanuel Church of Boston, Mass.

The questions discussed, also, showed a growth during the year.

Mr. Granville Staples spoke of the work of the "Social Committee," Rev. F. E. Clark on the "Relation of the Society to the Church," Mr. J. W. Stephenson on the "Experience Meetings," Mr. J. W. Van Patten, of Burlington, Vt., on "Ways and Means of Extending the Work," Mr. H. H. Burgess on the "Relation of the Society to the Sunday-school," Rev. S. W. Adriance on the subject, "Who May Become Members?" Mr. W. H. Pennell on "Our Rules," Miss Ada Sewall on "How May Young Ladies Assist in the Work?" and Mr. F. W. Hall on "Practical Experiences in Establishing a Society."

Some of the suggestions made at this convention are worthy to live in a permanent history of the organization, and will serve as rules for its guidance down to the latest time, I believe. For instance, Mr. Granville Staples, in speaking of the work of the social committee, urged that the *best* persons in the society be put on this committee, "not any one who happens to be able to make sport," and then, when they had their committee formed, he urged them to "pray about their socials as they would their prayer-meetings;" "to make a plan about

SECOND PARISH CHURCH, PORTLAND, ME.

their socials; to have a leader who is able to hold the reins and guide the social in the right way; to look out for the wall flowers; to give the older ones something to do in amusing the younger; and to keep good hours."

Seven better rules for the social committee could scarcely be formulated to-day.

Rev. Francis E. Clark, in speaking of the relation of the society to the church, urged the young people to get into the habit of thinking and speaking of "our church" and "our prayer-meeting" and "our minister" as well as "our society." There is a great difference between "our" and "your." Be sure and use the right pronoun when speaking of the church with which you are connected.

From that day to this the right use of the personal pronoun has not been forgotten, and an affectionate, deferential attitude of the society to the church of which it is a part, has always been inculcated.

In speaking of the relation of the society to the Sunday-school, Mr. Burgess, a Portland business man, said most truly: "The society does not aim to supplant the Sabbath-school in teaching the truths of the Bible, but rather to exemplify them in an earnest Christian life."

Rev. S. Winchester Adriance in discussing the question, "Who may become members of the Young People's Societies?" touched upon the somewhat vexed question of the age limit, and said, "Ordinarily the membership of these societies ought to consist of those between thirteen and thirty, and yet I should be very sorry if none of the brethren and sisters between thirty and forty and even older belonged to the society. The young need to feel that the older ones are interested in them and the older ones need some freshening intercourse with the young."

The matter could not be stated better after these years of experience, every one of which has exemplified the truth of Mr. Adriance's statement.

He then goes on to say that the pastor should always be a member, that only earnest Christians should be *active* members; that the associate membership should be made much of and enlarged in every possible way, as the first step to an active Christian life, and finally he gives some excellent rules concerning those who should *not* belong:

"First. All who do not wish to work for Christ.

"Second. All who are not willing to help the young.

"Third. All who cannot peaceably work with others.

"Fourth. All who cannot talk briefly.

"Fifth. All who are nothing if not critical.

"Sixth. All who are not willing to attend constantly.

"Seventh. All who are not willing to make any sacrifice whatever for Christ."

Mr. Pennell in speaking of "Our Rules" and answering the question how strictly they should be enforced, answered, "In a single word literally. Since there is no verbal reservation in any of the rules and requirements, there should be no mental reservation in the agreement to observe these rules."

Miss Sewall in her paper on the subject "How may young ladies assist in the work?" urges a modest, womanly, unselfish participation in all the meetings and in the work of the society, and this advice has been carried out by myriads and myriads of her sisters who since have been the mainstay of many a society throughout the world.

It will be noticed by all those who are familiar with the work of the society in later years that the ideas expressed in these pages are the same ideas that now prevail.

More than almost any other organization the Society of Christian Endeavor seems to have been born full fledged. Its principles were emphasized in that Convention of 1883, as they are to-day.

The careful report of the Secretary shows that while it was supposed that there was something like three hundred societies in existence, reports had been received from 56 such societies, with an active membership of 2,018 and a total membership of 2,870.

A list is given of the churches in which the society is established, from which it appeared that it had already found its way into the Methodist, Presbyterian, Baptist, Free Baptist, Dutch Reformed, and Congregational churches.

Of the 56 societies reported, five were formed in 1881, 24 in 1882, and 27 during the first five months of '83.

The five given formed in '81 are as follows, according to the records of that time: Williston Society, Feb. 2, 1881; Newburyport, Mass., Oct., 1881; Scituate, R. I., in the Christian Church, Nov. 22, 1881; Portland, Me., St. Lawrence Street Church, Dec. 1, 1881; Burlington, Vt., Winooski Avenue Church, Dec. 5, 1881.

I have since learned that the true date of the formation of the St. Lawrence Street society, of Portland, was Oct. 24, 1881, making it the third society, and that an Endeavor Society, which is still strong and flourishing, was formed in the Congregational Church, of Granby, Mass., on Dec. 14, 1881, making this the sixth society.

The largest society reported at this convention was the Williston Society, of 164 members. The next largest was in Oakland, Cal., which was formed Aug. 24, 1882, and reported 148 members. The smallest was in Acton, Me., the baby society, with only six members.

The reports which were given by pastors and others were most encouraging.

One reported "marked development in prayer and testimony, showing that it was a training school for the church."

Another, "much more interesting than the old way of conducting young people's meetings."

Another, "attendance at young people's meetings nearly trebled."

While still another says, "The interest manifested among young people is a surprise."

One pastor remarks, "The wonder is we did not realize before what a force we had." While still another said, "A year ago the time was taken up in this meeting by eight or ten members. Now it is not uncommon for seventy-five to take part." At this meeting the invitation of the Kirk Street Society, of Lowell, to hold the next convention with them, was cordially accepted.

Seventy-three dollars was raised by pledges from different societies for the expenses incurred in printing the minutes, etc. A bountiful collation was served, both at noon and at supper-time, by the young ladies of the Second Parish Church.

The convention closed by an earnest prayer by Dr. Small, of the First Baptist Church of Portland; the hymn which has ever since seemed to contain new beauty and sweetness, and which has told of our ever-increasing fellowship, "Blest be the tie that binds our hearts in Christian love," was sung, and the second convention of the Christian Endeavor Societies was numbered with the past.

CHAPTER XIV.

ENDEAVOR PIONEERS.

An Important Ally from Vermont—What He Did For the Society—A Prophecy and Its Fulfillment—Another Friend from New York—The Pioneer in the Dutch Reformed Church—A Beloved Leader of Congregationalism—A Helper from the Pacific—Some Early Friends from the Great Interior—The Free Baptist Pioneer—Good News from Societies Nearer Home—Mr. Adriance's Testimony.

OF some of these Endeavor pioneers I have already spoken, but the account of the second convention written in the last chapter affords me a good opportunity of mentioning the names of those who were identified with the society during the first two years of its existence, and who may fairly be called the Christian Endeavor Pioneers, though I would by no means deny this name to others who soon after this came into the work.

Of Mr. Dickinson and Mr. Stevenson, Mr. Burgess and Mr. Pennell, Mr. Staples and Mr. Agge I have already spoken. They were all prominent in this second convention. But in addition to these honored brethren we find some names that we have not noticed before in the records of Christian Endeavor.

One of these names is that of Hon. W. J. Van Patten, of Burlington, Vt., a prominent layman, connected with the Winooski Avenue Church, whose society stands fifth on the recorded list, being formed Dec. 5, 1881.

It was due to Mr. Van Patten's influence that this fifth society was formed, and ever since he has been a stanch friend of the movement.

At the convention already described he appears as a member of the finance committee most appropriately, for it was due largely to his generosity and ample

HON. W. J. VAN PATTEN.

pocketbook placed at the disposal of the society that its principles during its first two years were spread broadcast.

In his paper read at this second convention on "Ways and Means of Enlarging the Work of the Young People's Society of Christian Endeavor," Mr. Van Patten seems to have been gifted with almost prophetic foresight. He suggests that pastors should in their meetings, conferences, and conventions make the work of the young people's societies one of the subjects of discussion.

"What our pastors say about us," he goes on to say, "if in praise will be much more effectual than anything we can do or say."

In ten thousand cases since, without any knowledge of this suggestion, probably, the idea has been carried out and conferences and associations and minister's meetings everywhere have discussed the society and its work.

Moreover, he goes on to say, "There should be a committee on publication who should prepare papers and reports and have them printed for distribution, an idea which has been carried out by the United Society of Christian Endeavor which has always been simply a bureau for information and publication."

Again, he suggests, in this same paper, and this is the most conspicuous example of prophetic foresight, that frequent conventions be held, district, county, State, national and international, union and denominational.

It must be borne in mind that this was long before a local union or State union of Christian Endeavor had been established, and two years before the existence of the United Society.

Mr. Van Patten goes on to say: "I believe that these conferences would so fill us with the Spirit that we should go on from victory to victory."

This prophecy, too, has been literally fulfilled, for the conventions have been the great generators of enthusiasm for the Endeavor movement.

Mr. Van Patten elaborates his idea for county conferences and national and State conventions, and we all know how in later years these ideas have been carried out.

The word inter-denominational had not been invented in its application to Christian Endeavor Societies, but Mr. Van Patten touched the nerve of the subject when he said: "Our societies differ from Young Men's Christian Associations in this: We are denominational, while they are not. Work done for one of our societies is done for one denomination, while work done for an association is done for all denominations."

Mr. Van Patten, it may be well to say, is and always has been an earnest advocate and supporter of the Young Men's Christian Association. He has given a very large sum of money for the erection of a beautiful association building in Burlington, the city of which he is now the honored mayor.

Another name which we find in the list of vice-presidents of this second convention is that of Rev. Theodore W. Hopkins, D. D., of Rochester, N. Y., then the pastor of the church in that city which formed a society of Christian Endeavor on the 25th of April, 1882. Dr. Hopkins was an earnest advocate of the society, and still retains his love for it. He is now Professor in Auburn Theological Seminary, and is well known for his writings on theological subjects.

Rev. R. W. Brokaw also appears among the vice-presidents of this convention, though he was not present at this meeting. Connected then with the Dutch Reformed Church, his society in Belleville, N. J., was formed on the 24th of April, 1883.

Rev. Constance L. Goodell, D. D., of St. Louis, was also one of the earliest vice-presidents. His society was formed Nov. 2, 1882, and has always been an influential one in the southwest. Dr. Goodell himself

REV. R. W. BROKAW.

was one of the most influential ministers whom the Congregational Church ever knew, and his lamented death in the prime of life will be remembered by many. His eloquence and his devotion to every good cause are still fragrant memories in the denomination to which he belonged.

Rev. J. K. McLean, D. D., of Oakland, Cal., had the honor at this convention of being the pastor of the second largest Endeavor Society in the world. He is still the pastor of the same church, than which none is more influential or generous. His society is as strong and vigorous as ever, and has maintained unbroken its vitality during all these years. My readers who attended the St. Louis convention will remember that one of the eloquent addresses came from this honored pastor.

DR. C. L. GOODELL.

Among the other vice-presidents we notice Rev. E. L. Morse, then of Minnesota, whose society in Boscabell, Wis., a former charge, was formed Sept. 6, 1882, the first in Wisconsin.

At this convention he reports by letter: "I got a hearing with the young people through the society that I could have secured in no other way. In a town where the influence over the young was to make religion seem of very little account, I was able to make it seem the grand and glorious thing among at least a few people."

Rev. C. A. Towle, of Monticello, Ia., another of the vice-presidents, and a pastor of the earliest society in his State, was for a time superintendent of the work in Iowa, and laid the foundations of Christian Endeavor in that State.

Illinois was represented on the list of vice-presidents by Rev. L. L. Kneeland, of Kankakee. He was the pastor of a Baptist church whose society was formed in September, 1882.

Rev. J. M. Lowden, of the executive committee of that year, was the pastor of the Free Baptist Church in Portland, who very early tried the merits of Christian Endeavor. His devotion to the cause has never wavered since. He is now the pastor of the Free Baptist Church in Boston, one of the most influential in the country, and is also a trustee of the United Society.

REV. J. M. LOWDEN.

Of Rev. C. P. Mills, the pastor of the second society, we have spoken.

Though not present at this convention he sent word to it, "The present is full of achievement and the future looks big with hope."

Mr. H. T. Abbe, one of the youngest delegates to the convention, represented Immanuel Church of Boston at this convention. He is still in the work and is yet one of the *young* men of Christian Endeavor.

Rev. E. T. Pitts, of Limington, Maine, sent word that his society had steadily progressed in members and interest. He is now the pastor of a flourishing society in Everett, Mass.

Rev. G. B. Wing, then of Freeport, Maine, took part in the question hour of that convention. He has since passed to his reward, and was to the last a beloved pastor of a Christian Endeavor Society.

We find the names, also, of Brothers F. W. Hall, A. B. Hall, Harris M. Barnes, Oliver B. T. Wish, Rev. G. A. Lockwood, Rev. E. C. Andrews, Rev. A. Wiswall, of Norway, Maine, Samuel Seward, of Lowell, and Royal T. G. Brown, of Boston.

Some of these friends have "crossed the flood," but most are living, and all of them so far as I know are earnest in their advocacy of the Christian Endeavor principles after all these years of experience.

Another honored name which appears for the first time at his convention is that of Rev. S. Winchester Adriance, who reports "that the society has aroused a strong *esprit de corps* among the young people. It has developed an astonishing fertility in many a life that was barren before, and through its instrumentality over forty members have been added to the church."

We shall have occasion to speak of this devoted worker in another chapter, and we cannot better close this one than by quoting his closing sentence at this convention: "And so we all say God bless the society with the magic name Young People's Society Christian Endeavor."

CHAPTER XV.

THE EARLIEST LITERATURE OF CHRISTIAN ENDEAVOR.

Printers' Ink and What it Has Done for the Movement—A Convenient and Inexpensive Agency—Children and Church-Going—"Begin Early"—The First Article About the Endeavor Movement—"How One Church Cares for Its Young People"—How Wings were Given to this Article—*The Sunday-School Times* Contains an Article—The *Golden Rule, The Christian Mirror*, and the *Christian Union* Open their Columns—"How do the Boys and Girls Hold Out?"—*The Christian at Work* and the *Illustrated Christian Weekly* and Their Part in the Work—In Many Lands and Many Languages.

THE Christian Endeavor movement has always spread by use of printer's ink more than in any other way. There has never been a paid corps of secretaries or organizers whose business it was to establish Endeavor Societies, for it has been considered that it was a pastor's business to form such a society in his own church if he desires to have one, and not the concern of any outside party to form a society except at the request of the pastor.

But information must be given in some way, and the printed page has always been the best vehicle for this information.

Fortunately, having had some little experience in newspaper writing and editing on a small scale, I had in those early days, at the beginning of the movement, an entrance to a number of influential religious newspapers.

Referring to old scrap-books I find that my mind had long been considerably exercised on the subject of the Christian training of children, and that in May, 1881, an article was published in the well-known weekly, *Christian Work*, then called *The Christian At Work*, entitled "Children and Church-Going," in which a tabulated list is given of eight churches in Portland, Maine, with the whole number present at the morning services, the whole number in the Sunday-schools of these churches, and the number of children under fourteen years of age who were at the morning service.

From this it appears that on that particular Sunday morning there were present at these churches 1,764 persons, of whom only 248 were boys and girls under fourteen years of age, though 2,072 persons were connected with the Sabbath-schools of those churches. Less than one-seventh part of the members of the congregation could be reckoned as children. Less than one-eighth the number at church of the whole number in the Sabbath-schools, and yet Portland was an average city, above the average, in fact, in the number of its church-goers, and presumably in the number of children in attendance upon church services.

These facts and figures provoked disquieting thoughts, and led me to ask myself most seriously, Is there not a remedy for this state of things?

The Society of Christian Endeavor was already being tried as a remedy in one of those churches, but the time had not come to speak of it in print, as I did not feel that the success of a four months' old society was yet sufficiently assured. In the same month of May, 1881, another article of a similar nature was written for *The Christian Mirror*, entitled "Begin Early," in which I urged parents and teachers to begin earlier than they were accustomed to think was possible to help their children into the Christian life. The idea of the Junior Society was embodied in that article.

Later in the same year I felt that the Endeavor Society had long enough proved its right to live to warrant a brief description of it in the religious press, and so an article was sent to *The Congregationalist*, of Boston, which was published in August, 1881, entitled "How One Church Cares for Its Young People."

This was the first notice given to the world of the existence of a Society of Christian Endeavor. It may be of interest to my readers if I quote a few sentences from this first article. Here is the beginning and end of this article. The middle of it described the *modus operandi* of the society which has already been rehearsed in previous pages:

"We heard an eloquent minister say the other day, in the course of his address, 'I do not dare to bring too many children into my church; not because I do not believe in their sincerity and piety and fitness for church membership, but because there is no provision for their growth and nurture after they are in the church.' 'What shall we do for the children and young people of the church?' seems to be one of the pressing problems of the day.

"By the hopeful conversion of a large number of young people last winter, the writer of this article had this question thrust upon him as a practical matter, and the frequent inquiries concerning the plans adopted at the time tempts him to rehearse them, in the hope that they may be of some benefit to others. About 125 names are enrolled on the books of this society, most of them active members, and, with very few exceptions, the duties have been faithfully performed by all.

"The officers and committees have been most efficient and unwearied in their efforts. The pastor has attended all the meetings and sociables as one of the young people, and has thoroughly enjoyed and been benefited by them all. He has also had a Tuesday afternoon class, to which many of these young people have belonged, for the study of the church creed, the duties of the Christian life, and, latterly, the *Pilgrim's Progress*.

"The results of these endeavors have been the revival of a languishing young people's meeting; the constant and evident growth in grace of many young Christians, a large number of whom have come into the church, and some of whose voices are already heard in the regular church prayer-meetings; an intimate and affectionate acquaintance between the pastor and the young people, and the well-grounded hope that constant and increasing good will come of this organization in the future."

This article had still wider currency by being copied into *The Sunday School Times* and in many other religious journals both at home and abroad.

The next month, September, 1881, still another article on the same subject was published in *The Sunday School Times*, in which I say that since the appearance of the article copied into *The Sunday School Times* concerning one way in which one church cares for its young people, the pastor has had many requests from pastors in all parts of the country asking for further particulars and copies of the constitution. In this second article I urged that the society seeks to provide a natural and pleasant channel by which young people and even little children may acknowledge Christ; that it plans to look after its members when they become pronounced Christians and church members. In short, the object of the society is "to make a place in church work for young people and children. Not to form a separate church for them, but to make a place for them in their own church where they may spend their vitality and work as young Christians should, be trained for future usefulness, cared for and won back if tempted to go astray. It makes church membership possible for many who otherwise could not be safely received, and future usefulness more certain for many who but for this training would be drones in the hive."

The article closed with this piece of information: "After the long summer vacation the Williston Young People's Society of Christian Endeavor began its work September 1 with renewed vigor. All the young people were in their accustomed places, ready and anxious to begin their year's Christian labor; all the old voices were heard and new members are constantly being added to the society. Several of our New England States showed a decrease in the past year in the number of church members. How can this loss be arrested, how can the places of the fathers be made good, unless in some such way as this society seeks to provide, new life is infused into our churches from the ranks of the young?"

Other articles on the same general subject were published in *The Golden Rule* in December, 1881, and also in *The Christian Mirror* in the same month, while in an article published in *The Christian Union*, now *The Outlook*, in the preceding month of November, I attempted to answer the question, "How do the boys and girls hold out?"

The answer was: "Exceedingly well. None do better than the boys and girls. None are more hopeful, promising Christians. None live up to their covenant obligations better. If all older ones did as well there would be at least one model church in the land."

With the following words which show the growing faith of those who had most to do with the earliest societies in this method of Christian nurture the article closes: "Why cannot every church have just such an organization? Half a dozen young people, who are willing to pledge themselves to be faithful to it and its meetings, are sufficient to begin with; guided by some older and wiser head, they cannot fail to grow in numbers and in grace. The Williston Young People's Society of Christian Endeavor numbers over a hundred active members who are working Christians, a large proportion of them being boys and girls from twelve to sixteen years old. The Friday evening meetings average about a hundred in attendance, and nearly every one in the room takes part in every meeting; and already these young people have begun to be a help to their pastor, not only in these meetings, but in all church work."

Doubtless there are other societies, organized on the same basis, that are doing an equally good work. We do not give these particulars because there is anything startling or wonderful about them, but because the plan is so simple that it can be adopted everywhere; and because, for one church, it has helped to answer, in the right way, the question: "Will the boys and girls hold out?"

Another article by me appeared in *The Christian at Work* for an issue of December, 1881, on "The Church and the Young."

Another one in *The Congregationalist*, before the year closed, entitled, "Is there a better way?" declares, "the writer can say with renewed emphasis after four months more of trial that the Society of Christian Endeavor connected with the Williston Church, of which he is pastor, has been a blessed thing for the young people of one church at least. The boys and girls who are trained in this way do hold out. It is possible for the pastor and older Christians through this agency to look after and train the younger ones. Such a society as this does make it safe to admit young boys and girls to the church, and if its rules are lived up to, assures their nurture after they are in the church."

These articles, together with still another article of a similar nature, published in *The Illustrated Christian Weekly* for January, 1882, and a sermon on "The Conversion and Christian Nurture of Children," published in *The Christian Mirror* early in 1882, may be considered the pioneer literature on the subject of the society and its work.

From that day to this God has used the agency of printer's ink to bring the society to the knowledge of the Christian world. Tens of thousands of articles have been printed in many languages. The constitution has been translated and printed in a score and a half of the leading languages of the world. Newspapers, both secular and religious, have printed hundreds of thousands of columns concerning this organization, and all this printer's ink has had its influence in spreading the knowledge of the movement to the remotest boundaries of the world.

CHAPTER XVI.

THE FIRST BOOK ON CHRISTIAN ENDEAVOR.

A Little Tract, and What it Led to—The Work of a Summer Vacation—A Dedication from the Heart—Not a Sectarian Organization—Dr. Goodell's Testimony—Bringing in Honey—Growth Rather Than Conquest—A Lesson from Napoleon—Dr. Bushnell's Stimulating Book—Jerusalem Full of Boys and Girls—The Testimony of Eminent Divines—Practical Questions Answered—How the Book Was Circulated—Reprinted in England—Revised in 1887—A Significant Change—Principles Unchanged.

IN the spring of 1882 a tract seemed to be demanded to set forth a little more at length the work of the society, and so, at the request of the Congregational Sunday-school and Publishing Society, of which Dr. A. E. Dunning, now the editor of *The Congregationalist*, was then the efficient secretary, I prepared such a leaflet, entitled " The Children at the Church Doors."

This little tract of twelve pages sought to answer the question " Why the Society of Christian Endeavor is needed, and what it is designed to accomplish ?" My readers already know the answers given to these questions. The numerous inquiries started by these many newspaper articles alluded to in the last chapter, as well as by this tract, soon made it evident that there was a demand for a larger work on this subject—a demand which I attempted to fill in the summer of 1882.

During my summer vacation, which was largely spent at a seashore cottage at Pine Point, Me., near Old Orchard Beach, I worked diligently over a little book of 108 pages, which early in the fall of the same year was published. This book was entitled :

THE CHILDREN AND THE CHURCH;

AND THE

YOUNG PEOPLE'S SOCIETY OF CHRISTIAN ENDEAVOR AS A MEANS OF BRINGING THEM TOGETHER,

and it was dedicated

TO THE MANY MEMBERS

OF THE

Williston Young People's Society of Christian Endeavor,

WHO HAVE

SO OFTEN LIGHTENED THEIR PASTOR'S LABORS,

AND

CHEERED THEIR PASTOR'S HEART,

THIS BOOK

IS AFFECTIONATELY DEDICATED.

In a prefatory note the first article on the society is alluded to, and the correspondence to which it gave birth, and it further says: "It became evident that among pastors and other Christian workers there was a widespread desire for any light, however feeble, that might be shed upon the relation of the children to the church. This book is an attempt to answer the questions thus raised, and to solve the problems suggested, by stating as clearly as possible the needs and difficulties in the way of Christian nurture, and by presenting a practical plan for accomplishing this end, which in many cases has proved successful."

The preface goes on to remark: "The Young People's Society of Christian Endeavor is in no sense a sectarian organization. One of the first societies established was in a large Baptist Church in Connecticut. Many have been started in Methodist, Free Baptist, Baptist, and Presbyterian, as well as Congregational churches. It is hoped that no denominational lines will interfere with this method of bringing children and young people into the service of Christ."

Alas! this hope, so early expressed, was not destined to be altogether fulfilled.

The introduction to this book was written by that distinguished minister and beloved pastor, Rev. Constance L. Goodell, of the Pilgrim Church, St. Louis, who already had a society in his church. It is a strong and graceful introduction, and heartily commends the movement to all pastors.

"The method set forth in this volume," said Dr. Goodell, "is no longer an experiment. It has been very successfully tried by the author and by many others, who, adopting the suggestions of the author, are happy to attest their great practical value. The Society of Christian Endeavor, brought from Portland to St. Louis without injury, is one of the busiest bees in the Pilgrim hive. It brings in honey and comb and finds many wayside flowers that have been overlooked. It comes in every day rich with golden power. It is one of the special helps of the pastor. It is wings for him and flies all over the city."

This little volume does not describe simply the methods of the Society of Christian Endeavor.

As its main title indicates—"the Children and the Church"—it seeks to cover the larger ground of Christian nurture, and its central thought may be considered "growth from within, rather than conquest from without," as expressed in the chapter on Church Membership for Children.

"What nation," it says, "would neglect its own children and rely for growth on conquered foreigners? Even Napoleon, king of conquest though he was, was wiser than this. Though he laid every nation under tribute to France, his constant principle was: France must depend upon the children born upon her soil for her strength and glory rather than upon the annexation of alien nations."

"No nation can long thrive by a spirit of conquest," says Dr. Bushnell. "No more can a church. There must be internal growth. Let us try if we may not train up our children in the way that they should go. Simply this, if we can do it, will make the church multiply her numbers many fold more rapidly than now, with the advantage that more will be gained from without than now."

This quotation from Dr. Bushnell leads me to acknowledge my indebtedness to his most stimulating book entitled *Christian Nurture*.

Though it contains no hint of the *methods* of the Society of Christian Endeavor, it is the most thought-provoking and fascinating volume ever written on this subject of the Christian training of children. I wish that every parent, as well as every minister, might read it.

To begin at the beginning: The little volume of which we are speaking, *The Children and the Church*, devotes a chapter to "Child-life in the Bible," describes Jewish customs respecting child-life, the naturalness of child-life in the Bible, and insists that the Bible declares that the religious life of the child is a growth as much as his physical life—a very self-evident proposition it would seem—and yet there were some people then, and even now, who consider that a child at the very beginning of his Christian life should exhibit the mature graces and exercises of his grandfather and grandmother.

The second chapter of the book tries to answer the question, Is there a place in the church for the children? and to answer it in the affirmative, claiming that, as it is declared that Jerusalem is to be full of boys and girls playing in the streets thereof, so there should be a place in our earthly Jerusalem for the boys and girls, not for the occasional child, not for the one lamb among a hundred sheep, not only for the rare and precocious little saint, but for the great mass of average boys and girls who, by judicious training and careful Christian nurture, may be induced very early to give their hearts to God.

That there is such a place in the church is indicated by the nature of childhood, the nature of conversion and by the nature of the church, and the prophecy is hazarded that the church of the future here on earth will be full of boys and girls.

Chapter third shows the need of church membership for children as indicated by the sluggish and depleted state of our churches, the difficulty of impressing with religious truth persons of mature years. The opposition and indifference of pastors, teachers, and churches to early membership of children is dealt with, while the testimony of such eminent divines as Dr. Theo. L. Cuyler, Dr. C. H. Spurgeon, and Dr. Stephen H. Tyng, Sr., are quoted as enforcing the wisdom of early conversion and church membership.

Chapters fourth, fifth, and sixth go on to speak of the Society of Christian Endeavor as a practical means of bringing the church and children together; its object, its spirit, and its rules are discussed.

Its object is declared to be to promote constant confession of Christ and earnest Christian effort. Its spirit is the spirit of aggressive, evangelical Christianity. Its rules are simple regulations for the accomplishment of its object, and are not in any wise too strict or rigid.

Moreover the society is declared to be a half-way house to the church when parents and pastors are not willing that the children should at once join the church; a training-school within the church for all the young people; and a watch-tower for the church from which pastors and older members can see how the young disciples are progressing in the religious life, and what help they need in fitting them for larger service.

Then some practical questions are answered as how the society can be formed, what age limit should be imposed, whether or not the plan is fitted for small, weak churches, what "absolute necessity" means, etc.

After dealing with some misapprehensions, the book closes with a valuable appendix, contributed largely by Rev. J. G. Merrill, D. D., then of St. Louis, but now the editor of *The Christian Mirror*, of Portland.

This little book enjoyed a large circulation, and has since passed, we believe, to a third, if not fourth edition.

Through the generosity of Mr. J. W. Patten, of Burlington, Vt., 2,000 copies of a special edition in paper covers were distributed to pastors and Christian workers, and this did very much toward spreading a knowledge of the society.

An abbreviated reprint of this book has been republished in England, and the substance of it has been translated into a score of different languages.

In 1887 it was revised and slightly enlarged. One notable change was made in this revised edition, which indicates more clearly than anything else can do the progress of Christian Endeavor. During these few years the society had become a *Young People's Society*, and Junior societies had begun to be started for the children.

So it was necessary in bringing the book down to date, to go through it carefully, and substitute the words "young people" for the word "children" in most places where it occurred in the book.

However, the principles were unchanged, and this slight change of phraseology showed the expansion and growing power of the Christian Endeavor idea which had begun to take hold of the strong young men and women of the land.

CHAPTER XVII.

CHAINED LIONS.

Objections and Objectors—Honest Difficulties—Captious Criticisms—The Test of Time—"Bring Them All Into One Great Prayer-Meeting"—The Bold and Brazen Type of Piety!—Naturalness Cultivated—Scaring, Coaxing, Melting—Old Objections Reappearing—How they Melt Away—Time and Experience the Best Allies of the Endeavor Society.

IT is not strange that such an organization as this, with principles radically different in some particulars from any that had been applied to the training of young Christians in the past, should be misunderstood in many quarters. In fact, the strange thing about the whole movement is, that in the Providence of God it has been so well understood, and has excited so little factious opposition.

We have already had something to say about the objections and the objectors of the early days, in which the blind people who would not see any good in the movement were particularly considered.

There was another class, who really desired with all their hearts to adopt the best methods of Christian nurture, and who looked hopefully to this new movement as a possible solution of their difficulties, but who yet saw possible troubles and disasters which might arise from these somewhat radical measures.

Such persons have always been regarded by the leaders in the Christian Endeavor Society as real friends of the movement. Their objections have been carefully considered and by them we have often profited. In almost every case their misapprehensions have been removed and their fears allayed. But it is of interest to know just what these chained lions were that stood in the way at the beginning of the Endeavor Society.

The little book to which the last chapter was devoted, fortunately records some of these objections which otherwise might have passed out of our minds. Most of these may be grouped under two heads.

First, these young people's societies, it was said, will interfere with the church and detract from its pre-eminence.

Second, it is thought they would foster a forced, unnatural religious experience.

As to the first objection, the book answers: "The only test of this is experience, and so far as our experience goes it points directly the other way. Our church prayer-meetings have been better attended with a far larger proportion of young people and with much more active help from them since the establishment of this society than ever before. At least sixty whom we could not otherwise have expected to see join the church have joined within a year and a half, led to Christ and trained for Christ by the influences of this society.

"There are six organizations of the same kind in Portland, and every one has resulted in awakening a new interest in religious matters among the young and in bringing many into these different churches.

"The same is true in scores of different societies from which we have heard in different parts of the land. But some one says bring them all, young and old and middle-aged, into one great prayer-meeting and let us have no classification of age in the prayer-meeting. Very true, bring them all together, urge this upon them, keep it before them, that whatever happens they must never desert the regular meetings of their church, but, at the same time, if they wish to come together on still another evening when less embarrassed by the presence of their elders for mutual help, shall we forbid this, when all their practice will inure directly to the benefit of the church? Can we expect the child Christian to find its voice for the first time when two or three hundred older Christians are listening for his confession.

"As a practical matter, do we not need some fitting-school for the young convert, and, instead of regarding any such movement as antagonistic to the church, should we not welcome it as a most needed auxiliary?

"Another says in this same line of criticism, 'I don't believe in anything outside of the church. God appointed the church to accomplish the conversion of the world, and what is outside of the church is wrong in principle and practice.'

"But in what sense is such an organization outside of the church? No more than the Sunday-school, no more than the prayer-meeting, are outside of the church. It is carried on by the church and for the church, and for the purpose of bringing young people into the church, and of keeping them from falling after they are in the church. Surely nothing could have a more intimate relation with the church than just such an organization."

Another class of objectors took the ground that any such efforts, and especially such meetings as this society contemplates, will cultivate a bold and brazen type of piety; that it will brush the first bloom from the youthful Christian heart: in a word, that it will foster a forced, unnatural, precocious religious experience.

"The only answer to make to such objectors is the answer of actual experience, 'See if it does.' We have watched carefully for any budding signs of such unnatural religious precocity, and we have yet to find the first indications of it. And why should we expect this? Is there not a religious experience as germane to the boy as to the man? Is it not as natural for a Christian boy to speak as a Christian boy, as for a Christian man to speak as a Christian man? We have no doubt that some children could be flattered and cajoled into thinking that they were experienced veterans when they were but babes in Christ, and might put on unbecoming airs in consequence; but the vast majority will be so timid and modest and shrinking that the great problem will be how to bring them out rather than how to repress them in the expression they give to their religious life; and a very few kindly words will be sufficient to check the few too forward ones, if any such are found.

* * * * * * * * *

"It is an entire misapprehension that this society tends to make children prominent in public; that its prime object is to make a religious stump speaker of every boy or girl whom it can induce to join its ranks. Such an idea is so whimsical and so wide of the mark that it hardly seems worthy of serious answer; but it has been urged, and we wish to free the minds of all our readers of every such idea.

"This society contemplates no exhibitions, no display of the talent of its members for religious exhortation. The prayer-meetings are quiet gatherings together of young disciples. There cannot well be anything of the public declamation flavor to them; no exhibition of dress, no posturing, no stage effects are possible. What can be more natural or more childlike than the gathering together of young Christians to recite the words of inspiration, or the simple words God has given them to speak to each other? If recitations in public schools and Sabbath-schools are not open to this charge, we cannot well see how it can be laid at the door of the Young People's Society of Christian Endeavor.

* * * * * * * * *

"It is claimed with justice that much reproach has been brought upon child conversion and religious nurture by injudicious attempts to scare or coax or melt children into a religious mood. Such attempts, if they stop there, are often worse than useless. for the plant of Christian character, instead of being warmed into new life is often seared and burned, so that it never again easily responds to the vivifying influences of the Son of Righteousness.

"Against the prejudices thus created are all new plans for Christian nurture obliged to contend; but we desire to have it strictly understood that the methods we have described contemplate not this sudden, spasmodic, gusty work, but a quiet, watchful, long-continued, patient effort, extending through months and years to fit children for the church of God on earth and the assembly of the redeemed above."

Thus in the early days were these objections answered and these misapprehensions met. In every new land where the Society of Christian Endeavor has made its way the same objections have been raised and have gradually disappeared. I have come to know very well what difficulties will be raised and what objections urged where the society is new, and has not proved its right to exist by the work that it accomplishes.

But I am also glad to record that in every land the objections largely melt away like frost in the sunshine when societies have existed for a little while, and by the warmth and brightness of their fresh young religious life have shown their humble, persistent, and loving purpose to labor and pray in evil report and good report for the advancement of the cause of Christ and His church.

CHAPTER XVIII.

THE THIRD CONVENTION.

Outside the State of Maine—The Number of Societies in 1884—A Two Days' Convention—One Hundred and Forty-two Delegates—A Connecticut Pioneer—Massachusetts' Large Delegation—Proportionate Representation—The Society in Nineteen States, One Territory, and the Dominion of Canada—Massachusetts Now the Leader—Denominational Representation—The Constitution Not Too Strict—The Papers Read and Subjects Discussed—Can We Improve the Name?—Some Stirring Addresses.

S a result of the articles referred to in a previous chapter, and of the wide circulation of *The Children and the Church*, during the year 1883 and the beginning of '84 societies began to rapidly multiply, and when the time came for the third annual convention, in October of 1884, it was found that there were 156 societies recorded, with a total membership of 8,905. Undoubtedly there were many more societies from which no report was heard, but the gain in recorded societies in little more than a year had been exactly a round hundred.

KIRK STREET CHURCH, LOWELL, MASS., WHERE THE THIRD ANNUAL CONVENTION WAS HELD.

This was the first convention that occupied more than a single day, and, as will be remembered, the invitation of the Kirk Street Society, of Lowell, Mass., of which the Rev. C. A. Dickinson was then the pastor, had been accepted the year before.

This was the first convention which had been held outside of the State of Maine, and the only convention which has ever been held in the fall.

The printed list of delegates occupies two pages instead of one, and has exactly doubled, 142 being recorded this year in place of the 71 whose names were given at the last conference.

However, we will not place too much dependence on this list of names, for the recording secretary, in a foot-note to his report, naïvely remarks: "The committee on credentials carried away their report, and the mistakes in the above must not be laid to the recording secretary."

The list of delegates, too, indicates the widening sweep and scope of the society. Connecticut was represented for the first time this year in the person of Mr. Eli Manchester, Jr., of the Howard Avenue Society of New Haven—a young man whose faith and works entitle him to a most honorable mention among the pioneers of Christian Endeavor.

Massachusetts had a large delegation from twenty-one different cities and towns, representing twenty-eight different churches, and from that day to this the old Bay State has been nobly represented in every great Christian Endeavor gathering.

AUGUSTUS R. SMITH.

This year three Boston churches were represented, instead of one as last year: Immanuel Church of Roxbury, Phillips Church of South Boston, and the Walnut Avenue of Roxbury.

Cambridge, Charlestown (then a separate city), Salem, Marblehead, Concord, Auburndale, Lynn, and Wellesley, as well as other towns, we find upon the list.

From Lee came Augustus R. Smith, ten years afterward the efficient President of the Massachusetts union.

Lowell, the convention city, then had five societies—in the Kirk Street, Elliot, High Street, and John Street Churches, and in the Primitive Methodist Church.

From Maine, delegates came from Auburn, Bucksport, Grey, Kennebunk, and Woodsfords, as well as from the eight Endeavor Societies of Portland, which still, up to that date, maintained its supremacy as the first Christian Endeavor city of the country.

THE THIRD CONVENTION.

It sent at least thirty delegates from these eight churches, the West Congregational Church reporting eight, and the Williston Church as many more.

Three places in New Hampshire were represented—Great Falls, Hampton, and Newport; and two in Vermont—Chester and Burlington.

For the first time, too, at this convention, representatives were present from outside of New England. Two societies in Rochester, N. Y. (that early home of Christian Endeavor), representing the North Presbyterian and the Central Presbyterian churches, sent four delegates.

Doubtless there were others present who were as truly delegates as those whose names are recorded; but in the early days a more strict construction of the word "delegate" prevailed than at present.

The committee on representation at this convention recommended that every society, however small, should be entitled to one delegate; that if the society should number fifty members, it shall be entitled to two delegates; and that for every additional fifty members another delegate may be chosen.

This report was afterward amended so as to make the ratio of representation one to twenty-five, instead of fifty.

The secretary's elaborate statistical report showed that the society existed in nineteen States, the Territory of Washington, and the Dominion of Canada.

The leadership, in the number of Christian Endeavor Societies, had now passed from Maine, with its twenty-eight societies and 1,740 members, to Massachusetts, with its forty-three societies and 2,686 members. New York came third in the list, and was credited with seventeen societies and something over a thousand members.

Connecticut was fourth, with twelve societies and 689 members.

Vermont had seven societies, Illinois and Michigan six each, Ohio five, and New Hampshire four; while Iowa, Missouri, New Jersey, and Rhode Island had three societies; California, Colorado, and Washington, two each.

Pennsylvania, to-day the banner Christian Endeavor State, with its thousands of societies and tens of thousands of members, was then known to have but one society.

Indiana, Maryland, and Minnesota had just as many, while only one society, with but thirty-six members, was accredited to the great Dominion of Canada.

"The denominational representation," we are told, "remains in about the same proportion or disproportion as last year."

The Congregationalists were then far in the lead—a leadership which the Presbyterians soon took away from them. But there were thirteen Presbyterian societies, ten Baptist, seven Methodist, three Free Baptist, two Dutch Reformed, and one Christian.

The secretary pertinently remarks: "We desire it to be clearly understood that this is not a denominational organization. All evangelical denominations are cordially welcomed to its councils, and it is a source of disappointment that the disproportion of last year still remains.

"It is earnestly hoped that the denominations that are in a minority will make a special effort to reduce the inequality."

Most of the denominations, we are glad to say, have made this "special effort," but there is still room for a little more endeavor in this direction on the part of one or two.

At this convention an important step was taken in considering the matter of incorporation. It was recommended that the society become a permanently-organized body, and the matter was referred to the executive committee, the incorporation to take effect, as we shall later see, at the next convention.

The local constitution, too, was considered in some detail at this meeting, and we read the significant record that "the clause in our constitution which reads, 'If any active member of this society is absent and unexcused from three consecutive experience meetings, such a one ceases to be a member of the society, and his name shall be stricken from the roll'—*that this clause is not too strict, and, if carefully enforced, should save rather than add trouble to the society.*"

In the President's address Mr. Pennell makes some valuable suggestions in regard to withdrawal from the society, transfer cards, time of the conference, and so on.

Rev. F. E. Clark read a paper on the "Distinctive Features of the Society;" Rev. C. A. Dickinson on the "Uniformity of Name and Constitution," in which he wisely recommended uniformity of name for the societies, some of which had sprung up with different titles, though with the same principles and constitution.

"The Young People's Society of Christian Effort would not differ much," said he, "from the Young People's Society of Christian Endeavor, but so subtle is this influence of name that I have no doubt the two would be more truly one in sympathy and aim could they agree to come under a common appellation." . . . "Again, if we have the thing, we should not refuse to call it by its name," he most pertinently remarks; a remark which would be well for many societies which, for the sake of cheap originality and independence, have taken all the principles which have given vitality to the Society of Christian Endeavor and have ignored its name.

"Can we improve upon its name?" Mr. Dickinson goes on to say. "For one, I think not. It is both euphonious and expressive. To my own mind it expresses exactly the animus and interest of the society."

For the same reason he urges a uniformity of constitution, so far as its important principles are concerned.

Among other notable features of this convention was the paper of Rev.

James L. Hill, on "The Society as a Means of Home Evangelization;" of Rev. C. A. Towle, of Iowa, on "How Shall We Bring Our Work to the Notice of the Churches," and of Mr. Joseph T. Allen, of Rochester, Miss Ada R. Hartshorn, of South Boston, of Mr. Eli Manchester, Jr., Mr. E. H. Shattuck, of Lowell, and Miss Etta H. Stanwood, on "The Work of the Different Committees."

Rev. Michael Burnham, then of the Immanuel Church of Boston, Rev. A. H. Plumb, D. D., of Roxbury, and Rev. Alex. McKenzie, of Cambridge, made most

REV. ALEX. MCKENZIE, D. D., REV. M. BURNHAM, REV. A. H. PLUMB, D. D.

inspiring and eloquent addresses. Every one who has heard these gentlemen knows how they must have aroused the enthusiasm of Christian Endeavorers at this early convention.

That favorite convention song,

"Blest Be the Tie that Binds,"

was sung, the benediction was pronounced, and another milestone in the history of Christian Endeavor was passed.

CHAPTER XIX.

NEWS FROM ACROSS THE SEAS.

Foo Chow and Honolulu—Good News from Ceylon—Precious Pearl—Christian Endeavor Hens and Trees—Beginnings in Hawaii—The First Society in Honolulu—Its Vicissitudes and Its Victories—The Beginning of the Work in China—Mr. Ling and His Address.

A BRIEF paragraph in the report of the Third Convention informs us that "Rev. F. E. Clark told of the formation of societies at Foo Chow, China, and at Honolulu, S. I."

I well remember the thrill of interest and almost incredulous wonder with which we received the information concerning these earliest societies in missionary lands.

It had scarcely dawned upon the horizon of the most enthusiastic Christian Endeavorer that God could have any use for the society in circumstances so different and under conditions so strange.

If I am not mistaken, about the same time a letter was received from Miss Margaret Leitch, of Ceylon, telling about the formation of a society among the Tamil-speaking children of Jaffna. Her letter described the simple, touching faith of these far-off Endeavorers, and of their generosity, as well, for one of the first acts of the boys belonging to the society, according to her story, was to dedicate one of their cocoanut trees to the Lord's service, and to write upon the bark the letters, which, in Tamil, stood for Y. P. S. C. E.

All the cocoanuts which the tree grew were given to the missionaries for the advancement of the Kingdom; while the girls, who were too poor to afford a tree, devoted a hen to the same purpose; and all the eggs and chickens belonging to this biddy were sacred to the missionaries.

MISS MARGARET LEITCH AND PUPILS, JAFFNA, CEYLON.

Almost as soon as the society began to find its wings in America, it flew over to Hawaii and found rest, like Noah's dove, in the Fort Street Church of Honolulu.

Rev. J. A. Cruzan, now a pastor in Santa Cruz, California, but then pastor of this famous church of Honolulu, writes: " While serving in the Fort Street Church as pastor there drifted into my omnivorous scrap-book an article from the pen of Rev. F. E. Clark, entitled ' How one church looks after its young people.'

" Gracious revivals in 1881 and 1882 had brought a large number of new-born souls into the church. Many of these were young people, some of them young men who have since helped make history in that far-off, sorely tried nation.

" For the spiritual training of these young Christians there was organized a young people's meeting of the type so well known a quarter of a century ago, and of which in most cases it had to be sadly written ' Ye did run well, who did hinder you ?'

" Many things hindered this young people's meeting in Honolulu, and the summer vacation of 1883 proved a welcome opportunity to allow it to ' die decently.'

" In November, 1883, steps were taken to organize on Christian Endeavor lines, the invaluable scrap-book article furnishing the basis; and soon the first Christian Endeavor Society in Hawaii, and I think the first outside of America, was born. The number was small, the iron-clad pledge preventing many from joining. Nineteen names were enrolled and Miss Ella Spooner, Vice-Principal of Oahu College, was the first and the very efficient president. Failing health compelled Miss Spooner to lay down the work, and it fell into other and less efficient hands. The iron-clad pledge was pared down somewhat. The usual result which follows the removal of the spinal column, ensued—collapse.

REV. J. A. CRUZAN.

" But there was life in the society and it would not die. When the time was ripe, with a copy of that admirable little book, *The Children of the Church*, in hand, a thorough reorganization was effected on strict Endeavor lines.

" Hon. W. O. Smith, the present Attorney General of the Republic of Hawaii, was chosen president, and proved an admirable leader.

" From that time forth this society has been an efficient factor in the spiritual life of the church with which it is connected, of the city of Honolulu, and of the little nation.

" What proved helpful among the white foreigners, of course must needs find its way into the churches of other nationalities. The Hawaiian, Chinese, and Japanese churches have all tried the Endeavor idea, and proved it to be admirably adapted to the spiritual growth and efficiency of their young people."

All my readers will be glad to know that the original Chinese Christian Endeavorer, Mr. Ling, is alive and earnest and active in the Endeavor cause to this day. He was one of the prominent delegates at the first Chinese Christian Endeavor Convention, held in Shanghai in June, 1894, and his devotion, wit, and good sense can be judged from the following extract from his address at the convention. This report of it appears in the minutes of the first convention:

MR. LING.

"As the gospel has spread, the devil has had to retreat. Now that he has nowhere to stay in Western countries, he has come to China to live. In 1884 we started our first Christian Endeavor Society, the object of which is to drive him out of China. If we succeed he cannot go back to the West, but must be driven into the Eastern sea, where he will meet the fate of the Gadarene swine, who perished in the waters."

Other lands were not slow in following the example set by China, Hawaii, and Ceylon in forming, here and there, an Endeavor Society, though some years elapsed before there was any general movement looking to the establishment of the movement outside of America. The chief value of these occasional early societies in foreign lands, so far as the societies in America was concerned, was to prove the world-wide possibilities of the movement—possibilities which, in these later days, have been so fully realized.

The gradual development of the Endeavor idea in other lands, the world around, will be traced in later chapters of this book.

CHAPTER XX.

OUR EARLY FELLOWSHIP.

Inevitable and Natural—The Use of Anniversaries—Geographical and Municipal Lines—State Pride and Patriotism—Natural Divisions—The Earliest State Unions—The Beginning of City Unions—A Simple Program—Autumn Leaves in Vallambrosa—The Roots of these Union Meetings—"That they all may be one"—The Beginning of State and Local Unions—Their Prominent Place in Christian Endeavor—Where the First State Union was Formed—The First Little Convention—The Call of the Pastors and Presidents—How Mr. Manchester was "Loaded"—How the Name was Obtained—Dr. Twitchell's Account of the First Local Union—The Birthplace—How the Idea Spread—The Advantages of Local Unions—To God be the Glory.

THE early development of the fellowship idea in the societies of Christian Endeavor was as inevitable as it was natural.

Here were a number of similar organizations in different parts of the country, organizations with the same great purpose and underlying motive, the same methods and ways of working, the same name and pledge and consecration meeting and committees.

Inevitably, they demanded more knowledge of each other and more intimate fellowship one with another.

At the beginning, as we have seen, this fellowship was provided for in the annual convention, but this could hardly satisfy the wants of all.

The meetings were too *infrequent*, and the remoter societies were too far away to enjoy their benefit.

Then anniversary occasions were utilized to secure this fellowship and intimate knowledge, which the societies felt was so important. But after a little it was felt that these occasions were becoming too *frequent*, and the meetings burdensome with their demands upon the time of sister societies, whose great object always has been from the beginning to build up the interests of Christ's kingdom in their own churches.

Manifestly, it was not possible then for the societies to visit back and forth on anniversary occasions, after these occasions became numerous, without interfering with their proper work for their own churches; so the good inventive genius of the movement began to whisper into the ears of different Endeavorers, "Why not form local unions, organizations of all the Endeavor Societies within

151

a convenient radius, which shall have stated meetings two or three or four times a year for the inspiration and fellowship which we all so much crave?"

Naturally, geographical and municipal lines in many cases set the boundaries of these unions. The societies of a city would almost inevitably belong to one union. But for the sake of including in the fellowship the village societies and those in still more scattered communities, district or county unions were soon suggested and established in many places.

But State pride and patriotism are among the most amiable and charming features of American life. No wonder, then, that the young Christian Endeavorers, with a desire to win their respective commonwealths for Christ through the medium of the Christian Endeavor Society, in which they had come most enthusiastically to believe, began to group themselves into State unions, whose earliest meetings, at about this period in the history of the Endeavor movement, also began to be held.

And now we have, originated in this unpremeditated and entirely Providential way, the outlines of the Endeavor fellowship as it exists to-day; first, the National, or "International Convention," as it has always been called in America, since Canada and the United States have affectionately united in these annual celebrations without any thought of tariff walls or political differences. In fact, there has always been a strong and binding reciprocity treaty between the Endeavorers of the two nations.

Then the State, Provincial, and Territorial unions have held their annual conventions; the district or county union, for the sake of bringing the inspiration a little nearer home, has held its meetings once or twice a year, while the local union enjoys its fellowship gatherings from two to four times in the course of the twelve months.

Thus, without forming any burdensome tax upon the time or money of the average Endeavorer, their fellowship is preserved and their enthusiasm kept at a good temperature throughout the year, with the expenditure of not more than six or eight evenings out of the three hundred and sixty-five on the part of the average Endeavorer.

These union meetings of all kinds have been most stimulating and helpful. In fact, I can hardly conceive of the growth of the Society of Christian Endeavor to its present dimensions without these gatherings. In these meetings, some of which have now grown to enormous proportions, not only are the Endeavor principles discussed and maintained, not only are weak knees strengthened and feeble hands lifted up, but the community is impressed with a sense of the vitality and vigor of the Society and its importance as an evangelistic, Christianizing agency.

The newspapers have given great space to the conventions, national, State, and local; the news of the society and its work has been spread on the wings of the printed page to the very ends of the earth, and from every great convention, whether of the nation or of the State, the Endeavor Society has come forth stronger and more confident of its God-given mission, and to do humbly the work God has given it to do.

Connecticut has the honor of establishing the first local union of Christian Endeavor and the first State convention, and it is only fitting that those who had most to do with these early organizations should tell us the story, as they will do later in this chapter.

The earliest program of a regularly constituted Christian Endeavor Union which I remember attending is that of the Manchester, Conn., Union, held September 22, 1886, whose President was Mr. William H. Childs, so long and honorably known in the history of Christian Endeavor in Connecticut.

The Secretary and Treasurer of this union was Mr. Charles House, also known to all Connecticut Endeavorers.

The program was a very simple one, including the roll-call of delegates, three minute reports from each society, and an address and question-box by the writer of this history.

The brief and simple constitution of the union was also appended to this program, and provides that "it shall be composed of six delegates from each Christian Endeavor Society from Manchester and vicinity, and that the delegates be chosen for each quarterly meeting," although all the members of each local society are urged to attend all the meetings.

W. H. CHILDS.

Doubtless there were Endeavor Union programs printed before this, and I myself have programs of conferences of Endeavor Societies, but I find none of a regularly constituted local union, which it was my privilege to attend.

But from this time on the programs begin to multiply, thick as autumn leaves in Vallambrosa.

If no one else has profited by the Endeavor movement, it is safe to say that printers and paper-dealers should be grateful for the rise of the society. So many tens of thousands of meetings, with their tens of millions of programs, announcements, and circulars, have been necessitated by this uprising of the young people in behalf of a larger and more genuine fellowship than the churches had known before.

But we must not look for the chief significance of these numberless meetings upon the surface. Their roots run down deep into the soil of Christian character and Christian love. They show that the genuine desire for fellowship cannot be confined within the narrow borders of any one church or any one denomination, however great and good, but that there is a deep yearning, sometimes unconscious, but always present, in the hearts of earnest young disciples to fulfill our Lord's prayer, "That they all may be one." Like all the other developments of the Endeavor Society from the beginning, the good hand of God is manifest in the State and local unions. No one dreamed when the first local union meeting was held that this line of effort would develop in so many different directions.

ELI MANCHESTER, JR.

I have been fortunately able to secure from two men who were most influential in organizing these unions an account of the early days.

The idea of the State union seems to have preceded the local union. To Mr. Eli Manchester, Jr., I am indebted for the facts concerning these early meetings.

"Early in 1884," he says, "I suggested to the President of our society that it would be a good plan to try and find out how many Endeavor societies there were near us and to get together in some way. We decided to arrange for such a meeting and I tried in every way to find the societies. We succeeded in getting six societies represented by forty-nine delegates on July 2, 1884. We had an afternoon and evening session. At this meeting Rev. Erastus Blakeslee was chairman and I was secretary.

"If I remember rightly there were at this time three or four other societies in New Haven besides the one to which I belonged in the Howard Avenue Church,

HOWARD AVENUE CHURCH, NEW HAVEN, CONN.

where the first meeting was held; and a representative from each of them met with us, and we together arranged for the gathering. This little meeting was the means of bringing the societies into public notice in the State.

"From that time the work commenced to grow and societies were rapidly formed. This meeting, though a small one, was so successful that a committee was formed to arrange for another meeting of like nature. This second meeting was held November 18, 1885, in the Humphrey Street Church of New Haven." The call for this meeting is signed by the pastors of seven churches in New Haven and seven presidents of as many Endeavor societies, who said to their brethren to whom the notice went:

"Being greatly impressed with the importance of the work of the Young People's Societies of Christian Endeavor and the value of mutual consultation concerning it, we would hereby invite you to join with us and with the other societies of Christian Endeavor in this State in a State convention. We would suggest that each society be represented by the pastor of the church with which it is connected, its president, secretary, and treasurer, and one delegate for each ten members on its roll. These persons will constitute the voting power of the convention, and are cordially invited to the hospitality of the Humphrey Street Society."

But to resume Mr. Manchester's account: "In 1884 I was at Lowell, as you remember, and came back 'loaded,' and why not? I was the only one from Connecticut, and had to take in enough for all. Mr. Blakeslee and myself thought and talked it all over and broached the idea of a State organization, and at this meeting, in November, 1885, a preliminary organization was formed, only to be improved upon somewhat and permanently adopted in Bridgeport, Conn., the following year."

An interesting matter concerning the name "Christian Endeavor Union" has been told me by Rev. Erastus Blakeslee, who was the chairman of the first meeting, already described, and who is so well known in connection with new methods of Sunday-school work. The delegates were in some perplexity as to a good name for their new organization. Various names were suggested, but none seemed to be exactly the one desired. Mr. Blakeslee himself was on his feet with a suggestion, when his daughter, who was sitting by his side, whispered to him: "Why not call it the Christian Endeavor Union?"

It at once struck him as a happy name, and he suggested it to the convention, which adopted it forthwith, and henceforth, in Connecticut and in all the States, "Christian Endeavor Union" came to be the name for the organization of State, county, and city in Christian Endeavor work.

The local unions were of a little later birth, but the same goodly city of New Haven was the birthplace of this new development of Christian Endeavor as well.

Rev. Justin H. Twitchell, D. D., the pastor of the Dwight Place Church, of New Haven, who had more to do with the establishment of the local union than any other individual, must tell us the story of this happy thought. "When I assumed the pastorate of the Dwight Place Church," he writes, "in June, 1885, I found a large and flourishing Christian Endeavor Society. Meetings were held at an early hour on Sunday evenings and were full of interest. The young people of the church were in evident earnest in regard to work and worship.

"I began to study the peculiar features of this Christian Endeavor movement, and was not long in coming to the conclusion that something was being evolved which would be of great service to the church and world if the forces could be combined and wisely directed. When I asked the young people of my church how many other similar societies there were in the city and vicinity, and how they were progressing, I found that very little was known of them. The question, therefore, with me was, Cannot these various local societies somehow be brought together so that the members shall become acquainted with each other, interested in each other, and mutually helpful?

DR. TWITCHELL.

"Calling to mind a union young people's meeting organized in the Euclid Avenue Church, Cleveland, O., when pastor of that church, and remembering the enthusiasm of those large gatherings as they assembled from all over the city, the thought occurred to me that some sort of local union would be of service to each society and to the common cause.

"After consultation with a few leading members of our society, a committee was formed, and invitations were sent to all the local societies in the city to appoint each six delegates, who should meet in the Dwight Place Church on a designated evening to consider the wisdom of forming a local union, and, if deemed expedient, of accomplishing the same.

"About fifty delegates were present. It fell to my lot to speak of the young people's meeting in Cleveland, of the large attendance upon these gatherings, and of the great good accomplished as they planned and prayed together. I then outlined to these delegates a general plan of union and co-operation, which met with warm approval. The meeting adjourned, after appointing a committee to arrange details, and in January, 1886, the New Haven local union was formed—the first local union in the country. Other local societies in the city and vicinity soon sent members to learn of the movement, and one by one local societies joined the union, until at present thirty are members of it."

Word of course went abroad of what had been done in New Haven, and how a fresh impulse had been given to the Christian Endeavor movement. Ere long other local unions were formed, in every case found encouraging and helpful to the common cause, and so the work went on all through the land and across the seas. The Young People's Societies clustering together in cities and surrounding regions thus find fellowship and inspiration in local unions.

As Dr. Twitchell truly says, "It is not easy for any local society to have things always prosperous. Occasionally the tide seems to turn in organized as well as individual life, so that the ordinarily brave and trustful lose heart. The local union now meets very likely with the local society which is weak and waning. Fresh hope is inspired, fresh enthusiasm awakened, and so in cases not a few the local society has been kept alive when otherwise it would have died. All Christian Endeavorers may be truly thankful not only for the local society, but also for the coming together of local societies for mutual counsel, mutual encouragement, and inter-denominational fellowship.

THE DWIGHT PLACE CHURCH, NEW HAVEN, CONN.

"In the Providence of God it was left for some local society to move in this matter of local union. That society happened to be the one mentioned above. But here, as elsewhere and everywhere, let God have the glory, for no wise movement was ever made as to methods of Christian work and worship save as the Divine Spirit prompted and inspired."

CHAPTER XXI.

AN EPOCH-MAKING CONVENTION.

At Ocean Park—Two Hundred and Fifty-three Societies—Massachusetts Still in the Lead—Why the Convention was Memorable—The Beginnings of the United Society—A Matter of Far-reaching Influence—The Guiding Hand of God—No Forced Growth—No Preconcerted Boom—The Need of a General Secretary—The Chosen Man—How Mr. Hill Distinguished Himself—Generous Societies—The First President of the United Society—Passing into History.

THIS epoch-making convention was held at Ocean Park, Old Orchard, Maine, on the camp-ground belonging to the Free Baptist denomination, its sessions being held in the commodious pavilion, which amply accommodated the five or six hundred people in attendance.

This convention was held July 8 and 9, 1885, less than nine months, as it will be seen, since the last meeting of the kind, which was held in Lowell, as it was thought that the summer season, especially the early weeks of July, would accommodate more young people than any other season of the year, an opinion which we have seen no reason to change as the years have gone by.

A SCENE AT OLD ORCHARD.

The growth during this year had not been at all surprising, so far as the secretary's report shows. To be sure, only about eight months are included in this report, but an addition of only 97 societies is recorded. So far as known, they numbered in July, 1885, 253.

Massachusetts was still in the lead, with 88 societies; Maine came second, but a long ways behind, with 32, while New York had almost caught up with the Pine Tree State, for she recorded 25 societies on her list.

The Keystone State, however, reported but 5 societies yet—a gain, to be sure, of 500 per cent. over last year, but then she had a good opportunity to show a large

A VIEW IN THE GROUNDS OF THE FREE BAPTIST CAMP GROUNDS.

percentage of gain, an opportunity which her present enormous number makes impossible to-day.

In these 253 societies were nearly 15,000 members, and these 15,000 members were represented at Ocean Park by 161 delegates, representing 61 societies, though, as I have said, there were five or six hundred Endeavorers in attendance at the meeting, if my memory is correct.

I have called this "an epoch-making meeting," and so it was, not by reason of its attendance or enthusiasm, though that was all that could be desired, and the attendance was larger than it was feared it would be, as the experiment was tried for the first time of holding the convention at a summer resort.

Nor was the convention memorable chiefly on account of the papers read, though these were excellent and inspiring, but because of the action here taken looking to an organized work of Christian Endeavor and the securer establishment of a world-wide movement on broad, safe, simple, and brotherly lines.

It will be remembered that the committee on incorporation at the last convention made a report to the effect that "the society should become a permanently organized body," and that a committee be appointed by the Chair to carry into effect such an act of incorporation, to report at the next annual meeting.

This committee reported and fulfilled their instructions, and at once a corporation bearing the name of "The United Society of Christian Endeavor" was formed, during the progress of this convention at Ocean Park, under the

THE TABERNACLE AT OCEAN PARK.

general laws of the State of Maine. The object was declared to be, "to bind the societies closer together in a common interest, and to provide a responsible central organization through which the work of the society may be carried on in the way of raising, receiving, and paying out money, and giving proper custody for whatever property the society may acquire."

Annual membership in the United Society was obtained by those eligible by payment of an annual fee of $1.00. A payment of $20.00 at one time entitled any one to life membership and relieved him of the annual membership fee.

"Membership in the United Society," it was declared, "is not limited. Any person, young or old, who is in sympathy with young people, and desires to lend his aid to bring them to Christ and help them in their endeavor to form a good Christian character in His service, is earnestly and cordially invited to become a member of the United Society."

"In this way," it was said, "very many whose age or occupation prevent them from membership in local societies may become identified with the general movement and make their interest and influence count for much."

This was the action of this convention which had such far-reaching influence in the future of the Endeavor movement.

And yet it was all accomplished very quietly and unceremoniously, with the

THE INTERIOR OF THE TABERNACLE, OCEAN PARK.

help of a Portland lawyer who drew up the document in legal form, and was passed with the utmost unanimity by the convention.

Of the need and the development of the United Society, and of the simple but effective way which the organization has been carried on ever since, we shall tell in a subsequent chapter.

It is sufficient here to say that, as in all the other developments of the Christian Endeavor movement from the beginning, we can see in the formation of the United Society just at this time, and in the simplicity and effectiveness of its organization, the guiding hand of God.

As was natural, now that an organization had been provided, it was found necessary to have an executive officer who should make the organization effective, and a paper on the need of a general secretary was received with great favor by the convention.

In this paper I remarked: "One very patent fact concerning the Young People's Society of Christian Endeavor is that its growth has not been forced. In the popular phrase of the day, no one has attempted to boom it. As the Lord has led us on we have tried to follow; as He has opened one door after another we have tried to enter in. From the very beginning this is true of it. In a single church, in fearfulness and self-distrust, the work was started. It was considered for a long time a mere experiment, until God seemed to set upon it the seal of His approval. A single newspaper article, written without any thought of attracting especial attention, was widely copied and became a living seed, which sprang up in many places.

"One society after another was started, at first mostly in the city and vicinity of the original society. From mouth to mouth the story went; from church to church the news spread, until, in God's way and according to His plan, the little one became a thousand. But, of course, information was desired, methods of work were inquired for, constitutions were sought.

"To supply this information, to answer the hundreds of letters, became no slight task even during the first year of the life of the society. The work is growing every day; it requires more attention, more thought, more energy given to it every week. The Lord is opening the door wider and wider; shall we enter in?

"Apparently we have nearly reached the limit of effort under the present system. We are fairly pushed on by Providence to the consideration of this proposition: *We need a general secretary, who shall give his whole time and effort to the work of the Society of Christian Endeavor.*"

The paper then goes on to elaborate this proposition: first, we need such a secretary because the work has already outgrown the voluntary efforts of busy men; in the second place, because it has assumed such proportions as to fill the time and strength of any one who shall give himself to the work; third, because the work will inevitably lag unless such a forward step is taken; and, fourth, because the time has come when such an officer can be supported.

"Not for the sake of the Societies of Christian Endeavor," the paper concludes, "would I urge the appointment of a general secretary. The upbuilding of this organization is of minor and secondary importance, but for the sake of the young people in all our communities, for the sake of the church of God, for the sake of the cause of the Lord Jesus Christ, I would urge this forward movement."

This paper evidently voiced the sentiments of all present, and Rev. Samuel Winchester Adriance was unanimously and enthusiastically elected to the place, for it was felt that he filled the requirements, stated in the paper, that "the secretary must be an earnest, faithful, judicious worker, who has no crotchets, and who is not a constant fault-finder, one who loves the young, one whose life is devoted to Jesus Christ and His cause, and one who thoroughly and heartily believes in the Society of Christian Endeavor, its objects and aims."

One forward movement always leads to another, and if there was to be a general secretary his salary must be provided for.

In raising the money for the salary of the secretary, Rev. James L. Hill distinguished and endeared himself to Christian Endeavorers generally, for he not only undertook this somewhat ungracious task, but carried it through to a triumphant conclusion.

Many societies responded generously, eleven giving no less than $50 apiece. Their names should be recorded on this earliest financial roll of honor. Here they are:

The Second Parish and Williston Societies, of Portland; the Central Presbyterian Society, of Rochester, N. Y.; and the societies of the North Church, Lynn; Phillips Church, South Boston; the First Church, Burlington, Vt.; Humphrey Street Church, New Haven; the Second Church, West Newton; the North Church, Haverhill, Mass.; the Second Church, in Holyoke, and the Kirk Street Church, in Lowell.

Other churches gave $25, $15, and $10, many quite as liberally according to their

REV. JAMES L. HILL, D. D.

means, and many individuals subscribed generously. At the end of a memorable half-hour Mr. Hill found that $1,210 had been subscribed by that little company, and the modest salary of the Christian Endeavor secretary for the first year was insured.

There was also at this convention a report of a committee on a society paper, and *The Golden Rule*, of Boston, which had given more generous space than any other paper to the society, was thanked for its efforts. But the time had not yet come for the establishment of an organ that was worthy of the society, and the matter was put over for another year.

At this convention, too, we find the first mention of Christian Endeavor badges, and the following piece of information is recorded: that "the badges consisted of a little piece of white satin ribbon, with the interesting legend, 'Christian Endeavor Delegate,' printed thereon in red letters."

The following resolution, appended to the report of the committee on the advisability of recommending State conferences, was also of interest:

"*Be it Resolved*, That, in every State where there are more than two societies of Christian Endeavor, this conference recommends that there be an annual State convention; that this convention occur some time between the autumn and winter months, and that it remain in session not longer than one day."

The wisdom of at least a part of this resolution is indisputable, for there could hardly be a State convention in a State which contains less than two societies.

It will be seen later how quickly this general recommendation was adopted by all the States and Provinces and Territories.

But all wisdom is not given to any one convention, and the recommendation that this convention occur some time during the autumn or winter months, and that it remain in session not longer than one day, has been allowed to fall into innocuous desuetude.

Mr. W. H. Pennell, the first president of the conventions, was succeeded at this meeting by Mr. W. J. Van Patten, the former treasurer, and Mr. Pennell was thanked most heartily for the valuable services which he had rendered the cause from the beginning.

Mr. George M. Ward, of Lowell, was elected treasurer, and the Executive Committee, which served as the Board of Trustees for the newly-formed United Society, consisted of Rev. F. E. Clark, Rev. C. A. Dickinson, Rev. J. L. Hill, W. H. Pennell, Rev. J. M. Lowden, Rev. S. W. Adriance, Rev. R. W. Brokaw, and Rev. H. B. Grose.

REV. O. P. GIFFORD, D. D.

The reports from the societies continued to be as encouraging and as hopeful as ever.

The actual formation of a society was reported at Foo Chow, China.

Magnificent addresses by Rev. O. P. Gifford, Dr. Alexander McKenzie, and others gave literary tone to the meeting, and, late on the evening of July 9, 1885, this memorable convention passed into history.

CHAPTER XXII.

GAINING FRIENDS.

Why the First Secretary Resigned—Who was Chosen in His Place—A Faithful Friend—Mr. Hill's Address—Prophecy as Well as Definition—His Assistant Pastor—The Treasurer of the United Society and how he was Qualified for his Work—Mr. Grose and Mr. Brokaw—How Dr. Boynton Signalized his Advent to the Endeavor Field—Other Friends of the Movement—In the Cumberland Presbyterian Denomination—Men who Deserve the Thanks of all Christian Endeavorers.

THE epoch-making convention which we have just described was notable for the advent of several new friends, who, by their stanch support and earnest advocacy, have been a great source of strength to the cause.

Rev. S. W. Adriance has been already mentioned as the one who was chosen the first Secretary of the United Society upon its formation at the Ocean Park convention. For nearly two years previous to this he had been interested in the society, and his own young people's organization in the church at Woodfords, of which he was then the pastor, was among the earliest formed along Endeavor lines. For many years Mr. Adriance has been known and loved by the writer of this history. A college class-mate and an intimate friend, the acquaintance had ripened into still closer intimacy during the two years of our seminary course at Andover, where we were room-mates.

Afterward, being pastors of churches scarcely two miles apart, it was but natural we should talk over frequently and carefully this new effort to evangelize the youth.

REV. S. W. ADRIANCE.

Mr. Adriance's heart was wholly given to this work. He was a "young people's minister" in the best sense of the term. It was only natural, then, that the thoughts of all should turn to him when it was found necessary and possible to have a general secretary.

At first Mr. Adriance thought that he could accept the position, and, in fact, did occupy the place for several weeks, in the meantime sending in his resignation to the church in Lowell of which he had become the pastor.

But his church was so thoroughly attached to him that he found it impossible to leave them without injuring, as he felt, the cause of Christ in his own church, so, very reluctantly he relinquished the office of secretary, and Mr. George M. Ward, a young layman in the Kirk Street Church of Lowell, whose name appears in the minutes of the convention for 1885 for the first time, as treasurer of the new society, was chosen secretary in Mr. Adriance's place.

Mr. Ward was well adapted to the work of those early days.

GEORGE M. WARD.

With a winning and gracious presence and a pleasing address he was able to commend the cause to all with whom he spoke. He speedily became a great favorite with the young people of the societies and was in large demand at the conventions which then began to be held in different parts of the country. He traveled North, East, and South, and as far West as the Pacific Coast, and for four years served the society as its secretary.

Another most active Endeavorer, whose name we find for the first time in the minutes of the Lowell Convention in 1884, was Rèv. James L. Hill, who was elected one of the first trustees of the United Society and has ever been ready from that day to this to bear his share of the brunt and burden of the Endeavor battle.

His spirit and devotion were well shown in undertaking the somewhat thankless task we have already described of raising the first money for the work of the new United Society, but never did a cause have a better natured or more successful beggar.

At the Lowell Convention he read a paper on "The Society as a Means of Home Evangelization," and at the Old Orchard Convention a spicy address on the "Future of the Society" was given by him.

"There is undoubtedly an element," said he, "in this movement which is unique, and which is certain to give it a lasting place in all successful church administrations, and that is its provision that every young disciple shall, like young Timothy, exercise himself unto godliness.

"Mr. A. T. Stewart was fond of calling his store 'a place for training young men in business.' They learned to sell by selling. They were taught how to do things by doing them. One must get the pronunciation of a language by speaking it. Young men and women can be trained for the church work of committees by putting them on committees. Young persons can best learn church polity by becoming a part of the machinery and studying its working from within the work."

There is as much of definition as there is of prophecy in these statements.

The unique work and glory of the Christian Endeavor work is here defined, and there is a prophecy, too, of its future far-reaching success, which Mr. Hill has done not a little to bring about.

In his efforts Mr. Hill (now Dr. Hill) has always been seconded by a devoted and earnest wife (his assistant pastor, as he calls her), whose tongue and pen have never been idle in proclaiming the advantage of the Endeavor Society. "It is an ideal plan if it works," was a frequently quoted remark of hers, "and the beauty of it is—it works."

WILLIAM SHAW.

Another delegate to the Lowell Convention was Mr. Wm. Shaw, who, from that time to the present, has been an important spoke in the Endeavor wheel. A young business man, then a member of Phillips Church, South Boston, his former pastor can testify of him that in all church relations he was faithful to the smallest duty, and thus quickly qualified himself for larger duties.

He was one of the young men upon whom his pastor could rely not only in the young people's meeting, but in the church prayer-meeting as well, while the Sunday-school, the social gathering, and every good cause expected and received his support.

Naturally, when the Endeavor Society was formed in Phillips Church, he threw himself into the work most generously.

PROF. H. B. GROSE.

When Mr. Ward was chosen secretary of the new union, Mr. Shaw took his place in the treasurership.

From that day to this he has been the faithful and efficient treasurer of the United Society, and, as the publishing business increased, he was chosen business agent of the publishing department, an office which, together with the treasurership, has engrossed all his time.

When we come to the convention at Ocean Park, we find for the first time the names of several gentlemen who from that day to this have been prominent in the work of the society. Rev. H. B. Grose, then pastor of a Baptist Church in Poughkeepsie, N. Y., now Professor of Church History in Chicago University, and from the beginning a trustee of the United Society. His writings in *The Golden Rule*, his earnest advocacy of the society, and his constant championship of a broad, evangelical basis of fellowship for the society, as distinct from a narrow sectarianism, have endeared him to all.

Rev. Ralph W. Brokaw, then the pastor of a Reformed (Dutch) Church in Belleville, N. J., was another of the delegates, who dates his experience in Christian Endeavor conventions from the Old Orchard meeting. He was chosen at that time to represent the Reformed Church on the Board of Trustees, and, although he has changed his denominational affiliations since then, he is still a member of the Board.

REV. N. BOYNTON, D. D.

Rev. Nehemiah Boynton, then the pastor of the North Church, in Haverhill, Mass., signalized his advent in the Christian Endeavor field by pledging to the young and struggling society not only $50 for his society in Haverhill, but $5 for his little boy who was then three years old, and $5 more for the next oldest child, a boy of four weeks.

The early initiation of this baby of the society was greeted with hearty applause, and similar signs of approval have always followed Mr. Boynton's frequent appearances at national conventions and other Christian Endeavor gatherings since.

Dr. Boynton, too, from the beginning has been one of the trustees of the United Society. Rev. J. M. Lowden, the pastor of the Casco Street Free Baptist Church, in Portland, also figured in these early conventions, as we have before stated.

He, too, is one of the Trustees, and well represents his denomination on the Board. Among other names at this convention I find those of Mr. F. P. Shumway, Jr., prominent in Sunday-school work; Rev. J. J. Hall, pastor of the Free Baptist Church in Auburn, Me.; Rev. Dr. Hawes, of Burlington, Vt.; Rev. Erastus Blakeslee, then of New Haven, Conn., so well known in connection with the Blakeslee Sunday-school lessons; Mr. Joseph T. Allen, of Rochester, N. Y., an eminent layman, who teaches one of the largest Sunday-school classes of young men ever gathered in any church; Rev. L. H. Hallock, my successor in the Williston Church in Portland, who is now earnest in his efforts for the Endeavor cause on the Pacific Coast; Miss Alice Metcalf, who spoke for the young ladies most effectively and earnestly; Rev. W. J. Darby, of Evansville, Ind., who though not present at either of these conventions was known as an earnest Endeavor worker, and who now represents the Cumberland Presbyterian Church on the Board of Trustees; Rev. B. S. Everett, of Jamesburg, an early and tried friend of the movement, and Rev. T. W. Hopkins, of Rochester, N. Y., now professor in Auburn Seminary.

REV. DR. DARBY.

But what shall I say more, for time would fail me to tell of a multitude of these true and tried early friends of the Endeavor cause, and when we come to later years it will be impossible for me even to mention the names of a multitude who deserve an honored place in the annals of Christian Endeavor.

I have given particular notice to these early friends simply because they stood so near the beginning of things, not because their devotion or zeal has been any more marked or more worthy of praise than the names of those who have later come into the society and have given their heartiest devotion to its interest.

If this were the place and if I were the one to express these thanks I would in the name of Christian Endeavor most gratefully express the gratitude which the movement will ever owe to these friends, one and all, who with no hope of reward and with no thought of being conspicuous in the movement have unselfishly, in good report and evil report, stood everywhere for the principles, the methods, and the spirit of the Young People's Society of Christian Endeavor.

CHAPTER XXIII.

AN EFFECTIVE ORGANIZATION—THE UNITED SOCIETY.

No Ecclesiastical Functions—A Very Simple Organization—Not a Board of Control—A Bureau of Information—What the United Society has Done—The Movement Saved from Disaster—Business Reduced to a Minimum—Entire Harmony—Eminent Men who have Seen Eye to Eye—No Desire for Personal Aggrandizement—The First Quarters of the United Society—Subsequent Removal—The Board of Trustees and its Meeting—Other United Societies—Early Financial Struggles—Not Wrapped in the Lap of Luxury—Some Well-to-do Friends—A Generous Subscription—The Largest Contributors—Constituting Life Members—Precious Pearl a Life Member—The Ingenuity of the Finance Committee—The Deepest Financial Straits—A Dark Outlook—A Happy Thought and what Came of it—Christian Endeavor Day and its Contributions—What is Done with the Money—Modest Expenses—A Missionary Day—Living Up to Our Principles—Giving Through the Regular Channels.

IN a previous chapter I told something of the origin and earliest days of the United Society of Christian Endeavor, but this organization has proved so simple, so flexible, and so effective that it deserves a chapter to itself.

Like all the special movements which have blessed the Endeavor Society, the United Society is plainly of Providential origin.

We have seen already how quietly and unostentatiously it was begun; how it was evidently the outcome of a real need; how it could not be put off or postponed any longer. It was felt from the beginning, as it has been felt ever since, that the United Society must assume no ecclesiastical functions, must not attempt to rule or in any way control the local societies, but the Endeavor principle must be maintained, that the only source of authority and the only ultimate appeal for any Endeavor society was the individual church and pastor.

The problem naturally arose, then, how to form a central organization which should effectively accomplish the work of spreading the Christian Endeavor idea without usurping or seeming to usurp any office or work which does not properly belong to it.

The problem was settled by forming a very simple organization, whose duties should be limited to spreading the Endeavor idea chiefly by means of its literature. This original idea has been sedulously adhered to ever since.

The United Society from the beginning repudiated the notion that it was a board of control, that it sought or exercised authority over local societies, that it was set in Zion for the purpose of deciding difficult questions of discipline or morals or Christian casuistry.

It has had nothing to do with any of these functions. Its president has always refused to act as arbiter or judge in any question relating to a local society or its work. He has given his time to stating the principles of the movement, and these have taken care of themselves and the societies as well. In fact, the United Society of Christian Endeavor is just what it has professed to be from the beginning—a bureau of information, and nothing more.

It has published numerous leaflets and booklets concerning the society, innumerable topic-cards and programs. It has furnished the means for the translation and printing of the constitution into more than a score of languages. It has given information concerning this work in all the modern languages of Europe and many of the languages of Asia and Africa. It has collected annual statistics for the information of the society and for the world at large. It has provided the programs for the international conventions, and has published the reports of the proceedings of the conventions, which have been very influential in spreading a knowledge of the cause and its principles.

The question naturally arose at once, How should the society be constituted so that it should never become a governing board of direction or a controlling power? and in the simple formation of the United Society, avoiding the rocks of ecclesiastical politics, we see the good hand of God.

It was felt at once that if this were a *representative* body, and were composed of delegates from societies or from local unions or State unions, that these delegates would feel that they had delegated to them some power of oversight or supervision of other societies. Being elected by their societies or union, it would be almost inevitable that they should assume these functions.

Delegates naturally want to *do* something, to pass votes and make laws to justify their existence as delegates, and, if there is nothing for them to do, they usually cut out unnecessary work.

Hence, many representative ecclesiastical gatherings are anything but the places of quietness and concord and spiritual power which we could wish. But the Endeavor movement was saved from this disaster, because it was felt at the beginning that the United Society had no business with the control of local societies, and that, as it did not seek in any way to legislate for them or to guide them, and since it asked nothing from them, levied no taxes and demanded no fees, there was no one who could demand representation in the United Society.

Consequently, it was provided that any one who felt enough interest in the movement to pay one dollar, provided he was a member of an evangelical church, might become a member for that year of the United Society. If he felt sufficient interest to pay twenty dollars at any one time, he might become a life member without further payment.

In this way any one who desired could become a member. There was no cumbrous system of representation, which, as the society grew larger, would have been almost impossible to carry out; there was no temptation to representatives to legislate for others; but it was felt by these members, who were willing to pay their dollar, that their work was simply to promote by their dollars and by their influence in every way they could the growth of the Endeavor idea in all denominations and in all parts of the world.

The United Society, thus constituted, has for its executive officers eminent men from the different denominations into which Christian Endeavor had spread, and, from time to time since, new members have been added to the Board of Trustees to represent the other denominations that have joined the Endeavor ranks.

From many a disaster and tribulation, I believe, this simple, unassuming, but efficient form of organization has saved the whole movement, and difficulties which threaten the Endeavor cause in other lands, simply because the functions and duties of the central organization are not clearly understood, have been entirely averted.

It is worthy of remark, too, that entire harmony has always prevailed in the councils of the United Society. From the first day to the present there has scarcely been a ripple of dissent. More than a score of eminent men, representing various denominations, creeds, and forms of church government, have sat about the board of the United Society of Christian Endeavor, and, with almost absolute unanimity, have decided every question of importance. They have seen eye to eye as have few similar bodies of men in the history of the church. There has been no self-seeking, no desire for personal aggrandizement, scarcely any criticism, and the most lynx-eyed enemy of the Endeavor cause, and not a few have prowled about, seeking what they might discover, has been unable to find serious fault with the organization or its work.

After a year or two, the United Society, as originally incorporated under the laws of the State of Maine, became incorporated under the laws of Massachusetts, and its headquarters have ever since been in Boston.

At first it occupied very small quarters at 8 Beacon Street, Boston. In fact, its "quarters" consisted of a small corner in the office of the American Bible Society's room, scarcely large enough to hold an ordinary roll-top desk.

Afterward it moved to more commodious rooms at 50 Bromfield Street, and in 1892 to its pleasant and ample quarters at 646 Washington Street.

The by-laws of the United Society provide "that any person may become a member by the two-thirds vote of the members at any meeting; that each one shall pay an annual fee of one dollar; that the officers shall be members in good standing of evangelical churches, and that the trustees shall meet quarterly, and the United Society annually, in the month of July or August." This date has since been changed to the month of June, when the annual meeting is held, in Boston.

The quarterly meeting of the Board of Trustees is always an interesting occasion, though the attendance is often small, as most of the Trustees live at a distance, and are scattered throughout the country from the Atlantic to the Pacific Coast.

The principal Trustee meeting of the year, however, which is held in connection with the great annual international convention, always brings together a large number of these eminent men, and at this meeting much business is transacted and the work of the year reviewed.

In fact, but few of this widely scattered Board of Trustees are ever absent from this annual meeting. Other United Societies of Christian Endeavor have already been formed in Japan and China, and at the time of this writing are in the process of formation in England and Australia.

To all countries where the genuine Endeavor idea prevails, and which hereafter think of forming a United Society I can most unhesitatingly and heartily recommend the simple form of organization which has so admirably fulfilled its purpose in America.

It must not be supposed that this infant organization was wrapped in the lap of luxury, and had no struggle to find the ways and means of existence.

Like other children of poor but honest parents, it had to make its own way in the world and provide for its own living at a very tender age.

To be sure, it had some well-to-do friends who were greatly interested in its success in life. Chief among these was Mr. W. J. Van Patten, the first treasurer of the society, whose generous gifts I have before rehearsed.

Others, too, were willing to do all they could, but they could not be expected to support the society with its growing needs, nor would it have been so well for the child to have been thus tenderly cared for without any exertion of his own.

It has been seen how at the Old Orchard Convention the societies represented generously responded with contributions from $5 to $50, thus making a general secretary possible.

But the twelve or fifteen hundred dollars obtained from this convention were soon exhausted, and when the time came for another it was found that there was a deficit of nearly $300 in the treasury, though the strictest economy had been practiced.

Still more money was needed for the work of the coming year, and it was urged that more annual members join the United Society, and that the societies generally contribute to the expenses of the United Society.

AN EFFECTIVE ORGANIZATION—THE UNITED SOCIETY.

A year after this, two years after the United Society was formed, at one of the inspiring Saratoga conventions of which we shall speak later, Rev. James L. Hill, naturally after his first success the chairman of the finance committee, set forth in a clear and concise manner the exact condition of affairs, and made plain the urgent need of funds.

After an eloquent statement of the great good which might be done in the future could the requisite funds be obtained, he gave to those present "an opportunity to aid in the work," as the report modestly put it. The response was immediate and generous. For the next hour the work of raising money was continued until the handsome sum of $2,028 was reached.

The largest contribution to this fund, so far as the records prove, came from the North Congregational Church, of Haverhill, Mass., which gave $60. But there were several contributions of $50 each from other societies, and a number of individuals and societies clubbed together to make those whom they desired to honor life members of the United Society.

Thus Rev. H. B. Grose, Mr. W. J. Van Patten, Mr. W. H. Wood, of Burlington, Vt., and Rev. F. E. Clark contributed $5 each to the United Society, and thus made Mr. W. H. Pennell a life member.

Mr. J. L. Sedgely, Rev. J. L. Hill, and Rev. C. F. Thwing combined to honor Rev. C. A. Dickinson with a life membership, and still others made Mr. Brokaw, Rev. Erastus Blakeslee, Dr. Deems, of New York, Mr. Adriance, Mr. Eli Manchester, Jr., Mrs. Slocum of Iowa, the Misses Leitch of Ceylon, and Rev. E. K. Alden, D. D., the Secretary of the American Board, life members.

Dr. Alden returned the compliment by contributing $19 to make up the $20 necessary to constitute "Precious Pearl," one of the first members of the first society in Ceylon, a life member.

The "Do Without Club," composed of fifteen members, honored Miss Alldredge, of Rochester, N. Y., in the same way.

This "Do Without Club" promised to give up some one thing, like candy, ribbons, and so forth, and contribute the dollar to the advancement of the Endeavor cause.

I remember one member of the club, when asked what he was going to do without, pertinently replied that he expected to do without the dollar.

In all these ways, through the ingenuity of the finance committee, and the generosity of the societies and individual members, the United Society was kept alive during its early days of struggle, and the money used in its expenses was very largely raised at these annual conventions.

But it was felt, increasingly, that things could not always go on in this way.

As the expenses increased, some more certain and less emotional way must be found to provide the needed funds. The society could not always depend upon a finance committee that would touch the hearts and reach the pocket-books of the annual conventions.

It was the next year after this, in 1888, if I am not mistaken, that the society reached its deepest financial straits. The expenses had increased, and there seemed to be no means of providing the necessary funds. Business men in Boston were appealed to for a temporary loan, but none of them regarded the security which the officers of the United Society could offer as sufficient. Mr. Van Patton by that time was no longer president, for a poor pastor from South Boston at that time had taken his place.

Things, indeed, looked dark. I remember very well the meeting of trustees when the financial situation was considered, and when it seemed as if we must stop our publications and dismiss our secretary for lack of the necessary funds. Those of us who were particularly connected with the society had given everything we could in time and money. For a number of years before the United Society was formed we had borne the financial strain alone.

After much prayer and deliberation it was decided to send an appeal to the individual societies, asking them, so far as possible, on Feb. 2, which was suggested as Christian Endeavor Day, to contribute at least ten cents a member to relieve the pressing necessity of the work.

The letter asking for the money was sent out, and a most generous response was received, far more than the trustees had dared to hope for. Their little faith was rebuked. It was possible to carry on the publication of Christian Endeavor leaflets, to pay the general secretary his salary and traveling expenses, to translate the literature into different languages, and to enlarge the scope of the work in various needed directions.

This answered for once; but it was felt that it would not be wise *often* to make such an appeal. It was distinctly understood that this request was not in the nature of a tax of any kind. No society was under the least obligation to give anything. No individual need pay his quota unless he chose. It was simply a free-will offering given for love of the cause, but it was felt that just as soon as possible the society must become self-supporting.

To this end the expenses were reduced to the very lowest possible sum, the sales of constitutions, topic cards, and other literature was encouraged in every proper way, though at the same time an immense volume of this literature was constantly given away to meet the increasing demands for information concerning the society.

The sale of the badges, which about this time began to be generally used, contributed something to the funds, and after this first general appeal, if I am not mistaken, the society was never obliged to make another. It soon declared its independence, informed the societies that it did not ask for any contributions, and, after a little, even returned the money that was forced upon it by individuals and societies who had learned the blessedness of giving for the advancement of Christian Endeavor, and now for several years it has not taken a dollar for its own expenses. When money has been sent to it, the contributing societies have had it politely returned to them, and they have been urged to put it in their own denominational missionary treasuries.

Christian Endeavor Day, which is celebrated on the 2d of February, the anniversary-day of the first society, is now generally observed by a thank-offering in the various societies. This thank-offering is not sent to the United Society, is not given to extend the Endeavor cause as such, but is sent entirely and directly to the denominational missionary boards, both home and foreign, or is given to the needs of the local church, and is used for the extension of the Kingdom of God in all lands.

Thus the United Society has tried even in its monetary dealings to exemplify Christian Endeavor principles, that the movement exists not for itself but for the advancement of the Kingdom, to become a spur and stimulance to the generosity of the Christian Endeavorers as well as to their other virtues, and to turn this channel of benevolence, so far as it could, into the coffers of the church and the missionary treasuries to which each society should contribute.

To the present day the same principles of economy and carefulness of administration have been observed as in the earlier days of financial struggle. The expenses of the United Society are kept to the lowest point consistent with the advancement of the cause, and every cent that is expended is earned by the society.

While there is a considerable force of clerks necessary to carry on the work of publication and distribution of literature, there is, strictly speaking, but one paid officer of the United Society. The president receives his support from other sources, though he gives a large proportion of his time to the affairs of the United Society. The trustees receive no pay for their time, and their traveling expenses only to one annual meeting of the board.

Thus in every way the affairs of the United Society are administered with a view not only to the efficiency of the administration, and the advancement of the Endeavor cause, but to the principles on which the society was founded, and with a desire of training Endeavorers to give, as I believe they should, through the regular, accredited channels of their own churches.

CHAPTER XXIV.

THE FIRST SARATOGA CONVENTION.

Heaven-Breathing Devotion—"Do You Remember Saratoga?"—A Fragrant Memory—The Strength of Christian Endeavor—No Local or Provincial Affair—Eight Denominations in Christian Endeavor—From the Land of Steady Habits—Dr. Deems' Sermon—Some Notable Addresses—Keep Your Colors Flying—An Improbable Prophecy and How It Was Fulfilled—Self-Entertainment—The First Early Morning Prayer-Meeting.

THE name Saratoga Springs will always have an especially gracious sound in the ears of hundreds of Christian Endeavorers, who were privileged to attend the two conventions which were held at this famous watering-place in the summers of 1886 and 1887.

There was an air of spiritual refreshment, of peculiar heaven-breathing devotion which left its impress upon the life of every delegate, and when these fortunate individuals who were privileged to attend either of these

A SARATOGA STREET.

meetings meet each other to this day, they say one to another, "Ah, do you not remember the meeting at Saratoga, how our hearts burned within us as we talked one with another and with the Master?"

This specially fragrant memory which clings to these conventions was due in part, in fact largely to the fact, that they were among the earliest in which the Endeavor spirit was fully exemplified. There have been many just as good meetings doubtless since, and a multitude which have been far larger and more influential, but for the first time the genuine Endeavor flavor, so sweet and fragrant, was given to a young people's convention. It had all the force and freshness, too, of novelty and unexpectedness.

Moreover, these conventions were not so large but that all the members could greet each other and, to some extent, know each other, while the beautiful surroundings, the lovely scenery, and the life-giving waters of Saratoga added to the general joy of the occasion.

And yet it was with great hesitation that the committee decided to hold the convention of 1886 at Saratoga Springs.

Never before had the convention been held outside of New England.

The strength of Christian Endeavor was still within the six Northeastern States of the Union, and it was felt that it would be a somewhat risky experiment to take the convention so far from the centre of Christian Endeavordom.

But it was the purpose and determination of the leaders to make the

FIRST M. E. CHURCH, SARATOGA.

movement no local and provincial affair, and it was at last decided with a good deal of hesitation to go so far west as Saratoga. On the afternoon of July 6 the convention was called to order by Mr. Van Patten, and from the very beginning the doubts and fears of the faint-hearts were removed, for the attendance was much larger than was expected, and the spirit of devotion to the cause and love for the work was beyond all precedent.

Secretary Ward began his report by quoting a paragraph from the annual message of Secretary Stevenson at the Lowell meeting, which said that the report might be condensed into one word, "progress," and went on to show how large had been the progress since the last meeting. The 253 societies had become 850; the 15,000 members had become 30,000, while 2,067 had gone directly from the ranks of Christian Endeavor into the Evangelical churches during the previous year. Eight denominations were found to be represented, Congregationalist, Presbyterian, Baptist, Methodist, Lutheran, Christian, Reformed, and Episcopal.

The society had now spread into thirty-three States, Territories, and Provinces, and seven were reported in foreign lands.

REV. C. F. DEEMS, D. D.

It was stated that now there were twelve States having more than twenty societies each, and that in each of these States it would be feasible to hold a State conference, while the example of Connecticut was held up to the admiring view of the Endeavor world, because, as a result of its first State Union Convention, the societies had grown in fivefold ratio, so that now there were seventy-five Endeavor societies in the Land of Steady Habits.

Among the notable features of this convention was the opening sermon by Dr. C. F. Deems, the brilliant and beloved pastor of the Church of the Strangers of New York City, who from that day until his death was an enthusiastic and outspoken friend of the new movement.

The accession of such a man to the ranks of the advocates of Christian Endeavor was an event of no little importance. He gave the movement a standing and significance, which the advocacy of scarcely any other man could have given it, and the sermon preached by this honored father in Israel will be long remembered by every Endeavorer who heard it. It was on the importance of spiritual sight, from the text found in the 16th verse of the 6th chapter of 2 Kings, "And Elisha prayed and the Lord opened the eyes of the young man and he *saw*."

An important evening of the convention was given to the four cardinal principles of the society, which were declared to be Organization, Expression, Diversion, and Obligation.

The third division perhaps was not so happily expressed as the others, for it meant sociability and cheerfulness, good-fellowship and innocent amusement, and not diversion from the highest religious ideas.

It was ably treated by Rev. Mr. Dickinson, who brought out the true idea of the place of amusement in the religious life.

Rev. Nehemiah Boynton spoke on the importance of wise organization.

THE WORDEN HOUSE, SARATOGA.

Rev. James L. Hill on the idea of expression as a great aid in the development of faith and good works; and Rev. F. E. Clark on the fourth division, obligation, emphasizing, as I have always attempted to do from the beginning to the present day, the vital importance and necessity of the idea contained in the prayer-meeting pledge.

At this convention the society put itself strongly on record, as it has always done since, on the side of temperance.

Rev. W. E. Strong, of Beverly, opened a conference on the duties of officers, and the eminently wise suggestion was made for the first time that every society should have a permanent corresponding secretary to keep it in touch with the United Society and with sister organizations throughout the world.

Rev. C. F. Thwing, then of Cambridge, but now the president of Adelbert College and Western Reserve University, and a brilliant writer on educational topics, who was one of the earliest, as he has always been one of the stanchest, friends of Christian Endeavor, spoke on the subject, "How to Promote *Esprit de Corps.*"

His inspiring address promoted the spirit for which he pleaded—a spirit which has always characterized the movement and through which it has won its chief victories.

It was expected that the eminent divine, beloved by all young people, Dr. Theodore L. Cuyler, of Brooklyn, would be at this convention, but he was detained; and his place was abundantly filled by Rev. J. E. Rankin, D. D., then of Orange, N. J., and now the president of Howard University, of Washington. He made an admirable address, and also contributed a hymn to the convention, entitled "Keep your colors flying," which was one of the earliest favorites of the Christian Endeavor world.

REV. J. E. RANKIN, D. D.

As is well known, Dr. Rankin is the author of that most famous hymn of modern times, "God be with you till we meet again," which has probably been sung at more Endeavor conventions than any other hymn in the language.

Written a little before the beginning of the Christian Endeavor movement, it has been adopted by Endeavorers the world around. It has been translated into every language to which our missionaries have gone, and in our recent journey around the world it was always the refrain, with its blessed prayer and benediction, which was the last strain heard by Mrs. Clark and myself as we left the shores of every new land for a voyage across an unknown sea.

Dr. Justin E. Twitchell, of New Haven, was also one of the speakers at this convention, and he ventured the prediction, which then seemed most wild and extravagant, that at the end of five years the 53,000 members of the Christian Endeavor Society would number half a million, while at the end of a decade he believed there would be a round million of Christian Endeavorers. His prophecy, improbable as it then seemed, was far more than fulfilled, for at the close of the first five years from that date 1,008,980 Christian Endeavorers were recorded. In eight years from the time of the first Saratoga meeting over two millions were in existence, while the close of the tenth year will carry the numbers far beyond the line of two millions and a half, if not well on toward three millions of members.

One very important resolution which was presented by the committee at this convention reads as follows: "*Resolved*, That, in urging societies to hold State and local conferences, it is not the intention of this conference that these meetings be a burden on the hospitality of local societies, but that it is our opinion that the principle of self-entertainment adopted by the annual conference can also be adopted by local and State conferences to good advantage."

This idea from that day has been largely carried out, not only in the international conventions, but in most of the State and many of the district conventions, and always with the best results.

I have no hesitation in saying that much of the success of the meetings has depended upon this principle. It would be manifestly impossible for any city in the world to entertain an international convention, if the idea of free entertainment prevailed.

Many of the State conventions, in their present proportions, would also be out of the question.

This principle makes the delegates independent and self-respecting; it insures the right class of convention-goers, for none will attend such a meeting and pay their own way, even though the charge for entertainment be small, except those who have the spirit of Christian Endeavor in their hearts and a desire to enjoy the spiritual advantages of the convention.

In the rather meagre report of this convention I find no mention of the fact, but, if I am not entirely mistaken, the first early morning prayer-meeting was held in connection with this first Saratoga meeting. I well remember the look of incredulity and pitying regard for an enthusiast which involuntarily swept over many faces when I suggested a prayer-meeting at half-past six in the morning.

"You need not think that the young people will come out to a prayer-meeting at that hour of the day, after the late sessions of the convention," was said by more than one.

I did not think *many* would come, myself, but thought the experiment worth trying.

The sexton of the Methodist church, where the meetings were held, said that he could not get over to the church at that unearthly hour, but, if we wanted the key, we could have it.

So I took the key, and the next morning, being a minute or two late, I was surprised to find the whole sidewalk leading to the church crowded with Endeavorers who had left their beds and their breakfasts to attend the first early morning prayer-meeting of a Christian Endeavor convention.

Since then this early meeting has been one of the regular and most delightful features of Endeavor conventions in all parts of the world.

CHAPTER XXV.

THE SOCIETY'S MOTHER AND HER SISTERS.

The Traditional Stepmother—Part of the Mother's Life—Not a Poor Relation or a Young Relation—What is the Church?—Why the Constitution was Amended—Over-Tired Workers—Has the Sunday Evening Service Been Reinforced?—Is the Prayer-Meeting Stronger?—Facts and Figures Which Bear on the Subject—Some Sisters of the Society—A Hundred Years Ago—Robert Raikes and His Endeavor—The Sunday-School Committee and What It May Do—The Mission Circle—Enthusiasm for Missions—The Mothers' Endeavor Society—The Best-Loved Little Sister of All—A Brotherly Sister—The Y. M. C. A. and Christian Endeavor—The Brotherhood of Andrew and Philip.

THOUGH there may be some pardonable confusion of mind as to the exact number of the society's brothers and sisters, there is no possible question as to the mother of the Christian Endeavor Society. The Church of the Living God has always been acknowledged reverently and affectionately as the mother to whom it owes obedience and respect.

Sometimes, to be sure, she has treated the infant society more as the traditional stepmother is supposed to treat a child, but for the most part the affection of the child has been heartily reciprocated. Our motto—"For Christ and the Church"—is no empty formula. It is not a matter of printed letters or of fancy silk and worsted, but is a living legend engraved upon the hearts of millions of young disciples.

It has been seen from the history of the early days, already rehearsed, that the object of the society was to help one individual church, to aid its pastor, and to make the young people connected with that church more efficient in her service.

The object of the second society was the very same, and of the third and the fourth, and of the very last among all the tens of thousands was no different.

Some societies, to be sure, may have more fully realized the object of their being than others, and have more thoroughly filfilled their mission. But the real object of all has been the same, and, as they have come to realize the true meaning of Christian Endeavor, they have come to be more and more helpful to the church of which they are a part.

As the child is part of the mother's life, so the society is a part of the church.

It is of the church and for the church, and is to do the bidding of the church as much as the hand is meant to do the bidding of the brain.

The "relation" of the society to the church has been discussed innumerable times, sometimes by hostile critics, sometimes by friendly advocates of the society, and it has been too often assumed, without argument and without justification, that it is something apart from and one side of the church.

It is a "relation," a poor relation, a young relation, a relation that needs to be rebuffed, or a relation that needs a little patronizing approval. But until we find out what relation the child is to the family, until we can properly speak of the relation of the finger to the hand, we cannot with exactness talk about the relation of the society to the church.

What, pray, is the church?

I am speaking now of the local organization.

Is it a certain number of the older members? Is it the congregation that gathers to hear the pastor's Sunday morning sermon or to engage in the evening service? Is it the mid-week prayer-meeting?

Yes, it is all these and more. The church is the local body of Christ's followers who worship Sunday morning and Sunday evening.

The church is the people at prayer in the mid-week service.

The Sunday-school is the church giving and receiving instruction.

The sewing circle, if composed of Godly women, is the church working for the poor.

The missionary society is the church praying and giving for the advancement and extension of the Kingdom of God.

The Christian Endeavor Society is the church training and being trained for practical service in the kingdom.

Serious charges of disloyalty of the young people to the church—charges at least that could be maintained—have never been urged against the Society of Christian Endeavor to my knowledge.

But fault has sometimes been found with the young people because they do not all attend the Sunday evening service or the mid-week prayer-meeting as faithfully, it is said, as they attend their own young people's meeting.

To remedy any possible defect in this direction and to impress upon the youthful host the importance of maintaining the outward forms of grace, the following clause, not many years after the formation of the first society, was inserted in the Endeavor pledge: "I will make it the rule of my life to support my own church, especially by attending her regular Sunday and mid-week services, unless prevented by a reason which I can conscientiously give to my Lord and Master."

This clause, added to the rest of the pledge, constituted what is known as the "revised pledge."

It has been very generally adopted, and, I thoroughly believe, is very generally lived up to by the active members of the society.

Still it is sometimes said by pastors that the young people's meeting is more attractive than the Sunday evening service, and the young people attend their own meeting and go away immediately thereafter.

It never seems to occur to some brethren that possibly this meeting is quite as profitable, helpful, and necessary to the young disciples as the service that follows it.

It never occurs to them that a multitude goes to this meeting who would never go to any other, and that those whom they meet going away from the first meeting are often associate members or outsiders who could not be tolled within the church doors by any other bait than a live and vigorous prayer-meeting in which their companions took part.

Surely even the persistent critic of the society would not ask that the young people's meeting be closed, if there they obtained spiritual profit, in order that there may be a few more people to hear him preach. Yet some of the arguments against the young people's meeting sound very much like the wail of a misanthrope who is constantly disappointed by a thin and unresponsive audience, the responsibility for which he desires to lay upon somebody or something.

But I claim that it can be proved, beyond the shadow of a doubt, that while, undoubtedly, some young people go away from the young people's meeting without staying to a second service when the two follow each other in close succession, that these are very largely people who would not go to any service were it not for the young people's meeting, or else they are some over-tired workers, who conscientiously and prayerfully have decided that it is not their duty to attend the second service, but who find spiritual profit to themselves and much help to others in attending the young people's meeting.

In spite of these cases, too, I believe that the Sunday evening service and the mid-week prayer-meeting are far more largely attended than they would be were it not for the stimulus of the young people's society, and the constant reference of these questions to the individual conscience involved in the idea of the prayer-meeting pledge.

Participation in the mid-week meeting of the church has vastly increased, take it the country over, by reason of the training the young Christians have had in their society. Nor have I simply my own theories or prepossessions to urge in this matter, but facts and figures which have been gathered with much pains from a very large number of societies in all parts of the land.

Several years ago I found from inquiries, made by letter in all parts of the country, that the percentage of these active members who supported the other meetings of their own churches was *as nearly two to one,* when compared with all the members, old and young, of the same churches. Again, desiring to find out whether these statistics still held true, I sent out another list of questions to more than five hundred pastors and others in different parts of the country, representing churches of the Presbyterian, Baptist, Methodist Episcopal, Disciples, Friends, Lutheran, United Presbyterian, Congregational, Free Baptist, Reformed, Methodist Protestant, and Cumberland Presbyterian denominations, asking certain questions about the Sunday and mid-week services of the church, and also whether the Endeavorers were active in other church duties than those of their own society, and whether they were more or less active than before their society was formed.

These questions were sent, *not* to a picked company of friends, but in a most promiscuous and broadcast manner. They were sent out by a clerk who did not know my purpose in asking the questions. I knew my correspondents personally in scarcely a single instance, nor did I know anything about the churches, or the young people's work in the churches, to which my questions went, except in a very few instances. More than 500 replies have been received, representing Endeavor societies with 30,000 members, perhaps, and churches with nearly 100,000 members. These replies are remarkably similar to those received five years ago. They have been tabulated and averaged, and it is found that in all these many and wide-apart societies the average attendance of the active members of the Endeavor Society, at the Sunday evening service, is *seventy-six per cent.;* at the mid-week service, *fifty-seven per cent.* Of all the church-members, old and young, in these same churches, at the Sunday evening service, it is *forty-six per cent.;* and at the mid-week service, of all, old and young, it was *twenty-eight per cent.* These statistics have not been obtained by guess, but by careful count, by going over the roll of church and society, and considering each name.

It will be noticed that in the questions relating to the attendance of all the church-members, old and young, the active members of the Christian Endeavor Society are also included, and that these members very materially bring up the average of the whole church. If the question had been asked, "How large a percentage of the older members of the church, *aside from the Christian Endeavorers,* attend these two services?" the percentage would have been reduced to a pitifully small one in many churches. In fact, many of my correspondents volunteered the information that if it were not for the young people it would be impossible to keep up the mid-week service, while the Sunday evening service would be reduced more than one-half.

As to the other questions, they are answered with remarkable unanimity and emphasis in the affirmative. Are your leading active members also active in other branches of church work? "Yes," "Yes," "Yes," is the reply, with only two responses out of the five or six hundred of an equivocal character. Are the young people more or less generally active in church work than before the society was formed? "More active," "Decidedly," "Emphatically," "Beyond comparison more active," "Never were active before," "There is no comparison between the old times and these," "We can never cease thanking God for the activity of our young people," "The mid-week service is composed of the young people, with one or two exceptions."

I have not time to quote one in twenty of the glowing sentences which tell of the earnestness and devotion of the vast majority of these young disciples in all the branches of the work of the church. I did not ask these questions about the attendance of older church-members at these services for the sake of ungenerous comparison, but because it seemed necessary in estimating the faithfulness of these young disciples, which has sometimes been called in question, to have some standard of comparison, besides the absolute standard of perfect faithfulness, which I am confident it is their aim to reach.

Moreover, when it is remembered that many of the twenty-four per cent. who do not habitually attend the second Sunday service, and many of the forty-three per cent. who do not habitually attend the mid-week service, stay at home by reason of ill health, or to care for children, or to allow their elders to attend these services, the percentage of those who carelessly or willfully neglect their covenant vows, without an excuse which they can give to the Master, is very small. *At any rate, it remains true that nearly twice as large a per cent. of them attend the evening service, and more than twice as large a per cent. of them attend the mid-week service, as of all the church-members, old and young.*

One fact which is very noticeable is recalled by these statistics. Wherever the percentage of the attendance of the young people at these services is *comparatively* small, the percentage of the attendance of the older people is *lamentably* small. Evidently the *morale* of those churches is low throughout the entire membership. The sense of loyalty to the services, and to the work of the church, is weak and wavering, and even the strenuous pledge which the young people have taken is not sufficient to overcome the general demoralization of the church in these particulars.

Another thing is also revealed: where the attendance is particularly small, the explanation is often added that the pastor and older church-members take no sort of interest in the young people's meetings. They are left to drift and shift for themselves. Sometimes my correspondent tells me: "Our pastor never comes near our meetings, except to criticize us," "He never shows any interest in what we are trying to do, or encourage us by a word of sympathy," "Our church seems bound to freeze us out, or starve us out." I am glad to say that these are comparatively very few, but they account for some low percentages which have brought down the whole average of faithfulness.

THE SOCIETY'S MOTHER AND HER SISTERS.

But to turn to the sisters of the society. It is a fact worth noting that the birthday of the Christian Endeavor movement falls, almost to a day, just a hundred years later than the birthday of the Sunday-school movement. According to the best chronology, Robert Raikes gathered together the ragged children of Gloucester in the first Sunday-school in the year 1781.

A hundred years later, in 1881, another child of the church was born, which were it not for the discrepancy in their ages might be called a twin sister of the Sunday-school.

These two children of the church have always maintained a most intimate and affectionate relationship. The members of the Endeavor Society are, almost without an exception, found in the Sunday-school either as teachers or scholars, and the advocates of Sunday-school methods are for the most part advocates of Christian Endeavor methods.

In fact these two organizations have no excuse for estrangement or even for coolness one toward another, since they do not interfere with each other or overlap in their work, but are mutually supplementary of each other. The Endeavor Society has been well defined as the church training its young people, the Sunday-school as the church instructing its young people. The work of the society cannot be done in the Sunday-school, nor can the instruction of the Sunday-school be given in the society. There is an equally important place for both in every well-organized church.

From an Original Portrait in the possession of Major General Raikes.

THE FOUNDER OF MODERN SUNDAY-SCHOOLS.

One of the earliest committees formed after the three absolutely essential committees—the lookout, prayer-meeting, and social—was the Sunday-school committee, which existed very early in the Williston Church, and has been adopted by a multitude of other Christian Endeavor societies.

The object of this committee is to bring new members into the Sunday-school and to co-operate with the superintendent and trustees in every way to render the Sunday-school more efficient.

At one of the earliest conventions Mr. E. H. Shattuck, of Lowell, read a paper on the Sunday-school committee in his church in which he stated that, after six months, it was found that "the committee had given sixty personal invitations to attend the Sunday-school, forty of which had been accepted, and that the average attendance of the Sunday-school had increased from 225 before the society was formed to an attendance of 312, the largest for many years, and it seems safe to assert that the increase was due in a great measure to the influence of the Young People's Society of Christian Endeavor."

Similar testimony has come from a multitude of other Sunday-schools, but not only in increasing the attendance of the Sunday-school can the society be useful, but in finding teachers from among its older members who can be called upon by the superintendent for classes when needed. Many societies furnish a corps of teachers when needed by the superintendent. Others are able to aid him in preparing anniversary and concert exercises.

ROBERT RAIKES' HOUSE IN GLOUCESTER, ENGLAND.

Said the superintendent of a large school to me the other day, "Something happened to me recently which never occurred in all my experience as superintendent. A company of five young people from the Endeavor Society waited upon me, informing me that they were the Sunday-school Committee, and that they were ready to do anything in the world that I would let them do for the Sunday-school. Why," said he, " I was not only delighted, but overjoyed. There are plenty of things I can give them to do, and the fact that they offered so heartily and spontaneously makes the service doubly helpful."

Another sister of the society is the young people's missionary organization, and with this sister, too, it is on intimate and affectionate terms. Its object is to aid the missionary work of existing missionary societies both among the younger and older in every possible way, to increase their funds, and to enlarge their scope.

If, sometimes, a struggling mission circle has been absorbed into the young people's society, it has only been to enlarge the scope and the clientage of the missionary cause in interesting many more young people in praying for and giving to the missionary cause.

The great enthusiasm of late aroused by the missionary extension cause and by Christian Endeavor Day, which is essentially a missionary day, by the overwhelmingly enthusiastic sessions of the great conventions and in many other ways, proves the loyalty of the heart of the society to our Lord's great mission.

It would be almost a misnomer to call the Mothers' Meeting or the Maternal Association a *sister* of the society. If it were not that the Church of Christ is the only mother which the society acknowledges, it might more properly perhaps be called the society's mother, for wherever a maternal association exists, what object can engage its prayers more appropriately than the young people's society, where are the boys and girls, the young men and women, over whom every mother's heart yearns?

Of later years there has been a closer approach of the mothers' meeting, wherever it exists, to the young people's society. Many of these mothers' meetings are now called "Mothers' Endeavor Societies," and their special care is to pray for, sympathize with, and help the children gathered together in the Junior Society and the older ones of the Y. P. S. C. E.

We will not speak of that best-loved sister of all, the Junior Society, in this chapter, because it is not a relative, but an integral part of the Endeavor movement, and it deserves more than one chapter exclusively to itself.

The Y. M. C. A. can hardly be called a *sister* of the society without forcing language and bringing a smile to the bearded face of many a Y. M. C. A. *brother*, but yet the relationship between the Y. M. C. A. and the Society of Christian Endeavor has always been considered a *family* relationship.

They occupy different fields, and they both recognize the fact. The association is for the community at large, the society for the individual church.

The association is necessarily *undenominational*, the society is necessarily *inter-denominational*.

The association can acknowledge allegiance to no one church, the association must acknowledge allegiance to some one church; and yet, though they occupy different positions, each is doing an invaluable work which the other cannot accomplish.

The association, with its large expenses, its building, its reading-room, its gymnasium, and all its necessary equipment, is particularly fitted to cities or large towns, where it can be thoroughly supported.

The society can find its way into every hamlet which can support an evangelical church.

But, as I have said, they can in many ways mutually aid one another; as the receptions which are given by the associations to the societies, and by the societies to the associations, have often proved. Some of the best workers among the secretaries of the Y. M. C. A. have been trained in the Christian Endeavor Society for their future work, and some of the most earnest advocates and most eloquent speakers at Endeavor conventions have been leading Y. M. C. A. workers.

Mr. W. J. Van Patten, the most liberal friend of the Christian Endeavor movement in its earliest days, has always been known throughout his State of Vermont as a leading Y. M. C. A. worker, and the beautiful Association Hall in Burlington is largely a result of his liberality.

At the first Saratoga Convention, already described, Mr. David McConaughy, the well-known secretary of the Philadelphia Association at that time, afterward so used of God in planting the association work in India, conducted a Bible training-class which was one of the features of that memorable convention.

REV. RUFUS W. MILLER.

We cannot call the Brotherhood of Andrew and Philip, an organization of very recent years, a *sister* of the society, but we can call it a highly esteemed relative, which, wherever there is a special work for it do, especially among young men outside of any church, is heartily welcome.

In average churches, and particularly in smaller churches, as has been advised by the founder of the Brotherhood movement, Rev. Rufus W. Miller, who is also one of the trustees of the United Society, a Brotherhood Committee of the Endeavor Society answers every purpose, and prevents unnecessary multiplication of organization.

To all efforts to advance the Kingdom of God on broad and brotherly lines of inter-denominational fellowship, the Society of Christian Endeavor has always maintained a most hearty and cordial attitude. It wishes God-speed and desires to lend a helping hand to every brother and sister organization, and its prayer shall ever be, "God bless every man and woman in this wide world who is trying to do good."

CHAPTER XXVI.

THE SECOND SARATOGA CONVENTION.

Good-Natured Rivalry—Dr. Hoyt's Inspiring Sermon—Other Friends Added to the Movement—Rev. B. Fay Mills and His Address—High Ideals—Old Friends as well as New—An Important Action—The Trend of Events—An Unmistakable Call of Providence—Saying Good-bye to the Pastor—Twenty-three Hundred and Fourteen Societies Recorded—Six Thousand Dollars Raised—The Connecticut Penny—Another Pleasant Incident.

SARATOGA proved to be such a charming place for holding an Endeavor convention that with one voice, in 1886, the delegates voted to return in 1887.

The good-natured rivalry of half the cities in the Union for the next International Convention, which is now the source of so much interest and enthusiasm at each convention, was not then a feature of the meetings. The society was still but little known, and, by the great mass of the people, little esteemed.

Chicago and St. Louis, Minneapolis and New York, San Francisco and Boston, Louisville and Baltimore were not vying with each other for the entertainment of this somewhat obscure though growing organization of young people.

IN CONGRESS PARK, SARATOGA.

But Saratoga, a city of conventions and hotel keepers, was alive to the advantages of having a thousand or more young people poured into her streets during the weeks preceding the height of her busy season, and was quite willing to open her arms to them.

REV. WAYLAND HOYT, D. D.

Partly in default of other invitations, and partly because of the delightful memories and success of the first Saratoga Convention, the 5th, 6th, and 7th days of July, 1887, saw a still larger host of Endeavorers come together in the beautiful tree-lined streets of this famous watering place than the previous year had seen. Mr. Van Patten was in the chair, as he was the year before, and at this convention we find many of those already identified with the movement, as well as some new friends whom Christian Endeavor was glad to welcome to its ranks.

Chief among these was Rev. Wayland Hoyt, D. D., then of Philadelphia, who preached a most inspiring sermon on "The Unconscious Weight of Character"—a sermon which will long live in the traditions of the Endeavor movement, for its impressiveness, its power, and its peculiar adaptation to the youthful audience to whom it was addressed.

From that time to the present Dr. Wayland Hoyt has been an unswerving and unfailing friend to the Christian Endeavor cause. A trustee of the United Society, a voluminous writer on the subject, an eloquent speaker at many international conventions, his earnest voice and ready pen have always been at the service of a cause which he there came to love.

REV. J. T. KERR.

We find also the names of Rev. J. T. Kerr, of Elizabeth, N. J., an early president of the New Jersey Union, who has never wavered in his affection for the movement.

Rev. H. W. Sherwood, afterward the president of the New York Convention, reported that in New York State there were 267 societies, with 12,000 members.

Mr. F. J. Harwood brought greetings from distant Wisconsin, and told us that the movement was growing rapidly there.

From Iowa Rev. C. H. Towle told us that the membership had trebled.

Rev. C. W. Huntington, then of Providence but now of Lowell, told us that "the societies lived for the pastors' relief and joy: relief, because they made him hundred-handed, and joy, because they so facilitated his work."

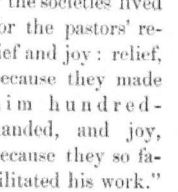

REV. H. W. SHERWOOD, D.D.

Dr. Deems, of New York, was again at the convention, and left this record in the report of his meeting, "I am a Christian Endeavorer all through and through and forever and ever, and I thank God for the society."

F. J. HARWOOD.

Rev. H. N. Kinney, then of Winsted, Conn., now of Syracuse, N. Y., who has ever since been identified with the movement wherever he has lived, and who has given special attention of late years to Junior work, was at this convention, and testified to the developing usefulness of the society.

Rev. B. Fay Mills, the evangelist whom God has so greatly honored, made his first appearance, but by no means his last, at this convention, and had for his theme "The Spiritual Aim in Christian Work."

REV. H. N. KINNEY.

Among many other notable speakers at this convention was Rev. Josiah Strong, D. D., secretary of the Evangelical Alliance, whose inspiring address was followed by another of equal inspiration by Rev. Lyman Abbott, D. D., on "The Equipments Necessary for Christian Work."

REV. B. FAY MILLS.

Rev. L. A. Crandall, D. D., was also one of the speakers at this convention, and a magnificent address he gave on "High Ideals."

Rev. N. B. Remick most happily emphasized the point that the Christian Endeavor Society is inseparable from the church.

Rev. H. W. Pope presented the necessity, or at least the wisdom and value of uniform prayer-meeting topics, while Mr. S. L. Mershon, who has since developed into a Boanerges on missionary themes, presented most ably the work of the prayer-meeting committee.

It is remarkable to notice how the Endeavor Society seems to bind to itself the sympathies of those who have once looked into its methods, and have put themselves under the spell of one of its great conventions.

Almost every one whom we have mentioned as prominent in this sixth convention, as well as a multitude of others who might be mentioned, is to-day a stanch friend, defender, and advocate of the Endeavor Society. Their voices are frequently heard down to the present time in cheering exhortation and counsel, and, though a constantly increasing number of eminent men from all denominations is drawn to the movement in connection with every international convention, these early friends are as stanch and stalwart in their attachment to the Endeavor cause as ever.

Moreover, there have been remarkably few cases of that very unpleasant and sometimes, so far as religious work is concerned, fatal disease which is vulgarly known as "sorehead."

As the friends of the movement have in-

MR. S. L. MERSHON.

creased, it is natural that some of the earliest promoters should not be so exclusively prominent as in the early days.

It has been necessary to draw new life into each of the conventions and to hear new voices, and sometimes the oldest and truest friends of the society have not been heard as all Endeavorers would like to have heard them; and yet, any suspicion of jealousy, ill-will, or chagrin has been the rarest possible thing, and very seldom has an early friend lost his interest in the movement.

One of the important actions taken at this convention was the choice of Rev. Francis E. Clark, then the pastor of Phillips Church, South Boston, where he had been for four years after leaving the pastorate of Williston Church, in Portland, Me., to be the president of the Board of Trustees of the United Society and the editor of the society's publication.

This was suggested in the annual address of the president, Mr. W. J. Van Patten, in the following words: "It will give you great pleasure to hear, as it does me to announce, that the man to whom we all look for guidance in this great work has been chosen president of the corporation and of the Board of Trustees, and that in the future even more than in the past he will give of his time and of his thought to the work. He cannot give more of his love and of his zeal, but we may thank God that we are to have even more than ever the benefit of his wise planning and his great executive ability."

These words, all too kind, were received with much enthusiasm, and when the committee on reports reported favorably on the President's address and nominated Rev. F. E. Clark, according to the report, the great audience arose, and indorsed the committee with cheers and round after round of applause, and then sang "Praise God from whom all blessings flow."

I speak of this action, though the account may seem immodest in a history which I, myself, am writing, because it seems necessary to tell of the circumstances which led to this important step.

For a number of months I had come to see that the trend of events was inevitably in this direction.

For six years and a half now the Endeavor movement had been in existence, and had been continually gaining strength and power.

The multiplying societies, and the increasing work, though the latter was generously shared by many helpers was coming increasingly upon my shoulders. Calls for addresses from different parts of the country were almost innumerable, and it was becoming plain, too, that there must be an official paper to represent the societies and that I must have not a little to do with its management and editorial supervision.

All these duties, combined with the care of a large and growing church, I came to see formed a heavier load than I could well carry.

Something must be given up. The work of the society I could not delegate to another, the historic development of the movement led a multitude of people to look to me, though I was no better able to give help or advice than many others, and I came to realize reluctantly that I must give up the pastorate of my beloved church and devote my whole life to this young people's movement.

I felt that it was a call of Providence which could not be disregarded, that God was speaking to me in even louder tones than I heard when I entered the gospel ministry.

So the decision was made, the election was accepted, and a few weeks later

A GROUP OF ENDEAVORERS AT HOTEL HEADQUARTERS, SECOND SARATOGA CONVENTION.

I resigned the charge of the church which from the first day of my pastorate to the last was an increasing joy, and said "good-bye" to a most affectionate and kindly people with very much of sorrow in my heart at leaving that particular church, and at leaving the pastorate which I had so heartily enjoyed for eleven years.

Another important action of this convention was the adoption of *The Golden Rule* as the official organ of the United Society of Christian Endeavor.

In this report a list of 2,314 societies were recorded, a very large gain, as we will see, over the 850 societies of the year before.

THE SECOND SARATOGA CONVENTION. 199

Every State in the Union by this time with three exceptions was represented, and every Territory but three, while in foreign countries societies were known to exist in Syria, China, Japan, Africa, Micronesia, Scotland, and England.

In our own country the secretary reported that the most noticeable growth had been in the Western States belting the Mississippi and on the extreme Pacific Coast.

In the East, the New England and the Middle Atlantic States had taken no backward steps. Over $6,000 was raised for the expenses of the coming year, and the good old Bay State of Massachusetts, through its delegates, gave $700 to pay the debt of last year.

Again, the life membership list was increased by contributions from those who were present, and we have never known more "cheerful" or, according to the strict translation, "hilarious" giving than at this convention.

Mr. Child's baby "Dick" was made a life member by eighteen different friends. Maude and Eugene Clark, the children of the new president, were made life members by other friends. Mrs. W. J. Van Patten and Mrs. Clark, Dr. Strong, Dr. Hoyt, Dr. Abbott, Mr. Mills, Mrs. James L. Hill, and Mrs. C. A. Dickinson by still others, all of whom seemed to vie with each other in helping along the Christian Endeavor cause and adding another name to the list of life members.

The famous Connecticut penny was here introduced. Illinois and Connecticut entered into a friendly rivalry as to which State should give the most money to the cause of Christian Endeavor. First the Nutmeg State was ahead, and then Illinois, and then Connecticut again, until, when the sum for each State had reached $300, President Holdrege, one of Christian Endeavor's veterans and most earnest workers, capped the climax by calling out: "Illinois pledges $300 and 1 cent." With that Miss Finch, of Bloomington, Ill., handed President Holdrege the one penny that afterward became so famous. Connecticut, good-humoredly, withdrew from the contest, and yielded to Illinois the palm for this occasion. This cent passed back and forth more than once between the States as a token of their mutual love for Christian Endeavor, and the badge of Connecticut was for some time a copper penny fresh from the United States Mint.

For the success of this convention, too, much credit is due to Rev. T. W. Jones, the pastor of the Congregational Church, who labored most assiduously for many weeks in advance to prepare for the coming of the Endeavor hosts. He combined in himself the numerous committees which have since become famous for their preparations for a Christian Endeavor convention, and it was due not a little to him, as the convention gratefully acknowledged, that the sixth annual gathering passed into history as the most successful of the series.

CHAPTER XXVII.

THE GOLDEN RULE AND OTHER ENDEAVOR PAPERS.

Mr. Boynton's Resolution—The Checkered Experience of a Newspaper—Things Which Cost Money—The Change from a Blanket Sheet—Early Editors and What They Did for the Paper—Large Accessions to the Editorial Force—The Junior *Golden Rule*—What the Papers Have Done for the Cause—Deacon Burnham's Connection With the Paper—Other Endeavor Papers.

AMONG the records of the convention which we have just described we find the following resolution offered by Rev. Nehemiah Boynton, of Haverhill:

"The Young People's Society of Christian Endeavor in convention assembled, recognize the utility of *The Golden Rule* as a worthy organ for the dissemination of their principles, and therefore resolved that *The Golden Rule* be adopted as the official organ of the United Society of Christian Endeavor."

It might be supposed at first glance that the Biblical precept, commonly known by this beautiful name, was referred to when the convention recognized the utility of "The Golden Rule," but a little closer inspection of the records show that the resolutions did not refer to the precept, but to a newspaper which had adopted the name of Our Lord's command and which was striving to exemplify it.

This paper had suffered a somewhat checkered experience. Started some dozen years before, it had known the various vicissitudes of a struggling newspaper.

Much money had been lost and very little made by its publishers, who were ready, for a consideration, to turn it over to the control of some of the leading spirits in the Endeavor movement, with the understanding that it should become, out and out and through and through, the organ of this new movement.

For more than a year previous to this convention, as will be seen from the record, the paper had served as the semi-official representative of the society. It gave at first a couple of columns weekly, and, after a time, more and more space to recording the news and to defending the principles of Christian Endeavor.

SECRETARY BAER'S OFFICE.

PROF. WELLS' OFFICE.

TREASURER SHAW'S OFFICE.

REV. FRANCIS E. CLARK'S OFFICE.

But it was felt that this was not sufficient; that it was necessary to have a paper exclusively devoted to the work, a paper which should be controlled entirely by those who were in the closest sympathy with the society.

But the question at once arose, how shall a newspaper organ be obtained? Even a paper with a small circulation costs money.

To begin one from the ground would cost quite as much.

Printers must be paid and editors cannot work for nothing.

The outfit of a respectable paper, such as would be worthy of the cause, would cost a great deal of money, and the expenses would constantly increase with the desire and purpose of putting it in the front ranks of religious journal-

A GOLDEN RULE OFFICE.

ism and making it more and more worthy of the growing movement which it represented.

Here was indeed a serious obstacle at the very beginning.

The United Society did not have money wherewith to purchase it. In fact, it took every dollar of its meagre resources to pay the necessary expenses of its literature and the salary and traveling expenses of the general secretary.

The very year before, as we have seen, the United Society had run into debt to the serious amount of $700, a sum which was generously made good by the delegates of the Bay State.

It was evident that not a dollar could be spared from the United Society treasury to purchase the plant, and that it could not become responsible for the very large expenses of a weekly paper, which for a long time at least could not be expected to pay its own way.

At this juncture some ardent friends of the movement came forward, several of whom risked their little all, borrowed from friends who were willing to lend, and purchased the paper that it might be forever a representative of true Christian Endeavor principles.

I felt very strongly then, as I have ever since, that I did not wish to receive my support as an official of the organization which I had helped to create and which was then dependent upon the contributions of Christian Endeavorers, but I was willing to receive a salary as editor of *The Golden Rule* from this company

A GOLDEN RULE OFFICE.

of gentlemen who had bought the paper, and to whom I should be responsible for its conduct and success.

Only on these conditions was I willing to accept the double office of President of the United Society and Editor of *The Golden Rule*.

At once the paper was changed in form from the old blanket sheet to its present quarto form, and for a time Rev. F. H. Kasson was retained as associate editor.

After a few weeks, however, he withdrew from the company and various assistants have been associated with myself since.

Miss Elizabeth Hanscom, whose literary work is recognized by all critics as of a high order, for a number of months was the associate editor.

Rev. John L. Sewell, now of Kansas City, was for a year the managing editor, and during one long absence of mine during a visit to Europe, ably conducted the paper.

Afterward Mr. Arthur T. Kelly became associated with the paper, and his unfailing accuracy and encyclopædic information have been of great assistance in making the paper the careful, trustworthy exponent of Christian Endeavor ideas that we all desire.

For five years Miss Lillian A. Wilcox, now Mrs. Charles Miller, pushed a facile quill in the interests of the paper, and later, in connection with *The Junior Golden Rule* became endeared as "AuntRuth" to a multitude of the younger generation of Christian Endeavorers. In 1892 Prof. Amos R. Wells, then a teacher of Greek in Antioch College, at Yellow Springs, Ohio, whose numerous contributions to the religious press and secular magazines had made his name familiar in the literary world, was persuaded to become the managing editor of *The Golden Rule*, and his accession to its force should be a matter of congratulation to every reader and to every Christian Endeavorer.

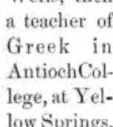
REV. J. L. SEWELL.

MISS LILLIAN A. WILCOX.

PROF. AMOS R. WELLS.

Most versatile in his literary labors, it has become the tradition of the office that there is nothing which can be done with a pen that Professor Wells cannot do. From a poem to an "ad.," from a spicy proverb to an elaborate argument in behalf of some neglected department of Christian Endeavor work, he is always equal to the emergency.

Moreover, his pen has been exceedingly busy in preparing manuals, leaflets, tracts, and books for the use of the Endeavor army in all parts of the world, and many of the most valuable publications of the United Society of Christian Endeavor bear upon the title-page his name as their author.

One of the later weeks of the year 1894 was signalized by the accession to *The Golden Rule* family of Mr. William T. Ellis, of Pennsylvania, an Endeavorer who has long been known for his earnest spirit and for his bright way of advocating the cause, and he has taken upon himself the work of Miss Wilcox (who, by the way, resigned her chair for a smaller and more select circle of influence), as well as other duties which he has found ready to his hand in connection with the ever-growing scope and influence of the paper.

In 1892 the Junior movement had grown so large and important and it was found practicable to give so little space to the work in the crowded columns of *The Golden Rule* that it was decided to publish a monthly paper for the children of the Junior societies.

The Junior Golden Rule, which has proved so helpful an ally of the cause among the younger people, was the result.

In a multitude of ways has *The Golden Rule* conserved the interests and saved the money of the United Society.

For one thing it has enabled the president of the society to give his time very largely to the interests of the movement, both in America and in foreign lands, without a dollar of salary being paid to him by the society.

WILLIAM T. ELLIS.

It has enabled the United Society to command the time and the ability of some exceedingly skillful literary workers with scarcely any cost to the society.

But more than all, it has conserved the true principles of the society by advocating every week the fundamental ideas on which it was built and for which it lives by keeping out of sight a great amount of cranky and ill-considered suggestions, for a paper is quite as valuable for what it does not print as for what it does, and by serving as the official exponent and authoritative messenger of the Christian Endeavor idea to the world.

That it has made so few mistakes; that it has maintained a most generous attitude toward other papers, particularly the denominational press, which in some instances have been inclined to look with a jealous eye on its growing circulation; that it has stood for Christian Endeavor principles pure and unadulterated, the society has abundant reasons to be grateful to my associates, who, in my frequent absences, have with much skill conducted the paper.

The early days of the paper were days of financial stress and struggle, and it has only been able to pay its way more generously of late years, because its growing circulation has made its advertising patronage increasingly large and liberal.

DEACON CHOATE BURNHAM.

The gentlemen who early bought the property have held to it through good and ill. More than once they have had to put their hands deep into their pockets to help it out of financial straits, but, for the love of the cause which it advocated, they were willing to do so, and while at the price at which it is given to subscribers it can never be a source of large wealth as some have supposed, it is probable that its days of serious financial struggle are for the most part over.

In this connection honorable and grateful mention should be made of Deacon Choate Burnham, who was the beloved senior deacon of Phillips Church, South Boston, of which I was for four years the happy pastor, and who from the very introduction of the society into his own church was its ardent friend and lover. Always present at the young people's prayer-meetings, though venerable in appearance with white hair and beard, his heart was young as the youngest, and his words were brief as the briefest. He was present at the convention at Lowell and at all the subsequent conventions until the one immediately before his lamented death.

From the beginning he was a member of the Board of Trustees of the United Society until God called him home, the first break in the ranks made by death. His death occurred while I was on the journey around the world in the interests of Christian Endeavor and the news came to me with a sense of personal bereavement such as I have seldom felt in all my life. This kindly, hearty, and beloved friend of Christian Endeavor was one of the owners from the beginning of *The Golden Rule*, and the only man of wealth among them, and it was due not a little to his financial credit and recognized standing among the merchants of Boston that the paper was tided over its early monetary difficulties.

The paper, as well as the society which he loved, will to its latest days be a monument to the devotion and the generous advocacy of Deacon Choate Burnham.

Others who should have most honorable mention in connection with the later history of *The Golden Rule* are Secretary John Willis Baer, who has been connected with the business management, and Mr. Geo. B. Graff, who will be remembered as one of the earliest Endeavorers of St. Louis, and who attended the Ocean Park Convention, the first delegate from beyond the Missouri River. In 1891 Mr. Graff became connected with the paper as manager of the subscription department, and has there done efficient and earnest work ever since.

Another indispensable factor in *The Golden Rule* office is Mr. Geo. W. Coleman, the manager of the advertising department.

GEORGE B. GRAFF.

A paper of the size of *The Golden Rule* with an exceedingly low subscription price must make both ends meet, if at all, by the advertising; hence the importance of having an energetic, enterprising, *persuasive* man at the head of this department. Mr. Coleman exactly answers to this description, and, moreover, is an earnest Christian Endeavorer, belonging to the Clarendon Street Baptist Church, of whose Sunday-school he is the superintendent. He has also been president of the Boston Christian Endeavor Union, and of the Massachusetts State Union, and his wife, Mrs. Alice Merriam Coleman, is prominent in Junior work and also is a most acceptable speaker on missionary themes.

GEORGE W. COLEMAN.

Others who should be mentioned are : Mr. Charles Brown, of the subscription department, a member of the First Baptist Church of Boston, and a musical composer of no mean ability, and Mr. Benj. Keeping, foreman of the composing room, whose faithfulness and extreme care account largely for the typographical excellence of the paper. In fact, if I should begin to enumerate all who deserve credit for making *The Golden Rule* what it is I should find it difficult to stop before the whole list of helpers was exhausted.

Other papers than *The Golden Rule* too have done good service for Christian Endeavor. My limited space forbids me to describe them at length, though allusion to them will be made in other chapters of this history. The name of State and local papers have been legion, but many of them have been short lived, for the editors and publishers have found oftentimes that it is easier to start a paper than to keep it up to a high standard of excellence and prosperity, however good the cause which it represents.

REV. G. BERNER.

Some papers having a wider circulation than a single State affords have been *The Endeavor Herald* of Canada, a paper which has well represented the Christian Endeavor interests in the provinces; *The Inland* of St. Louis, a newsy and enterprising monthly paper; *The Westminister Endeavorer*, published especially in the interests of Presbyterian Endeavorers.

The Mitarbeiter is a monthly Endeavor paper printed in the German language, in the interests of the hundreds of German-speaking societies of America, which are doing an admirable work, and which have a yearly convention of their own. This paper is ably edited by Rev. G. Berner, of Buffalo, and enjoys a large and constantly increasing circulation. It is also, to some extent, taken in Germany, and has aided not a little in the establishment of the society in the fatherland.

The lands across the seas, too, have their papers which have contributed largely to the interests of the Endeavor cause. Among them may be mentioned especially, *Christian Endeavor*, of England, of which the energetic secretary of the British Section, Rev. Knight Chaplin, is the editor, a paper with a very wide circulation, and one that is eagerly welcomed by Endeavorers throughout the United Kingdom as it makes its monthly visits to their homes.

The Golden Link of Australia, edited by the devoted secretary of Victoria Union, Mr. J. B. Jackson, is also a bright, breezy paper, as interesting as it is substantial, and wholly devoted to the exposition of Christian Endeavor principles in their purity.

I have also seen No. 1, Vol. I, of *The Golden Chain*, the Endeavor paper of South Africa, to which Dr. Andrew Murray contributes the leading articles.

The Christian Endeavor paper of Japan is under the care of Rev. T. Harada, and comes regularly to the office of *The Golden Rule* arrayed in its hieroglyphics so strange to Western eyes.

It should also be said in this connection, that many denominational papers and independent religious journals have done quite as much to advance the interests of Christian Endeavor as some distinctively Endeavor papers. The great majority of religious journals of the present day give not a little space each week to the Endeavor Society, especially to the exposition of its prayer-meeting topics. In fact it is quite often a more efficient way to help Christian Endeavor to use the freely-offered columns of already established journals than to start a paper distinctively in the interest of the society.

Among the ably edited State papers may be mentioned *The Convention Herald*, Milford, Del.; *The District of Columbia Christian Endeavorer*, Washington, D. C.; *The Christian Endeavor Echo*, of New Hampshire; *The Pacific Coast Endeavorer*, of California; *The Church Messenger and Rhode Island Christian Endeavorer;* *The Endeavor Banner*, of Montreal; *The Endeavor Herald*, of South Dakota; *The Endeavor Standard*, of Vancouver; *The Iowa Endeavorer*, published in Des Moines; *The Kansas Endeavorer*, the able State monthly published in Topeka; *The Keystone Herald*, of Pennsylvania; *The New Jersey Endeavorer; Our Union*, of Toledo; *The Oregon Christian Endeavorer; Once a Month*, published in Utica, N. Y.; *The Reflector*, of Omaha, Neb.; *The South Carolina Endeavorer*, of Charleston; *Sunshine*, of Tennessee, with its cheery cover; *The Washington Endeavorer*, of Seattle; *The West Virginia Christian Endeavor Banner; The Wisconsin Endeavorer; The Southern Chautauqua Journal*, of Florida, and a great number of local union and church Endeavor papers.

So far as I know, at the date of this writing, these papers named are all in existence; but I will not vouch for the life of all of them by the time this chapter is printed, and still more of them will have gone the way of so many good newspapers by the time this chapter reaches many of my readers.

It is no reflection on the zeal, enterprise, or literary ability of the editors and publishers that these papers are so often short-lived, for it takes large resources to continue the publication of a worthy weekly or even monthly paper; and if they are given up, I hope the editors and publishers will turn their enterprise to the very important task of giving to the denominational and other papers the latest news and the latest methods of Christian Endeavor.

In addition to papers already mentioned as published in other lands in the interest of Christian Endeavor, I may also mention *El Testigo*, a paper published in Spanish in Guadalajara, Mexico; *Our Young People*, of Santiago, Chile, and

The Chinese Illustrated News, of Shanghai, which has given much attention to Christian Endeavor matter. In a previous paragraph it should have been said that one of the brightest and best of Endeavor papers is *The Lookout*, published in Cincinnati by the publishing house of the Disciples of Christ and ably edited by Miss Jessie H. Brown.

Some local union papers have achieved a good measure of success, notably *The Philadelphia Bulletin*, which has recently become a weekly. Other Endeavor papers will doubtless be started, perhaps before this book reaches the public. May they deserve and command success.

The only paper in the Welsh language of which I know devoted to Christian Endeavor has been published in Chicago and rejoices in the following consonantal name, *Yr Ymdrechydd*.

REV. S. H. DOYLE.

One of the most efficient ways of reaching the public through the newspaper has been by means of the American Associated Press, for which Rev. S. H. Doyle, formerly the efficient president of the West Virginia Union, is the editor of the syndicate prayer-meeting articles which go far and wide throughout the land.

Many secular papers also give not a little space each week to the society and its work, and many Endeavorers do a quiet but very genuine service to the cause by supplying this weekly column with news and notes and prayer-meeting suggestions for the advancement of the cause. The press committees in many cities have been in this way most efficient in advancing Endeavor interests. To all fellow-laborers with the pen for the weal of Christian Endeavor I would like to record my heartiest appreciation and my earnest thanks for all that they have done and are doing by means of printers' ink and paper for the furtherance of our common cause. Whatever may be the decision concerning the old school-boy proposition for debate, it is certain that for the triumph of Christian Endeavor the pen is mightier than the sword.

CHAPTER XXVIII.

ENDEAVOR SONGS AND SINGERS.

At the Cross, at the Cross—"Faith is the Victory"—The Use of Hymn-Singing—Silence Not a Virtue to Be Cultivated—Dr. Rankin's Endeavor Hymn—Mr. Dickinson's Beautiful Hymn—How It Happened to Be Written—How They Sing in Australia—A Lesson Which America May Learn.

THE voice of song has ever been an inspiration of the Christian Endeavor prayer-meeting. Quite as important as the prayers and the testimonies have been the songs of our Zion.

A new meaning has been put into many a song by the tremendous volume and vast enthusiasm of many an Endeavor convention. Both in our own country and in Australia and in England as well I have heard Endeavorers going out from a meeting making all the dark air of the night vocal with the thrilling melody,

> "At the cross, at the cross, where I first saw the light,
> And the burden of my heart rolled away."

From the open windows of the Madison Square Garden with its crowded audience of fifteen thousand young people there came floating during the days of the New York Convention the triumphant tones of "Faith is the Victory" and "What a Wonderful Saviour," while ten thousand meetings have been closed with the sweet refrains of Dr. Rankin's hymn, "God be with you till we meet again."

Very early in the history of the movement the power of sacred song was recognized, and in the proceedings of the first Saratoga Convention we find a bright and witty paper by Rev. Charles Perry Mills on "The Use of Hymn-Singing in the Young People's Society of Christian Endeavor."

He claims that hymns have a use for the edification of the hearers, for exaltation, comfort, warning, exhortation. In short, we address and admonish one another in hymns.

> "God sent His singers upon earth
> With songs of sadness and of mirth,
> That they might touch the hearts of men
> And bring them back to heaven again."

Moreover, he claimed that hymn-singing has a use in our meetings to foster the emotions which our society seeks to cultivate. "Be it understood by all concerned, that the Endeavor Society is not a sentimental association. It has a policy. Neither is it a narrow conception, promoting a lean type of Christian character. Like the city above, it lieth four-square, the length, the breadth, the height of it being equal."

What, then, are the emotions which it aims to express and excite? Mr. Mills defines them as praise to Christ as our Redeemer and King; the idea of union and brotherly love and fellowship, the idea of the expression of our religious feeling.

"Silence is not a virtue to be cultivated. That grows without cultivation. We aim at the expression of religious feeling. And, finally, the principle of obligation and the spirit of aggressive work for Christ must be aroused by the live singing of live hymns like the grand martial notes of the church,

All hail the power of Jesus' name."

or,

"Stand up, stand up for Jesus."

These principles, we believe, have been exemplified and carried out with increasing power during the later years of the society. The first hymn, so far as I know, that was written expressly for the society was by President Rankin, of whom we have before spoken, and it was sung at the first Saratoga Convention. It is well worth quoting entire, for it is still sung, and will long, we believe, be a favorite with many societies:

Keep your colors flying,
All ye Christian youth,
To Christ's call replying,
Full of grace and truth.
Rise in strength and beauty,
In life's morning glow,
Answer to each duty,
Onward, upward go.

Life is all before you,
Where to choose your way;
Keep Christ's colors o'er you;
Watch and fight and pray.
With a firm endeavor,
Ev'ry foe defy,
True to Jesus ever,
Lift your colors high.

CHORUS.
Keep your colors flying,
Stand for God and truth,
Keep your colors flying,
All ye Christian youth.

Keep your colors flying,
Never think of ease;
Sin and self-denying,
Jesus only please.

Not for worldly pleasure,
Not for worldly fame,
Not for heaps of treasure;
Live for Jesus' name!

Keep your colors flying,
 Walk as Jesus did;
In Him, living, dying,
 Let your life be hid;

Hoping, trusting ever,
 Breathe this mortal breath;
You shall live forever,
 Christ has conquered death.

Another favorite Endeavor poet is Rev. Charles A. Dickinson, whose poetical contributions, though they have not been many, have been exceedingly choice, as the following hymn, written in 1891, while with the author he was crossing the stormy Atlantic, testifies. It has been sung in a multitude of conventions on both sides of the sea.

O golden days so long desired,
 Born of a darksome night,
The swinging globe at last is fired
 By thy resplendent light.
And hark! like Memnon's morning chord,
 Is heard from sea to sea
This song: One Master, Christ, the Lord;
 And brethren all are we.

The noises of the night shall cease,
 The storms no longer roar;
The factious foes of God's own peace
 Shall vex His Church no more.
A thousand, thousand voices sing
 In surging harmony;
This song: One Master, Saviour, King;
 And brethren all are we.

Sing on, ye chorus of the morn,
 Your grand Endeavor strain,
Till Christian hearts, estranged and torn,
 Blend in the glad refrain;
And all the Church, with all its powers,
 In loving loyalty
Shall sing: One Master, Christ, is ours;
 And brethren all are we.

Early in the history of the movement the necessity of a distinctive Christian Endeavor hymn-book was felt, and Rev. S. W. Adriance sought to supply this want by the publication of a small volume entitled "Hymns of Christian Endeavor."

Dr. Rankin, Mr. I. E. Diekenga, Rev. R. De W. Mallary, Rev. J. O. Barrows, Rev. Dwight M. Pratt, Rev. Joel S. Ives, Rev. A. Parke Burgess, Rev. T. S. Perry, Rev. C. H. Oliphant, F. W. Messe, Rev. H. N. Kinney, Mr. Adriance himself and others contributed original hymns or music to this book. The following are a few of the favorite hymns of this volume:

I PLEAD THY LOVE.
BY REV. J. O. BARROWS.

I plead Thy love, my gracious Lord,
 Thy wondrous love to me;
In sin's dark bondage I was held;
 But Thou hast made me free.

I plead the offering of Thy blood,
 Thy precious blood, for me;
For cleansing I have naught to do
 But look to Calvary.

I plead the merits of Thy life,
 Thy perfect life for me;
In what Thou wast I can behold
 What I myself may be.

I plead, dear Saviour, Thine own Word,
 Thine own sure word to me;
And need no more, for Thou hast said,
 "I'm all in all to thee."

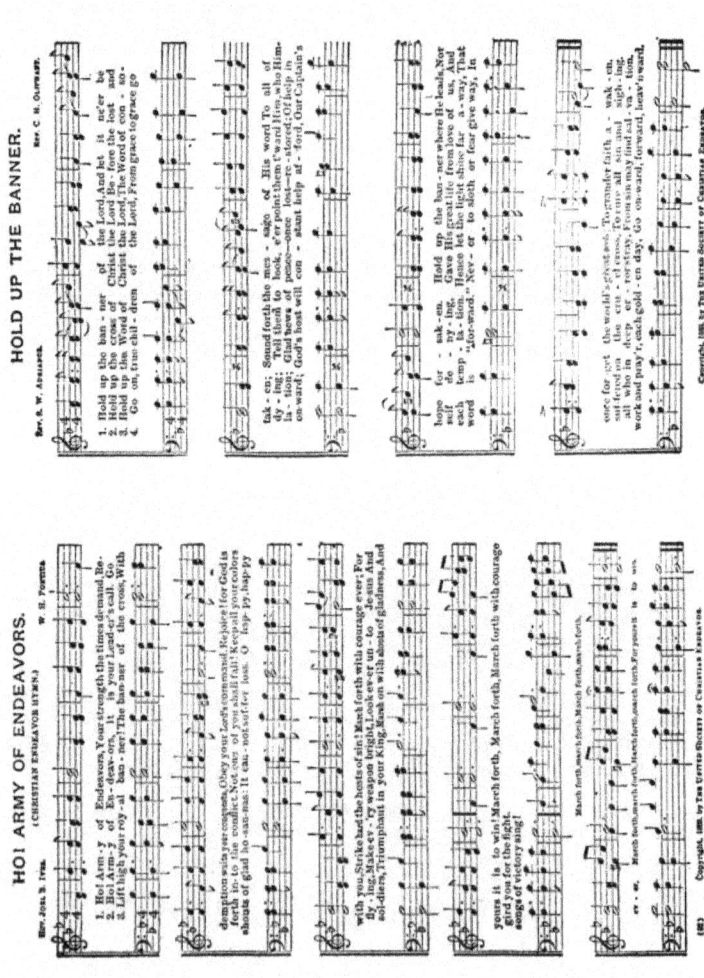

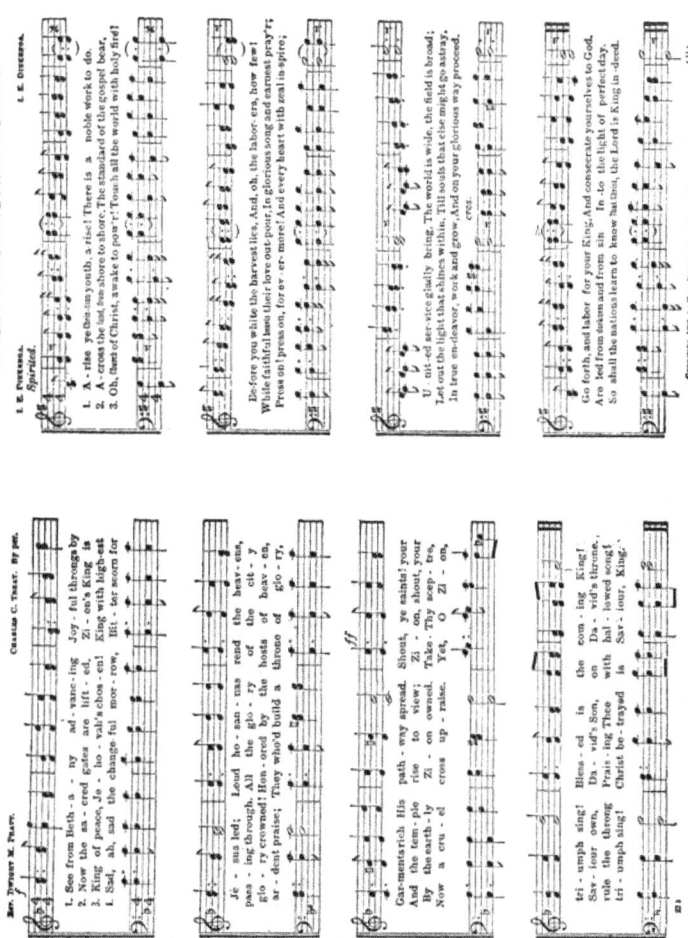

FOR CHRIST.

BY REV. ROBERT F. GORDON.

For Christ is our Endeavor,
  Our hearts to Him belong,
His presence cheers us ever,
  His love inspires our song;
We come in youth's bright morning,
  Obedient to His word,
And seek for our adorning,
  The beauty of the Lord.

In fullness of His blessing
  Good work for Him we do,
His name with joy confessing,
  His standard-bearers true:

And He will never fail us,
  Whatever may betide,
Though danger should assail us,
  In Him we safe abide.

So with youth's ardor glowing,
  We form a Christian band,
The mind of Jesus knowing,
  We for His honor stand;
For He is our Endeavor
  And to Him we belong,
Whose grace shall fail us never,
  Whose love inspires our song.

MISSIONARY HYMN.

BY REV. W. F. ARMS.

The voice of Christ, our Saviour,
  Rings through the Christian world;
Let gospel truth be spoken,
  My banner be unfurled
In every land and nation,
  Where'er man's foot has trod;
Go publish my salvation,
  Proclaim the Christ of God.

Baptized with heavenly wisdom,
  And lips aglow with love,
Speak to the lost and fallen
  The message from above;

Unfold with holy courage
  The grand and glorious truth
That speaks in benediction
  To every Christian youth.

The promise of the Master
  Crowns with its glorious light
Each faithful Christian soldier
  That strikes for God and right.
Go ye and preach the gospel
  In all its wondrous power;
Go, the Redeemer's presence
  Shall crown thine every hour.

Of late years Christian Endeavor poets have multiplied at a surprising rate, and some most admirable hymns have been added not only to the hymnology of the Endeavor Society, but as permanent contributions to the songs of the church in all ages to come, as I believe. But we must devote another chapter in a later part of this volume to these later hymns.

In Australia even more than in America attention has been given to the service of song. Much expression, tenderness, and pathos is put into many of the convention hymns. Some are sung with bowed heads. Sometimes while in the consecration meetings the members are on their knees; while some of the songs are bubbling over with gladness and adoration.

In the matter of congregational singing many of our societies, as well as many of our churches in America, have much to learn, but a live, energetic music committee is doing much in many societies to make the singing devotional, uplifting, and inspiring, and to improve the song service in a multitude of churches.

CHAPTER XXIX.

THE SOCIETY AND THE YOUNG MEN.

Incredible Statements—Young Men and the Endeavor Pledge—Young Men in the First Society—No End of Prigs—The Great Conventions and Young Men—"A Little Chariot for a Pony Team"—The Gap Between the Sunday-School and the Church—No Wheedling, Coaxing Tones—Not for Ice-Cream and Syllabub—"Pie and Cake Affairs"—Outspoken Devotion to Christ.

MORE often in days of yore than at the present time it used to be said that the young men were deserting the churches, that the religion of Christ was losing its hold upon the masculine element.

Scoffers rejoiced at this indication, as it seemed to them, that the old Gospel had had its day, and pessimistic Christians, with doleful faces, wailed and wept over the supposed defection of the young man.

I have even seen statements, wild and incredible always, and doubly so in the light of present facts, that only five per cent. of the young men of our country ever darken the door of a church, that only two per cent. of them are church-members, and that there are more young men in our State prisons than in our churches.

If there was ever a modicum of truth in these statements, I am very confident they are not true to-day, and it is not immodest boasting to assert that the Society of Christian Endeavor has had something to do with the great problem of winning and holding the young men to our churches.

There is something about the seriousness and strenuousness of the Christian Endeavor pledge, something about its high purpose and lofty ideas, which seems to appeal to the strength and vigor of young manhood, and from the beginning this element has been conspicuous in the great majority of societies.

It will be remembered that the first society in Williston Church had within its ranks quite a number of young men and big boys who were just developing into manhood.

The first and second president of the first society were not children by any means, but bearded men—young, to be sure, in years and young in heart, but men who were already fighting life's battles and winning life's bread.

From that day to this the society has attracted an increasing number of these earnest and faithful souls, and it has been a source of pleasure and just pride to the leaders of the movement to be able to point to the splendid specimens of young manhood which in almost every city and county of the United States are looked up to as the local leaders of these youthful hosts.

I remember that on my first visit to England in the interests of the society— a journey to which I shall soon devote a chapter of this history—a distinguished clergyman of the Church of England, who desired to know more about the Christian Endeavor movement, after listening patiently to an explanation of the principles and plans and methods of the society, looked up in my face and said, with a somewhat supercilious rising inflection, which perhaps was simply his English way of expressing dissent from the principles I had been advocating: "I suppose that your society raises up no end of prigs, doesn't it?"

I was glad to be able to say to him, promptly and unreservedly:

"No, sir, it does not develop that species of the human animal. I know something about the young people who are connected with this movement in almost every large city in America. I can call to mind the young men in Boston and Chicago, in New York and San Francisco, in Baltimore and Denver, in New Orleans and Omaha, in Philadelphia, in Portland, Maine, and Portland, Oregon, and I cannot recall among them all a single prig, a single smug and self-conceited 'cad' as you would call him in England. But they are strong, manly, devout, wide-awake young men; young men who will have the money of America in their pockets one of these days, young men who are influential in public affairs in state and church alike, young men whom you would not be ashamed to own as your brothers."

The great conventions are all notable for the conspicuous number of young men who attend. Fully half of the scores of thousands who now come to the annual Christian Endeavor feast from all parts of the country are young men.

The proportion at the local union gatherings possibly is smaller than that, because the young women are naturally in the majority in our churches, and in all such gatherings, but even there there is always a large proportion of men.

Those who have been most active in promoting the interests of the society in all lands have been the young men and the history of the Christian Endeavor movement from the beginning to the present day is one that has been made in good degree by them.

In an admirable paper read by Rev. James L. Hill at the Old Orchard Convention on "The Future of the Society," there is this statement, which in view of the recent interest in Junior work reads more like prophecy than exhortation.

"It has become a matter of common repute," he says, "that in the membership of our churches, women outnumber men in the proportion of two to one.

I see it stated that this is the great proportion in the denomination with which I am most familiar.

"In New England it must be confessed that the women outnumber the men in an even larger proportion. Now my observation and experience make me ready to affirm that the Society of Christian Endeavor can be greatly useful in correcting this abnormal condition.

"For a time church growth stood mocking us afar off. The provision for the wants of young men were altogether too scant. We lacked a little chariot suitable for working a pony team. Being unattached they are running wild, finding their own pasture.

"Much as it is to be deplored, in too many instances boys graduate from the Sunday-school. As a matter of fact they fall down and out between the Sunday-school and the church. That is the hiatus which this organization is designing to bridge.

"Hitherto we have gathered great multitudes of fishes only to lose them again. There has been a wide hole in the net. We should have commended ourselves as wiser fishers of men, if, like the early disciples, we had sooner pulled up to the shore and mended our nets. Since the organization of our society five-sixths of the male members who have joined our church have come from the society's ranks. Now, Mr. President, in the future of our work, we owe it to the churches to get hold of the boys, to introduce them young into our work, to interest them and develop them and Christianize them that they may become pillars in the temple of our God."

More than ever before, I believe, is the exhortation of this closing sentence being heeded to-day, and the Junior society furnishes just that "little chariot" for which Mr. Hill so wittingly pleaded.

Especially in England has the gap of which he speaks between the Sunday-school and the church been felt.

To win and hold the older scholars has been the great problem even more among our English brethren than among ourselves, for in their Sunday-schools, classes of young men and adults of the better classes, so common with us, have been far less common.

With gladness has the Christian Endeavor idea been hailed, because it has been felt that it would furnish the golden connecting link, which had so often been sought in vain. And why should not the Christian Endeavor Society attract the manliest young men? We should be surprised were the history of the past any different from what it has been, for there is something stalwart and uncompromising in the foundation principles upon which Christian Endeavor rests, something that appeals to the best that there is in a young man.

It speaks to him in no wheedling, coaxing tone. It does not plead with him to become a member of an organization for the sake of the trimmings and furbelows, for the sake of the ice-cream and syllabub, but in a flat-footed and unhesitating way it demands his best service for Christ's sake.

It writes to him "because he is strong." It asks that his largest powers, his best intellect, his scholarship, his business ability, his social tact, his power to win life's race, should all be consecrated to his Master's service.

At an early convention in New York State I remember hearing a young man express this thought in homely but forcible phrase:

"Before the formation of the Christian Endeavor Society," said he, "the church thought that the only way to win the young people was by giving them a great feed, but now," he continued, "when we have a pie and cake affair in our church," and his lip curled scornfully as he spoke of the "pie and cake affair," "you can hardly get a hundred of the young people together; but when we have an earnest Christian Endeavor prayer-meeting, as we do have every week, the vestry can scarcely hold them, for we have three times as many present."

This has been characteristic of the movement from the beginning. "Pie and cake," though not dispensed with by any means, have been relegated to the background, while manly confession and outspoken devotion to Christ have come to the front.

Naturally these qualities have won the young men.

CHAPTER XXX.

THE SOCIETY AND THE YOUNG WOMAN.

More Young Women Than Young Men—Prejudice Against Union Meetings—The Young Man of Constantinople and His Ungallant Remark—The Spiritual Tact of Women—Her Work on the Lookout Committee—The Young Woman and the Missionary Committee—Taking Part in Meeting—How a Heroic Young Woman Kept Her Pledge—Miss Sewall's Words to Her Sisters—Some Ladies Who Have Made Endeavor Meetings Memorable—New Chapters in the Acts of the Apostles—Dr. Wayland Hoyt's Memorable Address—How St. Paul Has Been Misinterpreted—The Evil of a Wrong Interpretation of Scriptures—Corinthian Women and American Women—A Typical Prayer-Meeting of Old—The Women Were Present—Do Not Let the Women Lal, Lal, Lal—Teaching and Usurping Authority—What She Actually Does in the Christian Endeavor Prayer-Meeting—Read Again the First Chapter of Acts.

LARGE and conspicuous has been the place occupied by young men in the history of the Christian Endeavor movement, but a still larger place perhaps should be given to the young women.

While the society has done something to rectify the disproportion between the numbers of young men and young women in the churches, the women still far outnumber the men undoubtedly, and perhaps always will.

Naturally, then, they have had a large and eminent place in the annals of Christian Endeavor.

It must be borne in mind that this is a young *people's* society; not a young man's society, not a young woman's society; but one of its glories and beauties is that it has brought both together, and with the utmost propriety they have worked side by side from the beginning for the advancement of this cause.

In the nations of the East and in Continental Europe, and, strange to say, even in some portions of our own country, a prejudice still exists to the union of young men and women in such religious efforts as the Christian Endeavor Society contemplates.

I remember at a Christian Endeavor meeting in Constantinople a representative from a society composed entirely of young men objected to the idea of having young women in the Christian Endeavor work, so thoroughly imbued was this young man with Eastern prejudices that even his Christian training and natural gallantry could not overcome the prepossessions of years.

In trying to reason him out of them I said: "A bird has two wings, and it must use both of them if it would fly; and so the Christian Endeavor Society has two wings, the young men and the young women. A man has two hands, the right and the left, and he must use them both in doing his work in the world."

"Ah!" said this young objector, "that is true, but then the right hand is so much stronger and more skillful than the left that it could do the work alone if necessary."

"Exactly so," I replied, "but I did not tell you which was the right hand and which was the left in the Christian Endeavor movement; and if I should tell the whole truth I should be obliged to confess that usually the young women are the right hand of this movement."

In a multitude of ways the society has developed and brought out the strength of womanhood. In very many cases, especially in the smaller churches and in not a few of the larger ones, a young woman has often been the president of the society when no prejudice in the church prevents her from accepting this office.

More often, still, is she the secretary, while the committees could hardly exist and do their work decently without her gracious presence.

Especially on the committees which have the more spiritual work of the society in their hands, like the Lookout and Prayer-meeting committees, has the young woman, with her greater fund of spiritual force, proved herself to be invaluable.

With tact and wisdom and spiritual insight, she has, in a vast multitude of cases, been able to win to the society those who would not otherwise come near its doors, and to win back to earnest Christian living those who have been inclined to slip away from its influences.

In the work of the Missionary Committee, too, she has had a most large and honorable part, while it is owing to her deft fingers in almost every instance that the Flower Committee has made beautiful the house of God, and has made glad the sick room of ten thousand sufferers.

But it is not only in these more delicate and personal ministrations that the young women have made themselves indispensable to every well-organized Endeavor society.

Her heroism and devotion, her outspoken fidelity has been appealed to as well as her brother's, and with equal courage has she met the test.

I remember very well, in the early days of the society, the case of an exceedingly bashful young lady who took the pledge and who meant to keep it.

She knew that it would be for her spiritual advantage and for her growth in grace to acknowledge her Lord more openly, but she shrank with a peculiar sensitiveness from taking her part in the prayer-meeting.

In those days it was not so common as it is now to hear the sweet voices of the former "silent partners" of the church in prayer and testimony.

This young lady thought she could not repeat even a verse of Scripture without fainting away.

In fact, she actually did faint the first time she essayed to take part in meeting.

But she bravely attempted it again. At first only the seat-mate who was next to her alone could understand what she said; then those in the very limited circle around could hear her; but at last she gained courage, until all in the room could hear her simple, modest, womanly testimony to the love of Christ, and always the meeting was thrilled and blessed by what she said.

I remember another case of a young lady who stammered and hesitated to such an extent that she could not trust herself to repeat the very shortest verse of Scripture, but she could sing, as many stammerers can, and every evening in the course of the meeting she would stand, and, by herself, no one joining with her, would sing a verse of some familiar hymn like

"Jesus, Lover of my soul,"

or,

"Nearer, my God to Thee."

That was her testimony to Christ's love. That was the way she fulfilled her pledge. Who can say that it was not more acceptable in the ears of the redeemed than the most eloquent sermon that was ever preached.

Here is a message that came to the young women from a young woman at the very first convention of which there is any extended report—the one that was held June 7, 1883, in Portland, Me. It was from Miss Ada Sewall, a member of the society where the convention met and one of the earliest workers.

"It is said that women possess," said she, "in a high degree the ability to make themselves agreeable, to inspire enthusiasm and courage in others. If this be true, here is the opportunity for using that gift which God has given them, by creating a clear, bright atmosphere wherever they are, and by doing their work in such a glad, happy spirit that others should feel the contagion, and before they know it shall find themselves also actively engaged.

"Dear young ladies, be enthusiastic. As you go about among your friends speak a word for the Society of Christian Endeavor. Put as much heartiness into what you say as you would in talking about your art society, your literary work, or a very delightful excursion you have planned for next summer."

Most appropriately she goes on to say, "We have in our ranks teachers who are accustomed to stand every day before thirty to sixty or more boys and girls, not to speak of the committee-men and visitors, and talk to them on almost every subject from the hyssop that springeth out of the wall to the great bodies that circle about us in space. They give to their scholars not only what they have taken from the storehouse of other minds, but thoughts which God has given them for their own.

MISS FRANCES E. WILLARD.

"Stand beside one of these teachers in her class-room as she gives an object lesson or leads her scholars along higher paths. There is no fear, no hesitancy, no stammering. The words come easily and carry conviction, because they are given with heartiness. Follow them into their Sabbath-school classes, or into the Bible-class, if they are scholars, and then into the sociables, and they are the same as in the class-rooms. But let the four walls of our little vestries close them in and they become dumb. Why is it? Is it because God, who gives to all liberally, has withheld from them all thoughts of Himself? Is it fear that has fallen upon them? Is the little company which has come together with the earnest desire to help and be helped more formidable than the class-room full of scholars provided with the full armor of criticism?

MRS. ALDEN ("PANSY").

"But there are many girls and young ladies who are not teachers, not accustomed to express themselves before a number, and who feel they dare not make an attempt for fear they should fail. To such I should say, try and put yourself out of your own sight. Think of Him who shrank from no suffering, if perchance He might save some. Your word, poor and unworthy as it may seem to you, may be just the word that some one else needs."

I have made this long quotation because it will show in the future years more clearly perhaps than anything I could myself write the obstacles and difficulties which in the early days the young ladies found in the simple service of the prayer-meeting.

It shows also the arguments used by the sanctified common sense of these sisters which have overcome their difficulties, and caused them to become among the foremost in work of the society, yet without brushing the bloom from their maidenly modesty.

At many conventions since have women spoken wisely and inspiringly.

Pansy, the charming writer for young men and women, whose stories have done more perhaps than any other one instrumentality to introduce the Endeavor Society to the notice of England, has read some of her charm-

MRS. ALICE MAY SCUDDER.

ing tales to the conventions.

Mrs. Alice May Scudder has been in great demand from the Atlantic Coast to the Pacific on all sorts of Christian Endeavor occasions, and has given her heart and voice to the upbuilding of the Junior cause, while her book for the Juniors, *Attractive Truths in Lesson and Story*, has been a most helpful manual for a multitude of Junior workers. Miss Kate H. Haus, of St. Louis, with a voice that can reach to the furthest end of the largest hall, has also spoken and written most instructively concerning Junior work.

But when we begin on this goodly list of women who have prominently aided the Christian Endeavor cause, where shall we stop?

MISS KATE H. HAUS.

To use the apostle's pardonable exaggeration, the world itself would scarcely contain the books that might be written

15

on this theme, and surely the limits of this volume will compel us to close this *written* chapter, though ten thousand young women, and ten times ten thousand of them all over the country are constantly writing quietly, unostentatiously, but none the less eloquently, in church and home and village and city, adding new chapters to this new acts of the apostles.

"Giving Holy Speech to Women," such is one of the sub-titles of an admirable address on "The New Prayer-Meeting," by Dr. Wayland Hoyt, at the Eighth National Convention, which was held at Philadelphia, and which is yet to be described in this volume.

But I know of no better connection in which to treat of this important subject, which has been so much misunderstood, and the misapprehension concerning which has doubtless hindered the growth of Christian Endeavor in some sections of the country very seriously.

The palladium of the opponents of the Society of Christian Endeavor, the last refuge into which they have often retreated, has been the thirty-fourth verse of the fourteenth chapter of first Corinthians: "Let your women keep silence in the churches: for it is not permitted unto them to speak; but they are commanded to be under obedience, as also saith the law. And if they will learn anything, let them ask their husbands at home: for it is a shame for women to speak in the church."

How often has this verse been thrown triumphantly at the Christian Endeavor Society!

How often, in certain sections, has the question-box been crowded to bursting with queries written, evidently by no friendly hand, and based upon this prohibition of Paul? But the obvious and sufficient and incontrovertible answer to this objection is, first, that Paul has been grossly misinterpreted, and, second, that the Christian Endeavor Society asks nothing but what a strict interpretation of Paul's words warrants.

It is a flippant begging of the question, and one which hurts the cause which it is meant to promote, to say, as has sometimes been said, that Paul was not inspired when he wrote this passage, as he confesses that he was not on another occasion, or to say that this is the grumpy utterance of a woman-hating bachelor.

If this is the teaching of Scripture, that women are to take no part in the weekly prayer-meetings, Christian Endeavorers will abide by it, though it might destroy their society and all its work.

But a little study of the context and of Oriental conditions will prove to any one that this was not Paul's design.

He did not have the modern prayer-meeting in mind, because there was no such thing in the Corinthian Church, to which he wrote; but there were noisy, turbulent, half-civilized women, who chattered and brawled even during the conduct of public worship.

Such women are found in Oriental churches to-day, as many a missionary testifies, and such a prohibition as Paul gives is in full force now as it was in the days of the Corinthian Church.

Any sensible preacher and leader under like circumstances would give a like command.

But what have the modest, quiet, thinking women of to-day, who, for the love of Christ, repeat a verse of Scripture, or read a hymn, or offer a sentence of prayer in a quiet prayer-meeting, to do with the noisy women of Corinth?

In the address alluded to on "the new prayer-meeting," Dr. Hoyt puts the matter so pithily and wisely that I must quote a few paragraphs from his brilliant paper.

Speaking of that early prayer-meeting recorded in the second chapter of Acts, he says: "That old, typical, New Testament prayer-meeting was a prayer-meeting which gave holy speech to woman.

"Look there! What is that? That shining, that strong, celestial wavering, gleaming tongue of flame? Behold it! It is on the head of Peter! Yes, it is on the head of James! Yes, it is on the head of Matthew! Yes, it is on the head of the son of Alpheus! Yes, it is on the head of Mary! Yes, it is on the head of Salome! Yes, it is on the head of Mary Magdalene! Yes! yes!

"In all that company there is not a single head unmitered with the celestial flame, as much on women's heads as on the heads of men. Unmitered in the prayer-meeting, women prayed for the gift, or they would not have received the gift; and when the gift came, it came to woman just as much as to man, for the shining, wavering flame was on the heads of all of them.

"Paul says: 'Let the women keep silence in the churches.' Yes: Paul does say that, and if I believed that Paul meant what is understood by many as the common interpretation of his meaning, I would submit to the apostle; I would not say that the world has outgrown the apostle. I believe in implicit and accurate and abundant submission to inspired authority; but because I am sure that the usual interpretation of that Scripture has been a huge misconception and blunder, I declare that the new prayer-meeting of Christian Endeavor is in close accord with the old typical prayer-meeting of the New Testament, because it gives to women holy speech; for do you know what the meaning of the words 'keep silence' is?

"Paul says, 'Do not let the women Lall, lall, lall.' Don't you see what he means? That is the Greek word *lalein*, which means to chatter, make a disturbance and a contention.

"Paul says 'Never let women do that.' The men had better take that to themselves as well. But Paul does distinctly say, ' When a woman prayeth or prophesieth, let her do it with her head covered.' That is, according to the custom of the times, ' in decent fashion.'

"Why, a woman may pray in the church. Why, prophesying is simply forthsaying your faith in Jesus and your love for Him and exhorting others to come to Him; and Paul distinctly allows that women find tongue for praying and for prophesying in the meetings of the church.

"Therefore, I declare that the new prayer-meeting of Christian Endeavor is in exact accord with the old typical prayer-meeting of the New Testament, because it does give to women and insists on giving to women, and God grant it may forever and continually insist on giving to women, holy speech. These miserable padlocks on the gracious lips of women ought to be unlocked and broken off and flung away forever."

But once more, it can be said, however Paul is interpreted or misinterpreted, that the participation of women in the Christian Endeavor prayer-meeting is a thing as much apart from his directions to the women of Corinth as the work of the mother in the home or the teacher in the school.

She does not *teach* in the prayer-meetings. She does not usurp authority over the man, but she simply repeats a verse of Scripture, a message which the Father has given her, a quotation from some sacred author, or in some way acknowledges her Lord.

She does not make a speech or deliver a sermon, but simply acknowledges the love of Him who died for her.

If, as in some churches, the pastor and church are not willing that she should offer her own sentiments in her own words, her pledge is fulfilled by repeating a verse of Scripture alone. This limitation does not in any way make a Christian Endeavor society impossible or destroy the spirit of the organization.

It is very strange, however, that any church which allows its women, young or old, to teach in the Sunday-school, should object to their modestly saying a sentence or two, which God has given them to say, in the prayer-meeting.

If Paul's prohibition refers to any feature of modern church life, it would seem to refer to the Sunday-school more than to the prayer-meeting, for in I Timothy 2 : 12, the only other passage which is quoted besides the one in Corinthians, we read " I suffer not a woman to *teach*." However, we believe that the whole spirit of the Gospel, Paul's spirit as well as the spirit of Christ, is in favor of just such quiet, modest, womanly participation as the Christian Endeavor Society cultivates.

Read over carefully and prayerfully the first chapter of Acts. Dwell upon that first prayer-meeting that was held after the resurrection; for we read concerning it, "These all continued with one accord with prayer and supplication *with the women*, and Mary, the mother of Jesus, and with His brethren."

Here we have our Scripture warrant for the modern prayer-meeting. On this most solemn and critical occasion in the life of the Christian Church they came together in prayer and supplication *with the women*.

It is a model for us to consider, not only because the presence of the women is distinctly indicated, but for many another lesson that we can draw from this passage.

With an eloquent quotation from the same address of Dr. Hoyt's, which I have already quoted, let me close this chapter: "Peter was not absent because it happened to be a little hot, and James was not away because it happened to be a little cool, and Bartholomew was not away because it happened to be a little wet, and Matthew was not away because his toga was a little worn, and Mary was not away because her veil had gotten to be a little out of style, and Salome did not refuse to fill her place because just then there happened to be a party in Jerusalem, and James the Less was not away because he thought Peter was taking too much on himself and was just a little officious; not for any reasons like these, or for any other reasons imaginable, was any one away. They were 'all with one accord in one place.' O, the enthusiasm of numbers! O, the holy contagion of religious elbow-touch! O, the power of presence; and this typical prayer-meeting had all these!"

MISS ELIZABETH M. WISHARD (INDIANA).

CHAPTER XXXI.

THE FIRST CAMPAIGN IN ENGLAND.

Slight Variations in Color and Odor—The Similarity of Christian Endeavor—The First Invitation from Across the Seas—" An American Fad "—" English Stolidity and American Precocity "—Some Pioneers in England—Christian Endeavor and Lawn Tennis—A Missionary's Testimony—A Meeting in the City Temple—Some Startling Figures from a Member of Parliament—How They Can Be Explained—The Meeting of the Boundary Lane Society—An Excruciating Pause—In Manchester—A Meeting in Acton—An Invitation from Mr. Spurgeon—What Amused the Students—The Sunday-school Union and Its Efficient Aid—The Earliest Champion of Christian Endeavor in England—Sympathetic English Audiences—A Brief Visit to Paris—Dr. McAll and Mr. Greig.

IT is not to be wondered at that a society that was making such rapid strides in the United States should attract attention in the mother country as well.

More and more is the Christian world coming close together. A successful plan inaugurated in one country is sure to be tried in another; tried sufficiently, at least, to see whether the root idea when transplanted to a foreign soil will bear the same fruit and flowers as in the home land.

Christian Endeavor has always stood the test of transplanting marvelously well. It has constantly surprised its friends by showing its adaptability to all circumstances and to every clime. Slight variations in the color and odor of the flower and in the flavor of the fruit perhaps there may be, but they are scarcely noticeable; and I have often remarked that if I were carried through the air with my eyes shut, and dropped down in the centre of a Christian Endeavor audience, I should scarcely know whether I was in New York or London, Melbourne or Philadelphia, Glasgow or San Francisco.

The same earnest light is in the eyes of young people in all parts of the world, the same eager questions are on their lips, the same intense desire to work for Christ and the church; and the little variations in methods or nomenclature only prove the adaptability of the seed to any soil.

In the spring of 1888 a cordial invitation was received by me from the officers of the British Sunday-school Union to go to London to address the annual May meeting of Sunday-school workers at the rooms of the Sunday-school Union, No. 56 Old Bailey.

Accordingly, on the 21st of April, 1888, I sailed from Boston in the "Cephalonia," and, after a pleasant passage of some ten days, reached Liverpool just in season to take the night train for London, where, the next morning, I addressed the Sunday-school workers and the ministers at one of the regular sessions of the Sunday-school Union anniversary.

I did not have time, I remember, to meet in advance the kind friends who had invited me to England, and I did not know their faces or they mine. Mr. Chas. Waters was in the audience, as was also Mr. Edward Towers, Mr. John E. Tresidder and others, all of whom were loved and honored by every Sunday-school worker in England, and all of whom at once became interested in the movement of which I had come to speak.

SUNDAY-SCHOOL UNION BUILDING, 56 OLD BAILEY, LONDON.

I remember that my good friend, Mr. Waters, who afterward became the first Honorary Secretary of the British section of the Christian Endeavor Society, made the way easier for me on that first evening by some personal explanations concerning the society from the English standpoint.

But, in spite of his kind offices and the sympathy of others, it was not the most enthusiastic of audiences to which I had the pleasure of speaking.

It was regarded evidently by the majority as an American fad, a fad which might do well enough for that pushing, young, and somewhat bumptious land across the sea, but which could scarcely be expected to find a welcome in more staid and conservative England.

CHARLES WATERS.

One good brother, I remember, remarked that he had heard much about the ways of young America, and was not altogether favorably impressed by what he had heard and read. "For his part, if he must choose, he preferred English solidity to American precocity;" and this seemed to be the opinion of quite a number in the audience.

However, my reception, personally, was most kind and cordial. Some were evidently expecting to see a rather bold and blustering fellow who had come over to England to cram down his notions, whether or not they were wanted; and when they found that my only desire was to make a modest plea for Christian nurture and to suggest the possibility of the usefulness of this new society, which had evidently been used so much of God in the daughter land, I could never ask for a kinder welcome.

REV. A. W. POTTS.

A day or two afterward I was asked to attend a meeting of the "Guilds' Council" of the Congregational churches of England and Wales, in Memorial Hall, the executive body of the young people's movement which was then making considerable headway among the Congregational churches of Great Britain.

At this meeting were several very earnest advocates of Christian Endeavor, but they were not in the majority. One of them was Rev. A. W. Potts, of Crewe, who already had a flourishing society, and who knew whereof he affirmed, and who stood up most valiantly for Christian Endeavor principles. Another was Mr. Benjamin Clark, the editor of *The Sunday-School Chronicle* and the beloved superintendent of the Home for Little Boys at Swansea.

His advocacy of the Endeavor movement in *The Sunday-School Chronicle* during the early days in England was most efficacious and encouraging.

But there were others in the meeting who seemed as utterly opposed to Christian Endeavor as these brethren were earnest in its favor.

I remember one brother minister, in particular, who heaped a good deal of ridicule upon the pledge and the strict prayer-meeting idea, saying that he did not think that it was always the duty of the young people to go to the prayer-meeting; that, if a lawn tennis party came at the same time as the prayer-meeting, it might be quite as much their duty to go to that as to the prayer-meeting, and he did not wish to have his young people bound by any hard and fast rules.

This gave the Endeavor advocates the opportunity that they wanted, and they poured in their hot shot and shell upon this palpably untenable position until its advocate was obliged to desert it.

"The trouble with too many of our English churches," said one of these advocates of Christian Endeavor, "is that they are too much lawn tennis and too little prayer-meeting; and the pernicious doctrine that one thing is as important as another, and that there is nothing peculiarly sacred or binding about the religious life, is eating into many of our churches like the dry rot."

To the defense of the Christian Endeavor idea also valiantly sprang forward an honored American missionary, Dr. Tracey, of Marsovan, Turkey, who happened to be in England, and was present at this meeting of which I am speaking; and his advocacy of the high religious ideal of the society and his knowledge of its working in America did much to turn the tide of sympathy before the meeting was over in favor of the strictly religious element embodied in the Endeavor movement.

Even my lawn tennis friend shook hands with me after the meeting, and implied that he thought the Endeavor idea was at least worth trying.

On May 11th I was invited to address a public meeting designed for young people in the City Temple, the famous church to which Dr. Joseph Parker has ministered so long.

Dr. J. McFadyen, whose death in the midst of his usefulness a few years later was so much mourned; Rev. J. R. Bailey, of Halifax, and Rev. Joseph Parker, D. D., were the other speakers. It was an interesting and helpful meeting, but did not have very much of a Christian Endeavor flavor to it, naturally, except that which I tried to impart.

In this respect I noticed a vast contrast to another meeting held in the same place a few years later, when the great audience-room was crowded with London Endeavorers who were ready to applaud with true English sympathy and heartiness every allusion to the principles and the success of the Endeavor idea.

I recollect well, too, the annual public meeting of the Sunday-school Union which was held in Exeter Hall on the 3d of May, to which I was invited. The Earl of Aberdeen was the chairman of the meeting, Canon Fleming and Dr. McFadyen made addresses, and I was asked to say a few words about the society.

I remember at this meeting, too, the address of a member of parliament who was in sympathy with Christian work, but who made the astounding statement, that everywhere else in the world except in England crime was increasing at a fearful rate. Especially did he marshal his figures to prove that in poor America all kinds of iniquity were on the increase, and the devil was getting the upper hands of every good cause.

Startling as were these statements, his explanation was still more marvelous, "for," said he, "it can all be explained by the fact that in America the Sunday-school is the luxury of the rich, while in England it is the necessity of the poor."

I could not help asking him, as I sat by his side on the platform when the meeting was over, if he did not think it possible that the vast emigration of millions of the lowest classes from Ireland and central Europe, as well as from the slums of London, did not have something to do with the increase of crime in America, even supposing that his facts and figures were all correct; and if he supposed that any country could stand it long to be the dumping-ground and the moral sewer into which all Europe should pour its vileness without showing an increase of crime and wretchedness?

However, my questions seemed to have but little effect, and I have no doubt that until this day he considers his explanation of the increase of crime in America as amply sufficient.

However, I must again repeat, that though I met with some such personages, my reception by the kind friends who invited me to England, and by others of whom I had not heard until my arrival, was exceedingly kind and cordial, and I shall always have the warmest place in my heart for some of these pioneer Endeavorers of the Mother Land.

This visit to England was a very short one, only about six weeks from shore to shore, and yet, as it was the first systematic attempt to plant the Endeavor idea in another soil, it deserves a little more extended notice.

I find in a scrap-book of this journey, that on May 9th I attended a social reunion of the Boundary Lane Society of Christian Endeavor, in London, and my memory of this meeting reminds me that though there were at this time a very few societies that were called by the name Christian Endeavor, yet the Endeavor idea had scarcely taken hold of all the organizations which had called themselves by this title.

To be sure, the society in Crewe was a vigorous, active, genuine Endeavor Society, and, doubtless, there were one or two others by this time which could be described in the same way. But there were still others to which the idea of service for all and by all, was still comparatively strange.

At this meeting of the Boundary Lane Society, the vigorous and earnest president said to the members, as they were assembled together before the inevitable "tea," "Now we will have a genuine Christian Endeavor prayer-meeting, and show our friend from America how we do it."

He made an admirable address of ten minutes, a young student from Mr. Spurgeon's college made another ten minutes' talk, the visitor from America was asked to occupy the time, which he did to about the same number of minutes, and then the meeting was thrown open to all.

But though the meeting was open, the mouths of the members were not. There was an excruciating and dreadful pause. The leader urged and urged in vain. No one would break the silence.

THE FIRST CAMPAIGN IN ENGLAND. 235

At last, in despair, he cried out: "Will not some one at least give out a hymn!" whereupon a trembling damsel arose and with evident trepidation said: "Let us sing number 75," and that, as I remember it, was the extent of the participation of the rank and file in that meeting.

But we all participated in the tea and in the delightful social hour which followed.

On this same visit, I heard of another society which called itself "Christian Endeavor," whose pastor told me that really they were so busy that they could not find time for the prayer-meeting, and he regretted that they had been obliged to give up that feature; but they had a tennis club and a foot-ball club, and a swimming school, and a sewing class, and a wood-turning class, and really they thought their Christian Endeavor Society was a very admirable thing.

I speak of these mis-named societies simply to call attention to the fact of the marvelous change and advance which has been made by the Christian Endeavor movement in England since those early years.

The Boundary Lane Society, if it exists, as I have no doubt it does, is now undoubtedly a model.

No foot-ball, tennis, swimming-club aggregation would now be called a Christian Endeavor Society in Great Britain.

The same loose ideas as to what a Christian Endeavor Society should be existed in America in the early days, ideas which, owing to the spread of our literature, it is now impossible should prevail in any part of the world.

On this visit to England I find also that I addressed the Ministers and Deacons' Association, of Manchester and Salford, in the school-room on Aytoun Street, Manchester, and also a special meeting for young people and others, in the Congregational Church, of Acton, near London.

Rev. W. F. Adeny, a well-known scholar, who prepared the revised helps for the latest edition of Bagster's Bible, was the pastor of the church.

I remember that evening with peculiar pleasure, and the kind attention I received.

I also received a note from Mr. J. W. Harrold, Rev. C. A. Spurgeon's private secretary, asking me to speak to the students at the college of the Metropolitan Tabernacle the next Friday afternoon at 4 o'clock.

With much interest I kept this appointment, and enjoyed speaking to the four or five score of earnest students, who weekly hung upon the lips of the great preacher as he opened to them his treasures, new and old.

Evidently very few of them had heard of the Endeavor Society, and when I began to speak of the different lines of committee work which the young people might undertake, and mentioned the Lookout, the Prayer Meeting and Social Committees, a visible smile overspread many faces.

They evidently were constantly expecting something good from the lips of their beloved instructor, some humorous anecdote, some facetious turn of thought, and they supposed that their visitor from America was indulging in the same exercise, and lighting up his address with a huge American joke.

As I spoke of the Missionary Committee, and the Sunday-school Committee, and the Flower Committee, the smile deepened into a grin; and when I went on to say that there might also be a Good Literature Committee, a White Cross Committee, and half a dozen others, the grin found expression in an unmistakable guffaw.

In fact, it was quite impossible to make the class understand that I was never more serious in my life, and that all such work was actually undertaken and well performed by societies in America.

Perhaps they shared Mr. Spurgeon's antipathy to committees, which I fully appreciate and sympathize with, if the ordinary do-nothing committee is referred to; but in many a church the Endeavor Society has put a new thought, a new seriousness and sense of individuality into the idea of committee work.

Mr. Spurgeon himself was present at this address, and afterward spoke to the students for a half hour with his usual simplicity and terseness of diction, and out of the deep wells of his experience and spiritual powers drew marvelously refreshing draughts for us all.

It will always be a pleasure for me to remember his kindly words and warmly expressed interest in the movement, both at this time and on other occasions when I saw him, and among my treasures I prize a kind autograph note which I received from him, acknowledging a little book which bore at least indirectly on the subjects discussed that day in the Tabernacle College.

THE FIRST CAMPAIGN IN ENGLAND. 237

Another important meeting held during this visit to England was also under the auspices of the Sunday-school Union, and held in their audience room at 56 Old Bailey, on the 17th of May.

The circular calling this meeting said to the superintendents and teachers of London Sunday-schools: "You are no doubt longing and praying for larger success in your work, and ready to welcome any means which will be likely to aid you and to conduce to this result. We therefore invite you to the conference with the full expectation that you will gain full and practical information."

HIGH TOWN CHURCH, CREWE, ENGLAND.

This meeting, if my memory serves me rightly, was even a more helpful one to the Endeavor cause than the first one in the same room; and not a few of the early Endeavor societies in England can be traced to the interest awakened by this helpful conference. I enjoyed, also, a pleasant visit to Crewe, the home of the original English Society of Christian Endeavor, and a cordial welcome from Rev. A. W. Potts and his wife. Mr. Potts was the earliest advocate and champion of the cause in Great Britain. His early death was a real blow to the movement.

Both in this meeting and in many others held during this visit to England,
16

I learned something of the splendid responsiveness of English audiences, a responsiveness which uplifts the speaker, and calls out the best there is in him.

The generous applause, the familiar "Hear, hear," even when it is clipped to the form almost unpronounceable by an American, "'Ear, 'ear," always helps a speaker to do his best.

Several succeeding visits have confirmed the impression I then received, that there are no such delightful audiences in the world to speak to as English audiences—none so generous, responsive, and appreciative.

DR. McALL.

I wish that American audiences, which are about the worst in the world in this respect—especially the staid, unresponsive, New England audiences, which do not at all tell of the genuine cordiality of individual New Englanders—could take a lesson from their friends across the sea.

After these meetings the work which I had laid out in England was largely done, but, having a few days at my disposal before my steamer sailed for home, I took a brief run to Paris to see the honored Dr. McAll, who had invited me to come to Paris to tell him something about the Endeavor movement.

I found this noble evangelist in feeble health, as he was for many years before his death, and overloaded with the cares of the great mission work in which he was engaged, but ready to listen to these new plans of Christian nurture in which he evidently saw something of help for the Protestant cause in France.

After taking dinner with Dr. McAll, I visited his devoted associate, Mr. Greig, who is now at the head of the McAll Mission. He was holding a meeting for the children in the Salle Philadelphia. After talking for a few moments to the children, with Mr. Greig for interpreter, I told him, at his request, something of the plans and methods of the Christian Endeavor Society.

At once he exclaimed: "How Providential! I have been thinking this very morning that we must have some better plans for winning and holding the young men and women whom we reach in our mission work. I have been praying earnestly over the subject, and asking God to open some door through which we might enter, and now you have come in answer to this prayer to tell me exactly the methods and exactly the society that we need."

Those who are familiar with the history of the Endeavor movement of late years need not be told that from that day to this Dr. Greig has been an earnest and consistent friend of the cause.

The society has been adopted not only in connection with the stations of the McAll Mission, but now by the general synod of the Protestant churches of France, and in the gay metropolis of the world there are something like a dozen earnest, devoted, and faithful groups of Christian Endeavorers.

On the 26th of May I sailed for home in the "Umbria," and after, for those days, a record-breaking passage, reached home on the first day of June, feeling hopeful that God had some work for the Endeavor Society to do in Old England as well as in New.

CHAPTER XXXII.

THE FIRST GREAT CONVENTION.

In Battery D—Forebodings and Headshakings—Westward the Star of Christian Endeavor—Some Magnificent Addresses—Pansy's Story—Encircling the Globe—New York in the Lead—Three Hundred and Ten Thousand Members—Reports from Different Sections—Our Emigrant Population—Five Million Boys Wanted—Systematic Bible Study—"Not to be Ministered Unto, But to Minister."

ABOUT a month after the events narrated in the last chapter the first convention, which, in the modern sense of the word, can be called a "great convention," was held in Battery D of the Armory at Chicago, Ill.

At the Convention of the previous year in Saratoga the following invitation was received: "Whereas, we have learned through the benefits derived from the meetings of this present convention of the vast benefits to be derived from union gatherings of societies of Christian Endeavor, whether State or national, Resolved, that we, members of this Illinois State Christian Endeavor Union, extend our heartiest greetings to the National Convention in session at Saratoga July 5 to 7; that we pray God's presence may be with them, and that they may be blessed in their work. Resolved, that we heartily extend an invitation to the executive committee to hold the next national convention of the societies of Christian Endeavor in Chicago, at the Union Park Church; that we feel that the cause of Christian Endeavor will thus receive a needed impetus in the West, and that the cause of Christ will be greatly advanced."

There were a good many forebodings and headshakings over this invitation when it was accepted, for it was felt by Mr. Faintheart and Mr. Littlehope that it was a great experiment to think of going so far west with an international convention.

New England still had far more societies than any other part of the country, if not more than all the rest of the country put together.

Certainly, with New York added, this was true, and this resolution, when accepted, committed the society to a convention a thousand miles from the centre of Christian Endeavordom.

However, it was felt by the committee that westward the star of Christian

BATTERY D, CHICAGO, ILL.

Endeavor, as well as of empire, must take its way, and so preparations were made for the seventh annual convention at Chicago.

REV. JOHN H. BARROWS, D. D.

Still Mr. Faintheart and Mr. Littlehope shook their heads, and all the rest of us feared, even though we did not express the fear, that this convention might be a failure.

However, when the time came for the meeting, faith and hope prevailed to the extent of engaging Battery D for the convention, for it was plainly seen that the Union Park Church, ample though it is, and generously as it was offered, could not contain those who would come together.

Before the day for the meeting actually came the hopes of all of us had revived, but none were prepared for the splendid attendance or the enthusiasm of that magnificent meeting, which will ever be memorable in the annals of Christian Endeavor.

To be sure, there were only about five thousand in attendance, a number which seems insignificant compared with the conventions of the present day; but for 1888 five thousand was quite as large a number as fifty thousand for 1895.

At this convention the "Royal Legion," a company of young men, Endeavorers from Boston and vicinity, made their first appearance. Attracted to each other on the excursion train to Chicago by mutual affinities, they proved most helpful as ushers and in many other ways throughout the convention. So congenial were these kindred spirits, that they have since kept up and enlarged their organ-

BISHOP FALLOWS.

ization. They are always represented at the National Conventions and enjoy an annual banquet together in Boston.

The rather barn-like structure where the meeting was held was prettily decorated with flags and streamers; the weather, except on one day which was insufferably hot, was all that could be desired, and the convention from beginning to end was an undoubted success. Among the notable addresses of this convention was one by Rev. John H. Barrows, D. D., pastor of the First Presbyterian Church of Chicago, who thrilled every one with his address, entitled "America for Christ."

Dr. Barrows' voice has often been heard since on important Endeavor occasions, and, as one of the Trustees of the United Society, and in many other ways, he has thrown his great influence always into the scale that makes for Christian Endeavor.

Bishop Samuel Fallows also appeared at this convention for the first time, urging the importance of the society as an element in Christian unity. He, too, for a number of years, has been one of the honored trustees of the United Society.

Rev. Arthur Mitchell, D. D., Secretary of the Presbyterian Board of Foreign Missions, also made an address, and Prof. W. R. Harper, then of Yale College, now the President of Chicago University, addressed the convention on "A Systematic Study of the Bible." President Harper, too, has always been known since that day as a warm friend of the Endeavor movement, and is a trustee of the United Society.

PRESIDENT HARPER.

Miss Frances E. Willard, the peerless orator among American women, made her first appearance on a Christian Endeavor platform, but by no means her last, at this convention.

Rev. Arthur Little, D. D., Rev. Nehemiah Boynton, Rev. E. Blakeslee, Miss Hattie Brown, of Decatur, Ill.; Rev. J. B. Wilson, of Muskegon; Mr. B. F. Jacobs, famous in Sunday-school work; Rev. A. E. Winship, of the *Journal of Education*; Rev. James L. Hill, Rev. C. A. Dickinson, and Rev. R. W. Brokaw made memorable addresses.

Another interesting feature of this convention was a story by "Pansy" (Mrs. G. R. Alden), entitled "Chrissy's Endeavor," a story which has since become famous in the annals of Endeavor literature, and which has had a very large influence, especially in England, in extending and commending the cause.

The report of General Secretary Ward was an encouraging and inspiring document, and told of more than a score of thousand of the associate members who had during the past year joined the churches of Christ. "In territory," he says, "the society has encircled the globe; every State and Territory long since yielded to its sway. Canada, Nova Scotia, Prince Edward Island, New Brunswick, Newfoundland, England, Scotland, Syria, India, Burma, Ceylon, South Africa, and China were lately added to our provinces.

"It has been a question of great interest each year, Where is the centre of the movement?

"In our answer to-night to this question we find that a strange thing has happened. The first year the centre remained in Portland. The next two or three years it swerved around from place to place in New England. Last year we found it had gone out to Buffalo, but this year, wonder of wonders, the centre is back again in Portland or Boston. Nor is this a retrograde step. No; it is the greatest stride of all, for in the past year our cause has gone completely around the globe, and we may select our own centre; and what so appropriate as the starting place, or the home office?

"In our own country the central point has moved still further westward, and to be anywhere near it we had to come out here to Chicago, where the centre has located itself.

"As regards growth by States, New York leads, with over nine hundred societies, followed by Massachusetts, with nearly six hundred societies.

"As the domain has increased, the recruits have come pouring in, and to-day the loud battle-cry 'For Christ and the Church' is raised from the throats of 310,000 loyal members of Christian Endeavor."

At this convention, too, reports were received from different sections of the country. Rev. S. W. Adriance reported from New England that there were 1,217 societies in the six New England States.

"We in New England are supposed to be cold-blooded and slow," he remarked, "but I want you to understand that we have trains called the 'Flying Yankee,' and both in business and religious work there is tremendous earnestness."

Rev. H. P. Grose, then a pastor in Pittsburg, Pa., reported for the Middle Interior States, and told us there were 1,899 reported societies in six of the Middle States, with a membership of 120,000, and he pointed with pride, as well he might, to the change in two years in New York State from 64 societies to 947, and from 2,400 members to over 60,000.

Pennsylvania then had but 249 societies, but she was destined to pass before many years her big sister, on her eastern border.

Ohio reported 245 and New Jersey 178 societies. Rev. E. N. Noyes, of Duluth, reported from the Northwest a constant and remarkable gain—195 societies in Iowa, 150 in Wisconsin, 100 in Minnesota, and so on—and he explained the difficulty of reporting for a territory so magnificent in distances and so rapid in Christian Endeavor growth by telling the story of an old farmer who was interrogated concerning his son's politics, which were of a somewhat variable nature.

The old man was asked one afternoon which way John was going to vote—with the Democrats, with the Republicans, or with the Greenbackers. "Well," said the old man, as he wiped his brow, "I don't know, I haven't seen him since breakfast."

REV. E. N. NOYES.

REV. J. B. THRALL.

And so Mr. Noyes had not heard of the Christian Endeavor returns from the Northwest since breakfast.

Mrs. Selden brought an encouraging report from Florida; Mrs. Perkins, of Missouri, from the South; Mr. Hedges, of California, concerning the advancement of the work there, and Rev. J. B. Thrall, afterward the beloved President of the Utah Union, then of Salt Lake City, but now of Albany, reported concerning the progress of Christian Endeavor in Utah.

M. A. HUDSON.

This convention was noted for the large number of brief addresses from young laymen, as well as from young ministers, many of whom had not previously been heard at Endeavor conventions. One of these was

Mr. M. A. Hudson, afterward the Secretary of the New York State Union, and one who did splendid work in the early days for the advancement of the cause.

Another was Mr. J. W. Howell, of Chicago, also prominent thereafter in Endeavor work. Another was Rev. J. L. Sewall, at one time in after years connected with *The Golden Rule*, and always a devoted Christian Endeavorer.

Rev. H. A. Scauffler also made an address on the "Work Among Our Emigrant Population," which will long be remembered; and the first recognition of

"THE ROYAL LEGION" AT CHICAGO

Junior societies in a convention was in an address by Rev. W. H. McMillen, of Oberlin, on this subject, in which he declared that there was a demand from the saloons for five million boys, and that the Junior society must make their claim for these five million boys before the saloons captured them.

The resolutions of this convention advised that the society hold to its own lines of effort; that it should not be made auxiliary to any other; that uniform topics be adopted for the prayer-meetings so far as the societies are willing; that a society badge be provided and be commended universally to our members.

Systematic Bible study was commended and urged, and also the observance of Christian Endeavor Day, the first observance of which in the early part of this year had brought in $8,000 into the empty treasury.

It may be remarked here, however, that this was the last time that the offerings of Christian Endeavor Day have been asked for the society.

After this the society became self-supporting, and the offerings are now all poured into the denominational treasuries.

Here are two resolutions which so exactly show the spirit of the organization from the beginning to the present, that I will close this chapter by repeating these ringing utterances :

"*Resolved*, That we commit ourselves to co-operation with the missionary organizations of our respective churches, and that we work through them in expressing our spirit and in applying our methods.

"*Resolved*, That we pledge our loyalty to the pastor of that particular church with which we are severally connected, and that we regard it as no part of our work to break down denominational ideas ; but that we go into that church with which we are allied, and there abide, doing our work in that place in the best way that may be disclosed to our united wisdom."

Over this convention Mr. J. W. Van Patten presided admirably and effectively ; but from that time on it has been understood that the President of the United Society was, by virtue of his office, the presiding officer of the convention.

On the 8th of July the convention adjourned, adopting for its motto for the coming year the one suggested by the President of the United Society, " Not to be ministered unto, but to minister."

The way in which Christian Endeavor takes hold of young men and the way in which young men take hold of Christian Endeavor is admirably illustrated by the Royal Legion, an organization of young men who live in Boston and vicinity. The original members first became acquainted with one another on their way to a Christian Endeavor convention, one of the Saratoga gatherings, if I am not mistaken. Their purposes and spirit were the same, and it did not take them long to become acquainted. As many of them as possible made a point of attending the annual conventions. They are always ready to serve in every way—as ushers, members of committees of arrangements, and messengers during the convention. A most happy combination this of religion and sociability. The Royal Legion seems destined to exemplify many of the characteristics of the Endeavor movement. Other annual gatherings are often held of those who have first become acquainted at Endeavor conventions, for there seems to be a peculiar and joyous comradeship in the idea, " You and I first got acquainted at one of the great Endeavor meetings."

CHAPTER XXXIII.

BADGES AND BANNERS.

The Badge and Its Significance—Mr. Grose's Story of the Badge—Mr. Woolley's Part—Ribbon Badges—The Badge-Banner and Its Significance—Captured by New York—Taken by Pennsylvania—Sent Across the Sea—Pennsylvania's Consolation—Oklahoma and Delaware—The Real Significance of the Badge-Banners.

RESOLUTION referred to in the last chapter as having passed the Chicago Convention refers to the badge which even then had been accepted by the society.

I think it is expressing no hazardous opinion to say that Christian Endeavorers will never want any other universal badge than this simple little monogram which so plainly tells of the organization to which they belong.

The letters C. E. tell their own story.

The two words of the title are made prominent. The C. embraces the E. The Endeavor is all within the Christ, and it was fortunate in my opinion that no involved or meaningless badge came to be adopted.

The United Society hastened in this matter because it was felt that for private gain Christian Endeavor badges would soon be upon the market. Already in fact badges had been forced upon the market, and were often weak and meaningless symbols. Various suggestions were made, but at last the badge as now worn was settled upon by the trustees.

Our readers will be glad to hear from Rev. H. B. Grose the story of the badge, since it originated with him more than any other individual. The credit for designing the exact shape in which it is now used must be given to Mr. Woolley, of Medford, Mass., an experienced draftsman. Here is Professor Grose's story of the badge: "In looking over some old papers the other day," he says, "I came across a half-sheet that at once struck me as of some historical interest in connection with the origin of that monogram pin which has now become familiar the world over. The characters rudely sketched on this bit of paper formed the basis, I believe, of the pin that we are proud to wear.

"Now for the accompanying bit of history. After the United Society was organized, one of the early matters pressing for action was the adoption of an official pin, in order to prevent the multiplication of styles otherwise inevitable.

BADGES AND BANNERS. 249

A little circle, with a star enclosed, had already made its appearance locally, as an earnest of what might be expected. Two or three designs were secured by the officers, and copies were sent to the trustees for inspection and suggestion, before the next meeting of the board. I was sitting in my study in Poughkeepsie when the letter was brought in to me. The designs were elaborate and beautifully prepared, one of them a shield, I think. My first impression was that they were too elaborate, and must prove expensive as well. My idea was that the simpler the pin, the better; and the backgrounds of shields and crescents and diamonds,

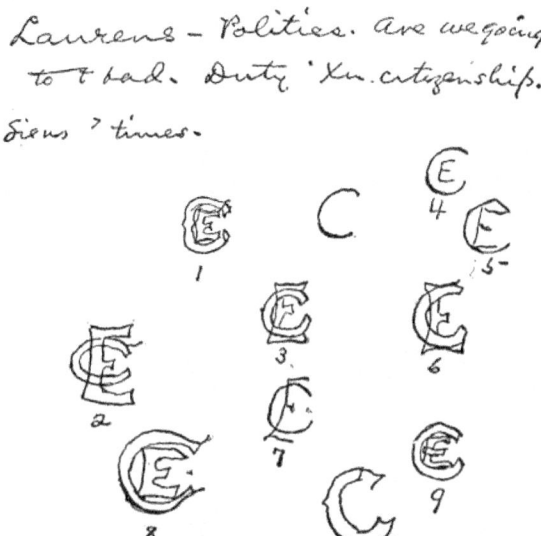

ROUGH SKETCHES FROM WHICH WAS MADE THE DESIGN OF THE CHRISTIAN ENDEAVOR BADGE.

and so on, had been used to such extent by one secret order or another that the open monogram occurred to me as more uncommon and capable of the greatest simplicity, combined with effectiveness and clearness. On the impulse of the moment I began to put the letters together, to see whether they would join gracefully. I have numbered the attempts in the order of their making. It will be noted that the first idea was the one finally returned to in the ninth outline, which, while very crude from the artistic point of view, still gives the form finally adopted. Satisfied that this was worthy of suggestion to the committee, I made a more careful sketch, and forwarded it, with the request that the artist, Mr. F. H. C. Woolley, who drew the other designs, be asked to prepare this in like finished fashion, for purposes of comparison. This was done before the board meeting, if I remember rightly. At any rate, at that meeting, November 8, 1887, the monogram pin was chosen with that unanimity which has been so marked and beautiful a feature of the trustee meetings, and within a short time the 'C. E.' pin was advertised by the treasurer, and began to be seen in Endeavor circles. The design was patented, so that any profits accruing from the sale of the badge should be used in the extension of the movement, and not go into the pockets of private individuals.

"How little any one dreamed in that day that it would, within a few years, be worn by tens and tens of thousands of loyal Endeavorers! Many emblems are more showy, more glittering, more ornamental, perhaps; but I see none that satisfies me so well, or that awakens so many feelings of affection, gratitude, consecration, and hope, as the strong, simple, speaking monogram in which the 'E' that means Endeavor is made sublimely significant by the encompassing 'C' that marks it all as Christian.

"These drawings were made on the sheet on which I was jotting down some points for an article at the moment the letter from Boston was brought in. I leave the points, too, because it seems an interesting coincidence that one of those points was that 'duty of Christian citizenship' which President Clark suggested and emphasized so effectively at Montreal, July, 1893, and which now has come to assume so much practical importance in the forward movement of the Christian young people of the nation. The awakening on this subject has come none too soon."

This account from Mr. Grose should be supplemented by the artist and draftsman, Mr. F. H. C. Woolley, who actually brought the Endeavor pin to its present perfection.

Concerning his part in the genesis of the badge he writes: "Several crude designs of various emblems and shapes with the letters Y. P. S. C. E. had been made by some party. These were shown me as not being suitable for the purpose, and I was asked to get up a design for the pin. I went to work with a will, being somewhat covetous of being the successful designer, and, after many hours thought, I submitted several sketches, combinations of the letters Y. P. S. C. E. on various backgrounds in monogram style. I am quite certain on one or more I made the letters C. E. most prominent. These sketches were shown the trustees, and suggestions came to me to work up in colors the simple C. E. without background. I made two finished designs in color, delivering them November 13, 1887, giving a good idea of how the pin would look when completed in gold, and also serving as a guide to the jeweler. I spent the greater portion of ten days time on sketches, designs, and interviews with the jeweler, regarding the possibilities of reproducing perfectly."

These "suggestions," of which Mr. Woolley speaks, are the same which Prof. Grose outlines in his account. In writing to Dr. James L. Hill about the matter a little later, Prof. Grose says: "The design is beautifully done. The only suggestions that I would make are that in the 'C' the outside points be clipped the least bit. Give my compliments and kind regards to the designer for his admirable work. If we get just the right pin it will be well worth the study and the experiment, and the designer's name will not be forgotten in Y. P. S. C. E."

Many States have adopted their own peculiar Christian Endeavor colors, and the fluttering ribbon badges flying from the button-holes of tens of thousands of Endeavorers form a picturesque feature, and add a very pleasant touch of color to the conventions, State and national.

Several years ago it occurred to that bright Endeavorer who is always prolific in new ideas, Mrs. Alice May Scudder, that a banner made of Christian Endeavor badges would be most attractive and interesting, and so, in accordance with this suggestion, the Secretary of the United Society invited the local societies, from far and near, to send to him their own ribbon badges,

THE OKLAHOMA BANNER.

for the idea had been adopted very generally of having local society badges as well as State badges to be worn at local meetings and on all similar occasions.

These badges poured in upon the secretary from the North and South and East and West, Juniors and Seniors vied with each other for representation upon the badge banner.

Very artistically and skillfully these badges were combined by Miss Addie

Gardner, of Medford, and this original badge banner has been for several years one of the attractive features of the convention.

It is offered each year to the State or province which has made the largest actual gain in the number of its Endeavor societies.

Pennsylvania has held this banner for two years, in the meantime sending it over to Ontario for a year.

In 1894 it was found that England had gained the largest number of societies, so the badge-banner was transported across the seas, much to the delight of English Endeavorers, and I have seen it there grace more than one convention with its brilliant combination of colors, which stand for so much earnest Christian work.

Pennsylvania consoles herself by remembering that it took a whole nation, and that one of the largest in the world, to get it away from the Keystone State.

Another banner of badges was offered to the State, Province, or Territory that made the largest relative gain. This was first captured by little Oklahoma, whose one society was increased several hundred per cent. before the convention at Minneapolis. But she had to yield it to Manitoba the next year, while the following year it came across the line again to New Mexico, which in turn relinquished it to West Virginia.

Another badge-banner for the largest relative gain in Junior societies was held first by Illinois for three years, and then passed over to Pennsylvania, while New York for one year held the Junior banner for the largest absolute gain, but in 1894 had to yield this one, too, to the all-conquering Keystone State.

The presentation of these banners forms a very pleasant feature of Endeavor conventions in these days, while others are given for good citizenship and for missionary zeal.

It is always understood, of course, that the banners in themselves are of little value, but the earnest work and faithful service for which they stand are of value beyond compare.

CHAPTER XXXIV.

THE SOCIETY AS AN EVANGELIST.

The Traditional Picture of Evangelist—How Many Endeavorers Have Joined the Churches—The Idea of Associate Membership—No List of Black Sheep—An Honor to Be an Associate Member—Yet Only the First Step—Are You Facing Up Hill or Down?—How Pastors Have Used the Pledge—A Large Pond to Fish In—No Extravagant Claim—Special Evangelistic Efforts—Pointing Young People to the Wicket Gate.

"THE man therefore read, and looking upon Evangelist very carefully said: 'Whither must I flee?' Then said Evangelist, pointing with his finger over a very wide field, 'Do you see yonder wicket gate?' The man said, 'No.' Then said the other, 'Do you see yonder shining light?' He said: 'I think I do.' Then said Evangelist: 'Keep that light in thine eye and go up directly thereto. So shalt thou see the gate, at which when thou knockest, it shall be told thee what thou shalt do.'"

Thus Bunyan describes one of the most interesting and benignant of his characters, who points young Christian, just as he is setting out on his long journey, the way to the wicket gate.

The traditional picture of Evangelist represents an old man, with a flowing white beard and upraised finger, pointing out to the youth the way of eternal life.

The Endeavor Society is not the typical Evangelist of old, but is rather a fresh-faced youth, who is trying to lead others like himself to the same wicket gate which the Evangelist of old pointed out; and that he has had some success with the blessing of God, in these efforts, is proved by the fact that over eight hundred thousand Christian Endeavorers, within the last half-dozen years, have joined the evangelical churches of America, influenced in some degree at least, it is believed, by the society and its evangelistic methods.

The very idea of the associate membership contains the germ of the evangelistic idea, which has always been so prominent in the society. A line is drawn between the active members and the associate, and it is no mere chance definition or arbitrary line.

The two classes of members were intended to signify that, in the opinion of the society, there is a difference between those who have accepted Christ and those who have not accepted Him—that there is a difference between Christians and those who are not.

Instead of shading off this difference and minimizing it and treating it as of little consequence, the society intends to emphasize it and make it sharp and distinct.

The active members, according to the first definition—a definition which has never been changed—are "those young people who believe themselves to be Christians, and who sincerely desire to accomplish the results above specified," namely, to promote an earnest Christian life among the members, to increase their mutual acquaintance, and to make them more useful in the service of God.

The associate members have always been defined as "young persons of worthy character who are not at present willing to be considered decided Christians, but who are willing to join the society as associate members. They shall have the special prayers and sympathy of the active members." The constitution goes on to say in its definition, "but shall be excused from taking part in the prayer-meeting. It is expected that all associate members shall regularly attend the prayer-meeting, and that they will in time become active members, and the society will work to this end."

And yet, while the associate members are of a different class from the active, they are no less really members of the society. They have their privileges and their opportunities for service.

The associate membership is no list of black sheep.

It is not, as some have erroneously thought, and, with a cheap kind of wit asserted, an "attempt to divide the sheep from the goats before the time."

It is an honor to a young person to become an associate member of the Society of Christian Endeavor.

The active members have always tried to make this list a most worthy and attractive one, because it is the first step to better things, and often a long step, when a young person is willing to put himself under the influence of Christian companions, and to distinctly ally himself with those who have chosen the better way.

On this account it has always been considered very unwise for a church member or any avowed Christian to join the society as an associate member.

Many have been tempted thus to join, even some of the more active church members, because the vows of the associate members are not so binding, and because attendance upon the meetings, though expected, is not absolutely required, nor participation in the service.

But this blurring of distinctions has often worked disastrously.

The associate membership has in such cases become a resort for the spiritually lame, halt, and blind, or the weak and the lazy, and, after a little, the young people who ought to belong are not willing to be associated with negligent and indifferent Christians.

It makes a great deal of difference how one is facing in his journey.

You may be on exactly the same slope of a hill as your companion, but, if he is facing up and you are facing down, you will come out at very different places.

The associate membership of the society is for those who are facing upward, from a life of indifference and worldliness or childish carelessness, to an Alpine height of Christian devotion; not for those who put their hands to the plough and are looking back; not for those who have made a profession of their love for better things and are looking down to the flesh-pots of Egypt.

Very often has the mere presentation of the pledge proved to be the turning-point in the life of many a young man or woman.

"Will you join the society as an active Christian, or are you not willing to make the decision which the pledge involves?"

Over and over again with trembling faith, but with an earnest purpose, the young soul has said, when confronted with the necessity of this decision: "I will be an active Christian. I will take the pledge which will forever put me on the side of Christ's active friends."

I know of more than one pastor who constantly carries with him the active members' pledge, which he uses as a means of bringing his young people to a decision for Christ and the church.

The associate membership is the great recruiting ground for Endeavorers.

Said Henry Ward Beecher to me one day, when I spoke to him with admiration of the large number of people whom he was about to receive into his church: "We ought to receive a great many, for we have a large pond to fish in."

So the Endeavor Society, with its hundreds of thousands of associate members, has a large pond to fish in. May every active member become a wise fisher of men!

Associate membership makes it comparatively easy to take the next step, and though some may be content to spend long years in the associate ranks, they come nearer the Kingdom than they otherwise would come, and are more likely to step over the dividing line.

From the very beginning we find large accessions to the churches from the associate ranks.

In the secretary's report of the very first convention whose minutes are printed, the one held in 1883, when there were but 673 associate members all told, we find that 253 were admitted to the churches from the societies, considerably more than one-third as many as all the associate members.

At the Old Orchard Convention the facts are even more gratifying.

At the first Saratoga meeting, when there were but 7,000 associate members, we learn that 2,067 had come directly into the churches during the previous year.

Thus the numbers rapidly increased until the secretary was able to report that tens of thousands and then hundreds of thousands of young people from the ranks of Christian Endeavor had made an open confession of their love for Christ by uniting with the several churches of their denomination, until at Cleveland it was reported that more than one hundred and eighty-three thousand had, within the previous year alone, taken this step.

I do not claim for an instant that the society brought all the influences to bear on these young people that resulted in their great decision. Other agencies were also at work with many of them. But it is not too much to say that the society was one influence with all these young people, and in many cases the predominant influence which led them to an open confession of Christ.

In many ways special evangelistic efforts have been undertaken by Christian Endeavor societies, either by the help of an outside evangelist or by holding special meetings themselves.

Of late in many sections, notably in the State convention of Pennsylvania Endeavorers, held in York in 1894, peculiar emphasis was given to evangelistic effort. The same efforts were made in the great international convention in Boston in 1895. Special services were held in factories, stores, and public buildings for the sake of leading the unconverted to Christ, and doubtless this distinct evangelistic effort will be more and more a feature of the society in a multitude of places, and an increasing host of youthful lives will every year be dedicated to the service of the Master, and make the final decision to serve Him, pointed on their way to the wicket gate by Evangelist Christian Endeavor.

CHAPTER XXXV.

INTERDENOMINATIONALISM.

A New Word—Not Undenominational—The Difference Between the Terms—Interdenominationalism "a Modern Fad"—What Sectarians Think of It—Looking Over the Denominational Fences—In Honor Preferring One Another—No Doctrinal Union—No Union on the Basis of Church Government—But a Union for Service—The Two Most Widely Sung Songs—Christ's Wonderful Prayer—When the Society Became Interdenominational—Sectarian Objections—Extraordinary Misstatements—Jaundiced and Untruthful Remarks—Their Refutation—The Denominations Which Lead—The Society Perfectly Adapted to All Denominations—Testimonies at the Pastors' Hour—A Glorious Consecration Meeting.

AMONG the new words which the Christian Endeavor movement may be said to have brought into prominence, if it has not invented, is the word "Interdenominational."

The older dictionaries know nothing of it; even the magnificent new Century Dictionary does not give it a place, though it gives some little space to a word which is often mistaken for it, the word "undenominational."

Though they sound very much alike, there is very little kinship between these two words. It is the hardest thing in the world, however, to make the general public see the wide distinction between them, and the Society of Christian Endeavor is constantly miscalled "an undenominational organization."

It is nothing of the sort. It is as distinctly denominational as any society possibly can be.

Each society, under normal conditions, belongs to some one church. It works for that church, seeks to upbuild it, aids its pastor, helps the Sunday-school, fills the missionary treasury, circulates the denominational literature, does just what the church and pastor demand, and only that.

But it exists in a multitude of churches and in many denominations to do the same service loyally and heartily for each church and denomination in which it finds a home.

Many most excellent organizations are necessarily undenominational. They have no particular church home, and cannot have. Their work is for the community at large, for the town, the State, or the nation, and they have no particular affiliations with any one church.

Not so is it with the Endeavor Society. The whole genius of the organization is distinct from this undenominational idea. It *must* work in some one place and for some one church, if there is a church to work with; and the few exceptions in public institutions, or in scattered school districts where there is no church, are only exceptions which prove the rule.

The first society was formed to do a special work for an individual church, and every other, formed according to the distinctive Christian Endeavor idea, has been established for the same purpose.

By those opposed to the society it has been sought to throw discredit upon the movement because it has existed in all denominations. It has been said, over and over, a multitude of times, till those who make the charge have doubtless come to believe it themselves, so easy is it to believe the things that we desire to believe, that this society, since it exists in all denominations, weakens the ties of the young people to their mother church, and makes one denomination seem as good as another to them. These people have sought in every way to apply the term *un*denominational to this organization.

Even some of the best friends of the Endeavor movement, not recognizing the vital distinction between the two terms, have said and written "un" when they meant "inter."

Now, however, it is getting to be generally understood that interdenominationalism contains a meaning and a truth almost as large as the word itself, and the enemy is beginning to train his gun upon this word and that for which it stands, to call it a "fad" and a craze.

One of the most sectarian journals in the country, whose interest it is to belittle the Christian Endeavor Society, and everything for which it stands, thus relieves itself in a recent issue: "Interdenominationalism is a modern fad, the logical outcome of which would be wide-spread demoralization to the church of God. The ——— has warm sympathy with all efforts to promote Christian fraternity, but for this interdenominational craze, which is being advocated so surreptitiously in certain quarters, we have only contempt."

Nevertheless, the great majority of Christian people are coming to consider interdenominationalism as anything but a fad.

As somebody has said, "The Christian Endeavor Society is not set for the breaking down of denominational fences, but it has taken the barbs off the wire, thank God."

People can come up to these fences and look through and shake hands across them, and wish each other God-speed in their common work for a common Master; while at the same time they stay on their own side of the fence and cultivate the flowers and fruits in the garden which God has given them to till.

Never again, we believe, will it be possible for the Christian people of

America among the Protestant sects to look upon each other with the jealous eyes and speak of each other with the acrid tongues of the past. Never again will these young people, who have touched elbows in the ranks of Christian Endeavor, regard those who are fighting a common battle with themselves with distrust and envy. Never again will it be possible for rival denominations to waste the Lord's money by planting weak and struggling churches so thickly together that they sap each other's vitality and die of mutual distrust and ill-will.

The Society of Christian Endeavor calls for loyalty to the uttermost to the individual church and the denomination with which it is connected. It yields to no one the palm for strenuous and devoted faithfulness to all the interests of the local church, and with this it combines the broadest and most delightful fellowship with all those who love the Lord Jesus Christ.

Its conventions, both the larger and the smaller ones, are object lessons of Christian fellowship and schools of spiritual Christian unity. "In honor preferring one another" is the thought of these conventions. No jibes nor sneers nor ill-natured jokes at the peculiarities of denominations are indulged in. But the devotion and the sincerity of all God's people are recognized.

No organic union is expected or desired. It is not supposed that all Christians will be massed in one great denomination, that all will have the same regimental colors. But it is believed that all may march under the banner of Christ, and that all may belong to the one great army, with its various divisions and corps and regiments and companies.

The union of Christian Endeavorers is not a doctrinal union, because they differ widely in minor points of doctrine, though all hold to the divinity of the Lord Jesus Christ and the great doctrines that centre around that truth.

It is not a unity based on forms of church government, for Episcopalians and Presbyterians, and Congregationalists all feel equally at home in the ranks of the society. But it is a fellowship based on a broad platform of service, love to Christ and work for Him. On this platform all can stand. It is broad enough to contain the millions of Endeavorers already enrolled, and the tens of millions whom we hope may yet take this name.

Every great convention and smaller gathering of a local union cements this fellowship and makes more enduring "the tie that binds." This beautiful spirit of interdenominational fellowship is surely in accord with the spirit of the age as well as with the spirit of Christ. Sectarians can no longer bind the hearts of God's people with their fetters, or shut them away from each other in the dismal dungeons of prejudice.

Wherever I have been, in all parts of the world, I have found this growing desire, which in many places is becoming an intense longing for larger spiritual fellowship among God's people.

The two songs which I heard more frequently than any other dozen songs the world around, the two songs which have been translated into every language and which have been sung by people in every clime, are songs which tell of this blessed fellowship and love:

"Blest be the tie that binds
Our hearts in Christian love,"

and

"God be with you till we meet again,"

and the significance of this fact is as hopeful as it is unmistakable. These songs are sung because God's people desire a closer fellowship and a truer unity, because they are ashamed of the miserable quarrels and wranglings of the past, because they are sick of disputations about old forms and ceremonies, about ecclesiastical laws and minor points and doctrines, and because they know that the united forces of the enemy of righteousness can only be overcome by the united forces of the friends of God.

They desire this fellowship, too, because they have learned the deeper meaning of Christ's prayer, which so long has seemed to be unanswered, as jangling sects have striven for the pre-eminence: " Neither pray I for these alone, but for those also whom thou hast given me, that they may be one as thou Father art in me and I in thee."

A wonderful prayer, a glorious petition, that the Christian world has been too slow to learn. May the Endeavor Society have some part in teaching the world to offer it in sincerity and truth, "that they may be one as thou Father art in me and I in thee."

It has been noticed, perhaps, that though the first three societies of Christian Endeavor were formed in Congregational churches, the fourth one, and that formed within less than ten months of the date of the first society in Williston Church, was in the church of another denomination.

From that day on it has been more and more distinctly evident that the society was designed by God to have for one of its missions, at least, the bringing of the young people of the different denominations nearer together. From that day on the multiplication of societies in all the evangelical denominations became the word more and more rapid.

Most of the denominations cordially accepted the society as a providential means of uniting the hearts of Christians without weakening the ties of church loyalty. The fact that the society was built upon two corner-stones of equal importance, on one of which was inscribed the word "Fidelity," and on the other the word "Fellowship," was thoroughly appreciated.

Other denominations, however, as the society grew strong, took alarm, and have done everything consistently and deliberately to crush out existing organizations of Christian Endeavor. The kind of arguments which have been used and the misrepresentations which have been indulged, are well indicated by the following extracts from articles published in one of the bitter anti-Christian Endeavor papers. The motive and animus of such articles are very plainly seen. I give space to these extracts only because in a history of this sort, which aims to be veracious and complete, some unpleasant things must be recorded as well as that which is altogether cheering. I will omit all reference to the name of the paper that publishes these extraordinary misstatements, as well as to the denomination in whose interest it is published. "For one thing," says this paper, "it (taking *The Golden Rule*) means that our young people, instead of supporting their own publishing house, send their money to support a Boston publishing house. It means, for another thing, that our young people, instead of encouraging and helping their own church institutions, are encouraging and helping the Congregational Church. It means, for another thing, that our young people read literature that is un———. Now these are serious things, especially in their bearing on the church of the morrow. The Congregational Church made a regular Stonewall Jackson flank movement when it started the Christian Endeavor Society under the taking title of 'undenominational.' For our part, we are ——— all through, and having promised to 'support the institutions of the church,' we cannot conscientiously give our adhesion to a society that silently but surely undermines the denominational life of the church.

* * * * * * * * * * *

"We oppose the Christian Endeavor Society in the ——— Church because we believe that under the plausible plea of being undenominational it gains access to our young people, and is a wide-reaching scheme of proselytizing.

* * * * * * * * * * *

"The Christian Endeavor Society is all right for the Congregational or Presbyterian churches. They started it, and it is run in their interests. As such we bid it God-speed, and have only words of praise for it. But when, under the plea of undenominationalism, it seeks to enter our fold, and silently subvert the faith of our fathers, and drive out our literature by one wholly beyond our control and outside of our church, we call a halt on it. Let our preachers everywhere stand by the church, and see to it that our young people are taught loyalty to our own glorious denomination."

* * * * * * * * * * *

It is painful to quote such jaundiced and untruthful statements from a religious paper. The historian of the twentieth century will wonder that they could ever have been printed; but truth compels us to acknowledge that they have been published, and many other statements equally misleading and false, and that in the last decade of the nineteenth century.

We will not here quote other similar articles, though many might be adduced, and are glad speedily to dismiss this part of our subject.

The only and sufficient refutation of these charges, did they need any refutation, is the fact that the society exists and flourishes, and is equally loyal and true to the interests of the churches of more than a score of different denominations.

In a later chapter will be found the record of the denominational representation of the society according to the latest available statistics. But these figures will soon grow old, and, with every month that passes, the adaptability of Christian Endeavor to every evangelical church is more and more clearly demonstrated.

It seems to be largely a matter of priority as to the denomination which leads in the number of Christian Endeavor societies. In New England, where the society began among Congregational churches, and where this denomination is very strong, there are more Congregational Endeavor societies than belong to any other one denomination.

In the Middle and Western States the pioneers of the movement were more frequently Presbyterians, and this denomination still takes the lead in these sections, and in fact in the country at large.

In other sections the Disciples of Christ very early recognized the value of the society and adopted its principles; consequently, in many sections the Endeavorers in this denomination are numerically the strongest.

In still other fields the Cumberland Presbyterians, the Methodist Protestants, the Quakers, and the Evangelical Association, have the largest number of societies.

In Canada, under the happy title of the "Epworth League of Christian Endeavor," the Methodist denomination is in the ascendancy in the matter of numbers.

In England, though the first society was formed in a Congregational Church, the Baptists have taken up the movement most vigorously and heartily, and are now in the lead so far as the number of societies go.

In Australia the Wesleyan Methodists, in some of the colonies at least, and I believe throughout Australia in general, have the greatest number of societies, and are in some respect the leaders in Endeavor work.

But all this only goes to prove the absolute and perfect adaptability of the society to all these denominations, and to all others which are on an evangelistic basis, and substantiates the claim that, with these foundation stones, "Fidelity and Fellowship," the society is in every sense of the word an interdenominational organization.

It is very interesting at national conventions to hear the reports of the delegates who represent the different denominations.

The denominational rallies are of great and increasing importance. The largest churches are crowded with the loyal young people. Oftentimes they overflow into one or two churches near by, so ready are they to show their thorough denominational loyalty at these meetings of interdenominational fellowship.

The reports of these rallies are always of the most stimulating and interesting kind. Denominational work is discussed and undertaken. Denominational missionaries are supported. Churches are built, and all lines of efforts are undertaken by Endeavorers, and, when the representatives of the denominations come to report to the great convention, they are not unlikely to dwell on the fact that the society is exactly adapted to the needs of their denomination.

The Presbyterian will say that "his church has always believed in the covenant. It has been a church of covenant keepers, and, in the Endeavor Society, it recognizes the substance of the old covenant, which has made the church a church strong and famous."

The representative of the Episcopalian Church will remark that "his denomination has always stood for child nurture and for Christian culture from the earliest days, and this they recognize as a distinctive feature of Christian Endeavor."

The Methodist will declare that "he finds in the Christian Endeavor meeting the fire and fervor of Methodism, and in the consecration meeting the old class meeting adapted to the needs of all denominations."

The Congregationalist will assert that "the self-governing principle of the Christian Endeavor movement, by which the young people obey their consciences and do what they believe is right in the sight of God, is in accordance with the genius of his denomination."

The Baptist will assert that "the way in which the Christian Endeavorer is sent to the Bible as his guide and to conscience as his mentor commends it entirely to him as a Baptist;" while the Quaker is not slow to assert that "the prayer-meeting idea of the Christian Endeavor Society is exactly in accordance with the spirit of his denomination, for with previous prayer and meditation and the stimulating effects of the pledge, the Spirit always works upon the heart of the young Christian Endeavor Quaker to testify according to the light that is within him."

This holy spirit of interdenominational fellowship was well illustrated at a great Australian Christian Endeavor convention not long since, when the delegates were seated by denominations and not by districts.

In one gallery were the Congregationalists and the Baptists. In another the Church of England young people and the Presbyterians. In the body of the great town hall of Melbourne were some of the smaller denominations, as the Bible Christians and the New Connection Methodists. Behind them was a great company of thirteen hundred Wesleyan Methodists.

The Episcopalians, when the time came in the consecration meeting for their testimony, arose and sang together the Te Deum.

The Presbyterians sang, to an old Scotch tune, an old Scotch version of the 23d Psalm.

The Baptists and the Congregationalists and the other denominations sang their special hymns of praise and consecration.

Then the Wesleyan Methodists arose, thirteen hundred strong, and they sang Charles Wesley's hymn, the first one he wrote after his conversion, beginning,

> "O for a thousand tongues to sing
> My dear Redeemer's praise."

Through the first and second and third verses they sang together, but when they came to the first line of the fourth verse,

> "He breaks the power of reigning sin,"

the Episcopalians joined with them.

> "He sets the captive free,"

and the Presbyterians joined.

> "His blood can make the foulest clean."

The Baptists and the Congregationalists could no longer keep silence.

> "His blood availed for me."

By that time all were singing.

This was a hymn of experience. It was too large for any one denomination. It told of the heart's love of all, and all must join in it.

Here is the real fellowship of the Christian Endeavor movement, a fellowship born of a common devotion to Christ, and of a common experience of His dying love.

CHAPTER XXXVI.

THE DEVELOPMENT OF STATE SPIRIT.

"Our State for Christ"—A Distinctive Feature of the Great Conventions—How the Badges and Banners Contribute—Maryland's Song—"Old Kentucky Home"—Washington's Invitation Song—"Tramp, Tramp, Tramp"—Baltimore's Song—The Massachusetts Christian Endeavor Hymn—A Stirring Convention Rally Song—Affectionate Pride in the State—"Our Country for Christ."

AS the State unions of Christian Endeavor began to develop and grow stronger and stronger, it is only natural that there should be developed a spirit of State pride and patriotism among Endeavorers. Our emotions must have some local habitation, some metes and bounds. It is difficult for most people to love being in general, or even to spread out their finest and most generous emotions over too large a territory.

To be sure, the cry of the Endeavor world has been "The world for Christ" and "Our country for Christ," and the aspirations of this youthful army have been no narrower than the conquest of the world.

Still it is not surprising that there should be born at the same time an intense love for their own locality, and especially for their own commonwealth embraced in the State union. This has been fostered, and, so far as I can see, without any evil results, by the State conventions and by the international conventions.

State rallies have come to be a distinctive feature of each great international gathering. State receptions, when the generous hospitality of the delegates from one commonwealth is offered to another, are among the most pleasing features of these conventions, and at the consecration meetings the delegates from the different States usually sit together and respond for the whole commonwealth, as it is impossible to hear from any smaller divisions.

Together with this spirit of State pride and loyalty has been developed among the young people an intense desire to win to Christ their commonwealth.

Everywhere I have seen this desire expressed, not only in the prayers and papers of the young people, but in the very mottoes and decorations of the churches where conventions are held. Even the letter paper which the unions use tell this same story.

"Missouri for Christ," "Kentucky for Christ," "Oregon for Christ,"

"Ontario for Christ"—these are the legends which I have seen in all parts of the land which tell of the deep devotion and intense longing on the part of the Christian Endeavorers to do their little best to make their section of our country Immanuel's land.

The different badges and banners which the delegates wear at the conventions emphasize the fact that they come from different sections, and that, while all are devoted to the union, they are, as they ought to be, especially devoted to the section from which they hail. Some of the State songs are of real merit and are the rallying cries for a great host of young Endeavorers.

When they come marching into the great convention halls with these songs upon their lips, the effect is sometimes thrilling, and when, at the great consecration meeting, the delegates from such a State as Maryland, for instance, rise and sing a verse of a hymn which tells of their desire to win their beloved commonwealth for King Immanuel, to the well-loved tune "Maryland, My Maryland," or when the delegates from Kentucky sing their song to the sweet refrain, "My Old Kentucky Home," there are few who can keep back the tell-tale moisture from their eyes.

Here are some of the best of these State songs, though the limits of this chapter will allow us to make a selection of few from the many good ones which might be quoted.

Here is Maryland's song, written by Miss Amanda Harker:

File into rank for Christ to-day,
O Maryland, dear Maryland;
Free to the breeze His banners play,
Maryland, dear Maryland.
Your noblest work for Him be done
From early dawn to setting sun,
Nor cease till latest victory's won,
Maryland, my Maryland.

"Christ and His church" your watchword be,
Maryland, dear Maryland,
Till time becomes eternity,
Maryland, dear Maryland.
His gospel spread through all the land;
His heralds, each Endeavor band,
And may they make a gallant stand
For Maryland, dear Maryland.

CHORUS.

Shout, shout for joy the glad refrain,
Maryland, my Maryland.
Our King shall claim His own again,
Maryland, my Maryland.

Oh, sound the call both loud and well,
In Maryland, dear Maryland,
For all who would His legions swell,
Maryland, my Maryland.
From mountain, river, hill, and plain,
Ring out the loud, resounding strain,
And bid the welkin ring again
In Maryland, my Maryland.

CHO.—Shout, shout, etc.

From Penmar's slope to Baltimore,
Maryland, my Maryland;
From eastern side to western shore,
Maryland, my Maryland.
Rise in your might, and put to shame
All those who would pervert the name
Of Him we gladly Master claim,
Maryland, my Maryland.

CHO.—Shout, shout, etc.

Kentucky's song was written by Miss Bessie DeMoss Ellis, Bellevue, Ky.:

Air: "Old Kentucky Home."

The valiant hosts of our great Endeavor band,
With banners triumphant unfurled,
Are gathering now at our mighty King's command
To bear His standard round the world.
With faith in God as our ever-shining shield,
With firmness, with patience, and love,
We'll stand for Christ till the world to Him shall yield,
And the flag of Union floats above.

CHORUS.

Shout a loud hosannah;
O, praise our God to-day!
"For Christ and the church," and our blest Endeavor bands,
In the old Kentucky home far away.

Begirt with truth we shall never weary grow,
Though sorrow and sadness assail,
For hope shall whisper of heaven as we go,
And give cheer when fainting hearts shall fail.
The night will come with its holy hours of rest,
When life with its trials are o'er,
The soul will sleep on the Saviour's loving breast,
And will bear the weary load no more.

CHO.—Shout a loud, etc.

When home ties call and the time has come to part
When lips breathe the tender good-bye,
When memories deep fill the caverns of the heart,
And the tears unbidden dim the eye,
We still shall sing of another happy time,
When mingled in union once more,
We'll chant the strains of that melody sublime,
That the angels sing for evermore.

CHO.—Shout a loud, etc.

Here is a battle hymn written for the Illinois Gospel Temperance Campaign by Mrs. Merrill E. Gates, wife of the honored president of Amherst College:

"Then said David to the Philistine . . . I come to thee in the name of the Lord of hosts . . . whom thou hast defied. This day will the Lord deliver thee into mine hand. . . . And all this assembly shall know that the Lord saveth not with sword and spear, for the battle is the Lord's. . . . So David prevailed over the Philistine." I Sam. 17: 45-50.

O Thou mighty God of battles,
Fight for us this fateful day!
For the foe is fierce and furious,
And has deadly power to slay!
Go Thou forth with our battalions,
Lead them on their conquering way,
"In the name of the Lord of hosts!"

CHORUS.

Glory, glory, hallelujah, glory, glory, hallelujah,
Glory, glory, hallelujah,
"In the name of the Lord of hosts!"

'Tis the gospel peal of triumph,—
Hark! the silver trumpets clear!
For the God of our salvation
"Saveth not with sword and spear."

Lo, our God is marching with us,
And His battle-cry ye hear,
"In the name of the Lord of hosts!"

CHO.—Glory, glory, hallelujah, etc.

O, be strong and of good courage,
For He says, "Be not afraid!"
Go ye up unto the battle,
Neither be at all dismayed!
Though the enemy defy Him,
On the Mighty help is laid,
"In the name of the Lord of hosts!"

CHO.—Glory, glory, hallelujah, etc.

O, the fight was fought by Jesus,
When He died for you and me!
None but Christ, the living Saviour,
Gives the power that sets men free!
So we follow our great Captain
On to certain victory,
"In the name of the Lord of hosts!"

CHO.—Glory, glory, hallelujah, etc.

Some of the brightest of these State songs have been born of the intense desire of the Christian Endeavorers to welcome a national convention. Here are three or four of these invitation songs. If any one thinks the meter occasionally halts a little, the tune to which the words are sung must be considered, and the tremendous energy and enthusiasm which the singers, when they are eager for the convention, put into the words. Some of the songs in themselves are stirring and inspiring poems. Here is

WASHINGTON'S INVITATION SONG.

Tune: " Tramp! Tramp! Tramp!"

From Potomac's lovely shore the historic hosts have gone,
Leaving tales of deeds so noble, great, and grand,
But once more we hear the cry of " On to Washington!"
From the great Endeavor army of our land.

CHORUS.

Washington in '96! Washington in '96!
We will bid you welcome there,
To the nation's home so fair,
Come to Washington, Endeavorers, '96.

Many thousands they will come, like an army to the fight,
From the prairies, from the mountains, and the sea;
To reclaim our dear homeland for the Master and the right;
Welcome, noble host of Y. P. S. C. E.

CHORUS.

Washington in '96! Washington in '96!
From the hilltops comes the cry;
From the valleys the reply,
" We are coming, Washington, in '96!"

It was a great disappointment to many thousands that Baltimore, instead of Washington, was not chosen for 1896. Here is Baltimore's invitation:

BALTIMORE, '96.

BY PAUL M. STRAYER.

Tune: " Hold the Fort."

North and East and West, we greet you,
Friends from far and near;
Open hearts and homes invite you
To our city dear.

CHORUS.

Baltimore, in '96,
O, make a glad acclaim!
Baltimore in 96,
Will greet you " in His name."

In our sunny South we need you,
Y. P. S. C. E.
Christ and church, enthroned, exalted,
In our land shall be.

CHO.—Baltimore in '96, etc.

Maryland repeats the welcome
To her friendly shore;
Come possess our State and city,
Come to Baltimore.

CHORUS.

Baltimore in '96,
" O come," our chorus still;—
Hear the glad triumphant answer,
" In His name we will."

One of the best of these invitation songs is Boston's song for '95, written by Mr. W. E. Allen, the President of the Massachusetts Union. Here it is:

"BOSTON, '95."

Tune: "Marching Through Georgia."

Come all ye Endeavorers, we'll sing another song,
Sing it with a spirit that will help the cause along,
Sing with exultation of the fifty thousand strong
  Who will come marching to Boston.

CHORUS.

Hurrah! hurrah! for "Boston, '95"!
Hurrah! hurrah! Endeavor hearts revive!
White and crimson banners floating free in '95,
  When you come marching to Boston.

See them come from ev'ry land beneath the rolling sun,
Come with songs of courage for the battles to be won,
Come with faith that fails not till the fighting-days be done
  Coming with praises to Boston.—CHO.

Bunker Hill invites you to its soil by heroes trod;
Lexington and Concord send their voices all abroad;
Faneuil Hall sends greeting in the name of Freedom's God
  To the hosts who march on Boston.—CHO.

Here the shades of Webster and of Franklin bid you come;
Paul Revere will hang aloft his lanterns one by one;
And over all will shine for you the stately gilded dome,
  When you come marching to Boston.—CHO.

Come all loyal friends of right, and capture our fair land;
Once again a standard raise on fair New England's strand;
Once again on Plymouth Rock shall kneel a pilgrim band,
  When you come marching to Boston.—CHO.

The Massachusetts State hymn was written by one of Boston's best known and most popular grammar-school masters, Mr. Granville B. Putnam, and it is worthy of him.

MASSACHUSETTS CHRISTIAN ENDEAVOR HYMN.

Tune: "Onward, Christian Soldiers."

Raise the gospel banner,
  March upon the foe;
Valiant be in battle,
  Conquer as we go.
From the hills of Berkshire
  To the Cape of sand,
Through the grand old Bay State,
  Wave the signal brand.

Other corps are marshalled,
  Maine to Oregon,
Soldiers of Immanuel,
  Pressing bravely on.
In this mighty army,
  Fighting man to man,
Let the sons of Pilgrims,
  Ever lead the van.

Christ claims our endeavor,
  Bids us loyal be,
Summons us to conflict,
  Pledges victory.
Onward bear the colors,
  Dare defend the right,
Join the shout of triumph,
  Win a gallant fight.

Though in lands benighted
  Darkness still holds sway,
Morning gilds the mountains,
  Dawns a brighter day.
Armed with faith and courage,
  Heart to heart as one,
Glory waits the victors,
  When the fight is done.

Here is Rhode Island's song:

"RHODE ISLAND FOR JESUS!"
(Christian Endeavor State Song.)
BY. MRS. CHARLOTTE LEAVITT SLOCUM.

We come with our banner, Rhode Island's own children,
Though least in Columbia's circle our State;
Our greetings we bring in His name who hath promised
Endeavor to crown and the small to make great.
The State Roger Williams for liberty founded,
For freedom in Christ shall expend her best powers;
The State that gave Perry, with courage undaunted,
Shall still meet the foe, and shall find they are ours.

When Washington led us to win Independence,
Rhode Island sent forth to the front every man.
From youngest to eldest, from sixteen to sixty,
They swerved not a line when the conflict began.
And shall we not rally for Jesus, our Captain,
And fight to the death a more terrible foe—
Bring young men and maidens, and old men and children,
Yea, all the wide world, our Redeemer to know?

CHORUS.

Rhode Island for Jesus! Rhode Island for Jesus!
In Him we are mighty, though evil be strong.
With faith for our anchor and hope for our watchword,
And love for our guide, we will vanquish the wrong.

Some others will be given in succeeding chapters. Again let me advise the poetical critic to reserve his literary criticisms for more pretentious literature. These songs are all singable. The spirit, the purpose, the earnestness put into these songs, as they are sung, redeem them from commonplaceness, and make them, in many cases, inspiring battle cries for the right.

To be sure, the "divine afflatus" can scarcely be said to have rested on the authors of all the State songs in very large measure. Some songs that have been perpetrated, it must be confessed, are but doggerel, and second-class doggerel at that; but such songs have but short life, even if they can be said to have any life at all. They are gradually weeded out, and in the end the result, I believe, will not be discreditable to the cause which the songs commemorate.

Who will say that there is anything unworthy in this spirit of loyalty and love for the Commonwealth when thus developed? Nay, who will not be willing to admit that this is one of the forces which makes for righteousness, which God is using to regenerate our land?

Out of this spirit of affectionate pride for the State or province has come, in no small degree, the movement for Good Citizenship which has been such a marked feature of the Christian Endeavor world of late. Corruption in politics and the spoiling of the State by those in power will not long be endured by young people who truly love their own Commonwealth. This spirit of affectionate pride will broaden into a strong and earnest desire for national regeneration.

"Our State for Christ" will not long satisfy them. "Our country for Christ" will surely be the watchword of those who have thus learned to pray and hope for their own State or province or colony. God speed the day when the devout prayers of this mighty host shall be answered and all nations shall become the peoples whose God is the Lord!

1. Junior Rally—Pennsylvania State Convention, York, Pa.   2. Michigan State Convention, '93
3. A Kentucky State Convention Hall, seating capacity 3,000, Hopkinsville, Ky.

CHAPTER XXXVII.

THE PHILADELPHIA CONVENTION.

Great Expectations—Over 7,000 Societies—New York Still the Banner State—A Cordial Address of Welcome—New Friends who have Since been Prominent—The Convention Sermon—Wonderful Progress in Every Direction—What the Papers Had to Say of the Convention—"The Largest Delegate Religious Assembly that Christendom Has Yet Witnessed"—The City Taken by Storm—The President and the Postmaster-General—General Howard's Address—Some "Philadelphia Mintings."

AFTER the convention in Chicago the Endeavorers of the country had come to expect great things of the next annual convention, which was to be held in Philadelphia from the 9th to the 11th of July, 1889. Nor were they disappointed in any respect, for this convention up to that date marked the high-water line of the Christian Endeavor movement.

The hall chosen for the convention was the First Regiment Armory hall, on Broad Street, and it was well adapted to accommodate the thousands of Endeavorers who came together, except that, by reason of the proximity of the railroad trains, it was somewhat noisy.

The "Committee of Nine" having the convention in charge, were highly complimented for their thorough preparatory work. The plan they adopted has been the model upon which many of the subsequent International Convention Committees have been formed.

REV. J. T. BECKLEY, D. D.

At this convention it was reported that there were in all 7,062 societies, with a total membership of 485,000 members, and it was believed that fully 45,000 members had joined the Church during the previous year. New York was then the banner Endeavor State, with 1,387 societies. Massachusetts came second, 742; Illinois third, with 541; Pennsylvania fourth, with 484, while Ohio was but a very few behind, for she reported 465 societies.

Connecticut and Iowa were the only other States that had gone beyond the 300 limit, the former claiming 352 and the latter 336 societies.

At this time Rev. J. T. Beckley, D. D., then the pastor of the Beth Eden

"COMMITTEE OF NINE" (PHILADELPHIA CONVENTION).

1. Walter B. Shumway, Chairman.
2. Lewis S. Lee (Treasurer), Finance.
3. Henry M. Bowers (Secretary), Reception.
4. Gustavos S. Benson, Jr., Hall.
5. John B. Scott.
6. Matthew Walker, Music.
7. William A. Bender, Park Meeting.
8. George M. Randle, Press.
9. Richard H. Wallace, Hotel.

Baptist Church of Philadelphia, but now of New York City, was the President of the Pennsylvania Union. He welcomed the convention in an admirable address, outlining the Christian Endeavor idea and the principles for which it stands.

Dr. Beckley's connection with the work of the society from that time to the present has been most intimate and important. He has traveled largely in the South and in the far East, and in his own State of Pennsylvania has always stood for the fellowship and methods of the Endeavor movement. No one has the faculty of making friends and of holding friends more than this much-loved pastor; and where he makes a friend for himself he is sure to make one for the Endeavor idea.

Bishop Nicholson, of Philadelphia, responded to Dr. Beckley's warm words of welcome, and from the beginning to the end this convention was marked by the delightful fellowship and affectionate, brotherly love to which these addresses gave voice. In this convention, too, I find the names of not a few who from this time on have been prominent in the work of Christian Endeavor. Among them is Mr. Tom C. Baldwin, of New Hampshire, honored and loved as few young men have ever been, and one whose lamented death while President of the New Hampshire Union was mourned by a circle far larger than even the young people of his native State.

TOM C. BALDWIN.

Rev. R. N. McKaig, D. D., of Minnesota, was also prominent in this convention. A Methodist minister was he who stood with all his heart for the interdenominationalism of Christian Endeavor.

Mr. E. E. Towner, of Vermont, who for many years has been Vermont's most efficient and active secretary, was also here.

E. E. TOWNER.

Miss E. D. Gates, of Massachusetts, who is known by Endeavorers throughout the Bay State and is most deservedly popular, was one of the delegates. Miss Elizabeth Wishard, of Indiana, was also at Philadelphia, and the amount of work which she and her devoted sister,

FIRST REGIMENT ARMORY, PHILADELPHIA (EXTERIOR).

Miss Harriet Wishard, both of whom have been secretaries of the Indiana union, have done for the cause of Christian Endeavor in their State and out of it will never be known.

J. S. SMITH.

I also find the name of Mr. John S. Smith, of Nova Scotia, another friend of the society, who by his untiring efforts has greatly advanced the cause in the maritime provinces.

Mr. A. H. Frederick, of St. Louis, was also at Philadelphia, and Missouri Endeavorers do not need to be introduced to him and to his work.

The sermons at the conventions had already become famous, and each one was looked forward to with eagerness. It was becoming increasingly evident from year to year that homiletics was not a dead art or science.

The sermons of Dr. Deems and Dr. Hoyt at previous conventions had made a deep impression upon all their hearers. At such a gathering the pulpit could hold its own with the lecture platform or the theatre as an attractive, drawing force.

The convention sermon of 1889, by Rev. Geo. H. Wells, D. D., then of Montreal, but now of Minneapolis, fulfilled the highest expectation aroused by the sermons of previous years.

The early morning prayer-meetings of this convention were full of inspiration and power. For the first time, if I am not mistaken, the different committees had separate meetings devoted to their interests, which were attended by those serving on those committees or especially interested in them.

In the Arch Street Methodist Church the work of the Lookout Committee was presented by Mrs. S. L. Selden, of Gainesville, Fla. In the lecture-room of the same church the work of the Social Committee was led by Miss Olive Blunt,

A. H. FREDERICK.

of Kansas City, now an honored and successful missionary in Japan, whom I had the pleasure of seeing with some of the native converts three years afterward in the Straits of Shiminosake. A conference on the Missionary Committee was appropriately led by Mr. S. L. Mershon. All these and others were held at 3.45 in the afternoon, while at 4.30 the same audience-rooms were crowded for conferences on prayer-meeting methods, local and State unions, Junior societies, and associate members.

Another interesting and novel feature of this convention was the three-minute reports from the States and Provinces by the leading workers in these different sections of the country.

In every instance the report was given of progress and wonderful gain, and this session was one of exceeding interest and power. The Pastors' Hour, conducted by Rev. B. B. Loomis, of West Troy, was also a memorable hour.

Pastor after pastor testified to the loyalty and devotion, to the courage and modest helpfulness of his young people, and, though but few of all the many pastors could be heard from, they all stood up at the close of this service to testify of their appreciation of the work which the society was rendering them in their churches.

I speak of these features because, though now they are common in national conventions, and in State conventions as well, they were then fresh and novel, and have proved, by their wide adoption and the continued interest that they excite, that there is a vital idea in them for Endeavorers

HON. JOHN WANAMAKER.

everywhere. In fact, every national convention, from the beginning to the present day, has developed new features and methods which have been very largely adopted in a multitude of other assemblies, larger and smaller. It is not too much to say that they have set the pace for young people's religious conventions of all kinds and in all parts of the world.

The religious press was full of pleasant things for this convention. More widely by far was it noticed by the secular and religious journals than any previous convention. Said *The Presbyterian*, of Philadelphia: "Among other things the late convention proves the possibility of large and enthusiastic gatherings in a noble cause."

The Congregationalist declared that "the recent annual convention of Christian Endeavor societies at Philadelphia is, so far as we recall, the largest delegate religious assemblage that Christendom has yet witnessed, and as such is a noteworthy event."

The Advance declared: "The Young People's Society of Christian Endeavor now represents the church in progressive and aggressive work. It is a method not so much for putting young people at work as for putting all people at work. This method is worthy and wise."

Said the *Philadelphia Press:* "Those who are beginning to bewail the degeneracy of the times and the decline in the influence and activity of the Christian church should visit this convention."

The *New Haven Register* declared: "The future of the society, if it continues to be guided divinely, as it seems to have been thus far, will perhaps secure the evangelization of the world."

The *Examiner*, of New York, remarked: "Philadelphia has been a willing captive this week to an army that never before took it or any other city by storm."

While *The Christian Union* declared: "To say that enthusiasm has marked the session is to convey but a faint impression of the ardor and inspiration that have been two characteristics of this remarkable meeting." For the first time at this convention, men who are prominent in political affairs took an interest in the convention.

GEN. O. O. HOWARD.

President Harrison sent a cordial telegram of greeting. Governor Beaver, of Pennsylvania, who expected to be present, but who was detained, sent also a kind message.

Hon. John Wanamaker, the Postmaster-General, who for many years has been a Trustee of the United Society, was present and gave a brief but very happy address, while Gen. O. O. Howard, the hero of Gettysburg, gave an address on "The Complete Christian," which awakened much enthusiasm. Among the strong addresses of this convention, too, was one by Rev. J. Wilbur Chapman, D. D., then of Albany, whose work as an evangelist has been so blessed of God. Clearly and forcibly he presented the idea of loyalty to duty as that for which the

REV. J. WILBUR CHAPMAN, D. D.

Christian Endeavor movement stands, and never was this fundamental truth more ably presented.

I cannot close the account of this memorable meeting any better than by quoting some "Philadelphia Mintings" coined by Rev. James L. Hill, which give graphic pen-pictures—snap-shots, as it were—taken by Mr. Hill's mental kodak on the spot:

"Two young ladies inquired the way to the Armory. 'Follow the crowd! Everybody's going!' was the reply from a Philadelphian."

FIRST REGIMENT ARMORY, PHILADELPHIA (INTERIOR).

"The delegates were as closely placed in that great auditorium as the rows of pins in a paper."

"And where were the cranks? Well, we suppose that there are few places so uncongenial for that ilk."

"The morning prayer-meetings were wonderful. Speakers stood waiting. Prayers were even coincident. Two hymns would sometimes be launched simultaneously in different parts of the house. . . ."

"In the reports of conventions in other organizations an omission of the sermon is suggested. It has always been with us of unsurpassed interest. We are not, some way, impressed by any decadence of the pulpit."

"The Armory was hard to leave. Its atmosphere was one of song and prayer. Earnest Christian life hallowed all our memories of it."

"The custom of starting a hymn as the audience was passing out of the great auditorium seemed new in Philadelphia and excited wide remark. Sometimes the tune was carried along for several blocks."

"After the greatest of our conventions our hearts beat quick with excitement as we anticipate St. Louis."

CHAPTER XXXVIII.

THE RISE OF THE MISSIONARY SPIRIT.

The World for Christ—Dr. Pierson's Remarkable Statement—Mr. Robert T. Wilder on the Missionary Uprising—Dr. Gifford's Stirring Words—Mr. Mershon's Missionary Sum in Arithmetic—A Great Awakening—Two Cents a Week for Missions—An Enthusiasm Which Never Wanes — $250,000 in 1893-4 — A Million for Missions —What the Societies Are Doing for Missions—A Montreal Society—Boys and Girls in Mission Schools and Colleges—A Revered and Beloved Leader—What a Society Did—Dr. Gordon's Plan—A Wise Suggestion—How the Denominations are Carrying it Out—Many Missionary Enterprises—The Significance of These Facts—Presbyterian Efforts—What the Reformed Dutch Endeavorers are Doing—Christian Endeavor Churches—The Disciples of Christ and Their Endeavor Enterprises—The Work of the Young Congregationalists—Sunday-school Endeavor Missionaries—At the Fountain Head.

THE convention just described was noted, among other things, for the large attention given to missionary ideas and missionary enterprises. Rev. Arthur T. Pierson, D. D., then the pastor of Bethany Presbyterian Church, in Philadelphia, gave a most inspiring address on "The World for Christ." His well-known eloquence and missionary zeal thrilled every one in his audience.

Here is an inspiring sentence or two from his noble address:

"The probability is that the next ten years will show discoveries, inventions, and the mastery of the elements of more importance in some respects than the fifty years that preceded. Look at what Mr. Edison has done in the last fifteen years for the development of the marvelous use of electricity. Just think of the phonograph as one of the ripest inventions of human times, an instrument which may yet be made so complete that it can take down accurately every word, articulate every utterance that is made in a colossal gathering like this, and put them in such shape that at another convention held one hundred years hence every one of the addresses made to-night might be repeated in the actual tones of the orators themselves.

"With these magnificent appliances before us, everything is moving, not at the rate of the old stage-coach or elephant team, but even beyond the speed of steam, with the rapidity of lightning, which Robert McKenzie says, in his grand book on *The Nineteenth Century*, represents the first of the last inventions of man, for, as he says, for once man has touched the highest summit of possible invention. There can be no transmission of intelligence that is more immediate than instantaneous; and it may be one indication of the approaching beginning of the end, that in one invention, at least, man has struck that principle of transmission of messages which cannot be exceeded, for celerity or rapidity or accuracy, by any method or agent known or unknown, for such a thing is inconceivable.

"We can hardly understand these things as we are in the presence of God and each other to-night, but I pray God to let me live long enough, after having given twenty years of the best of my life to the study and the advocacy of this great proposition, to see this enterprise of Christian missions taken up by the Young People's Society of Christian Endeavor, by the Young Men's Christian Association, by the Young Women's Christian Association, by the Young Women's Temperance Union, by the great Missionary Crusade in the colleges, as well as by the churches of Christ in general, with a determination that before this generation shall pass away the world shall have known that Jesus Christ died for sinners."

Another memorable address of this convention was given by Mr. Robert T. Wilder, now working in India, on "The Missionary Uprising." His name is well known as the leader of the Students' Volunteer movement, which has gone on side by side with the Christian Endeavor movement as a means of arousing missionary interest especially among the young men in our educational institutions. Here are some sentences that greatly impressed the assembled thousands:

ROBERT T. WILDER.

"Seventy-six years ago there was a division in the ranks of the Baptist Church, and some became anti-missionary. When they divided there were about thirty-five thousand in each body. According to the census of 1880, the anti-missionary Baptists numbered forty-five thousand, and the pro-missionary Baptists numbered two and one-half millions. 'There is that scattereth and yet increaseth; and there is that withholdeth more than is meet, but it tendeth to poverty.' Some one has said that the majority of us are not *anti*-missionary but *O*-missionary.

"I hope there is no one before me this afternoon who belongs to the *O*-missionary class. My prayer is the prayer of the stroke of the Cambridge University boat. He prayed that there might be such an outlet of men and money from his country that it would lead to an inlet of blessing from heaven. God grant that there may be such an outlet of men and money from the United States that it will be followed by a great inlet of blessing upon our country. The outlet is coming.

"Three years ago this month, two hundred and forty of our college men assembled near Mr. Moody's home, in Massachusetts. We gathered there to study the Bible. Twenty-three of us met in the little museum back of Crossly Hall and dedicated our lives to the work of foreign missions, and before that summer's school had closed there were one hundred men pledged to go into the foreign service unless God clearly blocked the way. It was deemed advisable that a tour should be made through the schools and colleges of our country, and two young men, one of whom is now in India, started out. They visited one hundred and seventy-five institutions, and, before the year closed, twenty-two hundred students signified a willingness and desire, God permitting, to be foreign missionaries. The movement has been increasing, until to-day there are three thousand nine hundred and thirty-eight enrolled on our list as volunteers for foreign service. Most of these are still two or three years removed from the completion of their courses of study; but I am very glad to say that we know definitely of one hundred and ten who have already sailed and are on foreign soil.

"It seems to me that I have seen that cloud the size of a man's hand; and now for one hundred Elijahs, each on his Mt. Carmel, crying to God for rain. The showers are coming, and the time is not far distant when our young men and women will go into this work by the thousands. Let us ask for it; let us expect it."

These addresses were not the only ones that aroused this intense spirit of missionary enthusiasm.

Rev. O. P. Gifford, D. D., then pastor of the Warren Avenue Baptist Church, of Boston, electrified the great audience with a magnificent address on "The World for Christ," in which were heard these thrilling sentences:

"There is no other secret of carrying Christ to the world. We must step out from the forests of our selfishness; we must get out of the mines of our self-seeking; we must yield ourselves absolutely to God, until, looking down upon us, He can say: 'My thoughts are your thoughts, my ways are your ways, and as high as the heavens are above the earth, so high have I lifted you into communion with myself, saith the Lord of hosts.'

"The great city is perishing in flame, the great reservoir is forcing its way through miles of pipe leading to disaster and conflagration. How shall the reservoir be brought to bear upon the burning city? The engine must give itself absolutely to completing the union between the reservoir and the city.

"Yonder on the mountains of light are the reservoirs of eternal life. Yonder lies a world wrapped in the flames of selfishness, perishing before God; and between God and the world must stand a busy, throbbing church, every power of its being surrendered to God in Christ that He may bring God in Christ to a world that needs Him and that will perish without Him."

Moreover, a conference on "The Work of the Missionary Committee," led by Mr. Stephen L. Mershon, provoked many to good works. In this conference the need of a Missionary Committee in every society was urged; a suggestion which has been very largely adopted by the great majority of Endeavor societies, I believe.

Among the suggestions made at this conference were the following:

1. Educate.
2. Interest.

3. Incite to individual effort.
4. Guide into practical channels of Missionary need.

Information + consecration — selfishness × by activity and ÷ by every individual Christian Endeavor = successful missionary effort.

I dwell upon the addresses and suggestions made on this line at the Philadelphia Convention because they resulted in such grand fruitage for the advancement of the kingdom.

Immediately after this there was noticed a vast awakening of interest on the part of young people in missionary matters. Missionary committees multiplied on every side. Missionary themes became favorite subjects for discussion at State and local conferences. Plans for proportionate and systematic giving were urged and adopted in many places.

Soon after this, Rev. A. A. Fulton, a beloved missionary from China, belonging to the Presbyterian Board, came back to America on furlough, and set the hearts of a vast multitude of young people on fire with the thought that with their limited means they could do something to hasten the coming of Christ's kingdom. Two cents a week was the modest sum which he asked from each Christian Endeavorer. Few felt that they could not give that sum. Wherever the idea was presented it was adopted, and before he went back to China, after a year of campaign among the Christian Endeavor societies, it was estimated that a hundred thousand Endeavorers in the different denominations were giving at least two cents a week in addition to what they would otherwise give for the advancement of the kingdom of Christ in the dark continents.

REV. A. A. FULTON.

From the date of the Philadelphia convention to this, missionary enthusiasm has shown no signs of waning. In fact, it has gained strength and power with every passing month. "As dull as a missionary meeting" is no longer true in Christian Endeavor circles.

Moreover, this enthusiasm is not a matter of sentiment alone, not a thing for conventions and union meetings, but it is an enthusiasm which materializes in dollars and cents. Christian Endeavor Day is now largely celebrated by a missionary thank-offering to one or more of the denominational boards with which the societies are connected.

In 1893 and 1894 it was estimated, from a very conservative standpoint, that at least two hundred and fifty thousand dollars had been given by Christian Endeavorers for missionary work outside of their own towns and churches, and perhaps as much more for the work immediately around them.

As we describe the succeeding conventions we shall show the development of this Christ-like spirit. At the Cleveland Convention those who were there will remember the stirring appeal of Treasurer Shaw for a million dollars for missions. A most cheering thought connected with this subject is that the missionary spirit is only still in the bud. The flowers and fruitage of this glorious plant are not yet seen. But the seed is planted in the soil of Christian Endeavor, and for centuries to come we hope and pray that it may bear more and more abundant fruit.

DR. A. J. GORDON.

Perhaps there is no better place than this present chapter to describe a little more in detail some of the efforts of Endeavor Societies to fulfill our Lord's last command, though we must necessarily anticipate somewhat the chronological order of events.

Even before this convention at Philadelphia many societies were doing noble work and making large sacrifices to fill the missionary treasuries.

For a number of years, for instance, the society connected with the American Presbyterian Church in Montreal had raised something like $1,500 for the support of a Canadian missionary who has gone out under the auspices of the American Board, Rev. Hilton Pedley, of Niigata, Japan.

Other societies perhaps had done quite as well, certainly in proportion to the means at their disposal.

In many places the societies have been grouped at the suggestion of missionary secretaries for the support of a missionary or native helpers or Bible workers when they were not able to provide the full support themselves. Many individual societies are supporting boys or girls in mission schools or colleges, have Bible readers, and other workers who look to them for support; have built churches on the home field, or furnished them with communion sets or pulpit Bibles, and have in a multitude of ways showed their interest in the great work of evangelizing the world. When that revered and beloved leader of religious work, not only in the Baptist denomination but in all America, Rev. Dr. A. J. Gordon died, the Society of Christian Endeavor connected with his church and in which he was intensely interested at once held a meeting, and from among its own members raised $425 as a memorial offering toward the debt resting upon the American Baptist Missionary Union. It is the splendid purpose of these Endeavorers of the Clarendon Street Baptist Church, we are told, to arouse the Baptist young people of the land to pay off the debt. They hope that their $425 will be increased by every Baptist young people's society in the United States in proportion as God has blessed the members. Whether this effort succeeds or fails, it is a noble attempt. In no better way could they honor the memory of the noble Christian minister and missionary worker who has left them pastorless.

WONG TSIN CHONG.

In this connection it is interesting to remember that Dr. Gordon himself described shortly before his death in *The Golden Rule*, in one of the last articles he ever wrote, a plan for obtaining far more money than has ever yet been contributed by the Christian Endeavor Societies. Suggestions from such a source are so valuable and the subject discussed is so perennially timely that we will quote this brief article entire:

" A significant service was held in the Clarendon Street Baptist Church, of this city, on the evening of October 3 (1894)," writes Dr. Gordon. " It was a farewell reception given to two young men that were about to sail as missionaries to China, under the auspices of the Society of Christian Endeavor, connected with that Church.

One of these young men was a Chinaman, and the other an American; and they go out together to labor in the vicinity of Canton in preaching the gospel to the people of China.

"In order to understand the significance of this event, it is necessary to give a brief account of the two men. Wong Tsin Chong, who came to this country from China about twenty years ago, was converted and received into the Clarendon Street Church some eight years since. He has proved to be a man of unusual character, so trustworthy and consistent as a Christian, and so wise and watchful in his oversight of the other Chinese disciples, of whom there are twenty-five in the same Church, that he has long borne the title of 'Deacon Wong.'

"His zeal for the conversion of his countrymen in America has been untiring. On every pleasant Sunday afternoon for three years he has been found in the Chinese quarter of the city, preaching the gospel in the street to the men of his nation, and to such others as have gathered about him to listen. In this out-door ministry he has had the constant assistance of Mr. Joseph D. Matthews, who now accompanies him to China.

J. D. MATTHEWS.

"Mr. Matthews is of Scotch blood, a young man of such sterling character and fervent piety that he has won the highest esteem of all his brethren in the Church. These two, after several years of successful experience in preaching the gospel to the Chinese in Boston, now go forth in company to labor for the Chinese in China. It is rare for missionary candidates to have enjoyed so thoroughly a testing at home before going forth to a foreign field; but it would be well if it were always the case.

"As illustrating the apostolic zeal of this Chinese disciple, I may be permitted to repeat the following conversation. A business man of the city said to me one day, 'Have you a Chinaman in your Church who preaches in the streets?'

"'Yes,' I said. "'Deacon Wong' we call him."

"'Well,' said the gentleman, 'my partner came in the other day, and said, "I have seen a strange sight to-day—a Chinaman holding forth in the streets of Boston. Noticing a crowd gathered, I came near, and saw a man reading from what appeared to be a Chinese Testament, and earnestly addressing his countrymen in their own language. Then he spoke a few words in broken English to the others that were standing about. After the preaching was over, I saw him talking very earnestly to a few that remained behind, till finally he drew one Chinaman aside, and, stepping into a narrow alley, I saw him kneel down on the ground and pray with the man. I confess I was rebuked; for, Christian as I profess to be, I have never had the grace to preach in the streets as I have seen a despised Chinaman do to-day."' Such was the story, and the reader will see from it what seal of apostleship this young Celestial has already won.

"The noteworthy fact in connection with this event is that the Christian Endeavor Society of the Church just named is to assume the entire support and direction of these, their fellow-Endeavorers, in their work upon the foreign field. This society, as well as its missionaries, has already had a preparatory experience. For two years it has sustained a missionary in Africa at an expense of six hundred dollars annually. In that instance it acted under the Baptist Missionary Union. Now it is to sustain two missionaries; and, as our board has no station in that particular field, it will assume not only the maintenance of the missionaries, but their oversight and direction as well.

"When the two left Boston a company of about one hundred and fifty of their fellow-Endeavorers went to the station to see them off. Though they did not so plan it, the train chanced to contain a large number of Chinamen, also bound for the Celestial Empire. The farewells were mingled with songs and prayers, and the society gave each of their missionaries a Christian Endeavor pin.

"I have given this account of a veritable new departure in the field of missionary enterprise with the sincere hope that the movement may extend far and wide among the noble army of Christian Endeavorers throughout Christendom. Who knows but deliverance may come from this quarter? Most of our great missionary boards have closed their financial year with an unprecedented debt. The demands of the foreign field are increasing enormously every year; the volunteers are coming forward by the hundreds; the money is the one human element that is wanting; but it is stolidly and doggedly withheld.

"Now the great requisite for meeting this deficiency the writer has long held to be a wider distribution of responsibility. 'The lift cure' develops extraordinary strength of muscle by first equalizing the strain and then putting on heavier and heavier weights day after day, till the man is able to lift like an ox. The lift cure is our only salvation in the present missionary crisis. Let the Endeavorers take up this work, and what may not result from their combined effort? I would not have believed it possible that our society could have taken such a financial burden and have borne it so easily. It is a simple fact that their annual missionary contribution for the last two years has been larger than that by the entire membership of some of our strongest churches. Yet they have raised it with the utmost ease.

"Our hearts' desire and prayer to God is that this movement may become general. Let the Endeavor Societies have each its own missionary, one from its own number, if possible; at least, one that is personally known and with whom constant correspondence may be maintained. The support of such a missionary will not be found difficult for the stronger societies, at least. In other cases let two or three combine. Let the societies by all means work under the boards of their respective denominations. The missionary boards will gladly co-operate in appointing and directing the laborer on the field, leaving with the Endeavor bands such responsibility as will make the work substantially their own. We think we see a bright light for the cause of the world's evangelization breaking from this direction."

Several of the denominations have made general appeals to their Christian Endeavor Societies for specific missionary objects. The Presbyterian, both on the home and foreign field, have received large help from the Endeavor Societies, and undoubtedly much more will be given in the future days, since Christian Endeavorers are only standing upon the threshold of missionary enterprises. Already thirty-six missionaries of the Presbyterian Board are supported largely, if not wholly, by groups of Christian Endeavor Societies, while the home field in that denomination is receiving quite as much aid for its work. The Endeavorers of the Reformed (Dutch) Church have for years sustained a Christian Endeavor missionary in India, Rev. W. I. Chamberlain, now of Vellore. Moreover, the Endeavorers of this denomination have built several Christian Endeavor churches; number one, at Edgerton, Minn; number two, at Wakonda, South Dakota; number three, at Johnston, N. Y.; number four, at Grand Rapids, Mich. We present the pictures of two of these churches, and the following is a brief history of church number two:

It is situated at Wakonda, South Dakota. In October, 1892, in this village of four hundred, twenty people organized a Reformed Church. Through the winter, without a pastor and under adverse circumstances, this infant church struggled along, maintaining a Sunday-school and other services in a public hall. They secured a subscription of over six hundred dollars and the gift of a fine corner lot.

"CHRISTIAN ENDEAVOR CHURCH NO. 4."
Bethany Reformed (Dutch) Church, Grand Rapids, Mich.

Vigorous work during the following summer, under the direction of Mr. C. M. Steffens, put the church securely on its feet. One of the most important results of Mr. Steffens's work was the organization of a vigorous Christian Endeavor Society, and the interesting in the church of the Christian Endeavorers all through the denomination.

The result is a beautiful little church 35x40 feet, seating about one hundred people. The bell in its spire is the first that has ever rung out the good tidings in that region. The church is painted in light, shaded with dark, olive green, significant of its title, "The Olive Leaf Reformed Church." Within, it is very cozy and inviting. Its total cost was sixteen hundred dollars, and there is no debt upon it.

At the dedication ceremonies, as was very fitting, both the Christian Endeavorers and the Junior Endeavorers had some part. One of the most significant things about the church is the fact that the Christian Endeavor Society has already made a generous gift toward the erection of Christian Endeavor Church Number Three.

The Cumberland Presbyterians have also moved in the same direction, and it is interesting to notice that on the very day when the General Assembly of the Cumberland Presbyterian Church at Eugene, Oregon, was resolving to ask Cumberland Presbyterian Endeavorers to combine for the building of a Christian Endeavor missionary church, the Cumberland Presbyterian Endeavorers of the distant State of Texas, meeting together at the State convention, were memorializing the General Assembly to be allowed to do that very thing.

Among the Disciples of Christ, too, not a little has been done along these same lines. Endeavorers of the Christian denomination in New England, we are told, are supporting a missionary in Japan. It is now proposed by the members of the denomination outside of New England to raise $1,000 for the support of a second missionary.

If I am not mistaken, the Christian Endeavor church built by this denomination in Utah was the first enterprise of this kind undertaken by any denomination. The society of the Central Christian Church of Dallas, Texas, has undertaken to sustain an evangelist for work in that State.

Among the Friends, too, similar efforts have been made, the Friends of Kansas, at their yearly meeting, appointing a Christian Endeavor evangelist to advance the good work in their State.

CHRISTIAN ENDEAVOR CHURCH No. 2.
"Olive Leaf" Reformed (Dutch) Church, Wakonda, South Dakota.

Among the Congregationalists many plans have been proposed to the young people of their churches, some of which at least have met with very generous response, and the sums given to Congregational missions, both home and foreign, are rapidly growing from hundreds to thousands, and from thousands to tens of thousands of dollars every year.

School-houses and churches on foreign fields have been built; native workers and Bible readers supported; a missionary ship in part built and in part sustained, while a very hopeful field has been presented to young Congregationalists of the interior who have been asked to contribute to the support of the younger missionaries on the field.

For this work much has been contributed.

Many societies in the Methodist Protestant churches have also contributed generously.

To return again to the Presbyterians, we read: Dr. James A. Worden, secretary of the Sabbath-school Board of the Presbyterian Church, now proposes to send out into the West Christian Endeavor Sabbath-school missionaries, to be supported by Presbyterian Endeavorers alone. These missionaries will report once in three months to the societies supporting them. They will found new Sunday-schools, and, wherever practicable, will organize new Endeavor Societies.

This chapter might be continued almost indefinitely, but the significance of it lies not in the enumeration of the work already performed, but in the fact that these efforts are the beginnings of an enlarged and more intelligent interest on the part of Christian Endeavorers in the mission work of their own denominations. The loyalty, the devotion, the missionary zeal, the denominational fidelity of Christian Endeavorers are all made evident in these simultaneous denominational movements.

Before this book is published a new chapter of the same general tenor might be added, and each year another chapter concerning the efforts and the results of Christian Endeavor denominational mission work. But these chapters are unnecessary to show the spirit and the purpose of the movement. These first seeds tell of an abundant harvest. We are standing at the fountain-head of a stream of missionary enthusiasm and service whose waters shall make glad the city of our God.

CHAPTER XXXIX.

WORK FOR THE BOYS AND GIRLS.

The Necessity of the Movement—Tabor, Iowa, and What Occurred There—The Germ of the Junior Movement—The Faithful Pastor and His Work—His Own Account of the First Society—Why Should There be Junior Societies—What the Junior Society is Not—Primary Sunday-School Methods Not Adapted—Not for Pouring In but for Drawing Out—Not Playing at Work but Work—Some Junior Leaders—A Leader in New Jersey—A Leader from St. Louis—A Wisconsin Leader—A Connecticut Leader Transplanted to New York—The Better Half Again—Too Numerous to Mention—A Splendid Society in Australia—Some Missionary Juniors—" The Dear Home Land Across the Sea"—The Junior Society of Two—The Prayer Shelf—Five Pennies as Good as a Nickel.

ABOUT this time in the history of the Endeavor movement we began to hear much about the Junior societies. To be sure, they were not new by any means, for the first distinctively Junior Society had been formed several years before in Tabor, Iowa; and more than that, the elements of the Junior Society were in the movement from the beginning.

It will be remembered that in the first society in Portland, Me., on the first evening of its formation, there were boys and girls as well as young women present. The youngest, probably, were ten or eleven, though the majority were verging on young manhood or womanhood, or had already left childhood's years some distance behind them.

Nevertheless, there was a place for the boys and girls in that first society. They were not left out of the plan of their elders, and something was at once given them to do. Before the first society was formed, too, there had been in the Williston Church a pastor's class for the boys and girls, as has been already narrated, and these boys and girls were asked to take a simple pledge, which committed them to the Christian life and which began with the familiar words, " Trusting in the Lord Jesus Christ for strength, I promise that I will strive to do whatever He would like to have me do."

Here was the germ of the Junior movement before any Endeavor Society was established. For a long time the boys and girls in the Williston Society met with their older brothers and sisters, took their share of the work so far as

SOME LADIES WHO HAVE HELPED THE ENDEAVOR CAUSE.

1. Mrs. Mary Montgomery (Adana, Turkey).
2. Mrs. J. W. Van Patten.
3. Mrs. Amos R. Wells.
4. Mrs. Dr. Farnam (Shanghai).
5. Mrs. George W. Coleman.
6. Mrs. Wm. Shaw.
7. Mrs. James L. Hill.
8. Mrs. Charles A. Dickinson.
9. Mrs. Neesima (Japan).
10. Mrs. John Willis Baer.
11. Mrs. J. L. Fowle (Cæsarea).
12. Miss Harriet J. Wishard.

MARCH OF THE NATIONS. JUNIOR RALLY, BOSTON CONVENTION.

TWO IN ONE.

This interesting picture is full of the spirit of Christian Endeavor, for it shows two societies uniting in the "C. E." monogram. The "C" is the Junior Society of the Christian Church, and the "E" that of the Presbyterian Church, of Yellow Springs, O. At the end of the "C" is Rev. O. W. Powers, and at the end of the "E," Rev. B. D. Luther, the pastors, and at the tip of the "C," Miss Amy Sizer, and of the "E," Miss Jennie Knox, the Superintendents of these societies, while Miss Gertrude Baker, the Presbyterian Assistant Superintendent, is at the centre of the "E." The societies are grouped on the front steps of Antioch College.

they could do it, occasionally led one of the prayer-meetings, and in every way were recognized as real members of the Endeavor Society.

So it was in a multitude of other societies. But after a time it began to be felt that some distinctive work was needed for the boys and girls, a work especially adapted to their more immature powers, and people began to say one to another: "If the society is a good thing for older young people, why should it not be equally well adapted to the younger young people? If young men and women need to be trained to speak and pray and work and give, is it not doubly important that the children should be trained in the very same way from the beginning?

"In the older society they are likely to be overshadowed by their elders. They cannot speak as well or pray as fluently or work as vigorously as the older ones, and it is likely that they will take the same place in relation to the older society that young people have for so long taken in relation to the church, unless they are brought together in a place where their individual needs can be consulted and their individual efforts used."

The credit for the actual formation of the first Junior Christian Endeavor Society must be given to the Rev. J. W. Cowan, pastor of the Congregational Church in Tabor, Iowa, who has now followed the course of empire and gone to the Pacific coast, where he is the honored pastor of a church in Oregon City. It will be more interesting to hear from his own pen the account of the formation of that first Junior society: "On the afternoon

REV. J. W. COWAN.

of March 27, 1884, at the close of school hours, a certain brick building in a certain Western town poured its usual noisy crowd of happy, careless children into the streets. And yet not quite its usual crowd, for a few had remained behind, and with serious faces were gathering at that moment in one of the upper rooms, with their teacher and with the pastor and Sunday-school superintendent of the church to which all but one of them belonged. There were eleven children present, and their ages ranged approximately from ten to fourteen.

"After preliminary devotions the pastor explained to them why they had been asked to remain, and ended by reading the constitution of an organization which it was proposed to form. If we could listen to that reading now it would have a peculiarly familiar sound, for it would rehearse substantially the text of the 'Model Constitution,' including the iron-clad pledge which has since been joyfully subscribed to by millions of Endeavorers the world over. But the words were less familiar then, and that pledge had never before been offered to children like these. It was offered not without some misgivings, for grave doubts had been expressed as to its Christian expediency. It was feared by at least one cautious counsellor that the pledge would prove a weary bondage to such young consciences, and that the prayer-meeting requirements would tend to cant and to artificial experiences; and in deference to such objections the organization had been postponed for several months after it was first proposed. And though they were now overruled by the enthusiasm of the teacher and the firm conviction of the pastor, it was felt that no sort of pressure ought to be brought to bear upon the children to induce them to enter into the movement, but that they should be left to do it, if they did it at all, with the utmost deliberation and freedom of choice.

"It was, indeed, hardly expected that it would seem best to organize at all that day. But the children seemed fully ready for it. They listened with the most thoughtful attention to the explanations given, and seemed to be deeply impressed with the responsibility of the step they were taking; but when the vote was taken, and, for greater freedom of expression, taken by ballot, every vote but one was for immediate organization, and when the pledge was passed from hand to hand every name but one was promptly subscribed.

"Thus was organized at Tabor, Iowa, the first Junior Endeavor Society. The ground for such a planting was not wholly unprepared, for the devoted teacher, Miss Belle E. Smith, who helped in the organization that day, and who was the soul and centre of the society for nine years afterward, had been training the children for many months previous in a weekly meeting for devotion and Bible study. Peculiar local conditions seemed also to mark out for us the course pursued, for it was a college town, and the young people whom the pastor would otherwise have organized into an Endeavor Society were already absorbed and well cared for in the college associations, and the children had to be organized, if organized at all, separately. So Providence seems to have designed and brought about the movement.

"For some months the society met weekly in the room where it was organized—afterward at the church. For a good while few knew of its existence, as no effort was made to advertise it or increase its membership. Rather, it was thought best to let it grow as quietly as possible, until the members were well established in Christian experience and trained in Endeavor ways.

"But, of course, it could not be long till the school knew what was going on, and some, who probably did not altogether understand the nature of the society, began to oppose. A series of children's parties were started, held at the same

WORK FOR THE BOYS AND GIRLS.

hour with the meetings, and the members were carefully invited. But it is not known that one of them ever accepted, or was absent from a single meeting for such reasons. The young soldiers stood solidly by their colors, and were so consistent and wise that soon opposition died out, and the society began to grow, and presently even older young people began to press into it, and it was necessary to organize a separate branch for them. This in time expanded so as to include even the college associations, which eventually changed their form and became Endeavor Societies.

"The ten original Juniors, with the possible exception of one, are, every one of them, Endeavorers still, in fact if not in name. The first of all to sign, Raymond C. Brooks, son of the college President, is just graduating with special honors from Yale Divinity School. He gives promise of conspicuous usefulness, and will be a worthy file-leader of the Junior hosts. Only two or three remain at the old, familiar spot. The rest are scattered from the Atlantic to the Pacific, and one is gone beyond the stars. It may interest the reader to see the names of the original ten, and they are given here:

"Raymond Brooks, Frank Baylor, Eugene Smith, Etta Gaston, Louise Fairfield, Anna Clark, Atha Newell, Almyra Peck (deceased), Anna Matthews, and Sarah Marshall.

"These early Juniors, according to their pastor's account, so far as he has been able to trace their history, have been faithful to their early vows, and have fulfilled their early promise. Raymond Brooks, already mentioned, preached

RAYMOND C. BROOKS.

for one year in Iowa, between the middle and senior years in the seminary, and was ordained. He expects soon to go to Oregon with a Yale band, and will doubtless do yeoman's work for the Master in the years to come.

"Eugene Smith is in business at Boise City, Idaho, is an earnest Christian, and is doing well, as his pastor informs us.

"Etta Gaston still has her home in Tabor, and is prominent and thoroughly useful in Christian Endeavor work.

"Louise Fairfield, a daughter of Prof. F. W. Fairfield, grew into a very sweet and bright young lady, graduated in due time at Tabor College, and was married to a fellow-student named Harris.

"Atha Newell (Heckendorn) is a devoted and faithful Christian wherever she has lived, and has been a bright and useful Endeavorer as she has had opportunity. Anna Matthews became a teacher, and is an active, positive Christian.

"One of the early members of the society, writing about the beginning of the organization, says: 'The first prayer-meeting was led by Miss Belle E. Smith, but the text none of us remember. Miss Smith was our leader for the first six months, after which time she would ask this or that member to occupy her chair, she always being present and near at hand to aid us in our trembling efforts to lead.'

"This early member speaks most affectionately of the work that the good pastor did with his Juniors. 'Through his kind, wise leading,' she says, 'we were made to feel at home, to be more free to speak of our temptations, our desires and hopes, and were thus helped onward to a truer life.'

"After a time, a cabinet, composed of the officers, with the several committees, was formed. The pastor was very necessary, and much depended on the members of this cabinet for several years. At the monthly meetings of the cabinet the roll was carefully gone over, member by member, and if any seemed to forget their pledge, failed in their duties, or seemed not to be living as they should, some one who had the most influence over them was chosen to speak kindly to them and to help them to improve.

"It was essential that great care be taken in choosing the officers and chairman to do this confidential work of the cabinet. Business was also talked over, to be brought before the society in as concise a form as possible. Although our ten has grown to three societies, Junior, Young People's, and Senior, we still have a cabinet with representatives from each, and find it necessary to the best work."

For a number of years but few Junior societies were formed. The necessity for this peculiar work was not understood. The usual young people's society helped the children to some extent, but as the young people grew older, more efficient and experienced, and the contrast between them and the younger ones became more marked, there began to spring up in various places Junior societies modelled on Christian Endeavor lines substantially like the Tabor Society.

The object of these Junior societies is exactly the same as the object of the older society, and their methods are very much the same. The Junior Society is not a primary Sunday-school class. It is not simply for instruction and for pouring in a fund of Biblical instruction into the little pitchers that are held up to receive it, but it is a place where the boys and girls actually pray and speak for Christ, and where they actually serve Him along the same lines as their older friends.

Lookout Committee and Social Committee, Prayer-Meeting Committee and Missionary Committee, Flower Committee and Music Committee, are just as appropriate and just as possible for a Junior Society as for any other.

WORK FOR THE BOYS AND GIRLS. 299

There is only one way to teach *any one* to work, and that is by working. If a child learns to use a hammer or plane he must learn to use it just as a man would learn, not by books, but by handling the tools; little tools perhaps, but yet real ones.

The greatest mistake I believe that is made by Junior superintendents is that of forgetting the distinction between the Junior Endeavor Society and the primary Sunday-school class. The Sunday-school class is largely for the purpose

JUNIOR SOCIETY, BETHEL PRESBYTERIAN CHURCH, EAST ORANGE, N. J.

of pouring in information. The Junior Endeavor Society is for the purpose of drawing out service.

Another mistake that is sometimes made of making it seem to the children like playing at work rather than like actual service. But Christian Endeavor work, whether Junior or Senior, is not play; it is not acting as little girls act with their dolls at housekeeping, it does not consist in getting up imaginary exercises for impossible children, but in recognizing the fact that boys and girls have as real a place in the kingdom of Christ as young men and women, and in giving them something appropriate and natural to do for Christ, something that really advances His kingdom and promotes the interest of His cause. This is the prophecy of old in part fulfilled in a multitude of Junior meetings to-day: "Out of the mouths of babes and sucklings hast thou perfected praise."

Far more than in the Young People's Society of Christian Endeavor does the success of the Junior Society depend upon one person, or at the most upon two or three persons. These persons are the superintendents, and the marvelous spread of Junior Endeavor during these recent years has been very largely due to the great company of devoted, unselfish, whole-hearted Junior superintendents.

Within the limits of this volume I can speak of but very few of these leaders, though we are tempted to extend this chapter indefinitely.

One of the earliest Junior leaders and one of the most efficient, whose heart is still as warmly enlisted in the work as at the beginning, is Mrs. Alice May Scudder, the wife of Rev. J. L. Scudder, of Jersey City.

Of fine presence and winning manners, Mrs. Scudder has always commended the cause of the Juniors wherever she has gone, and her services have been in the widest demand at State conventions, at local union meetings, and wherever, indeed, the interests and the work of boys and girls were discussed.

Miss Kate H. Haus, of St. Louis, an experienced and successful teacher in the public schools, is another one whose name is inseparably linked with the work of Junior Endeavor. Her vigorous voice has been heard on many platforms, pleading for more systematic and thorough efforts for the children, and her pen has been busy, as well as that of Mrs. Scudder, in writing concerning this subject which lies so near her heart.

Rev. W. W. Sleeper, now of Beloit, Wis., is another one who has given much time to the interests of the Juniors, and who is always a most acceptable speaker to the children as well as about them.

Mr. Thomas Wainwright, of Illinois, affectionately known as "Uncle Tom," is one of the most beloved of Junior leaders.

Rev. H. N. Kinney, whose name has before appeared in these records as connected with the work of Christian Endeavor in Connecticut, has also been enlisted heart and soul and voice and pen in this special form of work for the younger ones.

Mrs. Clark, the "better half," to whom I feel the necessity of making acknowledgment in every chapter of this book, has also been identified particularly with this branch of Christian Endeavor of late years, and has given much time to working out its problems, not only in conventions and union meetings, but more particularly with a company of Juniors in her own church. But time would fail me even to mention the names of those that come to my pen's point while I write, much less can I speak in detail of the valuable services that have been rendered to this department of Christian Endeavor by such workers as Mr. Wm. S. Ferguson; Miss Nettie Harrington; Miss Lillian A. Wilcox; Miss

PROMINENT JUNIOR WORKERS.

1. Rev. W. W. Sleeper.
2. Ida M. Middleton.
3. Miss Ida Bradshaw.
4. Miss May C. Merritt.
5. Thomas Wainright.
6. Miss Caroline M. Brookfield.
7. W. S. Ferguson.
8. Rev. A. W. Spooner.
9. Rev. Henry Nason Kinney.

Grace E. Hyde; Miss Belle P. Nason; Miss Mary C. Merritt; Mrs. E. C. Smith; Miss Bertha L. Hess; Mrs. M. L. Hagerman; Miss Daisy Dunnington, West Virginia; Miss Laura C. Preston, Oregon; Miss Frances M. Scuyler; Mrs. E. W. Darst; Mrs. George W. Coleman; Mrs. O. M. Needham, of Nebraska; Rev. A. W. Spooner; Miss Cora B. Berry; Miss Ruth Nash; Mr. C. J. Atkinson; Miss Margaret C. Sutton.

Of late years no International Convention is complete without giving half a day to the Juniors and at least part of another session to the Junior workers;

WESTMINSTER JUNIOR ENDEAVORERS.

and at Montreal, Cleveland, and Boston the Junior rallies have been meetings of exceeding interest and promise.

Few souls are so numb or dead that they are not stirred by the beautiful sight of thousands of boys and girls with their fresh young faces all animated with the purpose to serve Christ.

State conventions, and local union meetings, too, always in these days give ample attention to the Juniors, while Junior unions have been formed in many of the large cities whose meetings bring together hundreds and even thousands of children, and do much to fill them with the genuine spirit of Christian Endeavor.

In other lands than America, too, Junior Endeavor work is an important factor. One of the best Junior societies which I have ever visited is in Geelong,

Australia, a society to which that earnest worker, Mr. Howard Hitchcock, and his sister have devoted much time and prayerful attention. The amount of money that this society has raised, the number of sick rooms it has brightened with flowers, the number of errands run by the little feet, the amount of actual work really accomplished by the members would seem a marvel to any one unacquainted with the possibilities of a Junior Endeavor Society.

In Japan I remember a Junior society among missionary children which

JUNIOR SOCIETY, FIRST PRESBYTERIAN CHURCH, NORTH PLATTE, NEB.

interested me much. In Kyoto there is a large colony of American missionaries, and, in the families, are a number of little children who are still too young to be sent to America for their education.

I shall always remember with great delight a little meeting of these Juniors in the home of one of the Kyoto missionaries. At least twelve or fifteen Juniors were present, and, after they had repeated their verses and sang their hymns, we all kneeled down to seek God's blessing.

One after another the children offered prayer as well as a few of the older friends who were present. Simple, childlike prayers they were, while one little flaxen-haired girl especially voiced the feeling of all the rest in the petition: "O Lord Jesus, bless all the people in the dear home land across the sea, and make them all good Christian Endeavorers. Amen." This little girl, so far as I know, never had been in the "dear home land across the sea," but her simple faith and childlike petition taught me a lesson as to the real meaning of prayer such as many a longer and more eloquent supplication has failed to teach.

In Talas, a mission station in the very centre of Asia Minor, I saw another Junior Endeavor Society, composed of the missionary children belonging to two families of devoted workers. The oldest daughter, a girl of twelve or thirteen years of age, was the president; a ten-year-old boy was the Lookout Committee, the nine-year-old one was the Prayer-Meeting Committee, the six-year-old one was the Music Committee and gave out the hymns, while the little four-year-old one was the Sunshine Committee.

His touching prayer at his mother's knee one night, when he had not been quite a model Endeavorer, was, "Dear Jesus, help me to be a sunshine boy, and may I never belong to a thunder-cloud committee again."

The genuine devotion of little children to the cause of Christ has been proved a multitude of times, and, as hundreds of Junior superintendents have informed me, there is no greater joy in their lives than the development of these tender young plants in the Master's beautiful flower-garden. The freshness, the enthusiasm, the unfettered faith, the generous impulses of these boy and girl Christians is contagious, and spurs their elders on oftentimes to a deeper devotion. Whatever may have been the effect of the Junior movement upon the children, and I believe it has been altogether good, it has been marvelously productive in developing the Christian graces of thousands of superintendents chosen from among the older young Christians who have tried to lead the boys and girls into the way of life, and have thus been themselves led nearer to the Master.

I have no doubt that such instances of childlike, touching devotion might be multiplied ten thousand times over, and all would prove the capacity of the child-heart to open itself to influences that are pure, sweet, and true, and the desire of the child-heart to have Jesus, the King Immanuel, reign within.

The number of Young People's Societies of Christian Endeavor still far exceed the number of Junior Societies, but I do not believe that this will always be true. One of these days I think there will be a Junior Society wherever there is a similar organization for the young men and women. The great difficulty heretofore has been to obtain the right material for superintendents. It is still very difficult, in many churches, to find the right *one* who is willing to devote the time necessary to this work ; but in other places this problem has been solved by two or three, or even five, of the older young Christians, young ladies usually, joining together as co-superintendents to do this most Christ-like work.

It has been said by some one, that " five pennies are quite as good as a

BOYS' JUNIOR SOCIETY, BETHANY PRESBYTERIAN CHURCH, PHILADELPHIA, PA.

nickel," and while one individual who has the time and ability and skill and devotion, all combined, is not readily found, in almost every church can be found five earnest people who love children, and who know how to attract and win them, who are willing to do this blessed work for Him who took the little children in His arms and laid His hands on them and blessed them.

PROMINENT STATE WORKERS.
Plate No. 1.

PROMINENT STATE WORKERS.
Plate No. 2.

PROMINENT STATE WORKERS.

Plate No. 1

1. Rev. J. H. Barton, Caldwell, Ida.
2. Mr. W. L. Noell, Huntingdon, Tenn.
3. Mr. W. H. G. Belt, Baltimore, Md.
4. Rev. W. Hamlyn, Charlottetown, P. E. I.
5. Rev. Henry T. McEwen, D. D., New York.
6. Mr. H. H. Spooner, Chicago, Ill.
7. Mr. W. G. Bell, Austin, Tex.
8. Mr. W. H. Strong, Detroit, Mich.
9. Rev. A. E. Driscoll, Souris, Man.
10. Rev. W. P. Miller, Portland, Ore.
11. Mr. Robert Lawson, Cheyenne, Wyo.
12. Rev. C. H. Crawford, Hammond, La.
13. Mr. E. G. Chamberlain, Concord, N. H.
14. Rev. W. F. McCauley, Dayton, O.
15. Rev. Clarence H. Barber, Manchester, Ct.
16. Rev. A. D. Thaeler, Winston, N. C.
17. Mr. John S. Smith, Halifax, N. S.
18. Mr. T. P. Barber, Colorado Springs, Col.
19. Mr. John D. Ellis, Newport, Ky.
20. Miss Antoinette P. Jones, Falmouth, Mass.
21. Mr. H. A. Moulton, Montreal, P. Q.
22. Dr. Elmer E. Kelly, San Francisco, Cal.
23. Mr. G. Tower Fergusson, Toronto, Ont.
24. Rev. C. A. B. Jennings, Union, S. C.
25. Rev. William C. Daland, Westerly, R. I.
26. Mr. John H. Ganner, Russellville, Ark.
27. Mr. Charles E. Allen, Boston, Mass.
28. Rev. A. D. Kinzer, Perry, Io.
29. Rev. A. F. Richardson, Grafton, W. Va.
30. Rev. Harry O. Scott, D. D., Hasting, Neb.
31. Rev. J. C. French, D. D., Newark, N. J.
32. Mr. James R. Townsend, Augusta, Me.
33. Mr. William Blincoe, Guthrie, O. T.
34. Rev. C. D. McDonald, D. D., Grafton, N. D.
35. Mr. Robert Caskey, Salt Lake City, Utah.
36. Rev. Richard W. Lewis, Meridian, Miss.
37. Mr. C. C. Fuller, Bozeman, Mont.
38. Mr. John P. Hartman, Jr., Puyallup, Wash.
39. Rev J. T. McCrory, D. D., Pittsburg, Pa.
40. Mr. Thomas Jones, Kansas City, Mo.
41. Mrs. Mary R. Riggle, Socorro, N. M.
42. Mr. J. M. Wollam, Phœnix, Ariz.
43. Mr. Charles N. Hunt, Minneapolis, Minn.
44. Mr. W. I. Hulett, Aberdeen, S. D.
45. Judge L. J. Kirkpatrick, Kokomo, Ind.
46. Mr. Alton G. Leffingwell, Appleton, Wis.
47. Prof. D. S. Kelly, Emporia, Kan.
48. Rev. F. L. Nash, Carson City, Nev.
49. Rev. M. J. Williams, Muskogee, I. T.
50. Mr. L. A. Conner, Jr., Washington, D. C.
51. Mr. E. G. Osgood, Bellows Falls, Vt.
52. Mr. Fred. S. Ball, Montgomery, Ala.
53. Mr. R. A. Magee, Wolsley, N. W. T.
54. Rev. S. B. Meeser, Wilmington, Del.
55. Mr. F. A. Curtis, Orlando, Fla.
56. Mr. Edward Marsden, Alaska.

Plate No. 2

1. Mr. Frank A. Leach, Jr., Oakland, Cal.
2. Mr. Charles L. France, Toledo, O.
3. Mr. A. Gordon Cassels, Savannah, Ga.
4. Mr. E. E. Towner, Montpelier, Vt.
5. Mr. Roland Mellish, Halifax, N. S.
6. Mr. John B. Sleman, Jr., Washington, D. C.
7. Mr. Peyton Robertson, Nashville, Tenn.
8. Mr. H. H. Grotthouse, Dallas, Tex.
9. Mrs. Robert Collier, Denver, Col.
10. Miss Maude P. Douglas, Auburn, R. I.
11. Miss Mabel Milligan, Las Vegas, N. M.
12. Miss Nellie Whitfield, Kildare, O. T.
13. Miss Mattie E. Race, Jacksonville, Fla.
14. Mr. R. W. Timmons, Moose Jaw, N. W. T.
15. Mr. James McIntosh, Victoria, B. C.
16. Mrs. J. H. Darnell, Van Wert, O.
17. Mr. A. E. Kilbourne, East Hartford, Conn.
18. Rev. J. F. McCurdy, Bonshaw, P. E. I.
19. Mr. O. W. Stewart, Eureka, Ill.
20. Mr. Charles B. Dart, Kansas City, Mo.
21. Mr. Archie B. Warner, Atlanta, Ga.
22. Mr. Thomas H. Allan, Montreal, P. Q.
23. Miss Nellie C. Goodell, Spencer, Io.
24. Miss Mary F. Gipson, Caldwell, Id.
25. Miss Carrie A. Holbrook, St. Paul, Minn.
26. Mr. John A. Ewton, Russellville, Ark.
27. Mr. Frank O. Bishop, Pawtucket, R. I.
28. Mr. Ben. H. Soper, Oshkosh, Wis.
29. Mr. J. H. Burns, Wilmington, Del.
30. Miss Lillian M. Fisher, Bryant, S. D.
31. Mr. H. E. Dill, Moosomin, N. W. T.
32. Mr. Frank W. Lund, Nashua, N. H.
33. Mr. John Josten, Denver, Col.
34. Mr. J. H. Murphy, Boulder, Mont.
35. Rev. H. A. Thompson, Phœnix, Ariz.
36. Mr. A. E. Dewhurst, Utica, N. Y.
37. Mrs. M. Jolly Van Hook, Birmingham, Ala.
38. Elder M. F. Harmon, Jackson, Miss.
39. Mr. Thomas Morris, Jr., Hamilton, Ont.
40. Mr. H. N. Tolles, Salt Lake City, Utah.
41. Mr. Allan Nicholson, Union, S. C.
42. Mr. H. D. Boughner, Clarksburg, W. Va.
43. Mr. Louis Burt Hull, Grafton, W. Va.
44. Miss Jennie T. Masson, Indianapolis, Ind.
45. Miss Jeannette Prince, Spencer, Mass.
46. Miss Sallie M. Protzman, Baltimore, Md.
47. Miss Bessie E. Skelton, Kansas City, Kan.
48. Miss Lucy Jurney, Washington, D. C.
49. Mr. Paul Pratt, Richmond, Va.
50. Mr. George MacDonald, Altoona, Pa.
51. Miss Luella E. Holland, Saginaw, Mich.
52. Miss Myrtie Shively, New Orleans, La.
53. Mr. B. R. Hoobler, Bay City, Mich.
54. Mr. W. H. Morrow, Portland, Ore.
55. Mr. N. B. Fitch, Casselton, N. D.
56. Mr. W. R. Dawes, Lincoln, Neb.

CHAPTER XL.

THE ATTITUDE OF THE DENOMINATIONS.

Not Spoiled by Flattery—Beginning to Receive Recognition—The Harder Struggles of Sunday-Schools to Obtain a Footing—A Day of Fasting and Prayer Against Sunday-Schools—The Y. M. C. A. and Its Early Struggles—The Presbyterian Church and Its Attitude Toward Christian Endeavor—The Friends as Cordial Allies—The Reformed Presbyterians in Christian Endeavor—The Cumberland Presbyterians always Cordial—Methodist Protestants and Their Kindly Attitude—The Disciples of Christ and How They Accepted the Society—Denominational Leaders Identified with Christian Endeavor—The African Churches in the Movement.

THE discussions of the preceding chapter naturally lead us to the broader theme of the attitude of denominational authorities to Christian Endeavor. At first it could not be said that this attitude was one of excessive cordiality. The society has not been in danger of being spoiled by too much flattery from this source; but yet, all things considered, perhaps its reception has been quite as cordial as could be expected, even at the beginning.

It was something new and untried. It looked to many as though its purpose was to give excessive prominence to the young people. It was naturally feared that it would weaken their denominational ties and make them less true to their own churches. It is only natural that it should have been investigated with a good deal of critical care.

It was the very best thing for the society to be thus investigated. The natural conceit of youth did not have a chance to develop in this organization into abnormal proportions.

Much sooner, however, than could be expected did the society begin to receive recognition and even cordial support from denominational authorities and from some denominational newspapers. Much more readily and easily has the Endeavor movement been accepted and adopted by the churches than was the Sunday-school movement. Every one familiar with the history of Sunday-schools will remember how serious and determined was the opposition on the part of many churches and ecclesiastical authorities. One bishop of the Church of England is said to have issued a ponderous decree against this "unauthorized effort to teach the youth apart from the regular instructions of the sanctuary."

In New England it is said that a church of a leading denomination actually called the members together in solemn conclave for a day of fasting and prayer against the introduction of this "pernicious innovation" called Sunday-school.

In Scotland we are told the Assembly of the Scottish National Church condemned in severe terms the "unauthorized instruction of lay teachers," and some of the teachers were threatened with legal proceedings for violating the statutes by which teachers of religion were compelled to obtain a license and take oaths of allegiance to government.

Some ministers stated from the pulpit that Sabbath-school teaching was a breach of the Fourth Commandment, and others threatened to exclude from the communion of the church all parents who sent their children to the Sabbath-school. From some parts of Aberdeenshire Sunday-school teachers were marched into the city of Aberdeen, under the charge of constables to account before the magistrates for their presumption.

"But all the opposition came to naught. The civil authorities, on learning the nature of the new institution, wished the teachers God-speed, and church dignitaries soon became warm patrons of the school which at first they condemned. Those very religious bodies which passed resolutions against Sunday-schools now have annual statistical returns of their operations."

The suspicion and distrust with which the Young Men's Christian Association was looked upon in many high ecclesiastical quarters is remembered by many men who scarcely yet have reached middle age, and it is only surprising that the Christian Endeavor movement has had so little opposition from these quarters and by so many has been received with open arms.

In the great Presbyterian Church practically no rival society exists to the Christian Endeavor, and many Presbyteries and Synods have expressed their interest in the movement and have heartily wished it God-speed in their formal deliverances.

In the Christian denomination the society was naturally received as soon as it was known, not only without opposition, but with genuine enthusiasm, and has been very widely adopted by the churches.

The names of the Tylers, Rev. B. B. and Rev. J. Z., are known throughout America wherever the Disciples of Christ are known, and that is everywhere, and their great activity and influence in Christian Endeavor circles (the younger brother being a trustee of the United Society, and the chairman of the great Cleveland Convention) are equally well known.

The Congregational churches, too, accepted the society with little question, and at more than one of the Triennial National Councils, as well as at many of the smaller ecclesiastical gatherings, has the society been commended in no measured terms.

THE ATTITUDE OF THE DENOMINATIONS. 311

Among the Friends, Christian Endeavor has found the warmest friends, and but very few congregations now exist without such an auxiliary society, while the expressions of satisfaction and delight in the organization are unstinted.

The Reformed Presbyterians, too, have very heartily adopted the Christian Endeavor movement, and scarcely one of their churches is without its Endeavor society.

The Reformed Church in America is another denomination which very early welcomed this organization into its fold, and has carefully nurtured and cared for it ever since. Moreover it has given it a special work to do (as have several other of the denominations), by asking it to build churches, to support missionaries on the foreign fields, thus in the best and most emphatic way showing its confidence in this, its youngest child.

In many denominations leading editors or secretaries or denominational leaders in other lines have become heartily identified with the movement. As in the Cumberland Presbyterian Church, which has never from the first admitted a doubt as to the wisdom and expediency of the Endeavorer movement, the representative of the denomination upon the Board of Trustees of the United Society is Rev. W. J. Darby, D. D., who is also in one of the highest positions which the denomination affords.

To him and other leaders like him has been due very largely the fact that of all denominations in the country none have been more in entire harmony with the principles and methods and aspirations of the society.

Rev. J. W. Cowan, that well-known and delightful author, is another example of a denominational leader who is peculiarly identified with the Endeavor movement. The editor of the young people's paper of the Methodist Protestant Church has a large voice in the councils of this vigorous denomination, which has never desired any other kind of young people's organization within its ranks than Christian Endeavor pure and simple since it has found the society as loyal and true hearted as it is active and brotherly.

In the Presbyterian Church such leaders of missionary and denominational enterprises as Rev. Teunis S. Hamlin, D. D., Rev. John Henry Barrows, D. D., Hon. John Wanamaker, Rev. Wm. Patterson, of Toronto, are members of the Board of Trustees of the United Society, and many others who might be mentioned, have been prominently connected with the society for many years.

Among the Baptists the name of Rev. Wayland Hoyt, D. D., is as well known as that of any denominational leader. How staunch a friend of Christian Endeavor he has been all Endeavorers know. For many years he has been a trustee of the United Society; so have President Wm. R. Harper, Rev. J. T. Beckley, D. D., Rev. P. S. Henson, D. D., Prof. Howard B. Grose, while others no less influential have been equally prominent in other forms of Endeavor work.

Among the Congregationalists the secretaries of the Missionary Boards have always shown a great interest in the society and confidence in its methods, and the large contributions constantly received from the societies show that this confidence has not been misplaced, while the number of prominent names of the denomination that have stood for the society in evil report and good report is a very long one.

In the Methodist Church Rev. H. C. Farrar, D. D., and Rev. E. R. Dille, D. D., have represented the denomination for a number of years on the Board of Trustees, as has also Prof. W. W. Andrews, of Canada, and Rev. Gilby C. Kelly, D. D., of Owensboro, while many prominent Methodists, both in Canada and the United States, have frequently spoken upon the platforms of the International Conventions and have thrown their influence in favor of the society.

In the Lutheran Church no one is better known or loved than Rev. M. Rhodes, of St. Louis, of the Board of Trustees of the United Society Christian Endeavor, whose influence has always been for Christian Endeavor in his denomination, and whose graceful and glowing words have frequently commended it to his brethren.

The Reformed Episcopal denomination has always been heartily and thoroughly in sympathy with the Endeavor movement. Bishop Fallows represents it upon the Board of Trustees and Bishop Cheeny and others in high official position have graced its platforms. Rev. Rufus W. Miller is not only the founder of the Brotherhood of Andrew and Philip, but represents the Reformed Church in the United States on the Board of Trustees.

In the African Methodist Episcopal South, Bishop Arnett, the senior bishop, has on more than one occasion shown his devotion to the Endeavor cause, while in the African Zion Methodist Church the leaders of the denomination are equally in sympathy with the methods and plans of Christian Endeavor.

The society has as yet made comparatively little headway in the Protestant Episcopal Church, though the societies are constantly multiplying in that communion. Canon Richardson, of London, Ontario, beloved and honored of all, represents this denomination in the councils of the society.

Rev. H. P. Shupe, of Dayton, Ohio, stands as the representative of the United Brethren Church among the united brethren of Christian Endeavor.

Rev. J. W. Lowden, now of Boston, one of the earliest friends of the Endeavor cause, who was pastor of the First Baptist Church in Portland, Maine, at the time the Williston Society was started, represents his denomination on the Board of Trustees.

More and more recognition is constantly being given to the Endeavor Society by the denominations in their meetings and through their leaders and the society reciprocates this increased confidence by giving more and more attention to special denominational matters.

The denominational rallies at the great conventions are becoming distinct and most important features of these huge gatherings. Here plans are discussed, denominational projects are broached, denominational missions and their needs are considered, denominational churches are built by the money raised on such occasions, and denominational enterprises of all kinds are forwarded with loving zeal.

May the Endeavor Society in the good providence of God have some part, and an ever-increasing part, in advancing all true denominational interests, and prove, at the same time, that these are not inconsistent with the most blessed interdenominational fellowship and brotherly love.

CHAPTER XLI.

THE ST. LOUIS CONVENTION.

The Two Rival Claimants—How the Question Was Decided—From 7,600 to Over 11,000—The Graphic Report of the Opening Scene—The Sermon again a Great Event—Some Eloquent Addresses—The Advent of the New Secretary—His Introduction to the Work—The Marriage of the Flags.

WHEN the eighth annual convention met in Philadelphia, the trustees were in a strait betwixt two as to the place of holding the next convention, for two most pressing and importunate invitations were received from the young people representing the southwest and the northwest.

Minneapolis, or rather the twin cities of Minnesota, Minneapolis and St. Paul, sent a strong delegation to argue their case. The appeals of the young men were earnest, eloquent, and convincing.

St. Louis also sent an equally strong delegation to present her claims and the arguments of *these* young men were earnest, eloquent, and convincing.

EXPOSITION BUILDING, ST. LOUIS.

The trustees, in view of these urgent wooers, might have said:

"How happy would I be with either,
Were t'other dear charmer away."

At last they compromised the matter by promising to go to St. Louis in 1890, and by virtually agreeing to hold the convention of 1891 in Minneapolis. Since then it has been a recognized custom to decide not one year in advance but two, in order that the committees of arrangement may have ample time to prepare for a mammoth meeting.

Everything was auspicious at St. Louis for a delightful and inspiring gathering. The committee of arrangements had been indefatigable in their preparations.

In fact, the Committee of '90 ever since has been quoted as the model of business enterprise and has set the pace for other committees who have only

COMMITTEE OF '90 (ST. LOUIS CONVENTION).

1. W. H. McClain, Chairman.
2. A. H. Fredericks, Hotels.
3. J. M. Cannon, Correspondence.
4. J. W. Sheldon, Printing and Ushers.
5. L. F. Lindsay, Musical Director.
6. John H. Roth, Finance.
7. Ed. F. Israel, Secretary and Reception.
8. F. W. Tonner, Music.
9. Geo. B. Graff, Halls.
10. W. H. Hammon, Press.

exceeded it in their arrangements, because the succeeding conventions were larger and demanded preparations on a vaster scale. The history of the eleven months immediately preceding, too, was inspiring and at the very outset filled the delegates with great enthusiasm.

This convention, it will be remembered, was held in June, from the 12th to the 15th of the month, instead of July, in order to escape, as it was hoped, the great heat of the summer, so that a record of only eleven months was included in the figures for 1890.

These figures showed that the 7,672 societies of 1890 had increased to over 11,000, and the 485,000 members to 660,000. As many societies had been formed during the past eleven months as during the first seven years of the history of the society. Every month 17,000 had been added to the ranks, as the records say. Every week a corps of 4,000 young soldiers enlisted. Every day five full companies of new recruits had joined the army.

At this time New York was far in the lead, with 1,795 societies, while Pennsylvania came next and had less than half as many, only 818, Massachusetts with 813 societies and Illinois with 809, were close on the heels of Pennsylvania, while Ohio came next with 681 societies.

"Early on Thursday morning, June 12, heavily-laden trains, regular and special, from every quarter began to unload the bannered hosts of Christian Endeavor at the various stations of the city. About 3 P. M. the doors of Music Hall were opened and eager throngs began to enter," says the graphic report of the scribe of the convention, Rev. H. W. Sherwood, of New York, whose name is already familiar to us.

"Admission was gained on presentation of the Endeavor badge. Within doors everything was in readiness to receive the expected guests. Attentive ushers were waiting to conduct each one to his place. The location assigned to the delegations from the States, Territories, and Provinces were indicated by banners. The hall was tastily draped with festoons of red, white, and blue, flags with shields bearing the names of the States and Provinces adorned the gallery, front and sides of the building—a lovely sight to look upon; but great beauty and inspiration were soon to be added, for the delegations were steadily pouring in, rapidly filling the vast space with attentive faces.

"Some of the delegations formed outside and marched in bearing at the front banners of tasteful design and beautiful workmanship.

"When Iowa came with its white banner inscribed with Iowa's glory, 'A school-house on every hill-top and no saloon in the valley,' a hearty cheer arose from every part of the hall. The District of Columbia bearing a large banner with a fine painting of the capitol at Washington, is received with great enthusiasm. Others came and the volume of applause increases. Officers of the

United Society, the representative pastors of the different denominations have taken seats upon the platform.

"The President of the United Society and Governor Francis, of Missouri, enter, and are greeted with round of applause and waving handkerchiefs. The hour for opening the convention has come. The great stage curtain slowly rises, revealing tiers of seats to accommodate a chorus of nearly a thousand singers. Back of these is a great organ which peals forth the opening prelude.

"At a signal from Mr. Lewis F. Lindsay, of St. Louis, the director of the music, the chorus rises and sings, 'To the ranks, To the ranks,' and then after devotional exercises the chorus and convention rise and join in singing:

"'Blest be the tie that binds
Our hearts in Christian love.'

"The thousands of voices mingling in the righ harmony of this hymn, proclaim that this assembly is not a mass of diverse elements but one family in Christ."

But we cannot go on with this eloquent and vivid description. It is sufficient to say perhaps that the spirit, the harmony, and joyous enthusiasm of this first hour were continued throughout the whole convention. Governor Francis and the Rev. W. S. J. Nichols, of St. Louis, heartily welcomed the convention, and Rev. John H. Barrows, D. D., on behalf of the trustees, most eloquently replied.

Again was the sermon of the convention a great event. It was delivered by Rev. P. S. Henson, D. D., of Chicago, on the subject, "Truth as the Architect of Character," and every way sustained the high reputation which the sermon of the Christian Endeavor conventions had maintained for so many years.

Some of the notable addresses of the convention were those on the pledge. Rev. Otis H. Tiffany, D. D., pastor of the Hennepin Avenue Methodist Episcopal Church, of Minneapolis, spoke on the " Element involved in Private Devotion and the Support of Church Services."

It will be remembered that very soon after this convention this honored leader among the hosts of the people of God was called hence, to the great sorrow of Christian Endeavorers in his own denomination and the Christian public in general.

His closing sentence is worthy to be engraved on a tablet of gold with a pen of steel : " Every man is the best worker for the cause at large who is the truest and most faithful worker for the narrower field in which his lot is cast. A Methodist can best serve Methodism, I speak as a Methodist, by joining Christian Endeavor." His concluding sentences were never recorded for he was interrupted by such tremendous and prolonged applause that the reporters could not catch it, but this proved a happy and fitting close.

Rev. W. H. McMillen, D. D., of the Second United Presbyterian Church of Allegheny, Pa., spoke earnestly on "Public Confession of Christ" as involved in the pledge, and Dr. Wayland Hoyt as usual captivated the audience with his address on "Our Associate Members."

Another series of bright addresses was on the model society; "its Heart" was laid bare by Rev. David J. Burrell, D. D., now of New York city, then pastor of the Westminister Church in Minneapolis.

"Its Arms" were described by Rev. W. C. Bitting, D. D., pastor of the Mount Morris Baptist Church of New York city, who has often since spoken most eloquently and acceptably to Christian Endeavor audiences.

In speaking of the Social Arm of the society, he brought down the house as the saying is by the declaration: " I am a Baptist. Every bone in my body, every drop of blood in my veins, every atom of me is a Baptist. I can make this huge crowd angry in five minutes by talking about my ism. I am not here to do that. I stand here to say that I love you. All the way up, all the way down, all the way through, all the way round, from the heel of my foot to the top of my crown."

Rev. J. K. McLean, D. D., pastor of the great and active First Congregational Church of Oakland, Cal., spoke on the "Brains of the Society," and though he modestly claimed that he was there "to advocate brains and not to represent them," all felt that they were represented while they were advocated.

Another very happy series of subjects was on the happy theme "Growing Strong as Christian," divided into three divisions, "Good Food," "Good Air," and "Good Exercise." Rev. J. W. Ford, D. D., of the Second Baptist Church, of St. Louis, emphasized God's Word as the only proper food; Rev. M. L. Haines, D. D., of the First Presbyterian Church of Minneapolis, wittily insisted upon the importance of good air, spiritual, warm, and pure, and Rev. Teunis S. Hamlin, D. D., pastor of the Church of the Covenant, in Washington, who had just been elected to the Board of Trustees of the United Society, spoke happily on the equally important subject of good exercise in developing Christian manhood.

True Christian Union was happily treated by Rev. M. Rhodes, D. D., pastor of St. Mark's Lutheran Church, of St. Louis, and also by Rev. Geo. H. McGrew, pastor of St. Paul's M. E. Church, of New York city, who both claimed that this true Christian union is promoted, as is scarcely possible in any other way, by the interdenominational and international Christian Endeavor movement.

"The Young Christian's Duty to His Own Church" was the theme of Rev. J. M. Hubbard, pastor of the First Cumberland Presbyterian Church, of Nashville, Tenn., and was admirably handled; while "The Other Children of the Church" were treated in three splendid addresses: Rev. R. L. Greene, D. D., pastor of the People's Church, of Boston, speaking for the Sunday-school; Mr. R. P. Wilder, promoter of the Student Volunteers, for the missionary movement, and Rev. W. H. G. Temple, who had then become my honored successor in Phillips Church, South Boston, for the temperance movement.

REV. W. H. G. TEMPLE.

The convention closed with two notable addresses, one by Rev. H. A. Stimson, D. D., pastor of the Pilgrim Congregational Church of St. Louis, and one by Rev. B. Fay Mills, the eminent evangelist, an address which has been printed and widely circulated throughout all the country, and which was remarkable for its spiritual power and uplift.

Mr. Mills also conducted the closing consecration meeting, which will always be memorable in the hearts of those who were happy enough to be at the St. Louis Convention.

My limited space forbids me to speak of the very helpful conference meetings which were held in various churches, all of which were well attended, or of the reports from the different States and Provinces, which were of cheer. Nor can I describe at length as I would like the pastors' hour, which was full of good things, and which was conducted by Rev. H. C. Farrar, D. D., who had just been elected as another representative of the Methodist Episcopal Church on the Board of Trustees.

REV. HENRY A. STIMSON, D. D.

There are one or two special features, however, which we must not forget to record as we recite the history of this memorable convention. For the first time the State delegations were assigned to different churches, eight churches being used for this purpose, and some six or seven States and Provinces being assigned to each church.

This proved to be such a happy feature of the convention that it has been kept up ever since, though in these days a single State usually monopolizes a whole church.

JOHN WILLIS BAER.

Another event of this convention was the introduction to it of Mr. John Willis Baer, who, during the preceding spring, had been chosen the General Secretary of the United Society of Christian Endeavor in place of Mr. George M. Ward, whose uncertain health had led him to resign the office.

I cannot do better perhaps than to quote a few sentences from the introduction of the new General Secretary by the President of the United Society:

"I think we can believe now, as of old, that the Holy Spirit says 'separate unto me such and such a person,' and that He sends him forth to do His work in the world. A few months ago we saw in the State of Minnesota a young man who seemed to have the qualifications for this work. He had the spirit which we believe God will bless. He had been trained as a business man, and yet he seemed to be one who could put his business principles and habits into the Lord's work, to which he was called. And so, led, as we believe, by the Holy Spirit, Mr. John Willis Baer, of Rochester, Minn., was called to be the General Secretary of the United Society.

"It has been with joy that I have seen him take up the work. It has been with great affection that I have gone with him to some of our conventions, where we have tried to say something for this cause, which is dear to us all, and it is with great pleasure that I introduce to this Ninth Annual International Christian Endeavor Convention Mr. John Willis Baer, our General Secretary."

This announcement was received with applause, tumultuous and hearty, with a sea of white handkerchiefs waving the Chautauqua salute and the State call from the Minnesota delegation.

Mr. Baer responded happily and modestly, saying that at this his first International Convention, as he looked at the audience with its representatives from the entire country, he saw that which made him wish more than ever "to be the servant of the Endeavor Society, and under God's guidance to be used as you wish."

I rejoice to say that after these five years I have not seen occasion to revise my affectionate estimate of the man who was thus called to this office or to

THE EXCURSION STEAMERS AT ST. LOUIS.

believe that he was not set apart by the Holy Spirit for the work given him to do.

Another memorable feature of this convention was an excursion on two huge Mississippi steamers on Saturday afternoon. Five thousand went on this excursion in the steamer "Grand Republic," which had been chartered for the occasion, supplemented by the "City of Florence," from Peoria, which brought the Peoria delegates to the convention.

On the boat in the midst of the noise and the throbbing machinery, Rev. W. W. Andrews, then of Toronto, but now of Sackville, N. B., gave an inspiring address on the future of Christian Endeavor, while another episode in which Prof. Andrews had prominent part, must not be overlooked.

Owing to difficulty in procuring an English flag the Union Jack was at first wanting amid the decorations; before the first evening, however, a flag was obtained from the English consul, the omission was remedied, and a large

322   THE WEDDING OF THE FLAGS (ST. LOUIS CONVENTION).

Union Jack was affectionately intertwined with the Stars and Stripes in front of the speaker's desk.

Thereupon with ready eloquence and wit Prof. Andrews stepped forward and said : " This flag with the four and forty stars and the thirteen stripes—what means this crimson color? It is the sacred blood of your fathers and your brothers. No wonder you love it. What flag is this with the cross of St. Andrew and St. George? What means this crimson color? It is the sacred blood of your mother. Shall any man forbid the bans? I now call upon Dr. Clark, as a Canadian born and an American citizen, to pronounce the ceremony completed."

What else, then, could the President of the United Society, amidst the tumultuous applause of the assembled thousands say, except, " What God hath joined together, let no man put asunder."

Too much praise cannot well be given to the Committee of '90 for the success of this convention. Mr. W. H. McClain was its efficient chairman, and all the other names deserve to be recorded in lasting remembrance.

Mr. George B. Graff was particularly efficient in his services, but to mention one more than another would seem almost invidious.

PROF. W. W. ANDREWS.

Mr. L. D. Lindsay, of St. Louis, also proved himself equal to the occasion of leading the great chorus as he has at many a convention since, and his song, " The Endeavor Band," sung there for the first time, has become a great favorite in Endeavor circles throughout the land.

At last this magnificent convention came to a close, and the six or seven thousand delegates took the trains for their homes with a new purpose in their hearts to live up to their motto for the coming year, " One is your Master, even Christ, and all ye are brethren."

A GROUP OF DELEGATES ON STEPS OF CONVENTION HALL, ST. LOUIS, MO.

PROMINENT ENDEAVORERS.

Plate No. 1.

1. Rev. E. M. Hill, M. A., Montreal.
2. Rev. J. A. McGillivray, Montreal.
3. W. A. Coates, Montreal.
4. E. A. Hardy, Lindsay, Ont.
5. Rev. Wm. Shearer, B. A., Sherbrooke, Que.
6. C. J. Atkinson, Toronto.
7. R. W. Dillon, M. A., Ont.
8. G. Ward Siddall, St. John, Newfoundland.
9. Miss Bessie Thomas, St. John, Newfoundland.
10. Rev. W. W. Buwer, Charlottetown, P. E. I.
11. Rev. John McMillan, Halifax, N. S.
12. T. T. Fotheringham, St. John, New Brunswick.
13. Rev. Anderson Rogers, New Glasgow, Nova Scotia.
14. S. J. Jarvis, Ottawa, Ont.
15. Rev. Martyn Summerbell, D. D., Lewiston, Maine.
16. V. Richard Foss, Maine.
17. Rev. O. W. Waldron, Concord, N. H.
18. Wm. P. Fiske, Concord, N. H.
19. Rev. T. S. Weeks, Wolfboro', N. H.
20. Edw. G. Osgood, Bellows Falls, Vt.
21. Rev. E. K. Young, New Britain, Conn.
22. Rev. Lawrence Phelps, Boston, Mass.
23. Rev. J. B. Gordon, Pawtucket, R. I.
24. William C. Deland, Westerly, R. I.
25. Rev. G. A. Conibear, Westerly, R. I.
26. R. I. Morse.
27. Rev. J. H. Williams, Salem, Mass.
28. Rev. J. L. Fowle, Talas, Turkey.
29. Miss Carrie M. Schuyler, Little Falls, N. Y.
30. Mrs. H. T. McEwen, New York city.
31. W. D. Jackson, Buffalo, N. Y.
32. R. M. Sommerville.
33. Rev. John W. F. Carlisle, Newburg, N. Y.
34. Rev. W. J. Peck, Corona, L. I.
35. M. A. Hudson, Syracuse, N. Y.
36. Rev. Thorton B. Penfield, New York.
37. Rev. George W. Furbeck, Stuyvesant, N. Y.
38. Edwin F. Lee.
39. Rev. William Tracy, Philadelphia, Pa.
40. Rev. James A. Little, Hokendauqua, Pa.
41. Rev. N. F. Swengel, Baltimore, Md.
42. Rev. N. B. Grubb, Pastor First Mennonite Church, Phila., Pa.
43. Rev. J. C. Krause, Wilkesbarre, Pa.
44. Rev. J. H. Nabers, D. D., Sunbury, Pa.
45. Rev. D. F. McGill, Allegheny City, Pa.
46. Rev. C. J. Kephart, Lebanon, Pa.
47. Rev. A. L. Reynolds, New Brighton, Pa.
48. Rev. A. DeW. Mason, Boonton, N. J.
49. Rev. G. S. Sykes, Vineland, N. J.*
50. Robt. B. Sinclair, Newark, N. J.
51. Rev. J. Judson Pierson, Bridgeton, N. J.*
52. Miss Caroline B. Brookfield, Belvidere, N. J.
53. Rev. F. G. Ottman, Newark, N. J.
54. P. S. Foster, Washington, D. C.
55. Rev. Edward B. Bagby, Washington, D. C.
56. Rev. Alex. Proudfit.
57. John Silver Hughes, Baltimore, Md.
58. Mary E. Belt, Baltimore, Md.
59. Rev. Hugh L. Elderdice, Pocomoke, Md.
60. J. R. Whitney, Wilmington, Del.
61. Samuel C. Evans, Jr., Milford, Del.
62. Thos. J. Mason, Delaware.
63. Rev. J. C. Cromer.
64. Rev. Levi Rees, Indianapolis, Ind.
65. W. J. Lewis, Evansville, Ind.
66. Rev. Mary E. Mars, Greenfield, Ind.
67. Rev. M. M. Binford, Richmond, Ind.
68. A. B. Cristy, Cleveland, Ohio.
69. Elwood O. Ellis, Fairmont, Ind.
70. Rev. R. V. Hunter, Indianapolis, Ind.
71. Rev. Alfred C. Hathaway, Richmond, Ind.*
72. Rev. J. G. Fraser, Cleveland, Ohio.
73. Rev. Leander S. Keyser, Springfield, Ohio.
74. E. Lee Fleck, Dayton, Ohio.
75. Rev. N. F. Shupe, Dayton, Ohio.
76. C. B. Heldridge, Bloomington, Ill.
77. Ella D. MacLaurin, Chicago, Ill.
78. Thos. B. Nisbitt, Chicago, Ill.

* Deceased.

Plate No. 2.

1. Rev. L. F. John, Toledo, Iowa.
2. Rev. J. M. Lucas, Des Moines, Iowa.
3. C. C. McMill, Burlington, Iowa.
4. E. Belle Stewart, Cedar Rapids, Iowa.
5. P. E. Zartman, Sioux City, Iowa.
6. Rev. J. H. Wright, West Liberty, Iowa.
7. H. T. McIlfresh, Ex-Sec. W. Va. C. E. Union.
8. Rev. S. H. Doyle, Phila., Pa., formerly of W. Va.
9. F. C. Wheeler.
10. F. R. W. Porter.
11. Rev. E. P. Leeve, Tennessee.
12. Prof. J. R. McColl, Knoxville, Tenn.
13. R. J. Parnell, McKuzier, Tenn.
14. Rev. W. T. Rodgers, Nashville, Tenn.
15. E. A. Palmer, Chattanooga, Tenn.
16. Ira Landreth, Nashville, Tenn.
17. O. L. Stephenson, Bell Buckle, Tenn.
18. W. Watts, Louisville, Ky.
19. Mrs. Bessie DeMoss Ellis, Bellevue, Ky.
20. Mrs. Edith Meeker Waller, Louisville, Ky.
21. Wm. S. Waller, Louisville, Ky.
22. Frank H. Clark, High Court, N. C.
23. T. M. Johnson, North Carolina.
24. Dunbar Robb, Charleston, S. C.
25. Willard Eliot, Tampa, Fla.
26. Rev. S. F. Gale, Jacksonville, Fla.
27. C. H. Parsons, Salt Lake City, Utah.
28. Rev. H. G. Scudday, Longview, Texas.
29. William P. Taylor, Birmingham, Ala.
30. Miss Sadie E. Black, Montgomery, Ala.
31. Edw. Altemus, Missouri.
32. William H. Black, D. D., Marshall, Mo.
33. L. L. Roby, Topeka, Kansas.
34. Prof. A. W. Eshman, Miss.
35. Rev. C. E. Downman, D. D., Savannah, Ga.
36. Rev. W. O. Carrier, Wausau, Wis.
37. W. D. Gibson, Appleton, Wis.
38. Myra A. Manning, Oshkosh, Wis.
39. Alton G. Leffingwell, Appleton, Wis.
40. Rev. L. A. Morse, Tomah, Wis.
41. Charles F. Cutts, Pres. of the Union in Carson City, Nev.
42. J. H. Murphy, Boulder, Mont.
43. Mrs. Floyd N. Smith, Helena, Mont.
44. C. C. Fuller, Bozeman, Mont.
45. Rev. J. V. More, Helena, Mont.
46. J. D. Radford, Bozeman, Mont.
47. Miss Mary F. Gipson, Idaho.
48. F. P. Haskell, Jr., Tacoma, Wash.
49. Edwin S. Miller, Portland, Oregon.
50. W. H. Lewis, Seattle, Wash.
51. Margaret MacFarlane, Tacoma, Wash.
52. Rev. D. C. Garrett, Seattle, Wash.
53. H. L. Sizer, Seattle, Wash.
54. W. Willis Carr, Seattle, Wash.
55. W. Bench Wilcox, Spokane, Wash.
56. Joseph Chapman, Jr., Minnesota Union
57. C. L. Stevens, Ypsilanti, Mich.
58. Geo. Ransom, Ionia, Mich.
59. F. G. Langdale, Clark, S. Dakota.
60. Esther A. Clark, Yankton, S. Dakota.
61. Geo. A. Ragan, Sioux Falls, S. Dakota.
62. Rev. N. F. Richardson, Denver, Colo.
63. E. B. Clark, Denver, Colo.
64. C. Z. Merritt, California.
65. W. R. Guy, San Diego, Cal.
66. W. Stuart Merriam, Oakland, Cal.
67. Wm. G. Alexander, San José, Cal.
68. A. W. Lane, Nebraska.
69. O. M. Needham, Albion, Neb.
70. Mrs. O. M. Needham, Albion, Neb.
71. Rev. Harry Omar Scott, D. D., Nebraska.
72. Rev. A. J. Turkle, Omaha, Neb.

PROMINENT ENDEAVORERS.
Plate No. 1.

PROMINENT ENDEAVORERS.
Plate No. 2.

CHAPTER XLII.

TEN YEARS OLD.

The Tenth Birthday and How It Was Celebrated—Going Back Home—Williston Church on the Night of the Anniversary—The Cradle In Which the Child Was Rocked—The Early Prayer-Meeting—Some Admirable and Fraternal Speeches—Mr. Pratt's Address —Dr. Burrell's Famous Poem.

IT was only fitting that the tenth birthday of this vigorous organization should be celebrated in some fitting way. There was only one place in which it could be most appropriately celebrated, and that was in the city of its birth, so it was decided to have the chief celebration in Portland, Maine, though there were many minor recognitions of the day in other places.

The Portland societies entered heartily into the idea. The large City Hall was engaged for the principal services and for three days, Feburary 2, 3, and 4, 1891, "What Has Been," "What Is," and "What Is to Be," were the subjects of animated address and hopeful prophecy on the part of a large number of eminent speakers.

REV. DWIGHT M. PRATT.

Rev. Dwight M. Pratt, who had then become the beloved pastor of the Williston Church, welcomed the Christian Endeavorers who had come together from all parts of the country, as was most fitting, and the first services on the evening of February 2, were held, as was also fitting, in Williston Church itself.

Suspended in front of the pulpit was a huge globe with its colored map of the world and encircling it these words and letters, "The whole world for Christ—Y. P. S. C. E." "An ordinary date, a simple symbol," says Rev. J. L. Sewall in his account of the great anniversary meeting; "but between the two was encompassed the sum of the movement which was celebrated, and the substance of all that was said and done in the two days and three evenings of this memorable jubilee.

"How the people poured into the porticoes of that church and chapel which ten years ago was closed and quiet, the pastor's home alone lighted with the dawning glimmers of Christian Endeavor! As the magnificent strains of the pilgrim chorus pealed from the organ the crowds compressed themselves into every nook and corner and many were unable to find even a cranny in the wall from which to enjoy that delightful evening.

"True the gathering was in marked contrast to the last national gathering

WILLISTON SOUVENIR OF TENTH ANNIVERSARY.

of Christian Endeavorers, when the great Music Hall at St. Louis was thronged with its thousands for the closing service. But there was a coziness and home-likeness about this session which could not have been equalled elsewhere."

This meeting in Williston Church, was a kind of family gathering, and was made as informal as possible.

Mr. W. H. Pennell, Secretary Baer, Rev. James L. Hill, Rev. C. A. Dickinson, all made addresses as well as Rev. B. L. Whitman, of the Free Street

Baptist Church; Rev. C. P. Mills, of Newburyport; Rev. C. H. Barber, Prof. C. S. Nash, and Rev. N. Boynton, of Boston.

In the report of the proceedings of this anniversary some extracts are given from an informal address by myself which I will here reproduce, as they tell the causes which had led to the growth of this ten-year-old child as they appeared to me in the glow of that delightful anniversary:

"I have only some very informal things to say about that infant born ten years ago in that house over on Neal Street. Why was he born at all? and how came he to have so vigorous a growth as appears on this his tenth birthday?

"First of all, he was rocked in a good cradle. Williston Church was a good place in which to be born. We must look back into the old chapel, nay, into the school-house where the first Sunday-school was held, if we would understand the relation of the birthplace to the child. This church was not an aristocratic or a class church; it would have been impossible for this child to have been nurtured in such surroundings.

"Again, this child had its growth because a good woman rocked the cradle. The cradle needs a woman, you know, to keep it jogging by an occasional touch of her foot. There is one who has never had her proper credit for her help in starting and constantly caring for this society. It was the pastor's wife who gathered together that Mizpah circle, out of whose number largely came the original membership, and at whose meeting ten years ago this evening the society was formed.

"Another reason for the growth of the society was the kindly attitude of its older relatives in this church. The older brothers and sisters, you know, sometimes look askance at the little stranger; not so in this case. There have been churches where the other departments and members have been jealous and unsympathetic; but I never knew anything of the kind in this church.

"And this child had its remarkable growth and development also because of the kindly attitude of other relatives, less closely allied—I hardly know what to call them—the other churches in the city. One by one they adopted it as their own. I well remember that first conference, where one delegate was present from that distant city of Bath, twenty-five miles away; how strange it seemed that any one should come from so far as Bath to such a meeting! The sympathy and help of these other churches was a great aid in those early days.

"But the most important thing in the growth of this child was the good hand of God, the heavenly Father. God had a place for it in the world and in the church. The providential aspect of the movement is most marked. The increase has been gradual and unexpected at every point. There is no one person who has been responsible for it. It has come and grown and gone throughout the world because God had a place for it. The different lines of work have not been taken up until the hand of Providence has opened before us the doors, and we could not help entering. All that we can say to-night is with reverence, humility, and deep thankfulness, 'Not unto us, not unto us, but unto Thy name, O God, give glory! This is the Lord's doing, and it is marvelous in our eyes!'"

More formal exercises of the anniversary were opened the next morning in the City Hall. "Seven o'clock comes very early on a February morning," remarks Mr. Sewall in his account, "but there were a great many early birds who gathered in the Second Parish Church for spiritual food from the Father's hands."

The snow and rain began as promptly as the opening nine o'clock session in City Hall, and the delegates were favored with a large and varied assortment of Maine weather during the two days of the convention, but their enthusiasm was in no way dampened by the unpropitious elements.

The Mayor of Portland made a happy address, and the Governor of the State sent a cordial greeting in lieu of his bodily presence. Dr. George H. Wells, of Montreal, drew a glowing picture of the possibilities of the society in the future. Rev. Charles P. Mills eloquently and wittily sketched the origin of the society. He declared it was fathered by a revival and mothered by a necessity. "This is our syllogism. Necessity is the mother of invention. Necessity is therefore the mother of the Christian Endeavor Society. What necessity? Why simply the necessity of mothering.

REV. A. E. DUNNING.

"The Williston Church came in as an educated Christian woman to mother the young converts of the revival of 1881. She fashioned for it the Christian Endeavor Society, and said: Submit to the regimen of this society and accept its care; by it you will keep well; by it you will be nurtured with facts and principles into vigorous life and noble character. A capital incubator for babes in Christ to keep them warm and to supply them with vitality through a period of weakness is this Christian Endeavor Society."

Rev. Chas. A. Dickinson's happy address on "The Development of the Young People's Society Christian Endeavor," naturally followed Mr. Mills' account of the origin, in which he dwelt upon the timeliness of the movement as the secret of its surprising growth.

"A Retrospect and a Prophecy" was the title and indicates the scope of the address of the President of the United Society.

Dr. O. P. Gifford, then of the Warren Avenue Baptist Church, of Boston, gave an address on "The Society as a Means to the Great End, the Exaltation of Christ."

Dr. A. E. Dunning, editor of *The Congregationalist*, spoke sympathetically and helpfully on the relation of the Endeavor Society to the Sunday-school, while Rev. C. M. Southgate spoke cheeringly of the practical results thus far of the Christian Endeavor movement.

He said that, "The Christian Endeavor movement had demonstrated the winning power of duty. It has demonstrated that we have a living God in a living church. It has struck the true spirit of Christian unity, and declared that we look to the society to set the style and in spite of standards of blood, breeding, brawn, or bullion, to make the Christian youth the ideal of every boy or girl."

One of the most enjoyed addresses of this anniversary was that by Rev. Le Roy S. Bean, of the Free Baptist Church, of South Windom, Me., who told how the society meets the demands of the times in developing Christian workers, by the universality of its object, the reconciliation of the world to God, by its tendency to produce specialists in Christian work, and by its blessed spirit of unity.

Rev. Mr. Farnum, pastor of the First Baptist Church, in Salem, Mass., showed how the society was solving the social church problem.

"The whole work of every Christian Endeavor Society may be wrought out under the rule of the one divine and infallible motive, service for Christ's sake. That is genuine *Christian Endeavor*. Safety and success lie along that path. Let every effort swing on that pivot, and the barred gates of every difficulty will swing wide open.

REV. C. M. SOUTHGATE.

"There is no other successful method. Lord Nelson's advice to a subordinate officer, is good advice for Christian Endeavorers. The officer wanted to know how to engage his ship in a battle. 'Get alongside your enemy's guns,' was the response, 'and you'll find out how to do it.' So, with this problem, let any band of young people, anywhere on the globe, really bend their necks to the yoke of Christ's service, really catch the motive and inspiration of *true Christian Endeavor*—Service for Christ's sake—and every fibre of their being will feel the thrill of a new joy, and the girding of a new power. Handshaking, then, is found to have a divine element in it. A smile of recognition is the reflection of a beam of light from heaven. With this spirit there will no longer be any demand for broom-drills, or for exhibitions of Punch and Judy in the church of God. A toboggan shute from the pulpit to the deacon's pew will not be needed to attract and hold the people. *Christian Endeavor* endeavors to do something *Christian*.

"'This is the famous stone
That turneth all to gold;
For that which God doth touch and own,
Cannot for less be told.'"

Dr. J. G. Merrill, pastor of the Second Parish Church of Portland, enlarged upon the way in which the society meets the demands of the times. Dr. E. K. Alden spoke of the missionary idea as essential to large Christian thought, and Dr. A. H. Plumb, of Boston, preached a capital anniversary sermon.

Rev. Dwight M. Pratt throughout the meeting was helpful in every way, as were all the members of the Committee of Arrangements, and the closing sentence of his address of welcome happily reveals the spirit of promise and hope which the anniversary seemed to inspire in Christian Endeavor ranks everywhere·

"The church of to-day, with the eye of the prophet, seems, as never before, to be looking into the future. Isaiah stood and peered into the coming centuries until he saw the vision of the Child who was to be called Wonderful, the mighty God, the Prince of Peace. At a later day the Seer of Patmos stood in like manner, wistfully gazing into the future, and saw the New Jerusalem coming with its glory to earth. The church to-day stands between the prophecies of Isaiah and John, with its eager gaze along the same line of vision. It sees the consummation and the coming glory. It is laying plans for conquest as never before. It is inspired with hope, enthusiasm, and confident faith. Every new effort like that of Christian Endeavor is proof of new energy and wisdom, new power, devotion, and zeal. Let us plan and work and pray and make this new decade a new and glorious era in the progress of Christ's kingdom."

This occasion, too, gave birth to one of the happiest poems which the Endeavor idea has as yet inspired. It was by Rev. D. J. Burrell, D. D., now pastor of the Marble Collegiate Reformed Church of New York city, and was entitled "After Ten Years of Service." In no way can this chapter be closed and the history of the first ten years of Christian Endeavor as well, than by quoting these inspiring lines:

An angel came from heaven down,
  To speak one word and speak it ever,
To quicken hearts and kindle eyes,
And move dull souls from sloth to rise
And win a glorious renown,
  With one brave word, "Endeavor."

Ten years in service thus he wrought,
And then at heaven's gate besought,
"My Lord, what wilt Thou now?"
"Return," said He, "and ten years more
Proclaim thy message o'er and o'er;
Be faithful thou."

"And then?" "And then serve ten years more,
And ten years more, and so forever!
For angel ne'er had nobler task,
Nor of his Lord could nobler ask,
Than to proclaim forevermore,
  That potent word, 'Endeavor!'"

PROMINENT PHILADELPHIA UNION WORKERS. (See page 274.)

1. J. Howard Breed.
2. J. Burns Allen.
3. H. C. Lincoln.
4. Thomas R. Patton.
5. Mrs. L. V. C. Richardson.
6. W. W. Bitting.
7. W. L. Turner.
8. J. R. Robinson.
9. W. A. Gillespie.

CHAPTER XLIII.

ON ENGLISH SOIL ONCE MORE.

Slow Progress in the Mother Land—The Fostering Care of the Sunday-School Union—Another Invitation—A Run Through Italy—The First English Convention—Some English Endeavorers—An Address With the Right Ring—The Significance of this Convention—The Outlook for the Future—Some Devoted Endeavorers—The Two Weeks' Campaign—Going our Several Ways—Mr. Dickinson's Appointments—Mr. Boynton's Work—Mr. Hill's Tour—Coming Together in Cumberland—Under the Pines of Keswick—English and American Audiences—The Reflex Influence on America—The Endeavor Society No Temporary and Provincial Affair

DURING these years of rapid growth of the Endeavor movement in America, the society, though it had a foothold, was making very slow progress in the mother land. Perhaps this progress was as rapid as could be expected, and the growth of the plant was certainly healthy, if not rapid.

From the first the infant society in Great Britain had been taken under the kindly fostering care of the Sunday-School Union, and, so far as the honorary secretaries of the union and its branches of the union in different provincial cities could help on the work, the society found its way into the affections of the English Sunday-school workers.

Still, as I have said, the growth was slow, and it was freely predicted by some on both sides of the water that Christian Endeavor was not in accordance with the genius of English institutions, and that we need not look for any great growth in the mother land. Some of us believed, however, that the slowness of this growth resulted from lack of information rather than from lack of adaptability, and that all that was needed to secure a generous reception of the Endeavor idea was more light and fuller information. So, again, by the Sunday-School Union of Great Britain and Ireland, with three friends, I was invited to visit England for the purpose of attending some of the May meetings as well as the first Convention of Endeavor Societies of the British Section to be held in Crewe, in Cheshire, on the 13th of May.

Accordingly, on the 4th of April, 1891, my dear friend, Rev. C. A. Dickinson, and myself set sail on the steamer "Umbria" from New York for Liverpool. A week later we were on English soil, but we did not tarry long in the old country just then, for, being worn out with our duties at home, we had resolved to spend a little time in rest and pleasure-travel before beginning this English campaign. Our journeyings took us as far as Rome and Naples and Venice and, coming back by the way of the Riviera and the St. Gothard Tunnel, we had a little glimpse of Swiss mountains and lakes, and a breath of the invigorating breezes of the Alps before beginning in England the special mission for Christian Endeavor.

After getting back to England the days were crowded with a large number of meetings for both of us. I find the record of meetings that I attended in Macclesfield on the 9th of May, in Red Hill, South Surrey on the 15th of May, at Edmonton and Toppingham on the 21st, and in East London on the 22d.

But the most important meeting of this visit was the one already alluded to, the First Convention of the Christian Endeavor Societies of the British section.

Very appropriately this meeting was held with the parent society of Great Britain in the High Town Congregational Church of Crewe; just as the first convention of all was held in the Church of the parent society in Portland, Maine.

This First English Convention, though not large according to present standards, was a larger meeting than the First American Convention in 1882, and gave full promise of the larger things which were to follow.

Among those present I find the names of the following well-known English Christian Endeavorers: Rev. J. G. Morgan, of Chester; Mr. J. F. Hooke, of Birmingham; Rev. W. H. Towers, of Manchester; Mr. David Morris, of Marple; Rev. W. Bainbridge, then of Chester, and several others whose names are household words to English Endeavorers.

As was altogether appropriate, Rev. A. W. Potts, the original Endeavorer of Great Britain, gave the address of welcome, and a most hearty one it was. It so well indicates the spirit of hopefulness and of prophecy of larger things that pervaded that first meeting that I must quote a few sentences from this cordial address.

Not many months after this meeting this honored worker, who put so much of his life and abounding energy into this new movement to which he had given his allegiance to the uttermost, passed on to his reward, and the victory of which his closing sentence tells was fully his.

"In extending our welcome," he said, "to Dr. Clark and to the Rev. C. A. Dickinson, whom we are all both proud and pleased to see, and in extending our welcome to all the representatives of the societies under the British section, we are inspired by the lively hope that from to-day we shall make enlarged progress. We have watched with delight, and with increasing confidence, the growth and rapid development of this truly Christian movement. We accept the widespread testimony that Christian Endeavor has brought new life into the churches. It seems to have come for that very purpose. It sounds a trumpet call to obedience and service. It unfolds a banner that appeals to loyalty and motive. It wins the young people because it is their movement and because, in part, it has come to satisfy their claims.

* * * * * * * * *

"Welcome then! thrice welcome! for you have come to render personal service. Welcome! thrice welcome! for you have come to undertake this great Endeavor task. Welcome to all the fellowship of this meeting. Welcome to all the toil and the conflict of this great movement. Welcome to all the joy and the inspiration of it also. And in the end may it please God to welcome us all into heaven's higher fellowships, and to grant to us the final rewards of our labor and victory."

In addition to those whose name we have already mentioned as participating in this convention, Mr. Charles Waters, the early and always reliable friend of Christian Endeavor, also gave an address; Mr. Dickinson, as well as myself, spoke more than once, and at the close of the brief evening session the first English convention came to a happy end.

Its significance lay largely in the promise and outlook for the future, a promise which has been fulfilled a hundred times over during these later years.

Soon after this meeting at Crewe we were joined in London by two other personal friends and long-time supporters of the Christian Endeavor movement who had just come across the water. Their names have already appeared more than once in this history, Rev. Nehemiah Boynton, of the Union Church of Boston, and Rev. James L. Hill, then of Medford, Mass. If I were writing of them as they are to-day, the semi-lunar symbols of dignity must be affixed to their names, but we will try and observe the historic proprieties.

It was arranged by the secretaries of the Sunday-school Union that we should go to different sections of England, not two and two as went the apostles of old, but singly, in order to make our limited time and numbers go as far as possible in spreading the Endeavor idea.

Mr. Dickinson, as I have already stated, was my American colleague at the first English convention in Crewe already described. After that he went to Newcastle-on-the-Tyne, where he spoke at a Sunday-school Union meeting in the John Knox Church to a large and attentive audience.

Evidently he was not bringing coals to Newcastle when speaking on a Christian Endeavor theme. Later in the same week he addressed meetings in South Shields, Sunderland, Middleboro, and Waterloo. In all of which places he was greeted by large audiences.

He reported that, although the movement was quite new to his hearers and although some of their questions indicated a fear that the society would result in making the young people too precocious, he was able to allay their fears, for all were in earnest to do something for the young people, and the thought in every heart and expressed by all voices was "we must do something to interest our young people in the churches."

Rev. Nehemiah Boynton was assigned to meetings in the South of England, and spoke in Portsmouth, Bristol, Taunton, Tunbridge Wells, and Newport in Wales.

He brought back the same good report of large audiences and attentive listeners and exceeding cordiality on the part of the friends who came to hear about Christian Endeavor.

In Mr. Boynton's campaign one incident characteristic of the movement occurred. After rehearsing some details of the society, an objector arose to say that it was all very well, perhaps, for the young men, but he did not think it would do for the young women of England; that all the traditions were against their activity in prayer-meetings and such church work, and, in fact, they *could not* speak, even if the opportunity were given them.

No sooner had the objector sat down than a young lady from Boston, Mass., who happened to be in the audience, Miss Nellie Stark by name, arose and quite demolished the argument of the objector by showing, in a modest and womanly way, that a woman *could* speak in meeting, and speak quite to the point, and no less helpfully than a man, while her recital of what young women were actually doing in America was received with a hearty burst of applause, and by the complete subsidence of the critic.

Rev. James L. Hill addressed meetings in the interest of Christian Endeavor in West London, Boston, Barnesley, Huddersfield, Colchester, and twice more in London.

He writes to me, "This mission to England will always be of the deepest interest." At Barnesley the Mayor of the city presided, and an English paper describes Mr. Hill's remarks as "pointed and racy, and as listened to most attentively."

In writing to a home paper about this journey, Mr. Hill mentions some things which impressed him particularly. One of these things was that the atmosphere of the audience was "just right." Another, the heartiness of English hospitality. A third element in the success of the visit was its opportuneness. "In the conferences which followed the addresses many have voiced the conviction that action should be immediate. A bridge must connect the Sunday-school and Church."

Turning to study for a moment the condition of things as we found them, Mr. Hill noticed "the presence in the Independent churches of many who had heard of Christian Endeavor from friends on the sunset side of the sea; the influence of Pansy's books; the fact that ministers and young people being less brought together than in America, need to know each other even more than in America, and the character and dignity given to the meetings by the character of those who presided at the meetings, and who thus secured a good hearing for Christian Endeavor."

In another article Mr. Hill describes the different ideas which prevail in England concerning the prayer-meeting from that which prevails in America.

"Who makes the *address?*" he says is the question at the ordinary meeting. An elaborate discourse must be undertaken. This is the very thing our society discourages. Their earlier Christian bands were built up around one person, and when that person removed from town the whole fabric falls. We teach that it is the duty of leaders and individuals to make themselves unnecessary."

Again, Mr. Hill spoke of the multiplicity of organizations in the English churches, which many English brethren were beginning to feel might be united and "domed over" by Christian Endeavor. He also refers to the elaborateness with which the meetings closed, and the formal and sometimes stately vote of thanks, occupying fifteen or twenty minutes, which must be given to the chairman, and to which he must respond in equally set and lengthy terms.

I remember that one of our quartette was asked to move the vote of thanks to the eminent Lord Herschell, who presided at the annual Sunday-school anniversary in Exeter Hall.

Not knowing the English custom, he wisely declined the honor, and he confessed afterward that it was the luckiest escape of his life, for, if he had accepted, he would simply have arisen and said: "Mr. Chairman, I move a hearty vote of thanks to our honored presiding officer for the skill and grace with which he has conducted the proceedings of the evening."

But this would have seemed meagre and ridiculous in the eyes of an English audience, who would have expected at least fifteen minutes to be spent in moving the thanks, during which the speaker might touch on any points which he deemed pertinent to the occasion, while to the man who seconded the motion almost as much time would be accorded.

After these various meetings in different parts of the United Kingdom we all got together for a holiday in the charming lake region of Cumberland; and, while walking under the pines of Keswick and along the verdant shores of Grassmere and Ambleside, we talked over our experiences among our cordial English brethren.

We all agreed that there were no such audiences in the world to address, so far as our limited experience had gone, as English audiences. None so kind and sympathetic and encouraging to the speaker. The "Hear, Hear," the applause, the expressions of approval, so different from the stolid, disheartening silence in which many American audiences receive even an address of which they heartily approve, was a revelation and a delight to us.

We all agreed, too, that while doubtless Christian Endeavor had a future in Great Britain its growth would be slow for many years to come. We did not anticipate the rapid era of advance which would soon set in. In many ways I feel that the influence of my friends and colleagues wherever they went was greatly for the advantage of Christian Endeavor and in some of the places where we then found little to encourage, the movement has sprung up with great vigor, and is flourishing to-day in the same luxuriant fashion as in America. The reflex influence, too, upon the work in America was most beneficial. It began to be seen that the Christian Endeavor Society was no temporary and provincial movement, but that it had adaptabilities and capabilities that its friends had not suspected; that it had something to do for the youth of other lands beside our own; and this conviction strengthened the work at home and gave new courage to the workers.

I ought not to allow this opportunity to pass without saying that this trip was undertaken most unselfishly and generously by my friends, who took this long journey at their own expense, except so far as traveling expenses from place to place in England were concerned, because of their love for the Endeavor Society, and because of their desire to establish its principles in the lands across the sea.

CHAPTER XLIV.

THE CONVENTION OF THE TWIN CITIES.

The Actual Registration—The Opening Scene of the Convention—A Growing Task—Some Hearty Addresses of Welcome—The Secretary's Report an Inspiring Document—The Great Increase of the Past Year—Why the Color Came to His Cheeks—The Famous Pastor's Hour—Thrilling Addresses—Dr. Rondthaler's Open Parliament—His Flowery Remark—Dr. Deems on the "Soo" Line—"Beautiful Oklahoma"—The Next Convention—Good-Natured Montrealers—An Historic Thunderstorm—No Panic in an Endeavor Convention.

THE first decade of the Christian Endeavor movement was now well rounded out, and the societies were fairly started upon a new decade by the splendid convention which was held in the twin cities of Minnesota—Minneapolis and St. Paul.

To be sure, Minneapolis had the lion's share on this occasion, since it was necessary to have the principal meetings in some one place, but St. Paul shared in the preparations and in the entertainment, and an important meeting was held in that city on the Sunday afternoon of the convention, and it also shared, I believe, in the blessing which always comes with an International Convention.

This was by far the largest convention held up to this date. It was found that the actual registration was over 11,000, and it was estimated that at least 3,000 delegates were present who failed to register their names. "At half-past three o'clock," says the excellent report of this convention, "the doors of the hall were thrown open and the vast throng

DELEGATES ENTERING CONVENTION HALL, MINNEAPOLIS (EXTERIOR).

341

of delegates entered and took their seats. They found an auditorium, which, though crude in certain features, commended itself to all. The seats were arranged in the amphitheatre form, the speakers platform being midway the longest distance of the hall and in height a little below the level of the gallery."

Back of the platform rose the tiers of chorus seats, accommodating 800 persons. The hall was prettily decorated, especially about the platform, with bunting, foliage plants and evergreen. The only motto was a tastefully designed arch over the platform bearing the words, "For Christ and the

PLATFORM AND CHORUS SEATS, CONVENTION HALL, MINNEAPOLIS, MINN.

Church." This commodious audience-room was built by the energy and foresight of the efficient Committee of '91, in the great Exposition Building on the left bank of the Mississippi River.

But how shall the historian begin to tell of the good things which occur in a modern Christian Endeavor International Convention in the limits of a single chapter?

When the society was young and its meetings small and its programs covered but a single day, or, at the most, two days, it was a comparative easy matter, but it would take a literary hydraulic press to condense the good

COMMITTEE OF '91 (MINNEAPOLIS CONVENTION).

1. Franc B. Daniels, Chairman.
2. Willis M. McDonald, General Secretary.
3. Fred W. Dean, Treasurer.
4. William G. Brey, Assistant to Chairman Reception.
5. Trafford N. Jayne, Chairman Excursion.
6. Edward M. Conant, Assistant Secretary and Chairman Hotel.
7. J. E. Thwing, Chairman Transportation.
8. Harry A. Kinports, Chairman Reception.
9. Grove A. Grumman, Chairman Hall.
10. Lew A. Huntoon, Chairman Printing.
11. F. G. Atkinson, Chairman Music and Press.

things that are said at any modern convention into any reasonable amount of space. A volume is needed for every meeting, and we can only give a picture of the whole.

Among the attractive features of this convention were the addresses of welcome, all of which were full of wit and sense. Mr. F. B. Daniels, Chairman of the Committee of '91, briefly and happily welcomed the assembled thousands. This committee, by the way, covered itself with glory by the efficient service it rendered and in some important particulars set the standard for future committees. Rev. H. H. French, then of the Centenary M. E. Church of Minneapolis, on behalf of the pastors, offered the great audience "the freedom of our hearts and our homes," and offered it not in a casket of perishable gold, but "in the tried metal of Christian brotherhood impearled with the prayers and the best wishes of the pastors of Minneapolis."

REV. GEORGE H. WELLS, D. D.

Rev. Robert Cristy, D. D., of the House of Hope Presbyterian Church of St. Paul, made it very plain that it was a "Twin City Convention," and bade the Endeavorers welcome in the name of all those who believe that this movement has been endowed by the Lord Jesus Christ with power to say to the Church of the future, "thou dumb and deaf spirit, I charge thee come out of her and enter no more into her."

Mr. Elliot, of the Minneapolis Young Men's Christian Association, spoke in behalf of one of the elder brothers of Christian Endeavor, the Y. M. C. A., and Rev. George H. Wells, D. D., then of Montreal, replied to these humorous and hearty welcomes in one of the best speeches ever delivered on an occasion like this. In fact, the pages that report this speech are spotted all over with italicized words that tell of "*laughter*" and "*applause*" and "*applause and laughter*" and "*loud applause*" and "*renewed applause*." No wonder if, after this address, Montreal was not able to keep her eloquent son long within her borders, but was obliged to send him across the line in response to the loud and imperative call of Minneapolis.

The Secretary's report at this convention was an inspiring document, for he was able to tell of 16,274 societies, an increase of more than 6,200 during the preceding twelve months, by far the largest gain in any one year up to that time. New York was still in the lead, with 2,354 societies. Pennsylvania came next, with nearly nine hundred less. Ohio and Illinois both had passed the thousand line, and Massachusetts rejoiced in 918 societies, though she had now dropped from the first place to the fifth in the ranks of Christian Endeavor.

The work of the local unions was also particularly referred to in the report of the Secretary, and the aggressive missionary work in which they were engaged was commended.

It was found that Philadelphia had the largest union, composed of 182 societies; Chicago came next, with 160; New York third, with 80; St. Louis with 67, and Brooklyn with 65. At this convention I find the first report concerning "Floating Societies," four of which are mentioned.

The forms of aggressive work in which the societies were engaged were also

GREAT NORTHERN BRIDGE AND FALLS OF ST. ANTHONY, MINNEAPOLIS, EXPOSITION BUILDING IN DISTANCE.

enumerated by the Secretary, but, most of all, did he rejoice in the fact that 82,500 members of the societies had become church members within the year.

The President's address for this year dwelt upon the old subject of "Fidelity and Fellowship," which he felt were the two points still most to be insisted upon.

Dr. O. H. Tiffany preached an excellent sermon in the absence of Bishop Vincent, who was detained by illness, and other memorable addresses were by Rev. F. O. Holman, D. D., of Minneapolis; Rev. E. R. Dille, D. D., of San Francisco; Rev. J. A. Worden, D. D., of Philadelphia; Rev. J. S. McPherson, D. D., of Chicago, and Rev. Isaac J. Lansing, D. D., of Worcester.

At this convention the reports from the field were most encouraging and inspiring. Rev. W. O. Carrier, from Wisconsin, reported that Wisconsin's State's

Prison Society was one of the wonders of the age. "With about 500 prisoners, we have 116 members of the Endeavor Society."

Mr. J. W. C. Swan, from Manitoba, declared that his land was "not only the land of No. 1 hard wheat, but also the land of No. 1 hard Christian Endeavorers."

Rev. Thomas L. Johnson, from Africa, who, according to the report, was received with tumultuous applause and waving of handkerchiefs, declared that the hearty welcome he received made "the color come to his cheeks."

Moreover, countries that could not be represented by a delegate sent their greetings. A cablegram from London of hearty greetings and good wishes was received. From Melbourne, too, came the four words, "Australia rejoices with you," while the Japanese Endeavorers sent from Kobe the cablegram referring us to the Scripture passage which declared that "through Him we both have access in one spirit unto the Father."

The Pastors' Hour, conducted by Rev. J. S. Black, D. D., of Minneapolis, was also full of good things. Rev. Smith Baker, then of Minneapolis, speaking for the Congregational churches, said: "Several years ago a couple came from the country to me to be married. When I said to the young man, 'Do you take this woman to be your lawful wedded wife?' he replied, 'Course I do. What do you suppose I came here for?' Now, I represent the primitive, apostolic Plymouth-Rock Congregationalists, and that is just what we have come here for, to indorse this Christian Endeavor movement. As a mother takes her nursing child, looking into its laughing eyes and kisses it, each of our churches takes this Christian Endeavor Society, holds it to her heart, and kisses it as her most hopeful child."

The same spirit seemed to be echoed by all the eighteen representatives of the different denominations, who spoke on this most happy and fraternal occasion.

Other speakers and workers who added to the interest of this convention were Mr. Ira D. Sankey, the famous gospel singer; Rev. A. A. Fulton, from China, who, during the year, had created a vast wave of enthusiasm for missions as he detailed his two-cents-a-week plan; Rev. William Patterson, who, with genuine consecrated Irish wit, captured and held the audience while he discoursed on International Fellowship. President E. B. Andrews, D. D., LL. D., President of Brown University, gave a most strong and convincing address on "Interdenominational Fellowship."

President William R. Harper, of Chicago University, made a most effective plea for "Systematic Bible Study." Mr. Alonzo Stagg, of Springfield, the well-known Christian athlete, spoke on "The Young Man at Work," while the three addresses that were given on the Sunday afternoon of the convention will long linger in the minds that heard them. These were by Miss Margaret Leitch, of Ceylon, on the "Young Woman at Work;" by Mr. John G. Woolley, on "Gospel Temperance," and by Mrs. Alice May Scudder, on "The Child at Work."

In the evening Bishop Gilbert, of Minnesota, of the Protestant Episcopal Church, and Rev. J. W. Chapman, D. D., then of the Bethany Presbyterian Church, of Philadelphia, gave addresses, and Dr. Chapman also conducted the consecration meeting, which, like its predecessors and successors on similar occasions, was the crowning glory and chief joy of the whole convention.

The spirit of this meeting may be judged by the closing sentences of the report: "Dr. Chapman then asked all in the audience who would promise that, with God's help, they would try to lead at least one soul to Christ during the year to rise and hold up their hands. Nearly the entire audience arose, and, with uplifted hands, united in singing 'Alas! and did my Saviour bleed.' While they were still standing and his hands still uplifted, Dr. Wayland Hoyt led in the following prayer of consecration: 'O Lord Jesus, Thou didst utterly give Thyself for us. We do now utterly yield ourselves to Thee for this service. We will attempt to win souls for Thee. Accept our consecration. Give us souls. Put upon us the power of the Holy Spirit. Be Thou in us and upon us, O Thou Empowering Spirit, and, as never before, because we consecrate ourselves to Thee with earnest and full hearts. May Thy kingdom come, O Lord, through us to Thy glory. For Jesus sake. Amen.'"

Two or three more incidents should be recorded before the history of this convention is dismissed. The Open Parliament conducted by Dr. Rondthaler, of Indianapolis, who there gained the sobriquet of the Indiana cyclone, was a memorable occasion, and set the pace for many a future Open Parliament in State and local conventions the world around.

He kept the convention in supremely good humor from beginning to the end, and when he was through, like so many Oliver Twists, with united voices, all asked for more. One remark of his was heard a great many times afterward.

"I am going to make one little flowery remark," he said. "I, as a pastor, want to say that the Christian Endeavor Society is my heartsease. God bless it forever and ever. Oh! how I wear it upon my bosom in pride and in joy. How in the evening of the Sabbath days when discouragements have been many the Christian Endeavor is my heartsease, and I fall to sleep with the remembrance of what my young people have said and prayed as a sweet fragrance."

Dr. Deems was at the convention, and, as it can be well understood, he was not a silent partner either. In the course of this Parliament he told about the tribulations of the New York delegation in getting to the convention by the "Soo" Line. "We had seventy-two hours of continuous camp-meeting from

Forty-second Street, New York, into this Union Depot. I thank God for this, one of the most extraordinary experiences of my life. Glory to God, I know I have religion now. I have stood the 'Soo' railroad and still have hope

W. H. H. SMITH.

of everlasting glory, and I know that the rest of those people have religion. I know that Dr. Farrar has religion now. I know that Dr. Tyler has religion, though I suspected it before. Blessed be the Young People's Society of Christian Endeavor and blessed be all the obstructions that we met on the 'Soo' railroad."

"Sixty-three minutes," cried out Dr. Rondthaler, at the close of this little speech, "and sixty-seven speeches. Three cheers for the Young People's Society of Christian Endeavor that stands for brevity, sharpness, striking the nail on the head, spirituality and Christ."

Other Open Parliaments of great value and interest were also conducted by Mr. F. J. Harwood on the subject, "Souls Won Through the Committees;" by Rev. J. Z. Tyler, on "Souls Won Through the Prayer and Consecration Meeting;" by W. H. H. Smith, on "Souls Won Through the Influence of Local Unions," and by Rev. W. W. Sleeper, on "Souls Won Through the Junior Society."

For the first time at this convention, too, the badge banners were presented in accordance with the suggestion made at St. Louis the year before. Professor Andrews, in a witty speech, presented the banner, which represented the greatest relative gain in the number of societies, to Oklahoma. Miss Susie Griffith, a pretty young lady, of small stature, was the only one in the hall at the time to represent the Territory, and, as she came forward amid loud applause, Professor Andrews handed her the banner with the words "Little Oklahoma, wonderful Oklahoma, beautiful Oklahoma [great laughter and applause], take this banner and keep it as long as you can."

REV. GEORGE B. STEWART.

Rev. George B. Stewart, the President of the Pennsylvania Union, in a happy speech, received the other banner that went to his great commonwealth which, during the past year, had made the largest actual gain in the number of Endeavor Societies.

THE CONVENTION OF THE TWIN CITIES.

At this convention there was very great, though good-natured rivalry as to the location of the next one. New York and Montreal were the two most prominent candidates. Most of the delegates supposed that Montreal would receive the coveted honor. Montreal badges and streamers were everywhere, but the Trustees felt that it was more important that New York city should be stirred by a great convention, so, after much deliberation, it was decided that the meeting of 1892 should be held in that metropolis.

Undismayed by their defeat, however, the Montrealers simply changed one figure on their banner and flung it out again amid the applause of the great assembly, who admired their pluck and good nature, and now the banner read "MONTREAL FOR 1893," instead of *"Montreal for 1892."*

One incident in that convention will never be forgotten by any who were present on that occasion. Friday was an extremely hot and sultry day, and when the evening came the delegates had no sooner assembled in the great hall than it became evident that a fearful thunder shower was coming up. Some left the hall in hot haste, but most remained. The rain poured in torrents. The lightning flashed incessantly. The thunder rolled from one end of the heavens to the other. Suddenly a sharp clap of thunder was followed by the extinguishing of all the electric lights in the building, leaving the audience in total darkness.

The leaders feared that there would be a panic and a fearful scramble for the door, and that many might be thrown down and trodden under-foot and a horrible scene of carnage take place as has happened on other similar occasions. But there was no commotion or disturbance of any kind. No one left the hall. No one seemed frightened or dismayed.

At once Mr. Lindsay, the leader of the singing, started the hymn, "Blest be the tie that binds," and the great audience took it up with great enthusiasm. Again that first verse was sung in the total darkness of the hall and then once more. Then the electric light came back and the convention resumed its proceedings as though they had never been interrupted.

At an important meeting of the Trustees held during the course of this convention the following platform of principles was adopted which, while it contains nothing new, sets forth in most distinct and vigorous English the ideas for which Christian Endeavor has always stood, and which have given it its power and success in all parts of the world.

This platform was re-enacted with slight additions at the New York Convention, a year later. It is worth studying as an authoritative declaration of what Christian Endeavor stands for.

PLATFORM OF PRINCIPLES.

We reaffirm our adherence to the principles which, under God's blessing, have made the Christian Endeavor movement what it is to-day:

First, and foremost, personal devotion to our divine Lord and Saviour, Jesus Christ.

Second, the covenant obligation embodied in the prayer-meeting pledge, without which there can be no true Society of Christian Endeavor.

Third, constant religious training for all kinds of service involved in the various committees, which—so many of them as are needed—are, equally with the prayer-meeting, essential to a society of Christian Endeavor.

Fourth, strenuous loyalty to the local church or denomination with which each society is connected. This loyalty is plainly expressed in the pledge; it underlies the whole idea of the movement, and, as statistics proved and pastors testify, is very generally exemplified in the lives of active members. Thus the Society of Christian Endeavor, in theory and practice, is as loyal a denominational society as any in existence, as well as a broad and fraternal *interdenominational* society.

Fifth, we reaffirm our increasing confidence in the interdenominational, spiritual fellowship, through which we hope, not for organic unity, but to fulfill our Lord's prayer, "that they all may be one." This fellowship already extends to all evangelical denominations, and we should greatly deplore any movement that would interrupt or imperil it.

We rejoice in the growing friendliness of Christians throughout the world. We find reason for gratification in the fact that the Reformed, Methodist Protestant, and Cumberland Presbyterian churches, the Congregationalists, Disciples of Christ, Friends, and other denominations, have in their highest ecclesiastical gatherings indorsed and practically adopted the Society of Christian Endeavor, and that the Presbyterians in many synods and presbyteries have substantially done the same.

We rejoice, too, that the Baptist Young People's Union admits Christian Endeavor societies to all the privileges of denominational service, without any change of name or principle or interdenominational affiliation; that the Free Baptists recommend societies organized on the Christian Endeavor basis—"Advocates of Fidelity in Christian Endeavor;" the Evangelical Association, "The Keystone League of Christian Endeavor;" and the Methodists of Canada, "The Epworth League of Christian Endeavor;" and that the United Brethren in Christ recommend that when a society takes the prayer-meeting pledge, it should be called a "Christian Endeavor Society," thus guaranteeing, to those who desire it, our precious interdenominational fellowship as well as full denominational control.

We believe that *for the sake of Christian fairness and courtesy*, in all denominations and all over the world, the Christian Endeavor principles should go with the name, and the name, either alone or in connection with a distinctive denominational name, should go with the principles.

For the maintenance of these *principles of covenant obligations, individual service, denominational loyalty, and interdenominational fellowship, we unitedly and heartily pledge ourselves.*

CHAPTER XLV.

THE SIGNS OF NEW IDEAS.

Invented or Adopted—From the Standard Dictionary—"Endeavor," "Endeavorer," etc.—"Lookout"—"Sunshine Committee"—The Signs of New Ideas—Combinations of Words—"The Surprise Committee"—"Floating Societies"—"Barrack Societies"—Phrases of Work That Tell of Spiritual Energy—Endeavor Outside of the Endeavor Society—Introducing the Principles Into Other Church Work—What the Society Has Done for the Church Prayer-Meeting—Sometimes Saving it from Decay—A Christian Endeavor Church, not a Christian Endeavor Denomination—The Burlington Plan.

VERY great movement must have a nomenclature of its own. Whether it will or not some words become peculiarly its property. These words may be invented for its use or adopted from common life, but the new significance which is put into them or the new turn of meaning given to them makes them distinctly and peculiarly the property of the movement.

So it is with Christian Endeavor. It has attempted to establish no nomenclature of its own. It has aspired after no peculiar terminology, but as it has grown larger and stronger certain words which were not in the dictionary before, or which, if in the dictionary, had a minor place, have been added to the common stock or the commonly used stock of the English language.

The new *Standard Dictionary*, that marvelous compendium of words spoken by English tongues, has recognized this fact and has included, as has no other dictionary, some of these distinctly Christian Endeavor phrases. It thus defines "Christian Endeavor," "Endeavorer," "Lookout Committee," etc. :

YOUNG PEOPLE'S SOCIETY OF CHRISTIAN ENDEAVOR.—An organization first formed by Francis E. Clark at Portland, Maine, in 1881, membership in which involves certain pledged Christian service, now (1893) extended throughout the world in various denominations, and embracing more than a million members.

ENDEAVORER.—One who endeavors, or strives to do something; specifically, a member of the Young People's Society of Christian Endeavor.

LOOKOUT COMMITTEE.—A Committee in the Society of Christian Endeavor, whose duties are to bring in new members, to introduce them to the work, etc.

INTERDENOMINATIONAL.—Existing or occurring between religious denominations.

The word "lookout," as in the "Lookout Committee," has received, as we have seen, a new and distinct meaning from the Endeavor Society. There is probably no Endeavor Society in any land that has not such a committee as this, and all the similar organizations which are strictly denominational, for the most part have the same agency, though often called by a different name.

The idea of this committee is very plain. Its name defines its character and its duties. It is to look out for new members; to look out for the spiritual progress of the old members; to look out for those who lapse from their duties; to look out that they do not long remain members of the society if they are willfully negligent; in fact, to look out as best it can for the spiritual advancement of the whole society and all its individual members.

So it is with several of the other committees. Though old phrases have been used, new life and meaning have been put into them. The "Social Committee," the "Prayer-meeting Committee," the "Missionary Committee," the "Calling Committee;"—it is not too much to say that these old words have received a new meaning, so far as religious work goes, from the efforts of the society.

The word "consecration," too, has come to have a very definite and important meaning in connection with the Christian Endeavor movement. It stands for a definite and peculiar service held once a month in 40,000 societies the world around. It stands for the outspoken devotion of one's self to the Lord Jesus Christ at this monthly meeting. It stands for a renewal of the vows made by every Endeavorer when he joined the society, and a renewal of his allegiance to his Master.

The words "interdenominational" and "interdenominationalism" have already been commented upon. Until the Endeavor movement arose they were not found in any of our dictionaries. The society has given a new and important significance to a phrase which, if used at all, was very sparingly used before it arose. These words are not even found in the great *Century Dictionary.*

The "pledge," too, has come to mean much to a vast multitude of young Christians that the word never meant to the Christians of the former generation.

When *the* pledge is spoken of in Christian Endeavor circles a particular form of words, or, at least, the idea for which that form of words stands, is understood and recognized.

So, also, there are some combinations of words referring to the less-used methods of work which are distinctive in the Christian Endeavor movement, like the "Sunshine Committee," so popular among the boys and girls of many a Junior Society—a committee which is meant to carry sunshine wherever its influence extends.

The "Surprise Committee," which is to use its ingenuity in contriving some new and helpful way of aiding pastor and church that has not before been devised. The "Information Committee," whose duty it is to inform the societies of the chief events that have happened in the Christian Endeavor world since the last meeting.

Then, too, such phrases as the "Floating Societies," which describe so well the work among the seamen; the "Barrack Societies," which tell what is being done among the soldiers, and other similar phrases have been introduced and necessitated by the Christian Endeavor movement.

God grant that into all these phrases may be put spiritual warmth and energy, that they may be no longer words merely, but vital realities, telling of the work and service of increasing hosts of young disciples of our Lord Jesus Christ.

A study of the words thus introduced and emphasized shows that the influence of the Endeavor movement has been by no means confined to the societies actually formed. Large as are the figures which tell of the number of societies and the millions of members, they are not by any means adequate to describe the scope and indicate the force of the movement.

The denominational societies, already described, have owed their inception and their development in no small degree to the Endeavor Society. As many have avowed who are prominently connected with these societies, they have floated to their present success largely on the flood-tide of enthusiasm created by the Endeavor movement.

Many other organizations and societies, which are decidedly distinct from Christian Endeavor, have inevitably shared in this enthusiastic uprising of the youth of our land, and in many cases word has come to me of larger and more enthusiastic Sunday-school conventions, Young Men's Christian Association meetings, and religious gatherings of all kinds because of the resultant enthusiasm generated by the coming of the great Christian Endeavor Convention or the influence of an active local union.

The formation of Senior Societies is a direct effort to introduce Christian Endeavor principles into the other services of the church, for the members of the Senior Societies have no special meetings of their own, but apply the principles learned in their Christian Endeavor meetings to the mid-week services of the church and to all the activities of the church in which they may be engaged.

The affiliated members of the society, too, so far as they represent graduate active members, are supposed to carry their Christian Endeavor life and principles into their other work for the church, so that gradually the whole church in its work and worship, at least in many sections of the world, is being leavened by the Endeavor idea.

I should be afraid to quote here, lest it should seem to savor of an intolerable conceit, many of the things which have been written to me by pastors on both sides of the Atlantic Ocean in regard to what the Christian Endeavor Society has done for the church prayer-meeting. Some of the mildest of these admirers of the Endeavor prayer-meeting idea have told me that "it has saved the meeting from irretrievable decay," that "the dry rot had been arrested in the prayer-meeting," that "the infusion of fresh blood and the addition of new faces and young voices has saved the meeting from extinction, has re-converted it from a mid-week lecture to its original purpose of communion, fellowship, and inspiration."

But I will not quote these eulogies more at length, for they will seem extravagant to some, but I think it will be admitted on all sides that, in a greater or less degree at least, the Endeavor idea has permeated and blessed our evangelical Protestantism.

The Mothers' Society, which is a development of more recent years, and which will receive more attention in a subsequent chapter, is simply the carrying out this idea as related to another branch of church work, for it seeks to vivify and refresh and make more definite and effective than ever the maternal associations and the mothers' prayer-meetings which have been a blessed feature of some of our churches for many a long year.

In the missionary activities, too, of the churches, the Christian Endeavor leaven has been at work. It has made more clear than ever the fact that many a little makes a mickle. It has laid emphasis on the truth that even a child can give two cents a week to missions and that if enough two-cent pieces find their way into the treasuries the Boards will be troubled with no further deficit. The Missionary Committee has oftentimes brought new life to the struggling mission circle composed of half a dozen or a dozen faithful young ladies, and has extended their influence among the other hundred young people of the church who had perhaps previously voted missions a bore and missionary-meetings afflictions to be endured.

In still more marked ways has the Christian Endeavor Society made its influence felt in some churches, which, for the covenant of its members, have adopted substantially the Christian Endeavor pledge.

The admirable "Burlington plan" of church work is largely an adaptation of Christian Endeavor methods. This is the plan as described by Rev. Frank F. Lewis, of Vergennes, Vt., one who has tried in practical church work these methods. Here is what he has to say of the "Burlington plan:"

"One of the very earliest Christian Endeavor Societies was formed in December, 1881, in the First Church, of Burlington, Vt. A member of this church, Hon. W. J. Van Patten, was the second president of the United Society. It is natural, therefore, that this church should be friendly to Christian Endeavor principles, and should seek to extend the sphere of their application. We find here, therefore, the Burlington Plan of Church Work, in which the underlying idea is, by a system of committees, to enlist a large number of persons, and so divide the work that it shall not be a burden to any.

"During February, 1894, a series of revival meetings were held in Burlington, under the lead of J. Wilbur Chapman, D. D., with favorable results. A large number of people made confession of Christian faith, and many additions were made to the various churches of the city. It was evident to all who were engaged in the work connected with Dr. Chapman's meetings that his method of organization and of enlisting a large number of individuals in various phases of the work had much to do with the successful results. It seemed to some of the members of the First Church that the principle upon which Dr. Chapman's organization was based was applicable to regular church work. It was decided to take up the matter and see what could be done in organizing the work of the First Church along similar lines and on the same general principles.

"Heretofore a large number of churches have failed of their divinely appointed mission because only a small proportion of their membership have been engaged in active, personal Christian service. Churches have died of 'nothing to do,' not because there was no work to be done, but because there was no way of showing the members what to do and just how to do it. Pastors here and there have devised plans by which a portion of their church members were set to work, but the success of these plans has depended on the time and strength which the pastor could put into them in addition to his regular pulpit and pastoral work.

"The feature of the Burlington plan is that the initiative is taken by the lay members of the church, and while nothing is done without the pastor's approval, he is not burdened with details nor directly responsible for the success of the work.

"The Burlington plan does not present anything novel or untried. It lays no claim to originality, except in gathering into one harmonious system various lines of work that, singly, have had large success in many churches.

"In system lies success.

"The Burlington plan concentrates attention upon those things which ever must be centre and soul of the church work—the Sunday preaching services, the mid-week prayer-meeting, and personal contact with those whom we are sent to win.

"The mainspring of the movement is the Executive Committee, which is made up of a chairman, with three gentlemen and three ladies, and the pastor *ex-officio*. This committee meets regularly to plan for the work, make appointments, and to counsel with the pastor. It is chosen by the church at its annual meeting and serves one year. The pastor is *ex-officio* member of all committees.

"The Executive Committee enlists members in the Personal Workers' Band, and appoints the members of the Welcome, Outlook, Mid-week Prayer-Meeting, and District Committees.

"The Welcome Committee consists of four gentlemen, appointed to serve for one month or longer.

"The duties of this committee are to be present early each Sunday morning in the church vestibule and to endeavor to greet each comer with a word of welcome, a cordial grasp of the hand, or some token of recognition and pleasure at their presence.

"Especial care should be taken to greet strangers, and to see that they are promptly seated by the ushers.

"Each member of the Outlook Committee has the oversight of two or three pews in the church, greeting the occupants at the close of service, and reporting cases of sickness or absence to the pastor.

"The Sunday Evening Club enlists all men who are willing to join, and sets them to work to provide a service that has printed programs for all, with hymns and responsive readings, special numbers of vocal and instrumental music, an efficient corps of ushers and collectors, free seats, and short sermons. A prompt, varied, businesslike people's gospel service.

"The Mid-week Prayer-Meeting Committee co-operates with the pastor in arranging special meetings for the week-day service.

"The city is divided into districts containing twenty or thirty First Church families. A committee of gentlemen and three ladies in each district assists in pastoral work, and arranges for district meetings and socials.

"The Personal Workers' Band consists of those who are ready to do any religious work in which the pastor or Executive Committee desire help.

"The plan has approved itself to pastors and churches all over the country."

One of the most complete exemplifications of the Endeavor idea is found in the Congregational Church of Hardwick, Vt. It is a Congregational Church, pure and simple, like any other church of its sisterhood. It is a Christian Endeavor church in that the distinctive Christian Endeavor principles are applied to the whole membership, and not simply to the young people of the church. But Mr. Lewis, the pastor of the church, can describe it better than any one else, and I will leave it for him to tell of the inception and working of the plan, which simply shows how flexible and easy of adaptation are the Christian Endeavor ideas, and how they are good for older people, as well as for the younger people, and that there is nothing inimical, but everything that is helpful to the building up of a strongly individual denominational church. Here is his description:

THE CHRISTIAN ENDEAVOR PRINCIPLE.

"Young people are trained in their Society of Christian Endeavor to pledged attendance at prayer-meeting and participation therein. They are trained to take each his share of the common work through committees. Drones are not allowed in the hive. As these young people grow older and assume the responsibilities of the church, what sort of a church will they constitute? A partial answer to the question is attempted in the Christian Endeavor Church, organized at Hardwick, Vt., April 3, 1894.

"This village has lately risen into being to the music of clinking stone hammers. Here were found a number of young people, vigorous in Christian as in business life; young in spirit and trained in Christian Endeavor methods, desiring to form a church. Looking over the organized life of our churches, preparatory to forming the new church, two facts appeared. One fact is that in many churches there is a special service preparatory to the communion. This is one of the most important meetings of the church, but is often neglected, thinly attended, and without real power for those who need it most. A second fact is, that in many churches are members whose lives are correct outwardly, but who show little interest in the Christian life. They attend church services occasionally, never take any part therein, and although they are plainly violating their covenant vows they are unreached by present methods of church discipline.

"Further, these lapses might often be prevented if the first symptoms of decline were promptly treated.

"With these facts in mind the Covenant and Rules of the Christian Endeavor Congregational Church were formed. When members are received to the church, as the reading of the Covenant is ended, new members and old join in repeating the Christian Endeavor pledge, modified to apply to the church. Instead of the Consecration meeting is placed the bi-monthly Preparatory Service. Extracts from the By-Laws show still further the distinctive aim of the church. Thus, 'At the preparatory service the roll shall be called by the clerk, and the responses of the members present shall be considered as a renewed expression of allegiance to Christ. It is expected that if any one is obliged to be absent from this meeting he will send by some one who attends a request to be excused. If any member of the church is absent from the preparatory service and fails to send an excuse, the Standing Committee is expected to take the name of such a one and in a kind and brotherly spirit ascertain the reason for the absence.'

"Again, 'Any member of this church who shall be absent, unexcused, from six preparatory services of the church, shall be a subject for church discipline, and may, by vote of the church, be suspended or excluded from membership.'

"The council called to organize the church unanimously approved the new organization, at the same time regarding the Christian Endeavor features as 'experimental and subject to change.' No change has been found necessary as yet. New members have been received at every communion but one since organization, and no one has objected to the regulations as severe. Committees are organized as the need for them appears—Welcome, Missionary, Temperance, Social, and so on—the aim being that the church as a whole shall do the work which God has assigned, and that in carrying it on there shall be to every man his work."

CHAPTER XLVI.

ON SEA AND SHORE.

A Wild Prediction—Some Touching Stories—The Wreck of the "Galatin"—How He Saved His Pledge—The Japanese Society and the Floating Society—Miss Antoinette P. Jones and Her Work—How the Work Began, How It Extended—Another Clause in the Pledge—Introduction Cards—An Endeavor Social for Jack Tar—Throw Out the Life-Line—Ringing Them Up—Mr. Wood and His Mission—Junior Endeavorers of the Navy Yard—The Character of the Sailor.

IF, when the Christian Endeavor movement began in 1881, any prophet had predicted that within less than a dozen years there would be scores of faithful societies sailing the main, and that they would be found on almost every ocean where the American flag floats, he would have been considered a wild-eyed prophet indeed; and yet such were the facts, and the work among the sailors and on shipboard has developed into one of the most interesting and fruitful phases of Christian Endeavor.

Many touching stories have come to us from the sailor lads who are true to their pledge and true to their motto, and who live for Christ and the Church just as really as if they were not often ten thousand miles away from any church home, with only the tapering masts of their vessels to remind them of the heaven-pointing spires of their boyhood.

Most interesting is it to follow these wanderers from port to port, and to see how true they are to their obligations under most adverse circumstances. Pathetic is the story of the "Galatin," which was wrecked on the New Hampshire coast a few years since, and among whose crew was a floating Society of Christian Endeavor, some of whom were lost and some saved. One of the rescued sailors said afterward that he lost every prized possession that he had except his Christian Endeavor badge, and that was pinned to his shirt. Another mourned that he had lost his pledge card, "but," said he, "I have not lost my pledge, for that is engraved upon my heart."

Full of suggestiveness, because it tells how God's breeze carries a wind-wafted seed to the very ends of the earth, is the story of the Endeavor Society formed on a Japanese man-of-war among the Japanese sailors who came under the influence of a Christian chaplain in the navy yard.

Instinct with the spirit of our fellowship and fraternity is the account of the union meeting of the native Japanese society and the floating society on board of the man-of-war "Charleston" in the harbor of Yokohama, when the American sailor boys and the Japanese Endeavorers mingled their voices in the same hymns of praise and in common prayer to the Lord and Master, whom they had all pledged themselves to serve.

But the story of this type of Christian Endeavor should be told, not by myself, but by those who have been most assiduous in promoting it, especially by Miss Antoinette P. Jones, Superintendent of Floating Societies of Christian Endeavor, who has given of late years so much of her life and strength to the advancement of this cause. Here is her account of this most interesting work:

MISS ANTOINETTE P. JONES.

"The Floating Society of Christian Endeavor is a branch of the Young People's Society of Christian Endeavor, adapted to use on shipboard by men in every rank or service.

"Not limited to one ocean, or one class of men of the sea, it offers equal inspiration to its members, in consecration to Christ, training for His service, fellowship with His disciples, and personal endeavor 'afloat' and ashore; whether they are on man-of-war, ocean steamship, merchantman, coaster, or fisherman.

"It is Christian Endeavor always, interdenominational, international, intermarine—'floating' the world around.

"Floating Christian Endeavor is as surely God's plan for the men of the sea as the Young People's Society of Christian Endeavor is for the young Christian in our churches, and He owns and blesses this work in a wonderful degree.

"Quietly and providentially it came from the sea, not forced upon the sailor, God finding willing messengers.

"Early in 1890 the present superintendent was requested to prepare a pledge-card similar to the Christian Endeavor, for use by a seaman's missionary, through the desire of a recently converted petty officer on a Government vessel.

"Dr. F. E. Clark's sanction and approval was obtained for this apparently irregular use of pledge and constitution. His cordial interest then expressed, together with that of other officers of the United Society, continuing to the present time, has been an inspiration and support to this branch of Christian Endeavor.

"The printed matter issued in April, 1890, included pledge, covenant, and later, in July, a constitution.

"The pledge is the first form of Christian Endeavor active membership before the revision, with the insertion of a clause relating to pure living, total abstinence, and non-profanity.

"The pledge-card is gummed into the signer's Bible, the 'coupon' bearing name, ship, and a standing address, detached and kept on file.

"Originally arranged for enlisted men, the membership soon extended to changing crews on sailing vessels.

"The covenant which binds together the few, the constitution for the larger number, are each founded on Christian Endeavor principles, and except in phraseology but two points of divergence from the Model Christian Endeavor Constitution can be noted, those relating to pledge, form, and membership.

"The inserted clause in the pledge relating to temperance, etc., adopted by many floating societies is heartily indorsed by many seamen and other workers, and is intended as a declaration of principles rather than a discrimination against our brethren at sea, who, debarred from active participation in the numberless lines of Christian work enjoyed by young men ashore, may yet join in conquests on the sea, as 'knights of the new chivalry.'

"No provision has been made for associate membership, and the five years' trial has proved the decision wise.

"Active Christian Endeavorers on shipboard are called to heroic living, while men of mature years, not yet Christians, are rarely helped themselves, and prove a hindrance, by bearing the name.

"An 'intention,' or 'Christian life' card, such as evangelists advise, is profitably used instead of the associate member's card.

"Members carry the introduction card, helpful in fellowship; and wear the regulation Christian Endeavor monogram pin, a world-wide badge of recognition.

"In June, 1890, the United Society appointed Miss Antoinette P. Jones, of Falmouth, Mass., to be 'Superintendent of Floating Societies,' an office at that time more in prophecy than accomplishment.

"As the United Society assists the local society or union, so the superintendent, as the 'central,' has endeavored to put various and distant workers in connection, interchanging plans and methods, and by co-operation and correspondence receiving mutual benefit, and when providential circumstances open new work, assisting in organizing Floating Christian Endeavor Committees, societies ashore, or on ships.

"Floating Christian Endeavor Committees and societies report to the superintendent.

"Arranged primarily for shipboard a society on shore in church, mission, or reading-room, composed of sailor members, officered by Christian Endeavorers, is called a Floating Society, although the organization does not 'float.' Printed forms are applicable to both ship and shore societies.

"Representatives from Christian Endeavor Societies, or Local Unions in sea-

CHRISTIAN ENDEAVOR MISSION LAUNCH, VINEYARD SOUND MASS.

GROUP OF MEMBERS, NEW YORK PORT FLOATING SOCIETY.

ports, form a Floating Christian Endeavor Committee, from earnest young men and women; receiving the cordial and practical indorsement of churches and societies.

"These committees do not fail to honor existing seamen's missions, but are an inspiration and assistance.

"The Executive Board of this committee, whose members also form chairmen of sub-divisions of the work, according to local needs, directs the larger band of workers, in ship visitation; Gospel services on shipboard, dock and shore; Marine Hospital services; navy yard, receiving and training ships, and marine barracks; reading-rooms and boarding-houses; and distributing comfort bags and good reading, furnished by land societies.

"No time is wasted in offering saloon substitutes and rival attractions, but the social side of 'Jack's' nature is helpfully met in a typical Christian Endeavor social which can fitly begin with a praise service, and close with a brief, earnest consecration service, while crowded into the hour between, brightness, pure sunshine, and hearty good cheer, the recollection of which will follow the sailor lad many a day, a memory of true Christian gladness.

"The story of Floating Christian Endeavor might be called 'The Romance of Missions' if it was not also a record of plain, practical living and serving, on shipboard; of earnest planning and faithful effort toward the highest aim, soul winning and training for service, by Christian Endeavorers who 'throw out the life-line' from shore.

"Sixty societies on ship and shore and organized committees in unions, with two to three thousand members, report in good order, though some societies have unavoidably scattered.

"Each Floating Society, each band of workers, deserves a chapter.

"Let us 'connect' them and 'ring them up!'

"*Vineyard Sound, Massachusetts!*" The first pledges were signed here, and the first Floating Society organized on shipboard May 12, 1890. Membership among crews of government steamers and coastwise shipping. Mission launch flies Christian Endeavor flag, carries reading matter to be thrown aboard vessels, and brings sailors ashore to service.

"*New York Port Society, West Side Branch!*" The lady missionary obtained the first members among ocean line steamship men in August, 1892.

"*New Mizpah Reading Room, New York!*" More ocean steamship members. November, 1892.

"*Mariner's Church, New York!*" March, 1893, instituted a Floating Society among deep sea and coastwise seamen.

"*New York Seamen's Christian Association!*" Floating Society, number four, organized February, 1895. Among ocean steamship crews.

"*New York Floating Christian Endeavor Committee!*" Organized for service December, 1894.

"*Navy Yard, Brooklyn, N. Y.!*" Organized November, 1892. A large membership, including associate members, among naval men.

"*Cleveland, Ohio!*" Ring up the two Floating Societies among the 'salts' on the inland seas. Organized early in 1893.

"Shall we ring up *Boston*, and *Chicago*, and *Galveston, Texas*, and *Portland, Maine*, and the sponge fishermen of Florida Keys?

FLOATING SOCIETY DELEGATES, SOLANO COUNTY, CALIFORNIA.

ALAMEDA COUNTY FLOATING SOCIETY COMMITTEE, CALIFORNIA.

"Now the Pacific Coast. Call up the 'Sunshiners!' *San Francisco, San Diego,* and *Oakland, Cal.!* Organized Floating Christian Endeavor Committees in 1892. Splendidly equipped at each port, holding ship services, winning souls, furnishing reading-rooms.

"*Vallejo, Cal., Floating Society of Christian Endeavor!* Picked men for Christ's service from the naval men at Mare Island Navy Yard, March, 1894.

"*Tacoma and Seattle, Wash.!* Wonderful possibilities at this 'gateway of the North' for these Floating Christian Endeavor Committees.

"*Philadelphia Floating Christian Endeavor Committee!* Splendid field, fifteen miles of river front. Distributed over eighteen hundred comfort bags, Christmas, 1894.

"*Eastburn Church Floating Society of Christian Endeavor, Philadelphia!* Faithful and true, on land or sea. Organized February, 1894.

"*United States Naval Training Station!* The Floating Society fits the apprentices, fresh from home Christian Endeavor. Organized October, 1894.

"Now the British flag floats over Floating Christian Endeavor, ashore, as well as afloat!

"*St. John, New Brunswick!* The Floating Society of Christian Endeavor, organized November, 1894, already a blessing.

"*New Zealand, Wellington!* Floating Christian Endeavor workers realize joy of souls saved.

"*Australia, New South Wales!* Seeking 'best things,' adopts Floating Christian Endeavor.

J. M. WOOD.

"*England!* Floating Christian Endeavor for our hardy seamen in 1895!

"The many societies on shipboard, sailing the 'great and wide sea,' each deserve a chapter of details, their 'logs' full of heroic, devoted, faithful Christian Endeavor.

"Wonderfully touching are records of prayer-meetings held on shipboard.

"A society sails around the world, entering port of departure with increased membership.

"One holds meetings amid roar of cannon. Others hold nightly prayer service.

"A typical society attends services in a foreign land, receiving return visits from missionaries who assist in services aboard; conducts services, attended often by a hundred of the ship's company.

"Floating Societies, by correspondence and papers, keep alive to Christian Endeavor news in the world.

"Many Floating Endeavorers have joined the church of their choice, entered Christian work ashore, or consecrated life and means to missions.

"'And so the good work goes on!' But the three million seamen of the world are not all saved! 'One is our Master, even Christ, all ye'—seamen—'are brethren!'"

Another conspicuously good work in this same line has been accomplished by Mr. J. M. Wood, of the Brooklyn Navy Yard.

The following graphic account of Mr. Wood's conversion and chosen work of Christian Endeavor among the sailors, which I find in the Brooklyn *Daily Eagle*, will interest every one:

"Mr. Wood is a man with a strange history, and his experiences have been such as to fit him in a peculiar manner for missionary work among men-o'-wars men. One stormy night in October, 1890, he staggered into Jerry McAuley's mission on Water Street. He was on the verge of delirium tremens, and only a few days before had been discharged from the United States Navy, in which he had served for thirteen years, as an incorrigible drunkard. He had been drunk in almost every seaport city in the world, and after being discharged and paid off he determined to have one more spree and then throw himself into the river. It did not take him long to get rid of his money in the saloons along the Bowery and around Chatham Square, and then he started down Roosevelt Street toward the East River. On reaching the corner of Water Street he heard the people in the mission singing:

> "There is a fountain filled with blood,
> Drawn from Immanuel's veins;
> And sinners plunged beneath that flood
> Lose all their guilty stains.

"It recalled memories of his youth and of his mother, and it partially sobered him. Instead of carrying out his purpose to commit suicide he staggered into the mission, and 'Old things passed away and all things became new.' Shortly afterward the Seamen's Friend Society sent him to work in the navy yard as a missionary, and he is the only unordained man who has ever been called upon to work in the navy yard in that capacity. On the 20th of last October, the third anniversary of his conversion, Mr. Wood was the happy recipient of double congratulations when he visited the mission, as he had just married a beautiful Christian woman. Mrs. Wood is now almost as well known to the men of the United States Navy as her husband is. They have found her to be a wise and sympathetic friend and adviser, and the meetings in Library Hall would lose much of their charm if Mrs. Wood did not lead the singing. Mr. Wood's work in the navy yard has been very successful, and in no respect more so than when he enlisted the services of the members of the Christian Endeavor Union of Brooklyn to aid him in preparing the men-o'-wars men to resist temptation.

"Mr. Wood organized the first Christian Endeavor Society in the navy yard on November 1, 1892. There were seven members in the first society, including J. M. Wood, president; R. Stone, master-at-arms, vice-president; H. Elwood, ship's writer, secretary, and J. A. Caldwell, machinist United States Navy, treasurer. By referring to his books on June 19 of this year Mr. Wood found that the 7 had increased to 397, or 283 Senior and 114 Junior Endeavorers. The

Junior Endeavorers are naval apprentices. During the twenty months that have elapsed since the organization of the society, Senior and Junior members wearing the Christian Endeavor badge have left the Brooklyn Navy Yard on board the following vessels: 'Alliance,' 'Atlanta,' 'Bennington,' 'Baltimore,' 'Chicago,' 'Charleston,' 'Columbia,' 'Concord,' 'Cushing,' 'Detroit,' 'Dolphin,' 'Essex,' 'Fern,' 'Franklin,' 'Independence,' 'Monongahela,' 'Montgomery,' 'Monterey,' 'Marblehead,' 'Minnesota,' 'Miantonomah,' 'Newark,' 'New York,' 'Philadelphia,' 'Portsmouth,' 'Richmond,' 'San Francisco,' 'St. Louis,' 'Wabash,' 'Vermont' and 'Yorktown.' They are now scattered all over the world.

"It was very interesting to hear the Junior Christian Endeavorers who went away from the yard a short time since on board the 'Marblehead,' which was ordered South as soon as the loss of the 'Kearsarge' was received, tell of the difficulty they experienced in finding a place on board the white cruiser where they could hold their prayer-meetings. After trying various places they came to the conclusion that they could not do better than, as one of their number said:

"'Go right down into the hold, just over the powder magazine.' Then he added, 'That is where we shall hold our meetings all the time we are away.'

"Mr. Harry S. Shaw, chairman of the Navy-Yard Committee of the Brooklyn Christian Endeavor Union, assists Mr. and Mrs. Wood in the most energetic and enthusiastic manner. The ninety-four Christian Endeavor Societies in Brooklyn have an aggregate membership of 10,000, and out of that number Mr. Shaw can always count on from ten to fifty volunteers to attend and take charge of the religious services held in Library Hall every Sunday morning and every Thursday evening.

"The religious teachings of the government's small quota of chaplains is thus very largely supplemented by the missionary work of Mr. and Mrs. Wood and the evangelical labors of the Christian Endeavorers. It is now a very rare thing, indeed, for a ship to leave the navy yard without having a few Christian Endeavorers on board, and it is almost equally rare for the number not to be increased during the cruise. The testimony of the officers is that religious instruction tends to preserve discipline, and they do all in their power to assist Mr. Wood in his work."

Nothing, surely, could be more gratifying than to know of this development of the Endeavor Society among those who go down into the sea in ships and who do business on the great deep. As Dr. S. H. Virgin, of New York, happily says:

"The sailor is no more the natural child of evil than the landsman. He is often the favorite child of the household with vivid imagination and poetic soul and generous instincts and a roving disposition. His first experience of hardship is often on the sea. His knowledge of sin begins there; his first wicked stories are heard in the forecastle, and his evil training is after and not before he becomes a sailor. Many, however, yield to no such training, but preserve their purity and dignity of character through all the satanic enticements. Nature's noblemen are found among ship owners, who provide every comfort and every religious influence on board their ships, ship captains who preserve the family life and conduct family prayers and guard the young with parental interest, sailors who pour out their heart's adoration before Him who bought them with His own precious blood. They are often simple-hearted as children, swing in the cradle of influence as easily as in the ocean billows, passionate and impulsive as powder, dancing a hornpipe or singing a psalm according to the mood of the hour. They are as many hued as the pearls of the shells they gather and bring from afar as affectionate tokens of remembrance, and become thoroughly cosmopolitan from contact and association with people of every clime. It is significant that sailors were among the earliest disciples, and were made apostles."

In many places this work for the sailors has been taken up and carried on with great vigor by Endeavorers on shore. The Endeavorers of Brooklyn have been particularly vigorous in their efforts for their brethren of the sea, and the meetings they have held at the navy yard and with the floating societies have been most helpful to all concerned. On the Pacific Coast, too, by the Endeavorers of San Francisco, San Diego, and other ports, much has been accomplished.

In fact, from Portland, Me., to Portland, Ore., this movement has aroused the hearts of Christian young people to a sense of their kinship and their responsibility for those whose religious privileges are so restricted and whose opportunities for spreading the Gospel are so vast.

Among those most devoted to this form of Christian work should be mentioned Chaplain Tribou, who is now stationed at Boston, and who declares that Christian Endeavor has opened up a new and most promising field of religious enterprise among the men of the navy.

CHAPTER XLVII.

IN UNEXPECTED PLACES.

Neglected Mission Districts—In the Slums—A State Prison Society—A Pathetic Message—In Asylums and Hospitals—Among New York Policemen—Among the Life Savers—Some Earnest Workers—Christian Endeavor in the Army—Good News from the Frontier—Among the National Guards—Commercial Travelers and Their Endeavor—The Travelers' Union—What the Members Promise—A Touching Testimony—For the Deaf and Dumb—Among the Italians and Bohemians—Hungarians and Poles—Mexicans and Chinese—Mr. Ju Hawk's Address—"God Be With You" in Cree—Christianizing White People—What Some Christian Endeavor Indians Are Doing.

IF I had the data and the skill at my command I could write a most thrilling chapter on the struggles and triumphs of Christian Endeavor in unexpected spots, the victories won by humble souls in their efforts to begin and lead a new life, the attempts, the failures, and successes of those who have lost their place in the ranks of the world's respected toilers, and who have regained it through the influence of the society, or some kindly young soul connected with the society who has been led by the love of Christ to devote his life to the outcast and the downcast.

Many a society has been started in a neglected mission district; many a society has brought new life and cheer to a hard-worked city missionary; many a society has given workers and fighters to a forlorn hope; many a society has been hands to labor and eyes to see and feet to run on difficult errands for those who, almost discouraged, have been laboring for the uplift of humanity in the slums of our great cities, or the viler slums of some dark continent into which the light of the Gospel has only begun to pierce.

In other unexpected places, too, has the society made its way, and by its flexibility and adaptability has proved that it had a mission even there. I scarcely remember a more pathetic incident connected with all these years of the Endeavor movement than the telegraphic message that came to the St. Louis Convention from a Christian Endeavor Society of the State Prison in Wisconsin to the effect that the boys, in the only society in the world which could not be represented at the convention in person, sent their greetings. The story of this society can only be told appropriately by the chaplain of this institution.

"On February 2, 1890, the first Christian Endeavor Society ever organized within prison walls in this sin-darkened world was established in the chapel of the Wisconsin State Prison by Rev. Victor Kutchin, who had been deeply impressed by the methodical plan and practical workings of the Christian Endeavor from its inception by Rev. F. E. Clark at the renowned 'Williston Church,' of Portland, Me.

"The charter members consisted of 35 active and 23 associate. The highest membership at any one period is 204. Total membership, 724; present, 65.

"Owing to the expiration of their respective terms, it has proved impossible to regulate the numerical fluctuations; and the same influence has acted adversely upon some whom we have reason to believe would have been confirmed in a Christian course of life had they remained for a longer period under the elevating influence of the gospel truth, to which they were strangers upon their arrival at this institution.

"Still, we have cause to thank God for His manifest influence and resistless power which has sustained this little Christian Endeavor Society amid all the opposition, ridicule, sarcasm, and various hindrances with which it has had to contend. This opposition was more sharp, intense, and bitter than might be generally supposed by our kind friends in the outside world.

"Still, despite all the shadows which have clouded the course of this experimental society within Waupun's prison walls, we have kept on our way, and we can trust the Lord for still better results in the near future. We feel sure that the Christian Endeavor is about to be generally recognized throughout the land as a potent factor in leading many of the criminal classes to embrace that saving gospel of Christ which is so essential to their happiness, both in this present world and the world to come.

"By the working principles of the Christian Endeavor, in connection with the usual methods employed by clergymen having a prison congregation, we can easily arrive at the degree of spirituality wherein to grade our variously-minded individuals who, through this means, have become our special and more intimate charges. It is also a very convenient mirror in which the applicant for admission to the fold of the Good Shepherd reveals his earnestness, or lack of it, and that before he is scarcely aware of the possibility of our fully comprehending him.

"Where the conversion is actual, the changed demeanor from that common sadness or recklessness so prevalent in penal institutions to one of quiet and abiding trust peculiar to the genuine convert, is an indication which almost invariably indicates the new disciple of the Master."

Another such society is in the Connecticut State Prison, and the chaplain writes encouragingly of its work and its effect upon the men.

Other societies which have accomplished much good have been formed among the employees of asylums and hospitals, and one superintendent of a hospital has gone so far as to advise his fellow-superintendents everywhere to establish such societies; because, as he avers, the religious services and service of the society make the employees more kind, gentle, and patient with their charges, and greatly improve the *morale* of the institution.

To show how easily adaptable is the Christian Endeavor organization to all classes and conditions of men I quote the following account of a society among some glass-blowers of New Jersey, written by the manager of the works, Mr. Foster C. Moore:

"We have in our employ about two hundred men and boys. The glass industry is a very extensive one in Bridgeton. Some twenty factories are not identified with the church in any way—that is, the great majority of them. In our three factories, which we take pleasure in believing are something of an exception to this rule, we have quite a number who are active workers in Christian Endeavor. A few of us met about a month ago and decided to undertake this work. We organized as a regular Christian Endeavor Society with a full set of officers—a Lookout Committee, Prayer-Meeting, Music, and Special committees, taking only such as we felt the need of in the beginning. We held our first meeting last Monday noon, inviting many to bring their dinners on that day. We organized with thirty-five active members, and will have fully that many associate. There were thirty who took part in the meeting in twenty minutes. Much interest was manifested, and the behavior of all, especially the boys and those who are younger, was something remarkable. Fully as good order as could be expected in any church and as much attention—only a person who is employed in a glass factory can appreciate what that means. The singing was spirited and earnest. This is no hasty move with us, but the outcome of much prayer and thought. We believe much good can be accomplished by thus bringing many under the influence of the Gospel who otherwise would never hear it. We had an attendance of ninety at our first meeting. Already results can be seen of these meetings, and many who are not Christians have signified their willingness in any way to help, and are glad that such a work has been undertaken. This, you can see, means much to us. We use Gospel Hymns No. 6 and the union topics in our meetings, governed by the model constitution and by-laws, except a few changes to fit it to our work, but in substance the same. We have our topics from week to week nicely printed on a black-board and kept before them at all times. We try to make our meetings as much evangelistic in character as we can. The president of our society is Mr. Albus, a blacksmith. He asked me as vice-president to answer for him, as he was busy. My position as manager of the works throws me in contact with all these men, and I have a good chance to see the practical workings of the society."

Under the rule of Tammany the police department of New York city suffered grievously in the estimation of the world and became a stench in the nostrils of civilization. But that all the police of the city were not implicated in these unsavory revelations is shown by the fact that even while Tammany was in full sway a small but earnest Christian Endeavor Society was formed among the policemen of New York city. It was organized in 1893. Its membership includes a goodly number of men on the active force, together with members of their families.

It has a striking emblem, consisting of a picture of a policeman's cap, bearing the C. E. monogram, while below it is a policeman's club and a pair of handcuffs, the interpretation being, "Clubbed together in a Christian Endeavor to free policemen from the shackles of sin." Another important Endeavor work in an unexpected place is that among the crews of the life-saving stations on the Atlantic and Pacific coasts and on the shores of the great lakes, which will be described more at length in another chapter.

THE POLICE ENDEAVOR SOCIETY.

Still another spot where Christian Endeavor has unexpectedly taken root is in the army. Five army societies are known to exist, and very likely there are others of which I have not heard. These are found in Missouri, New York (Fort Hamilton), Illinois, and the District of Columbia. The one in Missouri in connection with Jefferson Barracks, of St. Louis, is the oldest one, so far as I am informed. This is a recruiting station, and every month about a hundred new men come in and about a hundred old men go out. For two years the only religious services they have had are the Christian Endeavor services, together with one held once a month by the Women's Christian Temperance Union.

Lieutenant E. H. Catlin, the President of the Army Society of Fort Riley, writes to *The Kansas Endeavor* the following cheering news:

LIEUTENANT E. H. CATLIN.

"In November, 1893, as there seemed to be a good number of soldiers ready to take and keep the obligations of the pledge, a Christian Endeavor society was formed with the writer as President. With all changes in membership, we have held our own, and count fourteen active and seven associate members. Four troops of the 3d cavalry left the post in September, and from the four troops of the 2d that took their place we have secured no new members.

"The only members of officers' families that attend the meetings (held Thursday evenings in the post chapel) are two officers, the chaplain and the wife of the

President, who plays the organ. Attendance is as high as twenty-five. The officers and four or five of the enlisted men can be depended upon to lead meetings. There is at the post a Sunday-school of about forty members, but conditions seem unfavorable for a Junior Society.

" We are conscious that our work is a small endeavor, but the meeting is an explicit witness for the Master; it affords a place of help for any one seeking to walk in the light, and for the giving of testimony. It will be a bright memory for those who have done their duty there.

" Last month we were cheered by the voice of a man lately recruited, who says that he has decided to return from his wanderings from the right path. He is now earnest in his efforts to influence others to come in with Endeavorers. How welcome are such unlooked-for accessions!"

The chaplain of this post for a time was Rev. D. R. Lowell, D. D., who is as warm a friend of Christian Endeavor as he is of the soldiers.

F. D. WING.

In this connection I recall most vividly an Endeavor meeting I attended in Allahabad, India, in the parsonage of the Methodist Church, of which Rev. Rockwell Clancy was pastor, and in which the majority of attendants and participants were English " red-coats," and a most delightful meeting it was.

The Endeavor Almanac of 1895 tells us that in addition to these societies formed in the barracks of United States troops the first society organized in a militia regiment was formed in connection with the Eighth Regiment, National Guards of Pennsylvania, in camp at Pittsburg. Forty members originated the movement, representing the Baptist, Lutheran, Methodist Episcopal, Presbyterian, and United Presbyterian Churches. Two captains and a sergeant-major are among the officers. This militia society, though its members of course retain their membership in their home society, will, when possible, meet quarterly, as well as during the annual encampment.

It is proverbial in business circles that there is no brighter class of men than are found in the ranks of commercial travel and none who are subjected to greater temptations than they.

Their number has been estimated to be a quarter of a million in this country alone, and, as has been said, " the very exigencies of their business would make them, if they were enlisted, incomparable couriers for the spread of the Gospel."

These considerations, together with the need of furnishing some organization for the many Christian Endeavorers who are commercial travelers, led to a remarkable gathering in Philadelphia November 14, 1892. At this time the Travelers' Christian Endeavor Union of America was organized with Mr. F. D. Wing, of Palmyra, N. J., as the President, and Mr. J. Howard Breed, of Philadelphia, as the Secretary. This organization uses the regular Christian Endeavor badge, bearing on the circumference the words "Travelers' Union." It includes besides commercial travelers, nurses, attendants at school, and all who may be compelled to be absent from their own church, and who wish to remain in connection with Christian Endeavor work. The regular pledge is used, except that instead of promising to attend meetings in connection with their own church, members of the Travelers' Union promise to attend Christian Endeavor prayer-meetings at least once a week and in their own denomination if possible. Mr. Wing writes:

"The work is of such an itinerant nature that it is well-nigh impossible to know of results. I do know, however, of a few societies that have been started by members of the Union while on their trips; Christian Endeavor literature has been distributed, and, in many instances, weak societies have been greatly helped in that way, and the words of advice given; I also know of a case, recently, where steps were taken toward the formation of a church by a member of our Union finding there was no church of his denomination in the town he visited, notwithstanding the fact that there were plenty of people there of that belief; it is too early to know just what the result will be, but I have no doubt the church will be formed.

"Talks have been had with fellow-travelers, and where an interest was manifested by an unconverted person he was followed up if possible through the Correspondence Committee; a few cases of conversion have been known of in that way.

"The attention of local societies has been called to the importance of placing a bulletin of church services in the hotels and other prominent places in the town, also of leaving personal invitations at hotels for all strangers who may be in town over Sunday. In some sections that is now quite generally done."

One of the touching incidents in more than one convention which I have attended has been the testimony given at consecration-meetings by the deaf and dumb. It would seem at first thought that they were the very last ones for whom there could be any helpfulness in the Christian Endeavor idea with its strong pledge for outspoken acknowledgment of Christ in the weekly meetings. And yet the deaf and dumb are not debarred from such a society. They have their own language, and on their fingers, if not with their lips, they can tell of the love of Christ which has made their souls if not their tongues sing for joy.

One of the developments of Christian Endeavor has been the establishment of regular societies for the deaf and dumb. In Columbus, Ohio, a young ladies' society of eighteen and a young men's society of eight was formed. At last accounts they had united and had obtained a membership of 133, besides two Junior societies had been established in the same institution with a joint membership of sixty-five.

In the institution for the deaf and dumb at Jacksonville, Ill., there are also two societies, one for the girls and one for the boys.

Much work has been attempted and successfully accomplished by Christian Endeavorers among the representatives of the various nationalities that seek an asylum on our shores, and Endeavor Societies are found among the Italians and Bohemians, the Hungarians and Poles, the Spanish Mexicans and the Chinese. All of the Chinese churches on the Pacific coast are said to have Endeavor Societies. These Chinese Endeavorers are received with great heartiness in the California conventions as they are everywhere, and few who were at the New York convention will forget the thrilling address of Mr. Ju Hawk.

In other parts of the country, too, Chinese Endeavor Societies are found, and here is a fruitful field for the Endeavorers of the future to till.

For a number of years some societies have existed among the North American Indians. At least two societies are known in Alaska, one at Juneau and the other at the Friends' Mission, on Douglass Island. A delegate from this society at the New York convention was received with enthusiastic cheers. Other Indian societies nearer home have also been formed among the Cree Indians by that devoted and talented Rev. Edgerton R. Young. Here is a verse of "God be with you till we meet again" in the Cree language:

> Man 'to ka wechawik eyekook,
> Mena ka nukiskatoyuk,
> Wechaomat oo mayatikwa
> Eyekook ka nukiskatoyuk.
>
> CHORUS.
>
> Eyekook, eyekook,
> Ka nukiskowuk Jesus;
> Eyekook, eyekook,
> Man 'to 'che nukiskowuk mena.

In Oklahoma, too, are some Indian Endeavor Societies, and a number are found in Nebraska, Dakota, Idaho, and Washington. The Sioux name for Christian Endeavor Societies, literally translated, means "Society of those who work for Jesus," which is a capital paraphrase of our usual designation.

One of the most effective Endeavor stories which I have ever heard is vouched for by a secretary of the American Missionary Association. He says that on one occasion, while he was visiting the field, he saw a company of Santee boys starting off on their ponies one Sunday morning for a gallop of twenty

SIOUX INDIANS OF SANTEE TRAINING SCHOOL, MEMBERS OF Y. P. S. C. E.

MEMBERS OF SANTEE AGENCY CHRISTIAN ENDEAVOR SOCIETY. (DAKOTA INDIANS.)

or thirty miles over the plains. When he asked them where they were going they told him they were all Christian Endeavor boys, and that they were going to attend a Sunday-school and Christian Endeavor meeting which they had established among some white settlers who had just moved into the outskirts of their reservation.

Surely, when we read of Indian Endeavorers so touched with the love of Christ that they are attempting to evangelize their white neighbors, we realize the power of the Gospel of Jesus Christ not only to subdue the heart of the dusky warrior of the plains, but to substitute the Bible for the tomahawk and the Gospel invitation for the war-whoop of the savage.

PROMINENT WORKERS IN TORONTO UNION.

F. D. Mills. Lottie E. Wiggins. E. C. Austin. W. G. Hawkins. S. C. Duncan-Clark. Anna U. Flaws. G. T. Graham.

CHAPTER XLVIII.

THE LATER LITERATURE OF THE MOVEMENT.

"Young People's Prayer-Meetings in Theory and Practice "—" Ways and Means for Christian Endeavor "—" Danger Signals "—" Looking Out on Life "—" The Mossback Correspondence "—" Christian Endeavor Saints "—" How " and " Why "—" The Philosophy of the Christian Endeavor Movement "—" Golden Rule Meditations "—" Social Evenings " — " Business " — " Endeavor Day Exercises "—" Foreman Jennie "—" Endeavor Doin's Down to the Corners "—Pansy's Books—" Our Town "—" The Iron-Clad Pledge "—Mrs. Hill's Works—" Attractive Truths in Lesson and Story "—" A Decade of Christian Endeavor "—Many Useful Pamphlets—The Society's Critic—The Hundredth Man—A Damnable Heresy—An Awkward and Meaningless Term—Unitarian Tendency—Perversion of Facts—A Theological Professor and What He Has to Say—Objecting to the International Bible—A Curious Leaflet—It Wags the Dog—Sectarian Criticism—The Impotency of Such Attacks—A Welcome Kind of Criticism.

THOUGH its history has been so short the Christian Endeavor Society has already been very prolific in literature devoted to its exposition. Not to speak of innumerable newspaper articles and of tracts almost beyond number, some of which have reached a circulation of millions, not to speak of the translations of the constitution and the pledge into scores of different languages; the bound volumes which have been inspired by the Christian Endeavor movement, and which relate to it, more or less directly, would make a very respectable library in themselves.

The first book devoted to the subject, *The Children and the Church*, has already been described in these pages. It has passed through several editions and has been reprinted in more than one language.

Another book which I wrote early in the history of the movement is entitled *Young People's Prayer-Meetings in Theory and in Practice*. This is a volume of one hundred and sixty-seven pages, and deals with the whole subject of the training of young converts, their training by instruction, by frequent confession of Christ, and by exercise in religious service.

The prayer-meeting idea in general is also treated somewhat carefully. An attempt is made to depose the prayer-meeting fetich, "edification," from his pedestal, and to substitute in his place what I believe is the true idea of the prayer-meeting. But naturally especial attention is given to young people's prayer-meetings; its place in the church, its dangers, the pastor's relation to it are all discussed. A chapter is devoted to the means of conducting it, and one also to the Sunday-school prayer-meeting, and another to the consecration meeting. The Society of Christian Endeavor and its relation to the prayer-meeting is also discussed, while some fifty pages at the end of the book are given to a large collection of prayer-meeting topics and Scripture references drawn from practical sources. This volume was published in 1886.

In 1889 the most extensive volume devoted to the practical methods of Christian Endeavor which has yet been published was issued. This book, entitled *Ways and Means for the Young People's Society of Christian Endeavor*, a book of suggestions for the prayer-meeting and all lines of Christian work adopted by Christian Endeavor societies, was a compilation of the best things which I could find which had been written by Christian Endeavor workers up to that date along all the lines covered by the society.

To dispose at once of the different volumes, for which I am responsible, and which have a bearing more or less direct on the Christian Endeavor Society, I may say that two companion volumes, entitled respectively *Danger Signals* and *Looking Out on Life*, the first a book for young men, and the second a book for young women, have been published and for several years have had a considerable sale.

Another book, entitled *The Mossback Correspondence*, was made up of letters published in *The Golden Rule*, under the *nom de plume* of "A. Mossback," who is supposed to be a shrewd country minister who has his opinions of men and things and who does not fear to express them, and who, not infrequently, has a suggestion for the young people of his own church and other churches.

Another volume which originated in the same way is entitled *Some Christian Endeavor Saints, together with some Golden Rule Receipts, Golden Rule Sermons, Golden Rule Epistles, and Pictures from Real Life*.

In this volume I have had something to say to Saint Sweet Temper and Saint Modesty, Saint Bright Side, and Saint Speak Well, as well as to many others whom I believe are represented in the Christian Endeavor Society.

Rev. W. F. McCauley has been a prolific writer on Christian Endeavor themes. His books, entitled *How* and *Why*, have deserved to take a high rank as manuals relating to the organization of the society, the duties of officers, business meetings, committee organizations, society extension, etc. They are compact, practical, helpful treatises which are bound to do much good.

Rev. Thomas Chalmers, of Michigan, is the only one so far as I know who has developed the philosophy of the Christian Endeavor movement and printed it in book form. His work is an original and unique little volume, in which he traces back the root principles of Christian Endeavor, which lie far under the soil, and which are not often exposed to view.

Prof. Amos R. Wells, the managing editor of *The Golden Rule*, as every Endeavorer knows, wields a most facile pen. Many of the tracts and booklets which the United Society finds most useful have been prepared by him. Especially has his book for social committees describing appropriate and captivating entertainments been very useful. His Endeavor day exercises and Christian Endeavor year books have been beyond compare in this species of literature, while his *Meditations*, two volumes of which have been reprinted from *The Golden Rule*, have expressed the deepest religious longings and aspirations of a great multitude of Christian Endeavorers. He has also prepared a large manual for Junior workers, which is the only exhaustive work of the kind which has ever been attempted, and is of great value to every Junior worker.

In the field of fiction, too, he has succeeded admirably. His story, *Foreman Jennie*, a capital Endeavor story, has been one of the most popular books of the kind.

When we come to fiction we find that the Endeavor movement is rich in works of this description.

Rev. J. F. Cowan, one of the trustees of the United Society and the popular author of the *Joe Boat Boys* and other stories, has written one of the most amusing, and at the same time practically helpful volumes that the Christian Endeavor Society has given birth to. It is entitled *Endeavor Doin's Down to the Corners*, which in quaint country dialect tells the story of Jonathan Hayseed and of his struggles to do whatever Christ would like to have him to.

MARGARET SIDNEY.

Probably no writer of stories for young people has been so popular or had so wide an audience as Mrs. G. R. Alden, whose pen-name, "Pansy," is known wherever English books are read. Her first Christian Endeavor story is entitled *Chrissy's Endeavor*. It has had a remarkable popularity, and has done more, perhaps, than any one agency to suggest the Christian Endeavor idea to the people of England and the English colonies.

Her next Endeavor story, *Her Associate Members*, has also been a great favorite, while *A Christian Endeavor Revenge*, and other volumes of a similar character from her pen, have spread a knowledge of the Endeavor cause far and wide.

That popular writer, Fay Huntington, has also written an admirable Endeavor story, *A Modern Exodus*, which was also published in *The Golden Rule*.

Margaret Sidney's story, entitled *Our Town*, is a very strong setting forth of the possibilities of an Endeavor society working amid adversity.

The Iron-Clad Pledge, by Jessie H. Brown, is a story whose admirable moral can be judged from its title. When it is known that Miss Brown is one of the leading Endeavor workers of Ohio the quality of the book, so far as it relates to Christian Endeavor, can be well understood.

Mrs. Grace Livingston Hill, another graceful and very popular writer for young people, has written more than one Christian Endeavor story, *The Parkerstown Delegate* being one, among others, that many of my readers will remember with especial pleasure.

MISS JESSIE H. BROWN.

MRS. GRACE LIVINGSTON HILL.

Miss Sophie Bronson Titterington's story, called *A New Endeavor*, is also one that is worthy of a place in our Endeavor library.

Mrs. Alice May Scudder was the pioneer author for the Juniors, and her book, *Attractive Truths in Lesson and Story*, has been found exceedingly useful by a great multitude of Endeavor workers.

Rev. Charles Roads, the beloved president for two years of the Pennsylvania Union, has also published a very attractive work for Junior workers and other teachers of children, entitled *Little Children in the Church*.

REV. CHARLES ROADS.

A valuable volume by Rev. Dwight M. Pratt should not be forgotten in this enumeration. It is entitled *A Decade of Christian Endeavor*, and is the first history of the society. It was published about the time of the Decennial celebration at Portland, and gives a graphic idea of the significance of the movement, its beginnings and spread, and also a brief history of the Decennial Anniversary, while it closes with an eloquent chapter, entitled "The Threshold of Another Century." It is happily introduced by Rev. Dr. Wayland Hoyt.

But from the beginning the great bulk of Christian Endeavor literature has not been found in bound volumes, but in leaflets and pamphlets, which have been sent out by the tens of thousands, and sometimes literally by the millions.

Next to the constitution itself, perhaps the most widely-circulated tract has been the one entitled *The Society of Christian Endeavor: What It Is, and How It Works*, by the author of this history. I have also published some score or more of other tracts and leaflets, which have been widely circulated, for the most part gratuitously.

Secretary Baer and Professor Wells have also been the authors of other leaflets which have gone far and wide; Treasurer Shaw has judiciously edited several of the annual reports, while others who have contributed to this branch of literature who should be mentioned are Rev. James L. Hill, D. D., Rev. Charles Roads, Rev. J. Berg. Essenwein, Miss Frances G. Patterson, Rev. H. W. Pope, Miss Kate Haus, Mrs. F. E. Clark, Mrs. James L. Hill, Rev. J. F. Cowan, D. D., Rev. Arthur W. Spooner, and Rev. W. W. Sleeper.

Millions of copies of the constitution and tens of millions of topic-cards have also been printed and distributed. Some of the Endeavor song-books have also had

REV. J. BERG. ESSENWEIN.

a wide sale. The first one was edited by Rev. S. W. Adriance; and later books by the famous singer, Ira D. Sankey, and also one edited by Rev. W. F. McCauley, have been widely popular. A Junior book, edited by Mr. Sankey, Secretary Baer, and Treasurer Shaw, has also gone far and wide.

Many of these leaflets and some of the books before mentioned have been translated into various languages. German, French, Spanish, Italian, Norwegian, Swedish, Welsh, Japanese, Chinese, Arabic, Turkish, Armenian, Bulgarian, Greek, Tamil, Telegu, Hindi, Hindustani, Urdu, Canarese, Bengali, and Marathi, are some of the languages into which Christian Endeavor literature has already found its way, while it is constantly being translated into new tongues which are spoken by millions of the human race. May these winged messengers carry to the young people of all the world the story of the blessedness of Christian activity!

There is another kind of literature which may also be called the literature of the movement, since it has been caused by the society, and would never have appeared had it not been for the aggressive earnestness of this organization, which, like every thought-compelling movement, has provoked opposition and hatred.

I devote a portion of a chapter to this literature, because it seems hardly fair to quote so many kind things and generous estimates of the movement without also quoting some of the objections and virulent criticisms to which it has given rise.

The critic of the society has seldom been mild, gentle, and generous in his criticism. Indeed, all such criticisms are welcome, and their lesson is, I hope, learned. The religious public has been divided into two classes very largely, so far as any interest has been taken in the Endeavor movement. On the one side has been the ardent and outspoken friends of Christian Endeavor, and this is by far the largest company. Nine out of ten of all Christian people—perhaps it would not be too much to say ninety-nine out of a hundred—who have investigated the claims of the society, and really understood its operations, have been its devoted friends, ready at any time to give a reason for the faith that was in them concerning the movement. The other one person out of a hundred, either by reason of temperament, disposition, or some unfortunate experience with an abnormal society, has been a bitter and violent opponent of the movement.

The future historian will desire to know what the one hundredth man says, as well as the opinions of the ninety-nine.

I have in my hand a leaflet printed by the *Gospel Echo Print*, of Palatine, West Virginia. Here is the cogent reasoning which this author employs against the society:

"Among the many heresies of modern times we have selected the Young People's Society Christian Endeavor, and will try to measure it by the Word of God. It is a society that boasts of its membership running up into hundreds of thousands. They claim that its growth has been 'phenomenal.' But I never heard of them trying to show that it is scriptural.

"Numbers are no mark,
That we shall right be found.
Eight souls were saved in Noah's ark,
While many millions drowned.

"If that society exists by the authority of Jesus Christ, certainly some of their members would be able to show chapter and verse.

"Peter says, 'Many shall follow their pernicious ways by reason of whom the way of truth shall be evil spoken of.' The way of truth is here in the singular number. There is but one way of truth. But 'damnable heresies' and 'pernicious ways' are both in the plural. If there were only a few that followed their pernicious ways, they could not exert the evil influence that they now do. It is almost impossible to find a church to-day but what has felt the blighting hand of that most damnable of all heresies, the Young People's Society Christian Endeavor."

Another brother, who " chooses to remain unknown," has written some long articles entitled " Westminster League or Christian Endeavor. Which ?"

He thought them of enough importance not only to publish them in a well-known paper, but also to put them in a leaflet form for wide distribution.

Referring to the society, which he calls " dangerous in its tendencies and aggressive in its methods," and one which threatens ere long to undermine all denominations, he says :

" Let me once for all say that this refers to the movement known as Christian Endeavor. It is such an awkward, meaningless term, that henceforth it will be referred to as the Christian Endeavor Society, or ' this society.'

" Can the Presbyterian Church look on calmly, when a foreign control comes in and surrounds its young converts, and binds on them pledge after pledge, many of them meaningless and trivial, to be sure, but so numerous and insistent that the religious life implanted by the Holy Spirit is in danger of being destroyed, and certainly is distorted and made sickly, by being held up continually for inspection? We are told by our Saviour that the Kingdom of Heaven is, in the heart, like a seed in the ground ; like leaven hidden in the meal, etc. Would seed grow if continually it was lifted up and examined ? No more can the spiritual life be properly nurtured if subjected to all the petty exercises these young people are expected, nay, are pledged to perform."

One of the special efforts of enemies of the movement has always been to prove that the society is a Congregational institution, because the originator, the President of the United Society, happens to be a Congregationalist.

They ignore the fact that the Congregationalists make up scarcely one-seventh of the members of the society, and that its leaders belong to all denominations. It is even often charged as a count of special importance against " this damnable heresy," that its headquarters are in Boston and so it must be of Unitarian tendency, despite the fact that there is not, nor ever has been, to my knowledge, a Unitarian Society of Christian Endeavor.

But this is the way in which the author " who chooses to remain unknown " tries to work upon denominational prejudices. It is a fair sample of many such attacks. Speaking of one of the denominational rallies at the Montreal Convention, a rally which was meant for Congregationalists and attended *only* by Congregationalists, a rally which was held simultaneously with twenty other rallies of different denominations, he thus speaks of this meeting:

"In the report of the convention in Montreal there appears a paragraph which uncovers the animus of the whole organization as nothing else so well could. On one day the societies, ostensibly under the care of the different denominations, held separate meetings. In most of these meetings the key-note for all the addresses was the Christian Endeavor movement. But the Congregationalist meeting is thus described:

"'To prove that they do not lack in eloquence, some twenty-two speakers were introduced in quick succession. To speak successfully in the open air one must conform to a rule that obliges him to say something every three minutes, but here, with such a theme, it was insisted that each speaker should say something every half minute, and stop; having, at that rate, said two things. Thus the speaking did not descend to a wordy drizzle. Having raised the temperature, it was kept up high until to the end. The speakers were exhorted not to travel too far to get a theme, but to take Congregationalism, and begin anywhere, and they could not fail to be eloquent.'

"This report of the meeting is copied from *The Golden Rule*. Particular attention is called to the sentence:

"'The speakers were exhorted not to travel too far to get a theme, but to take Congregationalism, and begin anywhere, and they could not fail to be eloquent.'

"Is it not clear that the aim of the movement is to spread the principles which underlie Congregationalism, and in doing so to destroy as far as possible the lines of denomination?"

Was ever a more falsely malicious charge made? Fortunately, they are scarcely calculated to deceive even the unwary.

Perhaps the strangest charge ever brought against the Society of Christian Endeavor was that *The Golden Rule* offered as a premium the so-called International Bible, a famous teachers' Bible (as my readers know), like the Oxford or Bagster, with notes by many eminent scholars. This critic, "who prefers to remain unknown," credits the editor of *The Golden Rule* with being the author of these notes, an honor which he regrets to say he has not the slightest claim to.

Then one critic goes on to say:

"Perhaps the International Bible, *with notes by the editor of The Golden Rule,* will explain to those who accept it as their standard, that our Lord did not mean what He said when He gave this advice to His followers: 'But thou, when thou doest thine alms, do not sound a trumpet before thee, as the hypocrites do in the synagogues and streets, that they may have glory of men. Verily I say unto thee, they have their reward. But thou, when thou doest thine alms, let not thy left hand know what thy right hand doeth.' Or, possibly it will be said by many followers of this new faith, that humility, and a hiding of self, was suited to the times before these, but that now each one should keep himself or herself prominently in view, lest any good deed, or meritorious act, go, by any chance, unnoticed.

"In conclusion, let me call the attention of all Christian people to the frequent omission of the one saving word in the name of this society. Again and again is it referred to by the editors of *The Golden Rule* as 'the Endeavor Society' and its members as 'Endeavorers.' And also to the fact that this Bible, *with notes by the man, specimens of whose writings have been shown in these articles*, is now an established fact. The December number of *The Golden Rule* was full of inducements and reasons why superintendents, teachers, and Bible classes should secure copies with the least possible delay. *The writer has not* seen this Bible. Perhaps it is just as well, or the editor might have to furnish space for another letter."

Italics are the critic's.

It is very unfortunate for the bitter opponents of the Endeavor Society that they are so often guilty in their statements of what seem to be deliberate perversions of facts. Every statement of the founder of the society is pounced upon by these critics, often twisted and perverted out of its original meaning, and then paraded as though it were a solemn statement of principles, authoritative and official. *The Golden Rule* is searched with a magnifying glass for any unhappy paragraph, in all of its eighty or a hundred weekly columns, which can be misinterpreted, and this paragraph is treasured up and sprung upon the public, perhaps months or years after it was written, wrenched from its surroundings and given an entirely new meaning.

I have frequently said that " the Endeavor Society never forces its way into an unwilling church. It always waits outside, until the door is thrown wide open and the church and the pastor invite it to enter;" of course, meaning by this figure of speech that a Christian Endeavor Society was never formed until a church was ready to welcome it. Yet a theological professor took this statement, which seems to me so plain and unequivocal, and thereby proved in the course of a long article, which is full of abuse of the Christian Endeavor movement, that Dr. Clark himself admitted that the society was sometimes outside the church, else if it were not outside it could not come in when invited.

This same writer, taking his text from the fact that in two or three denominations the Endeavorers have built a church at the solicitation of the Home Missionary Society of the denomination which, in honor of the donors, has been called a Christian Endeavor church, though of course it was as strictly denominational as any other in the country, finding also that a lay college to fit young men for Christian work and a hotel have advertised themselves in the papers as specially adapted to Christian Endeavorers, thus discourses against this favorite aversion :

" It has begun to run the regular church prayer-meetings, and even Sunday evening services. It has entered the field of Home and Foreign Missionary labor, has organized mission schools, and makes its own contributions to the missionary societies. It has even entered the field of moral reform, taking a hand in the largest and gravest questions, such as Temperance and the Lord's Day. The last development is a Christian Endeavor church, if a recent item in a religious newspaper is correct, which comes more quickly than I expected, but which I had been waiting for. Why not a Christian Endeavor church? The society has all the materials for it, a constitution, covenant, the substance of a confession, officers, committees—all it needs is a field. Naturally a Christian Endeavor Theological Seminary will follow, and that in a rough shape may be said to already exist, according to the following statement made last January in a religious journal of good Congregational repute concerning a certain institution: 'This is *distinctly* an Endeavor college, and all active Endeavorers who want to fit themselves to serve Christ and the Church should have the opportunity.' The writer says that one of these Christian Endeavor students 'goes sixty miles every Saturday to supply a church in the borders of Connecticut.' Plainly we are on the eve of Christian Endeavor candidates for the Christian Endeavor ministry. One would suppose that the limits of development were certainly reached at this point, but I learn as I write that a Christian Endeavor hotel, to be patronized only by Christian Endeavorers, has been established at Chicago, which shows at least how the *spirit of organization* has infected the society, and opens a wide perspective of business programs to the imagination. Really, it almost takes one's breath away to watch this movement, and see how easily it lays hands on every possible form of religious and social activity, as if 'all things' belonged to it. 'Whither does this tend?' we may well ask, with fear and trembling."

A curious leaflet, occasionally issued in Bridgeport, Conn., and entitled *The Eckford Press*, heads one of its issues thus:

"You-Pretty-Sweet-Child-Elimas. What and who are you, any way, if not an old bird in new feathers? You are a success spectacular! You are the tail that wags the dog! You capture and swallow at one gullup the whole city-full, pulpit and pew! You have come to stay! So come leprosy when it finds its affinity!! You have found a fat carcass!! You are covered with the dust, rust, and moss of ages!! You are simply an old bird in new feathers!! You are a bowing wall, etc.! You are a favorite of the world!"

And so the leaflet goes on through a whole page of incoherent abuse and hysterical exclamation points. The motive and object of such an attack I have never been able to fathom. But, fortunately, there is no occasion to attempt to answer such prejudiced and distorted views as those that have here been quoted. They carry their own refutation on their face. I quote them only in the interests of an accurate history, which should, so far as its limits allow, show all sides of the questions discussed.

By far the most determined opposition to the society, though not the most bitter, so far as denunciation goes, has come from a certain section of the denominational press of one or two denominations which have thought it necessary thus to bolster a strictly denominational society, and thus to prevent their young people from straying into the green pastures of interdenominational Christian Endeavor.

The object and animus of these attacks is very plain; but I shall not quote from any of them, for it is my sincere purpose in this history to set down no word which may arouse controversy or provoke bitterness; and it is with great joy that I record the fact that attacks of this sort on the Endeavor movement are growing less frequent and less violent as the years go by. The society is being understood in all quarters as it was not at the beginning, and even those who at first were inclined to criticise and distrust it have in some cases become its most ardent friends.

From none of these criticisms has the society really suffered, seriously or permanently, for its defenders have everywhere come to its support, have showed its true purpose and animus, and it is undoubtedly true that every violent criticism has vastly increased the number of its friends and has reduced the number of its opponents. Everywhere I believe Christian Endeavorers are ready to have their faults pointed out and a better way indicated, if only their critics will be appreciative and sympathetic, will allow for the mistakes of youth and the failures of inexperience, and will attempt not merely destructive criticism, but to lead the societies into larger and better and more fruitful service for their Lord and Master.

PROMINENT LOCAL UNION WORKERS.

PROMINENT LOCAL UNION WORKERS.

1. Miss MacRae................................Boston. See page 617.
2. Rev. A. DeWitt Mason.................New York City. See page 429.
3. H. M. Davis..................................Brooklyn.
4. W. W. Freeman............................   "
5. Henry W. Jessup..........................   "
6. Miss Gertrude L. Wood.................   "
7. Rev. Maltbie D. Babcock...............Baltimore.
8. Frederick Ohrenschall..................   "
9. William C. Perkins......................   "
10. Paul M. Strayer...........................   "
11. Dr. A. D. Mansfield......................   "
12. L. V. Denis................................Cleveland.
13. Miss Carrie L. Bacon...................   "   } See pages 489 and 570.
14. Elizabeth Marion.........................   "
15. F. H. Croxall..............................Denver.
16. John Jostin................................   "
17. W. E. Sweet...............................   "
18. R. L. Rigdon, M. D......................San Francisco.
19. Benjamin Bryon..........................   "
20. Rolla V. Watt..............................   "
21. Miss Bessie Scouler.....................   "
22. H. S. Blackwell, Pres..................   "
23. Lincoln Higgins..........................Chicago.
24. Charles W. French......................   "
25. Miss Jessie Williams....................   "
26. S. A. Wilson...............................   "
27. Miss Frances Patterson................   "
28. Frank E. Page............................   "
29. T. G. Anderson..........................Toronto.
30. Herbert W. Barker......................   "
31. A. Frank Wickson.......................   "   } See page 578.
32. Robert Kilgour...........................   "
33. W. H. Scott...............................Montreal.
34. Miss M. F. Lynch........................   "
35. Frank L. Horsfall........................   "   } See page 461.
36. Rev. J. R. Dodson, B. A., B. D........   "
37. W. H. Chapman..........................   "

CHAPTER XLIX.

THE NEW YORK CONVENTION.

A Magnificent Meeting—Opening Scenes—How the Endeavorers Came In—Some of the Distinguished Speakers—A Ripple of Excitement—Some Distinguished Statesmen—The Postmaster-General and the Secretary of State—Hon. Chauncey M. Depew—"Cleveland, '94"—The World Around—Simultaneous Meetings—Denominational Rallies—A Marvelous Consecration Meeting.

HOW shall we characterize this magnificently tremendous meeting? I do not intend to deal in superlatives, for I believe thoroughly "in the power of an under-statement;" but these adjectives are chosen deliberately. The meeting was magnificent in its size, in its spirit, in its enthusiasm. It was tremendous in the overwhelming throngs who crowded the Madison Square Garden day after day, from July 7 to the 11th. A conservative estimate placed the number of delegates at 30,000, to say nothing of the great multitude of those who took advantage of the reduced railroad rates to visit the city, and who were not registered as delegates.

As the introduction to the Eleventh Annual Report truly says: "The immense stock of souvenir programs, badges, and maps of the city which the committee of '92 had provided were exhausted almost before the first session opened. The great auditorium of Madison Square Garden, although the largest audience-room on the continent, seating 14,000, came far short of accommodating all who desired to attend the convention, and thousands of delegates were turned away at every session, unable to gain admission. It was also found necessary to increase the provisions which had been made for simultaneous meetings in adjacent churches, and this was done to such an extent that on Sunday evening mass-meetings were held in no less than eleven different places, including the Carnegie Music Hall and the Metropolitan Opera House.

"The presence of such a multitude of young people, actuated by a common religious impulse, made a most profound impression upon the city's life. That was manifested on every hand. The decorations of the hall were abundant and tasteful, and especially at the evening sessions, with the 4,000 incandescent electric lights lining the great steel arches of the roof, collected in rosettes along the wall, and culminating in a splendid monogram C. E. over the platform. The effect was very beautiful."

The amphitheatre being elliptical in form, the speakers' platform was placed at one end of the ellipse, with the choir seats rising immediately behind, and the reporters' tables on either side. "The sheep of the religious press on the right-hand and the goats of the secular press on the left," as one paper expressed it. The delegates were seated according to States, the larger delegations occupying the main floor and the others filling the side tiers of seats and the balcony, which extended entirely around the hall. Before the convention opened, for hours there

MADISON SQUARE GARDEN, EXTERIOR.

was much enthusiasm as the various delegations came marching into the hall, bearing their State banners and singing their State songs. It was conceded that Montreal should have the next convention, but Cleveland was after it for '94, and as the Ohio Endeavorers came in they were greeted with great applause, for they were singing to the tune of "Bringing in the Sheaves" the words:

> "Hear the tramp of armies, see the host advancing;
> Lift aloft the banner, tell its legend o'er;
> See the flashing colors, sunlight on them dancing;
> Hear the watchword echo, 'Cleveland, '94.'"

The Maryland delegation also sung, with fine effect, their State song to the tune "Maryland, My Maryland;" while Indiana marched in, singing to the tune of " Marching Through Georgia:"

> "Hurrah! hurrah! for Indiana's band;
> Hurrah! hurrah! for Indiana's band.
> We've come to bring you greeting and our offering to bring
> Of love and devotion to Endeavor."

Kentucky's delegation sung:

> "I will sing you a song of my old Kentucky home."

Canada responded with "Blest be the tie that binds," and the whole audience joined in singing, under the leadership of some other delegations, "Onward, Christian Soldiers."

Promptly at the advertised moment the convention opened, and promptly, when the time came for each speaker, he appeared. There was scarcely a break or a hitch in the program from beginning to end, while many features were introduced in the program which added much life and vivacity to the convention.

How can I begin to condense into one brief chapter, or even a dozen, the good things of this remarkable meeting! When we remember that the convention was addressed by such men as Dr. Russell H.Conwell, Rev. A. C. Dixon, D. D., Rev. Le Roy S. Bean, Rev. H. C. Mabie, D. D., Mr. Ira D. Sankey, Rev. Edgerton R. Young, Mr. John G. Woolley, Hon. John Wanamaker, then the Postmaster-General of the United States; Hon. J. W. Foster, then the Secretary of State of the United States; Hon. Whitelaw Reid, then the Republican candidate for Vice-President of the United States; Rev. Wayland Hoyt, D. D.; Dr. Joseph Cook, Hon. Chauncey M. Depew, and others no less distinguished, it will be seen that the task is quite beyond any historian who is not allowed to devote at least a whole volume to this remarkable meeting.

The effect on the city of New York of this meeting was most remarkable. Few of the citizens had been willing to believe that the predictions of the Endeavorers in advance were anything but the frothy extravagance of youth, and when they heard them talk about 20,000 expected delegates they discounted their expectations by about three-fourths. One hotel-keeper, when the Committee of Arrangements went to him to obtain the use of his hotel, offered to take in the whole convention, saying that he was used to providing for conventions, and that his hostelry would accommodate no less than 1,500 people. When the committee told him they expected ten times fifteen hundred, he regarded them with pitying incredulity.

A prominent pastor told me in advance that the convention would not make a ripple of excitement in New York city; that conventions came and went, and left no sign behind them. This opinion was probably shared by the great majority

INTERIOR OF MADISON SQUARE GARDEN.

"CROWDED OUT."

of New Yorkers and Brooklynites. But, when the delegates began to arrive, a different spirit was noticed. "Where have they come from?" "What are they doing?" "What does Christian Endeavor mean?" "What draws so many young people together?" were questions that were heard on every side.

REV. A. C. DIXON, D. D.

The tone of the newspapers plainly showed the impression which was made by the convention on the New York public. At first, with the exception of two or three of the daily papers, but little attention was given to the gathering. One or two papers even indulged in some sneering editorial paragraphs about these "beardless enthusiasts who had nothing better to do but to howl for a Puritan Sunday." But the tone soon changed, and during the last days of the convention almost all the papers gave large space and generous editorials to the convention.

In this chapter I can do little more than present a bare outline of this multitudinous meeting and the impression that it made, and allude to its more distinctive and unusual characteristics.

The opening hour of the convention was marked by the presentation to the President of the United Society, by the Rev. Dwight M. Pratt, the present pastor of the mother society, in a graceful speech, of a gavel made of black walnut from the original pulpit of Williston Church, and of granite from the corner-stone of that church. This beautiful gavel is preserved in the safe of the United Society as one of its treasures.

The addresses of welcome by Dr. Deems and Dr. Dixon, as can

PRESIDENT MERRILL E. GATES.

be imagined, were full of fire and spice and wit and earnestness, while President Merrill E. Gates, of Amherst, happily responded on behalf of the Trustees. At

THE NEW YORK CONVENTION.   395

the time of this convention the Christian public of America was excited by the efforts of unscrupulous directors to open the gates of the World's Fair on Sunday. The convention took very strong ground on this question, and every allusion to it was greeted with tremendous applause. Rev. R. V. Hunter, of Indiana, presented a report of the committee that had the matter in charge with great effect.

An unexpected feature of the meeting was the presence and participation of several men who are no less eminent in public life than in their religious duty: Hon. J. W. Foster, Secretary of State; Hon. Whitelaw Reid, Hon. Chauncey M. Depew, and Hon. John Wanamaker being four of these speakers.

With the exception of Mr. Wanamaker these gentlemen were not expected in advance, but, being in New York, and being present at the convention, they were earnestly called for by the assembled delegates, and responded most happily to the call. The Secretary of State in his remarks said: "We hear much from certain quarters in this day about the decay of evangelical religion and of the growth of agnosticism and the various forms of disbelief, which are to sweep off the earth our Bibles and our Christianity. Would that these critics could stand in my place to-night. They might be led to believe that faith in a risen Saviour and in the inspired Word of God were neither dead nor dying in this land."

Hon. Chauncey M. Depew, who claimed to be one of the earliest members of the Young Men's Christian Association, said: "The Young Men's Christian Association is the recruiting station of the churches, but you, as a Christian Endeavor Society, are doing the work in the interior of your own church. You are the citadel of the Christian camp inside the line. You keep the weak-hearted brother from deserting. You bring the deserter back into the fold. May you increase and grow in power, recruiting from the youth with the fire of youth urging you on, with hope to be realized before you and with Heaven's gate wide open to welcome you."

Hon. John Wanamaker, who was also received with great applause, said, in a delightful little speech: "I think one of the greatest surprises you have given to this wonderful city is the way in which you Christian men and women are taking possession of it. Who ever would believe that you would march on the city 30,000 strong. I think if you were to go out into the streets you would have to add 20,000 to that figure. I rejoice to-night that the Christian Endeavor movement has brought something to this age, not a local or temporary thing, but something that commands the heart and the good opinion of the whole world. In the simplest, and in the most practicable and in the most common-sense way on unsectarian lines, this the brightest star in the Christian world has risen, sending out its light and beneficence over the years of this closing century to usher in the dawn of a new century of the blessedness of Christian living all the world around."

Hon. Whitelaw Reid, in his brief address, awoke great enthusiasm when he said: "Our fathers, who laid the foundation of the civil and religious liberty which we enjoy, were men who planted their fortifications on every hillside as they advanced to the conquest of the continent. You know what these fortifications were, the school-house and the church. Let us guard them as our fathers guarded them, and we shall preserve the fair heritage we have received and transmit it in our turn grand and beneficent beyond their thought or ours to untold generations of men."

It so happened that all these men, among the most eminent in the public life of the Republic, belonged to one political party, though it was only by chance that this so came about. However, it is not to be supposed that the comic papers lost this opportunity for their quips and skids. One of the most prominent of them the next week represented all these eminent politicians in a boat fishing in a pond labeled "Christian Endeavor Fishing Ground," while a great many little fish with the Christian Endeavor badge upon them were nibbling at the tempting bait. But the Christian public knew that these men were invited to speak at the convention and accepted the invitation, not because they were statesmen and in public office, or desired future offices, but because, first of all, they were religious men.

Another happy feature of this convention was the addresses of representatives of other lands who had not heretofore appeared upon the convention platform. Mr. Sumantro Vishnu Karmarkar, a native Hindu of fine presence, wearing his turban and silken sash, was given a great ovation, and he spoke in excellent English on the subject, "Christianity for India." Mr. Ju Hawk, of St. Louis, a young Chinaman, thrilled the audience with his speech on Christian Endeavor for China, and Mr. Thomas E. Besolow, an African prince, made a happy address for the Dark Continent. A native of Alaska, also, Mr. Marsden, who is studying to go back as a missionary to his people, spoke most interestingly.

Thus a cosmopolitan flavor was given to this convention such as no previous meeting had had. Mission work, too, was given a warm place in this meeting, and the conference on mission work, conducted by Rev. Robert E. Speer, was one of the memorable events of the convention. The address of Rev. H. C. Mabie, D. D., of the Baptist Missionary Society, was a most able one, and Rev. Le Roy S. Bean supplemented it with an admirable address on "Systematic Giving to God."

Of course, temperance was not left out of the program, and Mr. Woolley's speech, as well as Mr. Murphy's, will be long remembered. One of the new features of this convention was the Denominational Rallies. They alone would have marked this meeting as an extraordinary one. Nothing like them had been attempted before, but they met with immediate and universal favor, and they have evidently come to stay among the features of our great international gatherings. These rallies were held by members of the Methodist Episcopal, Baptist, Presbyterian, Methodist Protestant, Reformed Dutch, Free Baptist, United Brethren, Congregational, Cumberland Presbyterian, Lutheran, Christian, Episcopal, Reformed Episcopal, Reformed Presbyterian, United Presbyterian, Disciples of Christ, Moravians, Friends, Seventh-day Baptists, and Evangelical Association, and, in almost every case, the numbers were large, the enthusiasm intense, and the spirit of devotion no less marked than in the denominational fellowship.

At this convention, too, the first International Junior Rally was held. This was held in the Broadway Tabernacle Church, and was under the charge of Mrs. Alice May Scudder. Dr. Deems, Mrs. F. E. Clark, Rev. C. H. Tindal, Rev. W. W. Sleeper, Rev. H. N. Kinney, and Mr. William Ferguson addressed the meeting, which was composed of hundreds of children who crowded into the Broadway Tabernacle and listened delightedly to the different speakers. This, too, has come to be one of the features of the international conventions, and thus in another matter did New York set the pace for the future.

As can easily be imagined, the tens of thousands of delegates could not all crowd into the Madison Square Garden, ample as is its audience-room, and so various churches and halls in the neighborhood were used for simultaneous meetings. Chief among these were the Madison Square Presbyterian Church, the Marble Collegiate Church, the Metropolitan Opera House, and the Carnegie Music Hall. These were not overflow meetings in the usual sense of the term, but were carefully provided for and furnished with speakers as eloquent and interesting as those who addressed the audience in Madison Square Garden.

Among them, in addition to those we have already mentioned, were Rev. J. B. Thomas, D. D., Rev. W. E. Park, D. D., Rev. D. J. Burrell, D. D., Rev. George H. Wells, Rev. William Patterson, Rev. G. C. Kelly, D. D., Rev. F. A. Noble, D. D., Rev. J. W. Lee, D. D., Mr. W. J. Van Patten, Rev. S. L. Baldwin, D. D., Rev. W. H. Black, D. D., Rev. W. H. McMillen, D. D., Rev. W. H. Allbright, Rev. G. R. W. Scott, D. D., Rev. W. H. G. Temple, Rev. W. F. McCauley, Rev. George T. Lemmon, Rev. J. Z. Tyler, Rev. James L. Hill, D. D., Rev. H. B. Grose, Rev. C. P. Mills, Professor Work, President Scoville, Dr. C. C. Creegan, and many others.

But even these numerous churches and halls were not sufficient, and "all out-doors" was utilized for a great public meeting on Union Square, under the charge of Prof. W. W. Andrews, at which some of the speakers already mentioned made most earnest and eloquent addresses.

The singing of the convention was one of the marked features which will always be remembered by those who were present. Mr. Sankey sang frequent solos, and the congregation was led by Mr. and Mrs. Geo. C. Stebbins, and by Mr. F. L. Lindsay.

The Committee of Arrangements, of which Rev. H. T. McEwen, D. D., was the chairman, is deserving of unlimited praise. The arduous duties that devolved upon them by reason of the unexpectedly large attendance, for the convention was nearly twice the size anticipated, were performed with great efficiency, and the memory of this committee will long live in the annals of Christian Endeavor.

The only sad feature of the convention was the fact that Secretary Baer was prevented by ill-health from attending the meeting. He was most active in preparing for it, and expected to attend until just before the convention was held; but sudden and severe illness kept him at home, much to his own grief and to the sorrow of thousands of assembled Endeavorers.

GEORGE C. STEBBINS.

Great was the excitement to know where the convention of '94 was to be held. Ohio, and especially Cleveland, were on the *qui vive;* and when Dr. Boynton, in a neat speech, after tantalizing the Ohio Endeavorers for a little while, announced that the next convention would be held in Montreal and the following one in Cleveland, the enthusiasm was beyond all limit. The Ohio delegates arose and sung, with tremendous effect, "Pass along the watchword, 'Cleveland, '94,' " in the chorus of which the whole audience joined. California and Denver, which were the two most serious rivals to Ohio, accepted the situation most gracefully and heartily, the Colorado delegation springing to their feet, even before Mr. Boynton had finished his remarks, to sing "Blest be the tie that binds," the rejoicing Ohio delegation taking it up and the whole audience joining. Then the California delegation proposed three cheers for Cleveland, which were given with a will, and Ohio responded with three cheers for Denver and San Francisco.

I cannot close the account of this marvelous convention without a word about the consecration meeting, which was the crowning service of it all. In fact, simultaneous consecration meetings were held, and the spirit never rose higher than in the Madison Square Garden, when State after State and country after

COMMITTEE OF '92 (NEW YORK CONVENTION).

1. Rev. H. T. McEwen, Ph. D., D. D., Chairman.
2. H. M. Davis, Printing.
3. J. W. Allen, Secretary.
4. A. V. Heely, Press.
5. James A. Cruikshank, Excursion.
6. W. F. Stevens, Hotel.
7. Parsells Cole, Correspondence.
8. Charles Caldwell, Reception.
9. Charles J. Frye, Jr., Music.
10. Josiah R. Wray, Treasurer.
11. Milton S. Littlefield, Jr., Music.
12. Levi S. Hulse, Hall.

country responded through their delegates as their names were called, all telling of their devotion and love to a common Saviour. Not only was every State and province represented, but Africa, Australia, India, China, Great Britain, and Japan, Mexico and Norway, the Sandwich Islands and Samoa, New Zealand and Switzerland, Spain and Turkey, and the West India Islands were all represented. The ends of the earth, it seemed, had come together in Madison Square Garden, and, in the solemn stillness and hush of that closing hour, after the responses had been given several spectators expressed their desire to begin the Christian life, and all held up their hands as an indication that they would try and lead one soul to Christ during the coming year. As the hands went up, in response to the request of the President they all joined in the old Roman oath of allegiance, "This for me, this for me."

"God be with you till we meet" was sung, the Mispah benediction pronounced, and the Eleventh International Convention, the greatest of the series up to this date, adjourned.

SOME WORKERS OF THE CLEVELAND UNION.

1. J. G. Warren.
2. Mrs. Josephus Craft.
3. Miss Netta A. Rockwell.
4. Rev. A. J. Waugh.
5. Miss Carrie L. Bacon.
6. Edward H. Kieffer.
7. Rev. John Doane.

CHAPTER L.

SOME CONVENTIONS BENEATH THE SOUTHERN CROSS.

An Invitation and What Came of It—Cordial Greetings Everywhere—Six Delightful Weeks—A Christian Endeavor Pennant—Elaborate Programs—The *Australian Christian World's* View of the Meetings—The *Golden Link* and Its Account of the Victoria Convention—Delightful Meetings in Adelaide—A Comparison with the Salvation Army—The Importance of the Pledge—A Pioneer of South Australia—In Queensland's Capital—The Singing of Australian Endeavorers—The Monster Tea.

T the convention in Minneapolis it was proposed by an enthusiastic Endeavorer that I should go around the world to tell the story of Christian Endeavor, and to stimulate interest in the movement in other lands, and it was also proposed that the Endeavorers should pay five cents apiece toward the expenses. This idea was vetoed, because it might seem to some like a tax levied upon members of the society. But the idea was not forgotten, and pressing calls from foreign lands gave emphasis to it.

The Australian Endeavorers were particularly desirous for a visit from the President of the United Society. Other invitations came from missionary lands, and before the New York convention it was decided that soon thereafter, with Mrs. Clark, I should start on this missionary journey. The United Society appropriated $3,000 to defray the expenses of the trip. When the statement was made in the Madison Square Garden that I was soon to start on this journey by Dr. McEwen, who said that he thought it an appropriate thing "to send our greetings of love and affection to our brothers and sisters across the sea in whatever land Dr. Clark may find them; if you approve of that make it manifest," at once the audience sprang to its feet, and by a vigorous waving of handkerchiefs and by loud applause showed its desire that I should carry their greetings with me.

The travel-story of this journey has been told in another volume, entitled *Our Journey Around the World*. In this chapter I will not rehearse any part of that story, but will simply tell of some Christian Endeavor meetings in the great island empire of Australia.

I beg that my readers will not think of our kindly receptions in the lands that lie beneath the Southern Cross as if they were of a personal character. We certainly were not so conceited as to give them this significance. We knew full well that the enthusiastic meetings were anything but purely personal in their character.

We understood full well that it was love for the Endeavor cause that was exhibited in all these receptions, and in these kind words that were so freely and generously spoken. It was because we represented the cause, and were on a world-wide mission in its interests, that we were received so heartily, and I trust that my readers will understand in any descriptions which are here given of these meetings that throughout these six delightful weeks this fact was borne steadily in mind.

For some time before this visit active and growing interest in the society had characterized the religious public of Australia. Into good hands had the society fallen. Influential ministers and well-known laymen had given time and attention to the subject. The religious papers had contained much concerning the movement, and many societies existed that were strong and flourishing. There were few carping critics to sneer at the society, and those who did exist were of slight influence. Everywhere, as we went throughout the colonies, we felt that we were in an atmosphere of enthusiastic religious earnestness.

Our very first greeting, before the "Mariposa," on which we sailed from San Francisco, was made fast at the pier in Sydney, on the 13th of September, 1892, was an indication of the welcome that never failed during six delightful weeks. While yet the great ship was steaming into the harbor, we saw a little steam yacht coming out to meet her. As she drew nearer, our hearts were stirred by the sight of the stars and stripes flying from one masthead, while, as she came still nearer, we saw that a pennant from the other masthead bore the well-known symbols, "Y. P. S. C. E."

Among those who were most active in making the meetings in this colony so conspicuously successful were Rev. William Scott, of Sydney, then the President of the New South Wales Union; Mr. George Gray, the Secretary; Mr. W. H. Barraclough, the Treasurer, beloved and honored of all, and since called to his reward; Rev. William Allen, Mr. J. Neale Taylor, and Rev. W. J. L. Closs, since then the very efficient President of the Union.

The care that was taken by the different committees of arrangements in preparing for these meetings is shown even by the programs, which were of the most elaborate character often, and printed in the highest style of the printer's art. The meetings in Sydney consisted of a welcome-meeting in the afternoon of the first day, a public reception and tea-meeting in the evening, a public welcome later, and an interesting convention packed full of good things on the five succeeding days.

AUSTRALIA.

1. W. H. Barraclough.
2. Rev. Alfred Bird.
3. Rev. W. Scott.
4. F. Kemp.
5. Rev. W. J. L. Closs.
6. George Gray.
7. J. R. Jackson.
8. W. B. McCutcheon.
9. Rev. Wm. Clark.
10. H. E. Wootton.
11. A. S. Wilson.
12. J. G. Thompson.
13. Randolph S. Gray.
14. Y.M.C.A. Building, Sydney.
15. Wesley Church.
16. Town Hall, Sydney.
17. Tea Meeting, September 12, 1892. 2,500 at tables at one time (Melbourne Town Hall).

I quote a few paragraphs concerning these earliest meetings on Australian soil, in the colony of New South Wales, from the *Australian Christian World*:

"During the Young People's Society Christian Endeavor Convention, which lasted from Tuesday the 13th to Monday the 19th of September, Dr. Clark gave eight set speeches, preached two sermons, and conducted a Christian Endeavor parliament and a consecration meeting. Mrs. Clark gave three addresses—two to Endeavorers and one to ministers' wives. Certainly Dr. and Mrs. Clark have not eaten the bread of idleness since they came to Sydney. Let it be noted, in regard to the Sydney convention, that it was a decided success. Indeed, considering that the number of enrolled Endeavorers in New South Wales is only sixteen hundred, and that the New South Wales Endeavor Union is not more than twelve months old, the public interest shown in the movement was really wonderful; so also was the enthusiasm. It comes as a surprise to many that, when you appeal to the young in the right way, you can awaken an enthusiasm for Christianity.

"There is such a thing as joy in Christ and joy in the felt union of Christian people in Him. It was this sense of the glorious devotion to the great Lord and the sacredness of the tie which unites His brethren to one another that gave the peculiar quality to the meeting."

I will not quote other of the kind things which were printed in the papers lest the praise should seem fulsome when read in cold type, or, at least, type that is not hot from the newspaper press.

After about a week spent in the capital of New South Wales, together with one or two friends from that colony and the indefatigable Secretary, Mr. J. B. Jackson, we went to Melbourne, the great and beautiful capital of the colony of Victoria. It was from this colony that the invitation to Australia had first come, but "geographical necessities," as the Endeavorers of Melbourne are fond of saying, brought us first to Sydney.

In fact, more than a year before this visit to Australia a formal invitation had been extended by the annual convention of the Victoria Union. "Early in 1892," said the *Golden Link*, "very active arrangements began to be made by the various unions which had been formed in South Australia, New South Wales, and Queensland for the anticipated visit, while the Victoria Union still maintained its position as the inviting colony. The local arrangements of each colony fell on the local union, and a common desire was manifested by them all to make this visit a memorable one in the history of Australian Christian Endeavor."

The first reception in Victoria came on September 21. This was followed by a welcome meeting on the next day, and for a full week in Melbourne and vicinity meeting followed meeting in quick succession. Ministers' conferences, social gatherings, consecration meetings, and Sunday-school gatherings came thick and fast, and each meeting had characteristics all its own, which made it a living memory with us for many a month to come.

The actual convention of the Victorian societies did not begin until Tuesday, September 27. For three days the convention lasted and closed with a most memorable consecration meeting. "This gathering," said the *Golden Link*, "will always be remembered by those who were present as the most sacred and significant religious meeting that it was ever their privilege to attend. The audience was a peculiarly impressive one, considerably over two thousand members of the society being present, and the zeal and enthusiasm was evidenced in the great fervor and readiness with which one and all took part. Only those present will ever be able to tell of the earnestness which seemed to possess every heart, and the peculiar and earnest way in which one and all in many forms, but with one purpose, consecrated themselves to Christ. It is not too much to say that never before in these colonies has a meeting been held so full of quiet earnestness, so rich in its hopefulness, or so potent in its inspiration as this consecration meeting, the climax and the glory of the three days' great convention of 1892."

Among those who had prominent part in this memorable meeting were Rev. L. D. Bevan, D. D., Rev. A. Bird, of the Baptist denomination, Mr. W. H. George, Mr. Howard Hitchcock, Rev. A. R. Blacket, Mr. W. R. McCutcheon, Rev. S. Savage, Mr. W. J. Piper, Rev. A. R. Edgar, and many others whom my space will not allow me even to mention by name.

Two other pleasant meetings which were held in connection with the Melbourne convention were those at Geelong, a thriving city of Victoria, thirty miles from Melbourne, which had a little convention of its own full of enthusiasm and power, and another meeting in Prahran, a suburb of Melbourne.

With one more quotation from the *Golden Link* I will close this chapter, a quotation which tells of the spiritual uplift which came to the young people of the colony by reason of this memorable convention:

"It is not too much to say that the fellowship which we enjoy in common will not remain a memory of the past, but will remain with us, a sweet and precious possession.

"But even above this priceless blessing, the individual spiritual life of our members has been profoundly affected. No one could have been present at those meetings without being impressed with the evident earnestness and sincerity of everything that was said and done. No one could have been there when at least three thousand hands were raised to God in solemn vow of service for Him, and earnest promise to win at least one soul to Him in the coming year, without feeling that deep down in the hearts of all there was a solemn purpose to redeem their vows and to keep their pledge. Will that purpose resolve into thin air, or remain only a faint echo of memory? We know that it will not. We know that every one will go back to the actual work of their own society inspired with more zeal than before to work for Christ there, to extend the glory and honor of His kingdom there, and to win more souls for Christ."

The Endeavor meetings in Adelaide were as full of stimulus and power as in the other colonies. The spiritual climate of Adelaide is as bracing and refreshing as the air which its fortunate inhabitants breathe. It is sometimes called "the religious city of Australia."

Every good cause here is heartily welcome and finds a congenial soil in which to grow. It can be imagined then that the Christian Endeavor meetings were not only well attended, but full of a peculiar spiritual flavor, and that they resulted in a quickened religious influence which for many weeks and months blessed the churches of Adelaide.

The welcome accorded the movement can be judged from some editorials which appeared in the leading Adelaide journal. Said *The Adelaide Advertiser*, comparing the society with the Salvation Army:

"Both have struck out new plans which have achieved extraordinary success going very different ways. The army has maintained an independent existence from the beginning and become, in fact, a separate religious sect, recruiting from older denominations as well as from persons who are outside. Whereas the young people's society has nestled close to the sheltering care of the churches where it has found a home, been fostered by them and repaid them for their care by enthusing into them something of the stirring vitality and fresh enthusiasm of energetic youth. Probably this accounts in a very large measure for the phenomenal growth which has been witnessed, and is still going on. In this respect nothing in the entire history of Christendom has equaled the Endeavor movement. . . . There is in the very title of the Endeavor Society a suggestion of its comprehensive and practical character. No doubt one of the binding and at the same time stimulating forces brought to bear is in the pledge, taken by every person who becomes what is called an active member. In every organization from Free Masonry onward the importance of some such obligation has been recognized, and in this case there can be no doubt as to the influence it exerts. It renders what was only dimly recognized before both tangible and concrete, thereby affording a constant impulse to the discharge of personal duties. At the same time perfect freedom is afforded for the play of individual temperament and for meeting the exigencies of local circumstances. The intellects of the youthful members are not exercised and perhaps puzzled over questions in theology, but their affections are appealed to and their sense of devotion increased. An American minister concisely expressed his approval in a characteristic way by the remark that the Endeavor Society manufactured cement and steam. . . . The Endeavor plan is to defeat the enemy by providing opportunities for practical work, thus additional interest is enthused into the life of whoever will embrace such opportunites, and his ability is cultivated in the most effective way. . . . The probability is that such an institution like the Sunday-school will come up to be regarded as part of the equipment of every church, thus additional machinery will be provided for doing what is regarded more and more as legitimate church work. At the same time the interdenominational bond will develop the charity and brotherliness which ought to prevail to a greater extent than they do. It rests with Endeavorers themselves to prove whether this forecast is verified."

I have given this extract from one of the admirably edited journals of Australia, because the principles of the Endeavor movement are not only clearly stated, but it shows how they were understood and fully grasped by our friends of the Antipodes. The meetings in Adelaide throughout were of a most encouraging and delightful character. Especially prominent was the evangelistic spirit of these meetings. Efforts were made to save souls, and these efforts were most successful. The sunrise prayer-meetings were full of the delightful fervor and well-regulated zeal. The consecration meeting will be long remembered, while the tea-meetings and other social gatherings brought the delegates together in unrestrained and delightful social intercourse.

Among other meetings was one with the ministers and lay preachers of Adelaide and vicinity, at which one hundred and thirty were present. Another meeting of much interest was for the university students of the colleges and private schools. At this meeting Hon. Dr. Cockburn, the Chief Secretary of the colony, presided, and the Premier of the colony showed much interest in the meetings.

So many names crowd to my pen as I write of these delightful Australian gatherings that I know not what names to record in the space at my disposal. A mere catalogue of names would not be interesting to most of my readers, and yet it would mean very much to me if these names were those of Australian friends who, during these brief six weeks, became forever dear. The faces of some of them I am able to show you, and the names of some to record, but many that have a very deep significance to me must be left unrecorded. However, if but one name could find its way into the account of these South Australian meetings it should be that of Rev. Silas Mead, D. D., pastor of the Flinders Street Baptist Church of Adelaide. At the time of my visit he was the President of the South Australian Union, and for months had been most active in promoting the interest of the Christian Endeavor Society. A patriarch in appearance and in length of service for this leading Baptist Church of the colony, his heart was as youthful and fresh as that of an unspoiled child. Unstintedly he gave his time and sympathy to the movement, and, associated with him were three daughters and a son, Dr. Cecil Mead, who is now a medical missionary in India, while Miss Lillian Mead is now the efficient and beloved Secretary of the South Australian Union, doing most effective work for the advancement of the cause.

After the last meeting in Adelaide we started immediately for Queensland. On the way to this progressive colony, whose capital is nearly eighteen hundred miles by rail from the capital of South Australia, we spent two or three more happy days in Sydney and attended a farewell meeting in Pitts Street Church. At this meeting most kindly and affectionate sentiments were expressed, and we were, metaphorically, wrapped in a beautiful fur rug made of a rare and almost extinct species of Australian possum, a present which told of the warmth of the Australian welcome.

The last Australian conventions which we attended were held in the capital city of Queensland. In Brisbane and vicinity, as well as throughout Queensland, the society was still small in numbers but vigorous in its activity. Though the first Endeavor Society in Australia is said to have been founded in Brisbane in consequence of the visit of Mr. Colby, there were still only about two-score societies throughout the colony. However, the meetings were enthusiastic enough and large enough to make one believe that there were ten times as many Endeavorers in the colony. The welcome was held in the City Tabernacle, where the first society was started, though it is claimed by other colonies that it was not at first altogether on Christian Endeavor lines. Mr. G. H. Buzacott, with whom Mr. Colby first talked concerning Christian Endeavor, was the chairman of the meeting, and, throughout this meeting, as well as in subsequent conventions, I was made once more to feel the warmth and glow of the religious fellowship of my dear friends in the Antipodes.

After two or three days, which were all too brief for the enjoyment of the many meetings planned during our stay, we sailed for China with only pleasant memories of the land of the Emu and Kangaroo; the land of sunshine and flowers; the land of hospitality and warm Christian Endeavor hearts.

Greatly impressed was I, as I visited these conventions, with the similarity of Christian Endeavorers in spirit and purpose and plans everywhere.

I have often said to myself that were I transported blindfolded through the air and let down through the roof into an Endeavor Convention, I should scarcely know whether I was in Philadelphia or London, in Boston or Sydney, Chicago or Adelaide, so striking are the resemblances of Christian Endeavorers the world around, so few and trifling are their differences. Little matters of pronunciation, matters of terminology, matters of dress or custom, are insignificant compared with the many common traits and common features of the religious life of both America and Australia. The singing struck me, as I have said before, as better in Australia than in America, more spontaneous, more varied. It seemed more devotional and more a part of the service. Frequently the members sang with bowed heads or upon their knees, and the hymn was a prayer, touching and reverential.

The social features, too, are somewhat different, clustering around great tea-meetings, as in Melbourne, where "A Monster Tea," as the papers advertised it, which was said to be the biggest affair of the kind ever held in the country, was enjoyed by three thousand Endeavorers, the tables being spread in the great City Hall more than once, and then cleared away with marvelous celerity for the public meeting which was to follow.

CHAPTER LI.

TYPICAL ENDEAVOR SCENES ON FOREIGN SHORES.

The Same Enthusiasm the World Around—A Glimpse in Canton—Some Beautiful Emblems—How Mr. Yeung Led the Meeting—A Glimpse in Shanghai—A Printers' Endeavor Society—No Printers' Devils—The Juniors of the South Gate—The Junior Society and the Baby Towers—A Glimpse in Japan—Some Things That a Traveler Learns—Is Christian Endeavor Fitted for Japan?—Some Reasons for Believing That it Is—A Glimpse in India—The Constitution and Its Translation—A Scene in the Woman's Union Mission—Some Endeavorers of Bombay—In the Land of the Sultan—Some Queer Hieroglyphics—How an American Endeavor Society Multiplied Itself—Think of the Possibilities—A Scene in San Sebastian—A Meeting in Paris—Union of French and English in Christian Endeavor—A Harmonious Variety.

AS the story of the journey necessitated by this year spent among Endeavorers in foreign lands has been told in another volume, I will simply present to my readers in this chapter glimpses of a few typical Christian Endeavor scenes in many lands. The scenes are disconnected, to be sure, and the glimpses but fragmentary; yet I believe they tell of the same spirit, the same enthusiasm, the same overmastering motive of love to Christ of which the movement speaks in all English-speaking lands.

A GLIMPSE IN CANTON.

It was a union meeting of the men's society connected with the Presbyterian school in Fa-ti and of the Second Presbyterian Society of Kauk-fu, both of Canton. The girls' society wanted to come, but it was thought scarcely proper for the young ladies to come so far in the evening. When we reached the chapel of the boys' school of the Presbyterian mission, where the meeting was held, all were in their places, about a hundred Chinese men and boys, and all rose while the missionaries and the visitors took their places.

The room was beautifully decorated with floral emblems in Chinese characters, which meant, as I was told, "Peace," "Prosperity," "Welcome," etc. From the centre of the hall went streamers of evergreen to the four corners of the room, and behind us, in Chinese characters, were two large scrolls, which were afterward given to us, and were translated as follows: "FA-TI [Flowery Region] CHRISTIAN ENDEAVOR SOCIETY [literally, Urge-on-in-the-service-of-salvation's

Lord Society] RESPECTFULLY PRESENT : MAY YOU TAKE THE BLESSED TIDINGS, AND PROCLAIM THEM UNTIL THEY FILL EVERY REGION WHERE WATER AND CLOUD REACH." The other scroll would have shocked our modesty, had we known what it meant, so complimentary was it; but we reminded ourselves, lest we should get too puffed up, that these Chinese knew very little of us, since we had been in Canton only two days, and that they are apt to deal in flowery compliments.

Mr. Yeung, who led the meeting, gave out a hymn, which was sung very heartily to the tune of "Silver Street." Then he called upon Rev. Mr. Noyes, of the mission, to tell why we had come together, and what my mission was. Then we sung another song, and Mr. Fulton was asked for a few words concerning the history and growth of the Christian Endeavor movement. Then, after a hearty prayer by one of the Chinese brethren, Mr. Yeung asked me to give them some words of counsel and advice, which I proceeded to do as well as I could for about five minutes, while Mr. Wisner, of the mission, translated what I said. I never knew better, however, the meaning of the phrase, " a few feeble remarks ;" for it is exceedingly difficult to speak with any force through an interpreter. I have no doubt, though, that Mr. Wisner made up in his translation for any lack of mine.

A CHINESE DOCTOR.

After these remarks, Mr. Tso, one of the native teachers, was called upon. He said that he regarded my visit as providential, because it might help them to spread abroad their detestation of the opium traffic. He said that a commission had already gone to England to present the claims of poor, opium-cursed China, and he hoped that I would ask the Christian Endeavor Societies everywhere to pray that the traffic might be abolished, and that China might be freed from her galling chains. This I promised to do, and I am glad to take this opportunity partially to redeem my promise.

After this Mrs. Clark and I were presented, by the society in Fa-ti, with two beautiful hand-painted fans, on one of which was printed in Chinese characters Dr. Rankin's beautiful hymn, " God be with you till we meet again," on one side, and, on the other the date, which reads as follows: " WESTERN CALENDAR, ONE THOUSAND EIGHT HUNDRED NINETY-SECOND YEAR, WHICH IS THE

SAME AS BRIGHT ACHIEVEMENT [name of reigning Emperor] EIGHTEENTH YEAR, NINTH MOON, THE LAST DIVISION OF TEN DAYS" (each moon is divided into three divisions of ten days each), all of which might be reduced to "November 17, 1892." Another column on this same fan reads as follows: "BEAUTIFUL NATION [the American] CLARK, TEACHER, CAME TO THE EXTERIOR EAST, FA-TI [Flowery Region] LOCAL SOCIETY [of Christian Endeavor]. ALL THE BELIEVING DISCIPLES REQUESTED FAK YAM [the given name of Mr. Yeung, who led the meeting] TO MAKE A RECORD, IT BEING A JOYFUL MATTER."

The next day, just as we were about to take the boat, the whole school, most of whom belonged to the society at Fa-ti, paid their respects, marching by, and each one making a pleasant bow on passing us.

Mr. Fulton and the other missionaries say that Christian Endeavor is splendidly adapted to the Chinese because they are used to guilds and associations, and the idea of the society seems natural to them. Moreover, they do not feel that they have really become Christians until they have taken part in meeting, so that the prayer-meeting pledge is not irksome. These societies in Canton are doing capital work. Every portion of this meeting of which I have written was planned and carried out by the native boys—decorations, scrolls, and all.

A GLIMPSE IN SHANGHAI.

In Shanghai are centered stations of the Presbyterians, Southern Methodists, American Episcopalians, English Episcopalians, London Missionary Society, and the China Inland Mission. There are probably few places on missionary soil on the face of the earth where more missionaries are congregated; and in respect to quality it was a rare audience of intelligent and earnest Christian men and women that greeted me in the Union Church of Shanghai. Many were the kind wishes expressed and predictions uttered that Christian Endeavor would yet have a large place in the Flowery Kingdom.

At once a self-constituted committee of missionaries volunteered to translate and print sufficient literature of the movement for present needs, and Shanghai will doubtless become one of the centres of Christian Endeavor effort for all the East.

The Illustrated Christian News, a monthly Chinese paper that has a large circulation among the native Christians, will devote much space to the society, and its editor, Rev. Dr. Farnham, told me that he proposes to make it "the *Golden Rule* of China."

Let us glance for a moment at the Christian Endeavor Society connected with the American Presbyterian Mission Press. Connected with this large establishment, famous throughout all China, are many Christian Chinese, who work as compositors and pressmen, as well as foremen of the several departments of the establishment.

These, under the leadership of Dr. and Mrs. Fitch, whose son and daughter are well known to Christian Endeavorers in Wooster, O., have formed themselves into a vigorous and efficient Christian Endeavor Society. They hold their meetings every Thursday night, and it was my pleasure to attend one of these meetings, to see the earnest faces of these printer Endeavorers, and to hear of the good work that they are trying to do for the Master.

This is the only society in the world, of which I know, that is connected with a printing office; but I certainly know some printing establishments that

A CHINESE JUNIOR SOCIETY.
Picture from a photograph of the Chinese Junior Society of Christian Endeavor in the South Gate Presbyterian Mission of Shanghai, showing Dr. and Mrs. Clark and their son Eugene.

would be all the better for a little more Christian Endeavor. When shall we hear of the first printers' Christian Endeavor Society in America? There would be no "printers' devils" among the members, but a happy transformation into printers' angels.

Now for a glimpse at the Junior Society at the South Gate.

Imagine yourselves in an old Buddhist temple converted into a Christian church. The blackened, carved rafters overhead, which used to echo with the sound of the Buddhist tom-toms and the incantations to heathen deities, resound now with children's voices singing Christian songs. "Work, for the night is coming," "Bringing in the sheaves," and "God be with you till we meet again," sound as familiar as in a Christian Endeavor convention at home, for the rhythm and the melody, the spirit and the meaning are all the same; only the words differ. In the audience are gathered the girls from the Girls' School, the boys from the Boys' School, some of the older Christians, and, most interesting to us, the Junior Christian Endeavor Society of the South Gate.

This society is made up of the boys and a very few of the girls connected with the day-schools, of which Miss Mary L. Posey, of the Presbyterian mission, has charge. None of these boys and girls have Christian parents; none of them have the slightest help in their religious life at home; none of them are as yet members of the church; but many of them are stalwart and earnest, and faithful to their duties as little Christian Endeavorers.

In the picture you will see their sober little faces; at the right hand of the group, in the background, you will see the devoted teacher, Miss Posey. Squatting on the ground in front are some of the very little ones, while their older brothers and sisters are standing behind them. These boys and girls have all taken the pledge, and faithfully live up to it. They pray and speak in the meetings, and do any service that the missionaries or their pastors wish them to perform.

Do you see that little fellow with the serious face, on whose shoulder Mrs. Clark is resting her hand? They call him "the little soldier," and they say that he is almost as good as a whole lookout committee in keeping a watchful eye upon the other members, helping them to remember their pledge, while he never neglects his own duties.

He and the other boys often go out with the lady missionaries and Bible-women, acting as guides to the native homes, helping in the singing and in any way that they can. In this work "the little soldier" is especially active, and will often suggest hymns, and offer prayer, and do his little utmost to make the meeting successful. May we not hope that as he grows older he will become one of the apostles, not only of Christian Endeavor, but of Christian faith and zeal in this great but sluggish empire?

If you will look closely at this picture, you will see the Junior badges that the members wear. They can hardly afford silver badges; and even the German silver Junior pins would be beyond their means, I fear; but a very pretty substitute has been chosen in the shape of a feathery red and white pompon, to which is attached a tiny little bell. These badges cost the enormous sum of five cash each, or about one-third of a cent in our money. I am not sure but some of our Juniors would think the Chinese five-cash badges were quite equal to the thousand-cash American gold badges that some of them wear.

On the way to the South Gate the most pathetic of sights are the so-called "baby-towers," into which are thrust unceremoniously the bodies of small children that die before they are a year old, and who are thus buried, "unwept, unhonored, and unsung." These children are not supposed to have souls until they get their teeth. So the little ones are thrust into these hideous octagonal towers, piles upon piles of them. When the towers are full, the bones are shoveled out, and again the tower is filled up with other bodies of babies.

What a contrast is presented by the baby-towers of Shanghai and the first Junior Christian Endeavor Society of this great heathen metropolis! May Christian Endeavor do something to abolish the awful disregard for infant life typified by the baby-tower. May it show to myriads of this nation the value of the soul of the little one, and inspire it with such love for little ones as He had who said, "Suffer the little children to come unto me, and forbid them not."

A GLIMPSE IN JAPAN.

If I were asked what I have learned concerning the religious life of Japan and the relation of the Japanese to the Society of Christian Endeavor, I would say I have learned that this quick, intelligent, high-spirited people cannot be led along any beaten track. They themselves must be the leaders in every movement, religious or otherwise, that has any hope of success. The missionaries themselves cheerfully recognize this, and are willing to decrease that Japanese Christians may increase.

Japan is like no other missionary country on the face of the globe. It is as different from many of them as a white-painted New England village is from a collection of Mexican adobe huts. The Japanese must be approached in the right way, must be their own leaders in religious enterprises, and must map out their own future.

FAC SIMILE OF TITLE-PAGE OF JAPANESE ENDEAVOR PAPER.

But the questions that most interest us just now are, What is their attitude toward Christian Endeavor? Do they want it? Will they adopt it as other Protestant Christians seem to be adopting it? Only time can fully answer this question, and we must leave it for time to prove.

I have had the pleasure of an acquaintance with many of the leading Japanese pastors, professors, and evangelists; among them, President Kozaki, of the Doshisha; Rev Messrs. Yokoi, Harada, and Honda, and Professor Ishimoto, of Tokyo; Rev. Messrs. Miagowa and Miyake, of Osaka; Rev. A. T. Fuwa, of Kyoto; and Rev. Messrs. Homma and Osada, of Kobe, and many others; and I have been assured, over and over again, by many such men, that there are many features about the Society of Christian Endeavor that admirably fit it for growth in Japanese soil. Some of these features are:

1. Its insistence on the supreme religious idea and the highest Christian motives commends it to the Japanese churches. Many of my Japanese brethren have told me that they have had enough of mutual improvement societies, debating clubs, and literary guilds, and that they want a CHRISTIAN Endeavor Society.

2. Its plans for service rejoice their hearts. The fact that the society strives to reduce noble theories to nobler practice; to give to every man his work; to solve the problem of the unemployed, which is pressing on the Church as well as on the State; in short, the fact that it is a Christian ENDEAVOR Society makes them like it.

3. Because it centres itself in the church, they like it. The Japanese churches, like others that I might mention, have had enough of organizations that dissipate and fritter away the energies of the young disciples, without concentrating and focalizing them for the building up of any particular church. They like Christian Endeavor because its motto is, "For Christ and THE CHURCH."

4. Because it is a self-governed, independent organization, they are interested in it. Because it acknowledges no authority outside of its own church and denomination; because it is ruled by no foreign pope, or bishop, or central board of authority; in other words, because it is under *Christ* and for *Christ* as well as the Church, they like it.

5. Once more, many have expressed an interest in the movement because it promotes Christian *fellowship*. If there is any place where sectarian rancor is out of place, it is on the mission field. If there is any place where a fraternal, and not a divisive society is needed, it is on foreign missionary ground. All the churches of the different Presbyterian boards—Cumberland, Northern, and Southern Presbyterian, and Dutch Reformed—have united in Japan. Any movement like Christian Endeavor, that brings together disciples of all creeds, without sacrificing any fundamental principle, is welcomed by intelligent, large-minded Japanese Christians.

If you will take an outline map of Japan, starting at Sendai, a city that you will find near the southeastern end of the large island of Hondo, you will find one Christian Endeavor Society there; then, following westward, at the capital city of Tokyo you will find at least two, and I think three, more. At Yokohama, eighteen miles further west, you could find three good societies if you should look them up.

Going still further westward, at Nagoya, the earthquake city, you will find a Young People's and a Junior society in the Methodist Protestant Church. When we get to Kyoto, the sacred city of temples, two societies, at least, will be found, besides a strong branch of the missionaries' children's society ; while at Osaka, forty miles or so to the westward, there are several more societies, one in the Presbyterian Japanese Church, and one, I think, in the girls' school. Kobe is only an hour's ride from Osaka by rail, and here are three more societies. Okayama, further westward, in its girls' school has the oldest society in the empire. Then look to the northern coast of Hondo, and you will see Tottori, where, under the care of Mr. and Mrs. Rowland, are found a good Young People's and Junior society. Then, following the map westward, you will find in the narrow strait between the islands of Hondo and Kiushiu, the town of Chofu, where Miss Blunt has her work, who told me that there would soon be two societies there, one for the young men and one for the young women. Further west still, on the island of Kiushiu, is the beautiful seaport of Nagasaki, where, Pastor Segawa assured me, Christian Endeavor would soon find a home in his church, connected with the Reformed (Dutch) mission. In the southern part of the same island you will find another society, in Miyazaki, a station of the American Board. Thus, from one end to the other, though not very thickly, to be sure, Japan is dotted with Christian Endeavor. There are many more Endeavor societies now, but the leading centres of the work can be judged from this outline. On all these dotted points in the great empire of Japan are our Christian Endeavor brothers and sisters. May our kinship with them lead us to open our hearts more widely, and to give more freely to all God's children, our brothers and sisters in Japan and all the world over!

TWO ENDEAVOR GLIMPSES IN INDIA.

We catch this glimpse in the compound of the Woman's Union Mission Orphanage and School, a splendid institution managed by some of the most enterprising and devoted of our American missionaries. Imagine a beautiful green lawn surrounded by cocoanut, guava, and tamarind trees, and beautiful flowering shrubs of every variety. The audience consists of bright-faced girls from the school (many of them Christian Endeavorers), native workers, catechists, preachers, Bible-women, and a few missionaries.

An address is made ; the pastor of the native Baptist church translates it into vigorous Bengalee ; a sweet Bengalee hymn is sung by the Christian Endeavor girls, and then tea and cakes and native candies are passed around for the refreshment of the inner man and woman.

All this time a juggler has been hovering on the outskirts of the assembly.

When the tea and sweets had been disposed of, the juggler draws near, and entertains us with all kinds of sleight-of-hand performances. How much many a social committee at home would give for an Indian juggler to put finishing touches on their bi-monthly sociables!

Another glimpse in India; in the American Mission of Biculla, Bombay. Here are gathered the representatives of the four branch societies that constitute the large Endeavor Society. Here were their teachers and pastors and several other missionaries. The singing by the boys and girls is most excellent;

SOME TAMIL CHRISTIAN ENDEAVORERS.

the address by the head-master, a native Christian who speaks fluent English, is very good; and then, after a speech by one of the pilgrims, comes the garlanding.

Do you remember that at the New York convention, after the Williston gavel of black walnut and granite had been given me, Mr. Karmarkar, who was once the President of this society, said, "When you go to India, Mr. Clark, they will not give you a stone and a piece of wood, but they will put beautiful garlands around your neck!"

Here comes a bright-faced boy with a great tray loaded with heavy garlands of yellow chrysanthemums, and every guest and teacher is thus bedecked; then our garlands are sprinkled with rose-water, a piece of betel-nut, wrapped in a green betel-leaf covered with gold-foil, is given us, and then, greatly to our surprise, a beautiful scarf-pin with a Christian Endeavor monogram was handed me by one of the Endeavorers, and a lovely little souvenir was given to Mrs. Clark by one of the girls.

The flowers will fade; the rose-water will evaporate; the betel-leaf will

RECEPTION TO PRESIDENT CLARK BY THE CHRISTIAN ENDEAVOR SOCIETY, MADANAPALLE, ARCOT, INDIA.
The Americans in this group are Mrs. Jacob Chamberlain, Rev. Lewis B. Chamberlain, Mrs. F. E. Clark, Rev. Dr. F. E. Clark, Master Clark, Mrs. W. I. Chamberlain, and Rev. W. I. Chamberlain.

wither; but one thing will not fade—the memory of this pleasant farewell reception, and of these earnest, faithful Endeavorers.

A GLIMPSE IN SYRIA.

I wish I could show you " Y. P. S. C. E." as it looks in Arabic.

What do those queer hieroglyphics mean? Nothing else, dear reader, than that with which you are so familiar. They stand for a society that I have found during the last eight months in the Hawaiian Islands and Samoa, in New Zealand and Australia, in China and Japan, in Ceylon and India; and here it is in Syria, for these sprawling characters show you how the name "Christian Endeavor" looks in Arabic.

There are only two organizations of the Nedwat el Ijtehad Messeahy in Syria, so far as I know; one in Tripoli, and one in Suq el Ghurb;—there is another jaw-cracker for you. I will leave it for you to pronounce. It is all I ought to be expected to do to spell it for you.

I hope that there may be many more of these organizations in Syria one of these days. However, if there are not many as yet, there is a splendid field here in which the Nedwat el Ijtehad Messeahy of America can work; and a few of the societies have invested in this most promising field. Let me tell you of a school that is supported by the Presbyterian Society of Rome, N. Y.

As we approach the door of the school Miss Saada Haddad, the teacher, greets us with a smiling face; for are not we a part of the organization in America that supports her and keeps her school running? Has not one of the societies of the Empire State not only sent the money, through its own denominational missionary board, to support the school, but has it not sent her a copy of *The Golden Rule* and the premium picture of the trustees of the United Society? To be sure it has. So she already knows how we look, and with a warm welcome we are ushered into her little school-room. It is neat and clean, and some fresh sprays of green over the doors and windows give it a holiday air.

In the room are about forty little girls from six to sixteen years of age. They are attired in their best; and very pretty and attractive many of them are in their red and blue dresses, their white clocked stockings, and their wooden clogs, very much, after all, like many little American girls that I have seen.

They sing their Arabic songs, and repeat the fifty-third chapter of Isaiah in English, and some other Scripture passages in Arabic, and go through with their pretty motion songs. Then two rows of them stand up facing each other, and one girl repeats a Bible prayer, and the girl opposite to her responds with a promise that contains an answer to the prayer. Then another prayer and another answering promise, until all have recited.

But we have not long to stay in this school, there are so many other places of interest in Beirut to visit; and after taking a glass of lemonade, flavored with orange-blossoms, we make our salaams to the girls and to faithful Saada Haddad, their teacher, and take our departure.

This school, this teacher, these forty girls, all this instruction, all these good influences, all the streams of blessing that flow out from this school, are dependent, for the time, on a little effort, a little self-denial, a little unselfish forethought, on the part of one Christian Endeavor Society in Rome, N. Y.

Multiply this school by twenty-five thousand, and you will know what the Christian Endeavor movement throughout the world might accomplish. Some could do more; some must do less; but I am confident that, *on the average*, all our societies might do as much as this, in addition to what they would naturally give in other directions.

Think of the possibilities! Twenty-five thousand glowing spots of gospel light and fire in this dark world, kindled by the societies of Christian Endeavor! Twenty-five thousand multiplied by forty are how many? Let us do that sum in mental arithmetic, and we shall find how many children in mission lands may be blessed by our efforts.

In all the mission lands that I have visited I have found all kinds of special work to be done, costing from ten dollars to ten hundred dollars. There is an infinite variety of opportunities from which to choose. The work fits the pocket-book of every society.

There are boys to be educated in schools, little school-houses and churches to be built, teachers to be supported, colporteurs and Bible-women to be adopted, mission stations to be manned and strengthened, missionaries to be paid—something for every one and every society.

A GLIMPSE IN TURKEY.

How many glimpses of Christian Endeavor in Turkey I could show, did my

"THE SMALLEST Y. P. S. C. E. IN THE WORLD," BROUSSA, TURKEY.

space allow; of the self-denying efforts of missionaries under the most trying circumstances; of patient continuance in well-doing in spite of the opposition and persecution of the government; of faithful societies that do not dare to wear the Christian Endeavor badge lest it be interpreted as the emblem of some secret political society, and subject them to imprisonment!

I would like to take my readers into the Endeavor societies of St. Paul's Institute, of Tarsus, the town of which its greatest resident once declared, that it was "no mean city."

I would like to show them the flourishing societies in Talas and in old Cæsarea, in Yozgat, in Adabazar, in Constantinople, and in other places.

I think I must introduce them, however, to the society which has the unique distinction of being the smallest in the world. It is situated in Broussa, Turkey, an ancient and famous city of the Moslems, where many of the Sultans are buried in magnificent tombs. The society consists of two members, Douglas Crawford, a missionary's son, and Louca, an Armenian boy, who faithfully have held their meetings week after week together, and observed their pledge in the letter and in the spirit as well. They have prayed and read the Bible together, and sung and taken up the collection, and done everything which a well-regulated society should do.

Once they had another boy in their society (three of them in all), but he was unfaithful to his pledge, and they rigorously, but lovingly, observed the rules about the exclusion of unfaithful members, though it reduced their society one-third at one blow.

Douglas Crawford is now in Robert College, Constantinople, but whenever he returns to his home, in Broussa, the meetings of the society are resumed. I am glad to show you a picture of the smallest Endeavor society in the world, because it is also one of the most faithful ones in the world.

A GLIMPSE IN SPAIN.

San Sebastian is most beautiful for situation.

The green, conical hills tower up on each side, a background of beautiful ramparts, whose feet are ceaselessly laved by the bright, sparkling waves of the "Bay of Biscay, O."

Right in front of us as we lift our eyes to look out of the window is the new summer palace of the queen of Spain, and at its foot the curved sandy beach, where on every summer day plays the little king, with whose face on Spanish postage-stamps you are familiar. King that he is, he can find nothing better with which to play than the clean, white sand of which every ragged little Spaniard can have as much as he.

But you and I are more interested in the mission, and the missionaries and the schoolgirls of the Institute of San Sebastian than in kings and queens, so let me introduce them to you.

As we enter the commodious house that is devoted to the mission, we are greeted by more than one familiar face, and see more than one familiar Endeavor badge. Here is Mrs. Gulick, our kind hostess, whose wise and energetic administration has made the school the far-reaching power that it is. Her Christian Endeavor badge pins a knot of white ribbon to her breast, a combination that I have often seen ; and I am reminded that Mrs. Gulick's sister, Miss Anna Gordon, is especially honored of all White Ribboners.

Near Mrs. Gulick stands Miss Barbour, whose Endeavor badge, if it could speak, would tell us that she is from Connecticut, the home of so many earnest Endeavorers. The early friends of the society will remember Miss Barbour at the second Saratoga convention, soon after which she came to Spain, where she has been working most efficiently ever since.

Then here is Miss Page, formerly of the Smyrna mission, whose friends in Haverhill, Mass., will be glad to know of the splendid work that she is now doing in this new field. Here, too, are other friends of many of my readers, Miss Webb and Miss Bushee, and the Misses Williams, and Miss Cutler, of Auburndale, Mass.

At the close of the roll-call of the Young People's society, the Juniors all stood together, and repeated their verses and sang their song. "A method worth transplanting," this, for an occasional union service of Young People's and Junior societies.

The American Girls' College of San Sebastian enjoys the unique distinction that every member of the school is a member, active or associate, of the Christian Endeavor Society. Can this be said of any other school in the world? Let us thank God for this splendid institution, the first school in Spain in which a Spanish girl could obtain a complete education, such as is open to American girls. Thus is America repaying her debt to her discoverers.

CHAPTER LII.

THE MONTREAL CONVENTION.

The Title of the Chapter—The Montreal Convention—The Preliminary Meetings—The Opening Session—The Wise and Witty Welcomes—The Booming Cannon, and What They stood For—Junior Society Work and Its Importance—The Statistics of the Past Year—Some Eloquent Addresses—The First Signer of the Junior Pledge—An Unhappy Incident—All's Well that Ends Well—Some Memorable Consecration Meetings—A Sudden Death—Generous Endeavorers—The White Caps, and What They Did—The Press Committee—A Delightful Excursion—A Happy End.

I HAVE chosen for the title of the chapters which relate to the great International Conventions the name by which they are familiarly known by Endeavorers everywhere. They are not spoken of as the Tenth Convention or the Twelfth Convention, but by the name of the city which extends its generous hospitality to the delegates. Moreover, to Endeavorers at least, the name is preceded by the definite article *the*. It is *The* New York Convention, The Minneapolis Convention, The Montreal Convention, as though no other convention had ever been held in these fair cities.

As a general description of this memorable meeting I cannot do better than to quote the graphic words with which the compiler of the admirable report prefaced his account of the Twelfth International Convention.

"Those who were present at the Tenth International Christian Endeavor Convention, held in Minneapolis in 1891, were deeply impressed with the eagerness of the Canadian delegates to secure the convention within their borders for 1892, and many sympathized with them in their disappointment when it was announced that the convention would be held in New York—a disappointment partly allayed by the announcement that Montreal had been decided upon for the convention of 1893. Such was the enthusiasm of the Canadian delegates on this occasion that it was confidently predicted that when the convention should meet in Montreal it would receive a rarely cordial welcome. This prediction was amply fulfilled. Long before the month of July arrived circulars of information were being sent repeatedly to all parts of the country, indicating a state of preparedness on the part of the Committee of '93 which augured great things for the coming convention. Every possible arrangement for the comfort and convenience of the delegates was made, and the work of the committee as a whole and of the several sub-committees received unqualified praise.

THE DRILL HALL, MONTREAL, AS THE ENDEAVORERS WERE ASSEMBLING.

"The incoming delegations were met by scouts from the reception committee at some distance from the city, giving ample time for 'billeting' and answering questions. A novel device adopted by the committee this year was the wearing, by every member of the reception committee, of a white yachting cap, thus readily distinguishing the members of the committee even in the midst of a large crowd. There were the usual scenes of interest at the railroad depots and steamboat wharves as the hosts of delegates arrived. The arrangements were so admirable, however, that everything connected with the preliminaries of the convention went smoothly and satisfactorily.

"Reasoning from the attendance at the New York convention, the committee had planned upon taking care of at least 23,000 visitors. Owing to various causes, however, chief among which were the severe financial stringency prevailing throughout the United States, and the failure to secure reduced railroad rates from the South and West on account of the World's Fair, the attendance was considerably less, the registry showing at the close of the convention a total attendance of 16,500. This, however, considering the circumstances, was a remarkably good showing, and stamped the convention as the largest yet held, with the exception of that at New York, which was altogether phenomenal.

"A novel feature of the convention this year was the division of the audience into two great assemblies for most of the sessions, holding simultaneous meetings with programs of equal merit. One place of meeting was the government Drill Hall, or 'Salle d'Exercise,' an immense stone building used as military headquarters, arranged to seat 9,000 people, and providing besides numerous committee rooms. The interior of this building was profusely and elegantly decorated with flags and festoons of bunting, the Union Jack and the Stars and Stripes being everywhere conspicuously interwoven. The platform at one end of the building was still further decorated with Christian Endeavor emblems and a huge pyramid of potted plants and flowers. The whole interior effect was rich and beautiful. The other place of meeting was a large tent on the Champ de Mars, or parade ground, on the other side of the street from the Drill Hall. This was arranged with chairs to seat about 9,000 people; and, while the conditions for speaking and hearing were naturally not so favorable as in the hall, it proved an acceptable audience-room, and its capacity was tested more than once.

"No souvenir program was issued this year, although mementos of Montreal and of the convention were to be had in great number. The United Society, however, furnished every delegate with a handsomely-prepared pamphlet of some sixty pages, containing, besides the program complete, a large number of selected Christian Endeavor hymns, Scripture selections, etc. The Committee of '93 also gave to every delegate an excellent map of the city and a convention badge, the latter consisting of a maple leaf in white metal with 'C E.' raised from an enameled background and backed by a red or blue ribbon."

For the first time in the history of these conventions, a feature which has now become a regular and important one was introduced. This was the preliminary services held on Wednesday evening, the evening before the convention proper began. It was reasoned wisely that the delegates would most of them be

COMMITTEE OF '93 (MONTREAL CONVENTION).

1. Mr. A. A. Ayer, Chairman.
2. Mr. H. A. Barnard, Music.
3. Mr. A. R. Grafton, Hall.
4. Mr. Arthur F. Bell, Reception.
5. Mr. Robert Greig, Treasurer.
6. Rev. S. P. Rose, D. D., Representative of the Local Union.
7. Mr. H. B. Ames, Press.
8. Mr. Geo. R. Lighthall, Hotel and Secretary.

on hand, that they would have an evening at their disposal, and if some churches were opened for these gatherings, with eminent speakers to address the audiences, all would be in good trim for the opening of the convention proper the next morning, and that, moreover, the people of Montreal who might be crowded out of the convention halls would have an opportunity to get some share of the good things of the convention.

This idea was carried out with much success, and addresses of great spiritual power and of an intensely practical character were delivered by Rev. J. W. Chapman, D. D., the eminent evangelist; Rev. Theo. L. Cuyler, D. D., the father in Israel who is beloved by young people everywhere; by Rev. J. Z. Tyler, who endeared himself to Endeavorers especially in the following year as chairman of the glorious Cleveland convention; by Rev. W. H. McMillan, D. D., by Rev. H. C. Farrar, D. D., of the Board of Trustees of the United Society, and others.

Ideal weather was vouchsafed to this convention for the opening day. "The delegates were early astir," we are told by chroniclers of the occasion, "and at half-past six o'clock prayer-meetings were held in five different churches."

The hour for the opening session was fixed at 9.45, but long before that time the delegates began assembling at the hall. Generous applause greeted the several State delegations as they came marching in with their State or local banners. The California delegates were especially welcomed as they made known their intention thus early to capture the convention for '95.

When the hall was about half full some one started the hymn "At the Cross." It was taken up at once with full volume. Director Lindsay and Cornetist Burleigh mounted the platform and joined in, and the old-time convention enthusiasm was immediately apparent. Hymn followed hymn. The famous Park sisters, of New York, with their cornets, joined their forces. It was gloriously inspiring.

Rev. J. McGillivray welcomed the delegates to Canada. "Citizens of every race and creed were eager to have you come," he said. "Our grand old river never ran clearer and swifter; and did you observe how, as you floated on its great bosom and neared our city, he became more eager to welcome you and shot you, as it were, the more rapidly into the arms of our hospitality? Nature lent her kindly hand and decked up our royal city in her queenliest robes. Every July leaf that quivers on Mount Royal whispers welcome to the young summer hearts before me."

This welcome, as witty as it was hearty, was followed by equally kind words from Mayor Desjardin, who declared, amid much applause:

"We believe in industry and progress and commerce, but we do not believe, as you do not, and in that respect we are in accord with you, that the whole goal of life is industry or commerce or merely the physical well-being of humanity.

"When you look at the top of one of our chimneys, you will see a cloud which prevents you from seeing above, but when you look at the spire of a church, that gentle finger pointing toward heaven, you feel, as we do, that we have something more—that we have another destiny which Providence has prepared for us. So amongst Christians there is now a great feeling that the old strifes must be laid aside, and that other occupations must engage our minds. The great battle now is not between creed and creed, but between believers and those who do not believe [*prolonged applause*], between those who go to church and worship their God and those who have made the earth the ultimate end of their ruling ambition. I think this great convention is to show that on this continent, where progress, where science, where activity and pushing enterprise have shown themselves developed to the utmost degree, we can find men and women by thousands and by hundreds of thousands, believing that they must not rest the whole of their ambition on things worldly, but that they must look above and beyond.

"You know that, for the time being, I have the honor to be the first magistrate of Montreal. As such, when I heard that a great army was going to invade Montreal, I felt a little uneasy [*laughter*]—an invasion by so many thousands. I was trying to remember some historical facts which would give me an instance of that kind. Would it be an invasion of the Romans, or a meeting of the Romans and the Sabines, or would it be something else? But when I saw the army and the gentle way in which it was managed, composed of so many young ladies and so large a number of gentlemen, I felt greatly reassured on that point, although I am not so sure now about that annexation question which was brought up here. [*Laughter and applause.*] You see, we have always been endeavoring to fight against political annexation; but there is another kind of annexation, and speaking for myself, I have felt that we have always been very weak in that line. That annexation in detail has been going on between the two countries pretty freely, to the great advantage of those who were led in that way and to the benefit of the two countries, which have gained by that social intercourse those friendly feelings which will stand always above any political question, and which will, I am sure, for a long time prevent any serious difficulty between us, and will make of these two peoples, not two distant or foreign peoples, but two populations whose traditions, whose aspirations, and whose Christian feelings are the same."

This address was memorable because it was delivered by a Catholic to an intensely Protestant audience. He did not speak as a religious sectarian, but in his capacity as the Mayor of Montreal; and yet he uttered Christian sentiments which every one could indorse, and which, if they had been shared by all the people of Montreal, the only unpleasant incident of this memorable convention would have been avoided.

The Mayor was received with great applause, and his address brought forth the abundant handkerchiefs in the Chautauqua salute. Then followed a striking incident as the report records. Director Lindsay started the English national anthem, "God Save the Queen," the audience joining in with enthusiasm. At the third verse he drew forth an English flag and beat time with it, the audience waving their handkerchiefs in response. Then he immediately started the hymn

"America" (the same tune)—"My country, 'tis of thee"—which was sung with magnificent effect. Again at the third verse he drew forth an American flag, and again the audience responded enthusiastically with their handkerchiefs, giving three rousing cheers as they resumed their seats.

A very happy address of welcome was also given by Mr. A. A. Ayre, a prominent business man of Montreal. His address was particularly appropriate in view of the fact that that was the wedding day of Prince George and Princess May. He recalled the wedding of Prince George's mother, when, on March 7, 1863, as the Danish princess, with ceremony of state, sailed up the Thames to meet the one she was to wed, Albert, the future king of England, children on the banks of the river sang an ode prepared by Tennyson:

> "For Saxon, or Dane, or Norman we,
> Teuton, or Celt, or whatever we be,
> We are each all Dane in our welcome of thee,
> Alexandra!"

So, to-day,

> Presbyterian, Baptist, or Methodist we,
> Congregationalist, Anglican, whatever we be,
> We are each all Christian in our welcome to thee,
> Convention of '93.

Who could respond better to these most hearty addresses than the wise and witty preacher of Chicago, the pastor of the First Baptist Church of that city, the Rev. P. S. Henson, D. D.? Here are his closing sentences, which were received with loud and enthusiastic applause:

"Brethren, we are beginning to utilize the forces of nature as never before. We are tapping the rock-bound earth, and the gas is spouting and the fiery flambeaux flame out upon the midnight air. We are tapping the earth and getting out the oil, and there are great gushing wells. And there is the subtile electric fluid that swings its splendors over our cities and drives our cars apace. We are getting at the latent resources of the earth. Do you know what we are doing at Niagara? We Americans and Canadians have a common interest there. Many a man, standing and looking into that awful abyss at Niagara, has had the feeling of that old countryman who said, 'What an awful waste of water-power!' But it is not being wasted so much as it was. They have constructed channels and turbine wheels, and now, by transmitted power, cities far away are to be illuminated. So, as we have looked abroad on Christendom, we have thought of the waste of power. 'Awake, O Zion! put on thy strength, O Jerusalem,' thy latent strength, thy unused strength, O Niagara of spiritual power! And I seem, in this Christian Endeavor convention, to hear the thunder of the Lord's Niagara that is being harnessed up to do service, and cities afar are to blaze with the electric light of the Gospel, and whole continents to be kindled with a new glory. God speed the day! I believe we are nearing it. I believe the time is coming, like unto that epoch in Switzerland's history when the invaders crept through the mountain defiles and no gallant Switzer appeared anywhere in sight, until at last there was a cry which rang out in the clear blue air as if it came from heaven, 'In the name of the Father, the Son, and the Holy Ghost, let go, let go!' The Switzers, up there among the everlasting crags, held mighty masses of stone in leash, and at the command of their leader they let go, and down the avalanche came with a roar of thunder, and buried the enemy. It seems to me I can hear already the thunder of the Lord's guns advancing to the last attack, the last charge, and I fancy that these Christian Endeavorers are come together for that great fight. May the Christian Endeavor banner wave in triumph on every hilltop, on every mountain, and in every valley, until all the world shall shout, 'Hallelujah! Hallelujah! The Lord God omnipotent reigneth!'"

During the closing portion of Dr. Henson's address, the booming of cannon on the parade ground was heard, making the speaker's reference to the thundering of the Lord's guns very effective.

The President of the United Society, at the close of the address, told the audience, so many of whom were from the United States, and did not know the meaning of the guns, that they celebrated the marriage of the heir to England's throne, and, as an appropriate proceeding, he called on Bishop Arnett to offer prayer invoking God's blessing on the future king and queen of England. Bishop Arnett is the Senior Bishop of the African M. E. of the United States, and the audience deemed it particularly appropriate that a colored bishop from the States on Canadian soil should offer a fervent prayer invoking God's blessing upon the future king and queen of England.

At this convention one whole afternoon was devoted to the Junior Society and its work, an afternoon over which Mrs. Alice May Scudder happily presided, and during which Rev. J. W. Cowan, in whose church was started the first society, told of its origin. Miss Kate H. Haus called the roll of Junior superintendents, Dr. Wayland Hoyt talked of the "Possibilities of the Junior Society," and Rev. H. N. Kinney conducted a Free Parliament on Junior methods of work, and Mrs. F. E. Clark spoke of Junior Christian Endeavor in foreign lands.

On this same day, too, Rev. Rufus W. Miller, of the Brotherhood of Andrew and Philip, gave an address on special work for young men, and Mr. J. Howard Breed conducted an open meeting on the same subject. Not a little attention was given to evangelistic methods of church work, which were treated by Rev. F. D. Power, of Washington, and Mr. P. S. Foster, of the same city.

As was very natural the President's address this year dealt with world-wide Christian Endeavor, as he had only returned a few days previously from his journey around the world, and he was able to bring greetings from Australian Endeavorers and Chinese Endeavorers, India's Endeavorers of many tongues, and black-eyed Spanish Endeavorers as well. French, English, Irish, and Dutch Endeavorers, all spoke through him. The Secretary's report was as encouraging as ever in the past, and told that there were 26,284 local societies in all the world, with a membership of 1,577,040. New York was still in the lead with almost 3,000 societies. Pennsylvania came second with 2,628, and Illinois third with 1,802, while Ohio only lacked 56 of Illinois's number.

He told us also that there were 600 societies in England, 525 in Australia, 71 in India, 41 in Turkey, 32 in Madagascar, and so on through the list. The model constitution had by this time been translated and printed in the following languages: English, German, Swedish, Norwegian, French, Danish, Dutch, Spanish, Chinese, Japanese, Tamil, Telegu, Hindi, Hindoostani, Bengali, Marathi, Arabic, Turkish, Bulgarian, Armenian, and Greek.

ANTHONY COMSTOCK.

Thirty evangelical denominations were represented in our fellowship. The Presbyterians still were in the lead with over 5,400 societies. The Congregationalists came next, then the Baptists, and fourth, the Disciples of Christ. One of the most cheering pieces of news was that during the past year it was believed that 158,000 of our associate members had given their hearts to Christ and had joined the evangelical churches.

How can I condense within the limits of any chapter of reasonable length the good things of this stimulating convention! Every hour was crowded with something fresh and vigorous. Every address was received with enthusiastic demonstrations of delight, and moreover it is scarcely too much to say that every address left an impression upon the hearts of a multitude of the thronging attendance.

I ought, however, at least to mention the titles of three or four significant addresses. One of these was by Rev. J. Q. A. Henry, pastor of the First Baptist Church, of San Francisco, on "The Bible in Our Work." Another was by Rev. Nehemiah Boynton on "Our Relation to the Sunday-school." A third was by Rev. David J. Burrell, D. D., on "Christian Citizenship." A fourth by Rev. S. L. Mershon on "Missionary Literature," and a fifth by Rev. W. H. G. Temple on "Missionary Money and How to Raise It."

But if I mention these addresses I certainly ought also to speak of that by Rev. George H. Wells, on "International Fellowship," and the powerful speech by Rev. J. W. Lee, D. D., on "The Raw Material of a Great Life," and also of the address of Rev. A. E. Dunning, D. D., on "The Religious Press and Its Part in Our Work."

Two more of the most memorable addresses were given by Rev. George Douglass, D. D., the blind Demosthenes of Montreal, and by Mr. Anthony Comstock, the man who so often has taken his life in his hand in his fight against the enemies of our youth. Social Purity was the theme of these two addresses, the former of which has been printed in leaflet form and circulated most widely. The theme of Gospel Temperance has never been left out of these conventions, and Mr. Thomas E. Murphy and Miss Belle Kearney did full justice to the subject.

One picturesque feature of the missionary meeting was by Rev. Gilbert Reid, a missionary of the Presbyterian Church to China, dressed as he was in full Chinese costume, and representing a mandarin of the upper classes.

Not only was there a session devoted to Junior societies, but there was a Junior rally of great interest, in which the children of Montreal were brought together in large numbers. At this rally the response to the address of welcome was given to Mr. Raymond C. Brooks, the first signer of the Junior pledge, then a theological student fitting himself for the ministry. This rally was happily presided over by Rev. John L. Sewall, and was a joyous occasion in every respect.

Only one event occurred to mar this magnificent convention, and of this event Rev. Sumantrao Vishnu Karmarkar was the innocent cause. In the course of his brief address, entitled "A Voice from India," which was published in the Montreal newspapers from advanced sheets, occurred this paragraph: "There is a remarkable correspondence between the Romish worship and Hindoo worship. Romanism is but a new label on the old bottles of paganism containing the deadly poison of idolatry. Often the Hindoo asks us, when seeing the Romish worship, 'What is the difference between Christianity and Hindooism?' In India we have not only to contend with the hydra-headed monster of idolatry, but also with the octopus of Romanism."

When it came to the actual address Mr. Karmarkar, warned of the strained and excited condition of feeling between the Catholics and Protestants of Montreal, left out this paragraph from his address. But it was too late to prevent disturbance. It had been published in the papers, and had been savagely commented upon by the French dailies of Montreal, which are under intense Jesuit influence.

Soon the mutterings of mob-wrath began to be heard. It was announced in private circles, and then news spread from mouth to mouth that a riot was to be anticipated; that the French Catholics were intending to assemble in force and attack the Christian Endeavorers; that the ropes of the great tent might be cut, and that thousands might be involved in the *mêlée*. The mutterings grew fiercer and hotter. Large bands of "plug-uglies" from the slums of Montreal were seen hovering around the drill hall and tent.

On Friday night of convention week some of the ropes of the tents were actually cut, but it was in the middle of the night, when the tent was unoccupied. On Saturday afternoon a fierce storm arose. The lightning flashed and the thunder rolled, and the rain poured down in torrents. Never, it seems, were the windows of heaven opened so wide or the cataracts of the skies so poured upon the earth.

By many this storm was deemed a most providential event, for the water stood several inches deep on the floor of the tent, and it was impossible to use it for the service on Saturday evening. The crowds that could not get into the drill hall were forced to go to the St. James Methodist Church. The howling mob knew that it could make no headway against the drill hall, and there was nothing in the dark and empty tent to attack. Moreover, they feared the vigilance of the police, who throughout the excitement acquitted themselves most admirably and afforded ample protection to the delegates. They were ready, with hose stretched about the drill hall, to play upon the excited religious fanatics and thus dampen, if they could not put out, the fires of bigotry and hatred.

The next day, Sunday, was a bright and beautiful day. The afternoon session in the tent was somewhat disturbed by the hootings and catcalls of the mob, but no serious damage was done. In the evening the chief of police decided that it was not safe to hold a meeting in the tent, and so the meeting scheduled for that place was held in the St. James Methodist Church, where an eloquent sermon was preached by Rev. B. Fay Mills; in the First Baptist Church, Erskine Presbyterian, American Presbyterian, and the Douglass Presbyterian.

In the drill hall a strong and able sermon by Rev. C. H. Lewis, D. D., President of Western Maryland College, an institution of the Methodist Protestant Church, was preached, and this was followed by a most impressive consecration service, which will be remembered by the tens of thousands of Endeavorers who participated in it to their dying day.

There was some fear that, as the delegates went out from the drill hall, they would be attacked by the mob, but the chief of police sent word that a large force of police was at the hall and that all would be amply protected. Moreover, a large company of several hundred Orangemen, many of them students in McGill University, with white handkerchiefs about their necks, formed in line about the hall as the delegates came out, and escorted them through the streets to their several hotels and boarding-houses.

Then the "white-necktie brigade," as they were called, marched to the Windsor Hotel, greeted the delegates quartered there, and were thanked for their kindness by the President of the United Society.

Another sad event of this convention was the sudden death of Mr. Rogers, one of the committee to receive the delegates, who fell dead of heart disease as he was conducting one of the delegates to his home. The generous sympathies of the convention were aroused, and the family of the young man received nearly $2,000 from the open purses of the generous Endeavorers.

The convention proper closed with the consecration meetings of Sunday night, but the influence of the convention and the happy memories of it still abide. The white caps were an original feature of this convention, and they were worn by the Committee of Welcome, some of whom went a hundred miles from Montreal or more to greet the incoming delegates.

Everywhere the white caps were found when they were wanted, ready to answer questions, or to show the delegates to their homes. So successfully was this idea carried out that I venture to say it will be copied by every succeeding convention.

The delegates were enthusiastic in their praise of the Committee of Arrangements. The Press Committee, Mr. H. B. Ames, Chairman, received an especial meed of honor. Never before were such complete and abundant facilities furnished for the press representatives, and never before were the daily papers, especially *The Montreal Star* and *The Montreal Witness*, so completely given up to convention news as on this occasion.

There were several private excursions after the convention to Quebec, the Lachine Rapids, Mount Royal, etc. But by far the most delightful event of this sort occurred on Monday morning, after the convention, when the Mayor and Aldermen of the city invited the officers of the United Society and other guests to a drive to the top of Mount Royal.

They assembled to the number of about one hundred in the City Hall, where they were welcomed by Mayor Desjardin in a very felicitous speech. Then they took carriages, a long procession to the top of Mount Royal, where tables were spread, and a fine lunch served in an open pavilion which looked down upon the magnificent view of city and river and forest below. The Mayor and Aldermen were assiduous in waiting upon their guests, and, to the expression of thanks by the President of the United Society, the Mayor responded in a gracious speech, first in English and then in French, which was received with three rousing cheers from the delegates. The company then joined in singing "God Save the Queen," followed by "America," and then, all clasping hands, this delightful attendant to the convention closed with the indispensable hymn, "God Be With You Till We Meet Again."

CHAPTER LIII.

THE GOOD CITIZENSHIP MOVEMENT.

How It Began—How National Conventions Sound the Keynote—The Keynote of the Montreal Convention—What Endeavorers May Do—Not Boycotters—Law-Abiding Citizens—"Go Tell That Tiger"—A Fluttering Bit of Paper—An Endeavorer on Duty—At the Dram-Shop—On Guard Respecting the Sabbath—"God is Marching On"—How the Fire Kindled—Dr. Parkhurst's Probe—Robert Ross, of Troy—Good Citizenship Clubs.

THE convention at Montreal was memorable not only for its immediate impressions, but because of forces then set at work which resulted in large attention given to matters of good citizenship and missionary extension. In fact, all the national conventions mark some advanced step. Some keynote is heard resounding from these meetings to the very ends of the earth. Some cry is taken up by the young people and echoed over hill and valley from the Atlantic to the Pacific and often across the sea.

The keynote of this convention, which was re-echoed in a thousand conventions in the year that was to come, was "Good Citizenship," "A Purer Political Atmosphere," "Our Country for the Lord Jesus Christ." It is not immodest, perhaps, to say that this keynote was struck first in the President's address on the first evening of the convention. It matters but very little, however, who speaks the word. If it is a word that needs to be spoken, it will be taken up and carried on by a million of Christian Endeavor voices. Here are the brief paragraphs in the President's address which refer to this subject. I will leave in the punctuations of applause, for they tell of the way in which the idea first struck the assembled thousands:

"One of these advance steps that we may take is the cultivation of a larger and more intelligent spirit of patriotism and of good citizenship. [*Applause.*]

"How shall this be done? By all joining, as a society, some one political party? Not unless we know of some party that embraces all the saints and none of the rascals [*laughter*]; one that is always right and never wrong. But whether you are a Democrat or a Republican, a Third-party man or a Populist, a Liberal or a Conservative, a Blue or a Grit, it can be done by bringing your vote and your influence—for your influence, fair Endeavorers, is often as powerful as your brother's vote—to the supreme test of the Christian Endeavor pledge. [*Applause.*]

"You have promised in that 'to do whatever He would like to have you do.' Then *vote* as He would like to have you vote. [*Loud applause.*] Then you will not knowingly vote for a bad man or a bad measure; and, if need be, you will sacrifice your party rather than your principles.

"When politicians realize that men with principles are watching their nominations they will not dare to put up a bad man for your suffrage [*applause*], for they will realize what so many of the secular papers expressed last summer after that wonderful Convention in New York City, that there is a new moral force in this country that must be reckoned with. Go to the primaries of your party, and take your Christian Endeavor pledge with you. Go to the caucus; get into the Legislature; stand for Congress or for Parliament; but, when you get there, for God and your Church and your country, do what *He* would like to have you do. [*Loud applause.*]

"So, in humbler ways, let your influence be felt for every right cause. I am glad, for one, of the stand that Endeavorers have taken for the Christian and the American Sabbath. I believe that the course of the society on this question has set an example that we may wisely follow in the future.

"We have proved, for one thing, that we are not boycotters, whatever ill-natured people may say. There is a suspicion of lawlessness in that word borrowed from the bogs of old Ireland. It is not our word, nor does it express our attitude. We protested and petitioned; we did everything that we could, as individuals and societies, to save the nation from the threatened disgrace; and now we, each one for himself, without judging others, will decide what *He* would have us do in regard to going to the Exposition, or staying away from it.

"Let it be understood that there is no power or wish in the Endeavor Society to compel uniformity, or to force the conscience of its members in regard to the World's Fair or any other subject.

"This convention can pass no votes or resolutions that are binding upon individuals or societies—nor can any State or local union—but it can and should lead us in this and every such matter more fully to recognize our individual responsibility as citizens as well as Christian men and women. Some phase of this very important subject of good citizenship, viewed from the Christian standpoint, may well occupy our attention at more than one of our society prayer-meetings, and at more than one local-union gathering of the year to come. How may we become better citizens? How may we be truer patriots? Let us give to these questions a worthy answer.

This thought was emphasized and enlarged by Rev. David J. Burrell, D. D., in his address on "Christian Citizenship." So much of this address entered into the lives of the Endeavorers throughout the coming year that it must be reproduced in part in this connection:

"I know that men who are without would be glad if we would have nothing to do with civil life. They are all the while saying to us, 'Content you with monopolizing heaven, and let this little rolling ball alone.' But your function as followers of the Lord Jesus Christ is particularly to have to do with the affairs of this little rolling ball, which is the vestibule of the everlasting life. Our Lord and Saviour Himself, when He stood between the pillars of the Temple porch, preached science and philosophy, physics and metaphysics, politics and theology, the science of this life and the science of the life to come. 'Go tell that fox,' said He—and if He had been in the city of New York to-day, He would have said, 'Go tell that tiger.' Our Lord did not hesitate to touch with a mighty hand any point of human life that needed it. He called for a penny, and said, 'Whose image and superscription is this?' and they said, 'It is Cæsar's.' His word was then, 'Render unto Cæsar the things which are Cæsar's.' And that injunction is as imperative as its complement, 'Render also unto God the things which are God's.' I say to you, young men, and I hope the time will come when it can be said to you, young women, also, Have to do with political life. Make your power as true Endeavorers felt in all the affairs of civil life. I am sorry that I cannot speak directly to the dear girls and women who are here, and say to them, 'Go attend also to the functions of your civil life;' but I remember the saying that 'the hand that rocks the cradle rules the world,' and I remember also how the wives and mothers fought during the Civil War, sitting in the chimney-corners knitting stockings for the boys who were far away at the front of the battle. So that when I speak to the young men, I may almost venture to say that I use the term generically as including the women, too.

"The word Endeavor is a gloriously significant one. It comes from two French words, which mean on guard or on duty. I dare not venture to pronounce those two French words here in the city of Montreal. It recalls the worn legend of the Roman knight at Pompeii, who stood in his place without flinching while the multitudes were flying from the molten stream of death which the great mountain belched forth, faithful among the fearful, on duty to the last. That is what it means to be a true Endeavorer. First of all, it devolves upon us to guard the rights of citizenship and the purity of the franchise; that is, to be on guard at the polls.

> "'There is a weapon better yet,
> And stronger than the bayonet,
> A weapon that comes down as still
> As snowflakes fall upon the sod,
> And executes a freeman's will,
> As lightning does the will of God.' [*Applause.*]

"This fluttering bit of paper in the citizen's hand is eloquent of the progress of freedom and equality. It means that Paul's manifesto on Mar's Hill is being realized, 'God hath made of one blood all nations of men for to dwell upon the face of the earth.' It means that, within bounds, every one is a king in his own might. But there is no privilege without a corresponding responsibility. The ballot suggests not merely that a man may exercise his franchise, but that he must do so. This bit of paper is the token of a freeman's sovereignty, and he has no more right to ignore or decline its responsibilities than Queen Victoria would have to cast down her sceptre in a pettish freak and refuse to govern her realm. In ancient Sparta it was the custom on election day for officers of the law to draw a vermillion cart through the streets. To bear the red mark was counted a misdemeanor. If you, young man, are an enfranchised citizen of the States or of the Colonies, go as a true Endeavorer, and stand guard over your citizenship at the polls on election day. One of the grave evils of our time is the withdrawal of a considerable class from the exercise of citizenship. The right to vote involves a corresponding duty, which no true Endeavorer will regard with indifference. It is our business to look to the education of the masses—that is, to stand on guard at the school-house door. In the freedom of the suffrage which prevails in all constitutional governments are involved not a few serious possibilities of danger. An ignorant citizen is like a reckless miner with an uncovered light on his visor. The fire-damp is all about him. John Milton wrote in the days of the English Commonwealth:

> "'There is a poor blind Samson in this land,
> Shorn of his strength and bound with bands of steel,
> Who may in some grim revel raise his hand
> And shake the pillars of the commonweal.'

"This blind Samson is ignorance. Wherefore our fathers wisely established the common school, insisting that as the people are princes they should be taught to rule. This institution is fundamental to our welfare. Withered be the hand that shall be raised to destroy it! The result of committing the elective franchise to the ignorant and unworthy was seen in the city of Chicago, a few years ago, when a body of anarchists, foiled in their efforts to possess themselves of the control of municipal affairs, gathered in the Haymarket and assailed the officers of the law with dynamite. Seven of them justly suffered the penalty of death; but that the infamous cause survives them is manifest in the recent pardon of their confreres by Governor Altgeld, of Illinois. The prime remedy for such abuse is in the education of the masses. This is our strong buttress against anarchy and kindred political heresies. It therefore behooves the thoughtful young who gather in millions within the charmed circle of Christian Endeavor to stand unitedly in defense of the public school.

"A true Endeavorer should be on duty close by the dram-shop. There is no more portentous menace to our liberties than this. In the city of New York there are 9,000 saloons. That fact alone is portentous, when we reflect that every one of them is an open doorway into the realm of darkness. But there are other considerations which give it a still broader and deeper significance. Five thousand, or more than half, of these saloons are under chattel mortgages, and these mortgages are, with scarcely an exception, held by a syndicate of twenty men—brewers, distillers, and wholesale liquor dealers. The full meaning of that statement is not grasped until we go on to consider that each saloon, at a moderate estimate, controls twenty votes, which gives to the rum-sellers of New York city the balance of political power. But it is a proverb that the vote of New York city determines the political complexion of the commonwealth, and, furthermore, as goes the commonwealth of New York so goes the nation! What, then, is the conclusion of the matter? The destinies of the American people are practically in the grasp of a group of less than twenty liquor dealers! Were it not for certain moral restraints put upon this formidable power by public sentiment, the outlook would be as black as midnight. As it is, it behooves every lover of law and order and national prosperity to use his utmost influence against the dram-shop. It is not for us at this point either to call in question or to concede the right of the individual to take a social or even a convivial glass. We are not talking about rights, but about Christian duties and privileges. There is a right which in the Christian life towers above all others; it is the right to surrender all rights for the sake of one's fellow-men. This is the mind that was in Christ Jesus, who, possessing all the inalienable rights of Godhead, emptied Himself and became of no reputation for us. This is the mind that was in the Apostle Paul also when he said, 'If meat make my brother to offend, I will eat no meat while the world standeth!' Never was a grander manifesto of human rights—never a sublimer declaration of independence than that! Oh! young men, to whom the welfare of the nation is presently to be committed, be 'on duty' just there.

"It should be the part of every loyal Endeavorer to be on guard respecting the sanctity of the Sabbath. Our minds revert in the instant to the opening of the gates of the Columbian Fair on the Lord's day. All praise to the noble army of American Endeavorers for the heroic stand they have taken in this matter. They have said, with a voice like the sound of many waters, 'If the gates of the exposition are open on the Sabbath we cannot attend it.' Let others call it a 'boycott' if they choose; a rose by any other name would smell as sweet. It was just such a boycott as was instituted by the Jewish youths in Babylon when they said, 'Because the king's meat has been laid on idol altars we cannot partake of it.' Such boycotts are in line with duty and principle. The Gospel of Jesus Christ pronounces, in behalf of the universal church, a boycott on every existing form of evil. The Sabbath has always and everywhere been the citadel of national piety, and by the same token, of national prosperity. No kingdom or commonwealth has ever persistently violated it and lived. We would therefore not be worthy of our Christian names, certainly not of the name of Christian Endeavor, did we not resent the opening of the Columbian Fair on God's holy day. The matter has a pivotal importance as being a new departure. For four hundred years America has regarded the Sabbath. It is now proposed to reverse all precedents, and make a new Sabbath policy for the nation. If this fair is a financial success it is safe to say that all similar expositions hereafter will pursue a similar course. If this one is a failure the experiment of Sabbath desecration will scarcely be tried again. It is respectfully submitted that thoughtful Christian people will not lend their influence to a movement which promises so calamitous a result. In any event, if there is a question as between duty and pleasure in this matter, conscience should have the benefit of the doubt. 'He that doubteth is condemned if he eat.' Our young Endeavorers have taken the right position. They feel that their principles are being put to the test, and they are willing that the world shall take note whether they have the courage of their convictions or not. God help them—clad in the full panoply of their profession—to withstand in the evil day, and having done all, to stand.

"The young men of the Christian churches are presently to bear the full responsibility of the welfare of the state. If they flinch or waver in the hour of trial, the generations of the future must suffer for it. If they quit themselves like men, upholding with stalwart steadfastness the institutions of truth and righteousness, the waste places of the earth shall be glad because of them, and the coming of the Lord shall be hastened in His time. They are already being put to crucial tests. God is asking, with respect to current questions of political ethics, whether they will be true or not.

"'He hath sounded forth the trumpet that shall never call retreat,
He is sifting out the hearts of men before His judgment seat;
Oh! be swift, my soul, to answer Him, be jubilant, my feet,
For God is marching on.'"

The meeting closed with singing "My Country, 'tis of Thee," and "God Save the Queen."

It is impossible to describe how the blessed fire of this idea caught in the wide prairies of Christian Endeavor, and how it spread from heart to heart throughout all the land. Many events and many necessities fanned this spark into a blaze. The growing sense of the power of young Christian manhood, the intensifying indignation against the horrid corruption of municipal politics which culminated in the startling disclosures of rotten Tammany, which about this time Dr. Parkhurst began to probe; the death of Robert Ross, of Troy, who was doing

ROBERT ROSS.

his duty at the polls as a Christian Endeavorer should, and who was murdered in cold blood by Bat Shea, a ward heeler of the lowest type; all these events, as I say, fanned the little spark at Montreal into a blaze, and from one end of the land to another Christian Endeavor meetings rang with Good Citizenship speeches, Good Citizenship Clubs were formed, leagues were established, and the study of the subject was entered upon. Under the auspices of *The Golden Rule,* Professor Graham Taylor conducted a series of valuable lessons in Good Citizenship, and in every way this blessed revival sped on its way throughout the land.

Some modest part in the glorious election of 1894, which was memorable not because of the defeat or triumph of any political party, but because of the triumphs of righteousness in New York and many other places, may be claimed for this revival effort begun in the drill hall of Montreal.

CHRISTIAN ENDEAVOR EXHIBIT AT THE WORLD'S FAIR.

CHAPTER LIV.

A MISSIONARY REVIVAL.

A Great Impetus to Missionary Earnestness—Another Important Enlargement—Come Over and Help Us—A New Crusade—Missionary Literature—A Missionary Meeting—Joseph and His Brethren—" Give, Give, Give "—Maintaining Our Institutions—Missions and Modern Civilization—The Missionary Extension Course—Golden-Rule Mission Clubs—Quarter of a Million Dollars for Missions—The Reflex Influence on American Life.

URING the months which followed the convention at Montreal a missionary revival among the young people went hand-in-hand with the civic revival. This could hardly be said to have begun at Montreal, for a growing interest in the subject of missions had been taking possession of the hearts of Christian Endeavorers for several years.

But it is certain that a great impetus was given to this idea by the events of the Montreal Convention. The President of the United Society had just come home from his long journey. His heart was full of rejoicing over the missionary heroism which he had witnessed and burdened with the sights of heathen degradation. He did his best to make the missionary feature one of the ideas of the convention, and in this he was seconded by all his associates and by the unanimous voice of the assembled thousands, as the following extract from the annual address will show:

"Another important enlargement for the year to come is an enlargement and more practical exemplification of the missionary spirit. [*Applause.*]

" I may as well confess it now and here—one great object of my long journey of nearly forty thousand miles across land and sea, a journey that has been no summer-holiday trip, has been to make, if possible, more concrete the demands of your brothers and sisters in all lands, to kindle your missionary zeal into a larger and brighter blaze, and to increase many fold your gifts to missions. If this might be the result I should feel that the journey had not been a mile too long. [*Applause.*]

"As I speak to you I can, in imagination, see myriads of heathen hands held out to you for your Christ, for your Bible, for your civilization. From the crowded house-boats of the Canton River; from the thronging wretchedness of the narrow streets of Shanghai; from the eager millions of Japan, who are deciding between Christ and Buddha and materialistic infidelity, for whom, as a nation some think that the great decision will practically be made before men date their letters January 1, 1900; from the dry, baked plains of Southern India; from the jungles of Northern India; from wretched, Mohammedan-cursed Egypt, Syria, and Turkey; from sunny Italy; from awakening Spain; from the pleasant land of France—from all comes the cry of unconscious need and want.

"If the needs of the one little province of Macedonia could appeal so loudly to the apostle of old, in what thunder-tones should all these countries speak to you, Christian Endeavorers!

"I would bring you their message; I would interpret their cry, 'Come over and help us; come over and help us.' If you cannot go, you can send. *You must go or send.* Money is as much needed as men and women, perhaps more, just now, for the recent great missionary revival has touched the hearts of consecrated young people more than it has touched the pocket-book of the average Christian.

"May it not be the glad mission of the Christian Endeavor Society to introduce a new era of benevolence, not to perpetuate the grudging dole that has been wrung from tight fists in the past, a meagre offering that will never evangelize the world, but to bring in an era of proportionate and systematic giving as God hath prospered us?

"Who will join me this year in a pledge of proportionate giving of at least one-tenth of what God may give us? Do you want a larger mission, Christian Endeavorers? Do you want a new crusade? Here it is. Could anything be larger? It reaches to the ends of the world. It embraces every nation and people and kindred and tribe. It means salvation, *yours* as well as theirs. It means the filling of our missionary treasuries; for we will always give, as we have done, through our own wisely directed denominational channels. It means that no worthy cause at home or abroad will suffer. In time, as we grow more numerous and richer, it will mean thousands where now there are hundreds, and millions where now are given thousands. It means obedience to our Lord's last command. It means that the twentieth century, yes, that this little remnant that is left of the old nineteenth, will usher in the glad era of an evangelized world which has heard in its remotest corners the gospel message."

Miss Ella B. McLaurin, of the Baptist Board, added to the impression by a vigorous address on missionary meetings and how they should be conducted:

"A missionary meeting is the place where you introduce Joseph to his brethren, and the 500,000,000 down-trodden, helpless, hopeless, prayerless women of heathen lands to their more favored sisters. These missionary meetings are the reservoirs from which our boards must draw in order to water the heathen world. At these meetings we become acquainted with those of our brothers and sisters who have not counted their lives dear that they might extend the boundaries of the Saviour's kingdom, whose blood has consecrated the soil of every land, and whoses names are written in letters of light in the blue heavens of every Christian denomination. Here we learn to love those who first scaled the almost inaccessible fastness of paganism and toiled on in the midst of discouragements and untold suffering until to-day that gigantic and hoary superstition is tottering to its fall. And here we come in deeper sympathy with those who, through self-denial and heroic purpose and sacrifice, have sought to do His will and have carried His Gospel to the nations that sat in darkness. Familiarity with these noble men and royal women will make us inheritors of their sublime faith and devotion. The contemplation of what God has wrought through them will kindle in our hearts a glowing gratitude, and a larger desire for the redemption of a lost race. The thought of what remains to be done will increase our dependence on the Divine Spirit. And it is here we learn the nature of their work, that it has to do, not with the relief of physical need and suffering alone, not with the diffusion of knowledge, not with the material progress of society, but rather with the peace, enlightenment, redemption of immortal souls and their restoration to the image of God—that their work is more than charity, and more than philanthropy and more than education; it is salvation, the very impartation of a new nature and a new and eternal life, the Christ life incarnate in the human soul."

"Missionary Money and How to Raise It" was the subject of a missionary address by Rev. W. H. G. Temple, in which he said:

"You ask me how to raise money for the Lord's work; I answer it in two words, Give it!

"My address this morning shall be an amplification of that advice. When God gets ready to sell salvation, it will be time for Him to purchase man's aid for the great purpose of His love. If I read my Bible aright, the All-Father has been sitting upon the circle of the universe from all eternity and doing nothing but give, *give*, GIVE. And if I have read the history of the race aright, man, ever since he had a being, has been doing little else than get, *get*, GET. God has put to shame every well-to-do and niggardly giver the world over by His magnificent benevolence.

"There is such a thing as the grace of giving. It ought to be put in the list as the tenth fruit of the Spirit. I have very little hope of the permanence of youthful piety until I see marked evidence of this estimable virtue. But like all other Christian virtues, it must be *enthusiastically* entered into and enjoyed to produce the best results. Prayer thus emphasized becomes communion. Service thus rendered becomes holy zeal. Giving in this spirit doubly blesses. It leaves its benediction alike upon both donor and receiver. It droppeth it like the gentle dew from heaven, blessing both him who gives and him who takes.

"This is the way God intended His kingdom to be built upon the earth. When the church has fully learned this divine principle, and has put it faithfully into operation, depend upon it, there will not be room enough to contain the Divine blessing that shall be hers. Give, then, generously, individually, vicariously, enthusiastically. Mark the initials of these, g-i-v-e! I close, then, as I began. How shall we raise money for the Lord's work? Give it!"

This series of addresses was closed by Rev. J. T. McCrory, D. D., who spoke on "The Reflex Influence of Missionary Efforts." With such sentences as these he stirred the hearts of the Endeavorers:

"The maintenance of our institutions and the perfecting of our civilization depends on the reflex influence of missionary effort. It is the person intelligently interested in missions at home and abroad who appreciates the degradation that ungodliness produces and fosters. Who but the true missionary knows, aside from those who directly suffer, the shuddering, withering, damning curse of the liquor traffic? He is the man who will lift his hand to heaven and swear eternal enmity against the overshadowing curse. So it is with all social and moral evils. He is the man, too, who appreciates the difference between the civil and political institutions of our own and those of heathen countries, and finds the reason for the difference in the religions of the people. And he feels the need and possesses the moral fibre for maintaining these institutions. The great battle for the preservation of the civil and religious institutions known across the line as the American Sabbath, which is being contested with such heroic persistence, is being fought with Christian men and women who are most interested in missions. You may count on this—the man who is not concerned to have the will of God made supreme in China will not be an enthusiastic friend of righteousness in his own land. It is the man who will send the Gospel to the Chinaman in his own country who will defend him against the unrighteousness of 'sandlot politicians' in our own country.

"It is the man who would strike to the heart that *monstrum horrendum* of modern civilization, the saloon, in old England and New England, who makes sacrifices to send the Water of Life to Africa and the New Hebrides, but execrates the shipment of 'double-distilled damnation' to those helpless millions. It is the man who is giving time, and thought, and means, to have the will of God done on earth as it is done in heaven who believes in the 'higher law' for his own country and hesitates not to use his influence for the suppression of anarchy of every kind, and the maintenance of liberty under the forms of law at any cost. Brethren, the great 'conflict of the ages' is upon us.

REV. J. T. McCRORY, D. D.

"The enemies of King Jesus are gathering their forces for one last desperate struggle. Our Revelation; our Christian institutions; our social customs; our civil liberties; all the attainments, in short, of these eighteen Christian centuries, are to be assailed by the forces of diabolism. The only force that can successfully contest the field with these mighty foes of mankind is that consciously led by the Omnipotent Lord, and reinforced by the angels and inspired by the assurance of glorious victory such as those only who are directly and heartily engaged in the mission work of the church can entertain. 'And who knoweth,' O missionary church, 'whether thou art come to the kingdom for such a time as this.' Amen and amen."

If my space allowed, many more stirring extracts might be given which would tell how the hearts of the young people at Montreal were fired with the missionary enthusiasm. But this is not the best part of the story, for, as a consequence of this convention, the same kind of a fire was kindled in ten thousand other places, and during the succeeding months it leaped higher and higher.

The Missionary Extension Movement which kindled the fires of devotion to Christ's world-wide cause was the direct outcome of this convention. It was soon inaugurated with earnestness in many States.

Moreover, this enthusiasm did not evaporate in thin air, but resulted in a genuine addition to missionary zeal. This interest is still as vital as ever, and is growing in power and intensity every day. A careful estimate founded on actual figures show that in the years 1893 and 1894 the societies of Christian Endeavor gave, through their own denominational boards, a quarter of a million of dollars, while the sum contributed in 1894 and 1895 reached nearly half a million of dollars. Constantly this missionary giving will increase, I believe, the enthusiasm will grow brighter and stronger, the reflex influence on the life of young Christians will become more potent, until in God's good time, and in some humble measure through the work of the Society of Christian Endeavor, He whose right it is shall reign as King of Kings and Lord of Lords.

FOUNTAIN LAGOON, LAKE VIEW PARK, CLEVELAND.

CHAPTER LV.

THE CLEVELAND CONVENTION.

Unfavorable Omens—The Hard Times and the Strike—Eugene V. Debs or Grover Cleveland—No Postponement—A Bitter Disappointment—A Graphic Report—The Preliminary Meetings—Governor McKinley's Welcome—Some New Features—Something for the Eye as Well as the Ear—Banners and Diplomas—The Roll of Honor—An Address in Chinese—Jonas Spotted Bear—The Sermons Once More—What the Papers Thought of It—Something More than Gush—Farewell Words.

IF ever a convention-day drew near clouded by unfavorable omens, it was the opening day of the Thirteenth International Christian Endeavor Convention. The superstitious felt that they had reason to be confirmed in their bad opinion of the number thirteen, and the hearts of even the bravest sank within them as the day approached.

In the first place, a year of intense business depression had been felt in all parts of the country. Many Christian Endeavorers who had hitherto been earning good salaries had been thrown out of employment altogether. The parents of not a few had been reduced almost to penury by the hard times, and it was thought that if there were no other cause operating to reduce the attendance it would be much below the average of recent years.

But worse than the hard times, shortly before the date of the convention the most extensive strike that ever paralyzed American industries was inaugurated at Chicago. For a little while it seemed that Eugene V. Debs, and not Grover Cleveland, was the ruler of the United States. The scenes of bloodshed and riot in Chicago, and in some other sections of our country, will be long remembered, and will cause 1894 to stand out in our history as a lurid and unhappy year.

The strike, starting in Chicago, extended sympathetically in every direction. Tens of thousands of miles of railroads were "tied up." Things grew worse and worse, and, just at the blackest hour of this night of industrial depression, before the dawning day of better things, came the week, from the 8th to the 15th of July, of the Christian Endeavor Convention.

The strike was at its very worst. The industrial condition of the country was the most hopeless. Delegates did not know whether, if they started from

THE CONVENTION IN SESSION (CLEVELAND), SHOWING AUDIENCE CONVULSED WITH LAUGHTER.

their homes, they could ever reach their destination; or whether, if they got to Cleveland, they could get home again.

An absolute embargo was laid upon all the delegates from the extreme west. No trains were running from the Pacific Coast, and no one could get through even from as far east as Colorado, unless they had started days in advance of the date of the convention.

As can be imagined the hearts of Endeavorers everywhere sank within them, and especially the hearts of the Committee of '94 and of the officers of the United Society, upon whom rested the responsibility for the convention. There was some thought of postponing the convention, and telegrams flew back and forth between Boston and various parts of the country on the wings of the lightning, asking whether the convention was to be put off. But it was manifestly impossible to make any change. The great Sængerfest Building had been engaged, the huge tent had spread its ample wings upon the chosen lot in Cleveland, the convention days had been advertised far and wide, the speakers were engaged and many of them were on their way to the convention. It was plain that nothing could be done, but to carry it out as well as possible.

The fact that, in spite of these difficulties and dangers, the Thirteenth International Convention has gone down to history as the largest and in some respects the most successful meetings of all the series, up to that date, is a proof of the inherent vitality and vigor of the movement which the convention represents, and a proof which could be given in scarcely any other way.

It was one of the bitterest disappointments of my life that I could not have the pleasure of attending this meeting. For months, as the result of a severe attack of influenza, I had been struggling with an illness which at the last prevented my attendance; though up to the very last day I had hoped to be able to go, and had made all preparations accordingly.

But a Christian Endeavor Convention is little dependent on any man, and everything moved on successfully and smoothly. Rev. Charles A. Dickinson was chosen to preside over the convention. Secretary Baer and Treasurer Shaw were most energetic and efficient in management; all the Trustees who could be present were assiduous in doing everything in their power to make the meeting the largest possible success, and the Committee of '94 was instant in season and out of season to make the meetings the grandest of all the series.

As I was not there to describe this meeting from personal observation, I will make use of the graphic account which prefaces the official report of the Thirteenth International Convention:

"White and gold everywhere! Flags, festoons, streamers, and banners decorated in profusion public and private buildings, business blocks, and residences. Storekeepers vied with each other in making displays of their goods

CONVENTION MEETING TENT (CLEVELAND).

INTERIOR TENT, CLEVELAND CONVENTION.

which should most beautifully combine the two colors. Florists filled their windows with white and yellow daisies, Japan lilies, and golden-rod. Jewelers devoted their show-windows to the most ingenious arrangements of silver and gold. Dry-goods dealers displayed a wealth of white and yellow silks, ribbons, and fabrics of all kinds. Booksellers gave a conspicuous place to their 'white and gold' editions. Some stores provided electric illuminations at night which emphasized the same combination; and even the fireworks at the 'Siege of Vicksburg' recognized the prevailing custom. Prettiest of all, great numbers of young ladies adopted for their home and street costumes white dresses with golden-hued belt and trimmings.

"White and gold are the colors of the Cleveland Christian Endeavor Local Union. The citizens of Cleveland took this method of expressing their welcome to the delegates who came to the Thirteenth International Christian Endeavor Convention.

"It should be said, also, that everywhere interwoven with the white and gold were the national colors. The great electric light mast in the Public Square, with its numerous stays, was heavily hung with United States flags. So, also, were the cross-wires of the electric street railway down town. Looking up almost any principal street there could be seen great stretches of color on either side, the folds of 'Old Glory' everywhere intermingled with white and gold.

"And all this exuberance and brilliancy of outward display was simply the threshold to the real, genuine, and substantial welcome which the delegates received.

"The Cleveland badge was one of the most beautiful which has yet been designed, consisting of two diamond-shaped pieces of white celluloid tied with a yellow ribbon and containing six sheets of fine paper, each bearing two photo-engravings of Cleveland views. The face of the badge bore the 'C. E.' monogram, surrounded by a laurel wreath, and on the back was a picture of the Garfield monument, with the lettering, 'Thirteenth International Christian Endeavor Convention, Cleveland, July 11–15, 1894.' The program, with covers in white and gold, was very handsomely designed, and contained, besides the order of exercises for the several sessions, a number of Scripture selections for responsive reading, and about sixty hymns selected from the new hymn-book, *Christian Endeavor Hymns*, by Ira D. Sankey.

"The convention, as at Montreal last year, divided its principal sessions between two places—the Sængerfest Building and a mammoth tent formerly belonging to Barnum's Circus. The Sængerfest Building, located at the junction of Wilson and Scoville Avenues, is an immense structure originally designed for great convocations of the German singing societies. The interior is arranged in the shape of a huge amphitheatre, or half-circle, the speakers' platform being in the geometrical centre, the choir seats rising immediately at the rear, and the seats for pastors extending on either side. The reporters' tables, accommodating one hundred representatives of the press, were on the floor of the hall, in front and on either side of the speakers' stand. The hall was very prettily decorated with the Cleveland colors and with flags of all nations, masses of palms and other potted plants being placed along the front of the platform. The speakers' stand was draped with the American and English flags and the Y. P. S. C. E. pennant which first greeted Dr. Clark in Australia on his voyage around the world. Over the choir gallery was hung an immense banner bearing the society's motto, 'For Christ and the Church.' The hall was provided with seating accommodations for 10,000 people, and the acoustic properties were for the most part very good.

"The tent was pitched at the corner of Wilson and Cedar Avenues, 'only three blocks from the hall;' but they were three of the longest blocks that most of the delegates had ever experienced. It was unfortunate that the cross-town street railway could not be completed in time for the convention; but the work was unavoidably delayed on account of the coal miners' strike, the company not being able to secure the rails. However, the delegates made the best of this inconvenience; and certainly the walk between the two auditoriums was a very pleasant one. The tent was 320x190 feet in size, and 55 feet high, seating about 12,000 people. The speakers' stand was at one end of the tent, the choir seats and pastors' seats being placed on either side. Of necessity, the decorations in the tent were less elaborate than in the hall; but the auditorium proved to be a very comfortable one, especially at the evening sessions, and the speakers were heard even more easily than in the hall."

To do justice to each international convention, as this history has proceeded, has become an increasingly difficult task. Even to mention the names of all the speakers at the Cleveland Convention, since they were numbered by hundreds, would fill a chapter, and a catalogue of names, however eminent they may be, is never interesting.

So, while the list of speakers was quite as famous as at any of the preceding meetings, and while the speeches were up to the fullest standard of eloquence, I can only mention the more unique elements of this convention which distinguish it from the others.

The preliminary meetings on Wednesday evening, meetings which had been inaugurated the year before at Montreal, were carried out with even larger success this year. There were no less than thirteen of these meetings; a convention in themselves they were, with such speakers as Anthony Comstock, Rev. M. Rhodes, D. D., Rev. Gilby C. Kelly, D. D., Rev. George Dana Boardman, D. D., Rev. Teunis S. Hamlin, D. D., and others equally famous.

Who could give the address of welcome so worthily as Rev. J. Z. Tyler, the Chairman of the Committee of '94, and a wise and witty orator?

"Our joy in greeting you is greater because of the dangers you dreaded when you left your homes to come. The great railroad strike made travel uncertain and even perilous. We gratefully recognize the fact that you were graciously preserved while on the way, and have been brought within our gates in safety. The flood of telegrams that came upon me as Chairman of the Committee of Arrangements, up to so late a date as yesterday, indicates that many thousands have been kept from coming because of grave apprehension as to the possibility of arriving in safety. Under favorable circumstances, and with open highways of public travel, who can tell what the attendance at this convention would have been? I trust you will not suspect that the enthusiasm of this glad hour has robbed me of my reason when I say that we would this morning have enrolled not less than forty thousand delegates and visitors. Possibly the great strike should be interpreted as a gracious interposition of Providence to prevent such an overwhelming flood submerging, not only the Committee of '94, but this entire city. This Christian Endeavor movement, although it numbers two millions, is yet in its infancy. A giant infant, this; but more wonderful than its size is the continued rapidity of its growth."

Governor William McKinley, the chief magistrate of Ohio and the famous advocate of a protective tariff, welcomed the delegates in the name of Ohio.

"It is a mighty cause," said he, "that could convene in any city of any State in the Union the splendid assemblages of people gathering in so many places this morning, in this city by the lake. No cause but one could have brought together these noble, earnest people; and that is the cause of the Master, and the cause of man. It is fitting that the largest convention of Christian Endeavorers ever held should be in the State of Ohio. I bring you the welcome of the State which you have honored with your presence—a State, the opening words of whose Constitution make grateful acknowledgment to Almighty God for our freedom; and it declares that religion, morality, and knowledge are essential to good government, and the law-making powers shall therefore protect every religious denomination in the peaceful enjoyment of its own mode of public worship, and encourage schools and means of education.

"I bring you the warm greetings of more than four million people of the State of Ohio who subscribe to that Constitution, and who were glad to have this representation of young, vigorous Christians of the United States. Your coming is hailed with satisfaction. Your stay will be to us a benediction. Your going will be to us the occasion of sincere regret. You are not strangers to us. The young men and women of Ohio are your associates in the great work in which you are engaged. The whole world knows you, for it has felt and profited by your influence and example.

"Mr. President, I have been peculiarly impressed with the significance and suggestiveness of the name of one of your committees—the lookout committee, or the committee on lookout. That is the most essential committee in human civilization. That is the most important committee that was ever raised, and every Christian Endeavorer, every citizen of the country, should be on that committee, and chairman of it. It is a useful and essential committee to all mankind. It ought to be adopted by everybody. 'Look out.' 'Look out for the breakers.' 'Look out for temptations.' 'Look out for sin.' 'Look out for pitfalls.' 'Look out for the enemy.' 'Look out for your associations.' 'Look out for yourselves.' Keep on."

Rev. Wm. Patterson, in the name of the Trustees, most happily responded to these addresses of welcome.

Then came Secretary Baer's report, which told of the mighty march of the

COMMITTEE OF '94 (CLEVELAND CONVENTION).

5. Rev. S. L. Darsie, Music. 6. F. Melville Lewis, Printing. 7. Norman E. Hills, Entertainment. 9. J. E. Cheesman, Hall.
4. A. E. Robter, Treasurer Finance. 1. Miriam C. Smith, Secretary. 3. A. W. Neale, Reception. 11. Rev. R. A. George, *Ex-officio*.
2. Rev. J. Z. Tyler, Chairman. 8. R. B. Hamilton, Press. 10. J. V. Hitchcock, Auditor.

Christian Endeavor troops. He was able to marshal in imagination 33,679 companies of Christian Endeavorers in all the world from which he had reports, of which 28,696 were in the United States. There were 6,809 Junior companies, with an enlistment of 365,000. Thirty intermediate societies were reported; 9 mothers' societies, and 6 senior societies.

New York, which for so many years had been in the lead, was obliged at this convention to accord first place to Pennsylvania, which, with her 3,458 societies, boasted of 138 more companies of Endeavorers than New York. Ohio took the third place with 2,274, Illinois fourth with 2,260, and Indiana fifth with 1,534.

SIGNING THE PLEDGE.
"*We come from every clime.*"

"We come from every clime, from every land," said the Secretary. "Our skins vary in color: 460 are red, 18,700 are yellow, 97,020 are black, and 1,907,620 are white, making in all an interracial and international army of 2,023,800."

He also made the glad report that so far as could be learned 183,650 had joined the evangelical churches during the year, and that during the last five years 614,150 had joined the churches.

His report also brought good news of the victories of the past year in the line of the three advanced movements suggested at Montreal—Good Citizenship,

Proportionate and Systematic Giving to Missions, and the Enlargement of our Interdenominational Fellowship.

In these vast assemblies, as can be well understood, it is often difficult for those in the rear of the room to hear the speakers. For this reason more was done this year to reach the eye than ever before. It was felt that those who could not hear could see, and so the presentation of the banners and of the diplomas and of the umbrella of state sent from China, by Rev. A. A. Fulton, were important features of the convention.

Pennsylvania took the beautiful Junior badge which Illinois for three years had held, but she was obliged to give up the banner for the largest absolute gain in number of societies to England, which had made the greatest increase.

Little Delaware took the Junior badge banner for the greatest proportionate increase, while West Virginia took the banner for the greatest proportionate increase in the number of older societies.

The umbrella of state, offered by Rev. A. A. Fulton for the largest number of those who give two cents a week to missions, was taken by New York, while twenty-five diplomas were given to the societies which had done the most respectively for Good Citizenship, for the distribution of good literature, in the way of systematic giving to missions, and for the enlargement of our fellowship.

It may be thought by some who read at a distance this meagre account of the presentation of these banners and diplomas, and who look at the matter in a cold-blooded manner, that it is a childish affair to offer and receive such emblems. But every emblem stands for service, every banner and diploma means hard work on the part of hundreds, and perhaps thousands of young Christians; work inspired not by the diploma, but represented by it; work inspired by the love of Christ and a desire to advance the interests of His church.

Another interesting feature of this convention was the "Roll of Honor," which was displayed in the Sængerfest Building. Upon this roll of honor were the names of five thousand five hundred and fifty-two societies from thirty-five States, seven Territories, seven Provinces, and four foreign lands. Each of these names meant that they had given not less than $10 to their own denominational home or foreign missionary boards for the cause of missions, while many had given much more. The total amount reported on this roll of honor was $138,205.93.

In addition to that it was found that $185,512 had been given by those same societies in other ways, mostly for local work, or for the maintenance of their own churches. This roll of honor, measured by the yardstick, was 465 feet in length; " but who can measure its real length and breadth," said Secretary Baer, " but He who guides us in all our endeavors."

Another very pleasant feature of the same kind as those just described was the presentation to the Cleveland Union of a beautiful banner by the United Society of Christian Endeavor in honor of those who had so self-sacrificingly prepared for the convention. After Mr. Baer presented it, Dr. Tyler and the other members of the famous committee came forward and were separately introduced to the audience amid tremendous applause.

Dr. Tyler, on receiving the banner in behalf of the committee, committed it to the custody of Mr. J. E. Cheesman, one of the most active members of the Committee of '94, and the President of the Cleveland Endeavor Union.

If I should attempt to make a catalogue of the eloquent addresses of this convention, I should speak of the brilliant address of President Tucker, of Dartmouth College, on "The Claims of an Educated Life;" of the forcible speech of Rev. John Potts, D. D., of Canada, on "Christ the Worker a Model for All Endeavorers;" of Miss Frances E. Willard's address on "Women and Temperance;" and of Mr. John G. Woolley's "Christian Endeavor *versus* The Saloon." In enumerating the orators of the convention, I should also speak of Rev. Joseph K. Dixon, D. D., who spoke on "Common Sense in Church Life and Church Work;" of Rev. Smith Baker, who spoke on "Christian Citizenship;" of Rev. A. C. Dixon, whose subject was "The Heroes of Faith;" of Rev. P. R. Danley, D. D.; of Rev. Wayland Hoyt, D. D., who discussed the great subject of "Interdenominational Fellowship;" of Rev. N. D. Hillis, who spoke on "The Strategic Element of Missions;" and of Rev. Maltby D. Babcock, whose address on "Glorifying God" will long be remembered.

But even now, with all this long list of speakers, I have not begun to exhaust the number, nor should I do so if the list were made twice as long. Some speakers representing other nationalities and unusual interests were Rev. Herman Warszawiak, who spoke on "The Movement Among the Jews Toward Christ;" by Rev. W. D. Johnson, who spoke of "The Negro and the Endeavorer;" of Mrs. Geo. H. Hubbard, a missionary from Foochow, China, who, dressed in full Chinese costume, gave a greeting in Chinese which her husband interpreted; and by Jonas Spotted Bear, who spoke of "Christian Endeavor Among the Indians."

It will be seen that subjects relating to missions, good citizenship, and temperance, as well as those directly relating to the methods of the Christian Endeavor Society, had the right of way.

Four open parliaments were conducted, on "The Benefits of Interdenominational Fellowship," on "Good Citizenship," on "Junior Societies," and on "The Pledge;" and the Junior rally was larger and more important than at any similar meeting yet held. Mrs. Alice May Scudder again prepared the exercise, and Dr. James L. Hill presided over the meeting, while Rev. H. W. Pope, Dr. Pauline Root, and Rev. A. W. Spooner addressed the children.

Again were the sermons inspiring and most helpful in their influence. They

EXTERIOR OF SANGERFEST HALL. (CLEVELAND CONVENTION.)

Taken about 7 P. M.

ARRIVAL OF MICHIGAN DELEGATION. (CLEVELAND CONVENTION.)

were by President B. F. Raymond, D. D., of Wesleyan University, Middletown, and by Rev. A. J. F. Behrends, D. D., of Brooklyn; and they led up to the crowning consecration meeting, and prepared the vast audiences for the stillness and seriousness of the closing hour.

The inauguration of the Missionary Extension Movement on a more elaborate scale than had heretofore been proposed was received with much enthusiasm and enlisted many earnest hearts. For this Mr. Mershon's stirring address at the Montreal Convention the year before had paved the way, and it received his persuasive advocacy at Cleveland.

It will interest my readers to know what some of the papers had to say about this great convention. I can only choose a few from a great number of testimonies of the same general character.

Said *The Examiner*, of New York:

"Big? The word is feeble. It is immense, stupendous; it is the megatherium of conventions. The most that is possible is to give a few impressions of such things as one man can see or hear; for such a convention is like a great battle—no one man sees it all, or can tell its whole story."

Said *The Interior*, of Chicago:

"The Committee of '94 receive words of praise on every hand for the admirable manner in which the arrangements for this convention have been managed. The city is gay with white and yellow, the colors of the Cleveland Union; they are seen everywhere, from the large convention halls and churches to the express-cart and the movable peanut-stand. We even noticed a beer-garden theatre decorated with Christian Endeavor banners, and the colors that stand for courage and purity; but this is only carrying out the Christian Endeavor spirit, which has the courage to enter even such places as these, and purify them in the name of 'Christ and the Church.'"

Said *The Cumberland Presbyterian* concerning the singing:

"Singing, cyclones, avalanches, landslides of singing. Singing on the train *en route*, on the street cars in Cleveland, in the hotels, in the halls, everywhere there were Endeavorers, and such songs! Multiply a good solo by 12,000, and add the inspiration and enthusiasm of the occasion, and you may form some idea of what the singing was."

Said *The Kingdom*, of Minneapolis:

"It is doubtless the fact that never before in the history of the world have such immense audiences assembled beneath one roof for a distinctively religious purpose, while the enthusiasm awakened by these conventions is something wholly unique in modern religious life."

The Outlook had these kind words to say, inspired by this great convention:

"An unkind critic said, some time ago, that the three main elements in a

Christian Endeavor convention were hosts, children, and gush. That critic was a little right and much wrong. The little that was correct in the criticism was favorable to the friends of Endeavor. They do mass the multitudes as no others do. No other organization of a religious kind on earth can bring together men and women as can Christian Endeavor. No organization of any other kind—labor, political, scientific—in Europe, Asia, Africa, or America, can present the testimony of enthusiasm and increasing interest, year after year, like this one composed of the friends of Jesus. The 'children' part of the criticism displayed great ignorance and misstatements, as well as unkindness. The hoary heads are seen, day by day, in these audiences by the hundreds. Christian Endeavor, under God, is manned by men and women, plus the young. The scientists of the day, the wise men of the times, the leaders of thought, the ornaments of the pulpit, the picked ones from the universities, the strong from the seminaries, the choice of the generation, are present, and enjoy and help on the conventions and the work they tell of and advance. And as for 'gush,' if it is to be found anywhere, the most unlikely place to look for it under the sun is at this convention. True, one hears the hyper-ornate in language and extra-analogical in presentation now and then. But from an extended experience in conferences and conventions of religious and secular kinds in this and in European lands, the testimony is soberly given that in an annual Christian Endeavor convention there is less of the unsubstantial than in any gathering of modern times that is numbered by the thousands. Take these Canadians who come down from the Dominion, these representatives who come up from the South, and these delegates who represent the districts lying between, and you have the 'pick' of the century. The leaders of genuine reform are here; the conservators of the best that now is are of the number; the churches' best workers are represented in convention; and here are they of whom the present workers, to whom the world owes a great debt, can say sincerely, 'The generation that is coming is better than ours that is passing away, because the God of the generations has bestowed newly and largely through this blessed agency of Christian Endeavor.'"

I may well close these kind tributes and the account of this great convention with the words of one of the convention city's leading secular papers, *The Cleveland Leader:*

"The great success of the Christian Endeavor Convention was assured in advance; but the immense proportions of the gathering in this city of the hosts which have made it their rallying-point was not to be understood until the tremendous meetings which marked the formal opening of the work to be done here by the representatives of a most wonderful organization.

"When the great tent and the big Sængerfest Hall were filled to the doors yesterday morning, and the churches in the vicinity were found too small for the overflow meetings, the true size and impressiveness of the convention became apparent. Now the whole city understands the tremendous size and power for good of the organization which is able, in hard times and in the face of a strike which would have destroyed many conventions, to bring together a host of enthusiastic and zealous young men and women, the like of which was never seen before.

The demonstration of the vitality and vastness of the forces enlisted on the side of religion and morals was calculated to move the most thoughtless and awe the most hostile.

"We congratulate the Christian Endeavorers, from the leaders to the latest recruits of their magnificent army, on the unbounded success of the convention of 1894. May they remember their visit to Cleveland with such pride and satisfaction as the people of this city feel as they contemplate the greatest gathering of any kind which has ever been seen in this part of the world at a meeting of any organization whatsoever."

THE TRUSTEES AT CLEVELAND (STILLMAN HOUSE).

CHAPTER LVI.

THE DEVELOPMENTS OF 1894.

A Year of Great Conventions—Secretary Baer's Journey—In the Far South—"The Best Convention Ever Held"—Nuggets from the Different States—England's Whitsuntide Convention—Denominational Endeavors—The Missionary Extension Course—Good Citizenship Work—A Break in Health, and What Came of It—Two Months of Complete Rest—Beginnings in Germany—A Visit to Scandinavia—In the Metropolitan Tabernacle Again—In Wales—In Ireland and Scotland—Home Once More.

THE year 1894 was, beyond all the years that had gone before, a year of great State and provincial conventions, as well as of the great International Convention. Early in the year the health of Secretary Baer, which for two years had not allowed him to be much in the field, permitted him to go to the Pacific coast on a tour of six weeks, attending conventions in many States of the far West. He was accompanied by Mrs. Baer, who spoke most helpfully at a number of Junior meetings.

Treasurer Shaw was able to attend a number of conventions in the Southern States and Canada. Many of the trustees were pressed into the work, and in the early part of the year I made one or two long trips, especially one which took in the State conventions in Kansas, Kentucky, Texas, and Oklahoma.

Both the spring and fall conventions of 1894 were exceedingly fruitful, attended by an enormous number of delegates, and exceeding anything that had gone before in impressiveness and influence. The report gets to be almost monotonous of these State conventions, so sure is it to come each year, "Larger and better than ever before."

In 1894 British Columbia held its first annual convention. In California the new "Parent Christian Endeavor movement" met with much favor. It was shown that during the year the Junior membership had doubled. No wonder that overflow meetings were the rule.

In Colorado, too, it was found that the Juniors had doubled in numbers. Connecticut reported the best and most practical convention of its history, with $20,000 contributed to missions. Delaware's State convention, too, was "the best ever held." Idaho's third convention was "its very best." One feature was a yard and a half of names sent by the 168 Nez Percés Indian Christian Endeavorers.

Illinois's meeting exceeded all previous conventions in numbers, enthusiasm, and spiritual strength.

Deep spirituality characterized the Indiana meeting. In Kansas 1,800 delegates came to Topeka from outside the city, and the total attendance rose to 6,000. Kentucky's fifth annual convention was attended by 5,000 people. Michigan's convention of '94, too, was the largest ever held in the State, and numbered 4,000 people in attendance. From Minnesota the report came "The tone of the convention was intensely spiritual." Mississippi held its first State convention this year. From Nebraska came the delightfully monotonous report, "The largest and best held, with a deep spiritual tone."

In New York, Practical Christianity was the convention theme. Three simultaneous meetings were required to accommodate the 4,439 registered delegates.

Pennsylvania's magnificent union rejoiced in the remarkable gain of 1,118 societies. Especially striking were the noonday prayer-meetings held by the Endeavorers during the convention in the factories, shops, hospitals, and jail. Tennessee's fifth annual convention, held at Nashville, was a remarkable gathering. Seventeen young men and women volunteered for missionary service. The Texas union had more than doubled during the past year, and its meeting was remarkable for its numbers and its enthusiasm.

In West Virginia the societies had grown from 96 to 240, and the Junior societies from 8 to 42; no wonder West Virginia obtained the banner. Nebraska, New Hampshire, North Dakota, and the Northwest Territories, Oklahoma, and South Carolina all reported that the Convention of '94 was "the best they had ever known."

From other lands, too, came the same good report. England's fourth national convention, held on Whitsuntide in 1894, brought together in London more than 5,000 delegates. Among the notable speakers were Hon. John Wanamaker, Rev. Thos. Spurgeon, and Rev. F. B. Meyer. Denominational rallies were held for the first time in the history of an English convention. There were then in England 1,453 in twelve denominations, the Baptists being the leaders; but at the date of the compilation of this book these numbers must be thoroughly revised and nearly doubled to state the truth.

The conventions in Victoria, South Australia, and New South Wales were also most encouraging. South Australia was found to have 324 societies, Victoria, 460, while New South Wales had increased hers 200 per cent.

In the different denominations, too, Christian Endeavor during this year had made great headway, as was indicated by many cheering circumstances. Among these facts may be mentioned the following: The Methodist General Conference of Canada gave its formal permission to its young people to adopt the name Epworth League of Christian Endeavor, thus putting them in affiliation both with the denominational Epworth League and the interdenominational Christian Endeavor Society.

A report presented to the General Assembly of the Canadian Presbyterian Church called the society a boon and a blessing, the means of mental stimulus and a spiritual blessing. In the churches of the Disciples of Christ, Christian Endeavor had made great headway, since this denomination had appointed a national superintendent for Christian Endeavor work for the denomination. The Mennonites held at Cleveland their first denominational rally. The Reformed Church in the United States support a missionary in Japan through their denominational board. The Lutheran Endeavorers at Cleveland formed a permanent organization of the Lutheran Endeavor societies. Almost all the Moravian churches are found to have Christian Endeavor societies.

In the Presbyterian Church of the North it was found that 725 societies are now supporting 30 Presbyterian missionaries through the Presbyterian foreign board. . Many Presbyteries have now appointed permanent committees on young people's work. The Methodist Protestants have a well-organized and very active Christian Endeavor Union. The Endeavorers of the Reformed Church in America have built four Christian Endeavor churches and their Christian Endeavor missionary league holds monthly conferences.

The Cumberland Presbyterian General Assembly has a permanent Christian Endeavor committee, and the Presbyteries are taking a hand in the organization of Endeavor societies. In the Baptist churches of America Christian Endeavor societies are growing, while in England and in some foreign lands they take the lead. The Welsh Calvinistic Methodist Church held a denominational rally at Cleveland for the first time. All but two of the yearly meetings of the Friends of the United States and Canada have organized Christian Endeavor societies.

The Missionary Extension Course it was found could not be carried on on the original basis without larger co-operation than it received from other interested bodies, and so, in the fall of 1894, it was committed to the State Christian Endeavor unions to make arrangements for missionary courses which, in many States, have been carried out with much success.

"It is impossible," says *The Christian Endeavor Year Book for 1894*, "when speaking of the effort to make better citizens, to sum up the Good Citizenship work undertaken so widely by Christian Endeavor workers through the country the past year. In Chicago at least 450 meetings were held during one week in the interests of the movement. All the important city and State unions now have superintendents of Good Citizenship work. Most of these have done preliminary service, sending out circulars, and holding inspiring mass meetings.

"Enforcement of temperance laws is one of the most obvious and popular of these undertakings. The State conventions have all been alive on this subject.

Good Citizenship pledges have been widely signed. Courses of Good Citizenship lectures have been inaugurated.

"In many places crusades against gambling-houses, lotteries, Sunday desecration, dance halls, low theatres, the sale of tobacco, prize-fighting, and similar nuisances have been successfully carried on. Everywhere young men have been aroused to a sense of their duties and responsibilities for better government.

But the year 1894 was not only a year of expansion and growth in our own land, but it was the beginning of Christian Endeavor work in some other countries where heretofore the society had not even obtained a foothold. And this was brought about in part by a good Providence whose beneficence at first I, at least, could not understand.

After spending the six weeks following the Cleveland Convention in complete rest and retirement, I was told by my physician that in order to regain my health in the speediest way I should go abroad. And so on the 1st day of September, 1894, with the primary object of rest and recreation, but with the hope that on recovering my health the way would open for the planting of the Endeavor standard in new lands, I sailed with Mrs. Clark for the other side of the water. The first two months in Europe the doctor's directions were implicitly obeyed, and the time was spent in Germany, Switzerland, and Italy in rest and recuperation. By that time I felt that I could again render some service to the cause of Christian Endeavor, and, as some meetings had been arranged in Germany by devoted friends of the movement, about the first of November we left quiet, dreamy Venice for bustling, wide-awake, modern Berlin.

On the way we stopped in the old city of John Huss, the capital of Bohemia, and here in Prague, through an interpreter, I addressed two or three audiences of Bohemians, and found a most receptive soil for the Christian Endeavor seed. Of the results of this visit, however, and in fact of all the work done in German-speaking countries, it is too early, as I write this history, to speak in much detail.

I can say, however, that I met with a much warmer reception in Germany for the Christian Endeavor idea than I dared to expect. Many Christian people, especially those belonging to the more evangelistic wing of the Lutheran Church, had already heard of the society, and were greatly interested in it. Such well-known men as Pastors Clemm, Stocker, and Stieglitz had written and spoken favorably concerning the movement.

The works of Pastor Berner, of Buffalo, in which he so ardently and effectively argues for the Endeavor cause, had been circulated to a considerable extent, and *The Mitarbeiter*, of which Pastor Berner is the editor, had also found its way into Germany.

Among all those who were enthusiastic for the cause none did more for it than the young Hülfprediger of a church in Bielfeld, Frederic Blecher by name. At his own risk he had imported much literature from America, had scattered it broadcast, and was instant in season and out of season in preparing for me a warm reception to "Fatherland."

While we were in Berlin three largely-attended meetings were held in the hall of the Berlin Young Men's Christian Association, and Count Bernstorff very kindly acted as my interpreter. His high standing in religious circles, as well as court circles, and his admirable command of English made him not only the ideal interpreter, but rendered his advocacy of the cause of great value.

Others who spoke and worked for the same cause, and who showed a great interest in the establishment of the work throughout Germany, were Count Rothkirch, the honored president of the Berlin Young Men's Christian Association; Count Pückler, Mr. Von Filius, secretary of the Young Men's Christian Association; Pastor Paull, an eminent evangelist; Herr de Neufville, of Frankfort-on-the-Main; Pastor Romann, of Liegnitz; Pastor Zacharius, of Leipsic, and others whom I might mention.

Not only in Berlin, but in Frankfort-on-the-Main, in Liegnitz and Dresden and Leipsic as well did I find most kindly audiences, and the deepest interest in the subject of which I had to speak, and I shall always remember, whatever the results are so far as the establishment of the Society of Christian Endeavor are concerned, these pleasant days in the Fatherland.

Afterward we spent a week in Scandinavia, addressing meetings in Copenhagen, Stockholm, and Christiania. In all of these places I found attentive audiences and earnest Christians who desired the accomplishment of such a work as the Christian Endeavor Society contemplates, though evidently in Scandinavia the time was not yet ripe as in Germany for the thorough establishment of the organization.

After these November weeks in the far north we crossed the North Sea to England, and spent ten very busy and very happy days in the Motherland. The great meeting of London Endeavorers drawn from London's two hundred and fifty societies in the Metropolitan Tabernacle I shall not soon forget, nor the delightful breakfast with the ministers of London in the Tabernacle, nor the cordial and sympathetic spirit shown. Almost equally large numbers greeted us in Bristol a few weeks later, where also the society has deeply taken root.

But, in fact, it is difficult to tell where the pleasantest or most enthusiastic meetings were held. With great delight we recall to mind the Endeavor rallies in Rhyll, in North Wales, and Cardiff, in South Wales, in Dublin and Glasgow and Edinburgh, and Wellingboro' and Darby and Blackburn as well.

Particularly gratifying was it to find the growth of the interest in the Endeavor Society in the capital of Scotland so marked. At first it did not altogether commend itself to the Scottish mind, but the meeting in Edinburgh in the Free Assembly Hall, under the chairmanship of the famous Prof. Simpson, showed that the society had come to Edinburgh apparently to stay.

On the 14th of December the last Endeavor rally was held, and a most enthusiastic one it was, in the city of Bristol, and on the 15th we sailed for home on the record-breaking "Lucania," reaching the home-land after a short and uneventful voyage.

Another event which should be recorded in connection with this journey is the establishment of Christian Endeavor in Switzerland. Two or three scattered and struggling societies had before existed in this sturdy little republic it has since been learned; but nothing was known of them outside of Switzerland, and Christian Endeavor may be said to have had its real beginning in 1894 in the city of Lausanne.

In the little Alp-begirt town of Bex, in Canton Vaud, Mrs. Clark and I met

three devoted young English ladies who lived in Lausanne, but who were summering in Bex; the Misses Jessie, Edith, and Mary Murray. They had read Pansy's story, had heard from other sources of Christian Endeavor, and not being able to interest their Swiss friends in the society, formed a household society of three. From this small beginning came the flourishing societies in Lausanne, the circulation of much literature among the French pastors, and the commencement of a general and wide-spread interest in the movement which will be described more at length in another chapter.

Altogether the leaders of the Endeavor movement have reason to feel that the year 1894, with its great international gatherings, its magnificent State conventions, and its wide extension of the Christian Endeavor idea, was one of the most notable for the advancement of the cause since its humble beginning.

CHAPTER LVII.

PRACTICAL WORK AND PRACTICAL WORKERS.

Saying Verses and Singing Hymns—No Mean Accomplishment—The Widening Scope of Christian Endeavor—Some Loving Efforts—Some Odd Committees—A Famous Sunday Breakfast Association—How it Works and What it Has Accomplished—Comfort Bags for the Life Savers—Many Services Sustained—A Good Idea from Rochester—Saving the Stranger—An Evangelistic Committee and its Work—What the Ushers Did—Helpers in the Song Service—A Jubilant Hymn.

IT is sometimes asked, with a suspicion of a sneer, not so often in these days, I am thankful to say, but frequently in former years, "What are these Christian Endeavorers doing, any way! It is about time for them to do something more than say verses and sing hymns in meeting."

There was never any reason for this unpleasant remark, for, if the society had done nothing but revivify the young people's prayer-meeting, if it had only taught the Christian young men and women to say verses and sing hymns and express their religious ideas and their love for Christ, the society would have accomplished a most worthy and blessed purpose. But it has always done more than this. Service has always gone hand in hand with confession. Religious *work* has always been the most distinctly recognized feature of the society. The very first society on the very first day of its existence provided room for the committee idea, and from that day to this no society has been formed without providing work for its members to do. It has been in deed, as well as in name, a training school for the church. But it has also undertaken a multitude of duties which at first could not have been contemplated.

As the society has grown, its range of vision has expanded. Its possible services have been better understood, and it has attempted larger and larger things for the Master, but always with strict deference to the Endeavor idea of doing those things, and only those, and always those things of which the church and the pastor at its head approve.

It is impossible, within the limits of one chapter, or in fact within the limits of a book much larger than the present volume, to describe all these forms of work. It would be impossible to tell of the visits to hospitals and sick beds, of the services held within prison walls and in destitute portions of our great cities, of the relief administered to those who are destitute and hungry, of the hope given to those who felt that the world was all against them.

I can only give in this chapter a few examples of work, but examples which might be multiplied a thousand times over without exhausting the story of practical, earnest service in which these multitudes of young people have engaged.

Here are some items gathered from a few weeks' scanning of the papers, telling of the loving-kindness of these young hearts:

"A potato social by which twenty-five baskets of potatoes were brought together for the poor;—a sewing-school opened in a poor neighborhood for the benefit of the women there;—an employment bureau, manned by Endeavorers, offered free of charge;—a free soup-house, opened in Kansas City, that fed 16,000 hungry men, using 4,000 gallons of soup and more than 10,000 loaves of bread;—

SUNDAY BREAKFAST ASSOCIATION, PHILADELPHIA, PA. (THE MORNING MEAL).

a Christmas dinner for 120 poor people, this being in England;—city missions supported for work among the poor;—a nurse hired for similar service;—fresh-air funds established;—a flour committee organized;—five thousand packages of provisions, each containing enough for a meal, given away by a Baptist society of Chicago;—four thousand dollars raised for the unemployed by the Endeavorers of St. Louis;—thousands of loaves of bread distributed by the Chicago Union to the suffering multitudes;—a 'can social,' held by a Methodist society of Philadelphia, to gather canned goods for the poor;—twenty-one barrels of provisions given away by a Disciples society of Cleveland."

The following are a few of the odd committees found in some societies, each one of which tells of the consecrated ingenuity and the resourceful devotion of young Christians in finding some new and useful form of service for the Master:

"A Messenger Committee, to run errands for the officers.—A 'Whatsoever Committee,' made up of all members without an office, to do everything that does not fall within the province of some other committee.—A Seating Committee, to get the members to sit up front.—A Pause Committee, to fill up pauses in the prayer-meeting.—An Improvement Committee, to suggest improvements to the society.—A Mid-week Prayer-meeting Committee, to interest members in the mid-week prayer-meeting.—A Thread and Needle Committee, to do sewing for the poor."

To go a little more into detail in regard to some of these efforts, we might take, by way of example, the Sunday Breakfast Association. The first association of this kind, if I am not mistaken, was formed in Philadelphia, and has done a grand work.

During six months, 1894-95, there were 323 meetings held, with an attendance of 91,903 persons, of whom 44,233 received a charitable meal, making a total of meals served during the sixteen and a half years of 496,337.

There were consumed 83,400 rolls, 104,608 rusk, 1,442 pounds of pressed corned beef, 1,444 pounds of coffee, 1,531 pounds sugar, and 1,716 quarts milk. There were made from the above corned beef and rolls 83,400 sandwiches.

One thousand one hundred and fifty-six persons signed the Temperance Pledge, making a total of signers to date of 31,011.

During the winter 5,222 were forward for prayer, asking God to pardon their sins, and seeking human help and sympathy in their efforts to lead a new and upright life.

During the breakfast season, meetings are held every night except Saturday, which is occupied in preparing the food.

The Wilmington (Del.) Endeavorers also have made a specialty of this form of service. Let me give the account of this blessed charity in the words of one of the foremost workers, Mr. J. H. Burns:

"The Sunday Breakfast Association," he says, "is a work undertaken and carried on by the Wilmington Christian Endeavor Union among destitute men to save souls and bodies. It was formally opened on the first Sunday of December, 1893.

"The original idea was to serve a breakfast to destitute, dilapidated, unfortunate men, such as are accustomed to spend the previous night in the very poor accommodations of the City Hall, in freight cars, in stables, or anywhere they can sleep, and to hold a gospel meeting as soon as the meal was partaken of.

"At the first breakfast, served Sunday morning, December 3, 1893, fifty-four poor, rough-looking, begrimed, dilapidated mortals gathered in the rooms provided for this purpose. In the gospel meeting, held immediately at the close of serving breakfast, there were twenty-six requests for prayer—and thus were we encouraged at the very beginning.

"After the work had been continued for a short time it was decided that the whole house wherein the breakfasts were served and gospel meetings were held should be rented and converted into a lodging-house to accommodate the redeemed men and to save them from their old life, habits, and associations. This was done, and the men were lodged at a cost of ten cents each to them. Later it was decided to provide meals for them in the house, and this was also done at a cost to the men of ten cents per meal. These ways of working proved very successful. Week-night meetings were soon inaugurated, and a sitting-room, with suitable reading matter, was provided at an early date.

REV. J. LESTER WELLS.

"During the summer months a gospel wagon was started, and, instead of breakfast, a tea was served on the return of the gospel wagon to the building. After tea had been served an evening service was conducted, with good results.

"When the cooler months returned the breakfasts were resumed and the teas were continued until now. Two meals are served each Sunday. A Bible school is conducted every Sunday afternoon.

"During the first year more than two thousand men were fed and had the gospel preached to them, not including those who heard it from the gospel wagon. During this time there were over five hundred requests for prayer and two hundred and thirty-five professed conversions.

"An industrial department has been added to the work, which has proved very successful and most helpful. A word as to the kind of men who come to the mission, and why they are there, may be of interest. They are from about every station in life. Men from the highest circles of society, of the finest education; one was familiar with seven languages; one had been the district attorney of Edinburgh, Scotland; one had studied for the ministry—besides lawyers, mechanics, laboring men; men of every profession and trade, and men of no occupation. Nearly every nationality in the United States has been represented.

"The association is organized by selecting two representatives from each Society of Christian Endeavor in the local union for the first twenty-five, and one for each additional twenty-five active members in each society. These representatives act as a committee of the local union, organize, elect their own officers, and appoint their own committees. Representatives serve for six months, and may be selected again. This work is in the direct line of good citizenship, and our local union of Christian Endeavor received a diploma at the Cleveland Convention on the strength of this work."

Another very useful work is that which is carried on among the Life Savers, which has been alluded to in another chapter. The secretary of the work, Rev. J. Lester Wells, thus reported concerning it at the Cleveland Convention:

"It was found that the wages of the life-saving crews were small; and among the first steps was one securing an increase in their stipend. Rev. S. Edward Young interceded with Congress, and secured better wages for their valuable service. We then issued a circular to Christian Endeavor Societies, especially to those adjacent to the stations, stating that as 'the surfmen were debarred throughout a larger portion of the year by the isolation of their lonely tasks, from home and religious influences, they, in general, would appreciate services of song and prayer, and that there was no organization that could take charge of the matter so effectively as the Christian Endeavor Societies. It was recommended that local unions along the ocean and lake fronts arrange monthly visits to the stations within their bounds, always remembering that the men are engaged in a work too important for subordination to the convenience of any individual or society.' It was also recommended that it would be well to confer by letter or in person with the keeper of each station regarding the most convenient hour for himself and the crew, with the understanding that stormy weather annuls the appointment, and the representatives have a general oversight of the religious meetings at the stations, in their districts.

"The Christian Endeavorers were also invited to send comfort bags, books, magazines, papers, leaflets, woolen wristlets—called pulse warmers by the crews—mufflers, mits, socks, yarn caps, and the like. In the comfort bags, which are made of strong ticking 12x14 inches, with a string shirred in at the top, so as to open and close

REV. S. EDWARD YOUNG.

at will, may be put buttons, needles, thread of different sizes, pocket scissors, knife, bandages, small bunch of white cotton, court and sticking plaster, coarse and fine combs, brush, pair of woolen wristlets, tooth-brush, automatic pencil, box of letter paper and envelopes, safety pins, a package of story leaflets, a Testament, and a bright cheery letter, written to the recipient. Anything may be put in the bag that will comfort the surfman, who daily hazards his life, far away from home, mother, and sister; or the lighthouse-keeper, upon whom ships freighted with precious lives depend for safety.

"In coming into communication with the societies I took immediate steps to come into correspondence with the stations and lighthouse-keepers, and so forwarded a circular with blanks, for answers to a few questions, stating in the prelude that the Christian Endeavor Societies, now representing two millions of young people, desired to give help and good cheer to the brave men of the life-saving stations, and would be glad if they would fill out the blanks and return answers to such questions as would inform us as to what could be done for their spiritual, physical, and intellectual good.

"It is gratifying to record that the most cordial letters with answers came from the keepers, and grateful thanks expressed to Christian Endeavorers for their kindly interest. Letters poured in by the hundreds from societies, inquiring concerning the work, and volunteering to help the life savers. As soon as possible I put the societies into communication with the stations in such a way as to distribute the help as equally as possible. Through the recommendations at Washington, comfort bags for the lighthouses and light-ships are sent through the inspectors of the different divisions in the United States. In the Dominion of Canada a similar arrangement has been made.

"It is impossible to record in detail the results of this noble work. In fact, the work is too new to look for large returns; and yet we have facts sufficient to show that the cause moves grandly on, and that it has the hearty interest of the United Society of Christian Endeavor. Of all the crews heard from only three thought it best not to hold meetings in their stations, and their reasons were considered satisfactory. Fifty-three stations the first year had regular services, two Sabbath-schools and one church organized. One station reported two meetings in two years and another only one in six years, and would be thankful for them every week. Some of the stations being in or near villages, the surfmen attend church there. Earnest efforts have been made along this line, and the workers in one instance went fourteen miles in a row-boat to hold services in a station.

"In the reports from the keepers the general feeling expressed is delight at the thought of having the Endeavorers come to them in songs and prayer, and cordially accept their thanks for all such visits. A large number of stations are almost inaccessible, owing to the fact that they are located so far away from any settlements; but the men appreciate the spirit of the young people in desiring to cheer and bless them. Owing to the trying times of the crews in severe weather, the young people have not been unmindful of their physical comfort. Four hundred and twenty-three comfort bags have been furnished and received with gratitude by the crews."

Another most useful practical work has been originated by Rev. G. F. Love, of Rochester, N. Y., whose heart was stirred by the fact that so many young men and women from the country are thrown among evil companions and get into evil ways almost unconsciously because of their surroundings, necessary surroundings, too, since they are obliged to take up their abode in furnished-room blocks, where they are at the mercy of unscrupulous human sharks, because suitable homes were not open to them when they arrived in the city.

Under his leadership, the Rochester Endeavorers are arranging to rectify this evil. They are arranging to establish a church boarding-house bureau, to be made a part of the work of all the city unions in the State, by which all church members who may be willing to take young men or young women into their homes are recorded at a central bureau. Communication is to be established with country pastors and societies, and whenever a young person leaves home for the city, his or her name is sent to the central committee, which at once sees that a home is provided the newcomer with a family of his own denomination.

As this work is proved to be practicable by the Rochester societies it will, undoubtedly, be taken up by other unions throughout the country, and a very great gain may be expected for the moral and the material comfort, as well, of a multitude of young strangers in our great cities.

Our chapter on this subject has already reached its full limit, but I cannot bring it to a close without speaking of the special forward movement by the Essex County local union of New Jersey. Under the leadership of the president of the union, who is also president of the New Jersey Union, Rev. J. Clement French, D. D., Rev. Ford C. Ottman inaugurated a most extensive and successful evangelistic work, which the Endeavorers were foremost in carrying out. As a result of the work it was found that 893 people professed conversion, and the church preferences of almost every one was obtained so that they might be followed up in the future.

The systematic way in which the work was undertaken in New Jersey will be seen from the following description of the usher committee and the music department:

"The work of this committee was undertaken with the thought in mind that the evangelist would be seriously hampered in his efforts, unless he could depend upon the ushers to approach each person with tact and sympathy, when the invitation was extended to the unconverted. In view of this a picked body of seventy personal workers was selected from the various societies, and additions were made to the list from time to time. To illustrate the methods pursued it is only necessary to describe the plans adopted in the first series of meetings which was held in the First Presbyterian Church, Newark. This church contains three aisles on the main floor and two large galleries extending the length of the building. The arrangement decided upon called for one usher to each forty persons in the audience, of eight men to each aisle and gallery. The entire body of seventy ushers, however, was assigned (fourteen to each aisle) so there could be no misunderstanding, and also to ensure having the requisite number every evening. A head usher and ten assistants were appointed, two of the latter in charge of each aisle, and if more than eight reported for duty those who were not needed were scattered through the pews to do personal work as opportunity offered. A room was set apart as an ushers' headquarters, and badges, acknowledgment cards and pencils were handed to each one as he entered. A record of attendance according to aisles was also kept on a large sheet, so the committee could tell at a glance whether the church was properly manned.

"Great stress was laid upon the ushers' prayer-meeting, held at seven o'clock each night, as from this service the men went to their stations with the consciousness of the presence of the Holy Spirit. Each usher had six or seven pews to look after, and, as soon as these were filled, he took his seat in the outer end of the pew of his block, where he remained until the distribution of cards was called for.

"In the organization of the choir for the evangelistic meetings we wrote to a member in each society asking for the names and addresses of such members as could read music and such as were accustomed to sing in choir or chorus, who would be willing to join the choir and pledge their regular attendance. In reply to these inquiries we received from two hundred and fifty to three hundred names, and a notice of our intention to form a choir, and of a preliminary rehearsal, was sent to each of these persons whose names were so received. On one of the stormiest nights of the winter we had our first rehearsal at South Park Church, with an attendance of nearly one hundred and fifty. Our average attendance in the choir at the first series of meetings held was about two hundred. We found for the most part that our Endeavorers were willing and glad to assist, and were faithful and constant in attendance and service. For the meetings at Bloomfield and Franklin we relied entirely upon local assistance, and it was cordially and enthusiastically given. In all our meetings the members of the choir have, at sacrifice to themselves, cheerfully and continuously given their assistance. A number of the members attended all of the series held in Newark, and from their efficiency and understanding of what was required, rendered valuable and effective service."

Many other local unions and county unions have done efficient work along the same general lines, though always it is understood, of course, that the full consent and approval of pastors and churches is obtained before any such work is undertaken. This approval of the churches is such an essential prerequisite to any such work, that I trust it will never be overlooked. Because the societies are subordinate and constituent parts of the churches, the State Unions very properly do not raise money for missionary schemes of their own, but use all their influence to fill the treasuries and enlarge the resources of the respective churches with which the societies are connected. Thus loyalty and fidelity are promoted as well as fellowship, and the State Unions are constantly producing more blessed results.

A GROUP OF ENGLISH WORKERS.

This picture will be full of interest to all our readers, for it shows the Council of the London Christian Endeavor Union, as they met—not quite all of them—in the garden of Mr. Charles Waters, the honorary secretary of the British Council. Dr. Clark is in the centre of the picture. Upon his right is the well-known writer, Rev. F. B. Meyer, who is the President of the London Christian Endeavor Union. Upon his right is Mr. Waters, the Chairman, renowned in Sunday-school labors, while upon Dr. Clark's left are the two secretaries. The three ladies at the back are the wife and daughters of Mr. Waters. This is the company of Endeavorers that has already accomplished such wonders for the cause of Christian Endeavor in the metropolis of the world, and is planning still more glorious things for the future.

CHAPTER LVIII.

CHRISTIAN ENDEAVOR IN EUROPE AND AUSTRALIA.

The Story as Told By the Workers Themselves—Early Days and Early Ways in Great Britain —The British Birthplace of the Society—A Christian Endeavor County—The Influence of "Pansy"—The First Christian Endeavorer of Great Britain—The Pathetic Letter From His Death-Bed—The Advance of Christian Endeavor in the Land of the Covenant— Progress in Ireland—Fitted to the Welsh Character—Beginnings in France—Great Advance of Recent Years—The Action of the General Synod—How the Work Began in Germany—Interesting Meetings in Berlin—Fitted to Hungary and Its Needs— Christian Endeavor in Spain—In Switzerland—Mrs. Gulick's Interesting Account—The Wonderful Advance in Australia—Endeavorers Under the Southern Cross—The Welcome to Endeavor in the Land of the Kangaroo.

IN another chapter some "glimpses" of Endeavorers and Endeavor societies in foreign lands have been given, but in this chapter and the succeeding ones those who have been most prominently identified with the movement in other lands than America tell their own story. I regret that these stories are sometimes necessarily fragmentary and incomplete. The fact is that the beginning of the society in many countries, as indeed it was in America, was such an inconspicuous and unheralded event that the earliest history has somewhat faded into obscurity.

However, Christian Endeavor in every land is making history, and future editions of this book can be supplemented with a larger and fuller account of the growth of the work. If disproportionate space seems to be given to some countries with few societies, and comparatively little to others with

REV. W. KNIGHT CHAPLIN,
Honorary Secretary British National Council.

more societies, it is because the accounts I have been able to obtain have sometimes been meagre and sometimes voluminous. I have thought it best that the workers in these lands should tell their own story, so far as possible. This chapter is devoted to a brief history of the movement in Europe and Australia, the Antipodes being thus brought together because I have felt that the wonderful advance in Australia among the peoples who speak our common mother tongue should be recorded in the same chapter which tells of the advance of the work in the mother country itself.

CHRISTIAN ENDEAVOR IN GREAT BRITAIN.

In other chapters of this volume considerable space has been devoted to the movement in the United Kingdom of Great Britain and Ireland, as I have seen it on the occasion of various visits to the mother country. In this brief account of the work, which of late years has taken on such large proportions, it is altogether fitting that the story of the early days in Great Britain should be told by Rev. Joseph B. Morgan, a prominent Baptist pastor of Chester, one of the earliest friends of the movement, conversant with the society from the first, and from the beginning a member of the Council of the British Section of Christian Endeavor Societies.

EARLY DAYS OF CHRISTIAN ENDEAVOR IN GREAT BRITAIN.
By Rev. Joseph B. Morgan.

America has sent England many good things, but certainly nothing better than Christian Endeavor. It took seven years for it to reach the old country. A prairie fire pauses at a river, and appears about to stop, but a breeze comes along that blows over a spark to the other side, and again it pursues its fiery course over wide-rolling plains. So it was with this fire of diviner glow and more benign influence. It paused seven years at the deep Atlantic, but a divine break wafted it to Britain's shores, and its career on this side has been as phenomenal as in the United States. To change the figure, it has found soil here quite as congenial to its development as in its first home. One of the most wonderful features of the movement is its remarkable adaptability. It is not confined by race or language. Granted evangelical principles, and you have suitable soil in which to plant a Christian Endeavor society.

It is not certain where the first British society called by the Endeavor name was started. Claims have been made in more than one quarter. Rev. Stanley Rogers, of Liverpool, a consistent friend of the movement, was possibly the very first, and there was at least one society in Glasgow in 1887. But even if some other city may claim to be the Bethlehem, Crewe is the Nazareth, and as the Saviour is called, not Jesus of Bethlehem, but Jesus of Nazareth, so to Crewe is due the honor of title town. There the society registered as "No. 1, British section," was formed; from Crewe as a centre it began to spread. It is in the truest sense the birthplace of the movement. It is the Mecca of British Endeavor, and the man to whom, above all other Englishmen, we are indebted for the insight that recognized its value, and for the determination and tact that brought it to the front, is, without doubt, the late Arthur Wilkinson Potts, pastor of Hightown Congregational Church, Crewe. The real beginning was the meeting that Dr. Clark addressed in Mr. Potts's church in 1888. How much the young people of Britain owe to that meeting!

It is difficult to trace the connection between place and place in the early stages of the movement. As in Macaulay's *Armada*, one sees the "twinkling points of fire" here and there, but the relationship of these beacon signals to one another is not easy to discover. Among the first fifty societies one finds Birmingham, Bristol, Balup, Bromley, Bollengton, Bridgenorth (these must have been the busy B's), Devonport, Portsmouth, London. Some of these are no doubt to be attributed directly to Mr. Potts's personal advocacy of the movement, as well as more indirectly through his speeches at Congregational association and Union meetings. One county seems, however, to stand out before the rest, and that is Mr. Potts's own county of Cheshire; and the old city of Chester was one of the early places to give the movement an enthusiastic welcome. Society No. 38 was formed in Grosvenor Park Baptist Church, and as a result of six years' work all the Nonconformist churches of the city, with one or two exceptions, have their Christian Endeavor organizations in full working order.

It may safely be said that the early workers in Christian Endeavor in Britain, like the founder of the movement, had small idea of its future. In wildest visions they did not dream whereunto this thing would grow. Probably the attitude of the majority might be set forth in the words, "It is worth trying as an experiment." They thought they saw good in it, as they certainly saw the need for some society, working on spiritual lines, to lay hold of the young people. But they certainly did not see all it meant to the churches. It took from 1887 to 1891 to gather 120 societies.

A great impetus was given to Christian Endeavor in Britain by the first convention, held in Crewe May 13, 1891. From that time, in a new sense, it became a national movement—a movement with cohesion, with organization. The Crewe Convention seems a small thing to look back upon—a hundred or so delegates, an audience of three hundred to four hundred. But in reality it was great—great in its possibilities, its promise, its outlook. In the circular announcing the meeting, signed in behalf of Society No. 1, by A. W. Potts and I. R. Jones, these words occur: "In arranging the program we have selected subjects which belong to the very foundations of our work, in the hope that at future conferences we may be able to build thereon securely and successfully." It was a memorable gathering, full of hope, possessing all the charm of novelty. Dr. Clark and Rev. C. A. Dickenson received an ovation. The young people were full of enthusiasm, and hungry for the best things. The highest calls were those most eagerly caught up and responded to. We were sure then with a holy certainty that Christian Endeavor had come to stay and grow.

During the year that followed inquiries poured in upon those that had taken part in the Crewe Convention, and the energies of willing workers were taxed to the utmost to tell the story, state the principles, and explain the methods of the Young People's Society Christian Endeavor. It was recognized that here was a force that must be reckoned with. The voice of the critic was heard in the land. The note of interrogation was in evidence. Rev. Hugh Price Hughes has said: "Every new movement passes through three stages—the pooh-pooh stage, the bow-wow stage, and the hear-hear stage." Christian Endeavor in 1891-1892 had a taste of all three. Slow-going Britishers objected to be taken by storm by this American bantling. Could the child teach the mother? But for the most part the reception was encouraging, cordial, if not enthusiastic. There was that great gap between School and Church, the perennial theme of conference discussions. It could not be blinked. If this new thing could do anything to occupy that ground efficiently, why come, and well-come. And it came and spread, the registered societies more than doubled in the year, and many others were known to be in existence that had not affiliated.

The Second Convention was held in Pepper Street Church, Chester, May 24-25, 1892. Dr. Clark was missed, but sent a stirring greeting to the meeting. Rev. A. W. Potts was lying "sick unto death," but from his bed of suffering sent a most cheering, inspiring letter. These vacant places could not quite be filled, but the presence of Mr. Ira T. Sankey gave the gatherings a public interest that they might not otherwise have commanded. From first to last there was a great wave of enthusiasm, full of high tone, aglow with consecrated purpose. Certain incidents of this convention stand out ineffaceably. One was the reading of the letter from Rev. A. W. Potts. It is surely worth producing here:

CREWE, May 23, 1892.

DEAR MR. MORGAN:

I write you as Chairman of Committee to express my deep regret in not being able to be present at the Second Annual Convention of the Young People's Society Christian Endeavor. The coincidence that the poet Longfellow, the poet of the people, was born at Portland, Me., led me to read some of his poems over again, and I could not help applying a line here and there to the whole Endeavor movement. We are reminded of what activities can be set in motion by a single good thought or a single workable idea:

"Ah! what a wondrous thing it is
To note how many wheels of toil
One word, one thought, can set in motion!"

And what has the Christian Endeavor thought set in motion? And how our churches are being changed from a state of indifference into cheerful hives of Christian industry!

We hope great things from these societies, because they speak to us of loyalty, service, love. And in speaking of these three sterling qualities, let me quote briefly once again:

"Ah! how skillful grows the hand
That obeyeth love's command!
It is the heart, and not the brain,
That to the highest doth attain,
And he who follows Love's behest
Far exceedeth all the rest."

Give that its deepest meaning, and put it on the highest plane, and no Endeavorer will ever want inspiration or incentive to life's noblest work. With kindly greetings, and with prayer for the success of the convention, and the whole of the far-reaching movement everywhere.

Yours very sincerely,

A. W. POTTS.

Mr. Potts lived to hear what a splendid success the meeting had been, and two days afterward, on May 26, passed to his rest. The closing consecration service of the Chester Convention was a never-to-be-forgotten experience. It was conducted by Rev. John Williams. The final appeal for decision and consecration had a most thrilling effect. "On His head be the crown," said the leader. A loud "Amen" came from the assembled hundreds. "On His shoulders be the government," said Mr. Williams. Again the loud response, "Amen." Once more, "In His hands be the sceptre," and once more the fervent, full-throated, full-hearted, "Amen" from the great audience; and with "God be with you," and the "Mizpah" the Convention melted into the past, but in its effects to live for many days.

The delightful reminiscences of the early days stand out very graciously in the perspective of the past. They will be a fragrant recollection through many years that are yet to come. We British Endeavorers are thankful for this movement, to Dr. Clark, to our American brothers and sisters, and, most of all, to God, from whose head we believe the movement originated, and from whom the inspiration came.

Mr. Morgan, in the above account, has dealt chiefly with the early days of the movement, and that in England alone. My space will not allow me to supplement his story at any length, but it certainly should be said in such a history as this that the cause of Christian Endeavor throughout all the United Kingdom has in these later years grown most surprisingly. Scarcely has its growth in

America been larger or more substantial. Indeed, for the last two years the banner for the largest absolute growth in the number of societies has gone to the United Kingdom, which in the year ending at Whitsuntide, 1895, added more than twelve hundred to the number of its Endeavor societies.

The conventions held in 1894, in the Metropolitan Tabernacle in London, and in 1895 in Birmingham, were remarkable gatherings and deserve whole chapters to themselves. The gathering of seven thousand young people in Birmingham for a Christian Endeavor Convention in 1895 was as remarkable in its way for England as the gathering of fifty thousand in Boston a little later in the same year.

Though England is the mother of Christian Endeavor in the United Kingdom, and is still the "predominant partner," the society is by no means confined to the country south of the Tweed and east of St. George's Channel; for in

SCOTCH NATIONAL COUNCIL.

Ireland, Scotland, and Wales, within the last few months, as remarkable advance has been made in Christian Endeavor as in England itself. It has been my great pleasure to attend enthusiastic Christian Endeavor rallies in Dublin and Belfast, in Glasgow and Edinburgh, in Rhyll in North Wales, and Cardiff in South

Wales, and in all these places I have found among Scotch and Irish and Welsh Endeavorers the same spirit, the same devotion to the leading principles of Christian Endeavor, the same blessed fellowship, and the same generous enthusiasm for Christ and the Church.

There are at this writing scores of societies in Ireland, two hundred or more in Scotland, and rapidly increasing hosts of Endeavorers in Wales.

In the land of Covenants Christian Endeavor seems to be entirely at home now that its principles and its pledge are fully understood.

The Scotch Convention, held in the spring of 1895, in Glasgow, was one of the most remarkable gatherings ever held in numbers, in the quality of the addresses given and its spiritual power.

The Irish National Convention, recently held, also was of very great value to the cause. All Protestant denominations throughout the Emerald Isle are represented in this work. The Wesleyan Methodists particularly, before whom the question recently came, distinctly and emphatically, "Shall we adopt the Christian Endeavor Society or the Epworth League?" decided heartily for Christian Endeavor.

The society seems to be peculiarly fitted, so I have frequently been told by Welshmen themselves, to the genius of the Welsh nation. The constitution has been translated into this consonantal language, and the future growth will doubtless be more rapid than the past has been. All these societies have now been happily united in the British Christian Endeavor Union, whose council is made up of representatives from different parts of the United Kingdom. This organization, I believe, will do much toward cementing the bonds of fellowship between Christian Endeavorers throughout Great Britain and toward promoting the work in all parts of the United Kingdom.

CHRISTIAN ENDEAVOR IN FRANCE.

Concerning the beginnings of Christian Endeavor in France, Rev. Charles E. Greig, of the McAll Mission, Paris, wrote as follows, some two or three years since: "In the *Golden Rule* for September 1, it is stated that, so far as the United Society knows, there are no Christian Endeavor societies in France. In 1888 my attention was directed to the phrase 'Christian Endeavor,' which I sometimes met in religious papers, and I said to a fellow-worker, 'Something like that is what we need.'

"Just then Dr. Clark looked in on us at the Sunday-school in our Faubourg St. Antoine mission hall, and explained to me fully about the American work. I explained to him the state of affairs in the French churches, and the difference in the customs of society, but asked him to send me literature. From the study of the papers he sent grew a little book, '*Sociétie d'Activite Chretienne Status.*'

"Any work of the nature of the Christian Endeavor movement will be hampered in France by the numerical inferiority of the Protestants (about 800,000, as against 37,000,000 Catholics) and by the customs of society. Even in Protestant centres, such as Nimes, and still more in Paris, you will not get any appreciable number of young people all living within a reasonable distance of a Protestant church of which they are members.

"Then, those who have to earn their bread are seldom free before 8.30 P. M., owing to the late hours at which workshops, etc., close, and those who belong to the more leisurely classes never go out at night, except under their parents' protection.

"A work so similar to that of the Christian Endeavor societies, that in the case of one of ours the two have merged together, is that of the Mission Interieure, the members of whose groups bind themselves to work actively for Christ and to stir up the apathy of those who surround them. A groupe de la Mission Intérieure, however, instead of being co-extensive with some individual church, is generally composed of members drawn from several, so that its effort is less concentrated."

Since the above was written the work has advanced greatly in France. There are at this writing, July, 1895, fully fifty Endeavor societies. The General Synod of the French Protestant churches has given much encouragement to the movement, and many French Endeavorers have been enlisted. Especially has Rev. Jean Sequestra, by his pen and his voice, not only in France, but in Switzerland as well, done much to advance the cause he loves.

CHRISTIAN ENDEAVOR IN GERMANY.
Translated from the German of Rev. Frederich Blecher.

Slow but sure, that is usually the way that new religious movements, which have become well known among you, are introduced here in Germany. Especially is this true of everything in the domain of the church and religion. Particularly when it comes from America, it is sure to be viewed with distrust in Germany. Like a Nathaniel, who said, "Can any good thing come out of Nazareth?" so many in Germany ask, "Can any good thing come from America?" Yet, at last, they realize its value. So was it with the temperance and Sabbath-school movements, and so it is with Christian Endeavor.

Through the writings of Pastor Berner, of Buffalo, N. Y., a theological student named Blecher, who in 1893 was Secretary of a young people's organization in Berlin, heard of the Christian Endeavor movement. He spoke of it to several pastors and friends, but they paid little attention and showed still less sympathy with it. "Quite good, but American," was the usual answer.

After Herr Blecher gave up his position in Berlin and became assistant pastor at Bielefeld, he published articles on Christian Endeavor in several religious, political, and Sabbath-school papers, in order to draw universal attention. In May, 1894, in the German *Evangelical Christian Times*, published by Hof Prediger Stöcker, a lengthy article appeared, called "Something that is Needed in Germany also." In June, in the Sunday-school paper for home missions, Director Engelbert Duisberg, at the head of home missions in Germany, published an article, and in July another article was published in the *Christian Monthly*, but no one appeared to be particularly interested.

REV. FREDERICH BLECHER.

At last, through the news of the Cleveland Convention in several of the papers, a few friends were won to the cause, who earnestly studied the Christian Endeavor literature.

Then it suddenly became known that Dr. Clark, his health having become impaired on account of overwork, was traveling in Switzerland to seek renewed health and strength. This opportunity of having the very man among us whom God had chosen as the leader of Christian Endeavor came to us in such an unexpected manner that we recognized the hand of God in it. The necessary preparations were quickly made and the following meetings, held: November 8, in Dresden; November 9, in Leipzig, and November 12, in the Young Men's Christian Association building in Berlin, which was very well attended. Herr Baron Rothkirch led this meeting and Herr Count Bernstorff interpreted.

Special interest was felt in a letter from Pastor Monod, of Paris, just received, in which he spoke of the great value of Christian Endeavor in the churches of France, and said that the local and General Synod had recommended the Christian Endeavor to all the churches.

On the 13th of November Dr. Clark was invited to Liegnitz by the Provincial Society for Home Missions in Silesia. Also the Young Men's Christian Association of Frankfort and Wiesbaden invited him to Frankfort-on-the-Main November 15, where two meetings were held. Unfortunately Dr. Clark had not time enough to allow him to accept further invitations from Baron von Gerningen at Gernsbach, Fräulein Romele at Freiberg, and the Young Men's Christian Association at Hamburg. Upon his return journey the friends at Berlin took the opportunity to appoint one more meeting.

At the first Christian Endeavor Convention in Germany Dr. Clark spoke on the two foundation principles of Christian Endeavor, and its practical value in Germany was emphasized by Rev. Mr. Haynes, from Yale University; Pastor Franklin, from Buffalo; Dr. Libby, of Portland, who was a member of the

FIRST ANNUAL CONVENTION, GLASGOW, SCOTLAND, 1895. PUBLIC MEETING IN GRAND HALL.
(Plate made in Scotland.)

first society in 1881. From that time people have gone on from talking to doing, until in April, 1895, there were sixteen societies in existence.

There may perhaps be fifty societies altogether in 1895. We Germans should call Christian Endeavor in our language "Christliche Entschiedenheit" (Christian Decision), for there is also need for Christian Endeavor here in Germany. It has been considered carefully on all sides. It has been investigated with almost microscopic exactness, and we praise the fruit of the Christian Endeavor tree, and we would be glad to have it planted here in Germany also. But we still wish to watch it a little more and examine the stem and look into the ground for the roots and inquire how it is nourished and strengthened.

Yet it is being introduced more and more, and still more frequently is heard the remark, "What I have long sought, have I at last found in Christian Endeavor." There is no region in Germany, Austria, Hungary, and even to Bukowina, where Christian Endeavor has not been heard of. So much is certain, and we hope to report larger things in future days.

CHRISTIAN ENDEAVOR IN HUNGARY.

The following extracts from a letter written by Rev. Theodore Biberauer, of Budapest, tells how the work has begun in the land of Kossuth. "I am very deeply interested," writes this earnest worker, "in the new movement of Christian Endeavor, and I am convinced that it will answer a great need in our Church, for it is admirably adapted to develop the spiritual life of our members. My son, a student of theology in Berlin, became the first Hungarian member of the Christian Endeavor Society in that city, and wrote a very interesting article about Dr. Clark's address at the Young Men's Christian Association in November of 1894.

"My son-in-law, Dr. A. Szabo, Professor of Theology of Budapest, takes likewise a peculiar interest in the Christian Endeavor work, and has published in two Hungarian religious periodicals articles about it, and communicates the subjects for the prayer-meetings every month to a journal for home missions. One result of this was that a pastor in a little country congregation in Nagy Kikinda resolved to begin a society on the basis of the model constitution. He gathered seven young people of both sexes in the first Hungarian Endeavor Society. May God speed it for His service. The Lord grant in His mercy that these may be the first rays of a rising sun for our poor land."

CHRISTIAN ENDEAVOR IN SWITZERLAND.

In another chapter a very pleasant meeting with a Swiss Endeavor Society of three sisters, English girls, living in Lausanne, has been alluded to. The President of this society, Miss Jessie M. Murray, who is also the Asssistant Superintendent of Christian Endeavor for Switzerland, shall tell the brief story of Christian Endeavor in Switzerland in her own words :

REV. M. C. JACCARD, LAUSANNE.
Superintendent in Switzerland.

"There are two distinct branches of Christian Endeavor in Switzerland, one among the Swiss themselves, the other among the large colonies of Americans and Anglo-Saxons in general who come to Switzerland. Of course these two branches will intertwine and overlap to some extent, but they are distinct in the main ; and, if you remember this, you will be able to take a much more intelligent interest in our growth than you otherwise could.

"The Anglo-Saxon branch promises to be the hardest to work, since the American and British population is continually changing, very few remaining more than a year at a time. Our great hope for these societies is that they will have continual reinforcement from the ranks of those that have already been Endeavorers in America, Canada, and the British Isles.

"The Swiss branch, called, as in France, the *Societe d' Activite Chretienne*, does not present the same difficulties, and we have hopes of its speedy growth into a great means of leading the young people of Switzerland to the Lord Jesus, and into the churches.

"At this point I want to introduce to you the man who has been raised up by God to direct and superintend the Swiss work, M. Jaccard, a minister of the *Eglise libre* (Free Church), and a man of deep spirituality and great zeal. I do not think that a more suitable man could have been found in all Lausanne. He has already done an immense amount toward making the society known in the French-speaking cantons; but you will hear more about him and his work soon, I hope. This is the time of sowing, so it is too soon to speak of results; but the first fruits are already being gathered, and formed into the first really Swiss *Societe d' Activite Chretienne*, in connection with the Swiss Methodist Church in Lausanne, the *Chapelle du Valentin*.

"Let me tell you one thing more. About two years ago, a young American girl, an Endeavorer, who had come from New York to study French in Lausanne, asked me whether there was a society of Christian Endeavor here. From that simple question has grown the present work. We cannot often trace the effects produced by what we thus say and do, but we do need to believe and to remember that our most trivial words and deeds are graven for eternity in the results that they produce, whether for good or evil, and that, if Christ is really working in us, He may often accomplish the greatest results when we are least conscious of doing any distinct work for Him."

GENERAL VIEW OF LAUSANNE, THE HEADQUARTERS OF CHRISTIAN ENDEAVOR IN SWITZERLAND.

Since this was written genuine progress has been made. Rev. Jean Sequestra, that devoted Endeavorer of France, has been to Lausanne, where he made a very helpful address and aroused much interest in the cause.

Several societies have been discovered in Switzerland whose existence was before unknown, much literature has been distributed, especially in French Switzerland, and there is promise of a most substantial work throughout this staunch little Republic.

CHRISTIAN ENDEAVOR IN SPAIN.

By Mrs. Alice Gordon Gulick.

Many years ago, I do not remember the date, a little society was formed among the girls in the boarding-school in San Sebastian for Christian Endeavor. We did not then know of the young society in America bearing that name.

The girls chose the name, *Hijas Leales*—Loyal Daughters. They had their meetings, in which all took part, and as there was very little money in their pockets they decided to give up some of the food they would otherwise have and devote the money to benevolent uses.

When we heard of the growth of the society of Christian Endeavor, and the fact that it was branching out into foreign lands, it seemed best to change the form of organization, and even the name for the sake of forming part of the great body of Endeavorers and receiving stimulus from their enthusiasm.

The society in San Sebastian, with its Junior branch, was therefore quite prepared to welcome Dr. and Mrs. Clark when, on their journey round the world, they also entered Spain. That visit was of lasting benefit. The girls realize their connection with the United Society as they could not have done otherwise.

The next society to be formed was in Madrid, under the leadership of two of the girls during vacation. That flourished for a time; but as the girls returned to school in San Sebastian, there was not enough force among the others to keep up the meetings, and after awhile they were stopped. We hope when there are some of our graduates permanently here, that a flourishing society may be formed.

Santander worked gradually up to a society. They held meetings and tried the temper of the young people, finally deciding to organize into a society. This has been very successful. The pastor writes to me as follows: "It is very pleasant to see various boys and young men, who have left the day-schools and whom we have not been able, hitherto, to attract to the preaching services—reached and interested and held by this new method of work among the young people. In such a community, special ways must necessarily be used to some extent; but nevertheless there is a true society of Christian Endeavor. It is delightful to see with what interest they study the Bible and sing the hymns, and take part in prayer in their meetings. Several of them have been led to attend regularly the week-day meetings of the church."

We also heard of a notable act of generosity on the part of this society. At Christmas time the Young People's Society of Christian Endeavor of Santander provided over two hundred pasteboard boxes filled with Spanish sweets for the Christmas tree of the school. Many of the young men were formerly pupils in the school, but are now employed in different ways, no one of them receiving a large salary.

We shall soon be able to report a new society, which may be already formed, by one of our graduates now teaching in Southern Spain. She has had wonderful success among a set of people utterly indifferent to religion "of any kind."

"Christian Endeavor" among the young in every city of Spain would re-create the nation and win it for Christ!

CHRISTIAN ENDEAVOR IN AUSTRALIA.

I wish that the limits of this volume allowed me to give a more extended history of the society in each of the colonies: Victoria, New South Wales, South Australia, Queensland, New Zealand, Tasmania, and West Australia. I would like to dwell upon the work of such men as Mr. George Gray, from the beginning the faithful, unwearied Secretary of the New South Wales Union; Rev. William Scott, the first President of that Union; Rev. W. J. L. Closs, the present President; Pastor Mead and his co-laborers in South Australia; Messrs. Jackson and Hitchcock and McCutcheon and Wootton, and others equally prominent in Victoria; Messrs. Scott, Buzacott, and others in Queensland, and many others in other colonies, to whose unselfish and devoted labors the cause owes more than any history can ever record. But it is true in Australia as in every other land, that many of the most deserving and most efficient workers are entirely unrecorded. Yet how little it matters to them! This history indeed would be the richer could all their names and unselfish deeds find place in it, but their work is done with no thought of record or reward. It has been its own exceeding great reward.

Some further account of their Unions and their great conventions will be found in a chapter devoted to my journey of 1892 in the colonies, and I can only add here that I know of no part of the world in which Christian Endeavor principles are better exemplified, and more earnestly and intelligently promoted than in those fair lands beneath the Southern Cross. Mr. Jackson shall tell the story in his own words:

A little haze hangs over the early days of the movement in Australia.

In 1888, in points so far apart as Brisbane and Adelaide, little bands were formed in Baptist churches bearing the (at that time) strange name of Christian Endeavor Societies.

Early in the following year branches were formed in leading Congregational churches in New South Wales and Victoria. The seed seems to have been dropped as it were from Heaven, as we can trace no connection between those four early societies, who, indeed, were not conscious of each other's existence until a considerable time had elapsed.

The new movement soon won for itself many enthusiastic and powerful advocates, and societies began to be formed with unexpected rapidity.

The leading denominations were approached, smiled blandly upon the new claimant for recognition, criticized kindly, asked many questions, waited awhile for results, and ultimately gave the Christian Endeavor cause official indorsement, and full recognition. Looking back now upon these early struggles it is pleasant to record an utter absence of unreasoning opposition. If criticism was vouchsafed it was kindly meant, and in general well deserved.

HOWARD HITCHCOCK.

The visit of Dr. and Mrs. Clark in September and October, 1892, marked a most important epoch in Australian Christian Endeavor history.

The help and inspiration they supplied cannot possibly be over-valued, and their memory will ever be kept green in Australian hearts. This memorable visit brought for the first time the leading workers of the various colonies into close touch with each other, and thus established that bond of unity that we now enjoy. Then, too, we began to feel conscious of our own strength, and to plan boldly great enterprises for Christ and His Church.

Our growth since then has been steady and sure. In a sparsely populated country like ours great figures cannot be expected; but to the great Endeavor host, we in Australia can at this time of writing add at least 1,500 societies, with 48,000 members.

This is by no means a small regiment, and it represents "leal hearts and true." Victoria leads with about one-third of the whole in societies and members, and the Wesleyan Methodists, as a denomination, have the largest number of societies.

In surveying the principal characteristics of Christian Endeavor work under the Southern Cross, chief place must be given to the help rendered to the missionary cause. Over fifty members of our societies are now engaged in the foreign mission field, and two at equally important work amongst the foreign element in our midst. These persons represent the cream of our workers, one chief prize being the Rev. A. R. Blacket, B. A., ex-President of the Victorian Christian Endeavor Union, and one of the ablest of Victorian churchmen, who felt constrained to go for his Master to Persia.

During the past year nearly £1,000 has been given to the various missionary treasuries by our societies, our Tasmanian friends leading with an average contribution per member of 27 cents. This is entirely apart from the usual missionary collections of the churches and Sunday-schools, to which our members fully subscribe.

A common plan adopted by societies is that they support in whole or part their own native teacher or missionary, and our missionary boards encourage this.

Of late an earnest and most successful effort has been made to secure the systematic *study* (not *reading*) of the Bible by our members.

Dr. Harper's course was adopted, and now nearly two thousand of our members are earnest Bible students, and carrying out diligently and intelligently a most exacting course of study. We mean to try for five thousand next year, and we are sanguine of success in gaining that number.

We believe that Christian Endeavor is synonymous with practical Christianity, and we aim at putting into practice the ethical teaching of our Master.

All the ordinary agencies of Christian effort are well supported, and in addition new ground has been broken in every direction. It is no exaggeration to say that we are developing an advanced type of Christian worker—earnest, consecrated, and—well-trained.

The loyalty of the societies to their respective churches has ever been most pronounced.

Careful statistics have been collected by the Victorian Union for some years past bearing upon the questions of church membership. These prove that eighty per cent. of our active members are also church members, and that the church membership rolls show a constant stream of recruits from Christian Endeavor ranks.

We believe that this result will hold good right throughout Australasia.

Just a word as to our official paper. *The Golden Link* still keeps its place in the affections of its readers, and, although only three years old, enjoys the distinction of having the largest circulation of any religious paper in Australasia.

Of plans for the future we might enumerate many. The first Australian Convention (as distinct from local conventions) will be held in Adelaide in August.

This is sure to be a great series of meetings. It is intended then to start the Missionary Extension Course, familiar to American Endeavorers.

Our plans are to extend still further the benefits of individual Bible study; to supply bright new music from time to time to our societies; to face the question of efficient visitation, and to advance in every possible way extension and sound consolidation.

CHAPTER LIX.

CHRISTIAN ENDEAVOR IN ASIA AND AFRICA.

Beginnings in China—The Story as Told by One of the First Endeavorers—Great Advances in Foo Chow—A Wider Outlook by the Secretary—Constantly Increasing Success—The Work in Japan—Told by the President of the United Society for Japan—"Wherever Formed They Prove a Blessing"—Christian Endeavor in India—An Evangelistic Committee and Its Work—In Madura and the Marathi Missions—Good News from Calcutta—The Interest of the Redcoats—A Few Words from Persia—From the Land of Persecution—The Sultan's Objection to Christian Endeavor—Beginnings in Africa—Good News from Cape Colony—How Christian Endeavor Flourishes in Liberia.

IT is with great satisfaction that I present in this chapter the story of Christian Endeavor in various countries of Asia and Africa, as told by those who have been most largely instrumental in introducing and fostering the society. Sometimes these workers have been missionaries of the Cross from our own land or England. Sometimes they have been natives of the lands about which they write. In any event I am sure my readers will be interested in the simple but interesting story which these workers have to tell.

It is altogether appropriate that the story of the beginning of Christian Endeavor in China should be told by Mrs. George H. Hubbard, who with her husband was instrumental in introducing the society in China.

> We arrived in Foo Chow, November, 1884, at a time when the mission was feeling specially weak, several of its members being at home on furlough, and those here were so weary with work, and somewhat cast down with the spiritual condition of the native church.
>
> The Christians, except those in mission pay, were doing next to nothing, in a social Christian way, for the advance of the kingdom. They seemed to have no idea of a happy voluntary effort to make those about them happier and better both for this world and the world to come. No wonder that missionaries and native preachers were much discouraged.
>
> It was just at this crisis that we arrived, and were besought to help devise something, if possible, to arouse our members to active Christian work. Papers from home were reporting the good work of societies of Christian Endeavor then being rapidly formed in the States, and as Mr. Hubbard had helped in the formation of a society the year before, and had in possession a copy of Dr. Clark's little book, *The Children and the Church*, he was prepared English-wise for the work in China. But, alas! only four months in Chinese found him but a babe in speech, and that indeed was a great obstacle. But Miss Newton, one of our missionaries, who has a special gift in this Foo Chow dialect, and can turn common English into forcible, convincing Chinese, was herself full of enthusiasm, ready and eager to do everything in her power, in putting this new movement to the test.
>
> Of course there was some "cold water" thrown upon the project, and such remarks as, "You can't make those ideas work in this country," "such and such requirement or regulation is utterly contrary to

PROMINENT FOREIGN ENDEAVORERS.

1. John N. Read, first President of the first Christian Endeavor Society in South America.
2. Rev. A. R. Morgan, Yokohama, Japan.
3. W. B. McCutcheon, Melbourne, Victoria.
4. Rev. Sumantra Vishnu, Karmarkar, B. D., Bombay, India.
5. Miss Mary Reed, Tasmania, China Island Mission.
6. W. Priestnal, Secretary Jamaica Christian Endeavor Union.
7. Rev. C. E. Randall, President, Jamaica Christian Endeavor Union.
8. Rev. H. S. Jenanyan, Tarsus, Asia Minor.
9. H. E. Wootton, Melbourne.

the Chinese mind, and they won't understand it," or "that sociability and freedom of speech is against Chinese propriety," etc., all of which, as may be easily imagined, was not conducive to the new missionary's encouragement.

However, we were bound to try and see if Christian Endeavor really would fail to work in this Celestial Empire; so after much earnest prayer and planning we gathered together the church members of the Church of the Saviour, also the girls' boarding-school to present our new ideas and plans for the future.

We met first in the apartments of the new missionary.

A desire to see and hear something new brought together a goodly number for our introductory meetings, increasing with each succeeding meeting, as we urged every one to bring in one other person. The first Chinese Christian Endeavor Society was formed at Foo Chow, March 29, 1885, after several preliminary meetings had first been held to give our Christians an idea of what would be expected.

The thing "took well" from the first, much better than we had dared to hope, and ere long our first rooms were too small and we adjourned to larger quarters in the girls' boarding-school. In the course of a year or two these, too, were outgrown, and it was found expedient to adjourn to the church where the meetings have since been held. The *social* aspect of these meetings at the church has been materially helped by the manner of seating. The prim order of the regular service is broken up by arranging the seats in a semicircle, bringing the leaders down from behind the pulpit-rail on a level with the audience, and thus the distance from one to another is made as short as possible.

It was difficult to choose a name for the society, but finally decided on one which did very well for several years. It was, however, changed for a better one at the Shanghai Conference in June, 1894.

In addition to the usual two classes of members, active and associate, we formed a third class called the honorary, which took in those who would like to take the full pledge to attend regularly, but cannot on account of age, or living at such a distance, or some other unavoidable hindrance.

The members of the various committees had for a badge and reminder a little picture frame, wherein was written their instructions, and these frames were passed on to the succeeding committees at the end of six months.

It was hard, up-hill work for a long time. There was so much of lethargy to be overcome, so much preconceived ideas to be reconstructed, so much of traditional manners and customs to be set aside. It was so difficult to make them think that one sentence of true, earnest prayer is just as acceptable as scores of words, though the many words may be prayerful, too; that a number of two-minute speeches is oftentimes much more edifying than only one in the same length of time; and that an Endeavor meeting is not the place for the few to show off their possible gift of speech, but for the many to speak to the mutual encouragement of all, and the increase of zeal for the salvation of souls.

But by time, patience, and perseverance many difficulties have been overcome, and we hear no skeptical remarks now as to the practicability of Christian Endeavor methods even for the Chinese.

It was my privilege last Sunday evening to be present at the consecration meeting of the first Foo Chow Society just ten years after they organized, and my heart was filled with surprise and gratitude at the contrast between *then* and *now*. They had invited two other societies to join with them for the evening service, and the spirit of enthusiasm and Christian cordiality was very manifest.

No one was to speak over two minutes; only a few take as much time as that. There was no waiting for one another, and those who took part seemed to regard it as a pleasure to do so. One woman especially, less than two years in Christian experience, stood up, and with a face radiant with the peculiar happy light, gave testimony of how her heart was filled with joy because that very day her husband had come out boldly on the Lord's side.

Then, too, the closing act of taking up a missionary collection, the *first* from them as a Christian Endeavor Society, was very significant.

"Comparisons are odious," but I could not help thinking that this meeting in its apparent life and Christian enthusiasm, was more than equal to the majority of like meetings which I attended during our recent furlough in the Home land.

Truly, no one can doubt that the tree of Christian Endeavor has struck its roots deep into the soil of old Cathay, and that its branches are going to increase both in number and strength year by year, more slowly perhaps than in some other countries, but yet none the less surely. Long may it live in this land, as also in the whole wide world around!

Praise be to God for the Christian Endeavor movement!

CHRISTIAN ENDEAVOR IN CHINA.

1. Chinese Delegates to California State Convention, 1895.
2. Rev. W. P. Bentley, General Secretary United Society of Christian Endeavor for China.
3. Officers of the Christian Endeavor Society of the Girls' Boarding-School, Foo Chow, China.
4. Rev. and Mrs. George H. Hubbard, Foo Chow, China.
5. Chinese Christian who led the Meeting when Dr. and Mrs. Clark were in Canton.
6. Rev. J. Nevens, President of United Society of Christian Endeavor for China.
7. The Officers of Foo Chow City Society, with Rally Banner.
8. First National Christian Endeavor Convention in China (June, 1894), Native Delegates.
9. Interior of Foo Chow City Church, the home of the largest Society in China. The Students from Banyan City Scientific College also held their meetings here.
10. Mass Meeting in connection with the First National Christian Endeavor Convention in China (June, 1894).

LATER HISTORY OF CHRISTIAN ENDEAVOR IN CHINA.

BY REV. W. P. BENTLEY, GENERAL SECRETARY OF THE UNITED SOCIETY OF CHRISTIAN ENDEAVOR FOR CHINA.

Christian Endeavor work in China is believed to have begun in the city of Foo Chow in 1885. This is only four years later than the organization of the first society at Williston.

So far as reported, the first Chinaman to sign the pledge was Mr. Ling, a very earnest and gifted Christian worker, who is still a power in Endeavor work.

Other work which was successfully prosecuted before organization took place was that inaugurated by Rev. A. A. Fulton, of Canton. A man full of zeal and of the Holy Spirit, and endowed with energy and tact, he fired his people with the new idea with results the most gratifying to himself and to all lovers of the native church. His latest reports show the good work going on to still greater achievements.

At a few other points work was carried on which, while it was not "Endeavor" in name, was so in method and spirit.

The second epoch was marked by the organization of the National Society at Shanghai May 15, 1893. Rev. G. Stevens, pastor of Union Church, Shanghai, was chosen President, Rev. C. F. Reid, D. D., was chosen General Secretary. Three Corresponding Secretaries were elected respectively for North, South, and Central China: Rev. G. S. Hays, Rev. A. A. Fulton, and Miss Laura White, to whose prayerful forethought the organization was largely due.

The work of organization has gone on until at present, besides the Central Society, called "The United Society of Christian Endeavor for China," there are acting Vice-Presidents in more than half the provinces, and at least one province has a complete provincial organization. After one year Dr. Reid resigned the secretaryship, and Rev. W. P. Bentley was chosen to fill the office. There has been a Chinese Assistant Secretary since last year.

The first and only convention we have ever held was in Shanghai June 23, 24, and 25, 1894. Delegates and friends were present from a wide region. The magnitude and success of this meeting was a surprise to every one. It is not too much to say that the influence and inspiration of this convention is felt to-day to the limits of this vast Empire among the ranks of Christian workers.

This was less than one year ago. At that time the number of societies was 38, and the membership 1,069. Since then societies have been formed in Nankin and other cities for the first time, and the number added to in other places, until there are, judging from reports at hand, 50 societies and a membership of 1,300.—[There are now over 70 societies.—ED.]

We must not forget that the Christians of China are not numbered by millions, but, at the most, perhaps number 55,000.

The propagandism of Endeavor ideas is with foreigners as yet. Our aim is to get the co-operation of foreign Christian workers, through whom this work can be introduced to the native church. Success is attending the effort. Inquiries for literature and information are more numerous. We hope the day may soon come when there may be found Chinese Christians to take over the work now of necessity done by foreigners, such as the presidency and secretaryships and other offices of the United Society.

The Committee on Literature translated the topic cards, pledges, and so on, and furnishes the Christian Endeavor literature in the native tongue. This literature is in considerable and growing demand.

Splendid testimony is at hand to show the blessings which have already attended "Endeavor" efforts in this great Empire. It has already proved a valuable ally. The number of its friends is constantly increasing, and north, south, east, and west there is steady progress.

CHRISTIAN ENDEAVOR IN JAPAN.

BY REV. T. HARADA, PRESIDENT OF THE UNITED SOCIETY OF JAPAN.

The Kyoreikwai, or the Society of Christian Endeavor in Japan, is much younger than the Young Men's Christian Association. Before the visit of the President, F. E. Clark, in 1892, a few societies were organized, three of which are still in existence. Dr. Clark's coming and his inspiring addresses in several places, resulted in the formation of over thirty new societies within a year. The oldest society now in existence is the Children's Society, connected with the Church of Christ of the American Board Mission. According to the latest statistics (May, 1895) there are 57 societies, with 1,470 members, representing the

FIRST JAPANESE CONVENTION.

CHRISTIAN ENDEAVOR GIRLS KOBE SCHOOL, JAPAN.

REV. T. HARADA.

Kumiai (Congregational) Churches, with 31 societies; the Church of Christ (the Presbyterian) with 15; Methodist Protestant Church, with 4; Methodist Episcopal, with 2; the Baptist, with 2; the Christian, Episcopal, and Union Churches with 1 each.

The United Society of Japan was formed at Kobe, in 1893, when the first National Convention was held in the same place. Before the convention Mr. A. T. Hill, of American Board Mission, represented the cause in Japan. The President of the United Society at present is Rev. T. Harada.

Most of these societies are based on the model constitution of the Endeavor Society in America. They are, therefore, more uniform and orderly in their organization than the Young Men's Association.

Some churches have two organizations, one for boys and another for girls, a characteristic feature of the Japanese organization. There are also a large number of older people who are active members of Endeavor Societies. Wherever these societies have been formed they have proved the means of much good for young people themselves and for the people.

CHRISTIAN ENDEAVORERS, TOTTORI, JAPAN.

CHRISTIAN ENDEAVOR IN INDIA AND CEYLON.

I had hoped to present my readers with an account of the Endeavor movement in India, written by one who is best fitted to describe its rise and progress throughout the empire, Rev. W. I. Chamberlain, of the Reformed Church Mission of Vellore. The account, however, has not reached me in season for publication in this volume, and I shall be obliged to give a brief, and I fear, an imperfect account from my own knowledge of the work in this country.

So far as I know the first or certainly one of the first societies in India was formed in the Reformed Church mission station of Madanapalle. This society was established some five or six years ago, and is still a most active and efficient society. In my journey around the world when visiting this society, I was much impressed by its earnest evangelistic spirit and its genuine zeal for the advancement of the Kingdom. Its

CHRISTIAN ENDEAVOR IN JAPAN.

1. Takashaski Young People's Society Christian Endeavor, Okayama, Japan.
2. President Kozaki and family of the Doshishra of Kioto.
3. A Christian Endeavor Family.
4. Second Annual Japanese Convention, Osaka, 1895.
5. Christian Endeavor Hall, purchased for the Okayama Orphan Asylum.
6. Okayama Church. The audience sits on the floor.
7. Okayama Christian Endeavor Society, 1895.
8. Kobe Kindergarten, where many Christian Endeavor meetings have been held.
9. Girls' School Christian Endeavor Society, Totiori, Japan.

CHRISTIAN ENDEAVOR SOCIETY, MADANAPALLE, INDIA (THE REFORMED CHURCH MISSION).

members would frequently go out into the outlying districts to preach to their unconverted friends, would ride in third-class railway cars from station to station because there they had an opportunity to speak for Christ, and in every way showed the delightful evangelistic zeal of the earnest young convert.

At one regular meeting of the society which I attended, the evangelistic committee reported that during the previous week its members had preached the gospel to eleven hundred of their non-Christian fellow-countrymen. I believe that this zeal and earnestness is characteristic of many other societies throughout India.

Not only is the Arcot mission of the Reformed Church a centre of Christian Endeavor work, but the two missions of the American board, the society of the Congregational churches of America, the Madura and the Marathi missions, are also centres of the same sort. Many societies are connected with the missions of both these stations, which are doing a good work and are heartily encouraged and sustained by the missionaries. Some of the pleasantest memories of my world-wide journey are connected with the work in these two stations, a more detailed account of which I have given in other publications.

JAFFNA NATIVE CHRISTIAN YOUNG MEN WHO HAVE BECOME LEADERS IN CHRISTIAN ENDEAVOR IN INDIA AND CEYLON.

In Calcutta, too, there is not a little Christian Endeavor interest. The Woman's Union Missionary Society, or the Doremus Mission as it was formerly called, under the leadership of Miss S. C. Gardner has taken most kindly to Christian Endeavor, and has exemplified its working force and power among the bright and interesting girls gathered in their school.

In Northern India, too, among the Methodists in the Telugu country, where the American Baptists have had such wonderful blessings, among the missions of the English Congregationalists and Wesleyans, the work has been taken up to some extent, and many missionaries express great hope that Christian Endeavor will do not a little to solve the problem of caring for the remote and feeble out-stations where but a few Christians can be gathered together, not enough to form a church or support a missionary, but enough to form the nucleus of an Endeavor prayer-meeting and a system of Endeavor committees, to work for their fellows who have not as yet come into the light of the gospel. They also express the hope that the society will do much to bring together the Christians of India of different denominations. Surely, if such fellowship is valuable anywhere, it is doubly valuable on the mission field. It ought to be added that in the Baptist mission of Burmah, the society has been particularly successful. In Rangoon and in other stations of the mission the society is carried on most successfully, and proves in many ways its special adaptability to mission work.

One interesting phase of Christian Endeavor work in India is that among the soldiers of the British garrison, who are found in the societies, devoted and faithful in many cases, ready, amid all the distractions and difficulties of barrack life, to stand up for Jesus. I cannot mention the names of all the friends in India who have done much for Christian Endeavor. They are scattered all over the vast peninsula. They are doing their work quietly and unostentatiously, but most effectively. May their prayer, "India for Christ," be speedily answered!

In other chapters I have spoken of the society in Ceylon and of the labors of those devoted and eloquent missionaries, the Misses Mary and Margaret Leitch. Probably the first society in missionary lands, if not the first outside of America, was formed in the Jaffna mission by Miss Margaret Leitch, who also thrilled one of our great International Conventions (the one at Minneapolis) with her appeal to the missionary spirit and heroism of the Endeavorers. This early society is still in existence, and those first Tamil Endeavorers are earnest and faithful Christians, doing much good in various parts of that wonderful island, whence "blow the spicy breezes." The missionaries of the American Board of the Jaffna station have always been warm friends and supporters of the movement. It is with much sorrow that I have recently seen a cable dispatch announcing the death of Miss Mary Leitch, one of the earliest advocates of Christian Endeavor on missionary soil.

THE HAMADAN CHURCH.

CHRISTIAN ENDEAVOR IN PERSIA.

When in our brief survey of Christian Endeavor in all lands we come to the Empire of the Shah, we find that there Christian Endeavor has entered before us. Miss Annie Montgomery, of Hamadan, Persia, writes: "We have had a Junior Endeavor Society for several years, which grew out of a prayer-meeting which four little boys asked me to start for them. We had at one time fifty-five members, but now we think that they are ready for the young people's organization which has just been formed, though we still continue our Junior meetings for the boys.

"Living in Persia we can only have separate meetings for the young men and women. When I see the great tree with branches spreading to all lands in the world, and think of the tiny shoot that had just appeared the year before I left America, I am amazed, and can only say, 'What hath God wrought.' Though I have never seen a Christian Endeavor Society in America, Miss S. S. Leinbach, who is with me in the Faith Hubbard School, was a most enthusiastic member of the society in America, and decided to become a missionary at a Christian Endeavor convention."

Thus the work spreads through the faithful missionaries who receive their first inspiration through some quiet home society, and who go out to the ends of the earth with their feet thus shod with the preparation of the Gospel of Peace.

CHRISTIAN ENDEAVOR IN TURKEY.

The following account of the Christian Endeavor movement in Turkey has been prepared by Rev. G. H. Krikorian. This story, too, should be supplemented like all the rest by reports of the devotion and heroism and genuine consecration to Christ among the Christian Endeavorers in many parts of the empire of the Sultan, which our brief space does not allow us even to mention.

Among the chief hindrances of organization were the prejudice of the people and the scarcity of young people in my church. Scarcely a half-dozen of these latter were available. It distressed me greatly, but none sympathized with my "American imported ideas." They were thought to be new, impracticable, impossible, even dangerous. Beginning in the Sunday-school, first, the start of a Primary department, followed by the Infant Class, furnished us the needed material, and the simple exercises after the lesson, consisting of Scripture texts, declamations, and orations (as the interest grew week after week). Having prepared the young people for Christian activity, our success was finally crowned with the organization of a Christian Endeavor Society. This was December 9, 1889.

Soon the society became a centre of life and love in our household of faith; "the rumor thereof" brought many letters of inquiry about Christian Endeavor methods. The following spring (1890) the subject presented to the Ministers' Conference, held at Cæsarea, found such favor that, upon the urgent request of the brethren and through kind assistance of the United Society Christian Endeavor, I set about preparing a Manual, and soon found myself surrounded by peculiar difficulties. I could not translate even the name Young People's Society

CHRISTIAN ENDEAVORERS OF HAMADAN, PERSIA.

Christian Endeavor safely. "Endeavor" had a military ring in it. "Society" was prohibited by an Imperial edict. Even "Christian" could not be used, while the term "Young People" was thrice altered. Finally the title read something like "Younger People's Brotherhood of Moral Activity;" even this was suppressed by the Turkish censors.

Despite these difficulties, the work has grown and spread. Seventeen societies have been organized by personal influence, some by correspondence. One of the members said to me, one day: "Pastor, we shall beat America." We may never realize the dream of this young Galatian Endeavorer as to numbers, but the spirit and degree of consecration, it would be difficult for any society to surpass them.

Let me recall a few incidents of our work. A society was organized in one of the roughest mountain villages with twenty-five members, brought together in a mission school. There was no church, not even a settled congregation; and soon after their teacher left—for lack of funds—in the midst of severe persecution of the villagers and threats of their own parents to expel them from home if they continued their meetings. These young men not only did not give up their meetings, but, by joining hands together, they also built a meeting-house, and requested the mission to send them a teacher.

The society at Injirli, one of the most difficult ones to organize, has become one of the most aggressive. The Temperance committee succeeded in securing the pledges of most of the men in the community. Besides their regular appointments this society has undertaken to carry on missionary work in a neighboring village, workers and the means all being furnished by them.

CHRISTIAN ENDEAVOR IN ASIA AND AFRICA.

In our society at Yozgat, the missionary spirit has been an instinct. First, the ladies started to support a Bible woman. This roused the young men, who assumed a share of responsibility in our Kindergarten. The Juniors support a pupil in the Galatia High School.

As to the future of the Christian Endeavor in Turkey, my own conviction is that it is safe as long as it is closely connected with the Church—dear to the Master "as the apple of His eye." He will not suffer any harm to befall her. He who has led her through darker ages and severer trials, will *surely* protect both the mother and her child from the greedy and expectant jaws of the Dragon.

In another chapter I gave some glimpses of Christian Endeavor in the Turkish Empire. It would be a great delight, did my space allow, to picture more fully the earnest Endeavorers whom I met in Tarsus and Adana, in Talas and Cæsarea, in Adabazar and Badezag, and Constantinople. Our work in the Turkish Empire is surrounded by difficulties and dangers which are entirely unknown elsewhere. More fortitude and heroism are required to be an Endeavorer in the land of the Sultan than anywhere else in the world, and the faithful Endeavorers of this country should receive a double meed of praise. Yet it is not for the praise of man that they faithfully persist in their work amid so many difficulties, and their reward is found in no record of their achievements on earth, but in the golden record of the Lamb's Book of Life.

CHRISTIAN ENDEAVOR IN NATAL.

In the great continent of Africa Christian Endeavor has made smaller headway perhaps than in any of the other great divisions of the earth's surface, unless it be South America, but even there, though the work is new, it is far from discouraging. Rev. Charles N. Ransom, of Durban, Natal, writes: "So far as I have been able to ascertain the first stream of Christian Endeavor in South Africa began to flow in Amanzimtoti (sweet water), a mission station of the A. B. C. F. M. Here Mrs. Robbins formed a society about the year 1886, which flourished for several years, until after the death of the beloved founder.

"A society was formed in the Long Market Congregational Church of Maritzburg, August 1, 1892. Maritzburg is the capital of the colony. This society still flourishes, and is under the influence of one of the most aggressive pastors of the colony, who heartily believes in Christian Endeavor.

"Durban is a flourishing seaport town, a gate to the gold and diamonds of the interior. A society was formed in the Smith Street Congregational Church, and two of the members were grandchildren of that great martyr and missionary John Williams. Afterward two societies were formed in the Berea Presbyterian Church of Durban, a Senior and Junior. One of the members of the Senior society writes that 'their meetings were like a deep breath of fresh mountain air after the steam of the week.'

A "Far Away Endeavorer."
HELENE RULIFFSON JENANYAN, TARSUS, ASIA MINOR.

"Two societies were formed in the Berea Congregational Church also, and have been a joy to pastor and superintendent. A wide-awake aggressive society was formed last year in the Baptist Church of Durban, while the pastor of the church in Ladysmith, where both a Senior and Junior society were inaugurated some time since, writes: 'I feel that nothing lays hold of the young life and energy in the church and turns it into useful channels like the Society of Christian Endeavor.'

"And now a word as to native societies. In the one in the Amanzimtoti church the average attendance is over fifty. In the associate ranks are twenty-five Kraal girls, who have run away from home and friends and braved persecution in their endeavor to do what Christ would have them do. Another society at Umvoti is in the field where the veteran missionary Grout lived and labored."

Mr. Ransom also writes: "We have in Durban a native church formed on Christian Endeavor principles. The church members promise to read the Bible every day, or at least to hear it read, as some of them have not yet mastered any book. They promise also to pay and to endeavor to give at least one-tenth to the Lord. They are a brave little church. There is no missionary with them in Durban, and a missionary can only occasionally visit them. Natives from all parts of South Africa attend the service. At our last communion service more than 300 packed the little chapel, and as many more sat in the sands near by enjoying the overflow meeting.

"These men and boys, for there are only one or two women among the church members, have wages ranging from five to fifteen dollars a month, but the Sunday contributions now are over seven dollars a Sunday. They sustain nine preaching services every Sunday besides the service at the centre, some going five and six miles from town to preach."

Mr. J. Baptist Rose, the President of the Baptist society in Durban, Natal, writes most encouragingly of that society, saying, "The net results of six months' work are twenty active members and eighteen associates, two of the original associates having become active members. The young women meet for prayer before each weekly meeting, and the meetings which follow gather in the blessing they have sought. The papers read are usually thoughtful and edifying, and the discussion which ensues most profitable for those present. We believe that there is by these means awakening in many young hearts a desire to walk with God, while the careless are kept in check by the restraining influence of their associates. The committees, equally divided between the sexes, comprise Pastor's Help, Lookout, Prayer-Meeting, Missionary, and Flower Committee. Several members have already been scattered to carry the seed of the movement far afield."

CHRISTIAN ENDEAVOR IN CAPE COLONY.

From the great colony which embraces the southern end of the continent of Africa, comes the following account of the movement, from Miss Lucilla Sprigg, the Secretary of the Cape Colony Union. Though small in numbers, it is certainly encouraging to know that the Union is aggressive enough to have regular meetings, to support a paper, and to plan for larger work in the future:

President Baptist Y. P. S. C. E., Durban, South Africa.

"The work of Christian Endeavor in this colony has not been much known, though there have been societies in existence for a good many years. The first to start was, I believe, one in connection with the Huguenot Seminary at Wellington, where Christian Endeavor was introduced by the American ladies there. About two years ago I read Pansy's book, *Chrissy's Endeavor*, and for the first time heard of Christian Endeavor. I made inquiries of various people but could find out nothing. No one seemed to know what it was. Soon after I met Mr. David Hunter, who had just come from England and who had worked in a society there. With his help we started a society in the Dutch Reformed Church, at Rondebosch, beginning with five members. For some months we were under the impression we were the only society in the colony. After some time we heard of three others, the one at Wellington, one at King William's Town, and one at Graaff-Reinet, and each of these societies thought they were the only one in the colony. A few of us talked the matter over and thought it would be well to have some sort of union and have the societies registered. I have been in charge of this and have now nineteen societies registered. Within the last few months several societies have been formed.

"In 1893, at the Wellington Convention for the deepening of spiritual life, the Christian Endeavorers met together for half an hour, three societies being represented, and agreed to form a Union. Last year at the convention we had another meeting, seven societies being represented, and a small executive was chosen: the Rev. Andrew Murray, President; Miss Bliss and myself, the Secretary. It was also decided to start a small quarterly paper in connection with Christian Endeavor. Miss Bliss and I are joint editors. The first number came out in January, and it is called *The Golden Chain*.

"I am afraid there is not much of general interest. The work is small at present, but I believe when it is once really known it will grow and be a great blessing.

"I ought to mention that besides the societies registered, there are a few others which have not joined us as yet."

CHRISTIAN ENDEAVOR IN LIBERIA.

By Rev. George P. Goll.

Generations of grossest darkness of mind and soul, filled with the most abject idolatrous, superstitious, and demoralizing training, which can scarcely be comprehended in this enlightened age of Christianity, education, and industry, constitute some of the greatest obstacles to Christian work in this country, and necessitate so much preliminary preparation as to make this field an exceptionally difficult one in which to labor.

Yet a more important field would be hard to find for the development of that distinctive feature of

CHRISTIAN ENDEAVOR IN LIBERIA.

1. Decorations of the Muhlenberg Chapel in commemoration of the Fourth Anniversary of their Christian Endeavor Society, January 6, 1895.
2. The First M. E. Church, of Monrovia, where the Liberia Christian Endeavor Union was organized, January 16, 1895.
3. Some of the members of the Granger Presbyterian Young People's Society of the Christian Endeavor, of Johnsonville. The white lady in the group is Mrs. Elizabeth C. Perry, President of the society and Corresponding Secretary of the Liberia Christian Endeavor Union. Many of the members of this society of twenty-five active and five associate members are of the Mashah tribe and also of the Bassa tribe. The picture was taken at Monrovia, and a very heavy rain prevented the rest of the members making the journey of some twenty miles.
4. Rev. George P. Goll, of Philadelphia, Pa., President of the Liberia Christian Endeavor Union. For seven years Missionary of the Evangelical-Lutheran Church in Africa.

the Young People's Society Christian Endeavor movement, training the young people who come into its sphere of influence, directly or indirectly, than Liberia; and the work of Christian Endeavor, since its organization in this country, has been, and still is, not only to point out the work to the young people, but especially to train them, in the most literal and practical sense of the word, how to do it after it was pointed out.

The first Christian Endeavor society was organized by Rev. George P. Goll and Mrs. Emma V. Day, in Muhlenberg Mission, of the Evangelical Lutheran Church (General Synod) of the United States of

America, on January 6, 1891, when twelve members representing the Golah, Bassa, Congo, and Pessa tribes, and several Liberians, were enrolled.

The second Christian Endeavor society was organized February 10, 1894, in the settlement of Johnsonville, on the Mesurada River, by Mrs. Elizabeth C. A. Perry, of the Granger Presbyterian Church, which has enrolled at the present time twenty-one active and five associate members, and is doing very good work, having already collected enough money to purchase a much-needed bell for their church.

Several months later Mrs. Perry persuaded some of the students of Liberia College to form a Christian Endeavor society, and twenty-five signed the pledge and constitution; but owing to some disagreement among the officials of the institution, the work has been somewhat hindered, many of the students having gone home to their respective counties. It is hoped that the Christian Endeavor seed planted in their hearts will prove as fruitful as that in their Vice-President's, Mr. Cassel, who is making earnest efforts to organize several societies in different settlements in his county.

About the same time Mrs. Perry was instrumental in organizing another society in Monrovia, which is not in a very flourishing condition, owing partly to inexperience and lack of knowledge of the workings of Christian Endeavor, which instruction and training will soon correct. They have seventeen active and twelve associate members on their roll-call. This number gradually increased as the years passed by, and though circumstances have made it necessary to drop many names from the roll, and has given about twelve of its members to organize another society of the same denomination, it has still an enrollment of forty-three active, two associate, and two honorary members.

It has taught its members to be more loyal, liberal, self-sacrificing, and bettered their lives in many ways, though there is still great room for improvement. As the only means of conveyance in Liberia is walking or riding in a canoe, the loyalty of the members who have to travel distances, some two, five, seven, and two twelve miles, to attend the meetings, can be more readily appreciated by those who enjoy the more modern facilities of travel.

This society has recently petitioned the President of Liberia for twenty-five acres of land on the St. Paul River, where they are desirous of beginning mission work among their heathen brethren, and have already a fund of money on hand amounting to nearly $30. Its "Flower Committee" has just finished a fine garden twenty-five feet wide and one hundred feet long. As soon as the finances of the society permit, these beds will be planted in choice flowers.

It was not until November 19, 1894, that another society was formed in Powellville, near the Junk River, through the efforts of Rev. T. A. Simms and Rev. J. J. Powell, who has charge of a prosperous mission of the Methodist Episcopal Church in that place. They have about forty-five members and are getting along very well.

Two days later, on the 21st of November, 1894, Miss Georgia E. L. Patton, M. D., organized a Christian Endeavor society in the Krootown Methodist Episcopal Church, in Monrovia, where she has been laboring for some time as doctor and missionary. The thirty active and fifteen associate members of this society are making slow but sure progress.

At the celebration of the Fourth Anniversary of the Muhlenberg Christian Endeavor, on January 6, 1895, at which several delegates from the other societies were present, the formation of a Union was suggested, and a committee of arrangements was formed for the purpose of holding a "Rally Meeting," at which the subject could be more fully discussed, and, if feasible, acted upon. The time set for the "Rally" was January 16, but before that time arrived the seventh society was formed by some of the members of the Muhlenberg Christian Endeavor living on the eastern side of the river, in the settlement of Harrisberg, where they have also built a neat church for themselves. This society is known as the Harrisberg Lutheran Society. This "Rally" meeting was most successful and resulted in the formation of the Liberia Christian Endeavor Union of which Rev. George P. Goll was chosen President.

A Junior society has also been formed at Muhlenberg.

We can but labor on trustfully, faithfully, and zealously for His dear sake, ever praying, in the language of the familiar hymn:

> Lead kindly light amid the encircling gloom,
> Lead thou me on.

CHAPTER LX.

IN MEXICO, SOUTH AMERICA, AND THE ISLANDS OF THE SEA.

A Natural Grouping—Pioneers in Mexico—Nine Years to a Day—Still Making Progress—A Creditable Periodical—Difficulties in South America—The First Society in Chile—The Spread of the Cause—In the Sandwich Islands—Good News from Honolulu—Societies in Honolulu's Schools—On the Other Islands of the Group—In the South Seas—The First Samoan Endeavor Society—Its Perils and Its Triumphs—The Blessings of the Prayer Chain—The Work Still Advancing.

A NATURAL grouping of Endeavor societies seems to bring those in Mexico, South America, the Sandwich Islands, and the Islands of the South Seas together in one chapter. Here is the story, as told by those who have the best right to tell it:

CHRISTIAN ENDEAVOR IN MEXICO.

In 1891 Mrs. Eaton wrote as follows: "The first society in Mexico, that of the Church in Chihuahua, formed about a year ago, has already sent four of its young men to the training-school at Juarez, as candidates for the ministry. These young men immediately set to work to form a society at Juarez, which is now larger than the one at Chihuahua.

"The work is of undoubted help to us here, serving as a training-school for young Christians and those who desire to become members of the church, although from the nature of the customs of the people here, the work must be more quiet and less aggressive than at home."

MRS. JAMES D. EATON, CHIHUAHUA, MEXICO.

The history of Christian Endeavor in Mexico has so far very largely centered around the Mexican Mission of the American Board. Rev. Mr. Howland, of Guadalajara writes: "There certainly is no question but that Mrs. James D. Eaton, of Chihuahua, is the one who should appear as the prime mover in Christian Endeavor in Mexico." Before her marriage she was Miss Gertrude Clifford Clapp. In 1875 she was married to Rev. James D. Eaton, who, in 1882, was commissioned by the American Board to take up the work in Mexico. The first Christian Endeavor Society, Mr. Eaton tells us, formally organized in Mexico, dates from February 2, 1890, in the city of Chihuahua, just nine years to a day, as it will be noticed from the formation of the first society in Portland, Me.

The society began to grow in Mexico in good earnest in 1895, when at a Union Sunday-school gathering, an organization was effected, and the United Society for Mexico was formed. The first convention, held in Zacetecas in June, 1896, was a most promising and inspiring meeting. It was my privilege to attend it, and though all of the exercises were conducted in (to me) an unknown tongue, I felt the enthusiasm and inspiration of the gathering. Some delegates, in order to attend the meeting, walked more than three hundred miles under the burning Mexican sun, a journey which took them eight days to accomplish. That of itself proves the devotion of Mexican Endeavorers. During the year the number of societies has more than trebled, and the prospects are most encouraging for the future. Missionaries of all denominations, except the Methodist Episcopal, were represented in this convention, and the society promises to be a great unifier of Christian forces in Mexico. Great credit is due not only to Mrs. Eaton, but to Rev. C. Scott Williams, the first President of the Mexican Union, for the advancement of the work, as well as to a score of faithful missionaries and earnest Endeavorers who have done so much for the cause throughout the republic.

CHRISTIAN ENDEAVOR IN SOUTH AMERICA.

In South America the Endeavor movement has made but little headway as yet. The reason is sufficiently obvious. The inhabitants of every republic on this continent are under the influence of the Catholic Church. Oftentimes these priest-ridden lands are ruled by Catholics of the most bigoted type. Protestant

SANTIAGO ENGLISH CHRISTIAN ENDEAVOR SOCIETY (SANTIAGO UNION CHURCH).

William Leason. Fanny Wilson. Carrie Manhood. James Macdonald. Chas. Gomien.
Thomas Sanderson. Fanny Buss. Rev. J. C. Wilson. Mrs. A. Hill. Mrs. J. C. Wilson.

missions have as yet made but little headway. But wherever they have gone Christian Endeavor societies have also gone. Societies have been started in Brazil, Peru, the Argentine, and some other countries, but I can only give my readers detail of the work in Chile.

CHRISTIAN ENDEAVOR IN CHILE.

By CHARLES R. JAMES.

The first Christian Endeavor society in South America was organized in Chile July 11, 1891. Rev. Jesse C. Wilson, the pastor of the Santiago Union Church, was the founder. He brought the enthusiasm, of course, from our sister Republic of the North, where he had already organized two—one in Yates Centre, and one in Carlyle, Kan., and been instrumental in starting a third in New Providence, N. J. The latter society, it should be said, deserves much of the credit of the work done here through its missionary spirit and constancy in sending, for more than two years, "used" copies of *The Golden Rule*. These were distributed where they would do most good.

The society began with but few members, ten in all (four active, six associate), who, with others, met to discuss and organize, if thought best (and it *was* thought best), in a pouring rain. The difficulty at organization was a symbol of the difficulties of the first two years. But then the clouds began to clear. The society now numbers: Active members, 19; associate, 14; honorary, 34; absent members, 15—total, 82. After a year's work, one of our members going thither, a society was organized in Concepcion, in Spanish. About the same time, another member going north, a second society was organized in Copiapó, in English. The work there has languished somewhat.

A year ago a third organization was made in the native church in Santiago, which is now one of the most flourishing. A fourth society was organized in the Valparaiso native church by Mrs. J. F. Garvin, out of a group of women whom Mrs. Garvin had taught to pray. The last organized was in the present year in Taltal, the far north of Chile, by Elder Castro, of the Valparaiso native church, who, in the interest of the Presbyterian work, made a trip to those parts.

The work and the experience in the native societies is as yet very crude. Sin is very deceitful always, but in Roman Catholic countries it takes on a deeper cast than elsewhere, owing to deep corruptions of the Roman Church. The difficulty in getting to the hearts is often quite discouraging. But there is bound to be some way, and we have the Holy Spirit to lead us thither.

None of the societies but the Santiago English have adopted badges. No conventions have yet been held. The distances are great, and the people among whom the work has taken hold are poor. The time does not seem quite ripe yet here for the convention idea.

A union meeting of the two Santiago societies was held in February, conducted in Spanish. To better express the unison of feeling a hymn was sung, "verse about," by the two societies. The native society could not have a better President than Rev. E. A. Lowe, who also is supported by a group of Presbyterian Christian Endeavor societies in Lima Presbytery, Ohio. The anniversary of the Santiago Spanish society was held April 20, 1895, the English society being also present by invitation.

CHRISTIAN ENDEAVOR IN THE HAWAIIAN ISLANDS.

By Miss Agnes E. Judd, Honolulu.

The first Christian Endeavor society on the Hawaiian Islands was organized in the Fort Street Church, of Honolulu, February, 1884. At its tenth anniversary the number of members in the society was 95, as compared with the original number of 25. As the society seemed too large for the most effective working, in April, 1894, a Junior society was organized, which in a year's time has grown from 19 to 35 members. May 17, 1894, the Senior society numbered 52 members, of whom 41 were active and 11 associate.

We quite often have the pleasure of welcoming to our meetings visiting Endeavorers from the United States. Sailors from men-of-war in port are frequently at our meetings. One evening we welcomed a number of Japanese and German sailors. During the ten months' stay in port of Her Britannic Majesty's ship "Champion," six of the sailors joined our society as active members. Recently three of Her Majesty's Ship, "Nymphe" men joined our number before the vessel left port. In April and May of 1894, the Christian Endeavorers of the Central Union Church, Honolulu, held short meetings Sunday mornings at eleven o'clock on board the United States Steamship "Philadelphia." Through this influence and that of other Christian people in Honolulu, a sailor who was afterward transferred to the "Charleston," started a Floating Christian Endeavor society on that vessel. The society has grown from 8 to 20 members, and is doing a noble work in starting a Christian Endeavor Home in Nagasaki, Japan.

The Young people's Society of Christian Endeavor of the Central Union Church contributes yearly to pay the rent of the Chinese Gospel Hall, which is situated in the heart of the "Chinatown" of Honolulu. A school for Hawaiian and Chinese children is taught in this room every morning. One evening a week, a band of Hawaiian children gathered from off the streets by a native, and drilled into something of a "Boys' Brigade," meets in this room. On other evenings in the week it is used for meetings conducted in the Chinese or Japanese language. We also support a Hawaiian boy in the Hilo Boarding-School, at

Hilo, Hawaii. At Christmas time we give money to help make a "Merry Christmas" for the children of the Mission Sunday-schools among the different nationalities in Honolulu. Some of the members of our Christian Endeavor society teach in these schools.

The second Christian Endeavor society on the Islands was organized in the Foreign Church of Hilo, Hawaii, January, 1892, with fourteen active and ten associate members. The membership at present is about thirty-five. There is a Junior society in connection with this society. Notices of the Sunday evening meetings are posted in the hotels and other conspicuous places in the town, and some strangers are in this way attracted into the meetings.

In September, 1892, the Young People's Society Christian Endeavor of the Makawao Foreign Church, Maui, was organized. February, 1895, a flourishing society of 20 members was reported. Some of the members come six or eight miles to attend the meetings. Most of these members are older than the majority of those in the Christian Endeavor societies on the Islands. A Junior society has lately been

YOUNG PEOPLE'S SOCIETY CHRISTIAN ENDEAVOR, OF KAMAHAMAHA SEMINARY, HONOLULU.

started. The money raised by the Makawao society goes toward work among the Chinese and Hawaiians.

There is a Christian Endeavor society in Kamahamaha Seminary, Honolulu, a school for Hawaiian girls. It was organized October 10, 1894, through the instrumentality of Miss Grace Wing, with 18 active and 13 associate members. The membership of the society is composed entirely of the girls themselves. Each Sunday a teacher helps in her preparation the girl who is to lead the meeting. Only the members of the society take part, though all the girls in the school attend the meetings. Every fourth Sunday a temperance meeting is held. Sometimes a friend is invited in to address the girls. The younger pupils of the school have a meeting at the same time, led by one of the teachers; this is not an organized Junior society. The principal of the Seminary speaks highly of the good influence of the Christian Endeavor society upon the girls. She says a great difference has been noticed in the behavior of some of the girls since the society was started.

The Mills School for Chinese boys, Honolulu, under the supervision of Mr. Frank Damon, has a meeting very much like that of a Christian Endeavor society, and it is hoped that they will organize before long.

The formation in the near future of a Christian Endeavor Union of the societies on the Hawaiian Islands is expected.

CHRISTIAN ENDEAVOR IN THE SOUTH SEAS.

By Rev. J. E. Newell, Malua, Upola, Samoa.

The first Young People's Society of Christian Endeavor in the South Seas, was established at the Malua Training Institution, Upola, Samoa, on July 10, 1890. The founder and first President of the society was the Rev. J. E. Newell, co-tutor with the Rev. John Marriott at the institution. The first Secretary of the society was a young theological student named Sā-anga. The first meeting was held in a small building used as an office and dispensary in connection with the Malua Institution. The Europeans who signed the roll and took the Christian Endeavor pledge were Mr. and Mrs. Newell and Mrs. Marriott. A few weeks after the first meeting the Rev. John Marriott joined the society with which from the first he had shown warm sympathy, and Fraülein Valesca Schultze. Of the Samoans there were two who then joined the society who have been elected year by year as Secretaries, viz.: Sā-anga (the first Secretary) and Imo. Both these young men have been recently appointed assistant tutors at the Institution. The former, viz.: Sā-anga, accompanied Mr. and Mrs. Newell to England in 1891, and was frequently seen on Christian Endeavor platforms in that country, and was a welcome guest at all Young People's Society Christian Endeavor festivals during his two years' residence in England.

At the first Christian Endeavor meeting held in Samoa 10 members were enrolled, but the numbers grew so rapidly that subsequent meetings had to be held in the large Institution class-room.

In January, 1891, another society was established at the village of Faleasiu, in the Aana District, and during the same year two more were formed at Saleimoa and Afenga, in the Malua District. The Rev. John Marriott became President of the parent society, and Imo Secretary of the society during the absence of Mr. Newell and Mr. Sā-anga in England. On their return in 1893, Messrs. Marriott and Newell became joint Presidents, and Messrs. Sā-anga and Imo, joint Secretaries of the society.

The Rev. A. E. Hunt, then stationed at Savaii, Samoa, established three societies in the district over which he had charge. With Mr. Hunt's removal to New Guinea during the present year these distant societies have lapsed for a time. During 1893 a society was established at the Samoan Girls' Central Boarding-School at Papauta, Upolu, which now numbers some fifty members. The joint Presidents of that society are Misses Schultze and Moore, and the Secretary is an able and energetic girl named Alisa.

Meanwhile the first members of the first Samoan society were getting scattered abroad to the work to which God had called them. Amongst these were two Ellice Islanders, named Panapa, and his wife Pesike, who were appointed as missionaries to the Island of Fakaofo, in the Tokelau Islands.

Since the establishment of the first Samoan society 258 members have been enrolled in that society alone. Of these no less than 13 have gone as missionaries to New Guinea—i. e., taking account of the young men and their wives, who were, and still are, corresponding members of the society. In the Tokelau Islands we have 2 of our original members; in the Ellice Islands there are 6; in the Gilbert Islands there are 4, thus making a total of 25 of those who avowedly received their impulse to missionary service from the meetings of the society.

The statistics of Samoan societies, as far as at present ascertained, are: Malua, active members, 82; Malua, corresponding members, 55; Faleasiu, active members, 30; Papauta, active members, 50; Fakaofo, Tokelau Islands, 56; Atafu, Tokelau Islands, 40; smaller societies in Samoa, 30—total, 343.

In addition to these upwards of 80 former members, who, whilst they have ceased any formal connection with the society, are actively engaged in Christian work in various parts of Samoa.

The fifth anniversary of the first Samoan society has just been celebrated in Malua with much enthusiasm. The meeting was the most successful ever held in connection with the movement in Samoa. A convention is not yet possible, and would in any case be very difficult in Samoa. Before the close of the present year, owing to the impulse which has gone forth with those who have recently left us for foreign work, our societies will be scattered over an area of one thousand miles of ocean. In Samoa alone the difficulty of transit is so great that the young people of distant societies could rarely if ever meet in a convention.

At the recent anniversary meetings addresses were delivered by Endeavorers on Christian Endeavor topics. The addresses were in all cases forcible and earnest and fervent. An address on "Bible Reading" by one of the younger members was so forcible and spiritual that it will be printed in the native magazine and a translation will probably appear in the *Silver Link* (London).

The greatest hindrance to all Christian work at the present time is the political unrest and misgovernment of the Islands. We can never hope to see the progress that so much prayer and consecration lead us to expect until the blessings of peace and good government are secured for the Islands.

CHAPTER LXI.

THE BOSTON CONVENTION OF 1895.

The Story of the Boston Convention—A Difficult Story to Tell—The Inadequacy of the English Language—Boston's First Great Convention—How Things Worked Together for Good—The Public Gardens and Boston's Decorations—The Convention Weather—The Boston Papers and Their Welcome—The Motormen and the Police—A Little Story from a Saloon—Historic Pilgrimages—The Jingo Spirit and Why it was Absent—Many Delegates from Abroad—The Wonderful Evangelistic Services—Christian Citizenship and Reform—A Missionary Convention—The World's Union and How it was Formed—A Brief Story of the Days—Tents "Williston" and "Endeavor"—The Growth of the Year—The Denominational Rallies—The Responsibilities of Success—Some Rare Excursions—A Quiet Sabbath—The Scholarship of the World for Christ—The Greatest of Conventions—" Arouse Ye, Arouse Ye, O Servants of God."

TO write the story of the Fourteenth International Convention as I am attempting to do immediately after its close is a difficult task indeed, without seeming to indulge in exaggeration and unwarrantable superlatives. And yet whatever the appearance may be to the cool-blooded reader who peruses this account a thousand miles from Boston and six months after the convention is over, it would, in reality, be difficult to indulge in unwarrantable superlatives about such a convention. Superlatives seem tame and the most glowing adjectives altogether inadequate to describe this magnificent gathering.

It is evident that it is not due to any professional partiality that I find the English language so inadequate to the description, for, as I read the many accounts of the convention in the secular and religious papers of the day, I find that my brothers of the quill are troubled in the very same way. The best that any of us can do is to give what seems to us a faint, tame, and colorless account of this hugest of all religious gatherings since the world began.

It will be remembered that it was decided in 1893 that the Convention of 1895 should be held in San Francisco if the railroads should agree to a sufficiently low rate in view of the thousands whom they would transport across the continent. This agreement was not forthcoming, however, and in October of 1894, it was decided that some other place must be found for the Convention of 1895. As can readily be seen this was very short notice, and afforded but

COMMITTEE OF THIRTEEN (BOSTON CONVENTION, 1895).

1. Samuel B. Capen, Chairman.
2. George W. Coleman, Vice-Chairman.
3. R. H. Magwood, Secretary.
4. F. F. Davidson, Auditor.
5. H. G. Dixon, Decoration.
6. Charles E. Allen, Excursion.
7. Charles H. Kilborn, Printing.
8. A. J. Crockett, Hall.
9. William Shaw, Finance.
10. E. A. Gilman, Reception.
11. F. W. Walsh, Jr., Accommodation.
12. George K. Somerby, Music.
13. W. F. Bartholomew, Press.

meagre time to make the vast preparations necessary for an International Christian Endeavor Convention.

Though for many years Boston had been the headquarters of the United Society she had never welcomed an International Convention.. In fact, she had kept her aspirations in this direction in the background, and it was felt by all to be only right that her wish should be granted, if she were willing in nine short months to undertake the task.

For this convention all things seemed to work together for good. There was no strike to frighten the delegates away from Boston, or to disturb the financial equipoise of the country. The Committee of Thirteen (no unlucky number by any means as it proved) profited by the experiences of their predecessors in this office who managed the splendid gatherings in Cleveland, Montreal, New York, Minneapolis, and St. Louis, and were able to accomplish wonders in the way of organization in a marvelously short space of time. In fact, too much cannot be said of the well-nigh absolutely perfect arrangements made and carried out by Hon. S. B. Capen and his very able lieutenants.

The city authorities of Boston and the merchants of the city were easily aroused to the magnitude of the coming gathering, and co-operated most heartily from the very beginning with the committee. Every reasonable request was granted them. The historic Common, which is almost sacred in the eyes of Bostonians, was given over to the Endeavorers for the time being, or at least so much of it as was necessary for the spreading of the largest tents ever constructed. The Public Gardens were decorated by the city gardener with choice Endeavor emblems and mottoes, and with the Boston colors of crimson and white. The merchants threw out bunting lavishly from their stores, and expended, in some cases, hundreds and thousands of dollars for decorations in electric lights and of other descriptions.

The press caught the spirit of the movement at an early day, and in advance devoted, in the aggregate, hundreds of columns to the coming convention, while their reports of the meetings when they occurred, embellished, as they often were, with colored plates and half-tone pictures, as well as with a multitude of illustrations of the ordinary newspaper variety, went far beyond anything that had ever been attempted for a similar gathering by American journalism in the past.

Not only did the Boston papers give voluminous reports of the convention, but those outside of the Hub evidently regarded it as a great event. One paper published in Chicago sent seven of its staff to Boston to report the convention and gave by telegraph three or four pages each day concerning the meeting; a marvelous feat in journalism indeed when it is remembered that it was a purely religious gathering that was thus recorded.

Another Chicago editor, not to be outdone in generosity and enterprise, tele-

INTERIOR MECHANICS' HALL (BOSTON), CONVENTION IN SESSION.

graphed to Boston an offer of $5,000 each year for three years if the United Society would move its headquarters to Chicago. This generous offer was politely declined by the United Society on the ground that it was already performing its work efficiently and satisfactorily, that it did not need large buildings or great funds to carry on its work, but preferred to do it quietly and modestly as in the past on the money which it could earn itself, and which with its very moderate expenses enabled it to perform all its duties as a bureau of information for societies in many lands and that speak many languages.

Not often, indeed, has the gift of $15,000 thus been refused by a society because it wished to subordinate its organization to its work, because it was "an influence and not an institution," but surely this is distinctly the spirit and true idea of Christian Endeavor from the beginning to the present day.

In the good providence of God this convention was blessed with the finest weather that an International Convention ever knew. All the days were cool and comfortable, and there was no suffering from the intensity of the heat within the buildings or without. Only one session, and that the open air session on the Common on Saturday afternoon, July 13, was interrupted by a shower, and in that case the convenient tents near by were soon thronged with an eager audience, only half the size, to be sure, of the audience without, but yet as many as could be reached by the stoutest pair of lungs, so that this patriotic demonstration was by no means a failure.

Not only did the merchants and the editors, the Christian Endeavorers, and the Christian people generally of Boston catch the convention spirit, but every one seemed to share in the genuine underlying ideas of peace on earth and goodwill to men, which make all such conventions memorable. It was remarked by all that the motormen on the electric railways were never so kind and obliging, though their work was vastly increased by the thronging thousands who came to Boston. The clerks and shop-keepers were politeness itself, and it would show an unwarrantably suspicious disposition to narrowly inquire how much of this politeness was induced by the spirit of trade and how much was due to the spirit of Christian Endeavor. Let us give Christian Endeavor the benefit of the doubt.

The police, too, in accordance with their instructions from the City Hall, were as polite and considerate in the performance of their arduous duties as policemen possibly could be. It was not the easiest task in the world to guard the doors of tent and hall from the persistent thousands who insisted on entering, badge or no badge, and who would have excluded the Endeavorers had they been permitted to do so—the persons who ought certainly to have had the first right of entrance. But all these duties were performed with as much suavity and kindness as possible.

The duties of the police, however, as guardians of the public peace and

CHRIST CHURCH.
Where the lanterns were hung for Paul Revere.

THE WASHINGTON ELM.
Under this tree, still standing in Cambridge, Gen. Washington assumed command of the Continental Army.

property were singularly light, and it was reported from headquarters that not nearly so many arrests as usual were made during convention week in the section of the city most largely occupied by Endeavorers.

The way in which these guardians of public morals entered into the spirit of the occasion is well illustrated by an incident which occurred during convention week. A brawny policeman saw in a saloon window the announcement, which was an insult to every Christian Endeavor delegate:

"CHRISTIAN ENDEAVOR PUNCH,'

in huge letters.

Going into the saloon he remarked to the proprietor, "You had better take down that sign."

"I guess not," answered the saloon-keeper. "I have a right to put up any sign I please."

"You had better take down that sign," again remarked the policeman.

"Why should I take it down?" demanded the saloon-keeper. "Have I not a right to put up any sign I choose?"

"You had better take down that sign," persisted the policeman. "In less than a year you will be wanting to have your license renewed, and if you outrage public sentiment in that way there will be precious little chance for you another year." Whereupon the obnoxious sign at once came down.

Thus every one entered into the spirit of the occasion, and all endeavored together to make the Endeavor convention as nearly perfect as possible.

Of course, it goes without saying that the historic sites in the neighborhood of Boston added much to the interest of the convention. They formed a prime source of attraction, especially to delegates from distant sections of the country, and these historic pilgrimages will long live in their memories. Cambridge and Salem, Concord and Lexington, and especially Plymouth, with its Rock and its monument and its hallowed memories, were visited by thousands of eager youth, who there renewed again their allegiance to their country and their country's God.

One afternoon of the convention, too, was given up to pilgrimages nearer the centre of the hub, and Bunker Hill and Faneuil Hall, Washington Elm, and the Old South Church, as well as the Old North Meeting-House, from which Paul Revere hung out his lanterns, were thronged with thousands of delegates from all parts of the Union.

Nor was the United States alone represented at these historic rallying points, for a multitude from Canada as well, and all the delegates from beyond the seas, visited one or another of these shrines, where addresses were made, not only by speakers from the United States but by orators from Canada and England, who drew the common lessons of patriotism and good citizenship and love of country from these historic surroundings.

An attempt had been made by one or two papers in Canada to arouse the sectional spirit and to show that these pilgrimages were deliberate insults on the part of the managers of the convention toward the Canadian delegates. But this attempt was a miserable failure. The jingo spirit could not be evoked. The delegates from both sides of the line met as brothers. They recognized that they had common problems to face in their respective lands, common foes to meet, and a common Lord to serve, that patriotism was the same thing on both sides of the imaginary mark which divides Canada from the United States, and all went home with a larger sense of the destiny of the North American continent with its English-speaking millions, and with a more brotherly sense of comradeship among Christian Endeavorers the world over.

The international features of the convention were especially emphasized by the presence of several well-known ministers from England, Scotland, and Ireland who had come, together with one delegate from Australia, especially to attend this convention. Though the limits of this chapter will not allow me to mention the names, even of the most prominent speakers, since the bare program alone would occupy more space than my publishers can allow me for the story of the whole convention, it is not unfitting that I mention the names of these gentlemen who came across the sea to attend the convention and who rendered it such generous aid during many of the sessions.

Rev. W. J. L. Closs, the President of the New South Wales Union, made the longest journey of any delegate, traveling half around the world to be present and returning home the second day after the convention closed. Rev. W. Knight Chaplin, the Secretary of the British Christian Endeavor Union, was also heard on more occasions than one, as were also Rev. John Pollock, of Glasgow, Scotland; Rev. J. L. Lamont and Rev. Henry Montgomery, of Ireland; Rev. R. Burgess, of Wales; and Rev. James Mursell, of England, all of them devoted Endeavorers, and all of them adding an element of signal value to the convention.

The evangelistic features of this convention should not be forgotten. This was the first time that these services had been attempted on a large scale. But it is safe to say that it will be by no means the last time. From every point of view they were an unqualified success. The convention was taken to a vast multitude of people who could not go to the convention, and on the wharves and at the car houses, in the great apartment stores and on the ships in the harbor, in some instances never-to-be-forgotten services were carried on and many souls were won to Christ. Moreover, at the noon hour of every day, simultaneously with this multitude of services in various parts of the city, old Faneuil Hall and

INTERIOR OF FANEUIL HALL, SHOWING THE PAINTING OF DANIEL WEBSTER DELIVERING HIS GREAT SPEECH IN CONGRESS.

Bromfield Street Church were thronged with people who listened to moving addresses from the most eminent evangelists in the world, and on Sunday, when no mass meetings were held, very many of these delightful evangelistic services took the flavor and the spirit of the convention into the nooks and corners of Boston that would otherwise have had little of it.

This fact that no mass meetings were held on Sunday was of itself a notable feature of this notable convention. It was felt that everything should be done by example as well as precept to promote the keeping holy of the Lord's Day. Many of the attendants upon the convention were quartered so far from the great auditoriums that it would have been impossible for them to reach the meetings without riding on the cars, and, while the convention wished to lay no undue burden upon the conscience of Endeavorers, it resolved to offer no temptation to any unwary soul. Hence, the convention hall and the tents were tightly sealed on Sunday, the 14th of July, while in hundreds of churches, some one of which were within easy reach of the attendants, services were held, the theme of every sermon and discourse being some phase of Christian Endeavor and its work.

I have already implied that Christian citizenship received a large share of attention, as, indeed, was inevitable in historic Boston. The atmosphere of the times, too, if I may so speak, made this element the more inevitable. The glorious reforms of the year in New York and Chicago, and in many lesser municipalities; the triumph of righteousness and good citizenship; the growing disfavor of the saloon power; the overthrow of the political boss and corruptionist during the previous year gave new point and force to allusions which are always forceful, and every reference to good government, to temperance, to righteousness, and the triumphs of the principles of Christ in the governments of the world was received with rapturous applause. Surely, Christian citizenship never had more strenuous advocates, and never received, in the same length of time, such a mighty impetus.

The same thing can be said of the importance given to the missionary idea. The Roll of Honor contained the names of nearly six thousand societies that had given $10 or more through their own denominational missionary boards during the past year, and this was only a fraction of the unrecorded gifts or of the gifts to and through the individual churches, which would swell the $150,000 found upon the roll to $425,000 if it were all recorded. Nowhere was the enthusiasm deeper or stronger than in the distinctively missionary sessions of the convention; and far from indicating any diminution or lessening of zeal for missionary extension, the thought of "the world for Christ and Christ for the world" was never such a pervasive force as thoughout the Fourteenth International Convention.

"No previous convention," it has been well said, "has exhibited so fine an interdenominational fellowship as this." At Boston an unprecedented number of religious bodies were represented, but all met as brothers in Christ. Misunderstandings in regard to the spirit and purposes of the Christian Endeavor movement have almost entirely passed away. There was at Boston no word regarding the organic union of Christendom, but many words regarding its spiritual union, and every such word was applauded with a vehemence that showed how dear was the thought to the multitude of pastors and young people present.

In this connection it seems appropriate to speak of the formation of the World's Christian Endeavor Union, which was effected on Friday afternoon, July 12. A large number of Endeavorers were present in the Mechanics' Hall, and almost all of those who had come from across the water were present at this session. The matter was presented by Rev. W. J. L. Closs, with whom the idea largely originated, and who also presented a proposed constitution for the new World's Union. It was unanimously voted to form such a union, the constitution, with possible modifications, was also adopted, and a set of provisional officers, with Rev. F. E. Clark as president, Mr. J. W. Baer as secretary, and Mr. William Shaw as treasurer were chosen to manage the affairs of the World's Union until the next convention at Washington.

Mr. Baer, who was not present at this meeting, afterward resigned in favor of Rev. W. J. L. Closs, of Australia, in order that the list of officers might be of a more cosmopolitan character. It is understood that all these officers are simply honorary, or non-salaried officers; that the World's Union shall have a meeting once in three years in connection with some national convention, and that its purpose shall simply be to draw together in closer bonds of fellowship those who believe in the Christian Endeavor idea.

To accomplish this all active Endeavorers and associate members are included in this World's Union, and there is also a class of certificate members, who, upon the payment of $1.00, shall receive a ticket of membership, and shall have voting power at all meetings of the World's Union. It is also distinctly understood that this World's Union, like the National and State conventions, has no authority over the local societies and no legislative functions of any kind. It is made up of individuals and not of societies. Among other blessings which it brings to the cause, it affords an opportunity for older people, or those who for any good reason cannot be active members, to be identified with the movement, and to remain thus identified to the end of their days. This, I believe, was one of the most far-reaching and important actions taken at the convention—an action from which only good can flow.

I have taken so much space to describe the general features and the peculiar

"BOSTON, '95."

1. Patriotic Meeting on Boston Common. 2. Tent Williston. 3. Tent Endeavor. 4. Interior Tent Williston. 5. Interior Tent Endeavor.

and memorable elements of this fourteenth convention that I have little room for its details, nor is this necessary. Through the daily papers published at the time, through a multitude of religious weeklies, and especially through the official report of the convention, which in itself forms a portly volume, any one who is interested in the details of these meetings can find abundant material to engage his attention for days at a time. I will not even mention any of the eloquent speakers who had part in these meetings lest the mention of one name rather than another, should seem invidious. It is enough to say that the speeches were of a remarkably high order. There was little or no clap-trap and few appeals to the galleries, but much earnest, stalwart common sense and much genuine eloquence found expression. By many old convention goers the exceedingly high average of all the addresses was remarked.

Three great audience-rooms were in constant requisition, and these, with their accommodations for thirty thousand, could not begin to hold the throngs who desired to enter, though for the most part Christian Endeavorers, who were admitted by badges, were able to find entrance at some one of the auditoriums. The Mechanics' Hall and tents Williston and Endeavor were crowded morning and evening at all the sessions. It is estimated that from one of the sessions, that of Thursday evening, fifteen thousand people went away from Mechanics' Hall unable to find entrance. Some of them succeeded in entering the tents, but many had to wait for the more favorable opportunity of the next day before getting within range of the speakers' voices. All took their disappointments good-humoredly, and the crank and the pessimist and the complaining croaker all were conspicuous by their absence.

The convention began on Wednesday evening, July 10, with twenty simultaneous meetings in the largest churches of Boston and its suburbs. At these meetings many of the most eloquent speakers of the convention were heard, and in the comparatively small audience-chambers an effect could be produced which was not altogether possible in the great halls, while on the other hand the thronging masses in the great halls produced another effect of strength and power and vastness which is impossible in any building of ordinary size. On Thursday morning hearty welcomes were given by the Governor of Massachusetts and the Lieutenant-Governor and the Mayor of the city of Boston by representative ministers of the city in behalf of the churches, and by the Committee of Thirteen, all eloquent and felicitous. At this session, too, General Secretary Baer read his admirable report. "Having in mind that the convention was at the Hub," as one account of the convention puts it, Mr. Baer entitled his report, "The Christian Endeavor Wheel," and with this metaphor made his statistics very entertaining. And what statistics they were! Seven thousand seven hundred and fifty new societies last year, and now 41,229 in all, with 2,473,740 members! Of these, 4,712 societies are outside the United States. And 9,122 Junior bands! Gifts to missions reported from only part of the societies, $149,719.09, and other gifts to the church, making $340,603.54 in all! Certainly, counting the societies that did not report, the Christian Endeavor gifts to missions last year amounted to $425,000. Best of all, Secretary Baer reported 202,185 as having joined the church from Christian Endeavor societies since the last convention! In six years 816,335 have joined the church from Christian Endeavor ranks.

As to States, Pennsylvania still leads, with 4,139 societies. Then follow: New York, 3,822; Ohio, 2,787; Illinois, 2,446; Indiana, 1,762, etc.

As to denominations, the Presbyterian, with 7,552 societies, is in the front rank; the Congregational stands next, with 5,898; Disciples, 3,549; Baptist, 3,487; Methodist Episcopal, 1,322; Methodist Protestant, 1,100; Lutheran, 1,043; Cumberland Presbyterian, 930, etc. This is in the United States. In Canada, the Methodist Episcopalians lead, with 1,179 societies, chiefly Epworth Leagues of Christian Endeavor. In England, the Baptists lead; in Australia, the Wesleyan Methodists.

The afternoon of this day was devoted to the Denominational Rallies, which, in their way, were as remarkable as any meeting of the convention. Three of them, the Presbyterian, the Baptist, and the Congregational, crowded the three great auditoriums, the Mechanics' Hall and tents Williston and Endeavor, with an enthusiastic body of young denominationalists, none of whom were sectarians, and all of whom at the same time were interdenominationalists.

It was said by representatives of each denomination that never did so many Baptists meet together under the same roof at the same time, never did so many Presbyterians gather at the same time, and never did so many Congregationalists assemble in the same room as in these respective gatherings.

The Methodist Episcopal rally, too, filled the great People's Temple, the largest church in the city of Boston.

The Protestant Episcopalians held their largest Christian Endeavor rally in the chapel of Trinity Church.

The Cumberland Presbyterians brought together 150 young people, every one of whom had to travel at least 500 miles to reach the convention.

The Disciples of Christ had a remarkable gathering, marked by missionary purpose and zeal for evangelization.

Sixteen States and 250 delegates were represented in the Lutheran rally, which was a notable one.

The United Presbyterians enjoyed a delightful reunion.

So also did the Reformed Presbyterians, the Southern Presbyterians, and the Canadian Presbyterians.

The Reformed Church in America had a meeting of much power.

The Christians had the largest and most important rally they ever held, while the Free Baptist meeting surpassed all expectation.

Two hundred Methodist Protestants assembled, all of whom had to come from a distance to join in this, their family gathering.

The Union rally of the African Methodist Episcopal and the African M. E. Zion Churches was full of enthusiasm and power.

The Mennonite rally, too, surpassed all expectations.

The Church of God enjoyed a notable gathering.

The Advent Christians were much encouraged by the gathering of 200 of their order, while the United Evangelical denomination in their rally brought out the fact that one-fourth of the entire membership of the church belongs to the Keystone League of Christian Endeavor.

The German societies also enjoyed a gathering by themselves, and planned for larger work in the future.

In the three great meetings in the evening of this day the President's address was read, the subject being "The Responsibilities of Success." He claimed that the success of the past year brought with it its own responsibilities, and that the success of the future depended upon meeting these responsibilities and learning the lessons of the past. These responsibilities and these conditions of future victory which the successes of the past force upon us are:

"*1. Humble, unselfish devotion to the cause we love, which is the cause of Christ.*

"We will have no bosses in the unions, as no bossism is even thought of on the part of the United Society. No use of the society for selfish, mercenary purposes.

"*2. Loyalty to the Bible and earnest study of it. Loyalty unswerving to all denominational interests.*

"*3. Clear appreciation of and adherence to the distinctive Christian Endeavor principles.* No form of words or uniformity of method is contended for, but to be an Endeavor society there must be a pledge, consecration meeting, and the principal committees. Maintain the standard! *Raise* the standard!

"*4. Follow the providential paths God has marked out for the movement.* These are our work along lines of better citizenship and missionary efforts. Christian Endeavor has done much already for country and the world. Advance, Endeavor! Do not rest till a Tammany in America is for evermore impossible! a missionary board debt for evermore impossible!

"*5. Seek fuller fellowship.* So far as we have been allowed by our superiors, we represent the undivided evangelical young people of America. Thank God that, in all denominations but one, this fellowship has been growing broader and more complete during the last twelvemonth. Never again will united wicked-

"BOSTON, '95."

1. The Bicycle Run—Reception at Secretary Bass's Home, Medford, Mass.   2. Mechanics' Hall (front).   3. Mechanics' Building, Showing Coalition Hall.   5. Some State Headquarters in Mechanics' Building.   4. Street Decorations.

ness triumph because Christians are divided. Never again will the devil laugh because Christians are busier fighting one another than they are fighting him.

"I have thought you might grow tired of our old annual motto, and I have tried to find another one as appropriate, but I cannot do it. The successes of the past year only emphasize it, for they are all of Christ and of Christian fraternity; so I must give it to you again for the coming year—the motto which tells of one Captain and of one fellowship; the motto which points backward to past successes; the motto which shows the only road to future victories; the motto which tells alike of our leadership and our brotherhood. Here it is. Take it, O Christian Endeavorers, take it, and live by it for another twelvemonth. 'One is your Master, even Christ; and all ye are brethren.'"

Three of the most eminent and eloquent speakers of the convention were heard on this evening, and it was felt that throughout the day the keynote of the whole convention was struck.

Each of the succeeding days had its own peculiar features, and it is difficult to say which was the most important, the most enjoyed, or which left the deepest impression upon the vast assembled throng. Friday, July 12, was devoted very largely to the distinctive features of Christian Endeavor, the principles of the society as viewed from an American, Australian, Irish, Scotch, and Canadian standpoint were discussed. In the afternoon committee meetings of great interest and importance were held, and in the evening Our Interdenominational Fellowship was the great subject of some of the most eloquent addresses of the convention.

Saturday was especially the International Christian Citizenship day, and the hall and the tents were vibrant with the eloquence of earnest speakers who demanded a purer political atmosphere and a deeper devotion and more unselfish patriotism. The afternoon of Saturday was marked by the most remarkable Junior rally that has yet been held. The Mechanics' Hall was entirely inadequate to the multitudes who desired to gain admittance. The children never acquitted themselves better, and, as arrayed in the costumes of different countries they represented a new children's crusade, they were received with the unbounded plaudits of their elders.

The Endeavorers who could not get into the Junior rally consoled themselves on this afternoon with sight-seeing and excursion-going; one of the most delightful of these excursions being given by the Mayor of Boston to the Trustees and some guests of their invitation, to the number of a hundred, down the harbor of Boston and among its beautiful islands.

In the evening the States held enthusiastic receptions, forty or fifty churches being used for this purpose, most of them thronged with eager guests, while in several instances overflow-meetings were held in neighboring churches or halls, as all could not be accommodated in a single audience-room.

To the Sabbath of rest and quiet and of services in the individual churches which followed I have already alluded. On Monday morning the whole convention came together again fresh and joyous for the early-morning prayer-meeting which on each day from the beginning had been meetings of wondrous power and at which reports of the stimulating evangelistic services of the day before were given.

At the usual hour we assembled again in the tents and the hall; the great idea of the day being the missionary thought of the whole wide world for our Lord and Master. The consecration of the scholarship of the world for Christ was the special theme in one of the tents, and this audience was addressed by some eminent college presidents. The missionary enthusiasm flamed high on this morning, and was not even outdone by the joyous pilgrimages to historic points in the neighborhood of Boston held in the afternoon of the same day and which I have already mentioned.

In the evening came the crowning session of all, the consecration meetings following the convention sermons in the hall and tents. Let me quote the description of one of these meetings as it was described by the graphic pen of one who was present:

"A silent prayer, followed by the singing of 'Just as I am,' is offered, and the leader, in a brief, earnest exhortation, asks that the sense of personal responsibility be kept uppermost by the delegates, regardless of numbers or appearances. Then comes that which teaches us more impressively than anything else the world-wide sweep of Christian Endeavor, and its deep spiritual foundation principles, namely, the roll-call of States and nations.

"Alabama would make Christ the passion of its life. Arizona aims to do more practical work, especially in exalting Christ in civil life. California sings a sweet invitation song to San Francisco in '97, and Colorado seeks to lift up its eyes to the hills.

"Connecticut, a great company, has a melodious song, and so has Delaware. The District of Columbia, in looking forward to next year's meeting, declares that it is 'not by might, nor by power, but by my Spirit, saith the Lord.' Florida, Georgia, Idaho follow in ringing consecrations. The Illinois delegation takes a pledge to renewed good-citizenship, missionary, and personal evangelization effort. Indiana's song is followed by prayer on the part of the convention for friends at home, and the delegate from Australia, who is farthest from home, leads the petitions.

"The roll of States cannot be repeated here. One after another the words of consecration, in song or Scripture, pour forth. Maine's missionary zeal leads her to take Carey's great motto. Mississippi, one of the newest of State unions, remembers that with God all things are possible, and Nebraska, by recitation and song, prays for the creation of a clean heart and a right spirit. New York's mighty host seeks to 'scatter sunshine,' and North Dakota's one representative, a young woman, aspires, with Paul, to 'press toward the mark.' Pennsylvania has a practical pledge, and the South Dakota delegation declares, 'We love our

Lord, we love our State, and it shall be our aim to bring the two loves together.' Tennessee sings sweetly, and Texas repeats a verse of its excellent State hymn. Canada upraises a beautiful banner, and with bowed head prays, 'Thy kingdom come.' Massachusetts is 'saved to serve,' and it sings 'Throw Out the Life-line.'

"Thus the long list goes, each response increasing the interest. Five delegates from the British Isles voice their consecration, and then—it was an inspiring moment—these sturdy Endeavorers stood on the platform, and sang in rich voices, 'E'er since by faith I saw the stream.' The representative from Scotland gives alone a verse of 'Scotland for Christ,' and then is heard Australia's message of faith. A Japanese in native costume, speaking for the group of Japanese on the platform, rendered a consecration in his native tongue, afterward translating it. China, Spain, Turkey, Burmah, Mexico, France, Palestine, Armenia, and India follow in quick succession with words that make the world's kinship in Christ very real indeed.

"The pastors and committees renew their vows, the Junior workers, the Sabbath-school teachers—and when this call came almost the entire house arose—the choir, the presidents and other officers, and the Floating society all take upon themselves afresh the service of the Lord. Now the last moment has come. 'Let us all, with uplifted hand, repeat to God the all-comprehensive first clause of our pledge,' is the spirit of Dr. Clark's suggestion. Slowly, silently, reverently, a mighty forest of arms point heavenward, and the Christian Endeavor *sacramentum* is taken. Dr. Hoyt makes audible the prayer of every heart, the tender strains of 'God be With You' are sung. 'Mizpah' is softly repeated, and the convention has left the great halls to take up its abiding-place in the lives of Christian Endeavorers everywhere."

Thus ended this greatest of all Christian Endeavor conventions. Acknowledging the marvelous blessings which have attended all those which have gone before, depreciating not by one iota their influence and vastness, it is not too much to say that in numbers, in enthusiasm, in interest, in its evangelistic, soul-winning spirit, in everything that goes to make up a great spiritual convention, the meeting of 1895 stands pre-eminent among the religious gatherings of the century, perhaps of all centuries.

With all these marvelous blessings in mind, the Christian Endeavor hosts turned their faces from Boston, some to enjoy the pilgrimages before mentioned to Plymouth, Salem, and Concord, others to go to Portland to visit the first home of the Christian Endeavor Society, and to hold an enthusiastic rally in Williston Church, and still others to return directly to their homes, but all with the spirit of Dr. Smith's grand hymn ringing in their hearts, a hymn (page 634) which was written for this occasion, and which has scarcely been surpassed since its honored author wrote "America."

ONE OF THE FLORAL DESIGNS IN THE PUBLIC GARDENS.

"COMMITTEE OF '96."

CHAPTER LXII.

WASHINGTON, '96.

Its Distinguishing Characteristic—Spiritual Power—Difficulties in the Way—The Wrecked Tent—The Registration—A Delightful Conference—Strong Resolutions—Mr. Baer's Eloquent Figures—How the Denominations Stand—The Roll of Honor—Before the Capitol—A Wonderful Sight—Men's Meetings and Women's Meetings—The Closing Day—The World's Unions—A Deaf and Dumb Forerunner—Crystallizations—Our Platform.

EVERY great International Convention is unique in itself. It is like every other, yet different from every other. It seems to have a distinct personality of its own. It has distinguishing characteristics and peculiarities which cause it to live in Christian Endeavor history. If I may summarize the characteristics of the Washington Convention in a single phrase, I would say, it was a convention of spiritual power. And this is not to be wondered at, for the keynote of Christian Endeavor for the twelve months before had been the quickening of the spiritual life, and the widening of the spiritual horizon. This thought was taken to the convention by thousands of delegates. Continually, for weeks beforehand, had prayer been offered for these results, and it is only by a natural sequence that we reaped at Washington what had been sowed throughout the land for many a month before.

THE CAPITOL

These most happy and blessed results, however, were not achieved without obstacle or difficulty, but rather in spite of obstacles and because of difficulties. Never, except possibly at the Cleveland Convention, did there ever seem to be so many hindrances in the way of our annual gathering. Washington has a reputation, and it must be admitted that to some extent it is deserved, of being a torrid city in July, and this fact prevented many old *habitués* of Christian Endeavor conventions from attending this year. Moreover, the country had been suffering from a year of extreme business depression, and many a Christian Endeavorer whose heart was at Washington was obliged to defer to the imperative demands of a lean pocket-book and stay at home this year.

Again the country was in the wildest throes of political excitement. The echoes of the convention of one of the great political parties had hardly died out, while the other was holding a most exciting session in Chicago during the very days devoted to our convention. The newspapers, outside of Washington, though giving a generous amount of space to Christian Endeavor, could not afford to devote their columns so lavishly to the story of Washington, when the more exciting story of Chicago also demanded their attention.

But, as though these hindrances were not enough, on the very night of the opening of the convention, the rains descended, and the winds blew, and beat upon the three great tents which spread their snowy canvas upon the White Lot, until at last one of them, Tent Williston, fell, and great was the fall thereof. The startling head-lines of the Washington papers on Thursday morning, the first great day of the convention, apprised the Endeavorers at their breakfast tables of the fact that one of the tents was "demolished" and the others "wrecked."

However, the actual results were not so disastrous as the scare-lines of the newspapers gave us to understand, and, though Tent Williston was rendered useless for two days, the others were made usable, and by half-past nine on Thursday morning, promptly at the advertised moment for the formal opening of the convention, the President's gavel fell, and the introductory words of Scripture told the great assembled audience that "God maketh small the drops of water; they pour down rain according to the vapor thereof. And now men see not the bright light that is in the clouds, but the wind passeth and cleanseth them. Fair weather cometh out of the north."

And so it proved, for soon the clouds were driven away, the sun shone, the face of nature seemed to smile upon all the assembled Endeavorers, and never was a convention, from beginning to end, more harmonious and more free from anxiety of any kind. All this simply goes to prove the inherent vitality of these great annual gatherings. Rain cannot drown them, wind cannot blow them away. Vast political interests and unbounded excitement cannot distract the attention of the young crusaders. Heat cannot melt their enthusiasm or untoward circumstances chill it. As a great Atlantic liner moves majestically through fog and rain and over tumultuous billows, avoiding iceberg and treacherous shoals, so there seems to be almost a living personality in these conven-

THE WHITE LOT, SHOWING TENTS WASHINGTON, WILLISTON, AND ENDEAVOR.

tions as majestically they march on from the opening day to the close without jar or friction, and in spite of obstacles that at first seem to forebode disaster. It is not too much to say reverently and to believe devoutly, that there *is* a living personality in these conventions; that the Spirit of God leads and directs, and that His presence makes them so successful.

But among the human agencies which must not be forgotten, a large meed of praise once more must be given to the local Committee of Arrangements. Never was a committee more indefatigable in carrying out its its well-laid plans than the Committee of 1896. From the beginning the machinery of the convention moved so smoothly that very few suspected that there was any machinery. Every one was housed and badged and registered and admitted to the convention without delay or disappointment. Every session began on time and closed within a few moments of the appointed hour. Very few speakers among the many hundreds whose names appeared upon the program disappointed the audience, and the places of these few were quickly and satisfactorily filled.

STREET DECORATIONS.

Better than ever before were the speakers heard at this convention. In fact, there was very little difficulty experienced even by those who sat in the remote corners of the tent in hearing every word. The reason for this was the fact that the tents were pitched upon the White Lot, a large park lying at the base of the Washington Monument, remote from any noisy street. The sod floor deadened the footfalls, and the courteous delegates refrained from talking and from moving about during the speeches. In this respect the convention was pre-eminently satisfactory.

The attendance at Washington was somewhat diminished as compared with the Boston Convention by the causes already enumerated. But still, with the exception of the Boston Convention, it was the largest ever held. Over thirty-one thousand delegates were registered; it was estimated by the Committee of Registration that fully nine thousand more came to attend the meetings who did not register, while the four thousand six hundred members of the choir brought the total attendance of Christian Endeavorers up to about forty-five thousand. At most of the sessions the tents were filled to overflowing, a large rim of humanity standing about the upraised sides, while many churches were often filled at the same time that the tents were thronged.

But in this brief story of Washington, I would lay more emphasis upon the quality than upon the quantity of the convention. It was a convention to be weighed as well as numbered. The keynote was struck in the preliminary meetings, held in the pouring rain of Wednesday night, which filled to overflowing twenty-two of the largest churches in Washington. The subject in every church was the same : " The Deepening of the Spritual Life," and, as has been said, this was the keynote of the whole convention.

In such a voluminous program, wherein the brief announcement of the names and topics of the speakers covers forty-eight pages of finely printed matter, it is obviously impossible for me, in the brief chapter devoted to this convention, to pick out speakers or addresses for special comment or detailed description. For a full report of this wonderful gathering, I must refer my readers who desire it to the official volume, which contains the leading addresses. In this chapter I can but give outlines and impressions.

One long step up our Mount of Transfiguration was taken on Wednesday, the day before the convention formally opened.

Not only did these preliminary meetings lead us upward, but for those who were privileged to enjoy it, the council held by the Trustees of the United Society and the State Presidents throughout this day, Wednesday, July 8th, was most inspiring and refreshing. For nearly six hours these representatives of Christain Endeavor, from many parts of the United States and Canada, talked together and prayed together concerning matters of most vital interest to the cause which we all love. In a surprising way, these representatives of different sections saw eye to eye, and agreed substantially, on every great principle of Christian Endeavor.

The most uncompromising hostility was shown by all toward every effort in the direction of institutionalizing Christian Endeavor. It was felt that during these fifteen years God had led us on, and that the principles which He had blest were those which might be called the fundamental ideas of the Christian Endeavor, the pledge, the consecration meetings, the organized work for the Master, and that all details of arrangement and management should be left to the local society and the local church. It was felt that the United Society and the Trustees, the State Unions and their officers, could do nothing better than to keep their hands off of the Ark of the Covenant. That it was not theirs to direct or control Christian Endeavor in the churches, but to simply maintain its principles, and to give information, wherever it was needed, concerning the work. So pleasant and profitable was this meeting that both the State Officers and the Trustees formally expressed the desire to hold similar meetings in the future years, and the opinions of the State Presidents on the general questions discussed were voiced at a meeting which they held subsequently in the following resolution:

The Presidents of various State and provincial Unions, or their authorized representatives, after a full and free conference with the Trustees of the United Society, a conference in which the Spirit of God was manifestly present in power, believe it to be for the best interests of the cause of Christian Endeavor that they make the statement which follows:

It is our conviction that, generally speaking, the conduct of the Christian Endeavor movement has been most wise, and in obedience to manifest providential leadings. The movement has been signally blessed in the self-sacrifice and devotion of those who, under God, originated and have so faithfully served it, as officers and Trustees of the United Society.

A SECTION OF STATE HEADQUARTERS, ARMORY HALL.

It is our conviction, further, that the officers and Trustees have not constituted a body assuming legislative functions, or the control of the movement, other than by directing it into channels of large development and usefulness as God opened the way. While they have been a conserving influence, we are confident that they have been and are of open mind and willing spirit, seeking only the best interests of the cause of Christ.

We recognize that Christian Endeavor has been a movement rather than an institution. The very simplicity of its organization, its freedom from machinery, combined with high character, sober judgment, and willingness to gain light from every rightful source on the part of the officers and Trustees, have done much to lift it to the high position of influence which, in the providence of God, it has attained.

We believe that the recent council of the Trustees of the United Society and Presidents of State and provincial Unions, in its combination of wisdom, gathered from a wide outlook and knowledge gleaned from an immediate contact with the problems of the different States and Provinces was a wise step in the progress of the movement, and that such a council might profitably be a permanent feature in connection with succeeding International Conventions.

The formal opening of the convention came as usual on Thursday morning, and the two tents which the wind had spared were filled with one of the most enthusiastic of Christian Endeavor audiences. Hearty welcomes were received from eminent men who spoke for the District, the churches, and the Committee of '96, appropriate responses were given, and the President and Secretary delivered their annual address and report.

Mr. Baer always knows how to make statistics interesting, and as he told of the Christian Endeavor tree, the growth of the mustard seed, within these fifteen years, filled all with joyful wonder. He reported the grand total of 46,125 branches on this Christian Endeavor tree. Of these Canada has 3,292, the United Kingdom of Great Britain and Ireland about 3,700, Australia nearly 2,000, France 66, Japan the same number, Madagascar 93, India 128, Mexico 67, Germany 25. Outside of the United States, in all there are nearly 10,000 Societies, the other 36,000 being found within the forty-five States and four Territories.

Pennsylvania is still the banner State in Christian Endeavor, with 4,500 Societies, including the Juniors. Again she carries off the banner for the largest absolute gain in the number of Junior Societies, though the banner for the largest relative gain of Junior Societies passes from Assiniboia in the north to Mexico in the south. Most appropriately the Land of Covenants obtains the prized badge banner for the greatest relative increase in young people's societies.

No one will begrudge the honor to Scotland, and all rejoice that once more England, the Mother Land, obtains the banner for the largest absolute increase of young people's societies. The States and Provinces, however, may well console themselves once more with the thought that it takes one of the greatest nations on earth to get and keep this banner from them.

More attention was given at this convention to Intermediate, Senior, and Mothers' Societies than ever before. One hundred and fifteen Intermediate Societies were reported by the Secretary; fifty Mothers' and twenty Seniors, Illinois leading in both these latter advance movements.

As to denominations, the Presbyterians are still in the lead, with more than 8,000 Societies, both Senior and Junior; the Congregationalists come next, with over 6,000; the Disciples over 4,000; the Baptists nearly as many; the Methodist Protestants with about 1,300; the Lutherans with 1,100; the Cumberland Presbyterians with as many more, and so on through the list. In the Dominion of Canada the Methodists lead, with 1,200 Societies; the Presbyterians come next, and the Baptists follow, while in the United Kingdom the Baptists lead, and the Congregationalists follow a close second. In Australia the Methodists are decidedly in advance.

But I cannot linger over these eloquent figures. I will simply quote a few lines from the Secretary's report, telling of the work done and the money given during the past year, so far as it can be summarized in statistics.

A visible demonstration of the work accomplished is seen in the presentation of the missionary Roll of Honor, a huge document over five hundred feet long, wound upon a great spindle, which was unrolled in each place of meeting, and which gave ocular evidence that the young Christian Endeavorers were learning to give as well as to pray.

Another evidence of this same sort was the presentation of a banner for the best local union work done in behalf of Christian Citizenship. Syracuse, New York, last year obtained the banner, but though it had done admirable work this last year, in the judgment of the Committee of Award, Cleveland surpassed her sister city, and received the banner. Hamilton, Ontario; Newark, N. J.; Janesville, Wisconsin, and Chicago, Illinois, all received honorable mention. New York City received the banner for the largest number of tithe-givers. Thus by these beautiful emblems which appeal to the eye, the facts which, presented to the eye alone would not have been so effective, were emphasized, and the practical nature of Christian Endeavor was demonstrated.

The denominational rallies held early in the convention were very largely attended, and were meetings of extreme interest and power. Many of the best speakers in the different denominations were present, and spoke strong words for Christian Endeavor and loving words for our interdenominational fellowship. A continuation of these denominational meetings was held on Sunday afternoon, under the same leadership, when missionary themes were especially exalted, and the appeals of the different denominational Boards were listened to.

Though the evangelistic note was often struck, and though the deepening of the spiritual life was the great theme of the convention, other subjects were not slighted. Christian Citizenship received deserved attention, and the fact that the meetings were held almost under the shadow of the Capitol gave added emphasis and point to the many addresses on this subject. Once more it was made plain that Christian Endeavor stands for good laws and good lawmakers, for temperance and for purity, for righteousness in municipal affairs, and for civic regeneration. Everywhere these sentiments were applauded to the echo, and the work actually accomplished at the different Endeavor Unions shows that the enthusiasm of the young people was not exhausted in applause, and that their Christian Citizenship ideas are something more than an echo of the different addresses.

The most impressive demonstration ever given at a Christian Endeavor convention of the patriotism of young people was that which took place on the Saturday afternoon of convention week at the east front of the Capitol. Here was massed together a vast throng of young men and women, fully as many, so said the " Oldest Inhabitant of Washington," as assemble on Inauguration Day. But it was not an inauguration crowd altogether. It was, for the most part, a gathering of young men and women, of Christian young men and women at that. The States and Provinces had been sifted to furnish the assembly. They came with high hopes and bounding anticipations for the future. Their pulses were thrilled as they thought of the historic ground on which they stood. As the westering sun descended the long shadow of

PATRIOTIC SONG SERVICE, EAST SIDE CAPITOL.

the beautiful dome of the Capitol was thrown athwart this vast assemblage of young citizens. Such a throng, at such a time and in such a place, must be dominated with thoughts of a redeemed nation and a nobler citizenship.

PATRIOTIC SONG SERVICE, EAST SIDE CAPITOL.

The most impressive feature of this impressive scene was the massing together of the great chorus choir upon the Capitol steps. Nearly, if not quite, four thousand voices were in this choir, and when their leader, Mr. Percy S. Foster, called for

"Holy, Holy, Lord God Almighty," it seemed to the listening throng as though the angelic choirs themselves were singing. More than a mile away this magnificent music was heard, while the music of the Marine Band, one of the best in all the country, was scarcely heard in the outskirts of the throng.

This was a patriotic song service rather than an occasion for speech-making. No human voice could be heard by one in ten of that vast company, and so no speech-making was attempted. The banner already alluded to, which had been won by Cleveland, was awarded, the national and international hymns were sung, and the simple service was over. But simple as it was, it will never be forgotten by those who had the good fortune to participate in it, nor will we ever despair of a country that can summon to its capital city such a vast company as was there seen of earnest Christian young men and women.

Throughout each of the later days of the convention the tide of earnestness and enthusiasm rose higher and higher. This was noticeable in the songs heard on the streets. At first but little singing was heard, but as the convention days wore on the delegates seemed to catch more and more the spirit of praise, and the public squares and busy streets and electric cars and hotel corridors resounded with their joyful songs.

INTERIOR OF TENT WILLISTON DURING THE JUNIOR RALLY.

The Sunday of the convention was spent, for the most part, in quietly attending the regular church services, many churches being compelled to hold overflow meetings, so great was the throng that attended them. In the afternoon, however, powerful evangelistic meetings were held in the tents for the citizens as well as for the visiting delegates.

One feature of this convention was the special provision made for the citizens of Washington. Several meetings were set apart for them, which it was not expected the delegates would attend, and in other ways the convenience and welfare of the hosts as well of the guests were provided for.

Another unique feature of this convention was the holding of a men's meeting and a women's meeting simultaneously in the great tents. These were very largely attended and proved of the deepest interest, while at the same time, in the other tents, an audience of nearly ten thousand listened to the exercises of the Juniors prepared under the careful supervision of Mrs. James L. Hill, which, as usual, was one of the most attractive features of the whole convention. The exercise was a most interesting one, and the Juniors carried it out with infinite spirit and gusto.

THE PLATFORM DURING THE JUNIOR RALLY.

In some respects, Monday, the closing day of the convention, was the crown of all. It was the first meeting held under the auspices of the World's Union, and a most cosmopolitan gathering it was. Tents Williston and Endeavor were devoted to addresses by representatives of Christian Endeavor from all parts of the world. England, Persia, Africa, India, Germany, China, Turkey, Liberia, Chile, Japan were all represented, some of them by more than one speaker. Visiting missionaries were introduced, and nearly forty student volunteers who had dedicated their lives to work in foreign fields, also stood upon the platform and moved the vast audience with the demonstration of their consecrated devotion. After the public session, a short business session of the World's Union was held, the amended Constitution was adopted, the officers elected, and it was informally agreed to hold the next meeting in London in 1900, in accordance with the invitation of the British Union. At the same time that Tents Williston and Endeavor were thus occupied, another meeting closely allied to the purposes and spirit of the World's Union was held in Tent Washington, in the interest of suffering Armenia. This burning question of the day was discussed by some of the most eloquent speakers of the country, and the audience was roused to the highest pitch of excitement against the supine governments which have allowed Armenia to be ravaged and ruined.

REV. W. J. L. CLOSS,
Secretary World's Christian Endeavor Union.

The evening sessions of the closing day were worthy of the traditions which cluster around the closing session of a great Christian Endeavor Convention, and were a worthy climax of the great days of spiritual uplift which had preceded them. In every case the sermons were inspiring and the consecration meeting most solemn and elevating. The responses from the States were unusually appropriate, and the vast multitude went away from the different auditoriums saying one to another: "Did not our hearts burn within us while He talked with us?"

Thus closed the Fifteenth International Convention, in some respects the most wonderful of all the wonderful series that had preceded it. If my space allowed, there are many incidents and special features of this convention on which I would like to enlarge. I have purposely omitted the names of the speakers, for the list is so long that if I attempted to give even a list of the chief speakers, this chapter would be little more than a catalogue of names. I would like to dwell particularly on the early morning prayer-meetings, which were unusually full of life and power, upon the daily Bible study from half-past eight to half-past nine, conducted by an honored college president so successfully that I believe this will be one of the permanent features of the convention; upon the evangelistic services carried on in many parts of the city, in which many a soul came out into the light. But for all these details I shall have to refer my readers to the full and voluminous report of this convention.

One of the interesting facts of history to which my attention was called at this meeting was that in 1875 a society by the name of Christian Endeavor was formed among the deaf mutes of Lawrence, Mass. This society, as I understand, had but a brief life, and soon expired; but it seems to have been one of the pioneers of the Christian Endeavor—one of the Endeavors before the Endeavor movement, like the many others of which I have spoken in the first chapters of this book. I have no recollection of having heard of it before, but it is quite possible that from these deaf mutes I received the suggestion of the name and some other words of Christian Endeavor nomenclature, instead of from the

Church of Christian Endeavor or other sources to which I have sometimes been inclined to ascribe them.

At the time of the formation of the first Young People's Society Christian Endeavor in Williston Church, I sought ideas concerning Christian work from every available source, but as I did not then suppose the origin of this society would be a matter of interest, I did not treasure up all these sources of suggestion, and am glad to have them recalled to my mind in these later days. It is interesting, to say the least, that one of the many forerunners of the Christian Endeavor movement, whose chief characteristic is outspoken devotion and a pledge to speak each week for the Master, was an organization among people deprived of the power of speech. May there be no deaf and dumb societies among young people whose vocal organs are in good condition!

Among the many pleasant excursions taken after the convention was one to Mount Vernon, which should not remain unrecorded. It was taken on the day after the convention closed, and was participated in by a large number of Christian Endeavorers. All paid a loving tribute to the Father of his Country, and, among other interesting exercises, a Christian Endeavor tree, grown from an acorn of the famous "Peace Oak" of Washington, was planted on a beautiful knoll between the tomb of Washington and the mansion house. Long may this Christian Endeavor Peace Oak flourish and grow strong to tell of the pacific patriotism of Christian Endeavor!

One chief characteristic of this convention was the crystallization of sentiment in regard to the real principles of Christian Endeavor. During the year preceding the society had been discussed more largely in religious circles than ever before. Many ecclesiastical assemblies had considered the subject with reference to adopting the organization, or, at least, of allowing it to have free and unrestricted course among their churches. In almost every case where the principles had become better known the society had won its way, and received the approval of denominational authorities. This was particularly the case in the Presbyterian General Assembly of 1896 and in several denominations in England and Australia. In the Methodist Episcopal Church of the United States alone the society made no headway, and the plan for affiliation approved by the joint committee of the Epworth League and Christian Endeavor Society was rejected by the General Conference.

But all these discussions concerning Christian Endeavor had cleared the air, and had made it evident to the religious public that the Christian Endeavor Society was a vital force, and that the movement rested upon definite principles which could be formulated and defended. So when the Fifteenth International Convention assembled it was only natural that these clear-cut principles should be defined and defended as never before. The President's address was largely devoted to setting them forth, and this address was adopted informally, but with much apparent enthusiasm, by a rising vote of the whole convention in the different auditoriums where it was delivered.

Perhaps I cannot better close this chapter than by quoting from this address, as it shows the principles to which Christian Endeavor was committed in 1896, the principles which God had peculiarly blessed for fifteen years, and the basis on which it proposed to go forward after its first decade of history to new conquests and victories. The address was entitled "WHAT GOD HATH JOINED TOGETHER," and attempted to show that the great purpose of Christian Endeavor was to bring together into a harmonious whole truths which had been disassociated in the past, but which were necessary for the uprearing of a symmetrical and well-rounded Christian character and life.

Here is our Christian Endeavor platform; here are the things which God hath joined together in weaving the Christian Endeavor fabric.

WHAT GOD HATH JOINED TOGETHER.

Our Christian Endeavor platform was built for us at the beginning by Providence. Its strength has been revealed by our history.

My task is an easy one, for I only need write in words what I believe God has written in deeds.

If I do not state our platform correctly, I do not ask you to stand upon it.

But if I can read our history aright, these are its chief planks:

First. Our Covenant Prayer-meeting pledge—the Magna Charta of Christian Endeavor.

Second. Our Consecration Meeting—guaranteeing the spiritual character of the Society.

Third. Our Committees—giving to each active member some specific and definite work "for Christ and the Church."

Fourth. Our Interdenominational and International Fellowship, based upon our denominational and national loyalty.

Fifth. Our individual Independence and Self-government, free from control of United Society, State or local union, convention or committee; all of which exist for fellowship and inspiration, not for legislation.

Sixth. Our individual Subordination as societies to our own churches, of which we claim to be an integral, organic, inseparable part.

Seventh. Our Christian Citizenship plank—Our country for Christ, but, as a Society, no entangling political alliances. Our missionary plank—Christ for the world.

Eighth. Our ultimate Purpose—to deepen the spiritual life and raise the religious standards of young people the world over.

For fifteen years Christian Endeavor has built upon this platform. The history of the Society which has wrought out in practice these principles may be briefly summarized, so far as words and figures can summarize a movement, as follows:

Forty-six thousand societies have been formed.

Five millions of Endeavors have been enrolled, of whom more than two millions seven hundred thousand are to-day members.

Two millions of others, Endeavorers in all but name, have probably been enrolled in purely denominational societies.

Ten million Endeavor meetings have been held.

Five million copies of the Constitution have undoubtedly been printed, in forty different languages, and at least fifteen million copies of the pledge.

Over one million of our associate members have come into the evangelical churches connected with fifty denominations, influenced in part, at least, by the Christian Endeavor Society; and it is certain that over two millions of dollars have been given in benevolence through denominational and church channels.

"The past at least is secure," we say. But ah! is it? Not unless we secure the future by learning the lesson of the past. The future stretches before us—ten times fifteen years of Christian Endeavor, please God, and ten times that. We stand yet at the beginnings, fellow Endeavorers. The stream is yet near its source. Our concern should be not to deflect it into any channels of our own choosing. Let God choose its way and direct its course, as He has done these fifteen years, and then the future, too, is secure. "We have but one lamp by which our feet are guided, and that is the lamp of experience." By the past what does God teach us for the future?

Let me try, as best I may, to draw out the lessons. Christian Endeavor, as our platform shows, is a practical paradox, a reconciler of irreconcilables. It has married opposites. It has brought into an harmonious family ideas which have been thought to be mutually exclusive. I am tempted to consider this the most important work of Christian Endeavor, in the future as in the past.

Our platform specifies some of the banns that have been proclaimed by Christian Endeavor.

First. It has married the ideas of denominational fidelity and fellowship between denominations, and has written on the door-posts of the home thus formed: "FIDELITY AND FELLOWSHIP, ONE AND INSEPARABLE."

These ideas have been thought by many to be inconsistent, if not hostile, one to the other. Hence, many ecclesiastics are to-day afraid of our fellowship because they believe it will weaken our fidelity. Christian Endeavor, sooner or later, will show them the groundlessness of their fears.

By combining these disassociated ideas, Christian Endeavor has created a new idea, which has required a new word—a word which is found only in the very latest dictionary—the word "interdenominational;" a denominationalism which is not sectarianism on the one side or care-nothingism on the other. Mind your prefixes, Christian Endeavorers; not "un," nor "non," but "inter."

Closely linked with this idea of Interdenominational Fellowship is that other great idea of International Fellowship. Look at these intertwined flags! They tell their own story. They tell of our intense love for our own flag—the Stars and Stripes, "Old Glory," if we live in the United States; the Union Jack, if we live in Canada or Great Britain. Interlinked as they are, they tell of our world-wide brotherhood. Our Society is an arbitration meeting which never adjourns, a peace-with-honor convention that is always in session. On these banners is written: "LOYALTY AND BROTHERHOOD, ONE AND INSEPARABLE!"

Second. Again, if our platform is correct, Christian Endeavor stands for a self-governed society that is yet wholly governed by its own church. I know of no way of developing responsibility except by bearing responsibility. That man and that society will always be a dwarf and weakling that is ever managed by some one else. In comparison with such a man, Mr. Caudle behind the bed-curtain will be independent and self-respecting.

Each society of Christian Endeavor is in a sense independent. It works out its own problems. It is responsible for its own success or failure. It lives or dies according to its own inherent worth. It manages its own matters. It elects its own officers. It plans its own campaigns. But it is always subordinate to its own church, and seeks to find out and obey the wishes of its own church and pastor.

Let me here take occasion to pledge myself to the Christian public, if I may be allowed to speak in any sense as a representative of Christian Endeavor. No United Society and no convention, no union, and no committee of evangelism, good citizenship, or missions shall legislate for or seek to control any society in the wide world.

More and more strongly every year is this principle of Christian Endeavor established, which, indeed, has been fundamental from the beginning—that each society owes allegiance to its own church. Some churches have taken advantage of this principle of subordination to compel their Christian Endeavor societies to commit suicide, to go out of existence, or to label themselves with a local or sectarian name. Is this entirely fair? I appeal confidently to the Christian public of the future, to the sense of justice in the Church at large, for my answer.

Nevertheless, and in spite of the advantage sometimes taken of this principle, Christian Endeavor has proclaimed the banns once more over these two apparently dissimilar ideas—self-government and subordination. It has married these disassociated thoughts, each of which is incomplete without the other; each of which is puny and weak without the other; each of which is complemented and supplemented by the other. It has married them, and has written on the lintel of their door, "OBEDIENCE AND INDEPENDENCE, ONE AND INSEPARABLE."

Third. Again, our platform embraces Patriotism and Humanity. Patriotism is a name that is used to cover a multitude of sins. "It is the last resort of designing knaves," said Johnson. It has been made to stand for partisanship and to mask hideous corruption. It needs to be married to another idea—the idea of humanity. This Christian Endeavor has attempted to do.

Our patriotic fervor was born at the same time as our missionary fervor. Good citizenship and missions have gone hand in hand. "America for Christ" had not ceased to echo before we took up the cry "Christ for the world." Good citizenship has too often meant in the lands where its slogan has been sounded, "America for the Americans," "Canada for the Canadians," "Great Britain for the British," "Japan for the Japanese." Christian citizenship means something more than this. It means our country for Christ, and Christ for the world. It means good rulers and good laws. It means the abolition of the saloon. It means prohibition wherever we can get it. It means Sabbath observance. It means inflexible opposition to all unrighteousness—not simply that America may be the greatest nation on which the sun rises, not simply that Britain's drumbeat may be heard around the world, but above all, that "His Kingdom may come, and His will may be done on earth as it is in Heaven."

By Christian Endeavor, then, we marry the too-often disassociated ideas, patriotism and humanity. CHRISTIAN CITIZENSHIP AND CHRISTIAN MISSIONS, ONE AND INSEPARABLE.

Fourth. Our Christian Endeavor platform, once more, stands for Organization, it stands for Spiritual Power. These two great ideas, alas! have too often been set over against one another. They have been divorced and sundered far. Come, Christian Endeavor, thou white-robed peacemaker, and pronounce the banns which shall make organization and spiritual power forever one!

Two wings are essential to the bird that would soar toward the sun. Organization is one wing, Spirituality is another. A poor, broken-winged eagle is that church or society that fails to use both wings.

Organization without spiritual power is the perfect engine standing upon the track with no fire under the boiler, no steam in the pipes. It is a dumb, dead, impotent thing.

Spirituality, without organization is the fire upon the prairie, kindling a blaze, but driving no wheels, turning no turbines, energizing no whirring looms or flying shuttles. This, too, is an impotent, evanescent thing. But Spirituality and Organization may move the world.

We have the organization practically complete—our covenant pledge, our consecration meeting, our committees, our unions. Our future conquest is a question of spiritual power, and that, O Christian Endeavorers, you must furnish. Spiritual power abides not in the machinery of itself, but it may be had for the asking. Listen to the promise, Christian Endeavorer: "Ask and ye shall receive; seek and ye shall find." Spiritual power is as free as the sunlight, as mighty as the tides. It is as abundant as electricity, but, like electricity, it must be generated. It is as omnipotent as God, but it must be applied.

The Christian Endeavor history of this past year is the story of this power. Its dominant note has been "Evangelism." "Saved to serve" has been its motto. The "new Endeavor" may be summarized as the evangelistic Endeavor, and wise evangelism is spiritual power applied.

O Endeavors, this is your supreme mission. Be the conductors of this spiritual electricity. Be the willing wires, the live wires, along which may run the power of God to every part of our organization. This is the one, the only, secret of true success—"Not by might, nor by power," not by organization or by perfection of machinery, not by committees, not by methods, "but by my Spirit, saith the Lord," working through committees and methods and organization.

Oh! that by some word of burning eloquence I might lay this thought on the heart of every Endeavorer throughout the world! This word is not mine to speak. It is not any man's to utter. Come, Holy Spirit, Heavenly Comforter, speak Thou the word that makes our organization live.

But I *can*, I do, urge you to make this the Christian Endeavor watchword of the coming year. Each year of the fifteen years has been noted for some advance step. Each convention has been signalized by some great thought. "Citizenship," "Missions," "Fellowship," have been our watchwords at conventions past, and they are our watchwords still; for a step once gained we will not lose. And here is the greatest word, and best of all: SPIRITUAL POWER. "Washington, '96"—may it live in history as the Convention of God's power! 1896-7, the year of God's energizing might in Christian Endeavor.

Then, as steel and copper, hitherto unweldable metals, are welded together by the mighty, subtle power of electricity in a union so complete that no human eye can find the seam, so, by the fusing might of God's Spirit in Christian Endeavor, will be welded together *fidelity that is true and fellowship that is large-hearted, responsibility that makes strong and loyalty that makes humble and gentle, patriotism and humanity, organization and spiritual power, now and forever, one and inseparable.* AND "WHAT GOD HATH JOINED TOGETHER, LET NOT MAN PUT ASUNDER."

CHAPTER LXIII.

"CALIFORNIA '97."

"Monotonous Superlatives"—Some Unusual Features—A Convention that began in a Hundred Cities at the Same Time—Fun on the Rails—Car Services and Wayside Meetings—A Widening Horizon—Do Conventions Pay?—How Love of Country is Stirred—Through Nevada—California's Greeting—The Decorations—The Audiences and Audience Rooms—The Banners and Who Received Them—Special Features—Historic Gavels—Banners from Distant Lands—The Convention Sunday—A Convention of Spiritual Power—Homeward Bound.

AS one convention succeeds another, it is difficult to avoid monotonous superlatives in writing their story. Even to old convention-goers, each new gathering seems to surpass those that have gone before it in some particulars, while to new-comers who reckon it as their first convention, it is always a surprising marvel of power, enthusiasm, and religious devotion.

"California, '97," had all the characteristics of preceding conventions which have made Christian Endeavor memorable, and it also had characteristics of its own which differentiate and cause it to stand out as a peculiarly interesting convention.

The unusual features of the convention of '97 were due largely to its geographical location. On the outermost rim of the Western Continent it was held. The beating surf of the Pacific Ocean, instead of the tidal roll of the Atlantic or of the Great Lakes was in the ears of the convention-goers. The convention seemed to partake somewhat of the boundless character and the sunny joy of the great commonwealth within whose borders it was held.

FIRST CALIFORNIA WELCOME—AUBURN.

A very large number of the delegates had traveled across a continent to attend the meeting. Their minds were expanded and their hearts were enlarged

CALIFORNIA, '97.

INTERIOR OF MECHANICS' PAVILION.

by the journey. They were in a mood to make the most of the mighty meeting. The long journey of a week or more had been a constant preparation. The convention really began, with a great many of the delegates, nine or ten days before the gavel of the presiding officer called the first session to order in the Mechanics' Pavilion.

This continental journey and everything connected with it, was a surprise not only to Christian Endeavorers but to the public at large, and none were more surprised than the railroad men who transported the thronging thousands.

When it was first proposed to hold the convention in San Francisco, Secretary Baer, and the leading workers on the Pacific Coast, had many a long conference with the railroad managers, trying to impress upon them the probable size of the convention and the importance of the business which would accrue to their lines in consequence, but they could make little impression upon them. When they ventured, modestly, to express the opinion that five thousand people would cross the mountains, attracted by the convention, they were summarily put down by a high railroad magnate, who peremptorily said to them, "cut those figures right in two, and then you will have them quite large enough!"

But instead of the five thousand people, whom they predicted would take the journey, nearly eight times five thousand were transported across the plains and across the mountains to the Golden West. Of these, probably fully one-half were either Christian Endeavorers or older church members who attended the convention meetings. As many more from California and the adjacent States came up to this Christian Endeavor Mecca during the days of our annual feast, and it is a very moderate estimate to believe that forty thousand different people attended the gatherings of whom more than twenty-six thousand were registered Christian Endeavorers, while the aggregate attendance on all the meetings during the five days of the convention could not have been less than 300,000.

But, as I said, the convention did not begin in San Francisco on the 7th day of July, as advertised on the program. It began in New York and Boston and Philadelphia and Baltimore and Washington and Chicago and in at least a hundred other cities, fully a week before the advertised time, when the clans gathered together at the different railway stations for the long continental journey.

Every spare Pullman and Tourist car in the country was impressed into the service. Many of them were decorated with Christian Endeavor colors and streamers. A chaplain was appointed for each car on every Christian Endeavor excursion train. Devotional services were held morning and evening, and frequently at the railway stations where the trains halted for a longer or shorter time. Thus a convention three thousand miles long and occupying a week of time was started from a hundred different points in the United States and Canada.

But though the religious and devotional features of these excursions were so marked, there was, as was to be expected, an abundance of fun and good-fellowship. Friendships were formed and cemented which will never be broken, and tens of thousands of people will look back upon this journey to California as one of the brightest spots in all their lives.

The occupants of each car became particularly well acquainted one with another, as was natural, but they did not keep their good-fellowship all to themselves, for they would organize themselves with their song and their State call, and then go through the train, making calls upon the other Christian Endeavorers who were journeying with them. As a specimen of the good-natured fun which prevailed on this long journey, perhaps I may venture to quote the Massachusetts "call," which resounded through many cars and was heard at a hundred stations in twenty different States:

> "Rub-a-dub-dub, rub-a-dub-dub,
> We're from the Hub, we're from the Hub,
> Plymouth Rock and Bunker Hill,
> Tea in the harbor, steeping still,
> Mass a-chu-setts!

Other States had equally appropriate verses, while the State songs, which are always of a religious character, were also frequently sung.

But it must not be supposed for a moment that this fun degenerated into frivolity, or this good-fellowship into giddiness. The spirit of devotion was never far away; it was always easy to bring the delegates back to the highest and deepest truths. A prayer service never seemed incongruous, and the spiritual song was more in demand than the college yell.

Another great blessing of this international journey was the broadening of ideas and the widening of the horizon of a great multitude of young people. To many of them, who had been away from home but little, it was worth a year's schooling. It opened their eyes to the vast resources and wide extent of their own country. It was a lesson in patriotism which they will never forget, and they will sing hereafter, as never before,

> "My country, 'tis of thee,
> Sweet land of liberty."

At the same time, it was a lesson in home missions, as well as patriotism, for it showed these ardent young Christians the needy fields of their own land; the great cities with their polluted slums; the lonely prairies, with their dugouts and log huts; the frontier life of the new settlers; and that everywhere there was need of aggressive earnestness in planting the Church of Jesus Christ, that our country may not be engulfed in the maelstrom of irreligion and godlessness.

Complaint is sometimes made by the inconsiderate that these conventions cost too much money, and that it might be more wisely dropped into the contribution box of the missionary society. Some good men go about with uplifted hands, saying like one of old, "To what purpose is this waste? It might have been sold for more than three hundred pence and given to the poor." But a little further consideration surely will convince any reasonable man that such conventions are worth all they cost many times over. It must be remembered that in this way tens of thousands of people take their annual holiday. They use their precious vacation week and spend the money which they have saved for their holiday in going to a religious convention rather than to the mountains or to the seashore. In other words, they spend upon a religious gathering what they would otherwise spend for mere pleasure at some frivilous summer resort.

Again, it must be remembered that sentiments of patriotism, love of country, love of God, and religious enthusiasm are stirred by such journeys and such conventions which can scarcely be aroused in any other way. In

EXTERIOR OF MECHANICS' PAVILION.

direct contributions amounting to hundreds of thousands of dollars the missionary treasuries feel the benefit of such a great convention, and the indirect benefits, which cannot be tabulated or reckoned in dollars and cents, are beyond compute.

This journey across the continent was saddened by two or three accidents, in which, though only one Christian Endeavorer lost his life, two or three older people, who were journeying with the excursionists, met with an untimely end. These accidents, however, occurred early in the great continental migration. They caused the railroads to take unusual precautions and especial pains in the running of trains, and because of the precautions there were no accidents of large magnitude, as might easily have happened with so many scores of special trains upon the same line of road at the same time.

It must be borne in mind that many besides Endeavorers took advantage of the low rate to make the journey to California, and that for the actions of all these excursionists Christian Endeavor cannot be held responsible. Fully half of those who crossed the continent were not and never have been Christian Endeavorers, nor did they go to attend the meetings, and though they may have worn excursion badges because they were on an excursion train, they in no sense belonged to the Endeavor pilgrims. But little complaint was heard of the non-Christian or indecorous behavior of these outsiders, and yet, in some cases, they were said to have brought discredit upon their companions when distinction between the two classes of travelers was not borne in mind.

INTERIOR OF WOODWARD'S PAVILION.

Most profitable and delightful were many of the little wayside meetings along the route. At many a lonely station the inhabitants told us they had not been able to attend a service for many months. They begged us to continue the prayer and praise, and more than one conversion resulted from these trans-continental wayside gatherings.

As the trains approached the California border, though still hundreds of miles from San Francisco, indications of the coming convention became more marked and evident. The stations were decorated with bunting and Christian Endeavor flags. The local Endeavor societies turned out in large numbers to meet the passing trains. Beautiful flowers and luscious fruits were often given to the tired and weary travelers to brighten their journey. Greetings were exchanged and services held, and sometimes, more than thirty times in a single day, the hospitable Endeavorers upon the platform heard from the vanishing train, as it rolled on westward, the familiar song, "God be with you till we meet again."

Nevada quite redeemed its reputation in the minds of Endeavorers by exhibiting an interest in something besides a bloody prize fight, for which, alas! it is most widely known by the outside world, for at more than one station, the decorated buildings showed the welcome of the inhabitants, and the songs and prayers indicated that there were Christian hearts, and many of them too, who desired to take "Nevada for Christ."

With increasing joy and intensity of welcome, the Endeavorers were made to feel at home when they crossed the beautiful green Sierras that separate smiling California from the sagebrush plains to the eastward, and when the trains rolled into Sacramento, such a vociferous and whole-hearted welcome as the Endeavorers received has never been surpassed. Scores of white caps there awaited the incoming trains. The station was ablaze with electric light devices of welcome and with the purple and gold of the California Union, and cheer after cheer went up for the Endeavorers from Yankeeland and from Dixie, from the Middle West, and all the States between. And yet, this welcome was only a foretaste of the glorious hospitality which awaited every Endeavorer when he reached his destination. The whole city of San Francisco had flung out its cordial greeting in flags and bunting, that decorated every street. A great arch of welcome spanned the middle of Market Street with huge Christian Endeavor emblems hanging from the centre, and the words, "MAINE, 1881— CALIFORNIA, 1897" on either pillar of the supporting arch. For months the flowers in the Golden Gate Park had been preparing their welcome, and in mottoes and emblems, they told of the cordiality and good feeling which seemed to reign in every heart.

Nor was the welcome only one of flowers and bunting and electric lights. The hospitality of the inhabitants was shown in quieter ways and in little acts of kindness innumerable and unrecorded. Every one remarked upon the politeness and good nature of policemen and motormen, of hotel clerks and shop assistants, as well as of Christian Endeavor ushers and white caps.

So well were the arrangements made in advance that everything worked smoothly in spite of the doubled delegations from all parts of the country. Everybody was housed and fed, and well cared for from a material point of view, and though the main audience room, the Mechanics' Pavilion, and Woodward's Pavilion were utterly inadequate in their seating capacity to accommodate the thronging thousands who desired to get in, yet other buildings and halls were obtained, overflow meetings were organized out of doors, and everything was done that was possible to accommodate the visitors.

One unique feature of the hall accommodations was the many booths used for State headquarters, for missionary societies, and for other similar purposes. The headquarters of California, of Alameda County, and of the Golden Gate Union, were especially unique and attractive, and were visited by tens of thousands of people, while the "Missionary Extension" room, under the charge of Miss Mindora Berry, was an object lesson to all who entered its precincts, in the cause of world-wide Missions.

THE ALAMEDA COUNTY DISPLAY.

The Auditorium, which had been constructed by the local committee, within the great pavilion, was most admirable in every particular. Of vast seating capacity, its acoustic properties were yet so good that almost all the speakers could be heard, while the smaller auditorium in Woodward's Pavilion was equally good, acoustically considered.

It becomes increasingly difficult, each year, to summarize or even characterize such a convention. To attempt to give even a list of the speakers would result in simply a long and bare catalogue of names. To attempt to pick out the most prominent and acceptable speeches would be an invidious and thankless task. I shall again have to refer my readers who may desire a full account of these later conventions to the annual portly volume which records the proceedings and addresses in detail.

I can only mention a few characteristics which made this convention memorable. In the first place, as was natural, much attention was given to the subject of Christian citizenship, a subject which has for four years past so wisely engrossed the attention of Christian Endeavorers the world over. Special problems confront the Christian people of the Pacific Coast, one of the most important being the rescue and preservation of the Sabbath.

AN OLD CALIFORNIA MISSION.

California is the only State in the Union without a Sunday law, if I am not mistaken, and yet the Endeavorers of California, by reason of their persistent and faithful effort for the preservation of the Lord's day, had won the banner offered by the Rev. Wilbur F. Crafts. This subject occupied the attention of Endeavorers at more than one session of the convention, and at the great out-door demonstration on Van Ness Avenue, where four platforms were erected, and where as many thousands gathered around each as could come within sound of the voices, this great theme of "Our Country for Christ" was uppermost in every address.

Another forward movement which received great impetus at this convention was that of systematic and proportionate giving to God. The plan inaugurated by the Tenth Legion of New York seemed to meet with unbounded and universal favor, and two extemporized testimony meetings in regard to the benefit of systematic giving indicated the ardor of Christian Endeavorers in this new field.

Nearly allied to this theme is the missionary idea, and even more prominence than usual, great as has been the place it has occupied in the past, was accorded to this theme. The missionary roll of honor showed that $400,000 had been contributed to missions at home and abroad during the last year. More than forty missionaries from all parts of the world were introduced to the audience on the Missionary Day. The addresses on this great theme were wise and strong, and the presence of twenty delegates from Hawaii and three from Alaska, besides missionaries from almost every land under the sun, made real and emphatic the thought that Christian Endeavor had much to do in winning the world for Christ.

The admirable report of the General Secretary, which every year is looked forward to with eagerness, showed a greater advance in foreign and missionary lands than has ever been recorded before, and the formation of the United Societies of Christian Endeavor in India, Burmah, and Ceylon, Germany, Sweden, and South Africa, in connection with the visit of the President of the United Society to these countries, showed more clearly than ever the world-encompassing character of the movement.

India, with a gain in societies of nearly a hundred per cent., came near to winning the banner for the largest proportionate gain, though Ireland finally carried off the coveted trophy. Spain secured the banner from Mexico for the largest gain proportionately in Junior societies, though Mexico had increased more than five-fold.

The banner for the greatest absolute increase in Junior societies this year went to Ohio, the Good Citizenship banner to Indianapolis. England carried back the banner for the largest absolute increase of societies which she has held for three years, and the beautiful emblem which stands for the most earnest promotion of the idea of systematic and proportionate giving was taken back, as was most appropriate, to New York city by the originators of the Tenth Legion.

A great advance in the number of societies and Endeavorers throughout the world was reported, and it was found that there were over 50,700 societies, with very nearly three millions of members.

All these facts and figures and addresses stirred the hearts of Endeavorers, and revealed to them visions of the time when He whose right it is shall reign from the rising of the sun until the going down of the same.

The Junior rally, as usual, attracted large numbers and awakened unbounded enthusiasm. Had the great hall held twice ten thousand people it would have been filled to overflowing by the eager throngs who wished to get within the doors. The Junior exercise was very sprightly and interesting, and the constantly increasing devotion of Christian Endeavor to the boys and girls was shown by the interest in all the meetings devoted to the Junior and Intermediate departments of the society. A new feature introduced this year was an evangelistic meeting for the boys and girls under the care of the General Secretary, which was addressed by some of the most eminent evangelists in the country.

THE FLOATING SOCIETY.

While speaking of this evangelistic effort I am reminded to say that never were the evangelistic efforts of a convention more wisely planned or effectively carried out. Many services were held every noon in great department stores and other places where men and women congregate as well as in the halls specially dedicated to these meetings. Evangelistic services were even held in the corridor of the Palace Hotel at the noon hour to the profit, let us hope, of all the guests, Christian Endeavorers and others, in this great caravansary.

Separate meetings for men and for women were held this year as they were in Washington with great profit; and new features of special interest were the meetings for pastors attended by nearly five hundred clergymen, and the great assembly of women interested in the Mothers' Society and its relation to the Juniors. This gathering was one of peculiar interest and power.

The denominational rallies this year, as heretofore, were meetings of remarkable enthusiasm and attracted large throngs. One of the features of special interest at the Baptist rally was the "Carey hammer;" the very shoemaker's hammer which William Carey, the great pioneer missionary of the nineteenth century, used in the days when Sydney Smith called him "the consecrated cobbler." This was the hammer with which this devoted hero of the mission field used to work at his bench, when he uttered the famous epigram: "My business is to preach the Gospel, I mend shoes to pay expenses." Though the Baptist Endeavorers naturally felt that they had the first claim to this historic relic, yet it was prized no less by the whole convention, and thousands desired to touch this famous bit of iron. It was loaned to the President of the United Society by Rev. James Mursell, of Derby, England, in whose family it had been for forty years, for the purpose of calling the Convention of '97 to order. Another historic gavel sent from India by the local union of Mussoorie, a hill station in Northern India, was used in another hall. This gavel was made of different kinds of Indian wood and into the head of the block on which it was struck in calling the convention to order, were let in rupees from Alwar, Nepaul, Ajmere, and other native States of India. A marble block with the Christian Endeavor monogram beautifully set in mother-of-pearl was also sent from Agra, in India, to be used with the "Cary hammer." Several banners had also been sent from India. Among them was a finely-wrought banner in Bengali characters, in which the Christian Endeavor pledge was displayed, and others in Hindi and Hindustani telling of the supreme desire of the dark-skinned Endeavorers of that land to win "India for Christ." These various gavels and banners added picturesqueness and romantic interest to the convention, and were each and all forcible incitements to missionary zeal and devotion.

A Christian Endeavor poem, "The Army of Daybreak," the best of the kind ever written, was read by a gifted young Massachusetts poet, and was enjoyed by all who heard it.

A few lines should be devoted to the State meetings held on Saturday night, July 11th. Gracious and delightful receptions were accorded to many State delegations by their hospitable hosts of the different churches of San Francisco. Owing to the large Chinese and Japanese population of San Francisco the Endeavorers of these two nationalities held separate rallies which were of very great interest and entirely unique, I believe, in the annals of Christian Endeavor conventions in America.

But the greatest gathering of this Saturday evening was the California

State convention which filled the vast auditorium in the Mechanics' Pavilion from floor to ceiling. Very wisely the State Union decided to hold its annual convention this year in connection with the International meeting, and, though the convention was all crowded into one evening, and many of the usual features were necessarily omitted, yet it was probably the largest and one of the most enthusiastic State meetings ever held in any State.

Sunday, July 11th, was one of the great days of the convention. The large auditoriums were used only in the afternoon, and the attention and energy of the Christian Endeavorers were concentrated upon the church services in all parts of the city. Never were the churches of San Francisco so crowded. Many of them had to organize one or more overflow meetings to accommodate the throngs.

CALIFORNIA CHRISTIAN ENDEAVOR MISSIONARY EXTENSION ROOM.

It was a day, too, throughout San Francisco of unusual quiet and freedom from crime. The daily papers of the next morning remarked that the pleasure resorts were comparatively empty, and the places of worship all full, and that seldom had San Francisco known so quiet and worshipful a Lord's day. The closing day of the convention Monday, July 21st, found every one at the highest pitch of quiet but intense enthusiasm, and the consecration meetings in the halls and churches will never be forgotten for their unusual depth, earnestness, and spiritual power.

In fact this was the key-note of the convention, a note more often struck than any other. Of late years each succeeding convention has seemed to surpass the others in quiet, intense spirituality and genuine depth and height and breadth.

This was peculiarly true of "California, '97," which was characterized by many an old convention-goer as "the convention of spiritual might." A "quiet hour" was conducted every afternoon by one whose name will always be connected with efforts for the deepening of the inner life and always called together more than the large church could hold. An hour of Bible reading by an eminent theological professor also attracted large audiences, and afforded another quiet hour for soul-hungry Endeavorers, while the early morning prayer meetings, as usual, gave opportunity each day for still and close communion with the Almighty.

In his annual address the President of the United Society ventured to suggest that two special Endeavors of the coming year should be the development of family religion and the dedication of "the morning watch," the first fifteen minutes of the day, to communion with God.

Those suggestions were most heartily received, and I trust will be carried out by multitudes of Endeavorers in the years to come.

Thus, with these deep, ineffaceable impressions, the convention ended as it began. The long months of preparation and the days of fruition bore their precious fruit of quickened hearts, renewed vows, stimulated zeal, and thrice ten thousand young lives dedicated anew to the service of Christ and their own Church, thus making them forever after more useful members of the Church universal and invisible.

It only remains to add that the impression made by the convention upon the Pacific Coast, and indeed upon the whole country, was profound and so far as can be judged, lasting. The papers of San Francisco did their utmost to give graphic, minute, and accurate accounts of the convention. The Associated Press dispatches were full and sympathic and people of every shade of religious belief seemed impressed with the fact that the religion of Christ is a mighty, resistless, and ever-increasing power in the world. The return journey across the continent was marked by earnest car meetings and delightful wayside services, as was the outward journey, and thus the eastward-facing excursionists took the convention back with them to twenty thousand churches and twice twenty thousand homes.

www.ingramcontent.com/pod-product-compliance
Lightning Source LLC
Chambersburg PA
CBHW031609160426
43196CB00006B/74